THE SOCIAL AND THE REAL

THE SOCIAL AND THE REAL

Political Art of the 1930s in the Western Hemisphere

Edited by
Alejandro Anreus, Diana L. Linden,
and Jonathan Weinberg

The Pennsylvania State University Press
University Park, Pennsylvania

Library of Congress Cataloging-in-Publication Data

The social and the real : political art of the 1930's in
the western hemisphere / edited by Alejandro Anreus,
Diana L. Linden, and Jonathan Weinberg.
       p.   cm.
Includes bibliographical references and index.
ISBN 0-271-02691-X (alk. paper)
1. Art—Political aspects.
2. Social problems in art.
3. Art, Modern—20th century.
I. Anreus, Alejandro.
II. Linden, Diana L.
III. Weinberg, Jonathan, 1957– .

N72.P6S64 2004
709'.181'209043—dc22
2004028709

CONTENTS

ILLUSTRATIONS

Trachtenberg

1 Walker Evans, Railroad Station, Edwards, Mississippi (February 1936). FSA.
2 Ben Shahn, Cotton Picker, Pulaski County, Arkansas (October 1935). FSA.
3 Berenice Abbott, "El," Sixth Avenue Line, 28th Street Station (10 November 1938). WPA.
4 Dorothea Lange, Nipomo, California, Destitute peapickers in California; a 32-year-old mother of seven children (February 1936). FSA.
5 Dorothea Lange, Nipomo, California, Migrant agricultural worker's family. Seven hungry children and their mother, age 32. The father is a native Californian (March 1936). FSA.

Martínez

1 Antonio Gattorno, "Decorative Panel" for the Pedagogical School of the University of Havana, c. 1929 (media, dimensions, and whereabouts unknown).
2 Antonio Gattorno and Gabriel Castaño, mural for Julio Antonio Mella (1933) (media and dimensions unknown; destroyed).
3 Arístides Fernández, *Manifestación con abanderado (Demonstrations)* (1933), ink and watercolor on paper, 472 x 366 mm. Museo Nacional de Bellas Artes, Havana, Cuba.
4 Alberto Peña, *El Llamado del Ideal (The Call of the Ideal)* (1936), oil on canvas, 95 x 82.5 cm. Museo Nacional de Bellas Artes, Havana, Cuba.
5 Carlos Enríquez, *La Invasión (The Invasion)* (1937) (fresco, dimensions unknown; destroyed).
6 Carlos Enríquez, *Campesinos Felices (Happy Peasants)* (1938), oil on canvas, 122 x 89 cm. Museo Nacional de Bellas Artes, Havana, Cuba.
7 Marcelo Pogolotti, *Paisaje Cubano (Cuban Landscape)* (1933), oil on canvas, 73 x 92.5 cm. Museo Nacional de Bellas Artes, Havana, Cuba.

Coffey

1 Diego Rivera, *Creation* (1922–23), encaustic and gold leaf, 109.4 x 109.4 m. Bolivar Amphitheater, National Preparatory School, Mexico City.
2 José Clemente Orozco, *Maternity* (1923), fresco, 10 x 8.5 ft. National Preparatory School, Mexico City.
3 José Clemente Orozco, *The Trench* (1923–27), fresco, 10 x 8.5 ft. National Preparatory School, Mexico City.
4 Diego Rivera, *The Liberation of the Peon* (1923), fresco, 4.38 x 3.48 m. Court of Labor, south wall, first floor, Ministry of Public Education, Mexico City.

5 Diego Rivera, *Our Daily Bread* (1928), fresco, 2.04 x 1.58 m. Court of Fiestas, south wall, third floor, Ministry of Public Education, Mexico City.
6 Diego Rivera, *The Hacienda* (1926), fresco, 3.84 x 7.70 m. Stairwell, second floor, Ministry of Public Education, Mexico City.
7 Diego Rivera, *The Mechanization of the Countryside* (1926), fresco, 3.52 x 5.67 m. Stairwell, third floor, Ministry of Public Education, Mexico City.

McKay

1 Louis Muhlstock, *William O'Brien Unemployed* (c. 1935), charcoal and brown chalk on paper, 68 x 51 cm. National Gallery of Canada, purchased 1974.
2 Laurence Hyde, *Still Life* (1937), medium, dimensions, and location unknown.
3 Charles Comfort, *Captain Vancouver* (1939), mural painting, 127 x 152 cm. Confederation Art Centre, Charlottetown, Prince Edward Island.
4 William Weston, *Beached* (1935), oil on canvas, 105 x 120 cm. Private Collection.
5 A. Y. Jackson, *Algoma, November* (1935–36), oil on canvas, 81.3 x 102.1 cm. National Gallery of Canada. Gift of H. S. Southam, Ottawa, 1945.
6 David Milne, *Ollie Matson's House Is Just a Square Red Cloud* (1931), oil on canvas, 46.2 x 56 cm. National Gallery of Canada. Vincent Massey Bequest, 1968.
7 Carl Shaefer, *Ontario Farmhouse* (1934), oil on canvas, 106.5 x 124.7 cm. National Gallery of Canada. Gift of Floyd S. Chalmers, Toronto, 1969.
8 Prudence Heward, *Sisters of Rural Quebec* (1930), oil on canvas, 157.5 x 106.7 cm. Art Gallery of Windsor.

Anreus

1 Antonio Berni, *Self-Portrait with Cactus* (1929), oil on canvas, 110.5 x 85 cm. Private Collection, Buenos Aires.
2 Antonio Berni, Photos of the unemployed (1933–34). Private Collection, Buenos Aires.
3 Antonio Berni, *Unemployed* (1934), tempera on burlap, 218 x 300 cm. Collection of Elena Berni, Buenos Aires.
4 Antonio Berni, *Demonstration* (1934), tempera on burlap, 180 x 250 cm. Collection of Dr. Eduardo and María Teresa Constantini.
5 Antonio Berni, *Tenant Farmers* (1935), oil on canvas, 200 x 300 cm. Consejo de Deliberación, Buenos Aires. Courtesy of Lilí Berni and the Estate of Antonio Berni.
6 Antonio Berni, *Midnight in the World* (1936–37), oil on canvas, 200 x 300 cm. Private Collection, Buenos Aires.

7 Antonio Berni, *New Chicago Athletic Club* (1937), oil on canvas, 184.8 x 300.4 cm. The Museum of Modern Art, New York. Inter-American Fund, 1943.

Weinberg

1 Hugo Gellert, *The Working Day; Struggle for a Normal Working Day Repercussion of the English Factory Acts on Other Countries,* 10 x 7 in., published in Hugo Gellert, *Karl Marx' "Capital" in Lithographs* (New York: Ray Long & Richard R. Smith, 1934), 37. Courtesy of Mary Ryan Gallery, New York.

2 Hugo Gellert, *The Working Day: The Greed for Surplus Labor,* 10 x 7 in., published in Hugo Gellert, *Karl Marx' "Capital" in Lithographs* (New York: Ray Long & Richard R. Smith, 1934), 35. Courtesy of Mary Ryan Gallery, New York.

3 Cesare Stea, *Assembling,* relief, Bowery Bay Pumping Station (1939), Queens, New York.

4 Hugo Gellert, *Cooperation,* 10 x 7 in., published in Hugo Gellert, *Karl Marx' "Capital" in Lithographs* (New York: Ray Long & Richard R. Smith, 1934), 39. Courtesy of Mary Ryan Gallery, New York.

5 Rockwell Kent, *Workers of the World, Unite!* (1937) wood engraving, $7\frac{7}{8}$ x $5\frac{3}{4}$ in. (20.1 x 14.9 cm.). Fine Arts Museums of San Francisco, Archenbach Foundation for Graphic Arts.

6 Paul Cadmus, *Pocahontas Rescues Captain John Smith* (1938), oil and tempera, 7 x 20 ft. Richmond Parcel Post Building (later transferred to the library of the Court House Annex, Richmond, Virginia.). Fine Arts Collection, Public Buildings Service, General Services Administration.

7 Jared French, *Stuart's Raiders at the Swollen Ford* (1938), 7 x 20 ft. Richmond Parcel Post Building (later transferred to the library of the Court House Annex, Richmond, Virginia). Fine Arts Collection, Public Buildings Service, General Services Administration.

8 Jared French, *The Farm (Vegetables)* (c. 1938), oil and tempera. Mural for New York State Vocational Institute, location unknown. Photo courtesy of DC Moore Gallery, New York.

Francis

1 Earle [Earl] W. Richardson, *Benjamin Banneker* (1934), oil on board, 12 x 19.75 in. Schomburg Center for Research in Black Culture, New York Public Library.

2 Malvin Gray Johnson, *Toussaint L'Ouverture* (1934), oil on cardboard, 12 x 22.50 in. Schomburg Center for Research in Black Culture, New York Public Library.

3 Earle [Earl] W. Richardson, *Columbus Soldiers— Estavanico* (1934), 12 x 22.5 in. Schomburg Center for Research in Black Culture, New York Public Library.

4 Earle [Earl] W. Richardson, *Harriet Tubman and Frederick Douglass* (1934), oil on board, 12 x 22.50 in. Schomburg Center for Research in Black Culture, New York Public Library.

5 Malvin Gray Johnson, *Nat Turner* (1934), oil on cardboard, 12 x 19.75 in. Schomburg Center for Research in Black Culture, New York Public Library.

6 Malvin Gray Johnson, *Negro Pharaoh—Eighteenth Dynasty* (1934), oil on cardboard, 12 x 16 in. Schomburg Center for Research in Black Culture, New York Public Library.

7 Malvin Gray Johnson and Earle [Earl] W. Richardson, *Negro Soldiers* (1934), oil on board, 17.50 x 23.75 in. Schomburg Center for Research in Black Culture, New York Public Library.

8 Earle [Earl] W. Richardson, *Art, Music, Literature* (1934), oil on board, 17.50 x 25.75 in. Schomburg Center for Research in Black Culture, New York Public Library.

Park

1 George Wesley Bellows, *The Law Is Too Slow* (1923), lithograph. The Art Institute of Chicago. Gift of George F. Porter, 1925.1567.

2 Philip Guston. *Drawing for Conspirators* (c. 1930), graphite, ink, colored pencil, and crayon on paper, $22\frac{1}{2}$ x $14\frac{1}{2}$ in. The Whitney Museum of American Art, New York.

3 Isamu Noguchi, *Death (Lynched Figure)* (1934), monel metal, 39 x $29\frac{1}{3}$ x 21 in. (without stand). Berenice Abbott/Commerce Graphics Ltd., Inc. Courtesy of the Isamu Noguchi Foundation, Inc., Long Island City, New York.

4 José Clemente Orozco, *Negroes,* or *Negros ahorcados* (1930) (print from *The American Scene, Series I,* 1933), lithograph, black ink, buff wove "France paper," $12\frac{3}{4}$ x $8\frac{15}{16}$ in. Milwaukee Art Museum. Purchased by George B. Perry Memorial Fund. © Estate of José Clemente Orozco/SOMAAP.

5 John Steuart Curry, *The Fugitive* (1935). Smithsonian American Art Museum. Peter A. Juley and Son Collection.

6 Wilmer Jennings, *At the End of the Rope* (1935), linocut, $8\frac{1}{2}$ x 11 in. Courtesy of the Kenkeleba Gallery, New York.

7 Hyman Warsager, *The Law.* From *New Masses* (9 January 1934): 7. Tamiment Institute Library, New York University.

Hills

1 Philip Evergood, *North River Jungle* (1933), pencil on paper, 18 ⁷⁄₁₆ x 22 ⁷⁄₈ in. Hirshhorn Museum and Sculpture Garden, Smithsonian Institution.
2 Philip Evergood, *Mine Disaster* (1933), oil on canvas. Private Collection.
3 Philip Evergood, *The Story of Richmond Hill* (detail), 1937–38, oil on canvas, 160 sq. ft. Queensborough Public Library, Richmond Hill Branch.
4 News clipping, "Theatres of War," source unknown. Philip Evergood Papers, Archives of American Art, Smithsonian Institution, Washington, D.C.
5 Philip Evergood, *American Tragedy* (1937), oil on canvas. Private Collection.
6 Philip Evergood, *The Artist in the New Deal* (1938), oil on canvas (original image later painted over). Reproduced in ACA Gallery catalog, 1938.
7 Philip Evergood, *New Birth/New Struggle* (1947), oil on canvas. Private Collection.

Lee

1 Diego M. Rivera, *Detroit Industry, North Wall* (1932–33). Gift of Edsel B. Ford. Photo © 1989 The Detroit Institute of Arts.
2 Diego M. Rivera, *Detroit Industry, South Wall* (1932–33). Gift of Edsel B. Ford. Photo © 1989 The Detroit Institute of Arts.
3 Diego M. Rivera, *Detroit Industry, West Wall* (1932–33). Gift of Edsel B. Ford. Photo © 1989 The Detroit Institute of Arts.
4 Rivera painting the south wall automotive panel with sketches pinned to the scaffold. He is watched by a group of unidentified men. Gift of Edsel B. Ford. Photo © 1932 The Detroit Institute of Arts.

Luckyj

1 Paraskeva Clark, *Myself* (1933), oil on canvas, 101.6 x 76.2 cm. The National Gallery of Canada, Ottawa.
2 Paraskeva Clark, *Presents from Madrid* (1937), watercolor over graphite on wove paper, 51.5 cm. x 62 cm. The National Gallery of Canada, Ottawa.
3 Paraskeva Clark, *Portrait of Mao* (1938), watercolor on paper, dimensions unknown. Collection unknown. The National Gallery of Canada, copy negative.
4 Paraskeva Clark, *Petroushka* (1937), oil on canvas, 122.4 cm. x 81.9 cm. The National Gallery of Canada.
5 Source for Petroushka: *Toronto Daily Star* (1 June 1937), sec. 2, p. 1.

6 Paraskeva Clark, *Evening Walk on Yonge Street* (1938), watercolor on paper, 40 x 34.5 cm. Collection of Mr. and Mrs. John H. Pollock, Toronto.
7 Paraskeva Clark, *Self-Portrait with Concert Program* (1942), oil on canvas, 76.6 cm. x 69.8 cm. The National Gallery of Canada.
8 Photograph of Paraskeva Clark, early 1930s. Private Collection of Clive and Mary Clark, Toronto.

Linden

1 Ben Shahn, *Jersey Homesteads* (1937–38), mural, full view, fresco 12 x 45 ft. Commissioned by the Farm Security Administration. Photo courtesy of VAGA. © Estate of Ben Shahn, licensed by VAGA, New York.
2 Ben Shahn, *Jersey Homesteads* (left detail). © Estate of Ben Shahn, licensed by VAGA, New York.
3 Ben Shahn, *Jersey Homesteads* (center detail). © Estate of Ben Shahn, licensed by VAGA, New York.
4 Ben Shahn, *Jersey Homesteads* (right detail). © Estate of Ben Shahn, licensed by VAGA, New York.
5 Ben Shahn, *Resources of America: Walt Whitman* (detail of center panel) (1938–39), egg tempera on plaster. Bronx Central Post Office. © Estate of Ben Shahn, licensed by VAGA, New York.
6 Ben Shahn, *Immigration* (1939), tempera on board, 5½ x 15½ in. Private Collection. Photo courtesy of Kennedy Galleries. © Estate of Ben Shahn, licensed by VAGA, New York.
7 Ben Shahn, *Immigration #2* (1939), tempera on board, 5½ x 15½ in. Private Collection. Photo courtesy of Kennedy Galleries. © Estate of Ben Shahn, licensed by VAGA, New York.
8 Ben Shahn, *The First Amendment* (1940–41), egg tempera on canvas, 8 ft. 6 in x 16 ft. Woodhaven Branch Post Office, Queens, New York. Photograph by David Linden.

Hemingway

1 Mitchell Siporin, *Endless Voyage* (1946), oil on canvas, 34.5 x 39.4 in. University of Iowa Museum of Art. Museum Purchase.
2 Anthony Toney, *Four Corners* (1946), oil on canvas, 37.75 x 51.4 in. Robert Hull Fleming Museum, University of Vermont. Gift of Dr. and Mrs. Arthur Kahn.
3 Philip Evergood, *Dream Catch* (1946), oil on canvas, 30 x 20.9 in. Hirshhorn Museum and Sculpture Garden, Smithsonian Institution, Washington, D.C. Gift of Joseph H. Hirshhorn.
4 Ben-Zion, *Seated Prophet* (c. 1950), oil on canvas, 17.1 x 12.2 in. Hirshhorn Museum and Sculpture Garden,

Smithsonian Institution, Washington, D.C. Gift of Joseph
H. Hirshhorn.

5 Joseph Solman, *Maurice Becker* (1951–52), oil on canvas,
36 x 28 in. Initialed lower right. Courtesy of Mercury
Gallery, Boston.

Stein

1 Photograph of Franklin Delano Roosevelt, with
retouching, circulated by Wide World Photos in October
1928. Stefan Lorant picture archive, International Center
of Photography. New York. With permission of AP/Wide
World Photos.

2 Double-page spread from M. Lincoln Schuster, ed., *Eyes
on the World: A Photographic Record of History-in-the-
Making* (New York: Simon & Schuster, 1935), 50–51.

3 C. C. Beall, "Find What Roosevelt Means to the U.S.A.
in This Picture," 1933. Reproduced as plate 523 in the
exhibition catalog edited by Alfred H. Barr Jr., *Fantastic
Art: Dada Surrealism* (New York: Museum of Modern
Art, 1936).

4 Louis Checkman, photograph of 1960 model in winning
plan by William F. Pederson and Bradford S. Tilney, as
reproduced in Thomas H. Creighton, *The Architecture
of Monuments: The Franklin Delano Roosevelt Memorial
Competition* (New York: Reinhold, 1962), 32.

5 Model designed by Marcel Breuer and Herbert Beckhard
for the Franklin Delano Roosevelt Memorial Commission
in 1966. Marcel Breuer Papers, Archives of American Art,
Smithsonian Institution, Washington, D.C.

6 Photograph of Neil Estern sculpture of FDR in the FDR
Memorial designed by Lawrence Halprin.

7 Photograph of demonstration in Washington, D.C.,
protesting the soon-to-be-dedicated memorial to
Roosevelt that included no representation of him "in a
wheelchair or braces."

8 Photograph of Robert Graham sculpture of FDR shortly
after its installation in the added forecourt of the FDR
Memorial designed by Lawrence Halprin.

ACKNOWLEDGMENTS

One recurrent image in the art of the Americas in the 1930s is that of many hands coming together, engaged in work, raised in protest and unity and cooperation. The spirit of this anthology parallels such imagery, for many hands have come together in its creation, with all the joys and frustrations of collaboration Americans of the 1930s knew so well. In recalling the friends, scholars, and colleagues who have helped us along the way, we can only hint at the depth of our gratitude.

Above all, the editors would like to acknowledge the contributing authors for their hard work and commitment to this project. Sadly, one of the authors, Natalie Luckyj, died before this book was completed. Natalie was not only a fine art historian but a gracious and generous person who is sorely missed. We thank her husband, Michael Bell, as well as Marilyn McKay and Anne D'Alleva for their assistance in preparing her manuscript for publication.

For helping us craft the introduction to this volume, we are indebted to Matthew Baigell, Lili-Ann Berg, Shifra Goldman, Barry Lord, Natalie Luckyj, Helen Langa, Virginia Hagelstein Marquardt, and Susan Noyes Platt. Frances Pohl, and Alan Wallach offered valuable support and feedback. Thanks also to David Brody, David Craven, Chris Garveau, Andrew Lee, Laura Malosetti, Angela Miller, Elizabeth Milroy, James Oles, Robert Panzer, Ezra Shahn, James Wechsler, Ellen Wiley Todd, and Rebecca Zurier.

We thank Patricia Fidler for initially approaching the three of us about writing such a work. We are in debt to Gloria Kury, our editor at Penn State Press, who enthusiastically embraced this book and made it hers. We would also like to thank Cherene Holland, the managing editor at the Press, and Suzanne Wolk, our copyeditor.

Last, but definitely not least, is the enormous support, patience and good humor we have received from our families, spouses, and children. Diana L. Linden would like to thank her parents, Joan and David Linden; her husband, Peter Ross, for living with this work; and her toddlers, Emily Rose and Alexander Daniel Linden-Ross, for being joyous distractions. Jonathan Weinberg thanks his ever-suffering partner, Nicholas Boshnack. Alejandro Anreus thanks his wife, Debra Blehart, and their children, David Rentkicwicz and Isabel Anreus.

Alejandro Anreus, Diana L. Linden, Jonathan Weinberg

INTRODUCTION

**Alejandro Anreus,
Diana L. Linden, and
Jonathan Weinberg**

The Social and the Real is the first anthology to deal with the painting, sculpture, graphic arts, and photography of the 1930s in a hemispheric context. We take as axiomatic Cuban poet, journalist, and political theorist José Martí's (1853–95) definition of "America" as a hemispheric, multiracial, and multiethnic entity in which the United States is one nation among many. Although many of the individual essays have a relatively narrow focus, as an aggregate they begin the process of forging a Pan-American perspective on the art of the period, encouraging the reader to compare and contrast the experiences of artists across national boundaries and reconsider familiar narratives. Thinking about art and politics in a hemispheric context expands the very chronology of social realism. Whereas scholars in the United States locate the origins of the movement with the economic crash of 1929 and conclude it with the advent of World War II, the story really begins in Mexico in the early 1920s and continues during the 1940s and 1950s throughout the hemisphere.

There were numerous threads of contact between artists throughout the Americas. These included artistic inspiration through the reproduction and dissemination of images, artists either traveling to, working in, or exhibiting in countries other than their own, or inviting foreign artists to work with them, as with the numerous artists who assisted or worked with the Mexican muralists in either Mexico or the United States. Artists' organizations were important sites of contact, among them the American Artists' Congress, which convened in 1936 in New York and whose twelve delegates included José Clemente Orozco and David Alfaro Siqueiros.[1] The Mexican Artists' Union inspired both the Artists Union and the Harlem Artists' Guild in the United States, the Union de Escritores y Artistas in Cuba, and the Artists' Union of Canada, whose members were involved with either the Communist Party or the social-democratic Cooperative Commonwealth Federation.[2]

It was at the 1936 American Artists' Congress that U.S. muralist Gilbert Wilson related how two summers before he had seen Orozco's extraordinary paintings for the National Preparatory School in Mexico City. "From that moment on I knew it was what I wanted Art to be—a real, vital, meaningful expression, full of purpose and intention, having influence and relation to people's daily lives—a part *of* life. Here was the first *modern* art I had ever seen. At least, it was the first creative work done in my own time that seemed to have any need, any excuse for being. I decided that murals, today, can contain one of two things, either the cruelty of emptiness or the cruelty of truth."[3] In contrast to the rhetoric of nationalism and isolationism that was gaining increasing currency in the culture of the United States by the mid-thirties, Wilson acknowledged that the contemporary mural movement had begun in Mexico and

that an art of social responsibility was in essence a Pan-American phenomenon. As artist and critic Charmion Von Wiegand wrote, "It is even
possible that they [the Mexican muralists] may give us a tradition from
which the American painters will draw. For, as their country like ours
belongs to the New World, their work seems to be a part of our actual
native expression."[4] As the essays in this anthology aptly demonstrate,
artists throughout the hemisphere shared Wilson's and Von Wiegand's
call for an art that was both responsive to the day-to-day struggles of the
working classes and had a wide appeal. Such popular understanding did
not mean sugarcoating reality; instead Wilson wanted murals that would
convey the "cruelty of truth."

It may still surprise some readers that Wilson used the word "modern" to refer to the work of the Mexican muralists who had rejected the
abstraction of the European avant-garde. The supposed antimodernist
quality of so much of the visual art between the wars has resulted in its
neglect by an approach to art history that still favors formal invention
over content, abstraction over realism. And yet all the artists discussed
in *The Social and the Real,* no matter what their nationality or style,
shared a belief that they were making art that was distinctly modern precisely because it responded directly to the political and social issues of
the times. But, as Paul Wood writes, "the mere depiction of recognizable
bodies doing recognizable things was not what made an art 'realist.'"[5]
In its most cohesive and authentic visual expressions, social realism
synthesized the formalist experimentation of the avant-garde with a critical interpretation of reality. Such artists as the Mexican muralists were
opposed to academic naturalism because it seemed to maintain conservative values. But they were equally opposed to avant-garde forms of
expression because of their supposed elitism and bourgeois individualism. Painters such as Stuart Davis in the United States, Paraskeva Clark
in Canada, and Antonio Berni in Argentina wanted to reconcile modernist painting with leftist ideology. The social dimension of reality and the
reality of social conditions are crystallized in the most powerful art of
this period.

Our focus on intrahemispheric exchange and artistic production
is a break from the dominant modernist paradigm that sees art of the
Americas as solely indebted and subservient to European art. This is not
to deny that many artists from Canada, the United States, the Caribbean,
and Latin America traveled to Paris and Berlin in the 1910s and 1920s
for training, camaraderie, and inspiration. But their travels to these European capitals were often taken after exposure to the Mexican muralists
or after having lived and worked in Russia and Eastern Europe. Artists
in Latin America and the Caribbean drew upon native radical political
movements, indigenous artistic traditions, and upon their own national

and popular heroes. In sum, the art of the Western Hemisphere represents a dialogue between politics and art both within the Americas and with European modernism and politics.

However, in emphasizing Pan-Americanism, and in particular the extraordinary influence of the Mexican mural movement, we cannot ignore the economic, military, and cultural imperialism of the United States. If artists outside the United States welcomed a certain amount of cross-cultural exchange, they also wanted to protect their native art production from the culture industry of their "good neighbor." The social and political manifestation of nationalism in Latin America and the Caribbean functioned on two levels: It sought to recover the historical past that reinforced the authenticity of indigenous artistic and social traditions (José Carlos Mariátegui's Marxism, for example, was rooted in Incan communal social structures); and it promoted a left-wing anti-imperialist nationalism, as evident in the politics of Peru's Alianza Popular Revolucionaria Americana (APRA), Nicaragua's César Augusto Sandino, Puerto Rico's Pedro Albizu Campos, and Cuba's Antonio Guiteras. These nationalisms throughout the Spanish-speaking Americas, as seen in the visual work of Mexican, Argentinean, and Cuban artists, absorbed rather than rejected the formal experimentation of the European avant-garde, which was then transformed into a national visuality that was neither chauvinistic nor nativist. The stylistic example of Diego Rivera, with its linear composition, bright colors, and didactic narrative, had repercussions in the Caribbean and the Andean countries. Rivera's heterodox politics (he evolved from Lovestone to Trotsky to Mao in a little more than a decade) was not as influential as that of Siqueiros, which was grounded in the Communist Party network throughout the Americas. Of the three great muralists (*los tres grandes*), Siqueiros traveled the most throughout the Americas, lecturing, publishing articles, and conducting workshops.[6] While his "dialectic-subversive painting"[7] alienated potential followers with its communist dogmatism, his sculptural sense of form found adherents in Berni (Argentina) and Mario Carreño (Cuba). In the end, the socially engaged realism found in Latin American art between the two world wars was pluralistic in both style and content.

Historiography

Our title, *The Social and the Real,* is derived from the term "social realism," which has become a standard catchall to describe the numerous public murals, graphics, and easel paintings produced between the wars that had some kind of leftist content. Social realist art tends to criticize the body politic or propose an ideal community. A term accepted both popularly and by scholars, it is vague and remains largely unexamined. The beginning of its use in the art-historical literature of the United States is hard to pinpoint.[8] During the 1930s artists in Canada, Latin America, and the United States never referred to themselves as social realists or to their art as social realism, a fact noted by many of the essayists in this volume; nor did the critics use the term. In Canada such leftist artists as Marian Scott, Fritz Brandler, and Louis Muhlstock, working in Montreal, referred to their imagery as "proletarian art." Charles Hill, in his *Canadian Painting in the Thirties,* discusses the "social function" of art with a decidedly working-class orientation.[9] It appears that the term social realism first appeared in the Canadian art-historical literature in Barry Lord's *History of Painting in Canada: Towards a People's Art,* published in 1974.[10] David Shapiro's widely read and referenced *Social Realism: Art as Weapon,* published in 1973, has resulted in the scholarly acceptance of the term to refer to leftist art in the United States, but it has since been adopted in studies of both Canadian and Latin American art of the period.

Despite the variability of the terms by which artists referred to themselves, through their political involvement, through their imagery, manifestoes, political networks, and public demonstrations, many artists engaged in debates over the artist's role in society, the role of the government in funding the arts, and how to create works that were both aesthetically and politically progressive. If Rivera, Siqueiros, and Orozco never used the term social realism, they always believed that art should have a direct political and social function, and they went so far as to embrace the word propaganda—a term always used negatively by modernist and antimodernist critics alike. As early as 1923 the manifesto of the Union of Mexican Workers, Technicians, Painters, and Sculptors declared: "The creators of beauty must turn their work into clear ideological propaganda for the people, and make art, which at present is mere individualist masturbation, something of beauty, education, and purpose for everyone."[11]

David Shapiro describes social realism in terms of socialist politics, and writes that "Social Realism attempted to use art to protest and dramatize injustice to the working class—the result, as these artists saw it, of capitalist exploitation."[12] Art historian Patricia Hills, a contributor to this volume, defines social realism as not so much a style but "an attitude toward the role of art in life" that emerged during the mid-1930s.[13] Cecile Whiting suggests a more inclusive definition that includes art with "social, though not sectarian messages."[14] These writers emphasize the message of the art rather than its formal vocabulary, and its potential to create class consciousness that can lead to social change. Most art historians insist on a clear distinction between social realism and Socialist

Realism, the officially sanctioned style of the USSR. First conceptualized
in 1932 by Karl Radek and Nikolay Bukharin, the doctrine of Socialist
Realism was presented to an international audience in 1934, when
Andrei Zhdanov, secretary of the Communist Party and Stalin's chief
cultural commissar, addressed the first Congress of Soviet Writers in
Moscow. Socialist Realism was official, academic, and controlled by the
Communist International in Moscow, and according to Zhdanov was the
only art appropriate to "the building of Communism."[15] The nomencla
ture social realism, by contrast, has some of the flavor of the ideals of the
Popular Front. Just as the Popular Front was an attempt to put allegiance
to communism aside so as to unite leftist artists and intellectuals in the
struggle against fascism, social realism as a construct brings together a
wide range of left-leaning artists regardless of their relationship to the
Communist Party. To paraphrase cultural historian Michael Denning,
social realists do not necessarily adhere to any one political dogma, but
they "labor on the left."[16] For every Hugo Gellert, a member of the Communist Party who illustrated the writings of Karl Marx, there were many
more artists like Paul Cadmus, who participated in events like the NAACP-
sponsored exhibition "An Art Commentary on Lynching," (13 February–
2 March 1935), was a member of the Artists Union, and signed the 1936
call for the American Artists' Congress. (As Jonathan Weinberg points
out, Cadmus said his politics were "pinkish" rather than red, alluding
archly to both his homosexuality and his political leanings.)

More troubling than the variety of terms used to describe the leftist art of the period—"social realism," social viewpoint," "social content,"
and "proletarian art"—is the vagueness of their meanings. In 1933 Meyer
Schapiro, writing under the alias "John Kwait," complained in the *New
Masses* about the lack of focus of the John Reed Club of New York City's
exhibition "The Social Viewpoint in Art":

> What is *The Social Viewpoint in Art?* It is as vague and empty as "the
> social viewpoint" in politics. It includes any picture with a worker,
> a factory or a city-street, no matter how remote from the needs of a
> class-conscious worker. It justifies the showing of [Thomas Hart] Ben-
> ton's painting of negroes shooting crap as a picture of negro life, or a
> landscape with a contented farmer, or a decorative painting labelled
> "French Factory." The mere presence of such "social" elements in a
> picture does not indicate any social viewpoint, since these elements
> are often treated abstractly and picturesquely without reference to a
> social meaning of the objects.[17]

Schapiro dreamed of a different exhibition, one that would include
"examples of cooperative work by artists,—series of prints, with a

connected content, for cheap circulation; cartoons for newspapers and magazines; posters, banners; signs; illustrations of slogans; historical pictures of the revolutionary tradition of America. Such pictures have a clear value in the fight for freedom." He called on the John Reed Club "to offer specific tasks, especially cooperative tasks, to the revolutionary artist." Jacob Burck defended the exhibition from Schapiro's attack, insisting that the goal was "to rally all artists whose sympathies are swinging leftward. It served its function well historically by making a thorough resume of this new development among the artists. Until the economic crisis, art (painting, sculpture) was entirely a snobbish, individualistic expression based on the 'gold standard' of bourgeois society. The 'social viewpoint' in politics, is of course absurd, but the social viewpoint in art is a *decided change* leftward from its former one of 'bananas and prisms.'"[18]

We find ourselves in sympathy with both positions. On the one hand it seems absurd to limit the discussion to works by those relatively few artists in the Western Hemisphere who were committed communist. At the same time, like Schapiro, we are worried by the vagueness of the terms used to designate and understand the art of the left. Recognizing that the term social realism was not contemporary, we wished to pull the term apart and examine its two separate components—the first indebted more to the realm of politics and sociology, and the second to nineteenth-century literary and artistic traditions.[19] And so we challenged the authors of this anthology to rethink some aspect of the crucial words "social" and "real." How did government and community function in the career of individual artists? What role did a conception of "the masses" or "the proletariat" play in the artist's understanding of his or her task? Do works of art from the period simply mirror powerful economic and social forces, or did they accomplish political work, causing people to think and act differently, creating a lasting impact on the social structure? To what degree was representation itself understood to be a matter of ideological struggle, so that the work of art conveyed not only the truth of everyday life but also the mechanisms of truth telling?

By inviting essayists to reconsider the meaning of both the social and the real, we asked that they broaden the social issues of the era beyond the dominant one of class and labor. In the end, such reconsideration brings into question the "realness" of the artists' social vision, which often projected utopian social ideals—active healthy workers at a time of mass unemployment, racially harmonious workforces despite heightened racial conflict, and the absence of images of women as wage earners and laborers. The contributors to this anthology explore how the representation of race, gender, and sexuality operates within the visual culture of the period and how these elements interacted with the class struggle.[20]

We have grouped the fourteen essays that follow into major themes to identify key issues raised by the authors. These themes should be considered borders to be crossed, as we encourage readers to draw their own connections between the essays. In Part I, "Representing the Nation: Reality and Authenticity," five writers consider what artists, audiences, and patrons perceived to be stylistic and thematic realism. While many artists were committed to social values that transcended that of the nation-state, their artistic production was still rooted in and informed by their country's immediate social conditions.

As Alan Trachtenberg writes in "Signifying the Real: Documentary Photography in the 1930s," during the Great Depression and the "breakdown of the world's greatest industrial society," photography emerged as the leading documentary medium. The "non-style" photographs by Dorothea Lange, Walker Evans, Ben Shahn, and others showing the destitute and the dustbowl came to define reality. Photography reached such prominence because the public needed to believe in the veracity of the artists' vision; photography, in turn, could not fulfill its documentary mission without the public's confidence. The task of documentary photography became to locate, recover, and preserve the "real" America in order to assure the nation's future.

Likewise, Cuban modernist artists, who shared with the rest of their generation a yearning for national sovereignty, sought to represent and define national culture by isolating what was authentically Cuban. They accomplished this, writes Juan A. Martínez in "Social and Political Commentary in Cuban Modernist Painting of the 1930s," by choosing as their subject matter Cuban peasants, the Afro-Cuban, the industrial worker, and such national heroes as José Martí. Sharing Trachtenberg's concern with the connection between artist and audience, Martínez questions the social role of images of "authentic Cuba," since these paintings primarily reached the white middle class and elite segments of society. Mary K. Coffey's "The 'Mexican Problem': Nation and 'Native' in Mexican Muralism and Cultural Discourse," examines postrevolutionary Mexico's identification of the nation with the native, and looks at how pre-Hispanic heritage—seen as the most authentic Mexican culture—came to signify revolutionary politics.

Although the Mexican mural movement influenced artists throughout the Americas, most governments, unlike Mexico's in the early 1920s, were not revolutionary and did not patronize leftist monumental wall art. Just as we lack an exact definition or application of the term social realism, we lack a single model for politically engaged imagery that can be applied throughout the Americas. "Canadian Political Art in the

1930s," by Marylin McKay, draws attention to artists who operated on the left but ultimately argues for a standard of political imagery internal to Canada. Overall, Canadian social realism displayed more "reserve and restraint," than that of other nations, writes McKay.

"Adapting to Argentinean Reality: The New Realism of Antonio Berni" likewise traces both the intellectual and stylistic formation of painter Antonio Berni against the backdrop of 1930s Argentinean social realities. Berni, as Alejandro Anreus writes, developed his vision of a critical realism based on his own brand of heterodox Marxism, which he derived from the necessary adaptation of Marxist principles to the realities of contemporary Argentinean life.

The visual culture of social realism was in large measure a masculine enterprise—most of the artists, critics, political leaders, government patrons, and officials were men; much of the cultural discourse centered on male achievements and on the symbolic and economic value of the healthy male worker. There were of course exceptions, such as Diego Rivera's depiction of his wife, Frida Kahlo, distributing rifles in his mural for the Ministry of Education (1923–24). The essays in Part II, "Men, Manhood, and the Male Body" explore the artistic representation of the male body and masculinity in social realist prints, paintings, and sculpture. Jonathan Weinberg's "I Want Muscle" can be considered a corrective to current art-historical literature, which acknowledges the centrality of the male worker image but circumvents the obvious erotic charge of such images. Regardless of the gender or sexual orientation of the artist, in a wide range of social realist productions there is a quality of muscular excess that suggests an emotional investment in the male form. What was the appeal of the hypermasculine worker during this period, asks Weinberg, and how was the lingering focus on the male physique seen as appropriate? Further, what was the tension between the representation of physical labor, which was valued as masculine, and that of artistic creation, which was deemed effeminate?

Jacqueline Francis draws attention to a never-realized mural project proposed under President Franklin D. Roosevelt's New Deal arts projects, entitled *Negro Achievement* (1934), by artists Malvin Gray Johnson and Earle W. Richardson. At the 1936 American Artists' Congress, painter Aaron Douglas, in "The Negro in American Culture," addressed the lack of attention paid to African American art and artists. "It is when we come to revolutionary art that we find the Negro sincerely represented," he wrote, "but here the portrayal is too frequently automatic, perfunctory and arbitrary. He becomes a kind of revolutionary prop, a symbol, vague and abstract."[21] It can be argued that the denial of artistic agency and self-representation was itself a negation of manhood and of the male privilege of functioning within the public sphere, albeit one more readily grasped by white men than African American men and women. In contrast to stereotypical social realist depictions of black men, Francis writes that Johnson and Richardson's proposed pantheon of black male heroes established history as "the decisive action of men," countered "accusations of black cowardice and passivity," and showed the two artists' investment in traditional notions of patriotism and manhood while simultaneously revealing racial violence in the United States.

An extreme example of that violence was the lynching of black men, which increased dramatically during the 1930s and which artists of diverse races and nationalities sought to protest through their work. The visual, legislative, and rhetorical discourse of both lynching and anti-lynching centers primarily on the black male body. Marlene Park examines two competing exhibitions, one organized by the John Reed Club and the other by the NAACP, that showed the response of artists to this epidemic of lynching and the fight for legislative reforms. The African American struggle for artistic and political self-representation informed both the images and the two exhibitions.

Two essays form Part III, "Labor and Labor Conflict." The worker stood at the center of leftist visual production, just as the condition of the worker stood at the center of Marxist and socialist theories. Artists on the left envisioned their imagery—which overwhelmingly displayed workers in heavy industrial labor—as stirring class consciousness while providing, to paraphrase literary scholar Barbara Foley, an "emancipatory message."[22] Patricia Hills, in "Art and Politics in the Popular Front: The Union Work and Social Realism of Philip Evergood," tells us that it was a police beating that radicalized Evergood, but that later, upon reading the news of the so-called "Memorial Day Massacre" at South Chicago's Republic Steel Plant, Evergood painted his sharpest social realist statement, *American Tragedy* (1937). This expressive painting of "determined class struggle" depicts a racially diverse workforce of both men and women. But unlike Evergood's direct statement of labor conflict and violence, Diego Rivera's *Detroit Industry* murals (1932–33), writes Anthony W. Lee, convey a leftist fantasy of the American worker that failed to confront American working-class racism and instead reveal Rivera's belief in an unalienated workforce.

Whereas class is a social reality and relationship that can change, race, gender, and ethnicity are "experiential realities" that inform class relations but cannot be eradicated.[23] Many of the essays in this volume explore the intersection of class with race, gender, and ethnicity in social realist art—Rivera's experiences with racially charged Detroit, for example. Yet the two essays in Part IV, "Voices on the Margins," focus specifically on marginalized identities as both producer and subject matter. Artist Paraskeva Clark, writes Natalie Luckyj, was a triple outsider to

Canadian society—she was a woman, an émigré (born in Russia), and a socialist, in addition to being an artist. Clark's paintings served as "contact zones" that enabled her to fuse public and private identities and to negotiate her outsider status. Further, Clark's status as an "exotic outsider" permitted her to challenge the Canadian status quo and social expectations.

As Diana L. Linden writes in "Ben Shahn's New Deal Murals: Jewish Identity in the American Scene," American artist Ben Shahn, who served as an assistant to Diego Rivera, was a working-class Jew who sought to represent Jewish historical experiences and political concerns in his New Deal murals. Public murals became for Shahn a forum both for representing the Jewish working class and its concerns and for literally painting Jews into the American Scene.

"Extending the Discourse," the concluding section of the anthology, invites us to reconsider the timeframe and the endpoint of social realism, and also to acknowledge its continued impact on visual culture. Andrew Hemingway's "Between Zhdanovism and 57th Street: Artists and the CPUSA, 1945–56," disproves the popular misconception that the cultural movement around the CPUSA disintegrated with the Nazi-Soviet Pact and that politically motivated art went into sharp decline. Hemingway draws attention to the "institutional base through which communist and fellow-traveling artists operated in the 1940s," and also establishes that artists and critics continued to be productive into the cold war era.

Focusing on representations of President Franklin D. Roosevelt, both during his tenure and since, Sally Stein discusses the issue of physical infirmity in the 1930s and how this was managed both semiotically and politically as America's need to stand strong and the president's physical barriers brought the body politic and the president's body into direct conflict. The controversies surrounding the creation of the FDR Memorial in the 1990s, which Stein charts, suggest that we are still coming to terms with the 1930s and its legacy of visual culture.

I REPRESENTING THE NATION: REALITY AND AUTHENTICITY

SIGNIFYING THE REAL:
DOCUMENTARY PHOTOGRAPHY IN THE 1930S

Alan Trachtenberg

It was in the 1930s, the decade of the Great Depression, that photography in the United States emerged as the great documentary medium of our era. Signs of economic collapse were visible everywhere, and a new visual culture arose in which images of "hard times" played a key role. In the 1920s the most common popular images, featured in advertisements in newspapers and magazines and plastered on roadside billboards, had trumpeted prosperity and a good life for middle-class families: new cars, new radios, a new variety of electric household goods, new fashions in dress and makeup, unlimited opportunities for pleasure on the installment plan. Now, in the 1930s, these images took on a bitter, ironic edge. As the trauma of the stock market crash of 1929 spread across the country, as banks failed and factories shut down and small farmers lost their land, the face of the nation changed demonstrably. As boom gave way to bust and, later in the decade, drought and dust storms hit the Great Plains, breadlines, soup kitchens, and migrant camps took the place of shining kitchens overflowing with food and gadgets. Images of idle workers, hungry children, ragged families on the road, the parched faces of Dust Bowl refugees fleeing not in swanky new automobiles but in broken-down old jalopies—pictures of a society on the edge now competed with the still-pervasive scenario of advertising photography, and "documentary" emerged as a contentious but undeniable presence on the American scene.

The breakdown of the world's greatest industrial society provided the spectacle, and the culture of photography developed the tools to record it. With the greater mobility and speed of smaller cameras, the use of flash bulbs, and the appearance by mid-decade of big picture magazines, photography was "fast being discovered," as Roy Stryker put it in a retrospective essay in 1973, "as a serious tool of communication, a new way for a thoughtful, creative person to make a statement."[1] With new openings for careers in photography, in journalism, book publishing, and government work, significant numbers of young artists, including many women, turned to the camera for their vocation. Whether working for government agencies or the new picture magazines like *Life, Look,* and *Fortune,* photographers captured scenes and faces that have survived in the collective historical record as indelible impressions of life in the 1930s. The Great Depression has been so powerfully portrayed by photography that it sometimes seems the invention of documentary artists like Dorothea Lange, Walker Evans, Ben Shahn, and their colleagues. Their pictures have come to seem definitive of the ways things were, of the very reality of the day.

By themselves, of course, even the best photographs cannot convey a full picture of a period, of its nuances and subtleties, its contradictions, the invisible lines of power in the economy and in the social relations that lie behind the look of the times. Like any set of facts taken in isolation, demographic data, for example, or unemployment figures, a photograph by itself stands as a lonely sentinel of the unspoken and the unseen, radically incomplete and possibly distorted as social knowledge. Arrayed on gallery walls or on the pages of elegant art books, documentary photographs of the 1930s may even interfere with historical knowledge, distracting us from a quest for underlying causes, from tracing visible clues to invisible meanings. If ever works of art demand to be understood contextually, restored in the imagination to their original times, seen and interpreted in light of the history they record, this is emphatically true of the documentary photographs of the Great Depression. As we come to understand the conditions and the circumstances out of which they appeared, we can better appreciate the aesthetic power many of them possess, a power that criticism seeks to connect to the historical knowledge they convey. For the great achievement of this decade in photography was to demonstrate that a photograph can be both a document and a work of art simultaneously, each dimension supporting and strengthening the other. The best works of Walker Evans, Dorothea Lange, Ben Shahn, Berenice Abbott, and others show that in the literalness of photography, its documentary function of showing the social world as it appears to the eye, lies the genuine aesthetic power of the medium.

That so many photographers chose to show a social world in a state of travail, distress, even upheaval, was itself a sign of a changed outlook among artists. Documentary photography was only one of the period's expressions of a revived concern with society as a subject of art and literature. If the 1920s, on the whole, were a time of experiment in the

arts, of high modernism, abstraction, and formalism, the 1930s were a
time predominantly of commitment to subject matter, of concern with
social truth in a mode of realism. Of course, like all generalizations, this
one says both too much and too little. Exceptions have to be taken into
account and qualifications made. The visual arts of the period were both
more complex and less homogenous than the capacious term "realism"
implies. But the fact that photography in a documentary mode or style
achieved such prominence in the period does suggest a strong desire
and need by artists and public alike for images signifying contemporary
reality—for a visual art based upon the "real," committed to identifying
and exploring exactly what could be recognized and accepted as American reality at this time. The sense of urgency was great, the compulsion
to know what was happening in the society that reached across so vast
a land, the undeniable visual facts of the here and now, exactly the kind
of subject matter photography, among all the visual arts, seemed best
equipped to convey. As photographs of social conditions filtered into the
popular media, confidence in photography as a means of defining reality increased strikingly. Another peculiar feature of the photographic
medium is that without public confidence in the truth of its images, the
documentary function could not possibly thrive.

The recognition of photography as, in the words of writer James
Agee, "the central instrument of our time" in helping us perceive "the
cruel radiance of what is," testifies to a state of mind, of hope and desire
and need in response to the social casualties of the Depression and the
collapse of American confidence.[2] For along with those visible material
casualties—no job, no pay, no food, old clothes, worn-out shoes, broken-
down cars—a major invisible casualty was the erosion of belief in the
old conception of the "real" in America: a happy, prospering society
of family farms and small towns, where hard steady work earned the
rewards of prosperity and security, a safe future for the children. For
many Americans the Depression destroyed confidence in the old slogans, the old illusions about reality, about what could be trusted as a
true account of things. For many, this loss of belief led to loss of hope in
the future, to anxiety, desperation, days and nights lived in fear of the
next catastrophe—loss even, in Horace McCoy's extraordinary novel
They Shoot Horses, Don't They? (1935), of the desire to live. The crippling
dance marathon depicted in that novel, its desperation, cruelty, and violence, its thrill-seeking mobs of spectators, became a powerful symbol of
hopelessness, cynicism, and entrapment. For some, loss of confidence led
to a new set of beliefs, a new basis for hope: in labor unions, in the "new
deal" offered by a new government led by that smiling symbol of hope,
Franklin Delano Roosevelt, or in even more radical hopes of a reconstructed society, a socialist America based on justice and fairness. At the

other pole a small but vociferous fascist movement appeared, spewing hatred at blacks, Jews, communists, and New Dealers. Conflicting views and incendiary passions fired up the climate of opinion in these years.

On the whole, documentary photography was the product of young artists committed to one or another of the more hopeful views, either liberal reformist, linked to FDR's programs for reviving the capitalist system by means of government assistance to farmers and small businesses, relief for jobless workers, greater controls over the economy and more reliable safeguards, or to the more radical programs for government intervention on the part of the labor movement and the socialist and communist left. While many photographers, working on their own or in groups like the left-wing Photo League of New York city, also adapted a documentary mode, the most important support for documentary photography came from New Deal government agencies, and the most important of these was the Farm Security Administration, the FSA, which undertook, starting in 1935, an epic project to record and thereby define American reality in photos. The FSA has become synonymous with documentary photography of the 1930s, and it is here that we will find the most influential account of its conception and practices at the time.

The FSA cannot be understood apart from the pressures, conflicts, hopes, and confusions of the times. "The American people," the writer Harvey Swados commented in 1966, "were as absolutely unprepared for the Great Depression as if it had been a volcanic eruption in Kansas or Nebraska, pouring red-hot lava from coast to coast and border to border."[3] A vivid, biting account of the shock of the collapse appears in a poem by Kenneth Fearing from his book of 1938, *Dead Reckoning:*

> But it could never be
>> how could it ever happen if it never did before and
>> it's not so now....
>
> But what if it is, what if it is, what if it is, what if the thing
>> that cannot happen really happens just the
>> same
>> suppose the fever goes to a hundred, then a hundred and one
>> what if Holy Savings Trust goes from 98 to 88 to
>>> 78 to 68, then drops down to 28 and 8 and out of sight
>> and the fever shoots a hundred and two, a hundred
>>> three, a hundred four, then a hundred five and
>>> out
>
> But now there's only the wind and the sky and sunlight
>> and the clouds,
>> with everyday people walking and talking as they

> always have before along the everyday street
> doing ordinary things with ordinary faces and
> ordinary voices in the ordinary way
> just as they always will
>
> Then why does it feel like a bomb, why does it feel like a
> target
> like standing on the gallows with the trap about to
> drop
> why does it feel like a thunderbolt the second
> before it strikes, why does it feel like a
> tightrope the second before it strikes, why
> does it feel like a tightrope walk high over
> hell
>
> Because it is not, will not, never could be true
> that the whole wide, bright, green, warm, calm
> world goes
> CRASH.[4]

The literal crash occurred on Wall Street in the fall of 1929. There had been economic crises before, losses of confidence, widespread unemployment, but never on such a scale and never calling so many of the assumptions of the market system into question. Along with the economic and social effects, we have to add the cultural effects of the crisis, responses that took the form of new ideas, new values, and new forms of representation, such as documentary photography. In the 1920s values had been keyed to the pursuit of individual wealth, the acquisition of goods not just for use but for prestige, a period when advertising emerged as a major industry with the sole purpose of persuading people to buy and enjoy. The downward spiral of the early 1930s led to a temporary revulsion against excessive consumerism and high living without regard for tomorrow. After the crash there emerged a struggle against the belief system, the definitions of reality itself, that had prevailed during the great bull market, what F. Scott Fitzgerald called in a story of 1931 "the big party."

"Well, the big party's over now," Fitzgerald remarked with a bitter smile.[5] Something had indeed ended, had simply fallen apart, and for some it wasn't only the bubble of prosperity that had burst but the whole supporting system of beliefs: faith in the market, in capitalism itself; belief in the Horatio Alger myth of the self-made man; belief in self-reliance itself, in acquisitive individualism as an appropriate ideal for the nation. The dramatically unequal distribution of pain after the crash, the vast lower end of the society suffering far more severely

than the upper end, brought home to many people how fundamentally
unjust was the distribution of income and resources in the first place.
Not surprisingly, a note of betrayal, a sense of having been cheated by
false promises, appeared in the outburst of personal writings of these
years, from essays and stories to personal memoirs and travel books
to the extraordinary letters from people from all walks of life—many
millions of them—sent to President Roosevelt and his wife. What did
we do to deserve all this, loss of job, loss of savings and property, loss
of security—even loss of the will to live?[6]

Some observers at the time were puzzled by the relative stoicism of
the bottom dogs of the society. Why did such widespread hardship not
lead to revolution? For some writers, like McCoy and Nathaneal West,
the escapist fantasies of mass culture seemed an explanation. In *Miss
Lonelyhearts* (1933) West writes about what his hero sees on the streets
of the city: "He saw a man who appeared to be on the verge of death
stagger into a movie theater that was showing a picture called *Blonde
Beauty*. He saw a ragged woman with an enormous goiter pick a love
story magazine out of a garbage can and seem very excited by her find."[7]
Another explanation is that the policies implemented by FDR in the first
hundred days of his administration, starting in 1933, did relieve the situation somewhat, if not decisively. At least the New Deal offered an image
of hope, and Roosevelt's extraordinary fireside chats, the soothing, convincing tone of his voice, his winning smile, did offer reassurance that
government, now in the hands of compassionate and caring leaders,
would do its best.

Some historians have ventured a more complex cultural explanation.
Even in the most difficult days, belief in a "bright, green, warm, calm
world" in fact persisted—an ordinary, everyday American world, the
true America, still intact beneath the debris of the crash, not only persisted but paradoxically gained strength. There was "an upsurge," Swados
observed, "of national self-awareness—not a patriotic fervor like that
triggered by war or invasion, but rather a reawakening of the consciousness that America was a unified land, that its problems were national
problems, that its misery was national, that solutions and resolutions
would have to be national."[8] It was an upsurge of belief that a nation did
indeed exist, if only we could find and identify it—that it existed as a
body, an entity that the mad, self-destructive quest for private wealth in
the 1920s had obscured. Even the Communist Party of the United States
adopted as a slogan, in its Popular Front period after 1935, "Communism
is Americanism."

A "search for the 'real' America," as historian Warren I. Susman has
put it, underlay most of the social criticism, the laments and complaints
of the period.[9] A rhetoric of commitment to the recovery of the body

of the nation, to a national community of equal persons, regardless of race or religion, to a body wounded but still vital, has been the most prominent cultural legacy of the 1930s. It reappears at times of national trouble, such as the civil rights and antiwar movements of the 1960s, and in the periodic revivals of interest in the documentary photography of the era, as in the 1960s and more recently in the 1990s. For, while much of that photography displays powerful evidence of crash and depression and can well be taken as an indictment of a cruel and unfeeling social system, documentary photography as a whole was very much part of the mainstream search for a "real," an authentic, American Way of Life. This is unmistakably true of the FSA, the major documentary project of the period. Under the directorship of Roy Stryker, the Historical Section of the FSA assigned to photography precisely that role: to serve as an instrument for the perception and recovery of a resurgent "real" America.

Looking back at the pictures of the 1930s from the perspective of the 1970s, Stryker grew nostalgic (as indeed he was even in the 1930s) for a "lost America." People "don't give a damn anymore," he wrote. "You look at these pictures before people lost—what? The ability to care. The ability to take simple pleasures. The ability to take life however it came. You could look at the people and see fear and sadness and desperation. But you saw something else, too. A determination that not even the Depression could kill. The photographers saw it—documented it."[10] A native of Kansas, Stryker had taken a degree in economics at Columbia in the early 1920s, then stayed on as an assistant to Rexford Tugwell. A prominent liberal economist, Tugwell became a member of FDR's "brain trust" of academic intellectuals who helped shape the initial recovery and relief policies of the New Deal, and in 1935 was named head of the Resettlement Administration, a government agency charged with helping struggling farmers adjust to new conditions. Tugwell appointed Stryker as head of the Historical Section of the RA (which a year later was changed to the FSA), with the charge to "direct the activities of investigators, photographers, economists, sociologists and statisticians engaged in the accumulation and compilations of reports," etc.[11]

Before long this broad charge became something much more sharply focused. "I'd tell the photographers," Stryker recalled years later, "look for the significant detail. The kinds of things that a scholar a hundred years from now is going to wonder about."[12] Enlarging the original purpose of the Historical Section, he instructed his photographers, in the famous shooting scripts he supplied, to photograph not only the routine official business of the agency, housing projects, farmers on federal aid, and so on, but everything they saw that revealed the American reality, people at work and play, towns, road signs, railroad stations, barber shops, the weather, the objects on top of a chest of drawers in Grundy

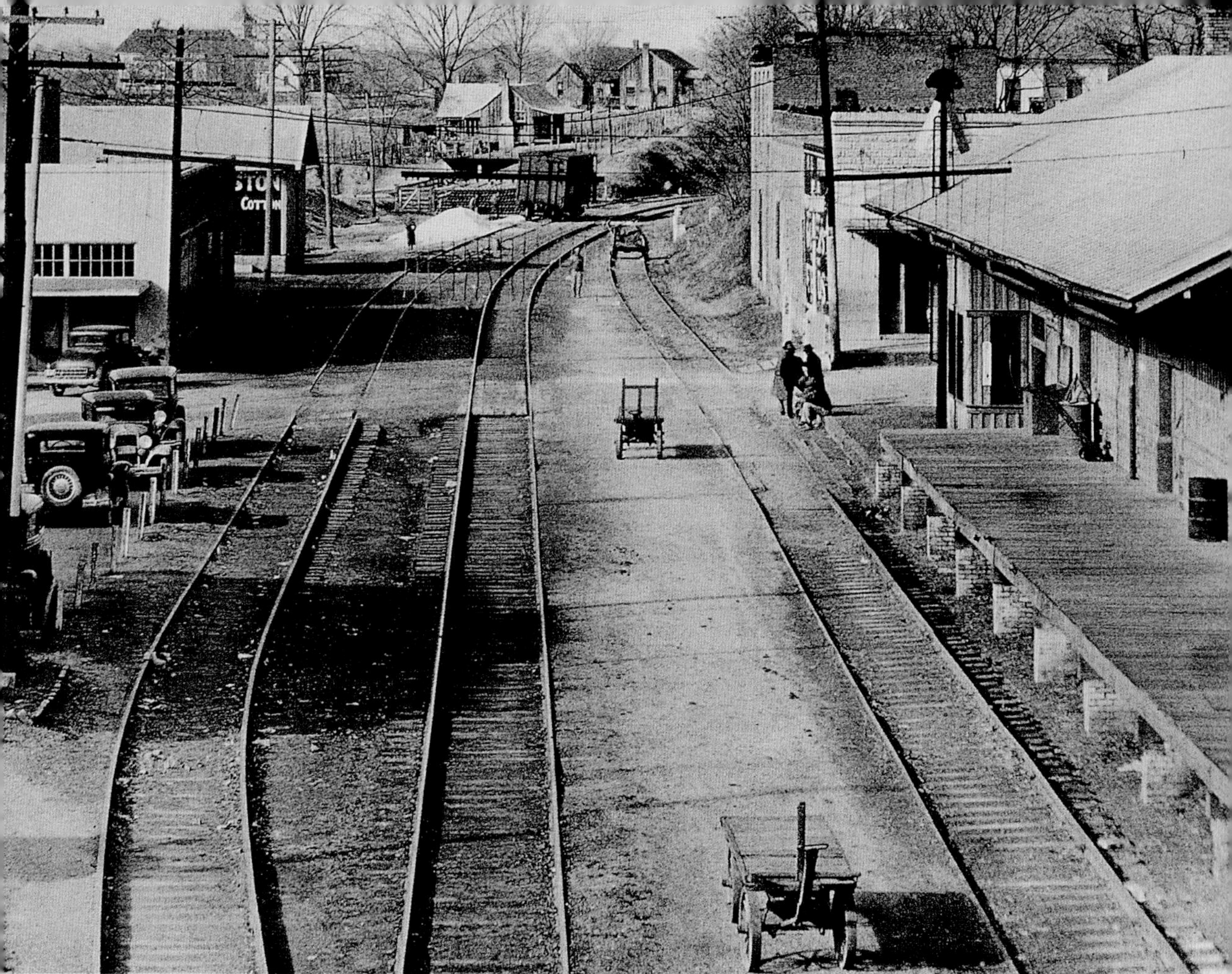

Co., Iowa. The expansion of the original charge owes something to a dream Stryker had cherished of producing an encyclopedic study of American agriculture in pictures. The family farm was already a fast-disappearing way of life, and the Depression sounded its death knell. Stryker wished to create a record of what was being lost. "I remember," he wrote in 1973, "Walker Evans' picture of the train tracks in a small town. ... The empty station platform, the station thermometer, the idle baggage carts, the quiet stores, the people talking together, and beyond them, the weather-beaten houses where they lived, all this reminded me of the town where I had grown up" (fig. 1).[13]

Walker Evans, one of the first photographers he hired for the project—Ben Shahn was another—provided something more than imagery for Stryker's small-town nostalgia. Evans joined the project in 1935 with an already carefully articulated and ardently advocated idea of what he believed photography could accomplish. In a 1931 essay he had described the kind of photography he wanted to achieve, based on what he had seen of the pictures of Eugene Atget and August Sander: "a photographic editing of society, a clinical process; even enough of a cultural necessity to make one wonder why other so-called advanced

1 Walker Evans, Railroad Station, Edwards, Mississippi (February 1936). FSA.

countries of the world have not also been examined and recorded."[14] Evans had a major impact on Stryker's conception of his new job. "I saw his pictures, I walked at night with him and I talked to him. He told me about what the photographer was for, what a photographer should do, and he gave me his rationale for pictures. It was extremely interesting because it was opening up a whole new field of ideas."[15] A year earlier Evans had described to an editor friend the kind of subjects he wished to explore in photography, and we can imagine his recounting these plans and hopes to his new boss in 1935:

> People, all classes, surrounded by bunches of the new down-and-out.
> Automobiles and the automobile landscape.
> Architecture, American urban taste, commerce, small scale, large scale,
> the city street atmosphere, the street smell,
> the hateful stuff, women's clubs, fake culture,
> bad education, religion in decay
> The movies.
> Evidence of what the people of the city read, eat, see for amusement,
> do for relaxation and not get it.[16]

In a letter to Stryker from the Pittsburgh region during his first assignment, Evans explained his "first objective" as "photography, documentary in style, of industrial subjects, emphasis on housing and home-life of working-class people. Graphic record of a complete, complex, pictorially rich modern industrial center."[17]

Eventually Evans and Stryker would part ways, but Evans's pictures and his ideas would prove to be essential components in the evolution of the FSA project, the grandest example of documentary photography in the period. For Evans, the desire simply to document by means of the camera was an end in itself, without reference to an explicit political view or principle of criticism of the faltering social order. "This is pure record not propaganda," he had written in a memorandum before accepting the job with Stryker. "The value and, if you like, even the propaganda value for the government lies in the record itself which in the long run will prove an intelligent and farsighted thing to have done. NO POLITICS whatever."[18] Resisting the subordination of his pictures to any use that might compromise their status as "pure record," Evans inevitably rubbed against Stryker's commitments as an administrator, as well as against his nostalgia and sentimentality about the "real" America. Tensions arose, and Evans was dismissed in 1938.

Whatever the personal issues, conflicts between the men signified a deeper tension within the project itself and within documentary photography as a whole in the 1930s—between the idea of the "pure record," and the needs of New Deal, or any reformist or radical political program. Evans's claim of "artistic autonomy"—Dorothea Lange, another major influence on the character of the cumulative FSA record made similar claims with equally antagonistic results—only partially accounts for the tension. Stryker attempted to serve two masters: his dream of an encyclopedic record of American reality, and his obligations as a New Deal bureaucrat. He encouraged his photographers to "photograph what they saw, really saw." At the same time he demanded pictures that promoted New Deal policies. This was a version of a larger tension experienced in the art of the period. Should the artist place a commitment to humanity, to social justice, to reform or revolution, ahead of a

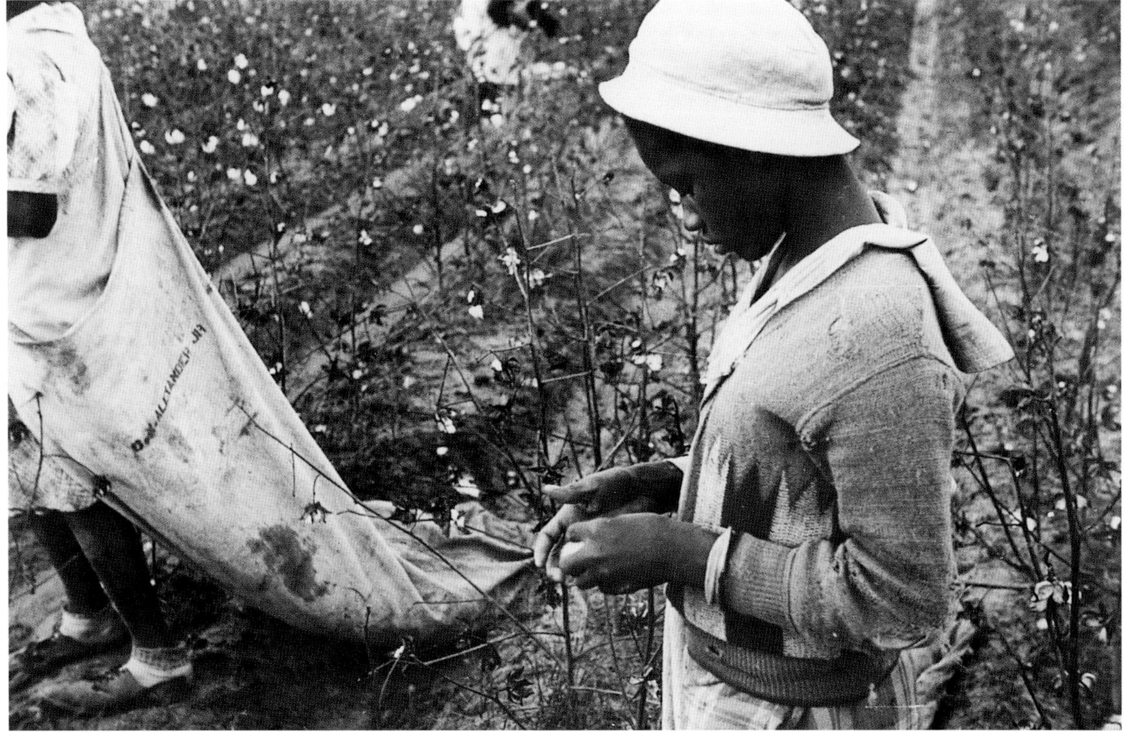

2 Ben Shahn, Cotton Picker, Pulaski County, Arkansas (October 1935). FSA.

commitment to art itself? We find traces of this dilemma in the literature, drama, and visual art of the period, in controversies over realism and modernism, surrealism and abstraction, the "proletarian novel," the relation of drama to political action, and the appropriate subjects and themes for mural art.

Tension between "pure record and propaganda" ran throughout the FSA project, and it is reflected in the monumental FSA file at the Library of Congress, as we can see, for example, in the work of Ben

Shahn, Dorothea Lange, and others (fig. 2). Documentary photographers of the era strove to close the gap by attention to craft and lucidity of style. Others include Berenice Abbott, whose documentation of "changing New York" (fig. 3) was sponsored by the WPA, and the twin brothers, Marvin and Morgan Smith, whose work in Harlem from the late 1930s through the 1960s presents a chronicle of street life, entertainment, politics, sports, and public events. The Smith brothers tried to avoid depicting downtrodden residents of slum areas, seeking instead to celebrate black achievement, especially in portraits of black celebrities. Their work deserves mention as documentary in a different register, a counterpoint to the FSA pictures, for example, which carry the angrier visual message of Richard Wright's *Twelve Million Black Voices* (1942).[19]

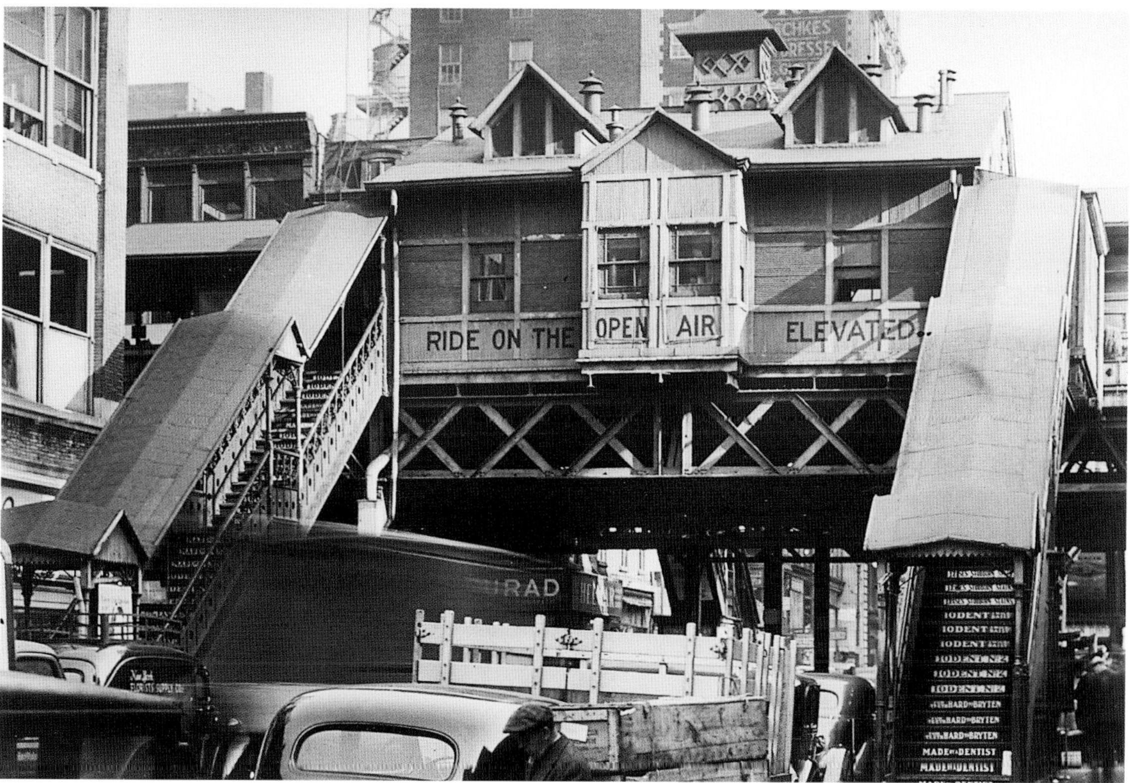

3 Berenice Abbott, "El," Sixth Avenue Line, 28th Street Station (10 November 1938). WPA.

How were the FSA pictures received and understood at the time? One notable reception occurred in 1939, when Edward Steichen presented a group of forty FSA images in that year's *US Camera Annual*. The pictures had appeared in an International Photographic Exposition held in New York to mark the hundredth anniversary of the birth of photography, thus taking their place within the history of the medium as, in Steichen's words, "the most remarkable human documents that were ever rendered in pictures." Steichen explained "documentary" as pictures that "tell a story." "Have a look into the faces of the men and the women in these pages. Listen to the story they tell." As if to enhance the story, or provoke the reader, Steichen included actual writing on the face of each image culled from written comments submitted by visitors to the exhibition. The comments show outrage, sympathy, sensitivity, and obtuseness. The words "Next time play up the other side" appears on the Russell Lee picture of four children standing before their grubby Christmas dinner. "Subversive propaganda" was written on Dorothea Lange's migrant mother.[20]

For Steichen, of course, the pictures told other stories. "Fierce stories of strong, gaunt men and women in time of flood and drought," he wrote. The events recorded in the pictures, Steichen wanted us to feel, took place "out there," in the real world. They belonged to a space that is not our space. In Steichen's version, the pictures were transparent communications of the story of those who suffer. The sympathy and pity and perhaps guilt we feel confirm for us that we have indeed heard a story, have had "a living experience." We ourselves are not among the afflicted; it is a crisis of the "lower orders"—uneducated, chronically poor blacks and whites, drifting migrant families—an order we can only look "down" upon in an act of self-ennoblement. The story Steichen tells is a "pastoral" one in that the downtrodden and lowly instruct us in dignity, humility, sorrow.[21]

Steichen's interpretation reveals one very characteristic response and use of documentary photographs in the 1930s, as a means of presenting and thus affiliating "low" subjects to ordinary middle-class viewers, a way of pointing to an elsewhere, out there, where reality occurs. The pictures brought reality from the outside to the inside. And it was their "realism," the assumption went, their commitment to "the real," that enabled this transference. But the word "realism" can be misleading. What we believe is "real" may well turn out to be something made up, a construction, a fiction—and yet, not necessarily any the less "real" as an indicator of a world outside the frame of the image.

One notion popular at the time was that what is real is true and timeless, typical and universal. The most famous of all the FSA pictures, Lange's "Migrant Mother" (fig. 4), is an instructive example. Countless pictures of migrant mothers and children made by many of the photographers appear in the FSA files, enough to call that configuration one of the key images in the entire project. But Lange's picture stands out; it has been treated as representative of the common trope in a way that reveals one of the underlying tensions within documentary photography as a whole. The "holy mother" theme captions the image, places it so that we can experience the universal in the immediate, the sacred incarnate

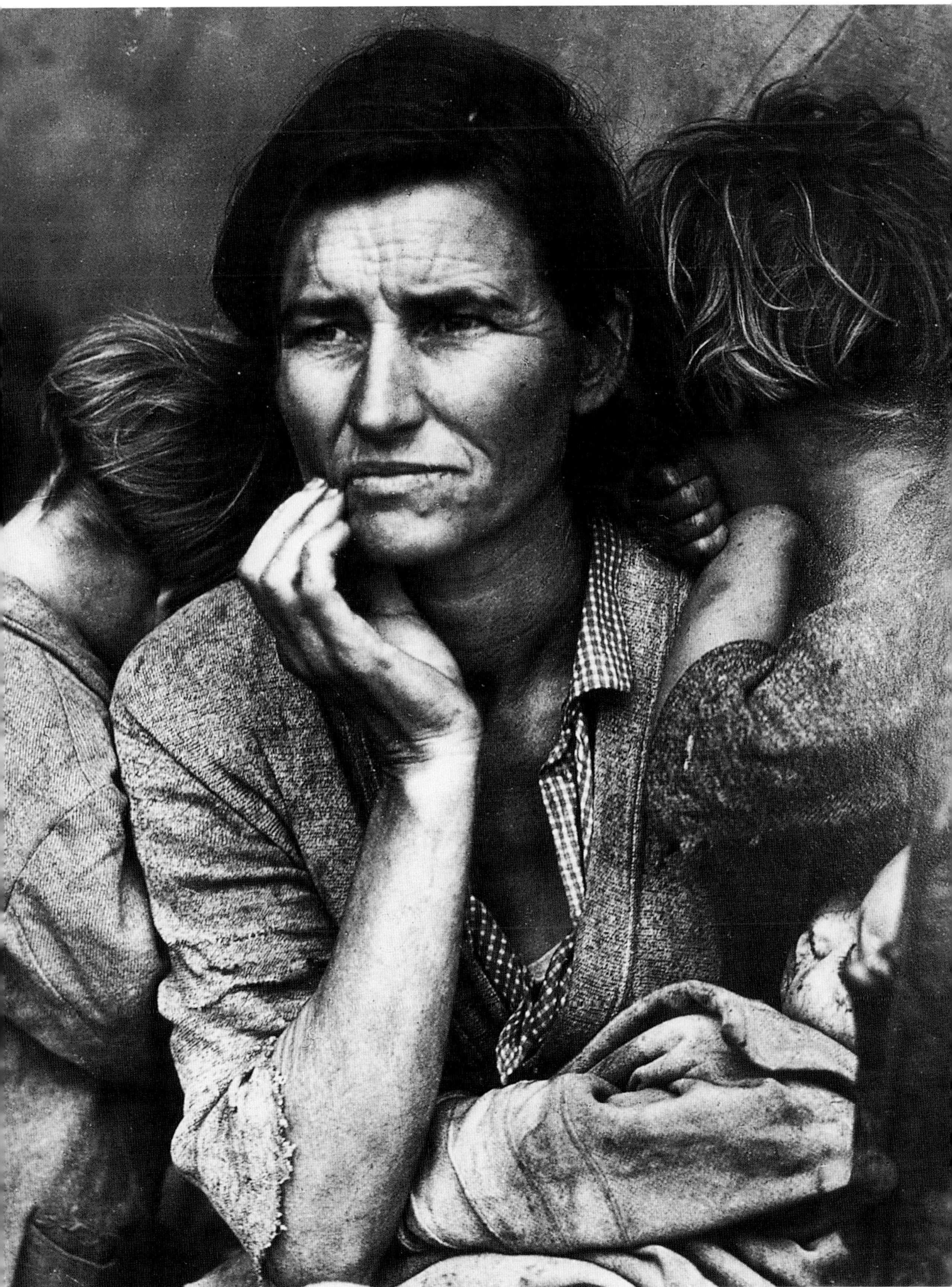

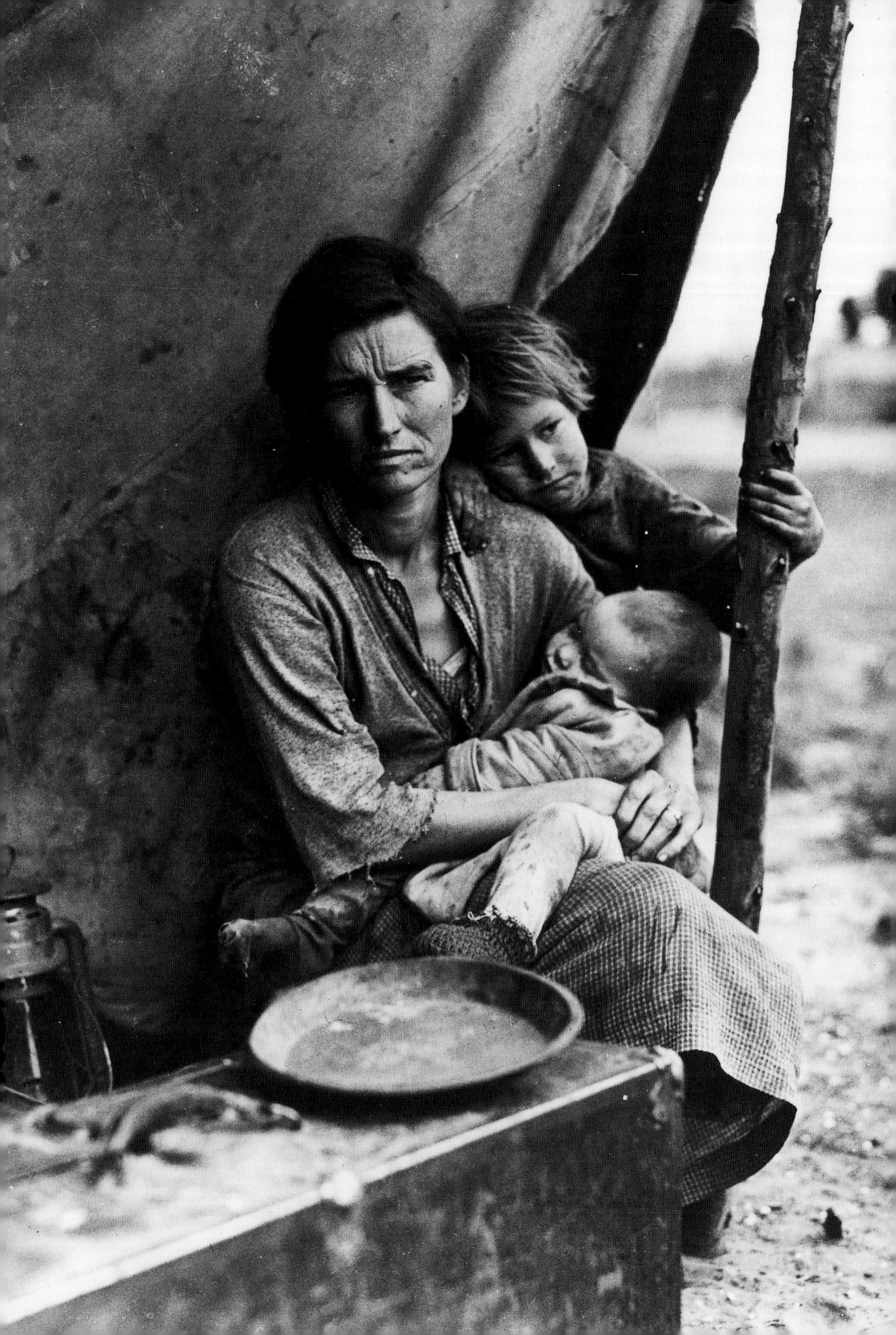

in the humble. We also notice dramatic differences from the traditional Madonna image. The mother wears a worried rather than a beatific look; the children cling for protection rather than loll in bliss. The differences produce a pointedly alienating and dissociated effect: how worn and beaten, how sorrowful, this holy mother, who takes upon herself the entire spiritual trauma of the times—the social destitution of the poor and outcast. If there is redemptive power here—the extraordinary fame of the image suggests it—one of its sources can only be the particularizing power of the camera, which makes Madonna seem a real creature of here and now, as frail against the storm as you and I and as inherently or "really" strong. But that is as far as the "Madonna" interpretation goes toward acknowledging the "reality," understood as *literal* factual truth, recorded in the image. Who the woman "really" is, her name and identity, what her personal circumstances are—the picture gives us none of this.

A different reading emerges when we see the image within a setting of other photographs made on the same occasion, in the context of a shooting sequence or assignment. "Madonna of the Migrants" is one thing; the same picture set within the sequence of five or six exposures made by Lange that particular gray afternoon near Nipoma, California, quite another (fig.5). We can take this group as a unit in itself, several perspectives on a single scene, Lange's camera selecting and excluding details and personae as it changes position. The mother remains the central point of interest in each, but less dominating in some than in others. The group of pictures can be read also as a sequence of "trial" takes leading up to the final image, as if the setting were a studio and Lange a director seeking a certain image, a special effect. Whether we read the group as a multiperspective account of a single scene, one of whose pictures stands out in pictorial strength, or as a kind of pyramidal process culminating in a masterpiece, the meaning of the Madonna has changed. It is no longer the Virgin in humble earthly guise, but a photograph capable of serving more than one meaning.

The lesson might be put this way: that while the motive in the 1930s to find and display the "real" America led to undeniably long-lasting achievements in documentary photography, that motive begs the question of fabrication in definitions of reality. Even the slightest adjustment in point of view, in lighting, in the type of film used, can produce a "reality" in a different register. Then there is the inescapable subjectivity of the photographer, differences in the vision, the quality of the eye, the instinctive sense of where to place the camera—all of which bear on what individual pictures give us to understand by "the real."

Differences are rarely as tangible in photographs as in other graphic media. We speak perhaps too unreflectively about a "documentary style," a favorite expression of Walker Evans. He meant the term simply as a certain straightforwardness, an absence of style, or an apparent absence, for the sake of visually lucid presentation of subject matter. We tend to use the term to refer to a whole period style, an "FSA style," by which we usually mean the subject matter of commonplace life rather than a distinctive principle of presentation. Evans also used the term "documentary style" to distinguish a kind of art from a kind of propaganda, a desire to show things without the clutter of an imposed rhetoric. In truth, it is often impossible, without prior familiarity with the image, to tell just who made what picture. Still, we can note differences, especially when we compare cases. A certain stilted air appears in Arnold Rothstein's Gee's Bend pictures against the unashamed openness, the informality and eye contact achieved by Ben Shahn in his pictures of Arkansas cotton field workers. Shahn's pictures give us a sense of movement and rhythm, of ease in the passage of the camera in and among the cotton pickers, a quality missing in Rothstein's more discursive pictures. In a group of pictures that may or may not have been made by Walker Evans on 61st Street in New York City (the uncertain authorship of these pictures illustrates the issue), the photographer's eye is drawn as much to the design of light upon façades (indicating time) as to the unconscious humor of a newsstand. The pictures convey space and time as integral, and 61st Street becomes less a physical place than a process of seeing, pausing, studying, passing, catching glimpses. We might say, but only provisionally, speculatively, that while Evans's eye is often lyrical and nonnarrative, Marion Post's is often novelistic, seeking the typical, images that burst with barely contained implication, verging at times toward the anecdotal. Lange works with people as if they were natural forces; she moves around them, toward them, under and above them, keeping a respectful distanced no matter how poor or wretched or foolish they may seem. Russell Lee appears usually as the clear-eyed reporter with an eye for "interest," for symbols of a communal moment, though next to Evans and Shahn and Lange and Post we miss a certain edge, a certain bite.

But on the whole, and this may be the most important thought, the closer to the reality of a time and place documentary photographs seem to bring us, the more distant we discover ourselves to be, distant from that fullness of being each image tempts us into believing lies complete and whole before our eyes. The reading of photographs reenacts the stubborn problem of historical memory itself: how to know a past in its completeness when all our records represent only someone's fallible and partial point of view. Rather than what Steichen called the "living experiences" of a place and a time, photographs in the end give us no more than someone's point of view, a perspective more or less intelligent, acute, knowing. As fictions, as stories, documentary photographs connect us to someone's past experience; they make that particular past seem present to us, present and real. But we can never forget the photographer within the photograph. These pictures are not scenes of history incarnate but personal propositions about reality. Reality, the sensuous and tangible apprehension of the real—certainly the documentary artists of the 1930s were in quest of nothing less. But the term realism misconstrues the accumulated Depression pictures. "Realism" imputes meanings, motives, and messages couched in honorific universals such as Stryker's remark: "There's honesty there, and compassion, and a natural regard for individual dignity; these are the things that, in my opinion, give the collection its special appeal."

The emphasis upon difference points to the self-evident but often forgotten lesson that the eye of the artist rather than the lens of the camera is finally responsible for what the photograph shows. Dorothea Lange described Stryker's shooting scripts in the following way: "No one was ever given exact directions. You were turned loose in a region, and the assignment was more like this: 'See what is really there. What does it look like, what does it feel like? What actually is the human condition?'"[22]

Photographs are not copies of the world but representations, not the measure of reality but part of the collective picturing of the real by which any culture takes its bearings. Like all representations, documentary photographs belong equally to the realm of the arbitrary, the realm of desire, as well as to the putative realm of the historical. An instrument of the eye and the will of the artist, the camera makes up stories about reality and then persuades us they are true. They invite us to see through them to a historical world they assume, but also, and at once, challenge us to see them as themselves, pictures made with particular intent and purpose and understanding, and, in the best of cases, with an infectious love of the real.

SOCIAL AND POLITICAL COMMENTARY IN CUBAN MODERNIST PAINTING OF THE 1930S

Juan A. Martínez

In Havana, on 7 May 1927, Cuban art and progressive politics first joined forces, opening the way for a decade of close collaboration between artists and left-wing intellectuals. On that evening, the Primera Exposición de Arte Nuevo (First Exhibition of New Art), organized by the cultural magazine *Revista de Avance,* opened at the Association of Painters and Sculptors' salon, launching the modernist movement in Cuban art. Earlier that day, the members of the Grupo Minorista (Minority Group), then Cuba's intellectual vanguard, wrote and signed a political and cultural manifesto known as the Declaration of the Minority Group, made public in the exhibition.[1] The advanced social program envisioned in the declaration and the paintings in the exhibition of Arte Nuevo were supposed to complement each other as the conceptual and symbolic guideposts to both a better Cuban republic and a more autonomous Cuban art.

Another event on that fateful day in Havana signaled the challenge for Cuban progressive politics and art in the coming years. The headline news that morning announced the return of President Gerardo Machado from a "victorious" visit to the United States, during which he received the continued blessing of North American business and the State Department and millions of dollars in loans to prop up the Cuban economy. Emboldened by these and other developments, Machado suspended upcoming elections in 1928 and appointed himself president for a new six-year term. Together these events set the stage for a decade of political violence and social upheaval, strengthening the alliance of many modernist artists with left-wing intellectuals and activists.

This essay aims to expand the discourse on a significant but little studied aspect of Cuban modernist art—the relationships between modernist painting, left-wing ideology, and Cuban politics in the 1930s. I am particularly interested in revisiting a significant selection of forgotten murals and somewhat better known easel paintings by Carlos Enríquez, Arístides Fernández, Antonio Gattorno, Alberto Peña (known as Peñita), and Marcelo Pogolotti, in exploring their original context and ideology, as well as their contribution to the intense cultural, social, and political debates in 1930s Cuba.[2] These debates centered on issues of Cuban independence vis-à-vis the United States, solidarity with Latin America, social justice and equality, education for all, and renewed efforts to define a Cuban cultural identity.

Cuban Modernist Art and Leftist Ideologies

The period from 1928 to 1940, from the second and self-appointed term of Machado to the inauguration of the second constitution, was a tumultuous decade in Cuban history. Near civil war, revolution, and nationalism marked the decade, including its cultural productions. The Cuban economy, closely tied to that of the United States, also underwent a depression beginning in 1929. The price of Cuba's two main crops— sugar and tobacco—upon which the entire economy depended, suffered a sharp drop due to the worldwide depression and the United States' (Cuba's dominant trading partner) legislation to protect its own markets. Unemployment soared and poverty was rampant, especially in the countryside. The political situation, affected by the economic depression, was just as harsh. The 1930s began with Machado's dictatorship (1928–33) and violent opposition to it from left and right, followed by a brief revolutionary government, the result of an unlikely coalition of a mutinous army and radical university students (September 1933–January 1934), and ended with another dictatorship, that of General Fulgencio Batista (1934–39), who ruled behind puppet presidents for the rest of that decade.

During the 1930s Cuban artists were divided into two main groups: academicians and modernists. This essay is concerned with the modernists, whose political views varied widely but tended toward the left. Modernism in Cuban art emerged in the late 1920s, the 1927 Primera Exposición de Arte Nuevo representing an important point of departure, and reached its first mature stage during the 1930s. This seminal modernist movement in Cuban art, today generally known as la vanguardia (the vanguard), or Grupo Moderno (Modern Group) was made up of a loose group of artists born at the turn of the century, about the time Cuba became a republic (1902). Most of them studied at Cuba's official art school, known as the Academy of San Alejandro (founded in 1818),

and the majority finished their artistic education in Paris in the late
1920s and early 1930s.[3] The artists I am concerned with in this group
were sympathetic to left-wing ideologies and produced in different
degrees a social and politically oriented art.

By those on "the left" I mean members of leftist organizations, from
the radical Left Wing Student Organization to the more conservative
Cuban Communist Party, as well as those, the majority of the artists,
who had socialist or anarchist leanings but were not affiliated with any
political party. As varied as the vanguardia painters were in social class,
political views, and artistic affinities, a fairly cohesive "generational"
social and political ideology took shape in the 1930s. This ideology can
be roughly defined by collective statements that political activists wrote
but that the artists also signed. In a few instances we also have the
statements of individual artists. Of the collective statements, the most
important are the 1927 Declaración del Grupo Minorista and the 1935
manifesto of the Union de Escritores y Artistas Revolucionarios de Cuba
(Union of Revolutionary Writers and Artists of Cuba, or UEARC).

The *minoristas* were a loose cluster of left-wing intellectuals and
artists, who from 1923 to 1929 met privately, and also in public at the
Café Martí in Havana, to discuss art, culture, and politics. The minoristas' personal political positions actually ranged from social democracy
to communism, and their differences eventually led to their breakup.
Although an elite within the middle class, they believed that they spoke
for most Cubans on social and political issues. This group had much in
common with other Latin American vanguards of the early twentieth
century in their self-image as a cultural-political revolutionary movement
that would lead the nation to a better future. They made their positions
known through public protests, collective declarations, editorials, and
articles that appeared, for the most part, in the magazines *Social* and
Carteles. The group's May 1927 declaration stated its cultural and sociopolitical agenda in concise terms. Both collectively and individually the
group's members were working

> For the revision of false and tired values
> For vernacular art and, in general, for new art in its diverse
> manifestations
> For the introduction and popularization in Cuba of the latest artistic
> and scientific doctrines, theories, and practices
> For reform in the public education system ... and autonomy for
> universities
> For the economic independence of Cuba and against Yankee
> imperialism
> Against political dictatorship in the world, America, and Cuba

> Against the excesses of [Cuba's] pseudodemocracy, the falsity of
> [Cuba's] suffrage, and for the effective participation of the people in
> government
> For the betterment of the Cuban farmer and worker
> For Latin America cordiality and union.[4]

Although only two of the vanguardia painters, Eduardo Abela and Antonio Gattorno, signed the declaration, much of the politically oriented
Cuban art of the following years—from illustrations in *Revista de Avance*
to easel and mural paintings—was motivated by the issues proclaimed
in the manifesto. The Cuban modernist painters were in favor of "the
latest artistic … doctrines, theories, and practices" and "vernacular art."
The former meant nonacademic and nonnaturalistic art, from Post-
Impressionism to Surrealism. The latter was evident in the self-conscious
nationalism of their subject matter. And these artists were also against
"Yankee imperialism" and "political dictatorship," and for the betterment of Cuban farmers and workers. Cuban social and political art of the
1930s addressed diverse issues that often blurred the lines between the
cultural and the political.

The UEARC was a short-lived organization of writers and artists that
published its own manifesto in the newspaper *La Palabra* on 3 February 1935. This newspaper and its editor, Juan Marinello, were associated
with the Cuban Communist Party and the manifesto was published a
few months before the major labor strike of May 1935, which signaled
the end of the most revolutionary tendencies within the reform movement that had begun in 1923. If the Declaración del Grupo Minorista
announced the revolutionary tendencies within vanguardismo, the UEARC
manifesto was its last hurrah. A more populist and radical document
than the minorista declaration, it was dedicated to Rubén Martínez Villena, the recently deceased founder of the Grupo Minorista, who led the
Communist Party at the time of his death. This manifesto read in part:

1. [We will] work to create a national art in its tone and accent, yet also
   universal and human, in tune with current cultural developments.
2. An art of these characteristics must forcefully unite with the
   aspirations of our popular masses, eternal repositories of national
   and human values.
3. [Create] a true, large-scale, and revolutionary art.
4. All work that expresses "that which is Cuban" has to carry the
   anguish throbbing in our people for a better world.
5. For Afro-Cuban art to have significance in Cuba it must rest on the
   social equality and dignity of the man of color and the end of his
   unjust oppression.[5]

In strong language, in which the imperative "must" dominates, the UEARC document called for an art of strong social content and context, privileging the popular voice and the underdog in the symbolization of the nation. In contrast with the 1927 declaration, there was no emphasis on "the new" or "the latest" per se, yet the commitment to "current cultural developments" was clear. The reference to a "vernacular art" in the earlier document was supplemented in the 1935 manifesto by a more specific and radical call for an art based on the aspirations of the popular masses. Surprisingly, the reference to "Yankee imperialism" in the 1927 document is conspicuously absent in the 1935, maybe because the hated interventionist Platt Amendment had been abrogated the year before.[6] The emphasis on Afro-Cubans rather than the generic peasant and worker may be a measure of the growing cultural and social space blacks were opening for themselves in Cuba. Finally, the call for a "true, large-scale, and revolutionary art" probably referred to the example of Mexican muralism. The manifesto was signed by a relatively large group of vanguardia painters: Jorge Arche, Enríquez, Gattorno, Amelia Peláez, Peñita, Domingo Ravenet, and Lorenzo Romero-Arciaga. But not all of the signatories' social activities and art supported the platform of the manifesto. Peláez did not produce art of social commentary, much less political protest. Arche, Gattorno, Ravenet, and Romero-Arciaga ventured only lightly into social commentary in their art. Only Peñita and some of the work of Enríquez parallel the tone of the UEARC manifesto.

Toward a Public Art

The most public, socially oriented, and revolutionary art of Cuba in the 1930s took the form of murals, some of which never got past the conceptual stage, while others were later destroyed.[7] From 1928 to 1937 groups of modernist artists approached public institutions and state and municipal organizations in Havana with plans for mural projects, most of which were ignored or abandoned.

The Mexican mural movement inspired Cuban muralism in the 1930s. Indeed, Cuba's strong cultural connections with Mexico go back to the Spanish Conquest. Spain's first three colonizing expeditions to Mexico (1517, 1518, and 1519) were launched from Cuba, and throughout the colonial period Havana was the port of call for all Spanish ships returning from Mexico. After Mexico declared its independence from Spain, many Cubans involved in their own liberation effort took temporary refuge in Mexico. By the early twentieth century, travel, trade, and cultural contacts between Mexico City and Havana were extensive. In the realm of the visual arts, the Mexican muralist movement was well known and respected among artists and intellectuals. Two of the magazines associated with the Cuban vanguardia, *Social* and *Revista de Avance,* regularly published articles on contemporary Mexican art and culture.[8] These magazines helped to introduce the main figures of the muralist movement, principally Diego Rivera, to Cuban audiences. Mexican publications such as *El Machete,* the official newspaper of Mexico's Artists' Union and, after 1924, of the Mexican Communist Party, also reached Havana. In addition, Cuban and Mexican artists traveled back and forth between the two countries. Emilio Amero and Carlos Merida, then assistants of Rivera, visited Havana, where they exhibited their work, in the 1920s.[9] In the following decade, such Cuban artists as Peñita, Mariano Rodríguez, Cundo Bermúdez, and Mario Carreño visited Mexico for the express purpose of establishing direct contact with the Mexican muralists.

At its most concrete, the contact between the Cuban and the Mexican avant-gardes in the 1920s and 1930s led many Cuban artists to advocate a socially oriented public art, preferably in fresco. In their repeated attempts to learn the fresco technique and to paint murals in public buildings, they were indebted to the Mexican example. To the extent that muralism is an unhappy chapter of the story of Cuban art of the 1930s, however, the Mexican influence remained, contrary to expectations, limited in scope; for even vanguardia painters committed to making social and political art were highly sensitive to their own national, historical, and sociopolitical circumstances, which were quite different from those of Mexico.

As one of the first modernist mural painters, Antonio Gattorno is a good case study for both the accomplishments and the limitations of muralism in Havana of the late 1920s and early 1930s. A 1921 graduate of the San Alejandro Academy, Gattorno spent the next several years studying painting in Italy and France. Not a follower of the latest trends, he gravitated in Italy to the art of the Quattrocento and in Paris to that of Paul Gauguin. From these models he developed his own primitivist vision of rural Cuba. Upon his return to Havana in 1927 he became active in such leftist groups as the Grupo Minorista, the UEARC, and the avant-garde publication *Revista de Avance* (1927–30). Gattorno's admiration for fifteenth-century Italian art and contemporary Mexican mural painting made him favor muralism at that moment in his career. "Painting," he wrote, "was born to decorate the most important spaces of a building, not to fill the corners of a room."[10]

The University of Havana awarded one of the few public mural commissions of the 1920s to Gattorno, for a "decorative panel" to be placed in its Pedagogical School. The painting represented a mother/teacher figure crowned by a laurel of banana tree leaves, reading informally to

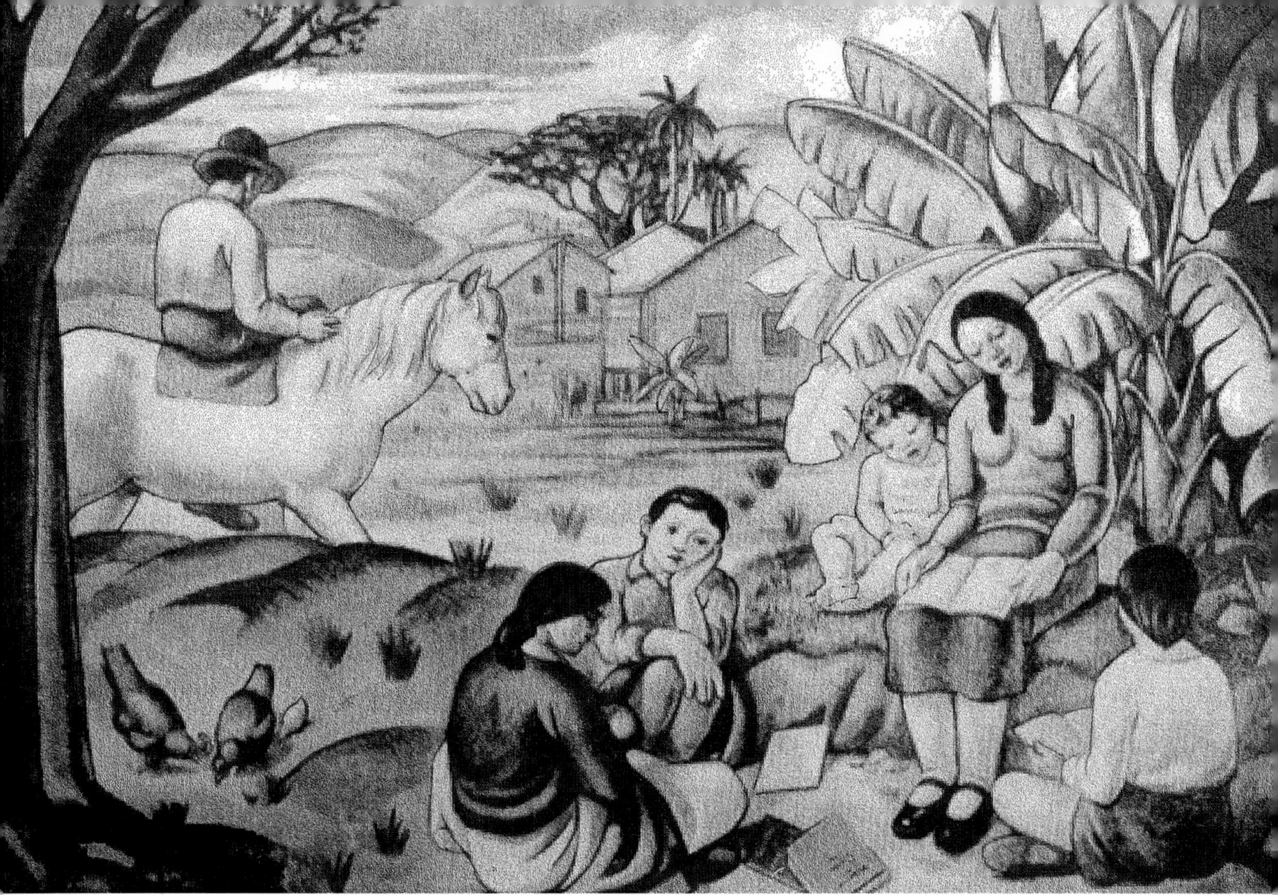

her students/children, as a farmer-father figure rides slowly by, all in the midst of a friendly and intimate landscape. Beneath the painting is written in bold letters José Martí's oft-quoted line on the value of education: "Trenches of ideas are worth more than trenches of stones," a fitting caption to Gattorno's idealized image of rural literacy (fig. 1). From the point of view of critical social commentary, Gattorno's mural is problematic in that it masks the fact of widespread rural illiteracy at that time. Rather than express the need for the "betterment of the Cuban farmer and worker" stated in the minoristas' declaration of the same year, which Gattorno signed, his painting suggests that all is well in the Cuban countryside. Gattorno's socialist views and his primitivist style were clearly at odds. He sympathized with the plight of the *guajiro*, or peasant, but represented him as living an Arcadian existence.

Gattorno was a muralist in the sense of the scale, placement, and function of paintings such as the one discussed above, but his style remained an extension of his easel paintings, and in fact all of his recorded murals are oil on canvas. Thus far, there is no indication that he ever painted a fresco. The fact is that Cuba's official art school, San Alejandro, did not teach fresco painting, and there was no tradition in Cuba of the use of such a technique. Cuban mural paintings, from Nicolas de la Escalera in the eighteenth century to Armando Menocal in the 1920s, were all done on canvas and hung on walls or ceilings.

Some modernist artists sought again to initiate mural projects
for public buildings in the immediate aftermath of Machado's overthrow in August 1933. A group of eight artists and one cultural activist
approached the government of Grau-Guiteras and proposed to "to paint
the walls of public buildings with the atrocities of the Machado regime
and the heroism of our people, the students, and other revolutionary
sectors," an honor for which they would not "charge one cent."[11] The signatories to this request were Eduardo Abela, José Manuel Acosta, Jorge
Arche, Romero Arciaga, Gabriel Castaño, Arístides Fernández, Jorge
Fernández de Castro, Antonio Gattorno, and Jorge Hernandez Cárdenas.[12]
Officials never responded to the petition, probably because the Grau-Guiteras coalition had their hands full with revolutionizing Cuban politics
and the economy in their brief hundred days in office. Nevertheless, one
mural project and one mural dating to that propitious time are worth
studying for the light they shed on Cuban muralism of the 1930s.

Gattorno and Castaño collaborated with the Cuban Communist
Party to paint a mural for Julio Antonio Mella's funeral, a politically
charged event that took place in Havana on 28 September 1933, at the
headquarters of the Anti-Imperialist League.[13] Mella was one of the
most radical figures of the Cuban vanguardia generation, a leader of the
university reform movement and one of the founders of the Cuban Communist Party. Imprisoned and then deported by Machado in 1926, Mella
took refuge in Mexico, where he kept active as a writer and communist
organizer until his assassination on 10 January 1929.[14] Soon after Machado's downfall, Mella's ashes were returned to Cuba for proper burial.
A somewhat faded photo, the only record of the event and of Gattorno
and Castaño's lost mural, shows an urn flanked by an honor guard and
behind it a high wall covered by a large painting (fig. 2). The mural features a large portrait of Mella's head in the center, flanked by students
on one side and workers on the other, both shown with raised arms and
closed fists. On stylistic grounds we may conclude that Gattorno painted
the Mella portrait and Castaño the lateral scenes. The artist based Mella's
portrait on the mural on Tina Modotti's much-reproduced 1928 photograph of him.[15] Modotti, Mella's lover and companion at the time of his
assassination, portrayed him as handsome, athletic, and intense. Her
photograph shows an alert Mella, head in sharp profile, a solid neck, and
a broad upper torso clothed in a worker's shirt. Gattorno amplified and
simplified the image, turning it into a bold representation of a visionary
leader. Most probably the context of the project and its patrons contributed to its unique qualities: the collaboration of two artists in the same
painting, its specific communist subject, and its graphic visual language.

Like the revolution that inspired them, never realized, the mural
projects of Arístides Fernández, known only through preparatory

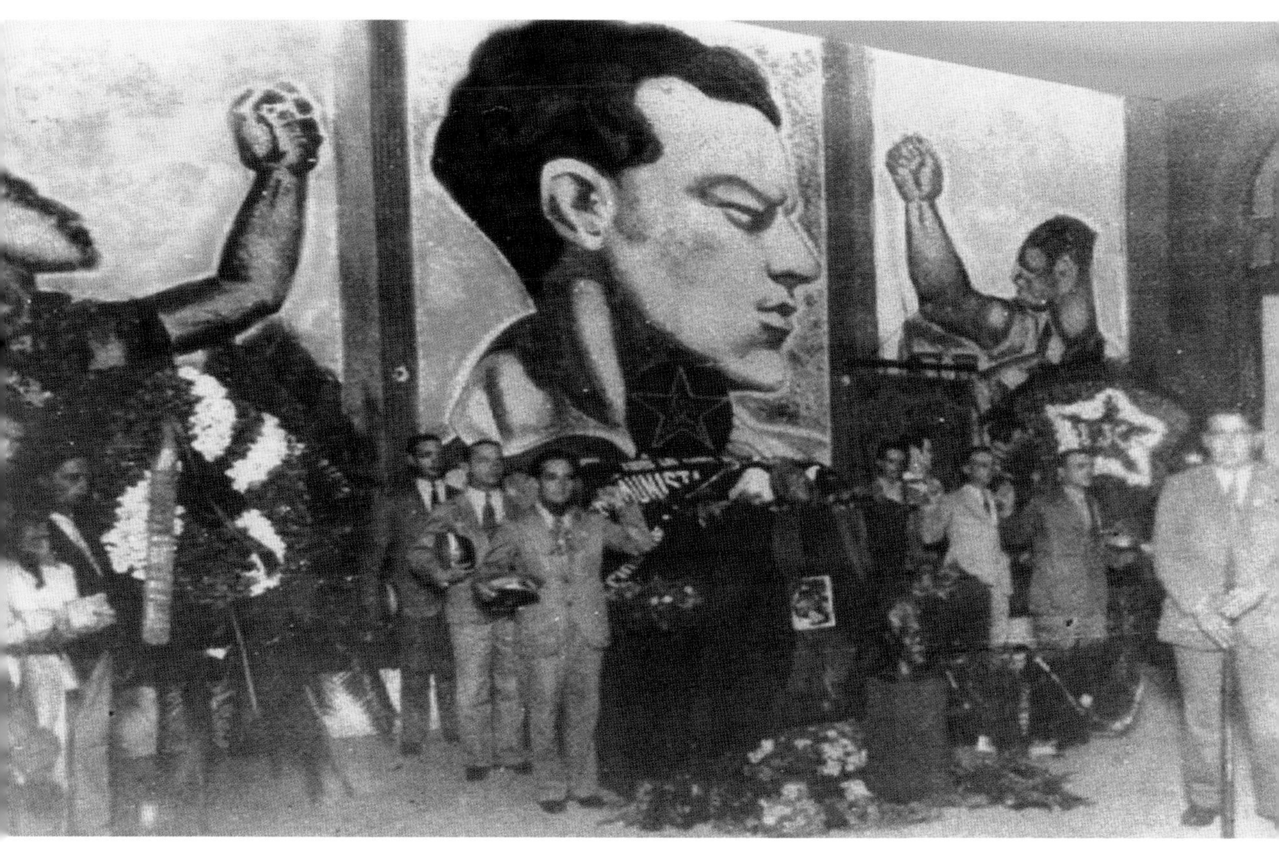

2 Antonio Gattorno and Gabriel Castaño, mural for Julio Antonio Mella (1933) (media and dimensions unknown; destroyed).

sketches, are worth examining as an indication of the Cuban vanguardia's frustrations and muralism's potential in the early 1930s. Fernández was a self-taught painter and writer of short stories who died at age thirty-four. He wrote most of his short stories between 1930 and 1933, and his artistic production dates to the last year of his life. He spent part of that time trying in vain to learn the fresco technique and making bold sketches for planned murals. He seems to have been deeply moved by the revolution of 1933–34 and, with the help of the Mexican mural movement, tried to give artistic expression to that significant event. His friend and promoter, the poet and novelist José Lezama Lima, wrote of Fernández at this moment in his life: "[He] scratched the walls ... looking for the possibilities of our muralism, as the masses were jumping around the city. When the romantic struggle against the tyrant ended in August 1933, Arístides Fernández believed that this political rift should have propelled its artistic parallel."[16]

A major stumbling block for those who wanted to follow the Mexican fresco model was the technique itself, which was difficult to learn. We have a poignant record of this difficulty in a letter from Fernández to Diego Rivera, which reads in part, "I have attempted several times

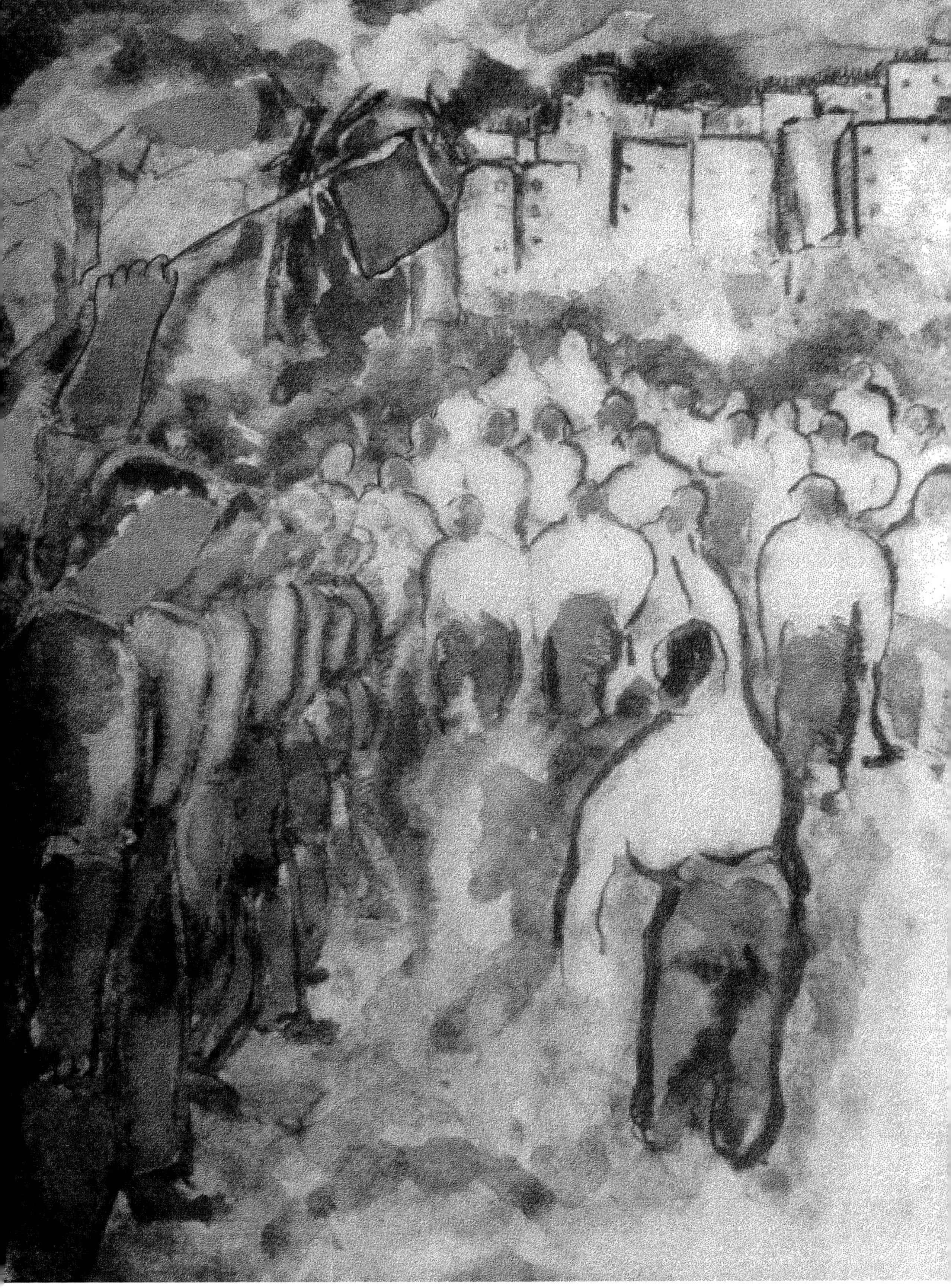

to make fresco painting and I have failed miserably; the technical part has detained me." After describing several failed attempts to master the method, he wrote, "I went to bookstores and libraries searching for a manual that would clear my doubts and found none. In all of Havana there is not a booklet on mural [fresco] painting!"[17] Although Fernández never learned how to paint frescos and his mural projects remained at the conceptual stage, his mural sketches are worth examining for their sense of monumental form (to the extent that this can be judged from a sketch), and strong sociopolitical content. In the summer and fall of 1933 he developed the theme of the massive demonstrations against Machado, in which he had participated and for which he did sketches in pencil and crayola entitled *Manifestaciones* (Demonstrations) (fig. 3). Although no more than a few square inches, the images project a sense of monumentality contrary to their actual size. Fernández's simplification of form, creation of a strong sense of depth, and concentration on a few motifs are ideal pictorial qualities for large-scale painting with a social message.

As one of the few artists of his generation who did not travel abroad, Fernández made the most of his second-hand (photographic) knowledge of the paintings of Gauguin, Cézanne, Rivera, and (perhaps) Giotto. He shared with these artists an attraction to pared-down form, strong, solid colors, and highly structured compositions. In regard to content, the *Manifestaciones* sketches are about documenting and expressing the "heroism of our people" as they took to the streets in massive demonstrations against the Machado regime. In a more universal sense, they are about the modern phenomenon of marginalized masses in an urban setting. As Enrique Carreño put it in his study of Fernández's writings, "the author presents man as the masses, victim of social marginalization."[18] Fernández manifests this sense of the urban masses through the representation of anonymous figures and their decisive, desperate, and collective action.

After repeated attempts, beginning in 1928, a group of the vanguardia painters were finally given the opportunity to paint a series of murals in a public building in 1937. "On the initiative of José Luciano Franco and with the support of the mayor of Havana," read a note in the magazine *Selecta*, "a group of Cuban artists, members of the Society of Modern Artists, has filled with mural paintings the classrooms, dormitories, and salons of the secondary school José Miguel Gómez."[19] This time the roster of artists included the most important names of the Cuban vanguardia: Carlos Enríquez, Víctor Manuel, Amelia Peláez, and Fidelio Ponce. Absent were Arístides Fernández, who had died in 1934, Antonio Gattorno, who left for New York around 1936, and Marcelo Pogolotti, who did not return from Paris until 1939.

By 1937 the modernist movement had gained momentum in
Havana, supported by a middle-class professional elite and by the Dirección de Cultura (Directory of Culture), a low-budget agency of the
Ministry of Education, recently created to promote the arts. The edu-
cated elite—lawyers, doctors, architects, journalists, literary writers and
poets—provided venues for exhibition (such as the nonprofit women's
organization, Lyceum), wrote for newspapers and magazines championing the modernist movement, and acquired artwork at moderate prices.
The state, during the brief tenure of President Grau San Martin (September 1933–January 1934) and his revolutionary administration, began
responding to long-standing demands by artists of all disciplines who
wanted official attention to and funding of the arts as part of nation
building. This renewed effort outlasted the hundred-day revolutionary
government and led to the creation of the Dirección de Cultura a year
later, and to its sponsorship of the National Exhibitions of Painting and
Sculpture. The modernist artists mentioned above figured prominently
in the first and second of these exhibitions, held in 1935 and 1938. The
modernist movement was also the subject of a major exhibition, with
an ambitious catalog, organized by the office of the mayor of Havana in
1937 and entitled the First Exhibition of Modern Art. That year leading
modernist artists organized, after many failed attempts, a free art studio.
During its brief existence, the Studio Libre represented the first alternative to the monopoly of the Academy of San Alejandro in matters of
art education. With minimal state, municipal, and private support, the
modernist movement in art had arrived in Havana's high culture by the
mid-1930s.

It is in this context that a group of modernist artists was commissioned by the office of the mayor to do a mural project in a grand new
public school named for a veteran of the War of Independence and later
president of Cuba, General José Miguel Gómez. The project had no overarching concept or theme, each artist selecting his or her own subject
matter, technique, and dimensions. In personal styles that in theme and
size were close to their easel paintings, these artists dealt with various
subjects—school, work, recreation, and history.[20] Peñita's and Enríquez's
murals offered the strongest social commentary.

Peñita, an Afro-Cuban from a working-class family, studied design
at the School of Arts and Trades in Havana and worked as a graphic
designer for the municipal government. His paintings represent the
artistic vanguardia at its closest to realism. Peñita's artistic production,
limited in part because he died at age thirty-eight, included protest paintings about class, racial struggle, and the plight of the worker. Inspired
by Mexican models, he developed a simplified naturalism to represent
and agitate on behalf of rural and urban workers in Cuba. For his fresco

at the José Miguel Gómez School, entitled *La llamada del ideal* (The call of the ideal, 1937), he used a dry fresco technique with a synthetic resin base recommended by David Alfaro Siqueiros.[21] The image (for the easel version, see fig. 4) centers on a representation of Martí's head, providing the ideological framework for the struggling figures represented in the foreground. The poet, prolific journalist, and prime ideologist of the War of Independence of 1895–98 is shown as a collective and inspiring vision to Cuban workers—men and women, black and white, urbanites and peasants—urging them to fight for their rights. The concepts of Cuban sovereignty and social justice for all, two major themes of Martí's political thought, were at the forefront of the vanguardia's political agenda, giving a nationalist slant to its leftist ideology. Like Gattorno and Castaño's Mella mural, Peñita's composition is centered on a large, rhetorical, and inspiring portrait of a nationalist leader.

In contrasting to Peñita's social realist approach, Carlos Enríquez's mural offers a complex visual language and subtle, if defiant, social content. Well-born bohemian, painter, and writer, Enríquez is one of the most original pioneers of Cuban modernism. His foray into socially critical art began in the late 1920s with biting illustrations for *Revista de Avance*,[22] followed in the mid- to late 1930s by a few easel paintings of dramatic expressionism. The bulk of his painting production from 1935 to 1940 consisted of a highly personal adaptation of modern European schools of art, from Expressionism to Cubism, and concepts such as primitivism, which he used to depict the Cuban countryside. He called these productions, which included a strong dose of social criticism, *romancero guajiro,* or peasant ballads. Enríquez's political ideology is complex, a combination of bohemian anarchism and independent left-wing views.

The bohemian side of his politics was defined by the artist himself in a 1936 article he wrote for the newspaper *El País,* entitled "El arte puro como propaganda ha fracasado plenamente" (Art as pure propaganda has redundantly failed).[23] "It is difficult to adjust art to a political mold," he wrote, "stereotyping a melodramatic theme until it becomes a poster, nullifying in this way art's creative purity and constructive anarchism, the essence of all artistic work."[24] Enríquez considered the emphasis on illustrative content detrimental to art and, by implication, to whatever restricted artistic freedom, which he conflated with anarchism. For him it was the artist's life and attitude that held the potential for the creation of revolutionary art: "The artist must go through life perverse, destructor and creator at the same time, as a harmful entity, without duties or obligations, without tradition and prejudices (as far as art is concerned), and thus produce true revolutionary work."[25] Posturing aside, Enríquez associated with the Cuban left throughout his adult life and was close to Pogolotti, Martínez Villena, Marinello, Nicolás Guillén, and Agustín

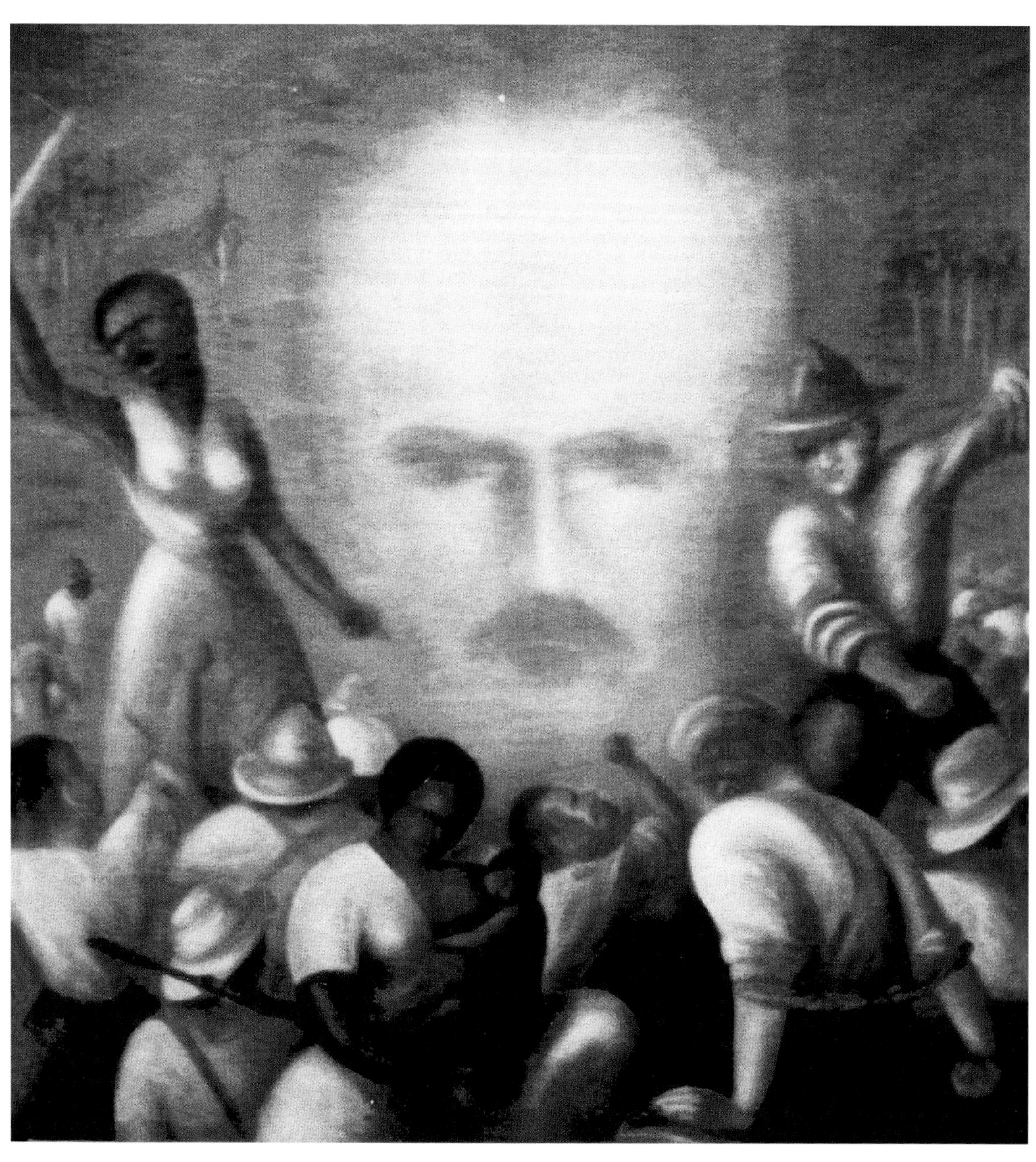

4 Alberto Peña, *El Llamado del Ideal (The Call of the Ideal)* (1936), oil on canvas, 95 x 82.5 cm. Museo Nacional de Bellas Artes, Havana, Cuba.

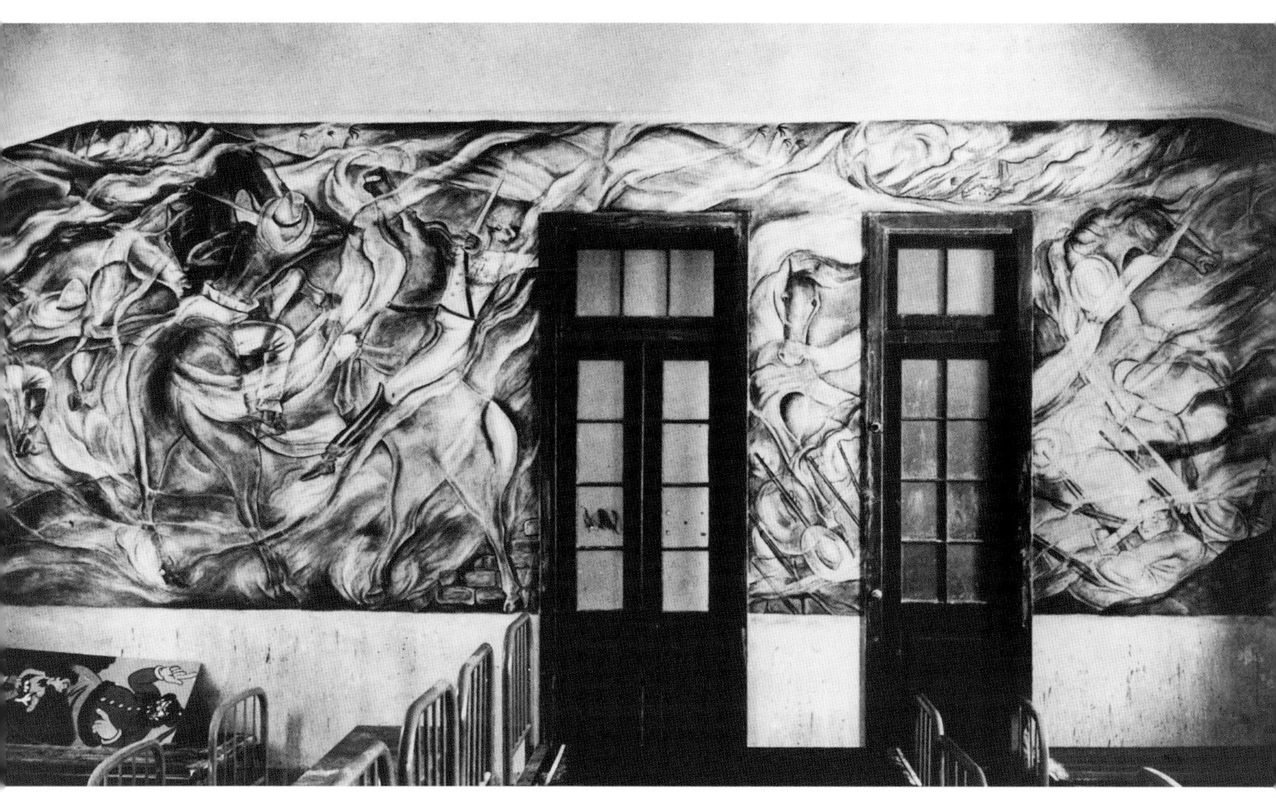

Guerra, among others. He also executed a number of paintings in the 1930s with strong social and political content. Enríquez combined a bohemian attitude toward life and art with leftist political views, a combination for which there is ample precedent in the history of modern art.

Enríquez, like Gattorno and Fernández, had a strong interest in mural painting. Unlike them, he did learn the technique of fresco and used it in a number of mural paintings he did in Havana from the late 1930s to the early 1950s. His most ambitious was the fresco for the José Miguel Gómez School, entitled *La Invasión* (1937), which, according to a surviving photograph (fig. 5), measured forty feet and covered the long side of a rectangular dormitory.[26] The destroyed fresco showed Enríquez's mature expressionistic language of dynamic, exaggerated, and transparent representational forms, used to imagine and memorize a scene from the most significant campaign of the 1895–98 War of Independence. In a sweeping movement from left to right, the *mambises,* or independence fighters, are represented on horseback, machetes in hand, combating the Spanish forces, which are shown for the most part as entrenched riflemen at the bottom right of the painting. The crowded composition, with its forceful curving and diagonal lines, strongly expresses the subject of battle.

Although Enríquez hardly dealt with historical subjects, he did a few very subjective paintings of figures and events from Cuba's War of Independence, the most significant of which are *El Rey de los Campos de Cuba* (The king of the Cuban fields, 1934), *Dos Rios* (Two rivers, 1939), and the mural in question. In the two easel paintings Enríquez concentrated on well-known, if very different, heroes of that war—Manuel Garcia and José Martí—with emphasis on the romantic notion of individual courage and action in the context of nationalism. *La Invasión* differs in that the nationalist cult of the hero is given a more collective slant. Its composition does not exalt the figure of a known leader but represents a group of evenly spaced anonymous fighters. On the social and political level, the significance of the painting's content is related to Enriquez's, and his generation's, view of the War of Independence as a defining moment in Cuban history—and also as an incomplete project, given Cuba's neocolonial relationship with the United States after independence from Spain. In the context of Cuban history and the artist's leftist ideology, *La Invasión* can be read as an inspirational painting aimed at keeping the flame of Cuban sovereignty alive, after the debacle of the revolution of 1933 and the island's deepening economic and political dependence on the United States. All of the murals at the José Miguel Gómez School were later painted over because school officials considered their artistic form and social message subversive. More recently, all of these paintings, but Enríquez's, have been restored.[27]

Among the vanguardia movement's contribution to Cuban art in the 1930s was its push for socially conscious public art, which was more or less achieved through murals. Vanguardia painters added the technique of fresco to the limited repertoire of painting techniques then practiced in Cuba and made a significant contribution to the development of publicly oriented art on a large scale. Owing to the lack of a strong muralist tradition in Cuba and to the absence of state support, mural painting in the 1930s was caught between promise and reality. Its production, thematic diversity, and social projection were limited but seminal.

Easel Painting, Social Commentary, and Protest

What the Cuban vanguardia could not fully accomplish in the field of mural painting it achieved in the more affordable medium of easel painting. Oriented more to elite consumption and with a long bourgeois history, easel painting is not the ideal medium for the creation of an "authentic, large-scale, and revolutionary art," as the UEARC manifesto put it, yet it served the Cuban vanguardia as the main vehicle for an art of social commentary and, at times, political protest. These easel paintings offer a more revealing sample of the vanguardia painters' range of artistic languages and socially oriented subject matter, as well as of their "true" audience—an elite within the Cuban middle class who befriended the artists, bought modestly from them, and organized exhibitions of their work with the help of the Lyceum (founded in 1929) and the Dirección de Cultura.

To the extent that those exhibitions can be reconstructed from catalogs and extant paintings in private and public collections, we know that there were a variety of artistic languages, more or less "revolutionary" in the context of Cuban art, and confluences in terms of subject matter. The same holds true for the more specifically socially oriented art within Cuban modernism. There are great distances between the gentle primitivism of Gattorno, the more crude primitivism of Fernández, the social realism of Peñita, the expressionism of Enríquez's paintings, and the purism of Marcelo Pogolotti, yet there are close affinities in their sociopolitical discourse. Certain popular and historical figures became dominant themes in imagining the nation at its most "authentic." The leading popular figures represented in modernist painting were the peasant, the Afro-Cuban, and the industrial worker, and the most often rendered historical character was Martí. The equation of the oppressed with the nation was one part of the leftist ideology of the 1930s in which these artists shared fully.[28] Such a view of the nation was appropriated locally from Martí and internationally from European socialism and communism.

The plight of the peasant was a major theme in socially oriented Cuban art of the 1930s in that peasants made up the more numerous and exploited sector of the working class and at the same time symbolized the "authentically" Cuban because of their closeness to the land. Some of the most significant social paintings of the decade—in which women and the family are well represented—address this theme: Fernández's *La familia se retrata* (Family portrait, c. 1933), Pogolotti's *Obreros y campesinos* (Workers and peasants, c. 1933), and Enríquez's *Campesinos felices* (Happy peasants, 1938) (fig. 6). These paintings are the first, in a tradition of representing the Cuban countryside that goes back to the nineteenth century, to present a problematic view of the life of peasants. The traditional picturesque view of the Cuban countryside is replaced in these paintings by images of poverty and work, presented by Enríquez as dire and harsh. They are pioneer images aimed at sensitizing Havana's white middle class to the conditions of the other Cuba—the island's interior.

The Cuban artist who most consistently dealt with the issue of class struggle, both urban and rural, from a Marxist point of view was Marcelo Pogolotti. A pioneer of the Cuban vanguardia in Havana in the late 1920s, he spent his brief mature phase, from 1930 to 1938, in Europe.

His career cut short by blindness, he returned to Havana in 1939 and became a successful writer. In Europe Pogolotti joined the Futurist movement while living in Turin, and after moving to Paris in 1934 he became a member of the Association des Escrivains et Artistes Revolutionnaires (Association of Revolutionary Writers and Artists).[29]

By the mid-1930s Pogolotti had developed his own semi-abstract but figurative visual language of precise geometric forms and finished surfaces. His style, in contrast to that of his Cuban contemporaries, imparted a certain intellectual slant to his protest paintings. Rather than invite sympathy for workers, it argues their case through the use of generic and hard-edged forms, and emphasizes the oppressive nature of industrial capitalism as a whole. Likewise, in an essay entitled "De lo Social en el Arte" (About the social element in art), Pogolotti argued the case for socially oriented art: "No, social painting is not a futile dream. But to realize it, it is necessary to bring down all limitations and restrictions, doing away with prejudices against anecdote, symbolism, figuration, and literature and using the magnificent resources offered by modern painting."[30] In his social paintings Pogolotti achieved a synthesis of modernist artistic language, traditional literary subject, and Marxist ideology.

Although living in Europe, he kept in close contact with events in Cuba, and in 1933, at the height of the revolutionary surge, he painted one of the most direct and critical references to the Cuban situation of the era in *Paisaje cubano* (Cuban landscape, 1933) (fig. 7). This painting represents the main players in the Cuban sugar industry—greedy foreign businessmen in dark suits, the U.S. Navy's big guns, an omnipresent national army, and able productive workers (agrarian and industrial, black and white)—which he rendered in precise figurative forms arranged in a collage-like space. The image offers a cool but blunt condemnation of the exploitation of the sugar industry by foreign capital, U.S. gunboat diplomacy toward Cuba, and the plight of the rural and urban workers (represented by the sugarcane cutter and stevedore, respectively).

Another recurrent figure in Cuban social painting of the 1930s is the Afro-Cuban, which made only occasional appearances in the "peasant" and "worker" paintings. Although they had had a strong presence in Cuba since the early nineteenth century, when brought as slaves from West Africa to expand the sugar industry, and later played a prominent role in the Wars of Independence, Afro-Cubans as a group were the least able to enjoy the economic and political benefits of republican life. Black and mulatto Cubans remained among the poorest and least represented sectors of society well into the republican era. On the cultural front, white hegemony and prejudice prevented their heritage from entering

6 Carlos Enríquez, *Campesinos Felices (Happy Peasants)* (1938), oil on canvas, 122 x 89 cm. Museo Nacional de Bellas Artes, Havana, Cuba.

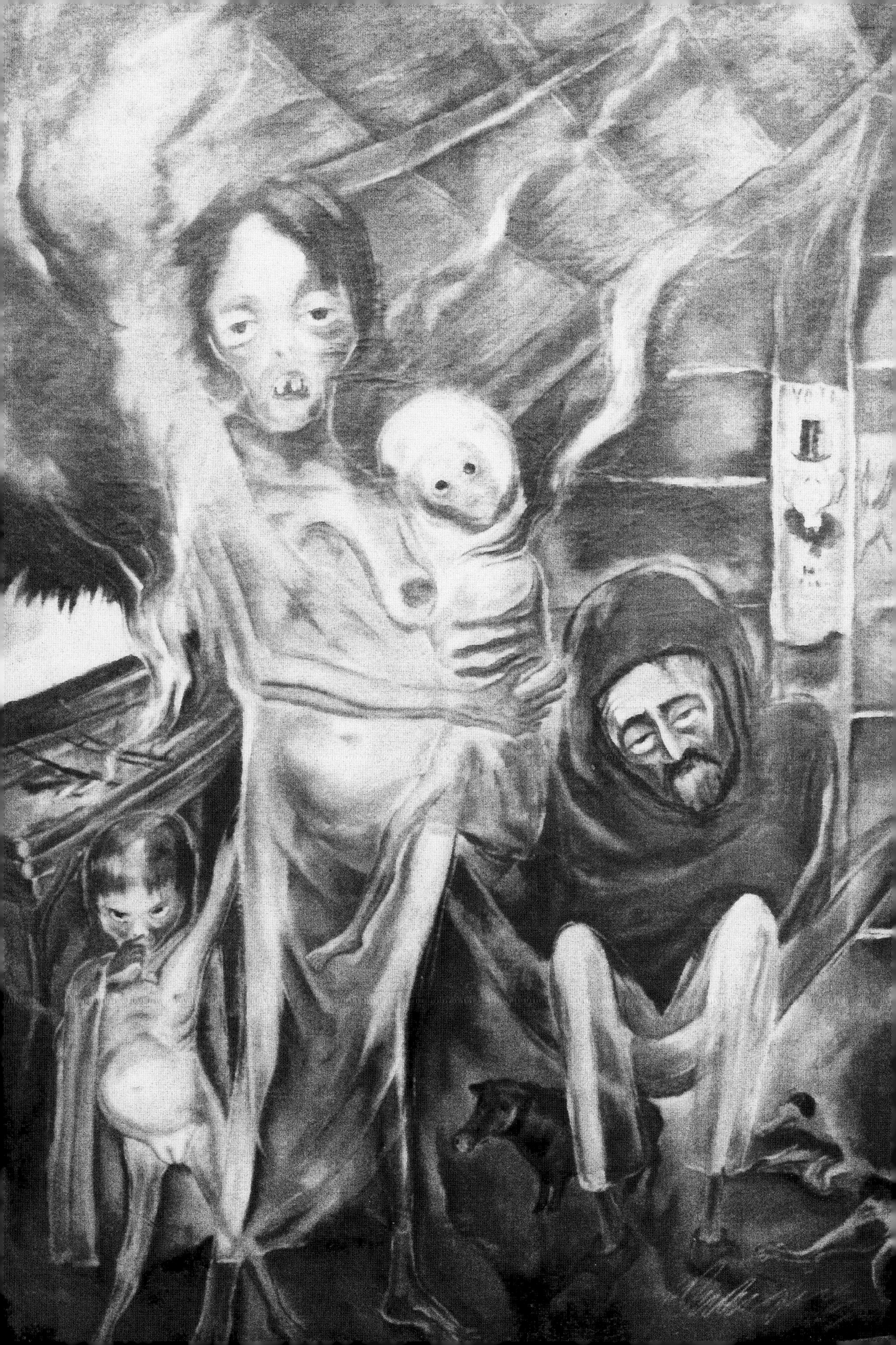

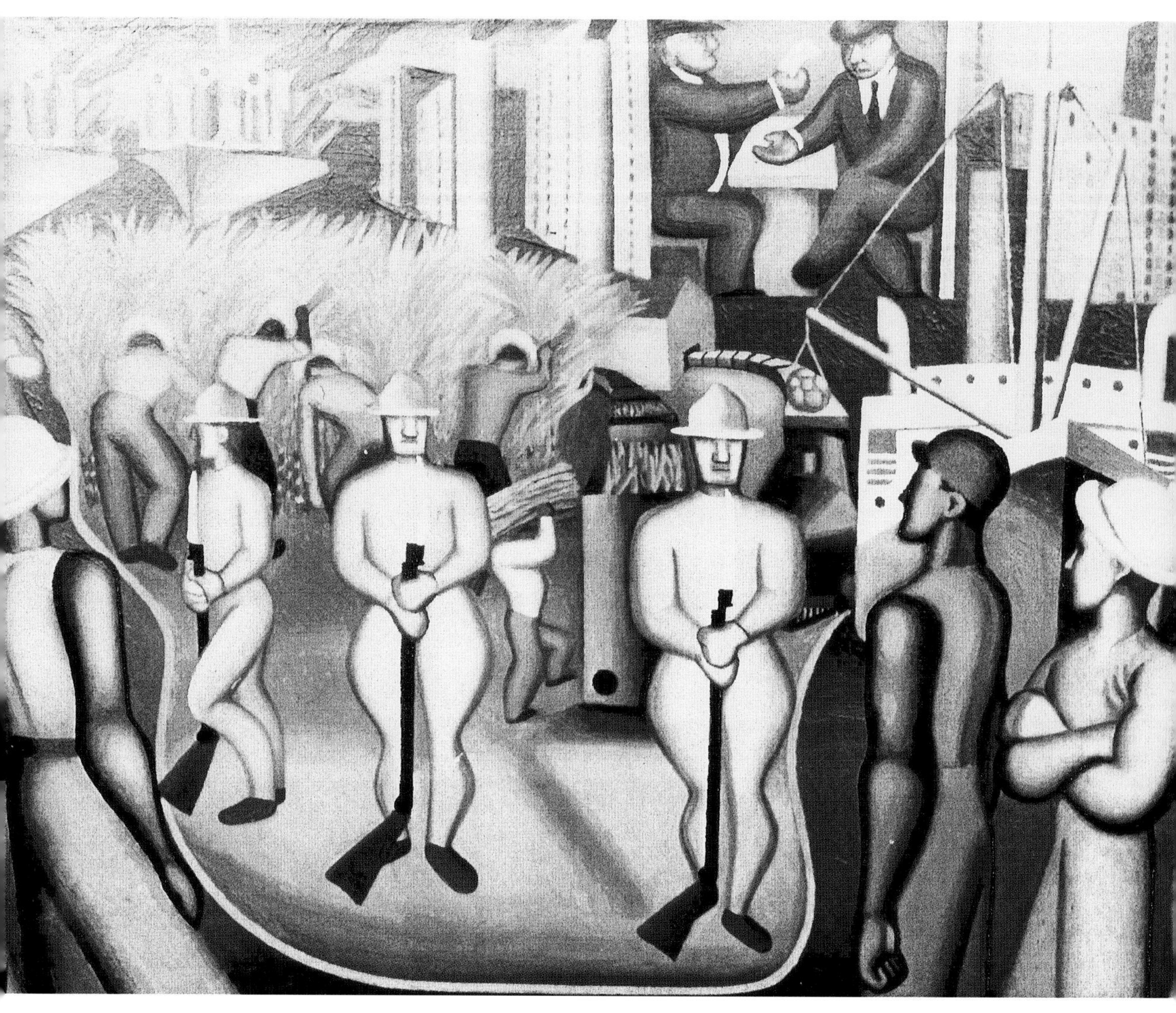

high Cuban culture until the late 1920s. At that time the literary, musical, and artistic vanguard began to make Afro-Cuban popular culture visible and audible to a white elite within the ruling class. Borrowing from popular culture, the Cuban modernist painters most often represented Afro-Cubans in the context of music, dance, and ritual, as seen in Eduardo Abela's *El triunfo de la rumba* (The triumph of the rumba, 1928) and Enríquez's *Tocadores* (Musicians, 1934). Although they presented a stereotypical view of Afro-Cubans, such images signaled the beginning of acceptance of African heritage as a bona fide and integral part of Cuban high culture. The mostly white middle-class vanguardia generation was the first to acknowledge and welcome the African contribution to Cuban life.

7 Marcelo Pogolotti, *Paisaje Cubano (Cuban Landscape)* (1933), oil on canvas, 73 x 92.5 cm. Museo Nacional de Bellas Artes, Havana, Cuba.

Finally, of all the leaders of the Wars of Independence fought by Cuba against Spain from 1868 to 1898, Martí slowly emerged as the foremost apologist for and symbol of that epic effort. The vanguardia writers in particular—Marinello and Jorge Mañach, among others—researched and published significant texts on Martí beginning in the late 1920s. In the visual arts Martí was usually represented as an icon, as for instance in Peñita's aforementioned *Llamada al ideal* (c. 1937) and José Arche's *José Martí* (1943). In general there was a tendency to immortalize him as a man of thought rather than action, whose guiding ideas on Cuban nation building survived him. A significant exception is Enríquez's *Dos Rios,* which represents Martí's death on the battlefield and can be seen as a metaphor for the fate of the revolutionary movement by the late 1930s. Cuban modernist art of the 1930s, in tune with international developments in modernism, openly addressed social and political issues from a leftist point of view. In most cases, Cuban social and political art of the decade did not serve a direct propagandistic purpose on behalf of a specific political party but aimed to call attention to social issues of the day. For the most part the Cuban vanguardia painters went for oblique political commentary rather than outright declarations. At its most effective, Cuban social and political art of the 1930s represented workers and peasants, popular culture, and leftist politics that had been excluded from symbolic representation in Cuba. At its least effective, modernist political art in Cuba failed to claim permanent public space, an arena in which the Mexican mural movement had succeeded, and reached only a small segment of the population, in contrast to the Cuban poster movement of the late 1960s and early 1970s.

THE "MEXICAN PROBLEM":
NATION AND "NATIVE" IN MEXICAN MURALISM AND CULTURAL DISCOURSE

Mary K. Coffey

Perhaps no art movement is as synonymous with national populism as Mexican muralism. Its images of indigenous peoples, popular traditions, and pre-Columbian mythology (see fig. 7) helped to construct and disseminate a national identity authenticated through the political values attributed to the revolutionary struggle. While the consistency of its artists' commitment to the Mexican Revolution (1910–17) has been questioned,[1] the articulation between native and nation evident in their work has been naturalized as a recovery of *México profundo* (deep Mexico).[2] Arguing that the word "revolution" is synonymous with "resurrection" in the Mexican context, Octavio Paz writes that the Mexican Revolution "revealed many previously unknown aspects of our country," and that its true "innovation was the rediscovery of the motherland, along with its popular arts and traditions."[3] By treating the revolution as a creative catalyst for popular expression, Paz divests this historical event of its status as a factionalized political struggle and crafts it instead as an eruption of an extant artistic impulse. Similarly, the rhetoric of "resurrection," "revelation," and "rediscovery" configure this expression as an essential rather than an invented component of the motherland. Nonetheless, if we grant that the identification between the nation and the native[4] has been fashioned over time, Paz's emphasis upon the revolution as the key

A version of this essay previously appeared in *Cultural Studies: A Research Volume*, vol. 5, ed. Norman K. Denzin (Stamford, Conn.: JAI Press, 2000), 147–89. I would like to thank the Tinker Foundation and the Center for Latin American and Caribbean Studies at the University of Illinois for sponsoring my research in Mexico. I am also grateful to Alejandro Anreus, Michael Bérubé, Jonathan Fineberg, Diana Linden, Katherine Manthorne, Cameron McCarthy, and Michael Palm for their editorial comments on various drafts of this essay.

inaugural moment is insightful, and it behooves us to ask why and how this identification was secured? Furthermore, why does culture, and more specifically the culture of indigenous peoples, come to signify the real success of Mexico's ten-year civil war?

The "popular arts and traditions" that Paz celebrates refer, of course, to Mexico's pre-Hispanic heritage, which was quite literally being uncovered by archeologists and anthropologists in the early twentieth century, and to the reappraisal of living indigenous peoples and their practices that ensued. While the identification of the nation with the native in postrevolutionary Mexico corresponds to the familiar mechanics of national narration that Benedict Anderson has so lucidly described, this idealization of indigenous culture is complicated by the assimilative governmental initiatives that were undertaken simultaneously.[5] Under the auspices of national progress, these initiatives employed culture and education to reorganize the affiliations and conduct of Mexico's indigenous populations into a homogenized citizenry that was predicated on the principle of *mestizaje* (racial and cultural mixing). Moreover, the authors and artists who celebrated the native contribution to national identity were very often also the social architects of Mexico's modernization. Discussing Mexican anthropologist Manuel Gamio's pioneering work, David Brading dubs this odd coupling of paternalism and patronage "official *indigenismo*" and argues that the "insistence upon the native roots of the Mexican people" evident in Mexico's cultural project is contradicted by a simultaneous "affirmation of the necessity of modernity."[6] Pace Brading, the promotion of folk culture as a component of social homogenization is not a contradiction, but rather part of the disciplinary logic of modernizing nationalism. This dynamic between modernity and tradition, assimilation and essence, paternalism and the subaltern, structures the discourses of philosophy, anthropology, education, and art in postrevolutionary Mexico. By examining the articulation of these fields of expertise through governmental initiatives, we can begin to understand how the popular truths of Mexican nationalism were produced and then translated into general political programs that targeted the conduct of specific groups, namely, mestizo and indigenous populations.

The identification of nation and native can only be understood through an analysis of the disciplinary agenda that underlay the "will to nation" after the Mexican Revolution. This agenda is manifest in the diagnostic literature assessing the "Mexican problem," as well as the assimilationist logic driving governmental initiatives to "Mexicanize" the Indian. The "aesthetic indigenismo" developed by the artists charged with constructing a visual iconography for the postrevolutionary nation proved instrumental in elaborating new figures for popular citizenship. The national community they imagined was predicated on the racial trope of the mestizo. However, a discursive gaze was focused upon the native component in particular, making the indigene an object of both knowledge and regulation, as well as the proscribed subject of national development. Over the decades of the twenties and thirties, Mexican artists, working for the government, developed an iconography and style adequate to the demands of a national art. The trajectory of individual careers as well as the "movement" at large have been well chronicled.[7] Often, however, mural art is treated in isolation from the discursive context that shaped its ideological coordinates and to which it contributed a compelling public face. By analyzing muralism with respect to the discourses of postrevolutionary nationalism, we can better understand how its artists consciously, and at times inadvertently, participated in the state's modernizing processes.[8] This necessitates a theory of culture and power that illuminates the productive capacity of visual representation as well as its function as a technique of governance.[9]

Questions regarding muralism's relationship to government are particularly cogent because this art form was inaugurated and developed as a didactic instrument of popular enlightenment during a period of intense concern over the conduct and welfare of Mexico's variegated population. Foucault's term "governmental" refers, in part, to the problematics of rule.[10] But, as Nikolas Rose points out, it also signifies a "mentality" or way of thinking about the exercise of authority that seeks to "realize itself as a *practice*."[11] Foucault's coupling of the words "govern" and "mentality" signals the extent to which the reflection of experts participates in the regulation of individual and group conduct. This helps to clarify the decentralized nature of governmental power while also indicating the part that thought plays in the translation of general political goals into effective and realizable practices. Govern*mentalities* incorporate both thought and practice, the ways in which humans have reflected on the conduct of themselves and others and have realized that thought through the establishment of governing protocols.[12] They encompass the myriad "authorities of truth" that affect the way in which we establish true and false accounts of who we are and what we should become.[13] Governmental initiatives link questions of being, personal conduct, and identity to questions of politics, authority, and citizenship.[14] Governmentality is therefore a political rationality with a moral concern for what is proper, an epistemological concern for codifying and knowing the subjects it seeks to govern, and a *style* of reasoning. Style here denotes those intellectual techniques that render the phenomenal world thinkable.[15] Social realism, for example, is one such technique. As a visual language, it attempts to elucidate political and social realities for the purposes of determining collective action. Throughout the period under consideration, the personal conduct of Mexico's indigenous populations was linked not only to the problem of national identity but also to political agendas and progressive government. And mural art was an important discursive site and "authority of truth" within the governmental projects of mestizo nationhood.

Diagnosing the "Mexican Problem"

At the close of the revolution, the national discourse in Mexico focused on the problem of a historically contentious population composed of "degenerate" indigenes, a large strata of mestizos (people of mixed racial heritage), and a minority of Spanish-descended people known as Creoles. Framed by the psychological and historical conditions of postcolonialism, Mexican national discourse seized upon the mestizo as the actual and metaphorical Mexican. In *The Cosmic Race* (1925), a pseudoscientific treatise on the future promise of "his people," José Vasconcelos elevated racial miscegenation to a transcendent eugenic principle. He argued that a "mixture of races accomplished through the laws of social well-being, sympathy, and beauty" would lead to a cosmic race "infinitely superior to all that have previously existed."[16] By converting racial impurity from a sign of shame into one of pride, Vasconcelos attacked the colonial legacy of inferiority attributed to miscegenated populations. Thus he concluded his tract with the emphatic prophecy that "we in America shall arrive, before any other part of the world, at the creation of a new race fashioned out of the treasures of the previous ones."[17]

Yet despite his celebration of mestizaje, Vasconcelos lamented the "race problem" in Mexico, stating, "whether we like it or not the mestizo is the dominant element of the Latin American continent."[18] "From our local point of view in Mexico," he continued, "I have started to preach the gospel of the mestizo by trying to impress on the minds of the new race a consciousness of their mission as builders of entirely new concepts of life. But if the mixed race is going to be able to do anything at all, it is first necessary to give it moral strength and faith in its own ability."[19] Vasconcelos reasoned that Indian blood was to blame for the mestizo's lack of "moral strength." For, as a "lower breed" without hope that "reproduces madly," the Indian languished in a state of degradation.[20] As the native "element" emerged as the difference through which a new mestizo identity could be elaborated, the "backwardness" of the living and breathing Indian remained recalcitrant, a perennial sign of Mexico's lack. Consequently, postrevolutionary national discourse was obsessed with the "Indian Question." In 1917 Mexican anthropologist Manuel Gamio founded the Department of Anthropology specifically to address this question. His department set out to study the racial characteristics, material and intellectual culture, language and dialects, economic, environmental, and biological conditions of the regional populations of present and past Mexico. Gamio insisted that this ambitious and holistic approach would guide the establishment of "official institutions" to "stimulate physical, intellectual, moral and economic development of the people," with the ultimate goal of "cultural fusion, linguistic unification and economic equilibrium," these things being integral components of a "coherent and ... true fatherland."[21] In his lecture "Incorporating the Indian into the National Population," Gamio concluded:

> It is unquestionably urgent, most urgent, to investigate the indigenous population of Mexico scientifically, for until this is done thoroughly, social contacts cannot be normalized and oriented authoritatively, a thing by all means desirable since it requires convergent racial, cultural, and spiritual fusion to secure unification of tongue and equilibrium of economic interests. This, and only this, can place the Mexican nation as a nation, upon a solid, logical, consistent, and permanent base.[22]

By 1940 this directive had become so commonplace that it was reiterated by Mexican president Lazaro Cárdenas at the First Inter-American Indigenist Congress, where he argued memorably for the "Mexicanization" of the Indian.[23]

In accordance with this sentiment, the Ministry of Public Education was retooled in 1921, immediately after the military struggles of the revolution subsided. President Obregón appointed José Vasconcelos its first director, and it was Vasconcelos's messianic vision that shaped the ministry's activities thereafter. In his autobiography, Vasconcelos states explicitly that the ministry's project was fivefold, with the promotion and development of schools, libraries, and the fine arts as its "essential" parts and "bringing the Indian into the current of Spanish culture and ... literacy to the masses" its "auxiliary activities."[24] For him, "ignorance" was a "plague" that afflicted the modern native population, and education was the "redemptive" agent of their inclusion within the Mexican nation. He equated his ministry with the work of Spanish missionaries who, in his words, "believed that they were saving not merely the bodies, but more important, the souls of their students."[25] As part of his mission, Vasconcelos allocated unprecedented resources to public education and inaugurated a national culture project.

Disciplinary Culture

Vasconcelos's belief in the utility and importance of culture was
nurtured during his participation in the Athenaeum of Youth, an organization of young intellectuals in Mexico City founded in 1909. These
young minds were united by a rejection of the positivism of the *Porfiriato* (the dictatorship of Porfirio Díaz, 1884–1911) and an interest in
humanist philosophy. While they advocated artistic individuality over
political participation, many were enfranchised by the postrevolutionary government as its policy makers and social programmers.[26] Art was
a vital component of the Athenaeum philosophy, as the writings of Vasconcelos and Antonio Caso, two of its most prominent members, make
clear. For both, art transcended the biological or material pursuits of
man, and each conceived of aesthetics as part of his ethics. Caso reasoned that, as an expression of the sublime, art was an avenue toward
moral and religious ideals. Those who contemplate art are not motivated
by self-interest, he asserted; thus they are better social beings.[27]

Likewise, Vasconcelos placed the "aesthetic" at the apex of his theory
of social and human evolution, according to which humanity progresses
through a series of stages: a materialist phase, an intellectual or rational-
ist phase, and finally an aesthetic phase. In the superior aesthetic stage,
the heterogeneous elements of existence are synthesized, man intuits the
"absolute" and is civilized through the purification of beauty.[28] Vasconcelos's privileging of the aesthetic as a synthesizing force over the material
and intellectual was a direct response to the scientism of the Porfiriato
and the capitalist values that rationalized U.S. investment in Mexico
at the expense of its inhabitants. The youths of the Athenaeum distinguished Mexico from the Protestant North by emphasizing a spiritual
disposition emanating from the Catholic tradition in Latin America.[29]
By heralding the aesthetic and equating it with the spiritual, Vasconcelos theorized a different standard for progress in which his homeland
was, by implication, ahead. And, by contrast, the rational and materialist society of the United States appeared to languish in an earlier stage
of development.[30] Vasconcelos's interest in aesthetics, therefore, must be
understood as both philosophical and political, for he believed that the
admixture of native and Hispanic characteristics in the Mexican people
made them more emotional and thus more susceptible to aesthetics than
their northern counterparts. According to Vasconcelos, "mixture," "synthesis," and mestizaje made up the fundamental components of Mexican
culture, and art embodied this in its most elevated state.

Formally, the Athenaeum disbanded during the Revolution, but
some of the members converted its philosophical insights into more
technocratic concerns through the Popular University, an extension

program that stressed the disciplining of the working classes through courses on hygiene, family, the work ethic, and art. In 1915 Antonio Caso presented a series of lectures at the university that emphasized the "civilizing role" of art based on his theory of disinterested pleasure.[31] What Caso advocated as an "aristocracy of virtue" became educational reform through the cultural renaissance orchestrated by Vasconcelos during his tenure at the ministry. As Mary Kay Vaughan has argued in her book on Mexican education and social class, the notion of art as a civilizing agent underlay the ministry's establishment of workers' cultural centers as well as Vasconcelos's gathering of Mexican artists, in 1921, to participate in a public art project.[32]

Returning to Vasconcelos's essay *The Cosmic Race,* we can better appreciate how public art contributed to his messianic vision of national development. As part of his celebration of the mestizo, Vasconcelos elaborated a theory of "aesthetic eugenics" that explicates the importance he placed upon beauty and the visual arts as an administrator. The optimal racial fusion he envisioned hinged upon what he called the "mysterious eugenics of aesthetic taste."[33] He writes:

> The laws of emotion, beauty, and happiness will determine the selection of a mate with infinitely superior results than that of a eugenics grounded on scientific reason. ... Where enlightened passion rules, no correctives are necessary. The very ugly will not procreate, they will have no desire to procreate. What does it matter, then, that all the races mix with each other if ugliness will find no cradle? Poverty, defective education, the scarcity of beautiful types, the misery that makes people ugly, all those calamities will disappear from the future social stage.[34]

The aesthetic was not merely a conceptual category, it was also a disciplinary principle with effects that Vasconcelos felt would be discernible in the behavior of all who came into contact with beauty. As part of his cultural initiative, Vasconcelos commissioned Mexican artists to paint large murals on public buildings, thus inaugurating the Mexican mural renaissance. To infuse these artists with a sense of their own cultural roots he encouraged them to look at and appreciate native and popular art forms. For Vasconcelos, however, the "classics" remained the epitome of beautiful and sublime artistic expression.[35] He writes in his autobiography, "I had recommended popular art as a basis from which to go on to the classics, without crossing over to the mediocre."[36] He envisioned murals based on literary themes with symbolic and allegorical representations of virtues, and theorized that the mere presence of this material in public space would enlighten and thereby lift up the populace.

While many artists participated in the mural project, *los tres grandes*—José Clemente Orozco, Diego Rivera, and David Alfaro Siqueiros—are its most famous representatives. The murals executed at the National Preparatory School, their first commission, reveal the extent to which these artists struggled to codify a national aesthetic and political platform without an adequate thematic or visual language in place.

Developing a National Iconography

In 1922 Vasconcelos awarded the indoor auditorium at the Preparatory to Rivera. The artist had recently returned from Europe, where he had mastered a variety of vanguard styles. Upon being commissioned to paint a large public mural, Rivera looked to the early Renaissance frescos in southern Italy as a model and drew inspiration from their iconography as well as their social function. Following Vasconcelos's advice, he toured Mexico's pre-Hispanic monuments and found a local mural tradition in the decorative remnants that survived at Chichen Itzá, Mitla, Monte Albán, and Teotihuacán.[37] Thus the reference to a "renaissance" in the Mexican mural renaissance is both a nod to the flourishing of culture in early modern Europe and a claim for a "rebirth" of pre-Columbian culture in modern Mexico, although the first paintings executed by muralists were more indebted to European precedents than to these local examples. The original Preparatory murals reflect an eclectic mix of religious fresco painting, classical allegory, and vanguard styles.

The theme for Rivera's first mural (fig. 1) was "creation." Its image radiates from a man emanating from the tree of life with his arms outstretched in a gesture that mirrors the rays of the sun directly above him. Rivera's equation of man and universe establishes a homology between micro- and macrocosm and is a subtle homage to Leonardo's *Vitruvian Man*. A nude couple, seated to the left and right of this universal man, are in "colloquy," with female allegories representing aspects of man's spirit: Knowledge, Poetry, Tradition, Prudence, Justice, Strength, Continence, Song, Charity, Hope, Faith, Wisdom, Micro- and Macrocosm, and Infinity.[38] These virtues are borrowed from the religious iconography and humanist philosophy of the Italian Renaissance, but Rivera augments them with markers of race and class drawn from the spectrum of Mexican society. Through hair and eye color, dress, and disposition, each female figure represents not only an aspect of "man's spirit" but also an essentialized aspect of the mestizo or "cosmic race." For example, in the grouping to the right, Rivera depicts a woman clad in a red *rebozo* (a shawl worn by Mexican peasants); her dark features and humble demeanor invoke the racial and social markings of an "Indian working woman."[39] Consequently, she signifies "Tradition." In contrast, the light-skinned and small-featured woman he depicts at the top of this grouping wears a simple tunic. She represents "Science," and it is no accident that one of Rivera's contemporaries described her as an "Aryan" who casts a "persuasive and possessive glance" at the figures below.[40] Perched at the peak of a subtle hierarchy of virtues, she embodies the ascendance of Western science, while her Indian counterpart, positioned on the left, allegorizes "Infinity."

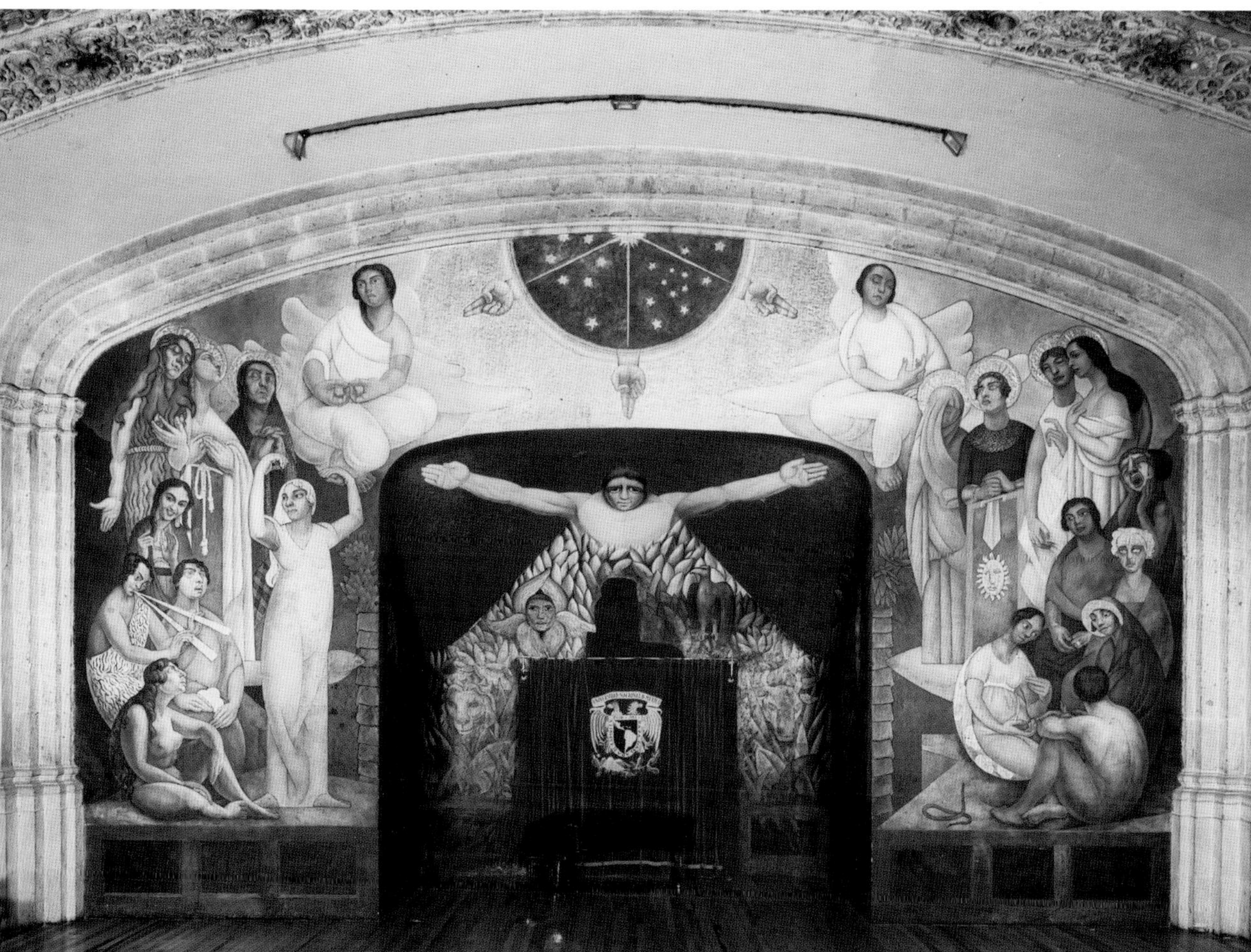

In addition to Native American and European figures, there are a variety of mestizo types identifiable by regional traits in their facial features and dress. While there is an even distribution of qualities and types, Rivera's allocation of intellectual and creative attributes to particular castes reveals his preoccupation with racial politics. In his attempt to speak to the specificity of his homeland, Rivera presented an egalitarian image of racial harmony. However, as Leonard Folgarait argues, his is an image of metamorphosis that uses "the history of stylistic developments in western art from the fifteenth to the twentieth centuries" to encode a progressive narrative of assimilation accomplished through education.[41] Folgarait notes that the nude male and female figures at the mural's base are rendered in a cubistic three-dimensionality, while the virtues that instruct them are flatter and more linear, not to mention clothed and "cultured." These rudimentary beings are linked formally to their "spiritual" consorts through a system of interlocking curves that move the eye upward from base materiality toward transcendence.[42]

Folgarait attributes the synthetic amalgamation of Renaissance art, cubism and "a hint of the naïf" to Vasconcelos's elitsm. Since Vasconcelos gave him the theme of "creation," Folgarait argues, Rivera was under the influence of his assimilationist agenda in this first mural.[43] But the stylistic eclecticism and the progressive narrative encoded in *Creation* are also present in Rivera's more politically radical murals at the Ministry of Public Education. Furthermore, the first public works by all of the muralists demonstrate a similar conservatism with respect to style and subject matter. Mexican artists had been given a public platform for their art, but they were not clear about what they were doing or how to do it. Naturally, they turned first to precedents from the history of "great" art. They had little knowledge of traditional Mexican culture and were themselves charged with inventing an authentic form of national expression. The murals executed at the National Preparatory School provide a visual record of these artists' initial trial-and-error approach.[44]

Between 1922 and 1925 Jean Charlot, Fernando Leal, José Clemente Orozco, and David Siqueiros all executed murals at the National Preparatory School.[45] Siqueiros began allegorical images of the four elements in the Colegio Chico at the end of 1922. Of these murals only one remains. It presents a winged figure with orientalized features surrounded by conch shells and other attributes of "water." Similarly, Orozco's *Maternity* (fig. 2), begun in 1923, presents a familiar trope of traditional civic allegory. As part of a proposed cycle of images—such as "virginity," "youth," and "intelligence"—describing the "Gifts of Nature to Man," *Maternity* depicts a seated mother and child surrounded by angels and a woman who offers a bunch of grapes (a reference to the maternal attribute of fecundity).[46] The flat red and black space behind the figures contrasts with their voluptuous nude bodies. A black triangle encompasses the central mother and child, a theme derived from the iconic figure grouping of traditional Madonna and child paintings and a commonplace in the national art of both liberal and conservative regimes. Like Rivera, Orozco combines motifs from Italian frescos (in this case Botticelli's) with cubist space, but *Maternity* is devoid of any references to race, class, or contemporary politics.

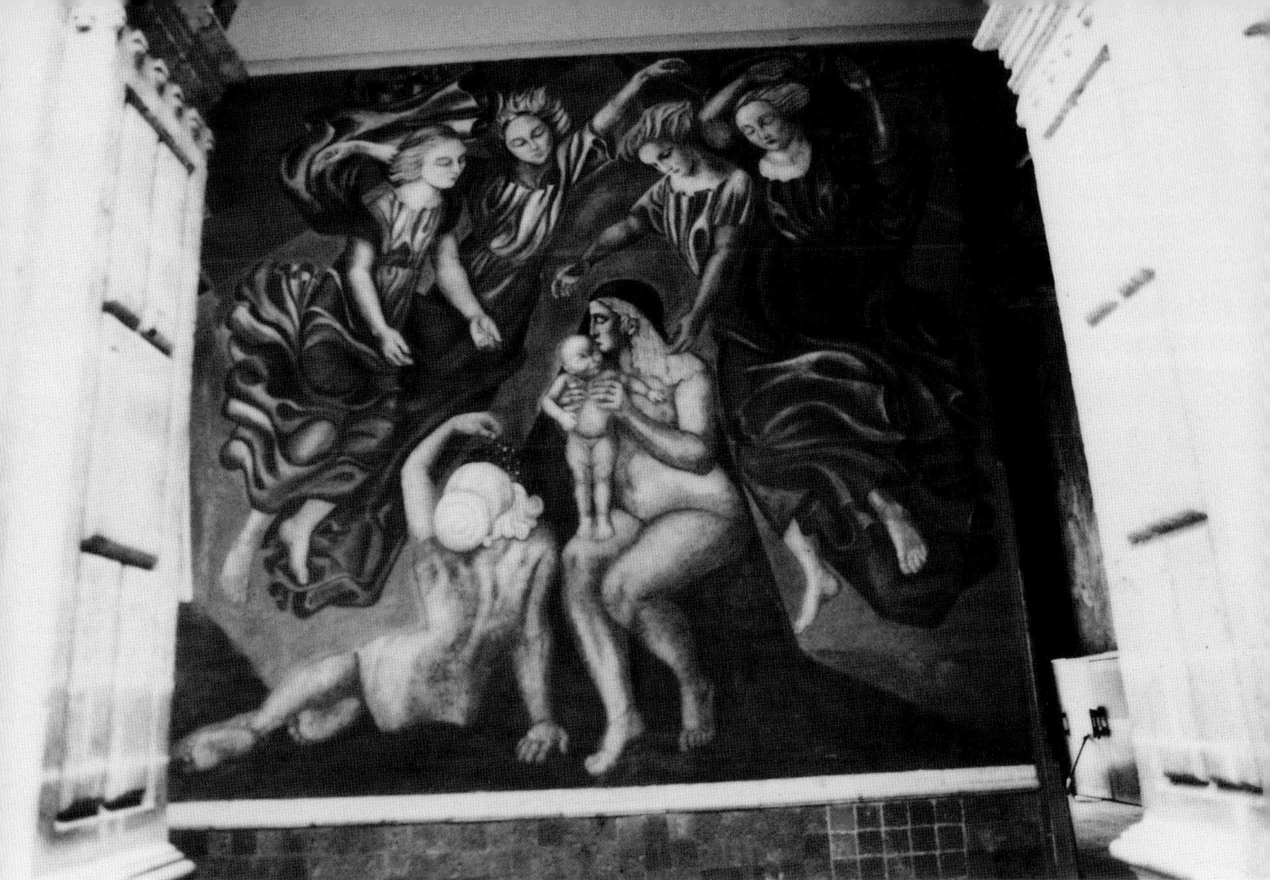

The murals by Charlot and Leal, by contrast, depict scenes drawn from Mexican history and folklore. In *The Fall of Tenochtitlán,* executed in 1923, Charlot re-created a scene from the Conquest in a cramped composition that emphasizes the overpowering force of the Spanish conquistadors. Aztec chiefs and warriors confront a cadence of arching horses and red lances. The visual rhythms and flat space of this mural are indebted to modernist styles, but the composition and many iconographic elements were lifted directly from Paolo Ucello's *Battle of San Romano* (c. 1445).[47] Leal's mural, *The Feast of Holy Lord Chalma,* also painted in 1923, represents a popular religious festival as a synchronistic layering of Christian and pagan rituals.

These early paintings were unsatisfactory to the muralists. Rivera characterized *Creation* as a "false start."[48] Siqueiros labeled his paintings and those of his compatriots "colonial" retrospectively.[49] Orozco scrapped his original cycle and, with the exception of *Maternity,* embarked on a completely different program. The rhetoric of derivativeness and inauthenticity deployed in these accounts betrays the anxiety these artists felt about their first efforts. Their retrospective historicization is all the more striking in its reliance upon the charged metaphor of colonization to discredit this period as a preliminary moment of indiscretion. The art-historical literature on Mexican muralism echoes this auto-critique.[50] The careers of these artists take the form of enlightenment narratives in which the "discovery" of their native heritage is a "recovery" of what was there all along. This naturalizes not only a historically constructed identity but also a historically constructed movement.

What these first commissions demonstrate is the very lack of collective values and the absence of any organized program on the part of the artists or their governmental patrons. Commenting on this period years later, Siqueiros explained: "There was no one to tell us 'do this and now do that.' We wanted to help the Mexican revolution, but we were doing a very bad job of it. What we were doing as public art might well have been interesting from the point of view of general culture, but from the point of view of what we were going through at the time it was hopeless."[51] Clearly the artists commissioned by Vasconcelos understood their practice to be part of the revolutionary struggle, but initially they did not know how to actualize their political convictions. Their early murals demonstrate that a specifically "national" iconography, style, or subject matter was far from obvious or given. Rather, it had to be developed, defined, and defended. Furthermore, culture proved to be a hotly contested political terrain, as various power sectors vied for the general acceptance of their interpretation of the nation, the revolution, and the people. The "invention of tradition" in Mexican art was characterized by constant professional and political competition, and only eventually unified through the rubric of a "movement."

Ultimately, the Mexican Communist Party (PCM), not Vasconcelos, offered these artists the direction they sought. Rivera and Siqueiros were both members (although Rivera was expelled in 1929). The party radicalized these artists and prompted them to join with others to form the Union of Mexican Workers, Technicians, Painters, and Sculptors. A socialist organization, the Union was dedicated to popular revolution and based in the tenets of communism, then understood as a contemporary rebirth of pre-Columbian social and political structure. Although the Union was clearly the brainchild of Siqueiros and Rivera, even artists skeptical about its affiliations with contemporary politics—such as Orozco—signed the manifesto they published in their journal *El Machete*. The manifesto declared war on "bourgeois individualism" and repudiated "easel painting and any other form of art emanating from ultra-intellectual and aristocratic circles."[52]

El Machete was a Marxist journal dedicated to "proletarian art" and an important vehicle for the elaboration and development of national culture. Socialism's alignment with the working class reinforced these artists' desire to put their talent in the service of the people. In their attempts to define a popular aesthetic and subject matter, they too turned to Mexico's indigenous populations as the solution to a crisis of Mexican identity. The identification between the nation and the native is clear in the manifesto, which reads in part, "the art of the Mexican people is the most important and vital spiritual manifestation in the world today, and its Indian traditions lie at its very heart."[53] The Union artists shared with their governmental counterparts a belief in the spiritual capacities of art, as well as in the centrality of Mexico's indigenous populations to the articulation of an autonomous identity.

The effects of this collective organization and mission were immediately visible in Orozco's Preparatory murals. Only *Maternity* survived the drastic changes in his subject matter and style, as he embarked upon the expressionistic images critiquing the postrevolutionary social order that we know today. Images from the completed cycle, such as *The Trench* (1926) (fig. 3), communicate a tragic perspective on the violence of the

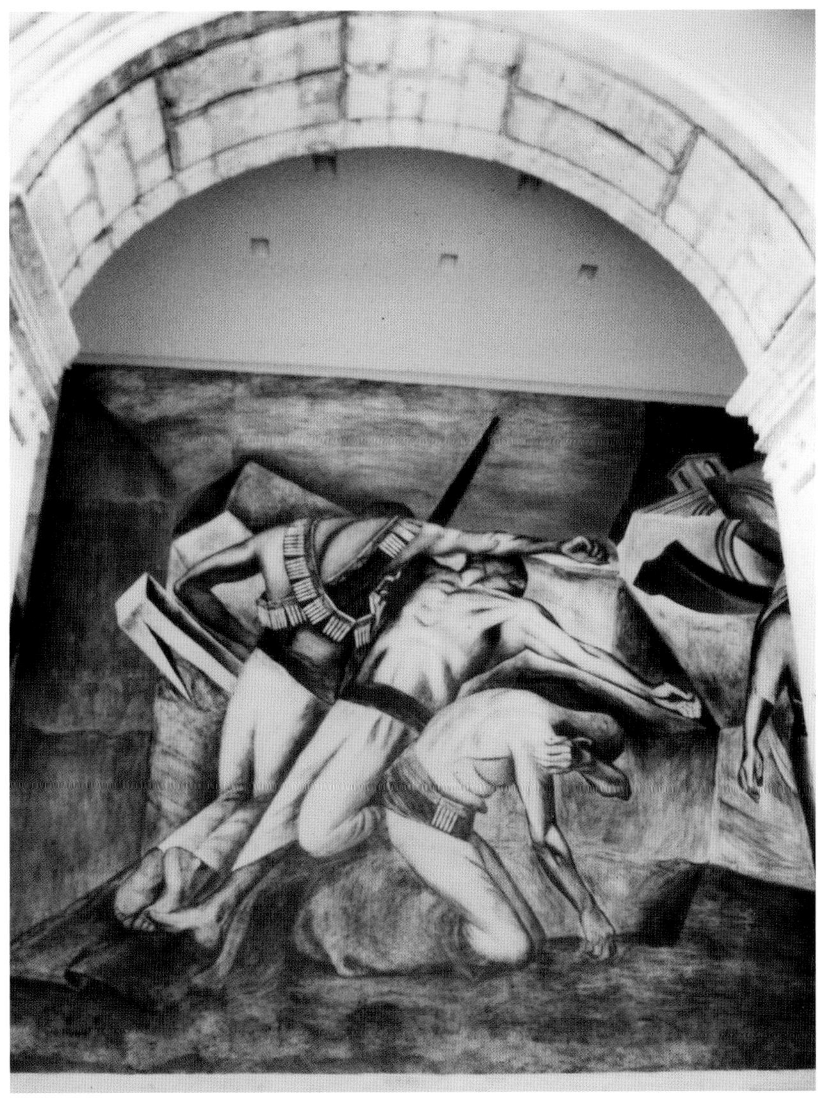

3 José Clemente Orozco, *The Trench* (1923–27), fresco, 10 x 8.5 ft. National Preparatory School, Mexico City.

revolution. Three soldiers form the center of the composition, one kneeling in a gesture of despair, another lying flat against a jagged rock, arms splayed in a posture reminiscent of the crucifixion, and the other collapsed upon him. Their peasant clothing and gun belts identify them as revolutionary soldiers. The red sky, jutting rocks, and bayonets describe a ravaged landscape in which no solace can be found. Orozco's image of martyrdom conveys the pain and loss of a long military struggle, accomplished largely through the sacrifice of Mexico's most impoverished citizens. His reference to recent events, although critical in tone, gives the mural a radical inflection that contrasts markedly with the Italianate *Maternity.* While Orozco's Preparatory murals represent the most striking and immediate effects of the Communist Party on mural art, the most enduring legacy of this influence is found in the careers of Rivera and Siqueiros. Despite the competing versions of proletarian art elaborated by each over his lifetime, both asserted the foundations of Mexican nationalism in an affirmative vision of indigenismo.

Cultural Mestizaje

In 1923 Rivera persuaded Vasconcelos to let him and other artists paint murals on the courtyard walls of the Ministry of Public Education.[54] Unlike his Preparatory murals, Rivera's ministry murals are explicit about his newfound political convictions, a militant socialism inflected by the values of *Zapatismo* that solidified over the five years he worked on them. Rivera writes in his autobiography that in these murals he wanted to "reflect the social life of Mexico as I saw it, and through my vision of the truth to show the masses the outline of the future."[55] His desire to reveal the "truth" to the "masses" in order to benefit the "future" recalls the disciplinary rhetoric of Vasconcelos and Gamio, and it finds its first visual articulation in these paintings. While Rivera asserts the native as the essence of the body politic, he reverses the moral hierarchy attributed to race in most of the diagnostic literature discussed earlier. However, by narrating a progressive movement from a rural and agrarian idyll to an urban and proletarian future, Rivera's murals promote the indigenous largely in the name of proletarianization.

While executing his murals at the ministry, Rivera was also at work on his Chapingo agricultural murals, in which he vividly expressed the reciprocity between the land, the revolution, and modern industry. In the Chapingo cycle, Rivera personified the Mexican landscape through nude women, enslaved by colonial forces and liberated through revolutionary struggle. The central and dominant nude represents the earth harnessed and exploited by man for industrial development. In other panels Rivera characterizes the land as a womb that houses revolutionary heroes who in turn nourish the soil with their blood. Responding to his location (an agricultural school), Rivera took up the subject of agrarian reform; consequently these murals directly engage an issue central to the revolutionary struggle. At the ministry, Rivera amplified the interdependence of land, people, and postrevolutionary nationalism. Thus his Chapingo murals provide a visual fulcrum between the classical symbolism in *Creation* and the "revolutionary" style he developed over the five years he worked on the ministry project.

At Chapingo, Rivera again used feminine allegories to represent Mexico. This time, however, instead of referring to abstract values, these monumental women are representations of the Mexican land. The central nude reclines in a posture that reproduces the contours of Mexico's territorial borders. These nudes fluctuate between allegorical and historical assignations. As symbols of the land, they conjure traditional associations between the female body and the gifts of nature. Within Mexico, however, the use of the female body to indicate "virgin," "fecund," or "exploited" territory recalls one of the most potent icons of Mexican colonization, the *chingada.* Based on the historical figure of Doña Marina, an Indian woman married to Cortés who then became his translator, the chingada or "fucked one" has become the figurative mother of postcontact Mexico.[56] As such, the women in Rivera's Chapingo murals are closer to the iconography of his ministry murals than to the feminized virtues of *Creation.* Similarly, at Chapingo Rivera first introduced overt references to revolutionary soldiers and heroes. Specifically, he paid homage to Zapata by depicting him in his grave, alongside Otilio Montaño (a professor and ideologue for Zapata). As with the nude women, these martyrs are literal and metaphorical representations. They refer to Zapata and Montaño's deaths but assert that they continue to nourish the nation with their blood. However, Zapata also represents México profundo (deep Mexico). Naturalized through an equation with the buried pre-Hispanic past, his racialized body represents the rebirth of the essential Mexico, and the revolution, the agent of its resurrection.

In the ministry murals the allegorical language evident in the Preparatory and Chapingo murals dissipates as Rivera develops a more realist and narrative style. The artist painted more than 150 panels from 1923 to 1928, literally covering every available inch of wall space on three floors of the colossal colonial building. The panels he painted during the first three years are sparse, open compositions, rendered in a naturalistic style that is often inflected by the pastoral and "primitivizing" tendencies of Post-Impressionist painting. The images he executed over the last few years are more uniformly cubist in style. Their dense compositions and shallow space convey complex political messages through economic formal means. Rivera's stylistic evolution mirrors his shift from subjects that literalize the agrarian values of Zapatismo to vignettes that emphasize the political potential of international socialism.

While most discussions of this complex project tend to treat individual panels in isolation, if one examines the cycle as a whole, a progressive narrative emerges that begins in a revolutionary past and moves toward a proletarian future.[57] Through his narrative use of architectural space, Rivera establishes the revolution as the foundation for Mexico's political future. Furthermore, he characterizes the revolution as a popular movement with the native Mexican as its agent. In the panels dedicated to this period, he emphasizes the landscape and idealizes indigenous communities and peoples, while in those panels representing socialist society he highlights industrialization and the equalization of race and social class.

Rivera's formal progression is attributable in part to the maturation of his style, but, like his eclectic mixing of visual idioms in *Creation,* this change elaborates a sophisticated symbolic narrative of national modernization. Implicit within this story is a cultural mestizaje that Rivera conveys as much through literal representation as through the formal language of style. Thus he renders the premodern native through the vocabulary of "primitivism," while treating the modernized citizen in the simplified cubist language typical of much social realism.[58] Throughout, Rivera makes sly references to the history of art. Most significantly, he intermingles pre-Columbian and modern tropes in order to express the promise of the cultural mestizo.

Rivera divided the subject matter of his cycle into two categories, the courts of labor and fiestas, which correspond to the two three-floor courtyards of the ministry building. In the former (painted in 1923), Rivera depicted the industrial and agricultural labors of the Mexican people on the first floor. He dedicated the second floor to intellectual labor, which he represented with grisaille renderings of professional insignia, while on the third floor he painted portraits of revolutionary heroes. The first-floor murals promote Zapatismo. Rivera exalts indigenous laborers and rural *campesinos* (agrarian workers or peasants) and condemns the exploitation of these figures by corrupt *hacendados* (proprietors of haciendas) or dangerous working conditions. In *The Liberation of the Peon* (1923) (fig. 4), revolutionary soldiers rescue a mistreated campesino. These same soldiers appear again in *The New School* (1923) overseeing the education of peasants. Rivera sets these images in vast landscapes that conjure the rich and diverse topography of the country and recall Zapata's revolutionary slogan, "tierra y libertad" (land and liberty). Furthermore, his paintings of volcanoes, magueys, and cacti, as well as identifiable architectural landscapes such as the hillsides of stacked housing typical of Guanajuato, elaborate an allegorical topography infused with political values.[59] By contrast, in panels dedicated to industrial labor, Rivera reinforces the theme of exploitation. For example, in *Entry into the Mines* (1923) he visually equates this dangerous work with death by rendering the mineshaft in the guise of a gaping skull that seems to ingest the approaching workers.[60] By juxtaposing these images of harsh labor with idyllic portraits of Tehuanas dying cloth or indigenous artisans decorating pottery, Rivera contrasts traditional communitarian modes of production with colonial and postcolonial forms of class exploitation and low-wage labor.

In the court of fiestas, Rivera illustrates popular religious and political festivals on the first floor, intellectual activities on the second floor, and revolutionary *corridos* (songs) on the third. On the first floor, amid panels describing native and popular festivals, he has placed three large murals representing agrarian reform, May Day, and the popular market. The latter is depicted as a modern embodiment of the ancient Aztec market—the *Tianguis*—for which it is titled. The physical placement of these three panels suggests the equivalence of each event. Similar in scale and located at equidistant intervals, these murals are the foci and visual anchors of the three painted courtyard walls. The homology Rivera endeavors to establish between native traditions, the agrarian revolution, and Soviet-style socialism is reinforced visually as well as physically through these spatial dynamics. His ideological disposition is clear in these panels, in which masses of soldiers, agrarian workers, and factory workers are unified culturally by local traditions and politically by the promise of socialism. Throughout the ministry cycle, his spatial distribution of individual mural paintings develops a narrative that is elaborated and communicated as much through representation as through the physical movement of the visitor around the building's courtyard. The progression from revolution to a proletarian society is conveyed throughout, but it is best illustrated through the narrative convention of the corridos on the third floor and the physical climb up the stairwell corridor. In both of these spaces, representations of indigenous peoples help to legitimize Rivera's vision of Mexico's past and future.

Rivera's conflation of the values of the Mexican Revolution and socialism is most evident in the third-floor panels, which are connected by a painted red ribbon upon which agrarian and proletarian songs are printed. These panels contrast bourgeois values with socialist ones. It is important to note that the critique of capital was multivalent in the Mexican context, where it called upon deep-seated resentment toward U.S. imperialism during the Porfiriato. Because U.S. investment during the dictatorship was viewed as a continuation of the colonial practices of Europeans, the "bourgeois" epithet is doubly insulting. It is both an

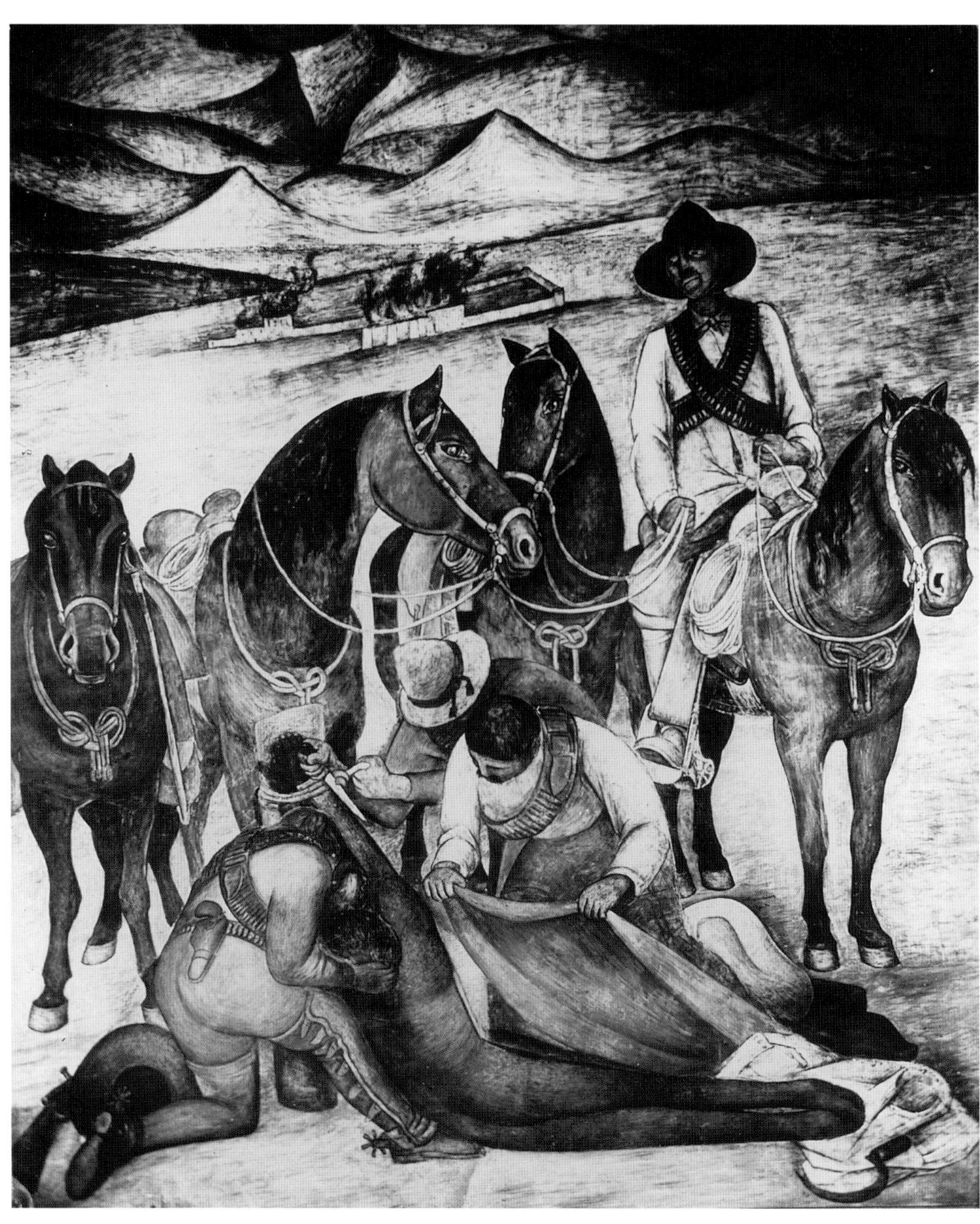

4 Diego Rivera, *The Liberation of the Peon* (1923), fresco, 4.38 x 3.48 m. Court of Labor, south wall, first floor, Ministry of Public Education, Mexico City.

attack on class affiliation through socialist political values and a critique of cultural affiliations through the politics of nationalism.

At the ministry, Rivera lampooned figures such as J. D. Rockefeller and Vasconcelos himself, while lionizing the communist worker and the revolutionary soldier. For example, in *Wall Street Banquet* (1928), he depicts wealthy Manhattanites dining on champagne and tickertape. In *Our Daily Bread* (1928) (fig. 5), Rivera portrays a humble table presided over by a worker in blue overalls, wearing the red star of communism and breaking bread as a Tehuana offers a basket of indigenous fruits. At the table are seated individuals gathered from across Mexico's racial and social classes, while a soldier and farmer stand nearby. Rivera sets the entire scene in front of a factory-scape—a motif that refers to the (vulgar) Marxist belief that technology would hasten the destruction of capitalist society and thereby social inequality (an issue relevant to Rivera's later *Detroit Industry* mural, as discussed by Anthony Lee in this volume). This kind of opposition occurs throughout Rivera's ministry murals, as socialism increasingly signifies the future of Mexican politics and inflects the popular struggles of the recent revolution.

Rivera introduces the third-floor images with *The Distribution of Arms* (1928), a painting that prophesies the proletarian revolution through its depiction of militant figures passing out weapons, and the worker's song that frames it. The opening line, "Así será la revolución Proletaria" (And so it will be, the Proletarian revolution), places the distribution of arms not in the past but in the future, and each subsequent image describes how the revolution will proceed. At the culmination of the song, an agrarian corrido begins, printed on the same tromp l'oeil ribbon. Through the iconographic continuity of each illustrated song, Rivera visually conflates the Mexican Revolution with a coming proletarian revolution and asserts that one follows logically from the other.

The Mexican Revolution has been historically distinguished from other revolutions (in particular the French, American, and Russian) because it lacked a collective political program or organization.[61] As a result it is often described as a "spontaneous" revolution, and its relative failures are attributed to the orgiastic nature of its eruption. In Rivera's murals, however, the "spontaneous" eruption born of a subjugated people's collective sense of injustice is tacitly modeled after the political organization of the international communist movement. Subsequently, the authenticity of the local event naturalizes an imported political agenda by asserting that both are structured by the same values.[62]

Rivera's metaphorical use of space and representation is best captured in his stairway murals at the ministry, executed in 1926. He painted the stairwell from the ground up with a symbolic landscape of social evolution that uses geological change to convey the sociocultural

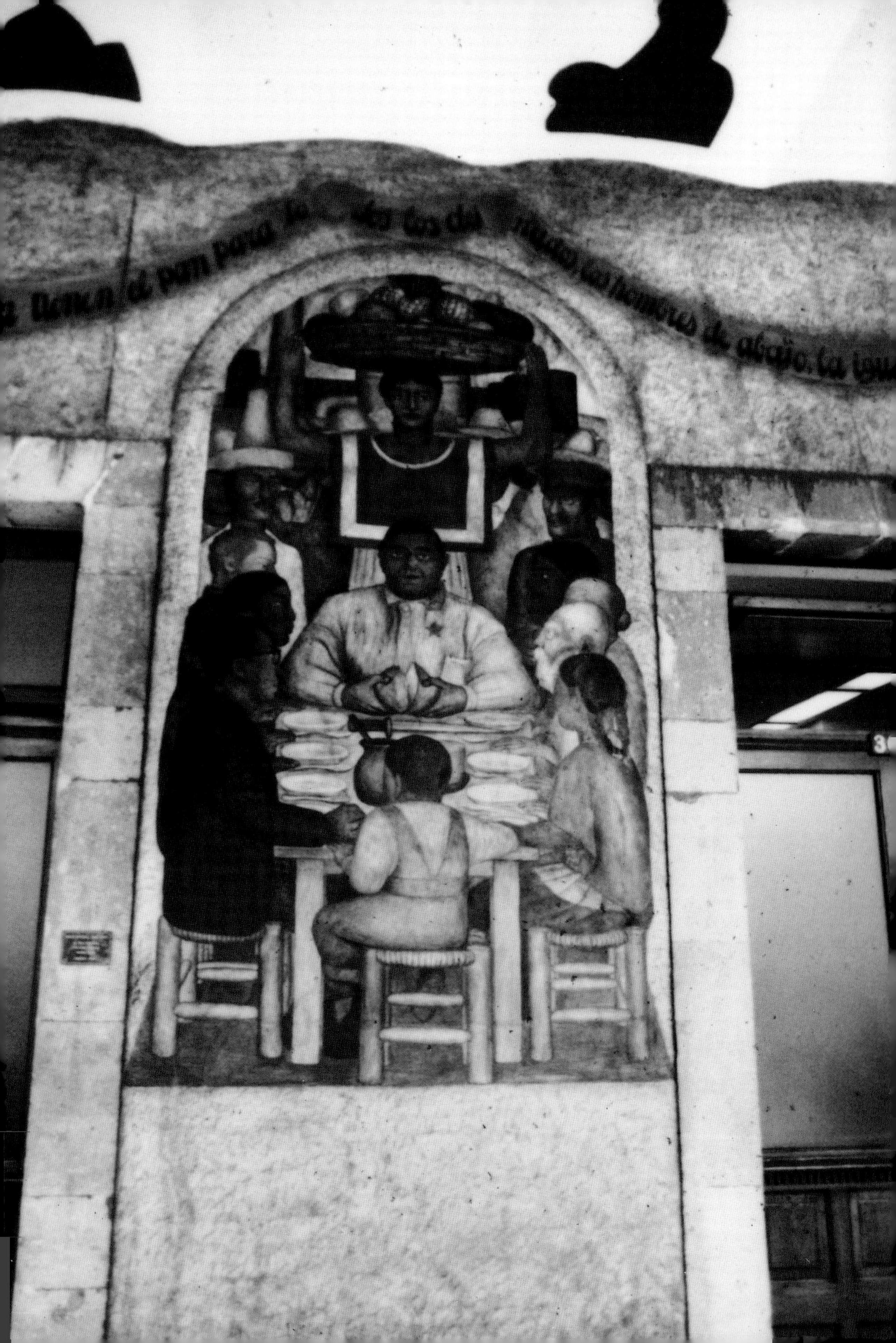

tienen el pan para la   los de   hombres de abajo, la igu

development of "peoples" from "pre-modern society" to a proletarian social order.[63] There is a general "progression" throughout the entire ministry cycle; as one moves from the ground floor to the upper balconies, the native symbolizes an essential yet primitive past and the communist worker signifies a socially unified future. The staircase images are both topographic and ethnographic. They present a cultural evolution from "subterranean waters" through the tropics, high plateau, and, finally, snow-capped mountains. Inhabiting these Mexican landscapes are allegorical nudes as well as native types from Mexico's past and present, such as the Tehuanas from the Isthmus of Tehuantepec. By mixing together past and contemporary native populations, Rivera suggests continuity from Mexico's pre-Columbian past to its postrevolutionary present. Nonetheless, there is a subtle chronological progression that converts his cycle into a political history lesson as well. Rivera's complex layering of topography, ethnography, and history makes sophisticated use of the spatial structure of a stairwell. As the viewer walks up the stairs he enacts a historical walk that simulates the passage from a primordial past to a modern future. Ultimately these paintings provide a comprehensive and politicized representation of national development in microcosm that encapsulates the narrative elaborated throughout the larger mural cycle.

The panels at the base of the stairs represent mythologized marinescapes inhabited by modern technologies. Ideologically, these images are ambivalent about the relationship between man, machine, and land. As one moves up from sea level into the tropics of Tehuantepec, the image of a sugar hacienda emerges, complete with lazy boss and exploited labor (fig. 6). Gradually, Rivera clothes the natives in these frescos, which suggests the encroachment of "civilization" along with conquest and colonization. He alludes to the revolution in *The Burial,* an image that recalls Courbet's famous *Burial at Ornans* (1849–50), as well as his own depictions of slain heroes at Chapingo. Finally, with the passing of the revolution comes *The Mechanization of the Countryside* (fig. 7), in which the trinity of exploitation—the church, capital, and the corrupt military—are struck down, while their counterparts, represented in the upper corner, augur a new society. In this new, advanced society, worker, soldier, and farmer are united. At the top of his historical narrative, Rivera depicts the artist (a self-portrait) as a technical worker along with the stonecutter and architect.

Throughout his stairwell murals Rivera samples an array of modernist styles and quotes specific motifs to reinforce the subject matter of each region and historical period. His representation of Tehuantepec doubles as an Edenic vision of pre-Conquest communal life. Consequently he stylizes the landscape through visual elements lifted from

Gauguin's paintings of Tahitian society (most notably in his treatment
of the trees and their red blossoms throughout the landscape). His use
of the bather motif in the same scene recalls the pastoral imagery that
was a staple of modernist painting from Impressionism through Expressionism. This iconography is not evidence of Rivera's derivativeness, but
rather a sly indexing of European "primitivism" in order to invoke preindustrial society within Mexico. Furthermore, his reference to Courbet
similarly inflects Rivera's realism with the socially progressive aesthetics and politics of the original modern realist. The nation's passage from
exploitation into modern autonomy is also accompanied by a stylistic
change from Post-Impressionism to a cubist rendering of space and an
iconography typical of social realist painting.

Rivera's stylistic facility and vast knowledge of modernist idioms
allowed him to convey his progressive vision of national history and
politics through diverse means. Not only does he explicitly describe this
process in the subject matter of these murals, he also encodes developmen-
tal concepts through a canny survey of the history of art, reworking it to
serve his didactic needs. This is reminiscent of his stylistic eclecticism in
Creation, but it is harder to see in his ministry murals because it is enacted

6 Diego Rivera, *The Hacienda* (1926), fresco, 3.84 x 7.70 m. Stairwell, second floor, Ministry of Public Education, Mexico City.

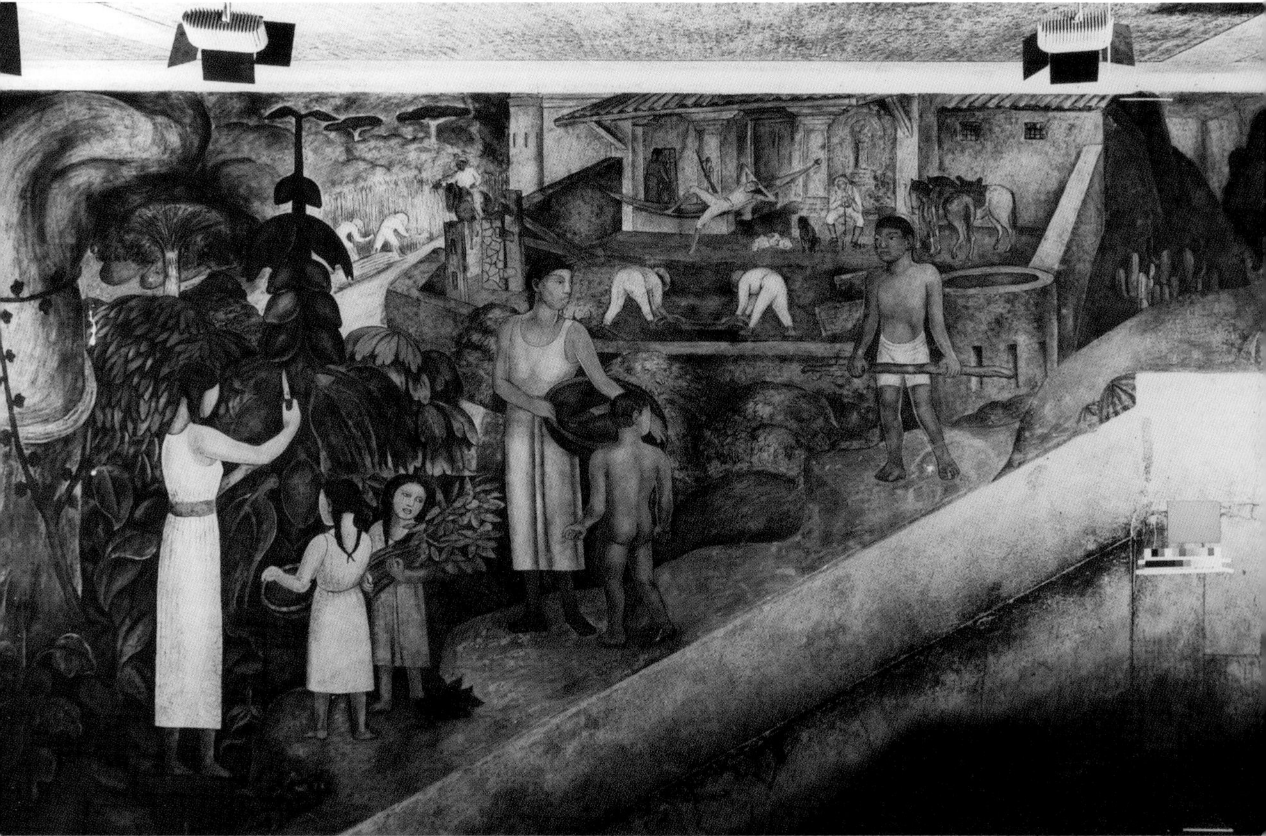

across numerous panels rather than encapsulated in a single iconic image. Nonetheless, just as Rivera used style to depict a progressive vision of assimilation through knowledge in his first mural, he uses it here to support a progressive vision of assimilation through political organization.

Dedicated to the Mexican people, their labors, and their celebrations, Rivera's mural asserts that the nation is founded in the native soil and native populations. Both ultimately undergo changes, however, as

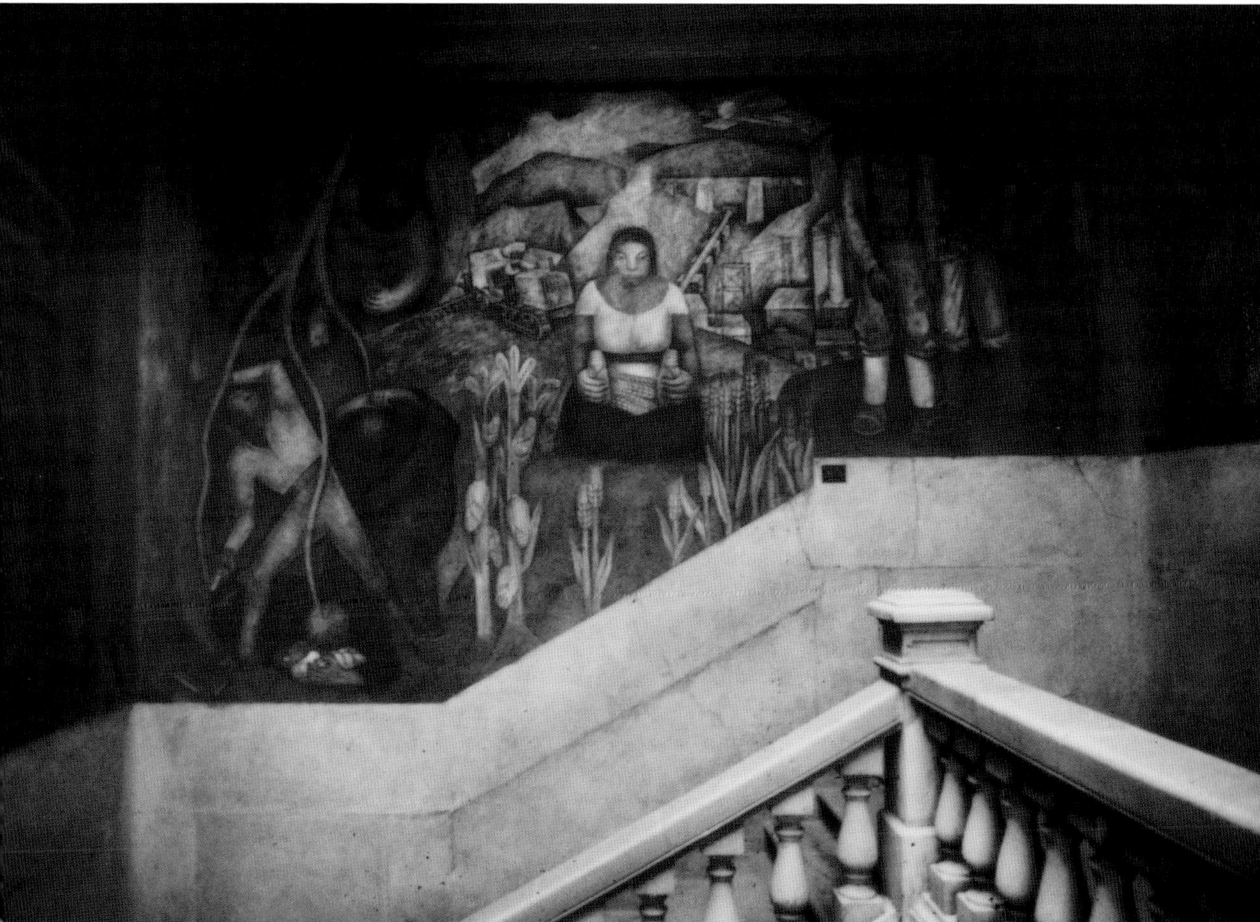

industrialization and Marxist social organization assimilate a disparate populace into a proletariat. By advocating this change in his murals, Rivera issues the same tacit mandate to the Mexican "masses" that Gamio endeavored to do in *Forging a Fatherland* and that Vasconcelos advocated in his educational policies. Native peoples and their practices are addressed as the essential Mexicans, all the while they are being asked to express their citizenship within the new nation by assimilating culturally and adapting to new collective values.

Nation and "Native"

By representing the Mexican nation through an equation of racial types
and landscapes, Rivera's ministry murals present a visual counterpart to
the contemporary literature on Mexican nationalism. For example, in an
essay entitled "Similarity and Contrast," Vasconcelos details at length the
topographical variety of Mexico and then equates this "land of contrasts"
with its various peoples and their characteristics.[64] The equation of
natives with their natural environment was also a component of Gamio's
research at Teotihuacán. Rhetorical appeals to the people and the land
are always an important part of the mechanism of nationalism, and
postrevolutionary Mexico is not unique in this respect.[65] However, the
particular qualities of the landscape identified as definitive of national
character in Mexico provided the basis for unique formulations of the
Mexican people and the "Mexican problem." The rugged terrain of the
"True North" provided a foundational mythology for Canadian national
character. In the United States, natural abundance and endless fron-
tiers have routinely been asserted as coordinates for collective national
personality, while in Argentina the *Pampa* figures significantly in the
popular imagination. In postrevolutionary Mexico, the vast contrast evident in the variegated topography of the country was seized upon as a
natural signifier of the "mixture" reflected in the nation's history and promoted through the racial figure of the mestizo.

As part of this discursive context, Rivera's murals illustrate the prevailing logic of early twentieth-century nationalism, both in his reliance
upon essentialist traits such as "race" and "climate" and in his enthusiasm
about the potential for social control through harnessing these "physical" determinants for a greater social good, future development, and
proper citizenship.[66] This logic appears in Vasconcelos's essay "Similarity
and Contrast" just as clearly as in Rivera's ministry murals. Vasconcelos
argues that Mexico is a "nation of contrast," its history "a series of layers
composed of materials that do not mix," its "social condition" characterized by a "compound of races that have not yet become thoroughly
combined," a place where a mere "glance at our physical structure will
only add to the puzzle of the Mexican problem." He speculates, "perhaps
the reason [for] social contrast lies in the varied physical, temperamental,
and historical factors that intervene in the making of our soul."[67]

Vasconcelos's analysis returns us to the crucial themes of postrevolutionary national discourse: the existence of an unassimilated and racially
variegated population and the difficulties of defining an autonomous
national identity within not only a postcolonial and postrevolutionary context but also one framed by historical and ongoing U.S. imperialism. Thus
in Vasconcelos's description, modern Mexico is a "nation of contrasts" com-

posed of "materials that do not mix" that has yet to realize its "soul." The crafting of the "Mexican soul" was the explicit project of postrevolutionary cultural nationalism. The "will to nation" expressed in this literature came to fruition with the concept of mestizaje, simultaneously producing and circumscribing indigenous peoples as objects of study, regulation, and representation. The emergent school of Mexican anthropology sought to know the native, while governmental programs endeavored to inculcate this disenfranchised population into the newly "imagined community" of mestizo nationhood. Furthermore, national culture seized upon the Indian as an object of representation and a producer of authentic Mexican art.

Manuel Gamio gave scientific credence to Vasconcelos's thesis when he added an analysis of the contemporary native peoples inhabiting Teotihuacán to his definitive archeological study of the area.[68] In addition to researching their folklore and medicine, his scientists surveyed their agricultural practices and diet, connecting cultural attributes to environmental ones in order to abet Gamio's conviction that a thorough study of the region's past and present would enable more effective assimilation policies. The institutional relationship between these fields of practice produced powerful popular truths about the nation, its heritage, and the conditions for citizenship.

Likewise, Rivera's ministry murals offer a "folkloric" appreciation of native life in the name of advancing modernization. While he asserts that the social organization of proletarian culture is based upon the communitarian social organization of pre-Hispanic Mexico, Rivera depicts modern Mexico as a mestizo nation in which racial and social distinctions no longer matter. In short, his vision of social egalitarianism is also a visual corollary of the disciplinary rhetoric of postrevolutionary nationalism. Rivera's murals are lessons in citizenship that rely upon the "natural" racial and territorial markers of a "nation of contrasts." While Rivera's mestizaje is cultural rather than racial (as Vasconcelos's was), the underlying principle of achieving a proper balance between the desirable traits of different racial and social sectors was based upon discriminate and selective criteria in the service of a modernizing national project.

Rivera's biographer, Bertram Wolfe, made this argument explicit in *Portrait of Mexico,* a book published in 1937 and illustrated with the artist's paintings and murals. While Wolfe is the primary author, the work was a collaboration between the two men. Rivera's illustrations account for more than half the pages, and Wolfe treats them as documentary evidence throughout his narrative. Rivera and Wolfe present a history of Mexico from pre-Hispanic times to the present, but they preface this with their own diagnostic take on the "Mexican problem." Wolfe begins by describing the diversity of the Mexican landscape; he then proceeds to the people, where, under the heading "Land of many tierras," he too lingers on the difficulty of unifying a population that in its cultural variety mirrors the incommensurability of its many regions. "Mexico's people and customs and ways of living," he argues, "are as infinitely varied as its landscape."[69] While Wolfe and Rivera value this diversity, they argue that it is rapidly becoming a thing of the past because "Mexico is a land in transition: it is in the process of changing from pre-capitalist to capitalist, from handicraft to machinofacture, from local to national-international economy—from a conglomerate of folks and regions into a nation."[70] They view this transition as inevitable and therefore insist that it be directed by the appropriate interests. As usual, it is the preindustrial native who needs to be brought into the modern era. This, the authors argue:

> would involve aiding them to construct a written language, to preserve ... what is *worthwhile* in their traditions and literature and dances and songs and decorative arts, and to lead to their *voluntary incorporation into a free union of peoples on the basis of a common national, and ultimately international, economy,* in which their immediate part in the national and world division of labor would flow from the climatic-telluric nature of their regions, the local fauna and flora, their special temperaments and aptitudes, and the application of the methods of modern science to the development of the possibilities latent in each of these factors.[71] (Emphasis added.)

While at times they suggest that the cultural practices that survive from the past can ameliorate the ills of urban life, whenever they address the future the corresponding surviving populations are the ones who need to change. Wolfe, in praise of Rivera's vision of Mexico's future, concludes his introduction by explaining that "Rivera is on the side of the machine;" thus his reverence for native folklore is always accompanied by images of the "esthetic beauties and human possibilities of modern machinery."[72] Rivera makes his interest in both evident throughout the ministry murals and his illustrations in this volume. Images of airplanes, tractors, and industrial plants coexist with pre-Hispanic statuary and *artesanías,* all set within Edenic landscapes. Through the combination of text and image, the authors argue that the preservation of certain elements of native life is desirable, but not those that interfere with modernization and an assimilated national identity.

Within the discursive practices discussed thus far, the native is at the center of questions regarding appropriate being or conduct and political reason or rule. The contemporary native is an object of study and therefore of knowledge, an object of moral reflection, an object of representation, and an object of government. The problematization of Mexico-as-nation produced statements of truth about the natives: that

in the contemporary period they existed in a degraded state that mandated intervention; that their culture was essential to the nation and the
only proper expression of their difference from the nation; that they
were in need of help; that they were the historical agents of national
becoming; that they had to assimilate to some new form of collective
or community.[73] The personal conduct of the native became essential to
the question of rule and representation, and these truths structured the
ways in which the native and nation could subsequently be framed. The
struggle over the nation was therefore a struggle over the native. The
allegiance of indigenous peoples was sought while they were simultaneously objectified as "the indigenous" through governing practices that
ranged from anthropological scrutiny to institutional representation. The
articulation of these many agendas through the national-culture project
took place over a number of years. While regularities occurred across
these discursive sites, it was the resonance between them that established the aforementioned truths about Mexico's indigenous populations.

We return to the contentious early history of muralism and *los tres
grandes*. Rivera's depictions of popular folk activities, native physiognomy, and revolutionary corridos prompted a conservative public
reaction that resulted in the threat of defacement of his and other murals
and the loss of Vasconcelos's support. Mural art was coming under attack
in the metropolitan dailies, where unsympathetic journalists argued that
they were a waste of public money and a defamation of Mexico. Rivera's militant revolutionary iconography prompted accusations that his
murals idealized "criminals" and encouraged assassination. All of the
muralists experienced a hostile reception to their work in these early
years. Their critics often objected to this art form on aesthetic grounds,
simply condemning it as "ugly." Others decried its depiction of *monos* (a
derogatory term for native peoples that translates in English as "mon-
keys") as displeasing. This criticism was lodged by the *gente decente* (the
"decent people," or upper classes) and abated only when the muralists
began to garner international acclaim. But there were recurrent demands
for the destruction of the murals, and in 1935 students attacked Rivera's
National Palace murals with acid.

Throughout the 1920s Orozco periodically halted work on his Preparatory murals because of student protests and attacks. The graffiti left
by these students are still visible today. Additionally, a few of his panels have been partially destroyed.[74] Despite the fact that Orozco was the
only deeply spiritual man of the three, the predominantly conservative
students at the National Preparatory School found his critique of clerical
corruption sacrilegious and objected to his austere aesthetics more than
to those of Rivera or Siqueiros. Siqueiros had a difficult time securing

commissions in the late 1920s owing to his political activities.[75] During
the 1930s he developed his mature style abroad and then engaged in
a public polemic with Rivera over who was the better communist and
therefore the more "revolutionary" artist.[76] All three criticized each other's work throughout their careers and fought to promote their vision
as *the* vision of Mexico and as a truly great and modern art form. That
these artists now peacefully coexist within a "movement" is the result of
the collusion of intellectual agendas, institutional arrangements, and historical retrospect. Nonetheless, revealing the contentious prehistory of
this movement by no means weakens its significance to the formation of
postrevolutionary national identity. On the contrary, it makes clear that
culture was a crucial front in the struggle over the nation.

Mexican muralism was inaugurated as part of a disciplinary program
for public education. Its development into an art movement has obscured
its status as expertise, a technique of government, and a style of reason.
As a technique of government, Mexican muralism sought to reorganize
the conduct of the Mexican population into a functioning national citizenry. While the muralists did not simply represent the political ethos
of the Mexican state, their vision of the Mexican nation would not have
been as effective as it has been without the network of authorities and
discourses that helped to reify their truth as popular art. Ultimately, the
"Mexicanization of the Indian" was accomplished through a plethora of
social and political initiatives, not the least of which was the construction
of a cultural infrastructure of museums, institutes, and heritage sites that
supported their claims to national representation through the authenticated practices of *México profundo*. Nowhere is this more evident than
in the crown jewel of Mexico's national culture, the National Museum
of Anthropology. Emblazoned upon its entryway are the words uttered
at its inauguration in 1964 by President López Mateos: "The Mexican
People raise this monument in honor of the admirable cultures that flour-
ished during the pre-Columbian era in regions that are today territories
of the republic. In front of the testimonies of those cultures, the Mexico
of today pays homage to indigenous Mexico, in whose example it recognizes essential characteristics of its national originality."[77] Nestor García
Canclini argues that the instrumentalization of indigenous Mexico within
this ritual space of national commemoration confronts the visitor with a
gentle mandate. "The watchword that governs this ritual," he eloquently
explains, "is 'become what you are.'"[78] As part of this complex process,
Mexican muralism not only made of its audience a similar request, but
it also helped to articulate the truth of Mexico's "national originality."
Perhaps, recalling Paz, this is the "truest innovation" of the Mexican Revolution. But to continue to celebrate it uncritically risks obscuring the
significance of culture to both discipline and government.

CANADIAN POLITICAL ART IN THE 1930s:
"A FORM OF DISTANCING"

Marylin McKay

Canadians were as adversely affected by the economic problems of the 1930s as anyone else in Western culture. They were also as deeply disturbed by mounting military aggression in Europe and Asia. It might therefore be reasonable to assume that a significant number of Canadian artists would have responded with a clear critique of the social, economic, and political troubles of this decade, just as many artists in other Western countries did. However, given the conservative nature and small size of French and English Canada's populations, as well as the repressive clericalism of French Canadian society, very few did. Indeed, French Canadian artists rarely if ever responded overtly in their work to the troubled times, and possibly made no covert responses either. In English Canada a small number of artists reacted critically, while a much larger number produced work that may reasonably be described as veiled critiques. In this way Canadian art of the thirties distinguished itself from the contemporary work of other American nations.

During the 1930s French Canadians were intensely focused on the maintenance of the "nation" of French Canada, just as they had been since the British Conquest of 1760. At that time the British had given control over education, social welfare, and health care to the French Canadian Catholic Church. Most French Canadians were generally content with this arrangement until well after the 1930s, for they believed that the Church, endowed with such powers, as well as with its traditional strengths, could prevent the annihilation of French culture by English Canada. In return the Church agreed to keep the French Canadian population from rebelling against British authority. The Church did, therefore, vigorously encourage politicians at municipal and provincial levels, almost all of whom were French and Catholic, to curtail criticism

of social and political life. The Quebec government complied, passing
(for one thing) the Padlock Law in support of Pope Leo XIII's *Rerum
Novarum* (1891), which instructed Catholics to shun any political party
or organization that rejected Christian teachings and traditional social
hierarchy. The law allowed for the imprisonment, without appeal, of
anyone who published or distributed tracts supporting communism or
bolshevism.[1]

In such an environment, art tended to be uncritical of social, economic, and political problems. The Catholic Church remained the
dominant patron of the arts, commissioning work to decorate its many
churches, monasteries, convents, schools, orphanages, and hospitals.
Secular art, such as the paintings of Berthe Des Clayes, Madeleine Desrosiers, Marc-Aurèle Fortin, and Ozias Leduc, often focused on idealized
images of rural Quebec, replete with rolling hills, lush farm fields, quaint
houses, horse-driven carriages, and tall church spires.[2] This work was
designed to aid in the Church's promotion of a rural way of life. Rural
life, or so the Church argued, would minimize contact with urban English Protestant Canada and thus maintain the French Canadian "nation."
French Canadian sculptor Alfred Laliberté upheld this goal in a more
explicit manner. Between 1929 and 1934 Laliberté produced eight small
plaster models of nude figures wrenched violently backward by modern
machines. Loosely based on the Greek myth of Ixion, these figures were
intended to deter French Canadians from becoming involved in English-controlled urban industry.[3]

In English Canada in the 1930s, by contrast, a significant number of
people formed associations with leftist and antifascist mandates, joined
the Canadian Communist Party, and took part in the strikes, marches,
and protests that these groups organized. They also established two
socialist political parties that promoted a welfare state. Some of these
Canadians were artists who used their work overtly to criticize social,
political, and economic conditions. For example, in 1937 Toronto painter
Paraskeva Clark stated that artists in particular should "preach revolution" because they possessed "added gifts of finer understanding and
perception of the realities of life, and the ability to arouse emotions
through the creation of forms and images." People who "give their lives,
their knowledge and their time to the social struggle," she argued, "have
the right to expect great help from the artist." Any artist who did not
help, Clark maintained, would be "blind to the forces which approach
to destroy that relative security in which he is permitted to exercise his
individuality."[4]

Clark's 1937 painting *Petroushka* (fig. 4 in Natalie Luckyj's essay in
this volume) was clearly designed to reinforce the social struggle. Based
on a recent labor dispute at Chicago's Republic Steel Corporation, in

which the police killed five workers, it represents an audience laughing at a puppet show and a policeman, urged on by a capitalist, beating a fallen workman. In the same year Clark painted two watercolors, *Portrait of Mao* (fig. 3 in Luckyj's essay), the Chinese Communist leader, and *Presents from Madrid* (fig. 2 in Luckyj's essay), a still life of items related to the Spanish Civil War that her friend, Dr. Norman Bethune, Canada's best-known Communist, had sent from Spain.[5]

Other English Canadian artists with leftist affiliations also made watercolors or drawings rather than oil paintings, as did many leftist artists in other Western countries, both because these methods were inexpensive and because they conformed to Marxist doctrine, which saw oil painting as elitist. Montreal artist Louis Muhlstock's *William O'Brien, Unemployed* (1939) (fig. 1) is a drawing of an elderly man whose emaciated face and sorrowful eyes are signs of economic deprivation. Toronto artist Laurence Hyde's *Still Life* of 1937 (fig. 2) warns Canadians against complacency about European fascism.[6] Montreal artist Fritz Brandtner made many drawings on the same theme, some of which appeared in a 1936 exhibition that Bethune organized under the sponsorship of the Canadian League Against War and Fascism. In these drawings and watercolors the compassion of the artists is obvious, as are stylistic and thematic influences from contemporary European and American artists with similar sympathies, such as George Grosz, Käthe Kollwitz, Joseph Delany, and Isaac Soyer.[7]

Many left-leaning English Canadian artists were also drawn to printmaking in the thirties, as were many artists in other Western countries, not only because, like watercolor and drawing, it was relatively inexpensive, but also because it responded to the Marxist call that art reach the general public. Leonard Hutchinson of Hamilton, Ontario, made *The Protest,* a block print, in the late 1930s as a sympathetic response to a recent picket line at a local steel mill. He made another block print that represents an impoverished family taking care of a small vegetable garden at the edge of an industrial site. The title, *Canadian Homes and Gardens,* turns the work into an ironic comment on the upper-class magazine of the same name.[8]

Some English Canadian artists who were not involved with specific leftist groups made similarly sympathetic works of art during the thirties. New Brunswick's Miller Brittain made many drawings and watercolors of local dockyard workers that were designed to evoke the viewer's compassion.[9] In 1934 Harold Haydon installed a mural in Pickering College in Newmarket, Ontario, in conscious imitation of Mexican and American political murals. One panel depicts a society overshadowed by force and oppression, another a society inspired by concepts of brotherhood and cooperation.[10] In the early 1930s Julius Griffith Jr.

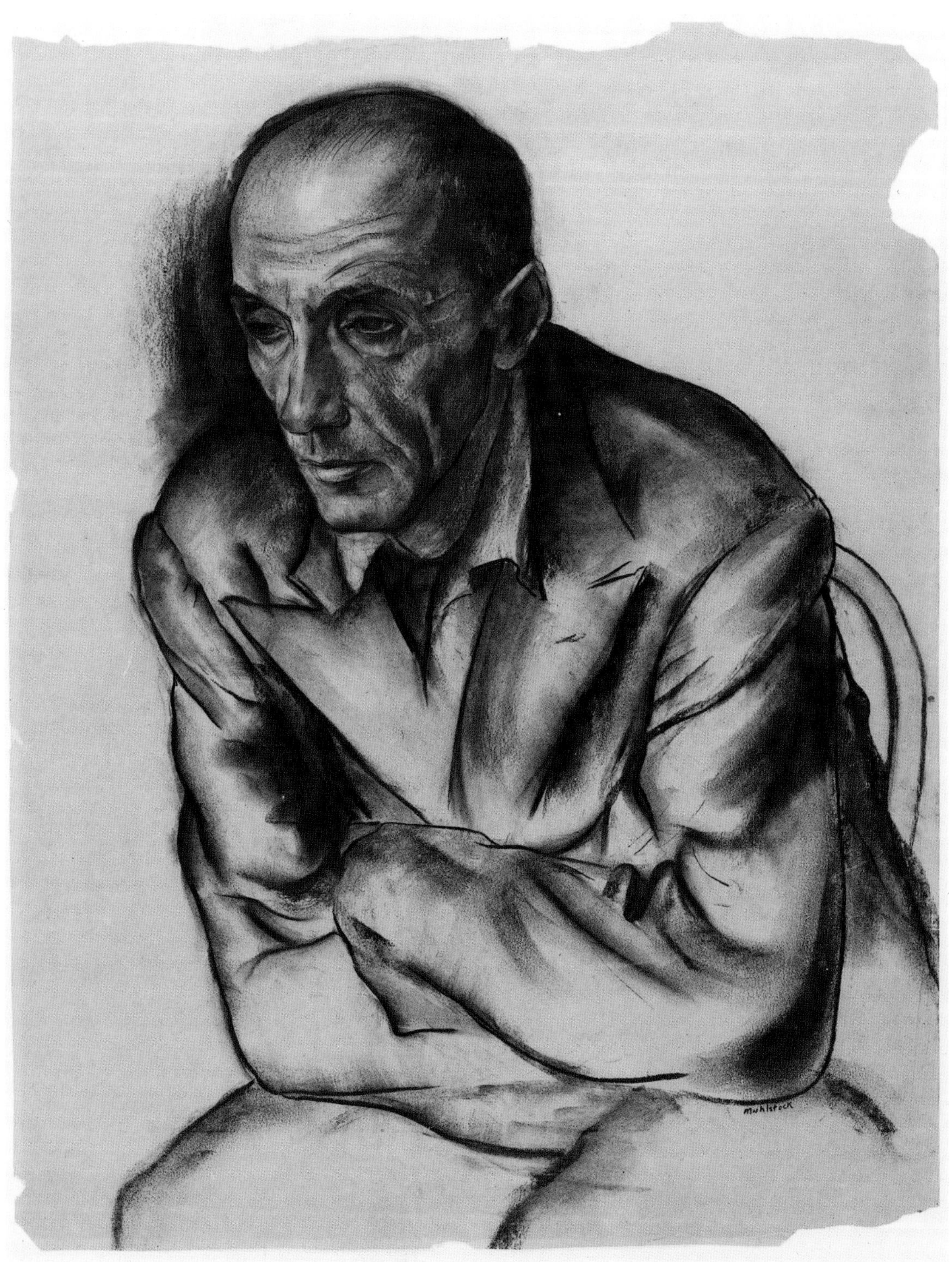

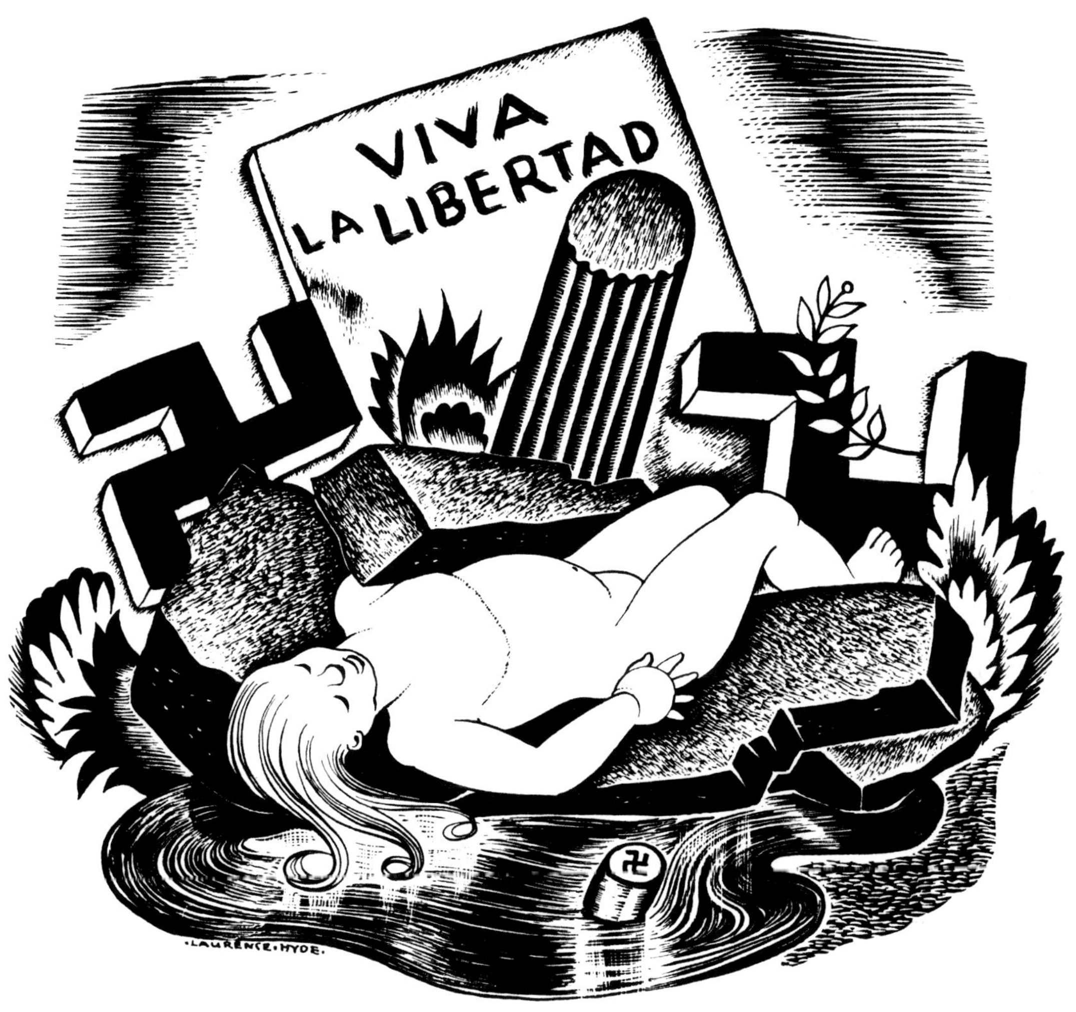

1 (opposite) Louis Muhlstock, *William O'Brien Unemployed* (c. 1935), charcoal and brown chalk on paper, 68 x 51 cm. National Gallery of Canada, purchased 1974.

2 (above) Laurence Hyde, *Still Life* (1937), medium, dimensions, and location unknown.

painted a mural with a similar theme for Shawnigan Lake School in Shawnigan, British Columbia. One of the panels illustrated scenes from the Trojan War, the other, various scenes of modern life, including warfare. As one of the students wrote about the mural: "Poverty and plenty are represented in [images of] the slums and factories ... the manual worker is large, showing the importance that he plays in the running of the world. The warships and aeroplanes show that we still live under the menace of war. ... [The mural suggests] that the [students] may feel the need of doing ... their share of setting things right rather than ... settling down to a smug life of money-making."[11]

This type of art received significant support in leftist Canadian newspapers and journals. Writing for the Communist Party's *Daily Clarion* in 1936, Neil Stuart stated that art for art's sake had led to a "divorce

of the cultural from social life [and] had caused art to fall into the arid
wastes of unrealism, byzantism [*sic*] and fads whose sole useful purpose
was to expose the uselessness and bankruptcy of the society which had
produced it."[12] John Fairfax, writing for the leftist *Canadian Forum* in the
same year, argued that the artist "should not be aloof from society, the
artist should serve his age ... it is necessary to cease pretending that we
live in [a perfect world], and face the facts of our times."[13] In 1932 the
Toronto branch of the communist-based Progressive Arts Clubs began to
publish *Masses* as a vehicle of support for, among other things, art that
would serve a proletarian society. In 1937 the communist-inspired *New
Frontier* was inaugurated in Toronto. It frequently included drawings
and prints by local artists. Here Paraskeva Clark published her impassioned article on the role of the artist in society and Laurence Hyde his
Still Life (fig. 2).

Apart from newspaper cartoons, however, the art I have just
described constitutes most of the overtly political work produced in
English Canada during the 1930s. Other art historians support this conclusion. As Charles Hill put it in 1975, Canadian painting of the thirties
had "little overt political or social content."[14] Eight years later Lorna Farrell-Ward wrote that "it would be reasonable to expect to find evidence ...
of the overwhelming social problems of the day [in Vancouver art of the
1930s], but this was not the case. ... There were no capitalists in silk hats,
and the noble worker was the familiar art school anatomy study."[15] In
1984 Esther Trépanier described artists in Montreal and Toronto in the
thirties as "ambiguous" about producing political art.[16] Eight years later,
in a study of Canadian women's art, Maria Tippett agreed, writing, "there
is little evidence [in the art of the thirties] of the social, political or economic turmoil that pervaded Canadian society at the time."[17]

Indeed, despite her political activism and her *Petroushka, Portrait of
Mao,* and *Presents from Madrid,* Paraskeva Clark mostly painted still lifes,
landscapes, domestic environments, and portraits of herself, friends, and
family in the 1930s. Nor did politically motivated art dominate the work
of Muhlstock, Hyde, Brandtner, Hutchinson, or Brittain. Also, the formats
that these artists regularly used for their politicized work (drawings,
watercolors, and prints) and the venues in which their politicized work
mostly appeared (leftist publications and exhibitions) did not receive
the serious attention given to oil paintings in public and commercial
galleries. At the same time, none of these artists used photography to
document the appalling conditions and events of the times, even though
many artists in other countries, whose work was known to Canadians,
did so with great effect.

Furthermore, overtly political English Canadian art of the thirties
did not suggest that the problems of the decade affected Canadians as a

whole. Often it was composed of single isolated figures, such as Muhl-stock's *Portrait of William O'Brien* (fig. 1), unlike the overtly political art of the thirties in other countries. For example, American artists regularly represented people crowded together in tenement houses, ghastly working environments, and welfare offices, while Mexican art often depicted centuries of oppression of the indigenous Mexican population as a whole. American and Mexican political art of the thirties also targeted specific institutions and individuals as the source of problems. Canadian political art rarely if ever did. Even Clark's *Petroushka* is removed from a specifically Canadian reality. Not only does it depict puppets rather than people, it also is based on a foreign labor dispute rather than one of the many that took place in Canada. Clark could have chosen, for example, to depict the bloody and well-publicized clash that ended the "On-to-Ottawa Trek" in Regina, Saskatchewan, in 1935. Here the Royal Canadian Mounted Police used physical force to prevent eighteen hundred unemployed men from riding boxcars to Ottawa to demand federal legislation to deal with unemployment.[18]

Other overtly political English Canadian art of the thirties is less than clear. Hyde's *Still Life* (fig. 2), for example, focuses on an oddly positioned nude who detracts from the serious reading that Hyde surely intended to make. Brandtner made an equally puzzling drawing, *Men of 1939,* in which two men and a pet dog, all wearing gas masks, stand and face the viewer as if posing for a comical photograph.[19] Possibly English Canadian artists were simply too removed geographically from foreign military activity to imbue this type of subject matter with greater horror. However, some artists who worked with politically sensitive themes that were very much a part of English Canadian life still made works of art that cannot be easily read. In Miller Brittain's oil painting of 1936, *Longshoremen,* dockyard workers are shown walking along a street in New Brunswick. One man's face has a troubled expression and another man is shouting; but two others are chatting and smiling. As Rosemary Donegan says of Brittain's work, "though Brittain was clearly fascinated by, and sympathetic to, his working-class subjects, there remains an ambivalence and skepticism."[20] Donald Andrus suggests that Brittain's work has "a form of distancing ... that must represent a desire ... to avoid any true emotional tie with the facts of the situation."[21]

On several counts Haydon's and Griffith's murals were quite unlike the Mexican and American murals that they were imitating. First, the schools for which the artists worked were private, so the murals did not reach the general public. Second, since Haydon's school was run by Quakers, he was essentially preaching to the converted. Third, Haydon volunteered his services and worked on inexpensive particleboard instead of using fresco or marouflage. Griffith, as a Shawnigan "old boy,"

probably donated his services, too, or reduced his price. Consequently
these murals did not receive the critical attention that professional commissions for public spaces did. More important, these were the only
murals produced in Canada in the 1930s with this kind of subject matter.

Some English Canadian artists who admired Mexican and American murals also demonstrated an extraordinarily naïve attitude toward
the foreign work. Toronto's Arthur Lismer, for example, argued that
his mural paintings of 1927–30 for Humberside Collegiate, a public
high school in Toronto, were much like those that Thomas Hart Benton
had done for the New School for Social Research in New York in the
mid-1920s.[22] Yet Lismer belatedly employed an impressionistic style to
depict classical personifications of Truth, Wisdom, and Beauty as over-
seers of British imperialism. Benton, on the other hand, employed a bold
expressionist style to represent the energy as well as the confusion and
tedium of the mundane activities of modern life. Remarkably, Lismer
also stated that the communist beliefs of Mexican muralist Diego Rivera
were "irrelevant to [Rivera's] artistic achievements."[23] In 1937 André Bié-
ler, a Kingston, Ontario, artist, made a similar remark: "Even when the
main themes of the [Mexican] frescoes are fiercely intense social questions, these remain fine works of art."[24] Even more astonishing was a
Vancouver critic's comparison of the Mexican muralists and the work of
Florentine Renaissance artist Fra Lippo Lippi. Both Lippi and the Mexicans, this critic claimed, had simply "freed [themselves] from art that was
strictly religious by a new involvement with nature."[25]

Given the comparative freedom that English Canadian artists of
the 1930s enjoyed (as opposed to the lack of artistic freedom in French
Canada), it is reasonable to wonder why English Canadians did not
make more overtly political art. In fact, many circumstances conspired
against the production of such art. First, despite the rise in leftist political activity, most English Canadians—including the two prime ministers,
Richard William Bennett and William Lyon Mackenzie King—regarded
such activity, even if it was only union membership, as radical and dangerous.[26] Legislation supported their position. Section 98 of the federal
criminal code, for example, made it illegal "to advocate governmental,
industrial or economic change ... by the use of force, violence or physical
injury to person or property, or by threats of such injury." This law was
frequently employed in the thirties to prevent leftist meetings, marches,
and protests such as the "On-to-Ottawa Trek."[27]

Furthermore, a significant number of leftist activists in Canada in
the thirties were foreigners or Jews (including Clark, Muhlstock, and
Brandtner), while Canada's dominant population, both Anglo-Saxon
and French Canadian, was openly xenophobic and anti-Semitic. Jews
and blacks were regularly restricted from private clubs, while quotas

kept them out of many public institutions. Signs in Toronto during this period equated Jews and blacks with dogs—"No Jews, No Negroes, No Dogs."[28] Some western Canadians even formed chapters of the Ku Klux Klan. As Canadian novelist Hugh Garner, writing about the thirties from the perspective of the 1950s, put it, "Inhabitants of Toronto believed in God, the Royal Family, the Conservative Party and private enterprise [and] were suspicious and a little condescending toward all heathen religions, higher education, foreigners and social reformers."[29]

As a result, even though membership in the Canadian Communist Party increased dramatically in the 1930s, it involved only a relatively small part of the population. By 1935 the newly formed Co-operative Commonwealth Federation (CCF), a socialist political party, had only 8.9 percent of the federal vote, and it did not form a provincial government until 1944. The Social Credit Party, another socialist political party formed in the 1930s, won the Alberta provincial election in 1935 and remained in power throughout the Depression and beyond, but it never did deliver the promised welfare state. Other leftist organizations in Canada did not attract large numbers in the thirties. For example, the League for Social Reconstruction never had more than a thousand members. Leftist publications such as *Masses* and *New Frontier* lasted less than three years, while others, like *Canadian Forum,* had a small circulation.

Then, too, there were no federal art programs in Canada, like those in the United States and Mexico, which might have given English Canadian artists the financial freedom to make overtly political art for public spaces. The prime ministers of the 1930s, Bennett and King, believed that the federal government gave adequate support to the arts by contributing to the National Gallery and the Royal Canadian Academy. They also favored art that represented stability and tradition or evoked nationalistic sentiment. King even openly criticized government-funded art in the United States. It made him "shudder," he said.[30] Presumably he meant that he feared the freedom that the American programs gave artists both to work in modernist styles and to pass judgment on government activities within public venues.

Some individual government departments at other levels and some public institutions in Canada did commission public art in the 1930s, but, on the basis of its subject matter and style, this work could just as well have been done in the 1920s. In 1931, for example, the city of Montreal hired thirteen French and English Canadian artists to decorate the chalet at Mount Royal Park as a "make-work" project in response to the Great Depression. The murals that the artists installed represent local historical events. Presumably to ensure that neither French nor English viewers would be insulted, the artists avoided the post–British Conquest (1760) period and said nothing about current social or political events.

English Canadian artists who wanted to produce political art for public spaces during the 1930s were not in a position to lobby for government support. In 1931 Canada's population was only 10,377,000, while its land mass was the second largest of any country in the world. Within this population there were only about three thousand artists, thinly spread across the country, as was the population as a whole. A critical mass of artists would not come together to discuss government support for the arts and the role of the artist in society until 1941. Significantly, they invited Edward Rowan, assistant to the director of the Federal Art Project under the Works Progress Administration in Washington, and American Regionalist and social realist artist Thomas Hart Benton.[31]

At the same time, most English Canadians of the 1930s, like their prime ministers, were content to see conservative art installed in public sites. They were also content to see equally conservative art in the private sphere. As working-class immigrants, or the middle-class offspring of working-class immigrants, most Canadians had no art education. Nor did they have an income that would have permitted the purchase of original art. Consequently art sales in Canada had never been high, and taste had rarely run to extremes of style or subject matter. The economic constraints of the 1930s and the concomitant decrease in sales further encouraged artists to produce uncontroversial work. As Miller Brittain, who had trouble selling his political art, stated bluntly, "Who on earth wants a picture of poverty hanging on their living room wall? … You paint your guts out, trying to tell them something and they want a pretty picture."[32]

Most English Canadian art criticism of the decade also encouraged conservative taste. Indeed, critics who wrote for publications that reached large numbers of Canadians had no particular art expertise. Rather, they reported on art exhibitions just as they reported on political, civic, and sports events. The *Toronto Star*, for example, the largest-circulation newspaper in English Canada at the time, employed English immigrant Ray Collett from 1929 to 1939 to write, among other things, a weekly art column. Collett was eighteen years old when he was hired, had a grade school education, and, in his own words, "knew nothing about art at all."[33]

Many Canadian historians and a significant number of American historians, such as Seymour Martin Lipset, have constructed a compelling but unverifiable theory that attempts to explain, among other things, how Canadian artists of the thirties approached their work. These historians have concluded that Canada's gradual progress toward independent nationhood, as opposed to a revolutionary route, produced a population that is relatively cautious and deferential to legal authority, government control, and social superiors and values order, hierarchy, and continuity. As these historians explain, in the late eighteenth century the population of English Canada increased dramatically through massive immigration of Americans who wanted to remain loyal to the British monarchy rather than live in the revolutionary colonies. At the same time, the clerical leaders of French Canada, who had a great deal of influence with the political leaders, sought to isolate French Canadians not only from English Canada but also from the anticlerical values of the French Revolution.

In 1867 Canada became a separate country, not in an act of defiance but because Britain wanted to end financial responsibility for the North American colonies and because Canadians, especially after the American Civil War, feared absorption by the United States. The Canadian "fathers of Confederation," therefore, envisioned a strong federal state that would provide capital for economic development and protect the French from the English and the French and the English from the Americans. This federal state was based in part on a strong link between church and state as well as on an executive/cabinet that could control the House of Commons. Final legal authority in all matters was left—until as late as the 1980s—with the British monarchy. As Lipset has stated, "Canada is a country of counterrevolution." Its citizens are "cautious ... concerned with order and continuity ... and have a deference for authority.[34] Logically, then, such a country would not produce much overtly political art.

Lipset based this stereotype of Canadian and American cultures on what anthropologist Clifford Geertz has called an "interpretive study." Geertz defines culture as a "historically transmitted pattern of meanings embodied in symbols ... by means of which men communicate, perpetuate and develop their knowledge about and attitudes toward life."[35] In using the word "interpretative" Geertz, like Lipset, acknowledged that such studies are not objective. Nevertheless, they seem to be supported by practical experience, and therein lies their appeal. Indeed, when I asked Ray Collett, the *Toronto Star* art columnist in the thirties, why English Canadians made so little political art during that decade, he replied simply, "Canadians just aren't like that."

If only a few English Canadian artists of the 1930s used their art to criticize their social, economic, and political situation, what did the others do? Some—such as John Lyman of English Montreal, Goodridge Roberts of Ottawa and Fredericton, New Brunswick, and Bertram Brooker of Toronto—simply rejected political organizations and political art and aligned themselves with international modernism, despite the fact that most English (and French) Canadians associated modernism with moral laxity and degeneracy. Roberts said that as an artist he was interested only in art's "plastic poetry." He would leave "to the sociologist social problems, to the historian the narrative, and to the psychologist psychological problems."[36] Brooker agreed: "Among fanatical Communists an artist who does not use his gifts to further the cause of the revolution is stigmatized as a sort of traitor to his generation." In Brooker's view, art "is not—and should not be—*useful* to society, *in any sense whatsoever!* ... The concern of ... the artist—is not with 'fact or reason'—with anything than can be argued—counted—measured. ... Art should be exciting; not persuasive. ... The job of economic stabilization is not the artist's business. ... The artist is concerned with the way God runs the universe and not with the way man proposes to run it."[37] The few French Canadian modernists of the 1930s adopted the same approach. Jean-Paul Lemieux said, "Too often present-day painting puts one in mind of the darker side of humanity and illustrates the driven, anxious quality of our era and the grim future that lies in store."[38] In a 1938 review of Lemieux's work, French Canadian critic Gérard Morisset happily wrote that it was "devoid of morose thoughts of any kind."[39]

Some English Canadian artists who did align themselves with international modernism *were* active in leftist political organizations. Still, they did not focus on making political art, nor did they explain why not. Presumably they supported Roberts and Brooker's position. Pegi Nicol, of Ottawa, Toronto, and Montreal, for example, was a close friend of Norman Bethune and active in the League for Social Reconstruction and the Committee to Aid Spanish Democracy. In 1935–36 she was art editor for the leftist *Canadian Forum.* In the December 1936 issue she published an antifascist Christmas card featuring people in gas masks pressed together to form the shape of a Christmas tree surmounted by a swastika "star."[40] The rest of Nicol's work, however, consists of happy family portraits, exuberant floral still lifes, cheerful street scenes, and domestic interiors.

At least one modernist artist was conscious of the discrepancy between leftist political involvement and nonpolitical art. Montreal painter Marian Scott was a good friend of Bethune's and active in the CCF and the League for Social Reconstruction (she was also married to one of the league's founders). In 1935 she designed the cover of the League's *Social Planning for Canada* and wrote, "I would like to be a proletarian painter." Yet Scott's work was never politically engaged in any overt way. Even her cover for *Social Planning* was composed simply of images of a family, a cityscape, a book, and grain. As Scott later said, "In spite of the time, in spite of the misery, the growing fear of fascism and war ... I found that I could not (or should not) use my painting directly."[41]

Even when the subject matter appeared to call for a political stance, many English Canadian artists of the thirties chose not to be critical. Representations of the working and living conditions of Canadian miners—which were abysmal—provide good examples. In 1931 Toronto artist Yvonne McKague Housser produced a view of an Ontario mining town, *Silver Mine, Cobalt.* But she excluded the inhabitants and painted the buildings in bright colors and at gently sloping angles so that the town has a quaint yet energized appearance. Deliberately ignoring the squalor that was certainly present, Housser wrote: "For me ... there is something romantic about a mining shaft against a northern sky with silver and black clouds racing by, and about the big mountain-like slag heaps beside the buildings, and all reflected in a large pond or little lake."[42] In 1936 Toronto artist Frances Loring sculpted *The Miner* as a portrait bust, a format that isolates the figure from the gruesome aspects of his life.[43] And in 1939 Alberta printmaker Margaret Shelton produced *Rosedale Mine Tipple,* a depiction of the massive machinery used to load ore at the entrance to a mine.[44] With none of the harried miners in evidence, the work glorifies the strength of modern industry in the manner of contemporary American artist Charles Sheeler. Yet some contemporary American artists, such as painters Joseph Hirsch and Fletcher Martin and photographers Walker Evans and Marion Post Wolcott—whose work was readily accessible to Canadians—produced scathing depictions of American miners' living and working conditions.[45] Canadian artists never did.

Other Canadian artists of the 1930s, such as Vancouver photographer John Vanderpant, produced idealized views of other aspects of modern technology. They too resemble Sheeler's contemporary paintings and photographs of the same subject matter. Karen Lucic believes that Sheeler's work may have been intended to represent "an oppressed, dehumanized technocracy."[46] Vanderpant could have had similar intentions, but if he did, then, in the words of Melissa Rombout, his work "was anchored in a spiritually driven utopian vision in which spiritual immanence and realization at the individual level would preclude the necessity of communal political and social reform."[47] In 1936–37 Charles Comfort provided the Toronto Stock Exchange with eight painted panels devoted to the industries whose stocks were handled at the exchange.[48] The workers in these panels appear remote and mechanical, as if they are part of the machinery with which they are intensely engaged. English Montreal artist Edwin Holgate took a similar approach to industry in the mural he painted for the Canadian pavilion at the New York World's Fair in 1939, as did Vancouver artists Orville Fisher, Paul Goranson, and Edward Hughes, when they provided British Columbia's pavilion at the Golden Gate Exposition in San Francisco in 1939 with fifteen painted panels.[49] Basing their work on photographs that the government supplied, the Vancouver artists produced images of well-dressed grime-free men under no apparent duress, bland expressions on their faces, at work in clean, orderly mines, railways, dockyards, and construction sites. Because they loom larger than the machinery they operate, Lorna

Farrell-Ward has described these figures as "Paul Bunyan–like" giants. Rather than being oppressed by their industrial environment, they are in complete control.[50]

Given that these murals were designed for private industry and government displays at world's fairs, this celebratory approach, even in the 1930s, is not surprising. But the Canadian muralists claimed that they were working under the influence of contemporary Mexican and American murals, and that is surprising, for many of the Mexican and American murals that depicted industry took a very different approach.[51] Diego Rivera's 1931 murals for the San Francisco Stock Exchange represent the richness of California's natural resources but focus on the humanity of the ordinary worker, without whom, as one contemporary critic put it, "California's riches would be dead matter."[52] John Langley Howard's *California Industrial Scenes,* installed in San Francisco's Coit Tower five years before Fisher, Goranson, and Hughes installed their mural at the San Francisco Exposition, represents an impoverished family living in a makeshift tent by a river in which they wash their clothes. In the background is the lucrative Shasta hydroelectric dam, presumably run by callous capitalists who exploited their workers.[53]

Many English Canadian artists of the thirties took the same approach to the representation of other politically sensitive subject matter. Depictions of black Canadians, for example, were as romanticized as contemporary depictions of industry. Clearly upholding a widely held Canadian myth that racism was an American problem, artists such as English Montreal's Marion Bond, Kathleen Daly, Edwin Holgate, and Prudence Heward, Toronto's Lawren Harris Jr., Will Ogilvie, and Dorothy Stevens, and Vancouver's Jock Macdonald depicted nude black women against a background of lush tropical foliage.[54] At a time when the representation of nudes was strongly censored in most parts of Canada, nude black models simply permitted artists to work with the exotic and the erotic. As a result, Canadian artists of the thirties produced no art that may be compared to American art such as Philip Reisman's *Forces Opposing the Negro* (1934) or Marion Post Wolcott's *Negro going in a colored entrance to movie house on Saturday afternoon, Belzoni, Mississippi* (1939). In Reisman's painting, death, the church, and the Ku Klux Klan terrorize the black sharecropper. In Wolcott's photograph a lone black man mounts a steep wooden staircase at the back of a theater, a reminder of racial segregation.[55]

Many English Canadian artists also romanticized Native Canadians, just as they had been doing for a century. Muralists in particular focused on the inability of the native people of Canada to cope with modern life. In this way they upheld a widely accepted Canadian myth—essentially a form of "wishful thinking"—that maintained that indigenous people were "disappearing."[56] In 1930–31 Toronto artist Charles W. Jefferys installed four mural panels in the writing room of Ottawa's Château Laurier Hotel. In one panel Native Canadians throw tobacco in the Ottawa River as a means of propitiating the spirit of the river. In another panel, meant to provide a contrast to the supposed ignorance and superstition of native beliefs, British soldiers use scientific instruments to build a canal to serve British commercial interests. The native men are no longer in the scene. Viewers were to assume that they had disappeared, and in a way they had.[57] By the 1930s the Canadian government had placed all native people on reservations as far away from developing urban centers as possible.

John Leman's mural of 1933, *Before the White Man Came,* painted for the rotunda of the Saskatchewan legislative building, represents a native village in the Qu'Appelle Lakes area. Its title tells us that it has the same subject matter as Jefferys's mural.[58] Charles Comfort's mural painting of 1939, *Captain Vancouver* (fig. 3), designed for the foyer of the Hotel Vancouver, also glorified racial imperialism. Here the late eighteenth-century English explorer is guest of honor at a potlatch, a traditional feasting ritual that established status in Northwest Coast native societies.[59] He is depicted with two of his sailors, who hold scientific naval instruments. All three are depicted frontally and in full-length. They appear to stand on a platform above three native men who offer them the gifts of the potlatch. Two of the native men are in profile; one has his back to the viewer; all three are "cut in half" by the lower frame of the panel. Thus they are rendered powerless. The mural seems to say that the potlatch had come under the control of the British, and in fact it had. Fifty-five years before Comfort painted this mural, the Canadian government had banned the potlatch on the grounds that it discouraged the development of desirable qualities like individualism and thrift, which would assist native people with assimilation into Western culture.[60]

At the same time many English Canadian artists were simply making art as a form of antimodernism.[61] For example, English Montreal artists Kathleen Daly, Ethel Seath, Mabel May, Kathleen Morris, and Albert H. Robinson painted quaint scenes of rural and preindustrial urban Quebec, not in support of French Canadian identity but to suggest that "the primitive" could provide a sanctuary from modern life.[62]

Most English Canadian artists of the 1930s, however, were involved in landscape painting. Speaking for a number of them, Toronto sculptor Elizabeth Wyn Wood wrote that Canadians "have not the appetite [for political art]. Then too in the civilization in which we live ... utter desperation such as is prevalent in Europe today is practically unknown to us by actual experience. Our way of life has some measure of social harmony, classlessness and racial cooperation than other countries. It offers

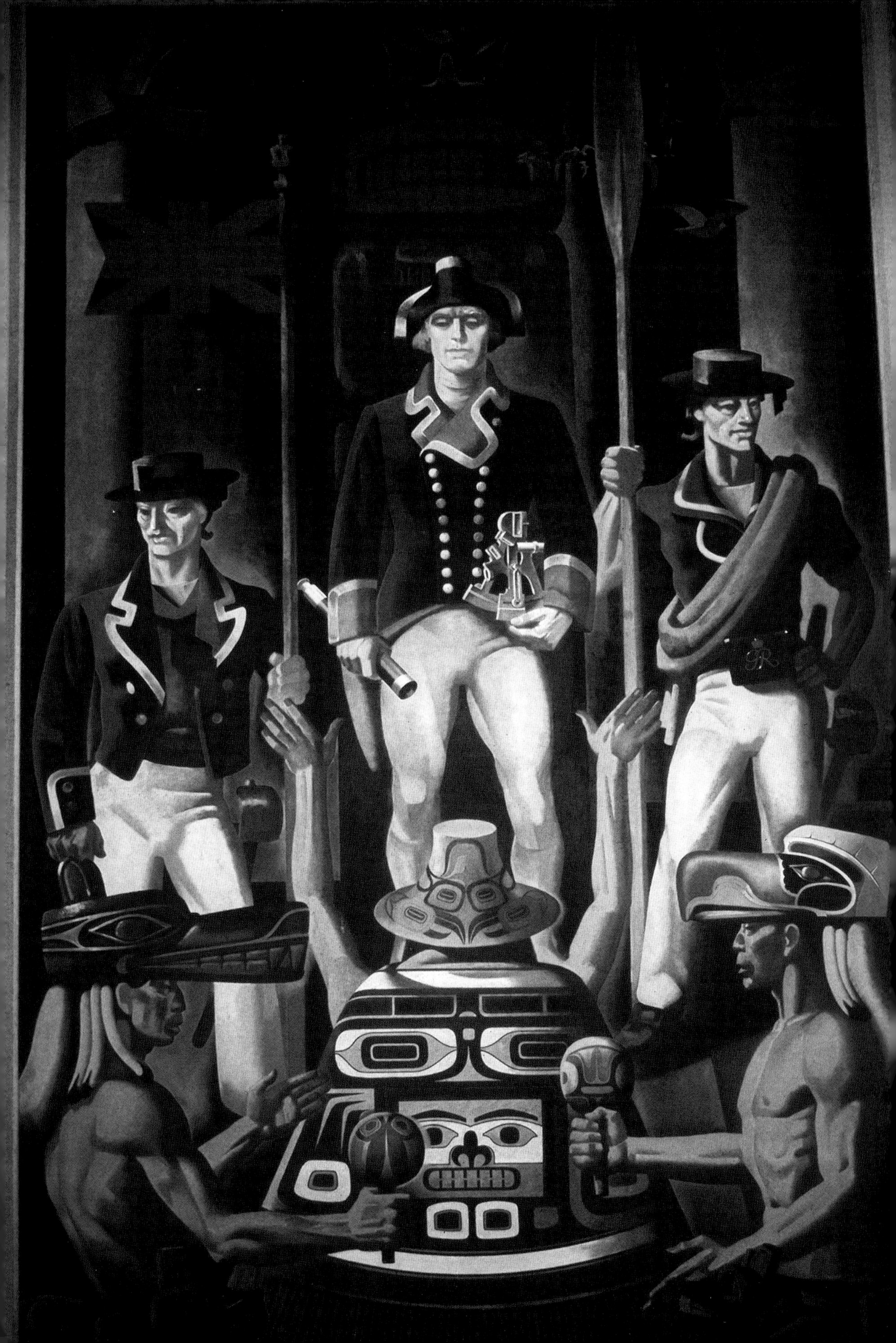

rare ground where art might conceivably function socially as art for all, for the first time in the history of the world, not for the propagation of an ideology but itself a treasure, an enrichment of life."[63]

Nevertheless, I would suggest that much of English Canadian landscape painting of the 1930s may have been produced as a covert response to the troubles of the decade, and I believe that the contrast between English Canadian landscape painting of 1912–1930 and that produced during the thirties supports this suggestion.

Just before the outbreak of World War I, eight Toronto artists began to produce what they described as a new type of landscape painting. Employing the loose styles and vibrant colors of European Post-Impressionism, these artists offered joyful images of uninhabited regions of northern Canada that had never been depicted before. In 1921 seven of these artists formed the Group of Seven. By the late 1920s the work of this group had not only attracted many imitators but was also frequently and approvingly described as English Canada's "national school," a description that is still frequently applied to it today, even though scholarly research has demonstrated that the regions were inhabited (especially by native people) and that the painting styles were anything but innovative. Nonetheless these landscapes became what Jacques Lyotard has defined as a *"grand récit,"* or "metanarrative."

The appeal of the work of the Group of Seven and its imitators during the 1920s lay in its ability to evoke nationalistic sentiment. For one thing, these paintings represented regions with untapped natural resources and so encouraged viewers to work toward material and cultural progress for the population as a whole. This belief in the necessity of progress was, of course, obsessively held throughout Western culture from the late eighteenth century to at least the mid-twentieth. Another basis of these landscapes' attraction lay in their representation of an apparently uninhabited North. In this way the landscapes appealed to antimodernist sentiment. They may even, as one art historian has argued, have permitted viewers to indulge the strong sense of xenophobia entrenched in English Canadian nationalism.[64] Furthermore, the artists imbued these landscapes with a religious morality by framing them conceptually within views of nature developed by Ruskin, the American transcendentalists, Walt Whitman, and the theosophists. The theosophical connection even gave support to what was and remains a key component of Canadian nationalism—anti-American sentiment. In 1928, for example, Lawren Harris, a Toronto artist, a leading member of the Group of Seven, and an ardent theosophist, wrote:

> We in Canada are in different circumstances than the people in the
> United States. Our population is sparse, the psychic atmosphere

comparatively clean, whereas the United States has filled up and the
masses crowd a heavy psychic blanket over nearly all the land. We
in Canada are in the fringe of the great North and its living whiteness, its loneliness and replenishment, its resignations and release,
its call and answer—its cleansing rhythms. It seems that the top of
the continent is a source of spiritual flow that will ever shed clarity
into the growing race of America, and we Canadians being closest to
this source seem destined to produce an art somewhat different from
our Southern fellows—an art more spacious, of greater living quiet,
perhaps of a more certain conviction of eternal values. We were not
placed between the Southern teeming of Americans and the ample
replenishing North for nothing.[65]

Significantly—when considering political art in Canada in the 1930s—
Harris's theosophical beliefs, which were shared by other Canadian
landscape artists and landscape art promoters of the 1920s, basically provided an ideological inversion of Marxism, preaching submission to a
higher power rather than inciting political activism.[66]

It is therefore not difficult to imagine why landscape art—which
had been widely promoted as a "savior" in response to English Canada's
obsession with nationalistic identity from 1867 to the 1920s—should
be maintained as a dominant art form in the thirties, a time when the
country was clearly in need of another "savior." However, a careful comparison of the work of the Group of Seven and that of their followers
in the 1920s and 1930s suggests that the landscapes of the 1930s are
fundamentally different from the earlier work. In particular, the joyful
quality of the earlier images has been replaced by an unstable and often
menacing edge, which may be interpreted as a response, albeit a covert
one, to the specific problems of the decade. Vancouver painter William
Weston's *Beached* of 1935 (fig. 4) represents a closely cropped view of
driftwood that acts as a visual barrier to the sea beyond the uninhabited
beach. Its abstract painting style makes one section of the wood look like
a cow's skull and others like flailing human limbs.[67] Toronto painter Isabel McLaughlin's *Grey Ghosts of Algonquin* (1933) depicts a small section
of dense wilderness forest. In the background is a single live evergreen
tree. In the foreground, blocking any route to what is "ever-green," is the
stump of a dead tree surrounded by many small dead trees with spiky
leafless branches.[68] The viewer cannot escape this threatening space. Vancouver painter Emily Carr's *Scorned as Timber, Beloved of the Sky* (1935)
represents one tall tree that reaches up to a sky composed of vibrat-
ing lines.[69] In *Algoma, November* (1935–36) (fig. 5), Alexander Jackson
employed grays and muted purples in a series of undulating horizontal
lines to represent the foreground shore, the lake, and the opposite shore

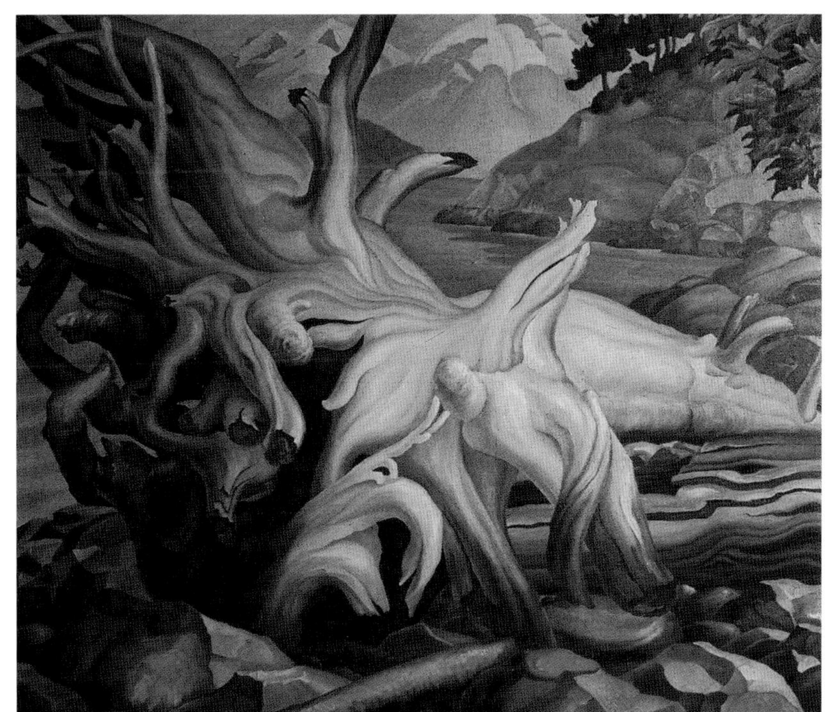

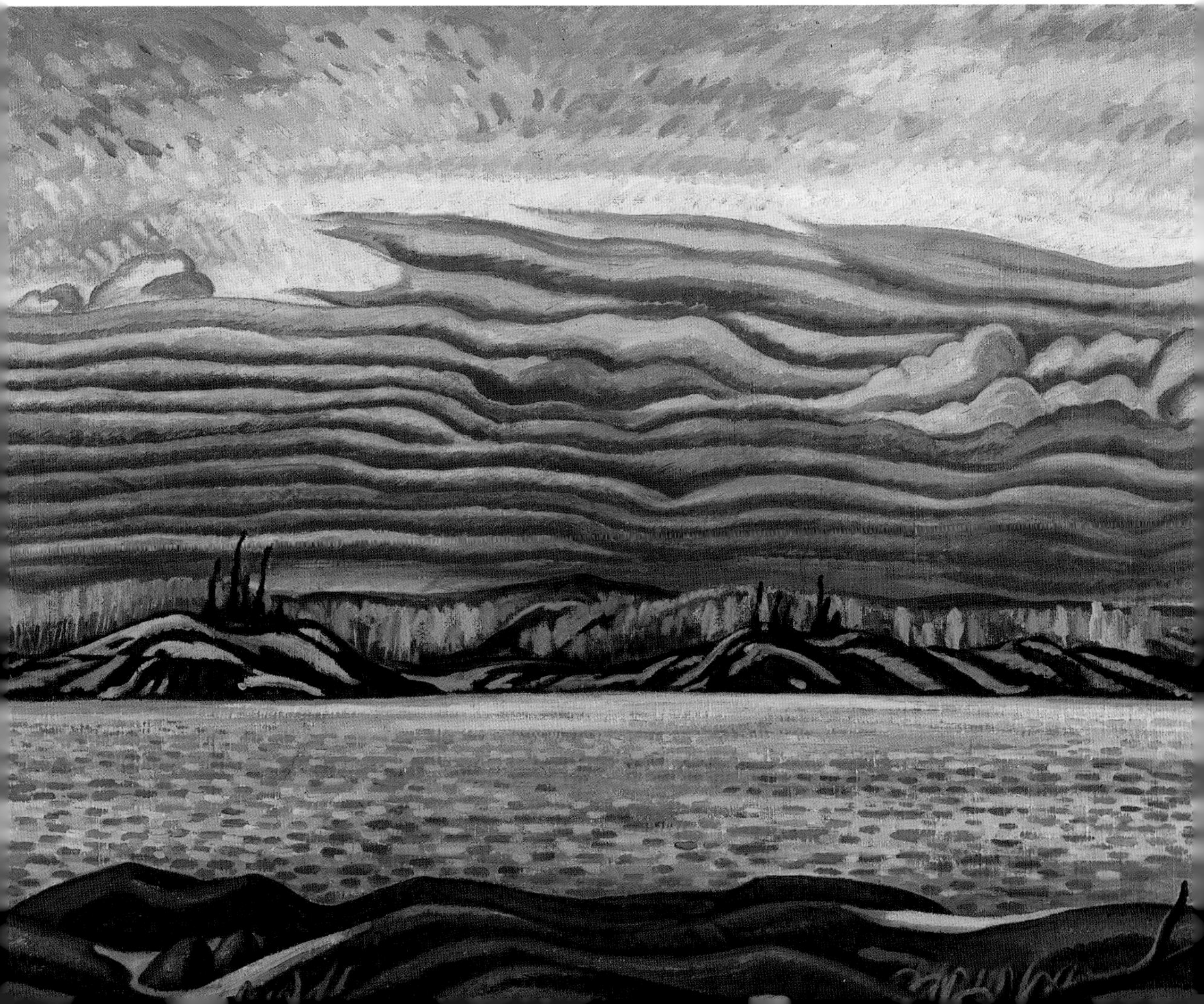

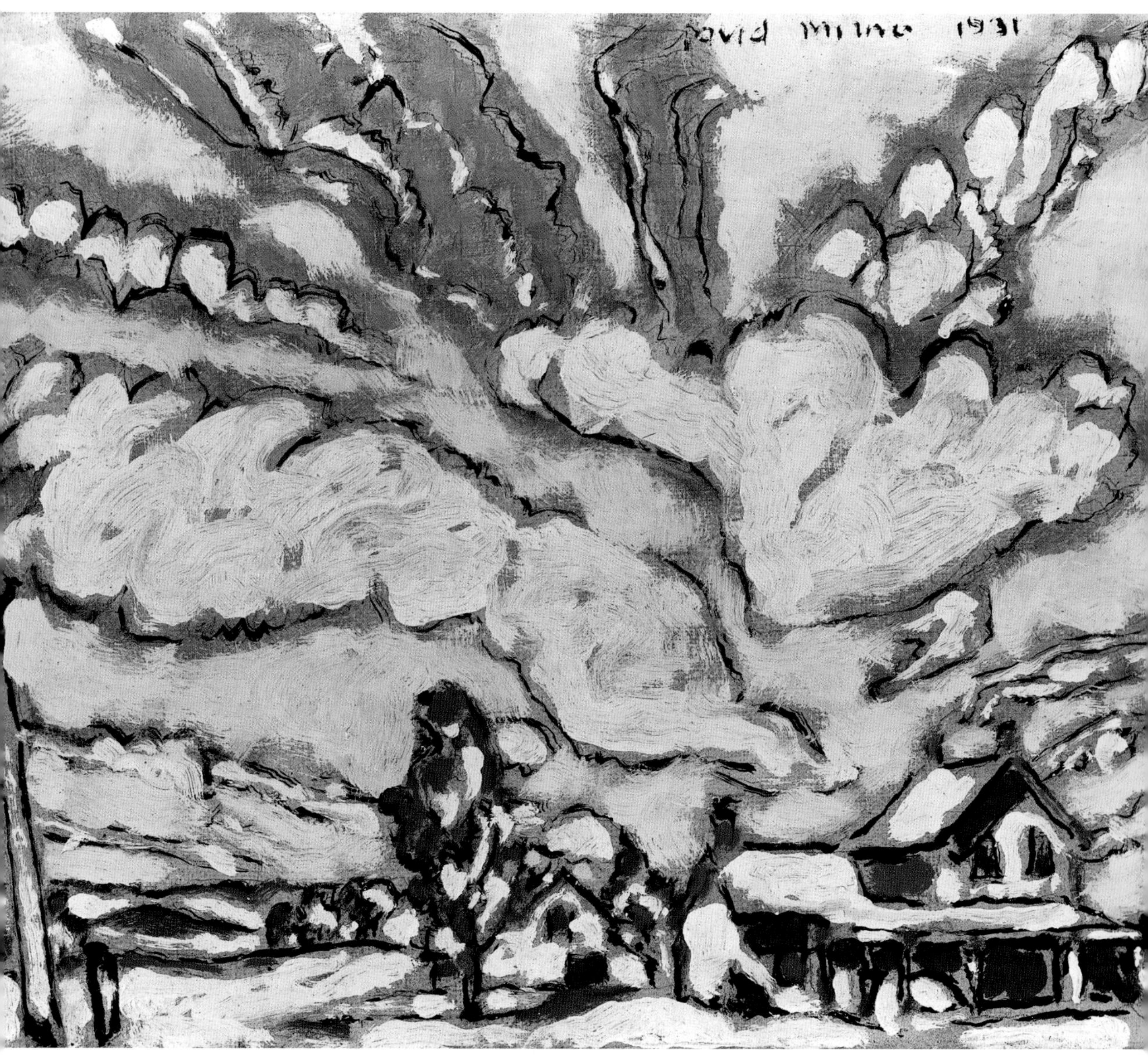

of an uninhabited wilderness setting during an approaching storm. The result is unnerving. Nothing in the painting stays still; there is no route that takes the viewer away from the intimidating site; and the rolling gray clouds suggest the destructive power of nature.[70]

Many English Canadian images of inhabited landscapes produced in the 1930s offer the same menacing views. Nova Scotia painter Marjorie Tozer's *Windswept* (c. 1931) is composed of a stark, steeply pitched rocky shoreline with a stormy sky above and a windswept sea in front. The only respite from geography and weather is a small fisherman's shack at the edge of the water. Precariously set on thin wooden piles, however, it

6 David Milne, *Ollie Matson's House Is Just a Square Red Cloud* (1931), oil on canvas, 46.2 x 56 cm. National Gallery of Canada. Vincent Massey Bequest, 1968.

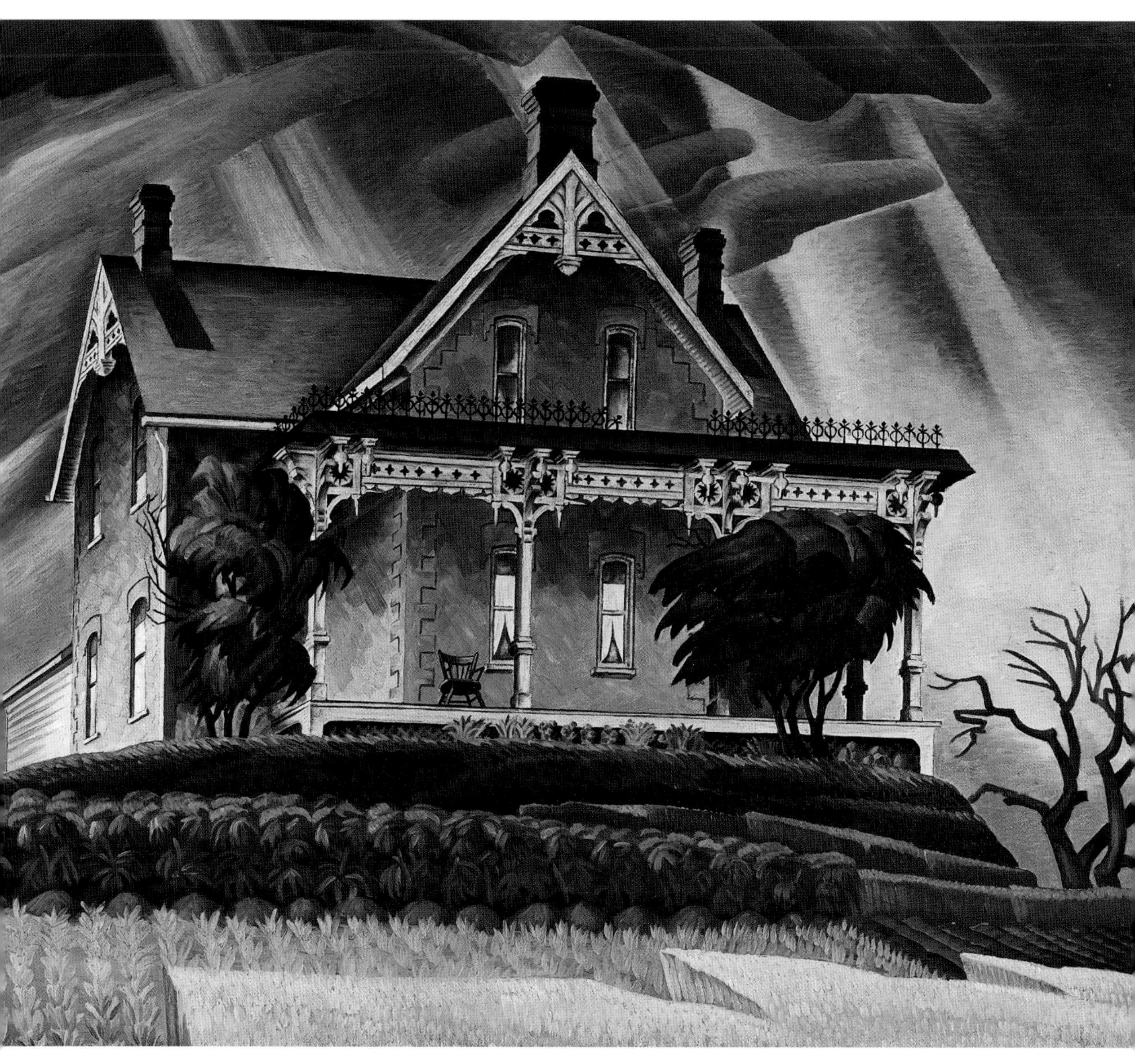

suggests that manmade structures provide little security.[71] David Milne, a painter living in rural Ontario, produced many inhabited landscapes in which lightning bolts rain down from the sky and funnel-shaped clouds move violently toward the land (e.g., *Ollie Matson's House Is Just a Square Red Cloud,* 1931, fig. 6).[72] In Vancouver artist Frederick Varley's *Dhârâna* (1932), a girl sits on the porch of a cabin in the mountains. She is rapt in the Buddhist metaphysical state of *dhârâna,* in which the mind frees itself from the body and becomes one with its surroundings; but her body is unnaturally elongated and her head at an uncomfortable angle.[73] In Carl Schaefer's *Ontario Farmhouse* (1934) (fig. 7), lightning forks out of the sky, not in thin lines, as it naturally would, but in broad, overpowering sheets above a stridently yellow farmhouse flanked by a dead tree, the limbs of which appear as spikes. An empty rocking chair on the porch suggests that the inhabitants have fled.[74]

Other English Canadian artists of the thirties, who were more concerned with the human figure than with landscape, made equally disturbing paintings, often with references to the land. *Sisters of Rural Quebec* (fig. 8), painted by English Montreal's Prudence Heward in 1930, is a good example. As art critics have noted, the portrait is "a profound exposition of the vulnerable as well as the heroic," a "kind of warfare, the battle of the human spirit against chaos."[75] But Heward's warfare is reserved. In the words of another critic, Heward's "empathy with her human subjects is clear but it should not be confused with the proletarian art of Kaethe Kollwitz."[76]

Charles Comfort's *Young Canadian* (1932), a watercolor portrait of Comfort's friend, Carl Schaefer, is similarly restrained.[77] Unable to find work in Toronto as an artist in the early thirties, Schaefer returned to the family farm. In the portrait he sits at some distance from farm buildings, with a box with a handle in front of him. In his left hand he holds an item (or items) that are not easily identifiable. His facial expression is serious. It is possible for a viewer to conclude that Schaefer is waiting on the side of the road with his suitcase for a ride to a place where he can seek better material circumstances. His serious expression and limp hands may suggest that he thinks the quest is futile. It is also possible to interpret the "box" as a paint box, the unidentifiable objects as paint brushes, and the thoughtful expression as part of a decision-making process regarding a work of art that he is about to make. Indeed, unless viewers knew that Comfort's figure was unemployed—and most would not—the latter interpretation is more likely. Certainly the title gives no hint of Schaefer's particular situation. Many other English Canadian artists of the thirties, such as Jack Humphrey of St. John, New Brunswick, Edwin Holgate, Lilias Torrance Newton and Jori Smith of English Montreal, and Frederick Varley of Vancouver, made similar images.[78]

English Canadian social critics of the 1930s who embraced leftist politics were naturally critical of art that did not openly critique specific problems of the decade. They were particularly annoyed by the large amount of landscape painting. Frank Underhill, president of the League for Social Reconstruction, wrote: "There is not much sign that Canadian artists have been moved by the phenomenon of a civilization dissolving before their eyes. ... Wouldn't one feel happier about one's country if the note of rustic rumination were not quite so dominant among its artists in this year 1936?"[79] In her 1937 plea for more political art, Paraskeva Clark insisted that "It is time [for landscape artists] to come down from your

8 Prudence Heward, *Sisters of Rural Quebec* (1930), oil on canvas, 157.5 x 106.7 cm. Art Gallery of Windsor.

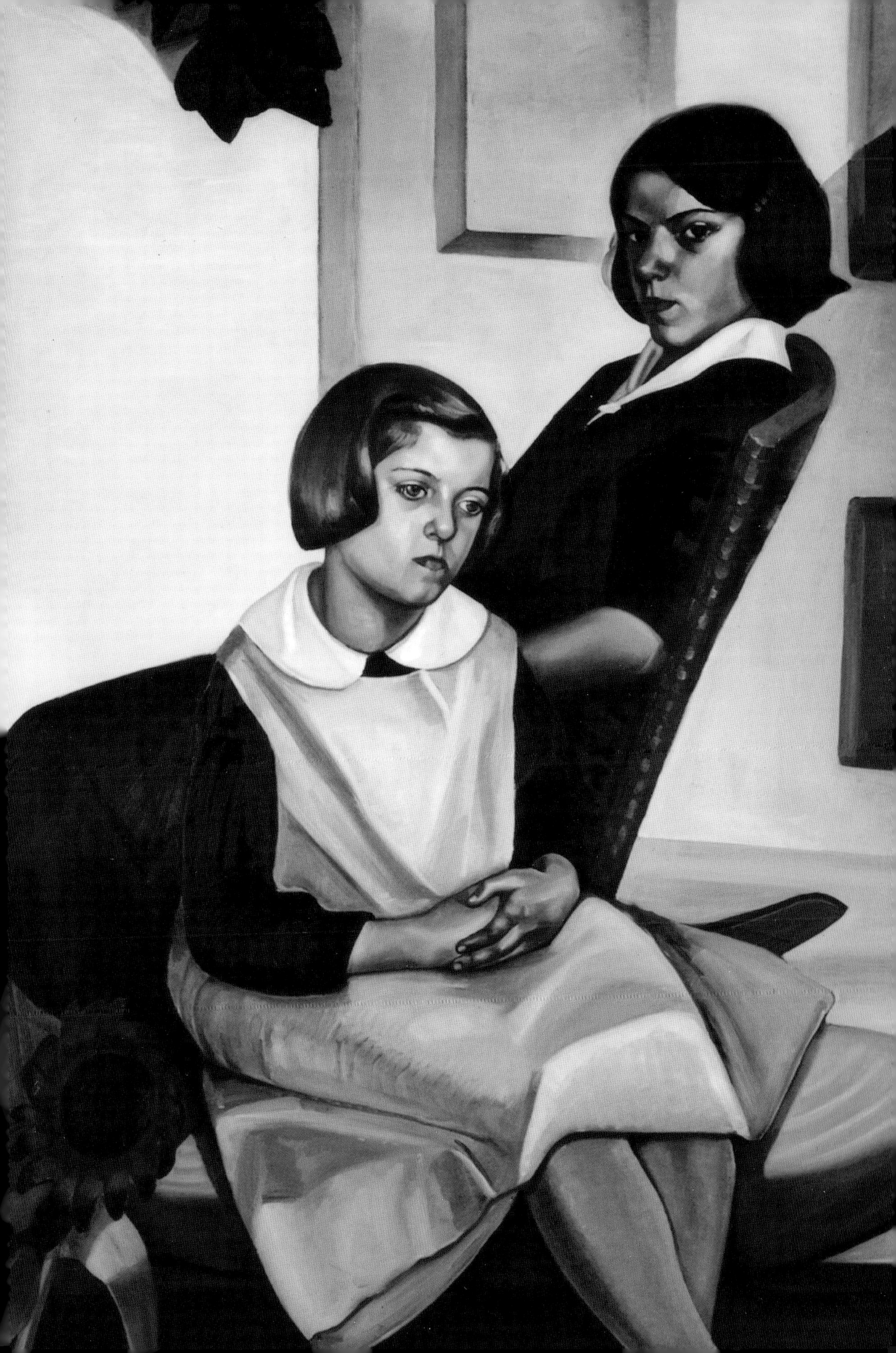

ivory tower [and] to dirty your gown in the mud and sweat of conflict. ...
It is to enable you [to paint landscapes] that castles are tumbling in
Spain."[80] Two years later Barker Fairley of the University of Toronto called
for "the painting of humanity to take priority [over landscape] ... especially
in this age of intense human conflict and suffering and innovation."[81]

Writing with the benefit of seventy-odd years of perspective, I
would respond to such critiques that many of the English Canadian artists of the 1930s may have intended to imbue their work with a sense of
social and political concern, if only covertly. The landscapes and portraits
I have just described could well have been designed for this very reason.
Frances Loring may have produced *The Miner* as a portrait bust to make
a favorable comparison between the miner and statesmen and literary
heroes, who were regularly depicted in this format. Margaret Shelton's
apparent glorification of industry, *Rosedale Mine,* grew out of a rift
between wealthy mine owners and impoverished workers in northern
Alberta mining towns; so her work may have been intended as an act of
sympathy on behalf of the miners.[82] And Emily Carr's *Scorned as Timber,
Beloved of the Sky* was certainly inspired, at least in part, by her concern
with the industrial logging practices of the region.[83]

Still, this art is not clearly critical of specific conditions that political activism might reform. It does not openly express sympathy for the
particular problems of any individual or group of individuals. The people who might have occupied the canvases' empty houses and industrial
sites, or experienced the storms in the wilderness and farmlands, and
for whom sympathy is presumably being evoked, are absent; and no reason for their absence is given. Even when human figures are the focus of
the work, as they are in *Sisters of Rural Quebec* (fig. 8) and in Comfort's
Young Canadian, the artists do not explain the sombre expressions of
their subjects.

Several decades ago Canadian art historian Charles Hill mounted an
impressive exhibition of Canadian painting in the thirties. In the well-
researched catalog Hill summarized the work by stating, "The thirties in
Canada lack a definite image in the history of Canadian art."[84] Presumably Hill meant that Canadian art of the thirties lacks the overtly political
content of other Western art of the 1930s. I would argue, however, that
Canadian art of the thirties does have a definite image—one of reserve
and restraint. As such, it distinguishes itself from the art of other American nations.

Painters and sculptors, we are working to create in Argentina and in Uruguay (perhaps in all of South America) the bases of a monumental pictorial movement, open and multi-exemplary for the great popular masses.

We intend to take pictorial work out of the aristocratic sacristies, where it has been rotting for more than four centuries.

We are going to liberate painting and sculpture from dry scholasticism, from academicism and the solitary cerebralism of art for art's sake, to take it to the tremendous social reality that surrounds us and is already wounding our foreheads.

> — David Alfaro Siqueiros, "Call to Argentinean Artists," (Un Llamamiento a los Plasticos Argentinos), in *Palabras de Siqueiros*, ed. Raquel Tibol (Mexico City: Fondo de Cultura Económica, 1996), 86–87, my translation. Originally published in the Buenos Aires daily *Critica* on 2 June 1933.

Mural painting cannot be more than another of the many forms of expression of popular art. To want to make of the mural movement the battle horse of the art of the masses in a bourgeois society is to condemn the movement to passivity or opportunism. The bourgeoisie, in its progressive move toward fascism, will not cede its monopolized walls for proletarian ends; not even the very contradictions of the regime will arrive at a point where the bourgeoisie would, out of its own volition, place the weapons in the hands of its class enemy, in order to be defeated.

> — Antonio Berni, "Siqueiros y el arte de masas," *Nueva Revista Política, Arte, Economía* 1 (January 1935): 14, my translation.

ADAPTING TO ARGENTINEAN REALITY:
THE NEW REALISM OF ANTONIO BERNI

Alejandro Anreus

Antonio Berni (1905–81), painter, muralist, graphic and installation artist, was well known in his lifetime in his native Argentina as well as throughout the Spanish-speaking Americas. Yet Berni's life and work remain little known in the United States. This essay will examine Berni's early life and work (1920s–1937) in relation to his development of a socially engaged figuration.

Antonio Berni returned to Argentina in 1930, with his French wife, Paule Cazenave, and their newborn daughter, Lilí. He had been living in Europe since August 1925. The Argentina to which he returned was in the midst of its second year of economic depression; a coup had deposed President Yrigoyen, and a cycle of military governments that would last ten years had begun.[1] Berni, like most Latin American artists of his generation, returned home for several reasons. The threat of fascism in Europe was one, the "patriotic" need to contribute to one's native culture, another. Finally, there was a more mundane reason: lack of funds.

Who was Antonio Berni? Born in Rosario, a province of Santa Fé, Antonio Berni was the youngest of three children of Italian immigrants; his mother, Margarita Picco, was a housewife and seamstress, his father, Napoleón Berni, a tailor.[2] In 1915, at the age of ten, Antonio started an apprenticeship in a stained-glass workshop in Rosario. That year his father departed for Italy on family business. While in Italy, Napoleón Berni was drafted into the army and was killed in action during World War I.[3] By 1916 Antonio was studying drawing and painting with Eugenio Fornels and Enrique Munné at the Centre Catalá in Rosario,[4] a working-class club that practiced the ideals of the late Catalonian educator and anarchist Francisco Ferrer and his "Escuela Moderna": an integrated education for the children of the working class that emphasized the arts and humanities. A hotbed of political radicalism, the

Centre may have been where Berni first came into contact with anarchist and socialist ideas.[5] In 1925 the Rosario Jockey Club granted Berni a scholarship to continue his art studies in Europe; he arrived in Madrid that August. Two years later he was settled in the outskirts of Paris, at Arcueil, where he met fellow Argentinean painter Lino Enea Spilimbergo (1896–1964), who became a lifelong friend. With Spilimbergo Berni shared both stylistic concerns regarding painting and left-wing political ideals.[6] In 1928 the provincial government of Santa Fé granted Berni a scholarship to continue his art education; he enrolled at the Grande Chaumiére, where he studied painting with André Lhõte and Othon Friesz. In 1928–29 Berni met and befriended the poet Max Jacob (who introduced him to the technique of etching), the young sculptor Paule Cazenave (former secretary to communist activist and novelist Henri Barbuse), who would become his wife, and members of the Surrealist movement.[7] He also befriended the Surrealist poet Louis Aragon, though the two men drifted apart when Aragon became an adherent of Stalinism.[8]

Of all Berni's friends at this time, however, the philosopher Henri Lefebvre (1901–91) had the most profound intellectual impact.[9] Lefebvre introduced Berni to the writings of Sigmund Freud and, more important, to the writings of Karl Marx. A professor of philosophy at a Parisian lyceum, Lefebvre was only four years older than Berni. The two met at each other's homes or in cafes to read and discuss Marx. For Lefebvre, Marxism was a framework for thought, and a dynamic framework at that, rather than a fixed ideology. Lefebvre argued for a nondeterministic Marx, a Marx who had not been placed in the straitjacket of the so-called orthodoxy demanded by the French Communist Party of the late 1920s. Over time Lefebvre used Marxism as a basis for a move into sociology, which informed his structuralist and differentialist philosophical position of the 1960s and 1970s. Berni maintained the friendship with Lefebvre until his death in 1981. Every time he visited Paris, and when he briefly lived there in 1975–76, Berni always saw Henri Lefebvre socially.[10] Thanks to Lefebvre's influence, Berni approached Marxism critically, and from a non-Stalinist position. In the larger context of Marxism in Latin America, this is quite exceptional, as is the critical, independent Marxism of Peru's José Carlos Mariategui. By the time Berni met the Mexican muralist and communist David Alfaro Siqueiros in Buenos Aires in 1933, he had already acquired a Marxist basis for interpreting society, and a highly independent one at that.

In addition to meeting Lefebvre, it was during his stay in Paris that Berni met the Brazilian painter Candido Portinari (1903–62), read the *Second Surrealist Manifesto,* saw the Giorgio de Chirico retrospective of 1928, and viewed both Sergei Eisenstein's *Strike* (1924) and Luis Buñuel and Salvador Dalí's *The Andalusian Dog* (1928). He also became inter ested in photography and, as his daughter later recalled, "he bought a small Leica in Paris, which he really put to use after his return to Argentina."[11] These diverse cultural and visual experiences expanded Berni's notions of art and experimentation—he became, and to the end of his life remained, open to change, to the use of diverse elements in the construction of his art, both formally and conceptually, as long as the social discourse, the political engagement, was there.

Before his trip to Europe, Berni's student work in Argentina had affinities with Post-Impressionism, not just in terms of subject (still lifes, landscapes, and an occasional nude) but also in its consciously distorted drawing and application of color. The Parisian work evolved out of his encounter with both Surrealism and the neoclassicism of such painters as Derain and the Italians of the Metaphysical School. The influence of Giorgio de Chirico's paintings, which Berni saw in 1928, with their strong modeling of forms, dramatic chiaroscuro, and use of perspective to create "an infinite and melancholic space,"[12] is clearly evident in such Berni paintings as *The Bald Bullfighter* (1928), *Napoleon III* (1928), *Objects in the City* (1929), and the notable *Self-Portrait with Cactus* of 1929 (fig. 1).

Berni's *Self-Portrait with Cactus* is one of a handful of self-portraits that the artist executed.[13] Berni represents himself from the chest up, his right arm leaning on a gray wooden table, where a small pot contains a cactus. Wearing a salmon-colored shirt without buttons, his skin color ranges from olive to sienna, and he stares at the viewer with sober intelligence. Behind his figure, Berni painted the gray walls of buildings on a street in one-point perspective, which runs into a pale blue sky. The environment in which Berni represented himself is possibly a street remembered from his native Rosario. The modesty and isolation of the background may indicate that this is a working-class neighborhood. According to his daughter, Lilí Berni, the cactus in the painting was commonly found in the Argentinean countryside. Berni paints himself without any of the trappings traditionally associated with the figure of an artist. To the contrary, this self-portrait proclaims his identity as a member of the working class.

Stylistically, Berni's *Self-Portrait with Cactus* reveals the influence of de Chirico, as well as of the many artists who returned to a neoclassical idea of the real after World War I, among them Gino Severini, André Derain, and Pablo Picasso.[14] Berni's friend and fellow painter Lino Enea Spilimbergo had been painting under the influence of Severini's neoclassical work of the period. Ideologically, the classicism of these artists was both a rejection of the constant experimentation found in much of the painting and sculpture that preceded World War I and a reflection of the chaos of the war itself. Once he returned to his homeland, this search for

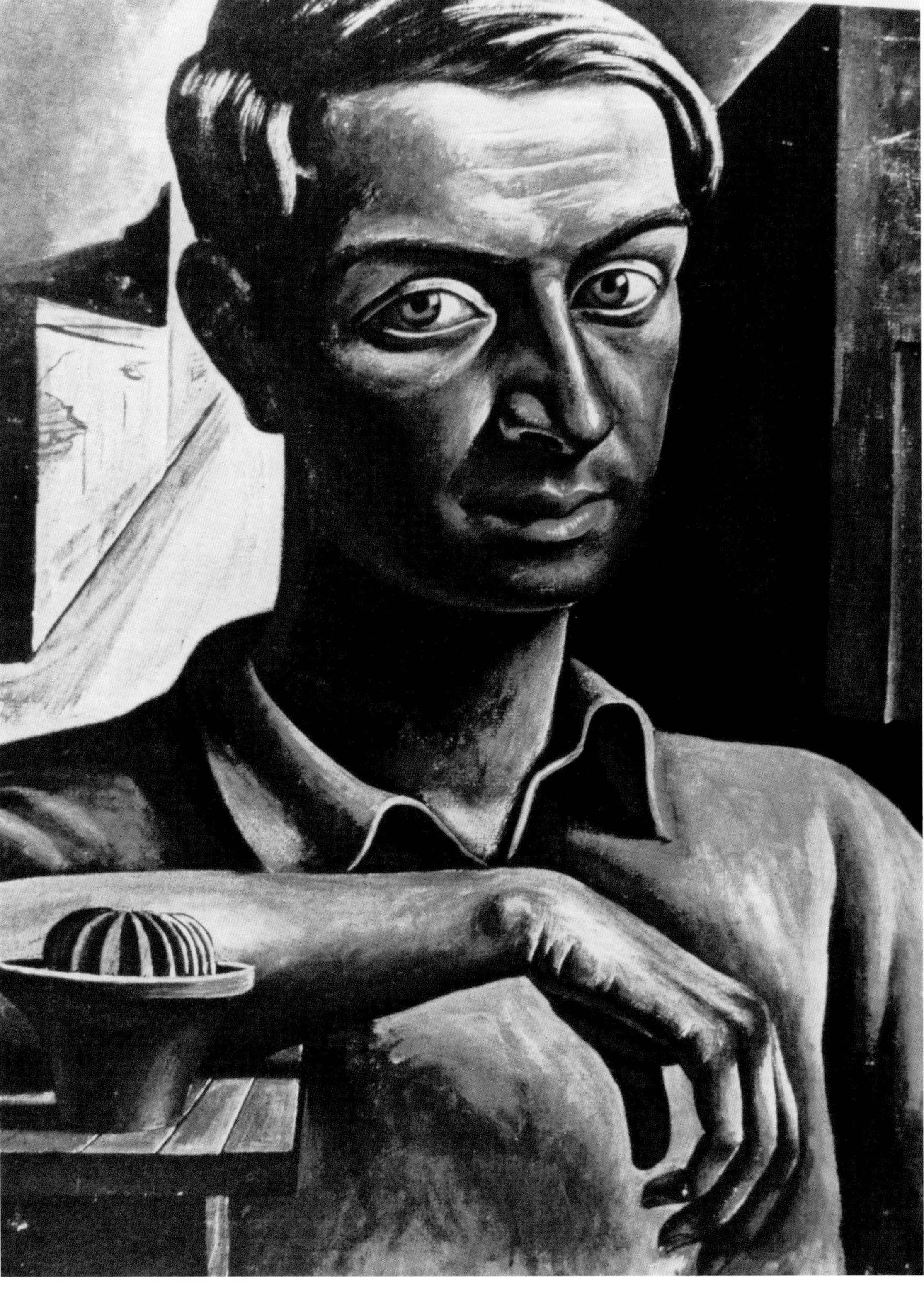

a clear and solid visual vocabulary served Berni well in his Marxist interpretation of Argentinean social reality.

Argentina was in a state of turmoil in the 1930s, and the worldwide economic crisis was felt throughout the country. In September 1930 the Novecento exhibition took place in Buenos Aires (Asociación Amigos del Arte), which presented the work of Italian artists concerned with neoclassical clarity of form as well as with clear narrative content. In 1930, the year of Berni's return, liberal president Hipólito Yrigoyen was deposed by a military coup, immigration ceased by order of the government, and the anarcho-syndicalist labor union Confederación General del Trabajo was founded. On the cultural front, playwright and director L. Barletta created the proletarian theater group Teatro del Pueblo, and a group of left-wing intellectuals (among them the art critic Julio Payró) organized the Free School of Superior Studies for the education of the working class.[15] The Argentinean Socialist Party had been founded in 1896; in 1918 a dissident group broke with the party and in 1920 became the Communist Party of Argentina. Both parties were very active in Argentinean life throughout the 1930s, in the labor movement and electoral politics as well as in intellectual circles.[16] The military regime persecuted all progressive elements in Argentinean society, from students to labor activists to intellectuals.

Antonio Berni settled with his wife and child on a small tenant farm (*chacra*) in the countryside near Rosario. In 1931 they moved into Rosario, where Berni took a menial job working for the municipality. Soon Berni joined the Communist Party of Argentina. According to his daughter, he never forgot the hostility he experienced during this period. "On the one hand," she recalled, was "the hostility of the respectable citizens of Rosario, because he had joined the Communist Party and was openly a 'red,' and on the other hand the hostility within the party because he wanted to be an independent artist, with his own interpretation of Marxism. Lefebvre told him this would happen."[17] Berni resigned from the Communist Party the following year. For the rest of his political life he associated himself with various groups on the left, ranging from anarchists to socialists, and with all sorts of independent Marxists as well as labor unions. He occasionally took positions similar to those of his "fellow travelers," but he strove to preserve his independence and to keep his distance from the Communist Party.[18]

In 1932 Berni exhibited the paintings he had done in Paris under the influence of Surrealism at the Amigos del Arte association in Rosario. The press practically ignored the exhibition.[19] Although Berni believed that his Surrealist-inspired work had no context in the Argentina of 1932, he nevertheless felt a need to exhibit the work of his European period.[20] At the same time Berni started to use his Leica to photograph the brothels in Rosario, the unemployed (fig. 2), labor demonstrations, and the deplorable and inventive architecture of shantytowns. These photographs were a great resource for some of the paintings of the 1930s; the brothel and shantytown photos also appeared in his best work of the 1960s: the Ramona Montiel and Juanito Laguna series. For Berni, the photo documentation of the impoverished areas and social problems of Rosario served to create a series of unmediated visual references that could be used as a "real" point of departure in the creation of his paintings.

David Alfaro Siqueiros (1896–1974), the youngest of *los tres grandes* of the Mexican mural movement, arrived in Argentina in the late spring of 1933.[21] Siqueiros lectured, granted interviews, and wrote articles in Buenos Aires on behalf of mural painting and against the Plutarco Calles regime, then in power in Mexico.[22]

While in Argentina, Siqueiros published his "Call to Argentinean Artists," which had a strong impact on Berni and his contemporaries.[23] Similar to the 1924 Mexican manifesto, the 1933 "Call" was both an attack on bourgeois notions of art, easel painting in particular, and a demand for mural painting that portrayed the realities of contemporary life and served the interests of the working class. Shortly thereafter, Natalio Botana, the owner of the newspaper *Critica* (in which the "Call" had been published) and a patron of the arts, commissioned Siqueiros to execute a mural in his country residence "Los Ganados" in the town of Don Torcuato.[24] Siqueiros invited Berni, Spilimbergo, Juan Carlos Castagnino, and the Uruguayan painter Enrique Lázaro to assist him.[25]

Plastic Exercise (1933) was the product of a true collaboration, with all the painters contributing equally to the overall design and execution. Painted in a space the shape of a tunnel, on the walls of the home's wet bar, *Plastic Exercise* was an unorthodox fresco. The paint was applied on wet black cement, using an overhead projector and airbrush. The images are variations on the female form, as if reflected through a prism.[26] The formal experimentation of this project was important for Berni, but even more important was the experience of working on a mural for the first time, as part of a team of artists, in an experimental medium (airbrushed fresco) and with untraditional tools. After the team completed the mural, they wrote and published a text in which they discussed the work's technique, its method of execution, and its purposeful lack of social content. The lack of social content was a conscious decision on the part of the team, since they wanted this first mural project to be purely experimental work.[27]

The following year, 1934, Siqueiros and Berni engaged in a public debate regarding the nature and patronage of mural painting in Argentina. Siqueiros called on the Argentinean government to offer the

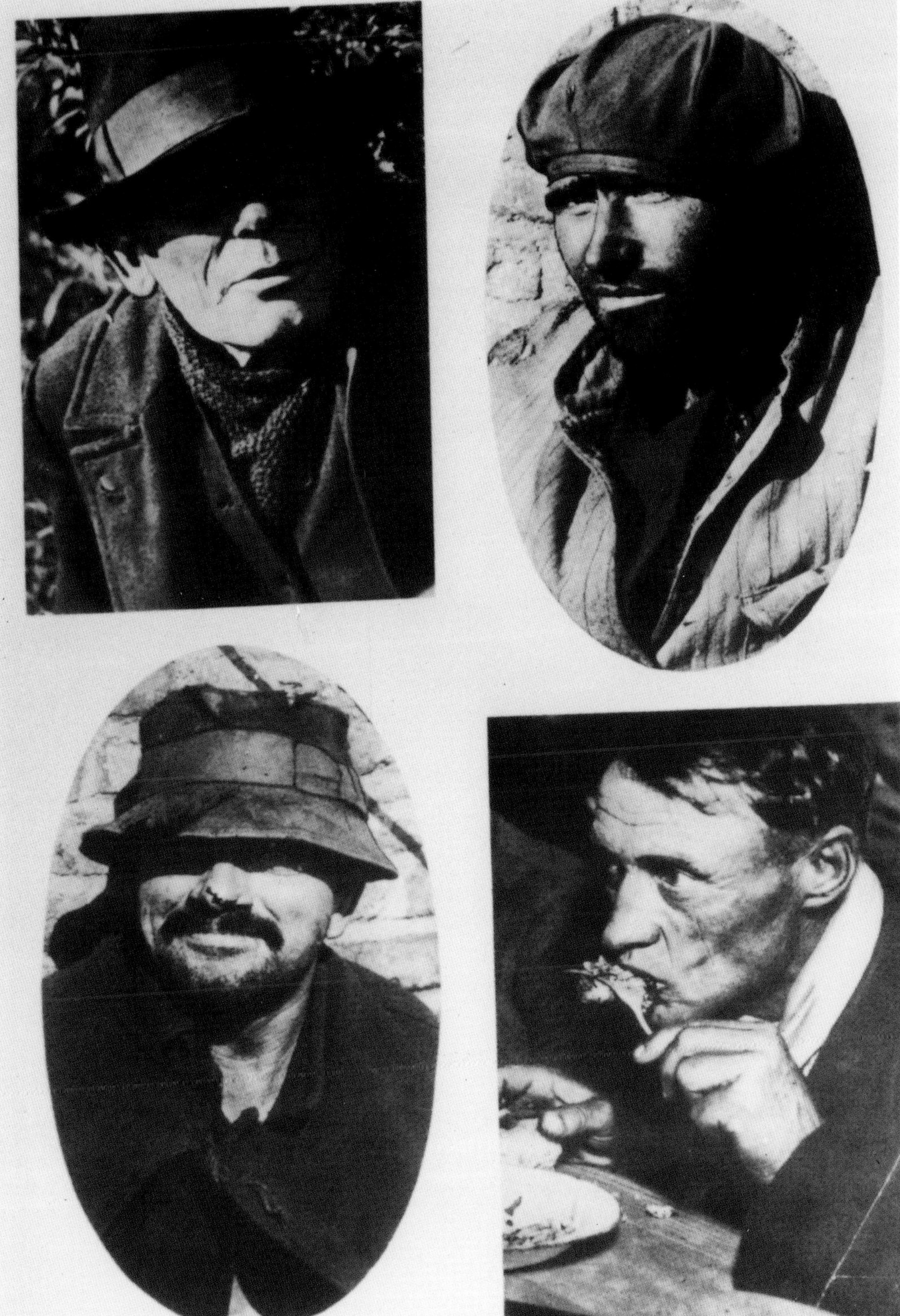

walls of public buildings to its artists. On these walls, Siqueiros argued, the artists could celebrate the past of the nation and call for change in the present and revolution in the future.[28] Berni responded that because Argentina lacked a social revolution comparable to Mexico's, the conservative (and at the time military) government of Argentina would not offer public buildings to potential muralists. Instead, Berni insisted, Argentinean artists had to adapt to their immediate reality; this meant temporary murals, or mural-sized easel paintings, executed with the most available media (in Berni's case, tempera on burlap), to document the problems of the moment: unemployment, strikes, and political repression. At this time Berni was also thinking of the print as the most practical and portable replacement for the mural as a means of mass communication.[29] Yet it was also in April of 1934 that Berni, in spite of his debate with Siqueiros, founded the school/workshop Mutualidad Popular de Estudiantes y Artistas Plásticos, which was derivative of Siqueiros's ideas about collaborative artistic production, in Rosario.

Siqueiros left Argentina later in 1934, and after his departure his friendship with Berni became distant, owing to ideological as well as aesthetic differences.[30] At this time (1934–35), Berni worked with a team of artists to produce banners and temporary murals for labor unions and various political organizations of the left, most notably *The Wounded Man* mural (a collaboration with Anselmo Piccoli, airbrush and pyroxilyn, destroyed) at the Teachers Union building in Rosario.[31]

In 1939 Berni and Spilimbergo painted the murals for the Argentinean pavilion at the World's Fair in New York City, and the following year Berni painted a mural for the Teatro del Pueblo in Buenos Aires (both destroyed).[32] No preparatory drawings for these two projects are in existence.

But it was between 1934 and 1937, when Berni painted a number of easel works of mural proportions, that he defined his social realism in the context of Argentinean art and culture. Although Spilimbergo and Castagnino shared Berni's pictorial and social concerns, these two artists never achieved the clarity and force found in Berni's work. This was due in part to individual temperament and talent, Berni being the strongest of the trio in these respects. Yet it is important to emphasize here the difference in social class and intellectual makeup among the three artists. Spilimbergo and Castagnino both came from the middle class. Politically, Spilimbergo was a nonaligned leftist with communist sympathies, and Castagnino was a lifelong member of the Communist Party who was content to follow its dictums. Berni, by contrast, was of the working class, possessed an independent formation in Marxism, and had belonged to the Communist Party of Argentina only briefly.[33]

Two principal groups, the grupo de Florida and the grupo de Boedo, dominated the cultural climate of Argentina between the world wars. The first consisted mostly of poets like Jorge Luis Borges, Ricardo Molinari, and Leopoldo Marechal, who were middle-class, sophisticated, and liberal. The second group was made up of essayists and novelists like Roberto Mariani, Luis Emilio Soto, and Bernardo Verbitsky, who were working-class admirers of popular culture and socialists or anarchists. In time the grupo Florida became associated with the literary magazine *Sur* (founded in 1931), and the grupo Boedo with the socialist periodical *Claridad* (founded in 1927).[34] Although Berni developed friendships with both Manuel Mujica Lainez of *Sur* and Bernardo Verbitsky of *Claridad,* he always maintained his independence, aesthetic and political, from these groups. Antonio Berni was an independent painter, someone who could have solidarity with social causes but was solitary in his work as an artist.[35]

Among the forty-odd easel works that Berni painted between 1934 and 1937, five stand out as exemplary of his pictorial and social concerns. These are *Unemployed* (fig. 3), *Demonstration* (fig. 4), both from 1934, *Tenant Farmers* (fig. 5) from 1935, *Midnight in the World* (fig. 6), painted 1936–37, and *New Chicago Athletic Club* (fig. 7), from 1937. A significant iconographic and conceptual source for these paintings is the work *Sin pan y sin trabajo* of 1893–94 by Ernesto De la Cárcova (1866–1927), a nineteenth-century Argentinean painter who depicted working-class subjects and who also influenced painter Carlos Alonso in 1968.

Unemployed, like other important pictures from this period, is a mural-sized easel work executed with tempera on burlap. It depicts a group of nine figures in the foreground and five other figures in the middle ground. The background consists of an austere landscape containing a cliff, the sea, and a ship on the horizon. Most of the foreground figures are lying down, sleeping. The only female figure in the composition, a mother who holds a sleeping child, stares off to her right with a look of exhaustion. In the middle ground five men sit on the curb; some of them seem to have fallen asleep. Their dress suggests they are working-class, with the exception of one figure in the foreground, sitting on a box. He is dressed in a hat, tie, vest, pinstripe trousers, and overcoat. His head is thrown back—he, too, is asleep. He may represent a lower management functionary, who, like everyone else, has been thrown out of work by the Depression. His shoes, their laces untied, are a metaphor for a social situation that has come apart. The name Santa Fe is visible on the box on which he is sitting. The scene is obviously provincial; we are not in urban Buenos Aires. The picture conveys an air of melancholy and inaction. The palette is generally cool, the only warm touches being the reds of a dress and a couple of sweaters. The forms of the figures are solid, drawn forcefully and with a strong emphasis on the heads and hands.

The sculptural way in which the figures are painted, with their dramatic foreshortening, brings to mind Siqueiros's work, but also some of Berni's favorite painters: Piero della Francesca, Mantegna, and de Chirico.[36]

This painting does not sentimentalize the working class; on the contrary, it shows it exhausted, stupefied by unemployment. It also raises questions: What is the ship's destination, if the Argentinean government has stopped immigration? Is it a cargo ship? If so, why are the unemployed men not hired to unload the ship? Will they be hired? This possible note of hope is counterbalanced by the landscape's aridity, which reflects the dead-end situation of the economic crisis. These figures are lost, suspended in a state of irresolution. They are waiting for something, but this "something" is not about to happen. *Unemployed* was rejected by the jury of the Salón Nacional in 1934 because of its politics.

In *Demonstration* (fig. 4) which depicts a crowd, Berni based the faces of the unemployed on his earlier photographs (fig. 2), a strategy similar to that of U.S. painter Ben Shahn. The painting represents a group of unemployed men (and a few women), marching down the main street of what may be a town in the provinces. A hand-painted sign above the crowd demands bread and work. Featured in the foreground are the faces of ten men of varying ages, two women, and a child; they are up against the picture plane, pressed against the viewer. As in the previous picture, Berni paints these in a sculptural manner, with a dramatic use of light and shadow, and a great deal of detail in the drawing of the individual faces. The painting is abundant in yellows, oranges, and reds, which are in turn balanced by blues and greens. The buildings in the background, drab with their brick, ochre, and brown colors, stand against a blue-gray sky, charged with turbulence. Some of the faces express exhaustion and despair, others, defiance. A clenched fist is about to emerge from the crowd. Several faces are looking upward, possibly at policemen on horseback. The painting captures the moment in which the crowd is about to be repressed. The dialectic of this picture is complex; these are individuals united in a crowd—unemployed workers painted with all their wrinkles and grime, powerful as a unit, yet not idealized or falsely heroic. The key to this demonstration is the solidarity of the dispossessed, expressed through their very human faces, their worn and calloused hands.

If *Unemployed* and *Demonstration* depict the social unrest of provincial towns during the Depression, *Tenant Farmers* (fig. 5) is a picture of agrarian solidarity. This work is the product of Berni's experience living on a chacra upon his return to Argentina from France. In it, tenant farmers are gathered for a meeting during the early evening. They are positioned under an arch in what is obviously a meeting place in an agrarian town. Behind a table sits the tenant farmer who is apparently

3   Antonio Berni, *Unemployed* (1934), tempera on burlap, 218 x 300 cm. Collection of Elena Berni, Buenos Aires.

4   Antonio Berni, *Demonstration* (1934), tempera on burlap, 180 x 250 cm. Collection of Dr. Eduardo and María Teresa Constantini.

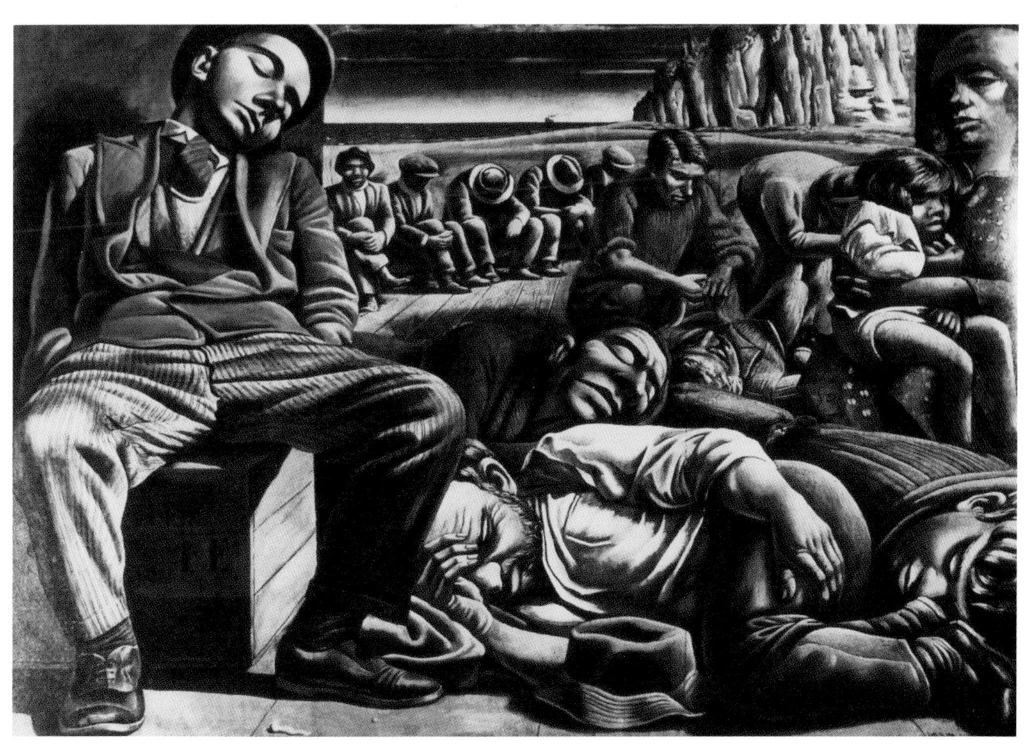
PAN Y
TRABAJO

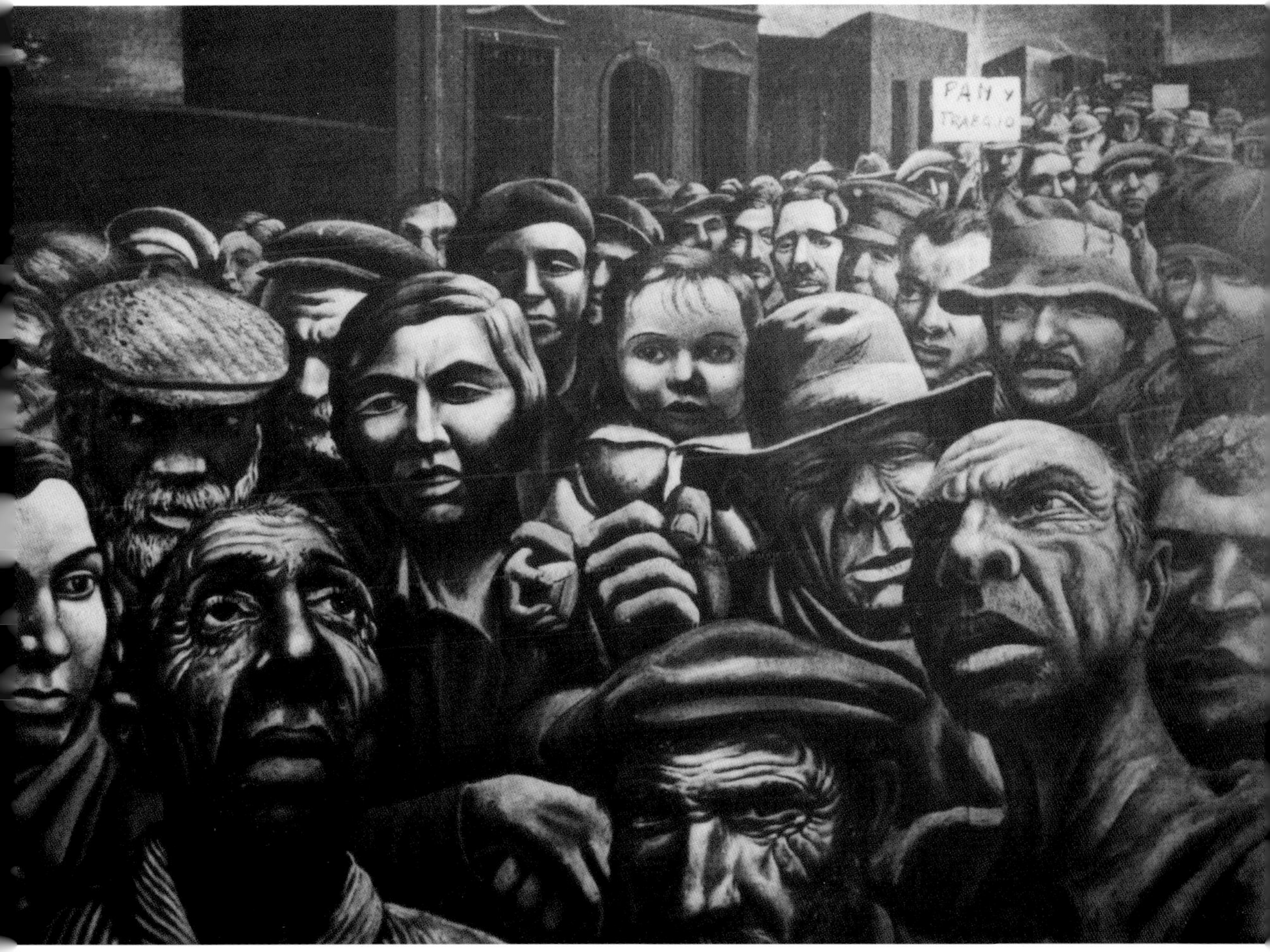

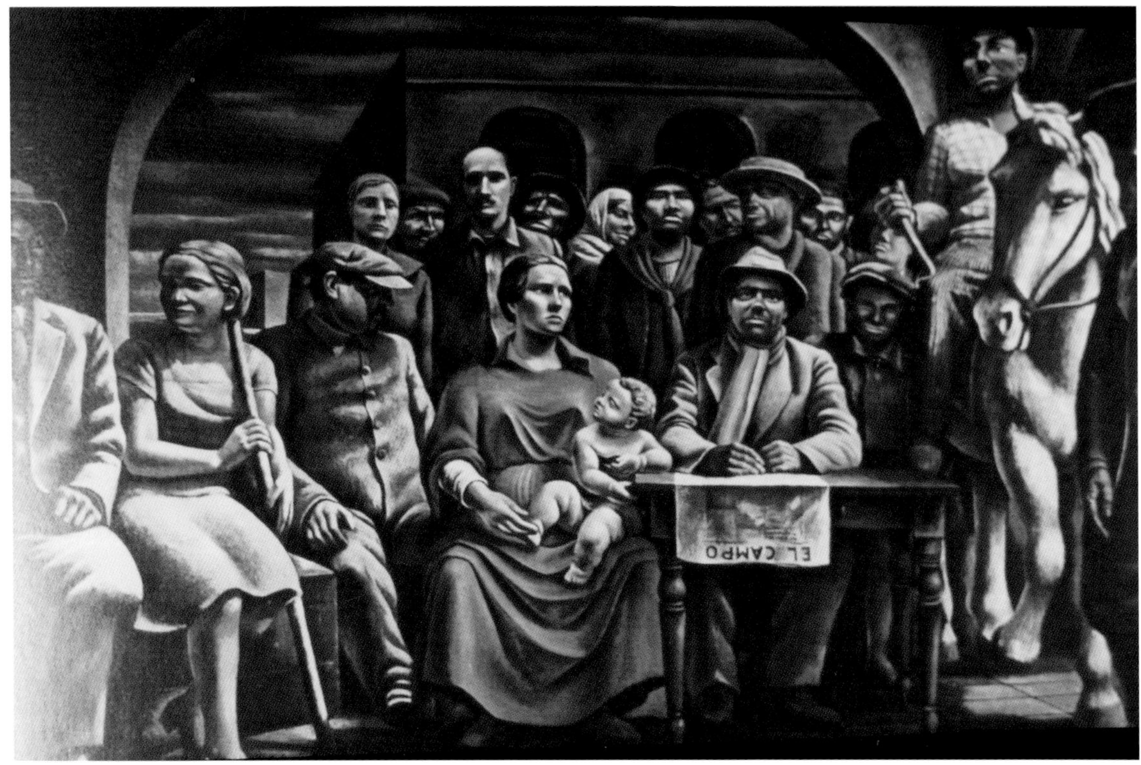

the leader; on the table, beneath his hands, is a newspaper entitled *The Countryside*—perhaps a left-wing periodical that supports the farmers' position. This figure is surrounded by eighteen others, all of them tenant farmers: a young woman with a baby, another woman holding a staff, young and old men, other women who are older, and a child. Both genders, and the ages of man, are represented. One tenant farmer sits astride an Ucello-like white horse. Some of the figures are dressed in their best clothes—hats, jackets, even a suit. Two Indian faces stand out among the group, which is a bit odd when we consider that the Indian population was practically wiped out by the end of the nineteenth century in most of Argentina. Perhaps through these figures Berni is making a statement about the marginality of people of color in the Americas, even within the lower social classes. All of the forms are sculptural, the colors both bright and neutral against a dark background of gray and earth-colored buildings.

The composition evokes Renaissance paintings of a *sacra conver-zasione,* or a Last Supper, or civic activity, and the mother and child bring to mind a Madonna and child. It is in effect a secular adaptation of a Renaissance work. The horse and rider evoke a traditional equestrian figure from Italian art of the fourteenth and fifteenth centuries. These symbolic references give the tenant farmers a certain grandeur. The bodies are tense within the space that contains them. They are also

5 Antonio Berni, *Tenant Farmers* (1935), oil on canvas, 200 x 300 cm. Collection of Consejo de Deliberación, Buenos Aires.

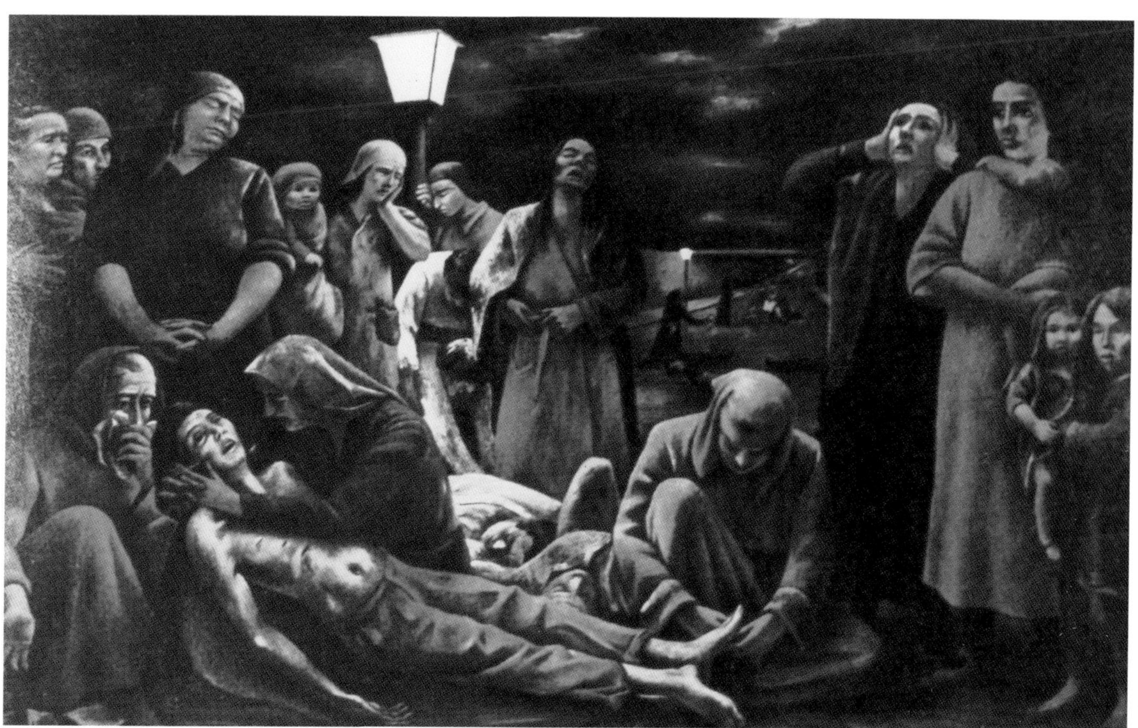

assured, self-contained in their poses. These tenant farmers are about to negotiate, to make demands of the landowners. Behind them the desolate Argentinean countryside stretches out. Most of them stare out at the viewer—whose physical position in relation to the picture is that of the landowners. The group stands as a unit of solidarity.

Midnight in the World (fig. 6) is the one painting from this period with obvious allegorical overtones. Painted in 1936–37, it is Berni's direct commentary on the Spanish Civil War (1936–39), in which the fascists ultimately achieved victory. This war had a powerful impact on the Spanish-speaking countries of the Western Hemisphere; committees of solidarity with the Spanish Republic sprang up in several countries, as Spain was after all the "mother country"—the source of language, religion, and culture. Berni, like other artists in Latin America (such as Siqueiros), was moved by the conflict to paint a particularly mournful work in *Midnight in the World*.

A large horizontal picture, *Midnight in the World* is a secular version of the deposition-of-Christ theme. Like Rivera, Orozco, and Siqueiros before him, Berni used the established visual culture of Roman Catholicism as a reference point, which allowed him to communicate culturally with a Roman Catholic audience. By secularizing the subject, he updated it and invested it with the politics of his historical moment. The background of the composition depicts a desolate nighttime urban landscape, with two solitary streetlights. The streets are populated with corpses and grieving figures. The sky is stormy, the light from the moon barely visible. In the foreground lies the Christ-like figure of a dying man, shirtless and without shoes. His trousers are red, perhaps symbolic of the revolutionary dimensions of the struggling Spanish Republic. His body rests on the lap of a Mary-like figure who is shrouded in blue. They are surrounded by weeping women and children, their expressions reflecting either horror or stoicism. The humility and poverty of their dress identifies them as the poor. The corpse of another man lies in the middle ground; behind it another male figure carries the corpse of a third man on his shoulders. The paint is applied in a more painterly, scumbled manner than in the previous works, giving the overall picture an expressionistic quality.

This is a painting of absolute mourning, even despair. Only such a devastating reference to grief—the death of Christ—can evoke the brutality wrought by fascism on the Spanish people. The picture depicts the remains, the aftereffects, of a particularly brutal assault. This work was painted within the specific political context of Argentina at the time; the working classes, and a minority within the intellectual class, were the only elements in society solidly behind the Spanish Republican cause. (During World War II the government of Argentina remained neutral, although with a strong pro-Axis sentiment.)

Berni's most life-affirming social realist statement of this period is his *New Chicago Athletic Club* (fig. 7), in the collection of the Museum of Modern Art in New York. "New Chicago" was a working-class industrial area on the outskirts of Buenos Aires named for its physical similarity with the industrial sections of Chicago, Illinois. The boys in the painting are probably the children or grandchildren of immigrants—their roots are not just in Spain but possibly in Italy, Ireland, and other European countries. Their soccer team, the "Club Atletico Nueva Chicago," with its eleven players and six substitutes, is posing as if for a formal team photo. Behind them is a landscape endowed with the usual metaphysical and melancholic qualities of Berni's outdoor scenes. All of the forms in the composition are modeled sculpturally, recalling once again the paintings of the Italian Quattrocento. The colors are intense and bright. A luscious still life of watermelons, grapes, and pears occupies the lower right corner of the picture. The faces of the boys are all painted with individual details. Different types of hair and skin color are evident, reflecting the diverse ethnic background of the team. Yet these boys are undoubtedly Argentines, linked together by a love of the sport as well as class solidarity. They are strong, alert. Through them Berni celebrates an aspect of working-class leisure—according to Henri Lefebvre, organic leisure activity helps break down industrial alienation and build genuine solidarity. In this case the leisure happens to be the national passion of Argentina:

soccer. But in this painting these boys also represent the future; their reliance on one another and their individual, forward manner are qualities that make them "ready for anything."

These five paintings show us Berni's social subjects and social realist style, which he defined as *nuevo realismo*. They depict moments of abandonment and revolt, brutal persecution, but most of all solidarity among the oppressed elements of society; the working class, the urban and agrarian poor. The formal devices of Berni's style were derived not

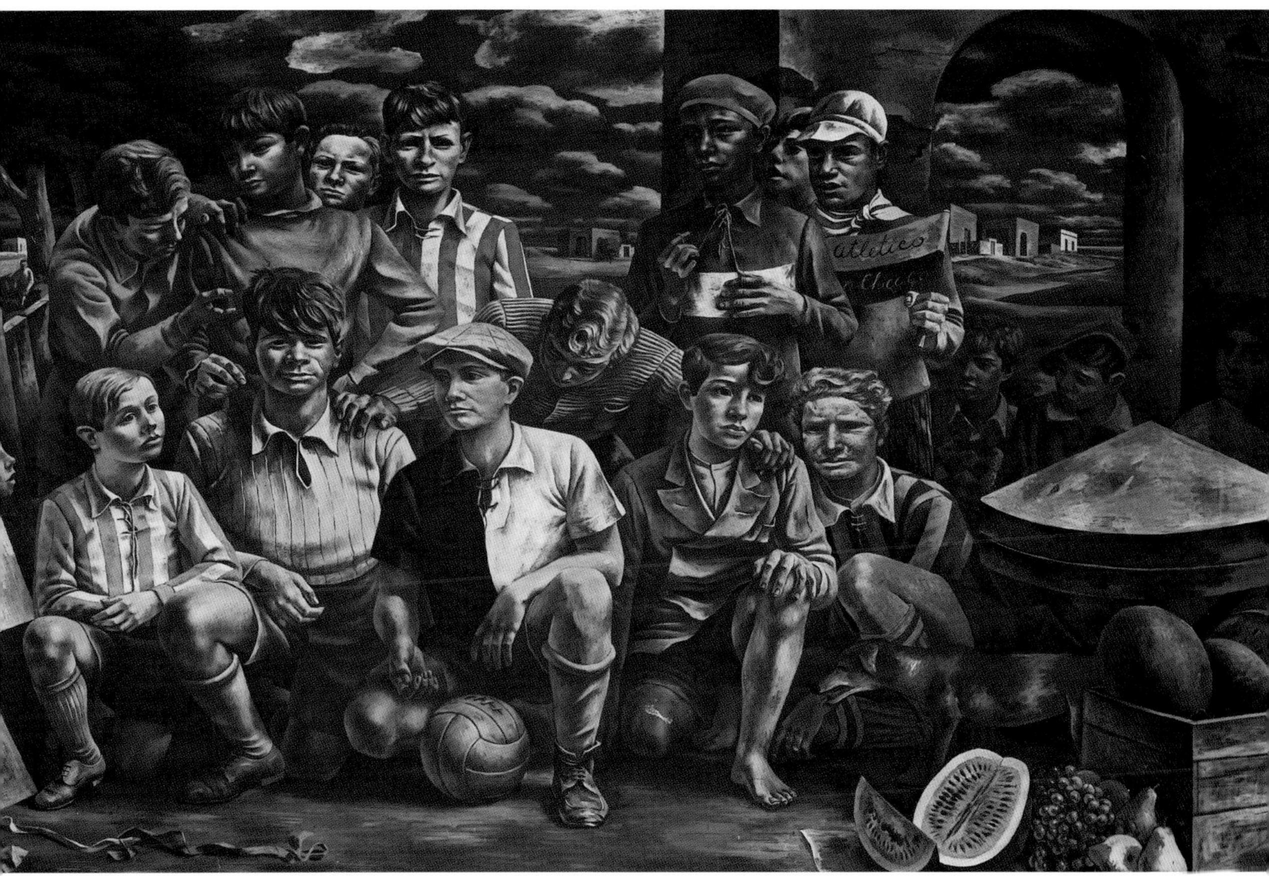

7 Antonio Berni, *New Chicago Athletic Club* (1937), oil on canvas, 184.9 x 600.1 cm. The Museum of Modern Art, New York. Inter-American Fund, 1943.

just from the modernism that he encountered in Paris but also from the "sculptural" painting of the Italian Quattrocento. Photography, for Berni as for Siqueiros, was an important resource for painting. At the same time, Berni rejected Siqueiros's dogmatic call for murals in public buildings as the only strategy of communication, as well as the Mexican's optimistic, monumentalist style—a style that became increasingly official in both the fascist and Stalinist sense. Politically, Berni also diverged from Siqueiros, repudiating the notion of the artist as a loyal, unquestioning member of the Communist Party.

In 1936 Berni published the article "El nuevo realismo" in the August issue of *Forma* magazine (Buenos Aires). In it he called for a new realism that represented "the new hero and the new drama in a universal visual language of apparent formal modernity."[37] Three years later, together with Spilimbergo, Castagnino, and others, Berni founded the short-lived Taller de Arte Mural (Mural Art Workshop). Yet the decades of the forties and fifties were difficult ones for Berni. Like many artists, leftist and otherwise, he opposed the fascistic regime of Juan Domingo Peron. The Peron regime persecuted socialists, communists, and other leftists. Still, Berni did not opt for exile but remained in Argentina, painting. His work of these two decades suffered both stylistically and in terms of content. Of course, there are exceptions, such as the powerful *El obrero muerto* (1949), in which he secularized Andrea Mantegna's *Dead Christ.* His depictions of the "insulted and the injured" of society became at times sentimental, his colors dull, his forms flat. At their worst, the paintings of this period are mannered and repetitive, having much in common with the paintings of a less talented artist like Candido Portinari of Brazil. Yet by 1960 Antonio Berni had returned in full force with a powerful body of work—the Juanito Laguna and Ramona Montiel series—based on elements of his early social realist period, a bold reworking of the collage technique, and a renewed critical Marxist vision, this time humorous and even erotic. These works deeply influenced the newer generation of artists, including the draftsman Carlos Alonso and the Otra figuración painters Noé, Deira, Maccio, and de la Vega.

Antonio Berni understood early on that murals could be large easel paintings that could be moved from one end of the country to the other according to need, and that printmaking offered another means of mass visual communication, one more adaptable to the reality of a conservative society like Argentina's. For Berni, the construction and definition of a style was open, as long as it was true to a particular reality, even when this reality reflected melancholy and despair. What was important in putting forth a narrative through a style was clarity. This clarity he achieved in his best work through a sculptural (but never falsely monumental) figural vocabulary. For Berni, the political position of the artist would always be that of a heretical Marxist, unsentimental, critical, realist, and independent.

Berni defined his "social" vision of reality as "being modern, not through a simplistic imitation of the style of a Cézanne or Picasso, but in interpreting, the way they did, one's own era with its new phenomena and realities, the spirit and originality of the moment ... being empirical, never diminishing the real with an ideology, but adapting that ideology to the reality, and through it radically revising the real."[38]

II MEN, MANHOOD, AND THE MALE BODY

I WANT MUSCLE:
MALE DESIRE AND THE IMAGE OF THE WORKER IN AMERICAN ART OF THE 1930s

Jonathan Weinberg

In March of 1934 readers of the *New Masses* were greeted with an advertisement announcing, "Good News! The management of the Daily Worker is glad to announce that by special arrangement it is able to offer as a PREMIUM and PRIZE in the Daily Worker Circulation Drive the year's outstanding book … KARL MARX 'CAPITAL' IN PICTURES. Sixty pages of original text. Another sixty pages devoted to original, creative LITHOGRAPHS drawn by the internationally known proletarian artist HUGO GELLERT."

The reader was given a choice. Purchase a subscription and book for $7.00 or sign up five subscribers and get the book free.

According to the advertisement, "the text and original illustrations give you the necessary material for the understanding of the fundamentals of MARXISM."[1] Whether or not one approves of Hugo Gellert's highly abridged selections from Karl Marx's *Das Kapital,* they do manage to convey Marx's arguments about the relationship of labor and production in a capitalist economy. Stranger than Gellert's project of abridging the vast *Das Kapital* to sixty pages of text was his attempt to illustrate complex and abstract concepts like the "twofold character of the labor embodied in commodities" or "the repercussion of the English factory acts on other countries" in his brutally direct cartoon-like style. Particularly odd is his emphasis on the naked and near-naked bodies of male laborers.

The Hungarian immigrant Gellert was one of the founding editors of the *New Masses,* the leading communist-leaning magazine of the

A more extended version of this essay appears in my book *Male Desire: The Homoerotic in American Art* (New York: Harry N. Abrams, 2005). I would like to thank the Mary Ryan Gallery. I would also like to thank Sally Stein and my fellow scholars at the Getty Research Institute for their suggestions, as well as my co-editors, Alejandro Anreus and Diana Linden.

thirties.[2] His illustrations were ubiquitous in its pages as well as in the
Daily Worker. Several of these images were reused in *Capital.* For example, a picture of a Caucasian and an African American laborer, back to
back, was published in November 1932 in the *New Masses* above the caption, "Labor with a white skin cannot emancipate itself when labor with
a black skin is branded."[3] This picture reappears in *Capital* to illustrate
"The Working Day" (fig. 1). Both figures wear overalls without a shirt
underneath, thus exposing their enormous biceps. Their taut, muscular
bodies pressed against each other, along with the prominence of their
phallic tools—a pick and a wrench—give the image a strong homoerotic
flavor. But at least these men wear clothing. In several images in Gellert's
Capital, the workers' hard hats, shirts, dungarees, and work boots have
been stripped away. To illustrate the concept of "primary accumulation,"
in which Marx discusses the repeal of English laws against strikes and
trade unions, two naked men carry sledgehammers in one hand while
they make the sign of victory with the other. The concept of "cooperation," in which a "considerable number of workers effects a revolution
in the objective conditions under which the labor process is carried on,"
is illustrated by five men in bikini briefs pulling a rope in unison. And
Gellert's picture for "the greed for surplus labor" seems created to titil-
late the viewer rather than castigate capitalists. A completely naked man,
arms and legs splayed apart, muscular buttocks exposed, awaits the lash
of a foreman whose tight clothes reveal an equally well-developed frame
(fig. 2). Gellert's illustrations would not look out of place in the oeuvre of
the openly gay artist/pornographer Tom of Finland.

How do we explain Gellert's repeated and seemingly inappropri-
ate focus on the male body? I want to avoid making assumptions about
Gellert's sexual identity. It is not the possible homosexual longing
embedded in Gellert's imagery that fascinates me, but rather how it was
that such imagery was thought appropriate for the task of illustrating
Marx. And how was it that the publishers of the *Daily Worker* and the
New Masses thought such pictures would help them in reaching a larger
audience? Why was the erotic male body a locus of desire in art of the
1930s for male artists and their audiences? I use the word desire in the
broadest sense. A man may desire another man as a sexual partner, but
he also may project onto the male body fantasies of potency and power.
Once the work of art leaves the artist's studio, it takes on new meanings
that depend on its audiences. Women may find pictures of half-naked
workers protective or threatening, seductive or simply ridiculous. Men
may find in these figures compelling models for emulation, a comforting
sense that the traditional values associated with masculinity, strength,
and control were still being embodied in the unyielding musculature
of construction workers. If the viewer is a homosexual male, murals of

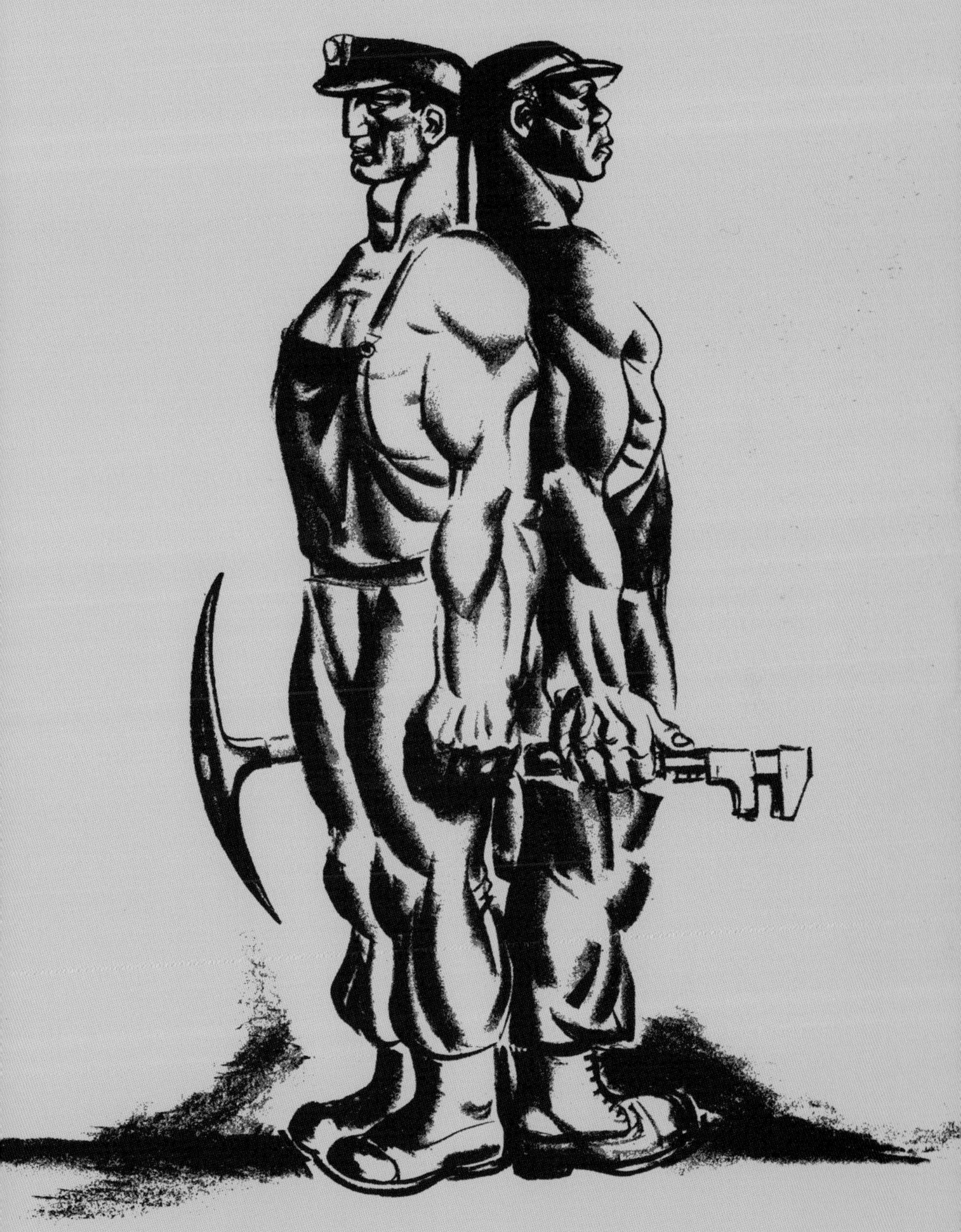

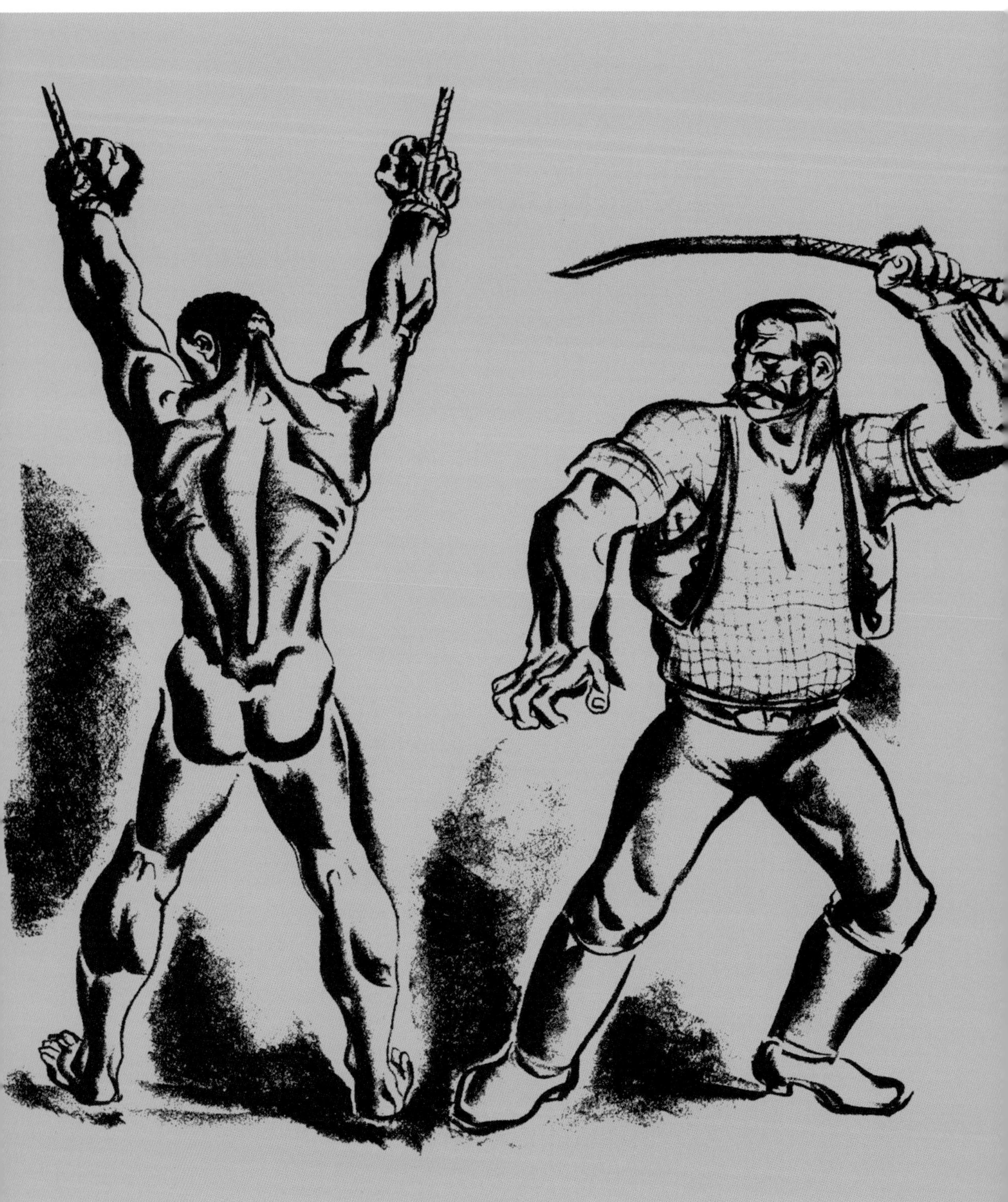

scantily clad laborers might provide the unexpected pleasure of gazing in public at the beautiful male physique without the repercussion of homophobic reprisals.

Gellert's laborers may be unusual in terms of their nudity, but the hypermasculine male, with bulging biceps and accentuated buttocks, is a staple of 1930s art. Of course, the thirties did not discover the pumped-up worker as a fit subject for American art. In the nineteenth century there were paintings like John Ferguson Weir's *Forging the Shaft* (1877) and Thomas Pollock Anshutz's *The Iron Workers' Noontime* (1880), but these images were exceptional in the careers of these artists and in American art in general. Workers continued to be depicted in the early part of the twentieth century by the painters of the so-called Ash Can School, yet their depiction was usually based on an assumed difference between the class of their subjects and their middle-class audiences. For the most part, the worker was not so much a hero as an object of compassion. The situation began to change in the 1920s. Both the sculpture of Max Kalish and the photography of Lewis Hine made the laborer a model of American action and integrity.[4] This idealization of labor accelerated in the thirties so that the muscular body of the industrial worker became a central icon of American culture. A shirtless African American laborer in the guise of a sculpture by Heinz Warneke (with the assistance of Richmond Barthé) guards an entrance at the Harlem-Macombs Housing Project (c. 1936); a dock hand, also shirtless, and massively built, holds a pole as if it were a spear in Barthé's own bronze, *Stevedore*; bare-chested steel riggers, their pants so tight they appear almost naked, raise a bridge over the Oakland Bay in Arthur Murray's *Steel Riggers-No. 4–Bay Bridge* (1936). Street workers, their sleeves rolled up and their backs bent over, battle with their jackhammers in Reginald Marsh's *End of the 14th Street Cross Town Line* (1936), and construction workers, their bodies taut and hard, scale the side of a riverbank in William Gropper's *Construction of a Dam* (1937).

Given their ubiquity, it would be unreasonable to talk about such images of muscular laborers in terms of latent homosexuality. It makes more sense to introduce the postmodernist concept of the "homosocial." The intense male bonding that is conveyed in so many 1930s images of manly men conveys what Eve Kosofsky Sedgwick identifies as the hegemonic interchanges and negotiations between males that exclude women.[5] For the most part, images of labor tended to be rigidly gendered, so that women were usually excluded from pictures of industrial work. For example, in Gellert's *Capital,* there are no pictures of women working in factories. Instead, females play the role of mothers or wives. In one of the illustrations, a male wraps his arms protectively around his female partner while she suggestively holds her breasts, as if to say that women's role is one of sexual and domestic bounty. According to

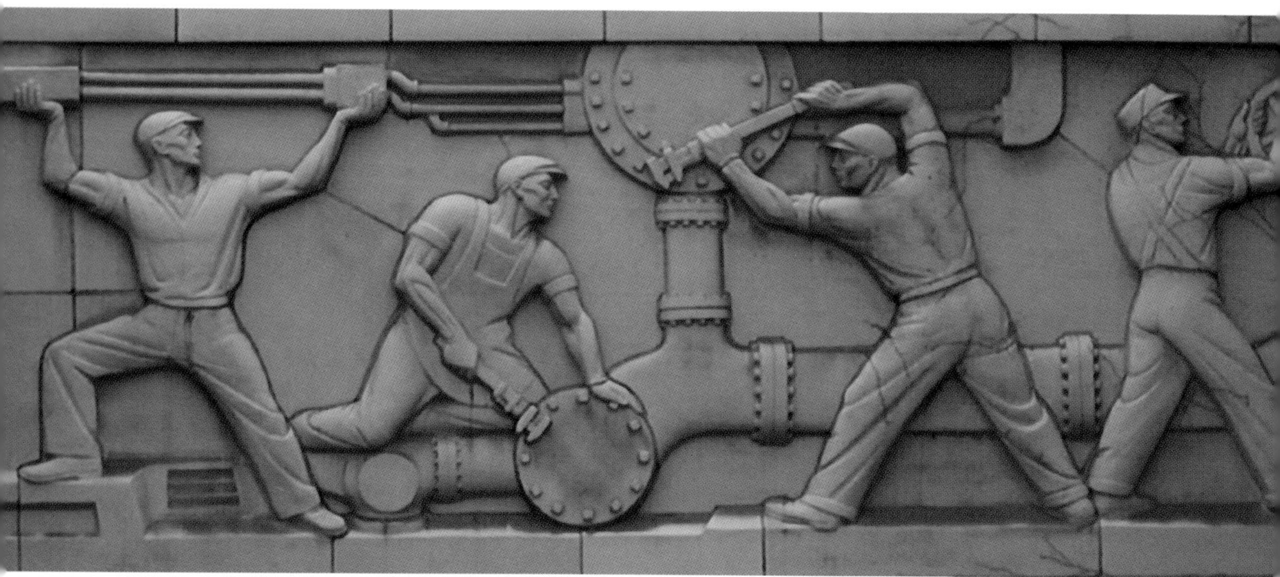

Sedgwick, the homosocial, by bringing together men in close companionship and collaboration, usually incorporates elements of intense homophobia and misogyny. The intense bonding of men in the locker room or workplace is always in danger of crossing the line into a sexual relationship, or at least of being mistaken for sexual desire. It therefore becomes necessary to distance such bonding from homosexuality. In its most extreme forms, this distancing takes the form of violent action against gay men. Or it may merely be a matter of asserting the heterosexuality of the participants by making allusions to the desirability of absent women. The very inclusion of this nude couple in the midst of the mostly male *Capital* may be such an indication of Gellert's anxiety about the homoerotic content of his book. Yet a more pervasive check against the possibility of a homosexual reading of images of labor in the 1930s was the very muscles of the workers. We need to keep in mind that, given contemporary stereotypes that equated homosexuality with effeminacy, it was unlikely that the brawny male worker would be identified as gay. On another level, the male worker's hardened body appears inviolable, there to be looked at but not possessed. The muscles of Gellert's heroes are simultaneously seductive and aggressive. If one of Gellert's proletarians might give a fellow worker a good-natured slap on the behind, he might also punch an unwanted admirer in the face.

This emphasis in the art of the 1930s on brawny men has been attributed to a "crisis of masculinity" that began in the nineteenth century, as work and family structures underwent major changes. Above all, women increasingly made inroads into what had previously been male occupations. Martin Berger has wisely questioned whether the word

3   Cesare Stea, *Assembling*, relief, Bowery Bay Pumping Station (1939), Queens, New York.

"crisis" is the best characterization of such transformations, since gender is always inherently unstable.[6] Nevertheless, men's insecurity about their manhood was intensified by the widespread unemployment of the Depression as well as by anxiety about women entering the workforce. Significantly, the industrial laborer became a major hero of thirties art at exactly the moment that America's heavy industries were laying off workers in unparalleled numbers.[7] The image of men with enormous biceps drilling or welding pipes was a response to the fear of losing such jobs. Ben Shahn's *Riveter* (1938) does not take up his tools for a few days; he rivets forever. Form gave permanence to an unstable job market. Government sponsorship actively encouraged artists to create such pictures of labor. As New Deal policies attempted to put men back to work, it encouraged imagery that suggested that the American male was already hard at work in traditionally masculine occupations. At the same time, as Melissa Dabakis reminds us, the increasing organization of workers into industrial unions in the 1930s legitimized images of labor that emphasized both the individual and the collective.[8]

Cesare Stea's 1939 relief *Assembling* (fig. 3) for a sewage-disposal plant in Queens is typical. It shows four men working together on a length of sewage pipe. Their shirtsleeves are rolled up and their pants are tight, so that their muscular frames are accentuated. Their bodies are massive, and angular like the section of pipe they are working on. Such an image clearly is meant to celebrate the New Deal's emphasis on putting Americans back to work, and its egalitarian rhetoric. Whereas in the past such lowly activity as sewage treatment would be disguised by classical motifs of a suitable nature—the labors of Hercules comes to mind—here the work of the sewage plant is depicted directly. In this sense we can argue that Stea's relief is *real*—in that it responds to the actual function of the plant. But its *social* message is ideal, or *unreal*. It cleans up the messiness of such work (what could be more filthy than sewage work?), removing any signs of spillage or the possibility that the strain of labor relations will upset the flow of the waste that is hidden from view. The difficulty of such labor does not register on the men's faces. Their huge muscles do not stand for the brutality of their job but for their fitness for the task at hand. The workers' different positions along the pipe—the first featured front on with hands raised high, the second kneeling, wielding a wrench, the third and fourth standing with their backs facing us, heads turned in profile—sets up a rhythm. Their job is to make sure there are no stoppages along the sewage pipe route. But even as they keep the plant going, the plant regulates their movements. They are ordered by the structure of the pipes and the frame of the frieze. The potential for working-class solidarity and labor unrest built into the celebration of the laborer is suppressed by the relief's

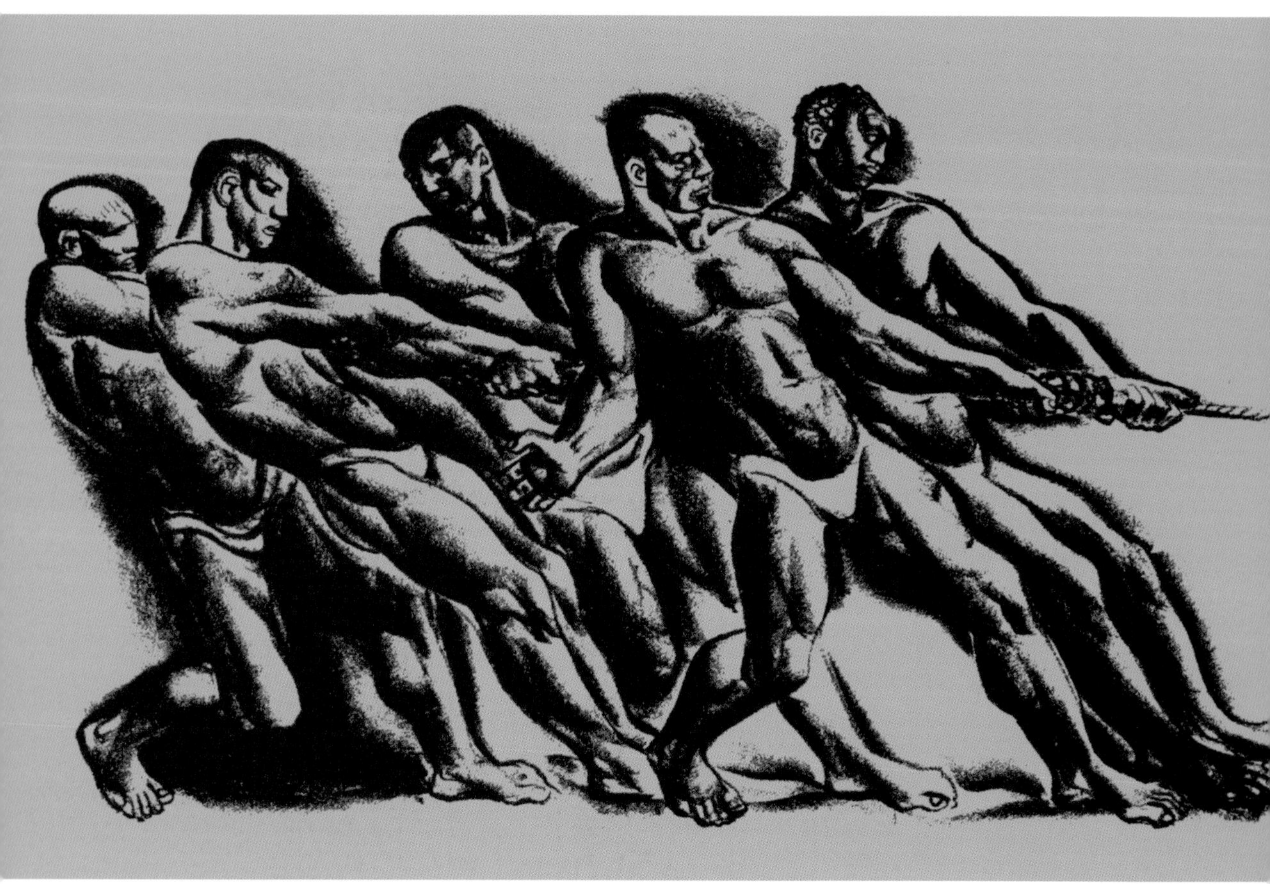

sense of clock-like routine and the almost automaton-like quality of the workers' movements. Probably only unconsciously, Stea's frieze presents another threat to masculinity, that posed by the machine. Charlie Chaplin made this threat central to his extraordinary film of 1936, *Modern Times,* in which the hero is a victim caught in the wheels of a monstrous machine.

Gellert's vision of the manly worker is not nearly as contained as Stea's. Take Gellert's illustration for "cooperation," in which a group of men join together in a tug of war (fig. 4). By stripping their clothes away Gellert emphasizes their enormous muscles and their impossibly narrow waists, but it also suggests liberation. Since they are participating in what is ostensibly an athletic contest, workday clothes are unnecessary. But in stripping down to their underwear they seem liberated from all constraints of work. Unlike Stea, Gellert does not frame his figures. He prefers to leave the background blank or sketchy, allowing the action to almost float on the page. Where the line of pipe and its valves in Stea's image regulate the movements of the laborers, so that they seem like machines, Gellert's figures grab the rope in a variety of fluid gestures.

4 Hugo Gellert, *Cooperation,* 10 x 7 in., published in Hugo Gellert, *Karl Marx' "Capital" in Lithographs* (New York: Ray Long & Richard R. Smith, 1934), 39. Courtesy of Mary Ryan Gallery, New York.

Their task does not master them; they, through cooperation as a group, master the task.

Gellert had little interest in anatomical accuracy. His bodies are excessive. The arms of the laborers are so pumped up that they verge on the grotesque, and their hands are equally enormous, with fat wrists, so that they look like the branches of massive trees. These anatomical distortions differentiate Gellert's figures from the fascist images of the male body being made in Germany and Italy at the time. And, while they are closer in spirit to the sculpture being produced in the USSR at the same time (in particular the sculpture of Vera Mukhina),[9] Gellert's instinct is far more consciously anticlassical than such Socialist Realist art.

The enormous muscles of Gellert's male nudes are meant to suggest the latent power of the proletariat, even when he is made to do the work of the industrialist. Factories are represented in *Capital* in two ways. Gellert uses several images of clocks to represent the idea of assigning value to labor. Such images seem critical of the assembly-line system in which workers are forced to structure their activities. Yet in other images he celebrates the potential of the factory to provide the kind of wealth necessary for the revolution. The muscular body of the worker was a way for Gellert to reconcile this seeming paradox. Even when doing the hardest work, Gellert's laborer is never crushed. For Gellert, capitalism would bring itself down by inscribing resistance onto the body of the proletariat. Labor itself becomes the means of liberation, and so even when the foreman lashes the body of the worker he remains unscathed, his beautifully muscular body taut and ready for action. And although Henry Ford towers above his factory plant in one memorable picture, he meets his match in the figure of a workman who stands before him, exuding physical confidence. Gellert's workers may do their job for the present, but only because they will soon own the plant. Indeed, in one of the final images of *Capital* the Soviet flag has replaced the image of Ford above the smokestacks of the factory.

Barbara Melosh writes that the U.S. government was careful to make sure that public commissions focused on "typical" workers code for workers of northern European ethnicity.[10] Stea's figures are so abstract and without individual character that it is hard to assign a racial type to them at all. In contrast, Gellert goes out of his way to include figures with stereotypically African American features and dark skin in his work, including his illustrations for *Capital*. An African American leads the rope line in his illustration of "cooperation." Gellert's intention in putting a Caucasian and an African American worker back to back in the November issue of the *New Masses* was to suggest both the tension between these groups—they are turned away from each other—and the need to bridge the distance between them. But their very proximity adds an erotic charge to the picture, suggesting less an ideal of racial harmony than a dangerous dynamic of attraction and aversion. The possibility of a sexual union between men of different races is at once suggested and negated in the way they are pressed up against each other. They could not be any closer, and yet they remain completely apart.[11]

The advertisement for Gellert's edition of *Capital* called him a proletarian artist, as if there were no separation between his images of labor and his life as an artist. Can we equate what Gellert does with brush and pen with the work of the laborer? Is the artist a worker? In contrast to building a skyscraper or mining for coal, making art may not seem like manly work. Indeed, it may not seem like work at all. Yet a common theme of artists and art professionals across the political spectrum of the 1930s was the idea that making art was a job like any other. The anti-modernist critic and champion of Thomas Hart Benton, Thomas Craven, writes in his book *Modern Art,* "The painter must cease to esteem himself as only a delicately attuned receptive instrument; he must become a workman again ... let him get down to work; and in possession of all the resources and instruments of his craft, break his back to do something that shall stand in its own right, independent of verbal exegesis."[12]

There was a pragmatic dimension of the association of art with work. The various New Deal programs that supported artists—such as the Federal Art Project of the WPA—were predicated on the idea that artists, like any other unemployed workers, required assistance. Jonathan Harris writes, "The Project was constantly forced to fight against claims, made by a variety of opponents, that art was not real work and that artists were not (and could not be) authentic workers."[13]

But how was an artist to represent in his work the hard labor of his own craft? Realism itself could allow such a representation. Undoubtedly for Craven, the conservative art critic, the careful vivid depiction of the world-out-there imbues a picture with a sense of labor. Yet this was not the only way to suggest that the artist was a worker. Making pictures of laborers and taking up their plight made Gellert a "proletarian artist." For Gellert, the radical artist was supposed to identify with the worker because labor was the essence of life. As he put it, "To be isolated from the worker is to be isolated from the only vital, progressive force in society today."[14] Yet Gellert's style itself is hardly *labored.* He applies the litho crayon in bold strokes. Instead of carefully modulated shadows, he uses the side of the crayon to suggest depth and light. However long it took him to make the actual prints, they appear to have been done spontaneously. As a result, they have an immediacy and brusqueness usually associated with the working class.

Rockwell Kent

The crudeness of Gellert's style stands in stark opposition to the artistic approach of his fellow leftist artist, the painter and illustrator Rockwell Kent. Like Gellert's, Kent's politics can be read into his images of the beautiful male body, but it is a very different body from Gellert's. Kent's most overtly communist image, *Workers of the World, Unite!* (fig. 5), appeared on the cover of a 1937 issue of the *New Masses*.[15] In this wood engraving a young man (he could be in his teens) in tank top and tight jeans raises a shovel above his head to protect himself from two disembodied bayonets that plunge at him from the right. In the background are smokestacks, but the boy's bare feet and the surrounding landscape give the print a rural flavor that is unusual in such an overtly proletarian picture. The youth's body is delineated in one long sensuous line from his left hand, which grasps the shovel, up around his bare arm, shoulder, and head, and down the length of his other side to his feet. A few parallel hatch marks accentuate his muscles, giving his body a shiny sleekness. Where Gellert's men are muscle bound, Kent's boy is limber, as if his power were less a matter of brute strength than an ability to outmaneuver the enemy.

The title of Kent's image suggests solidarity, yet his picture shows a single beautiful boy facing off against unseen adversaries. The picture emphasizes the individual's response to oppression rather than collective action.[16] As Frances Pohl writes, Kent joined the Socialist Party in 1904 and was dedicated to the labor movement throughout his life. He joined the International Workers of the World (IWW) and the Artists Union, among many other workers organizations, and he was active in Vermont politics.[17] But even as he actively participated in political organizations that emphasized working-class collectivity, his art and writing tended to celebrate rugged individualism and the relationship of man to nature. Kent seemed most himself when he was fighting the elements alone in a bleak northern landscape or sailing on the sea. It is no surprise, then, that this picture calling for proletarian unity focuses on a lone figure.

The worker's youth and body type relate to a series of pictures that Kent made for a very different purpose: the national advertising campaign for the American Car and Foundry Company in 1930–31. These woodcuts feature a naked young man in rapturous communion with the sea. He is so intensely connected to the water, sky, and light that he seems unaware of his nakedness and vulnerability to the viewer's gaze. In the picture *Hail and Farewell*, Kent's youth stands naked on a rope ladder that hangs from the mast of a ship. The legs and rungs of the ladder frame his buttocks. He raises his arms to the sky as if the light of the heavens were penetrating his prone body. In *Fair Wind*, we are again

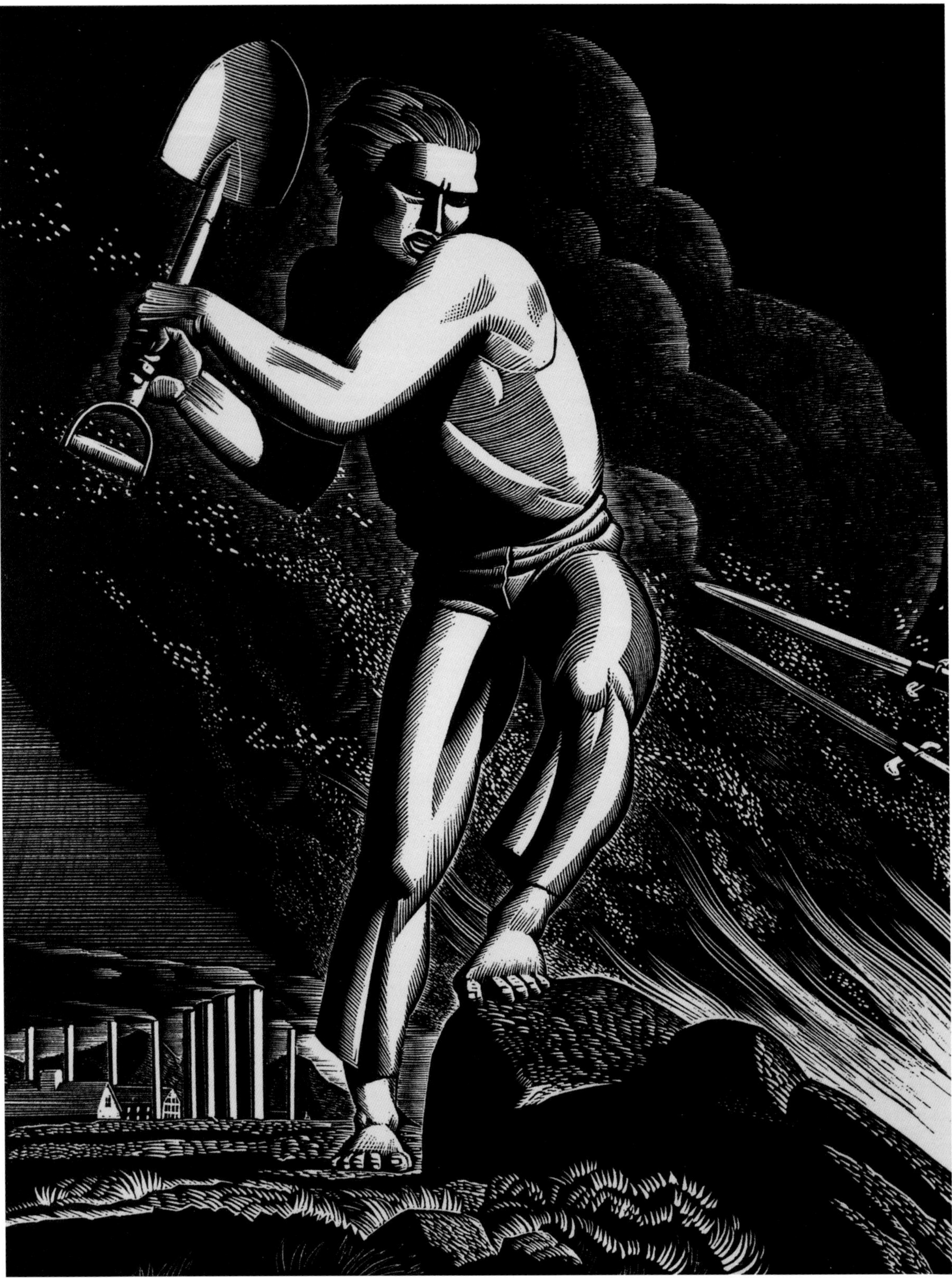

invited to contemplate the rear end of the male youth, who now sits on the bowsprit of a sailboat. The boy's bottom hangs over the phallic bow as if he were offering his body to the prow's masculine form. In *Sea and Sky* Kent's boy wraps his body around the mast as if he were making love to it. The cruciform mast juxtaposed against a sunburst evokes Christian rapture even as its phallic shape can be read as a surrogate for the young man's erection.

When *Workers of the World, Unite!* is placed next to Kent's woodcuts of the naked youth and the sea, we get a greater sense of his peculiar radicalism. Like his heroes, William Blake and Walt Whitman, Kent wants to free the body from the confines of middle-class respectability. Kent's adventures in Greenland and Alaska, retracing the route of Jack London, were all part of his emphasis on rugged individualism and hypermasculinity. Nudity suggests freedom from bourgeois constraints and reconnection with nature. His figures appear absolutely relaxed in their nakedness, and so they do not resist the gaze of the viewer. His boys are often lost in reverie, allowing us to view their naked bodies without fear of reprisal. Even when the worker takes up the shovel to fight off the phallic bayonets, his legs and genital region are surprisingly unprotected, as if his body were meant to be penetrated, if not by the weapons then by our eyes.

Kent's prints seem far more self-consciously homoerotic than Gellert's illustrations. Given his circle of acquaintances in the New York art world, it is difficult to believe that he was unaware of their potential appeal to a homosexual audience. Lincoln Kirstein, who was to be so instrumental in supporting the careers of such gay artists as Paul Cadmus and Jared French, commissioned Kent to design the Harvard Contemporary Art Society's insignias, which Kirstein described as "two nude [male] youths, one riding a curveting Pegasus, or Bellerophon, the other restraining it."[18] In the case of Kent, however, the homoerotic figures not necessarily as the choice of the artist but as a way to suggest freedom from traditional social norms. The homoeroticism of Kent's image gives his otherwise elegant black-and-white engravings a hint of the scandalous. He may have hoped that by suggesting illicit desires his pictures might have revolutionary potential, even when they were being used by the American Foundry Company to sell auto parts. But why would an auto parts company want them? My guess is that Kent's patron saw their stylized eroticism as a means of differentiating his product from others. If I am right, then Calvin Klein was not the first to use a whiff of the "perverse" to sell products. The decorativeness and stylishness of Kent's pictures, his serpentine line and emphasis on pattern, made it easy to accept sexual ambiguity as part of the sales pitch. After all, the automobile itself manages to be both a feminine object (it is often referred to as a "she") that the male consumer *rides* and a sleek phallic instrument that extends his power.

So far I have deliberately avoided the subject of the artist's actual sexual identity in discussing the role of hypermasculine men in American art. As it turned out, the period's emphasis on masculinity may have provided a kind of cover for exploring aspects of gay identity. The most famous case is Paul Cadmus's *The Fleet's In!* (1934). As I have written elsewhere, the navy removed the picture from an exhibition at the Corcoran Gallery of Art in Washington, D.C., in 1934 because of its depiction of a homosexual pickup.[19] Slightly downstage from the interchanges between women and men, an elegantly dressed gentleman with red tie and painted lips (symbols of a "pansy") offers a cigarette to a smiling seaman.

As is often the case with censorship, the suppression of the picture only made it more famous. "For every individual who might have seen the original," *Esquire* claimed, "at least one thousand saw it in black and white reproduction" when it appeared on the front pages of major newspapers across the county.[20] What is fascinating about the various editorials attacking the navy for its censorship is how the homosexual pickup is never mentioned. Indeed, the navy itself described the picture's immorality only in the most general terms, probably because it did not want to draw attention to the issue of male hustling by naval personnel during shore leave. Admiral Rodman claimed that the picture "represents a most disgraceful, sordid, disreputable, drunken brawl, wherein apparently a number of enlisted men are consorting with a party of streetwalkers and denizens of the red-light district."[21] But for the *Daily News* the very impropriety of the sailors was a sign of their virility. In an editorial entitled "Should Sailors Be Sissies?" the newspaper declared, "If most of our sailors have come to the point where they hurry alone to the Public Library or the museums on shore leave, instead of finding themselves some girl friends and doing a little drinking, dancing and the rest of the things the he-men do when they want to relax, then it's too bad for us and our Navy."[22] The key concept here is that being "he-men" protects sailors from the potential degeneracy of their civilian counterparts. The sissy's attraction to a man in uniform, if noticed at all, would be just another sign of the comparative virility of sailors. Cadmus had found a way to depict a homosexual encounter and yet, because of the way the sailors' muscles were read as a sign of masculine vitality, that encounter did not tarnish the sailor's image in the mainstream press. The navy officials, who were far more familiar with the reality of sexual cruising and hustling in the military, read Cadmus's picture in a different light.[23]

Cadmus continued to risk scandal. His mural for the Richmond Parcel Post Building, *Pocahontas Rescues Captain John Smith* (fig. 6), was considered indecent because of his treatment of the fox's skin that

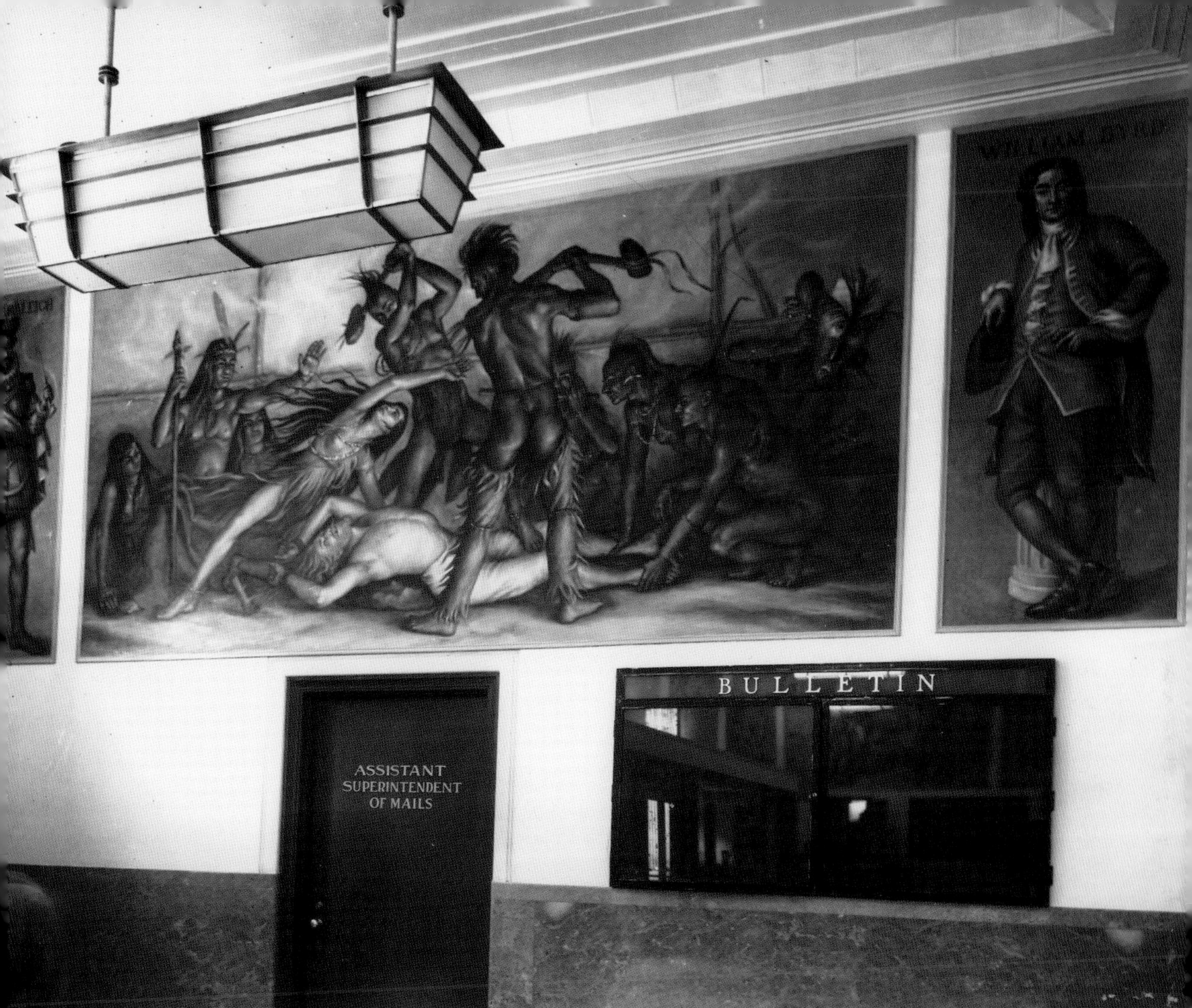

6 Paul Cadmus, *Pocahontas Rescues Captain John Smith* (1938), oil and tempera, 7 x 20 ft. Richmond Parcel Post Building (later transferred to the library of the Court House Annex, Richmond, Virginia.). Fine Arts Collection, Public Buildings Service, General Services Administration.

covers the genitals of the central Native American, who raises an axe to kill John Smith. The long nose of the fox originally appeared precisely where his penis would be. Cadmus was forced to alter the mural so that the face of the fox was omitted and replaced with a limp tail. Yet Cadmus's lewd joke may have only been a ploy to shift attention from the unusually intimate relationship of two warriors on the right, one of which is supposed to be modeled after Lincoln Kirstein. Although the two are in the midst of holding down the struggling Smith, one fellow is relaxed enough to drape his arm around the other. John Smith himself was modeled after Cadmus's lover, Jared French (Cadmus's sister, Fidelma, who was to marry Kirstein, was the model for Pocahontas).[24] The picture's conflict, in which the central character is "saved" from the clutches of half-naked men, could be read as Cadmus's wry response to French's recent marriage to the painter Margaret Hoening in 1937. This image of imminent violence—stopped only by Pocahontas's entreaty— provided an opportunity for Cadmus to explore the physical and emotional connections in his circle of intimates.

Perhaps the penis-like fox head was deemed obscene because it consciously or unconsciously raised the prospect of Smith's rape. After all, just what exactly is Pocahontas saving John Smith from in Cadmus's version of the story? The horizontal composition, showing Smith stretched like a rope between Pocahontas on one side and the two embracing Native Americans on the other, suggests a tug of war between heterosexuality and homosexuality. Is it possible that, before they bludgeon him to death, the Native Americans will ravish him? In a curious reversal, Cadmus had to cut off the head of the fox—a kind of ritual castration—to quiet the fear that Smith's body was going to be penetrated (that is, unmanned) by his male attackers.

Once the fox head joke was removed, the authorities were satisfied. Undoubtedly the veiled homosexuality of the image was cloaked by the hypermasculinity of the male figures. Another factor is the depiction of "exotic" Native Americans, who were allowed to act strangely and appear almost naked because of their very otherness. Scantily clad Indians were ubiquitous in the decorations of government buildings as symbols of America. Many of the earliest nude and seminude male images in American art were of Native Americans. When Cadmus designed his mural he certainly was aware of John Vanderlyn's *Death of Jane McCrea* (1804), which depicts a white woman about to be scalped by two seminude Indians.

Cadmus's lover and artistic collaborator, French, also had to deal with censorship. His original submission for the Richmond Parcel Post Building included several scantily clad male figures. He carefully chose his historical subject, *Stuart's Raiders at the Swollen Ford* (fig. 7), because it plausibly allowed for nudity. In the end, by modulating the degree of nakedness, French was still able to depict a group of handsome men doing nothing much but standing around in various states of undress. The conceit of the picture is that such naked swimming was necessary to a Confederate maneuver by Stuart around McClellan's army, but in fact Stuart managed to find a bridge to cross. And so French really commemorates an inconsequential moment whose glory is not some act of violence but the unexpected unveiling of male bodies. Their stripping is more a function of the artist's need to picture the muscular form of beautiful youths in close proximity to each other than of the needs of historical memory. It was also a way, perhaps, to get around what may have been French's distaste for commemorating a Confederate victory. After all, the men are not fighting; they are only taking their clothes off. All of this was all right with the federal government and Richmond as long as French's men didn't take too much clothing off. As Karal Ann Marling suggests, the unbreakable taboo was full frontal nudity.[25] The sexual desire of men for each other seems not to have been

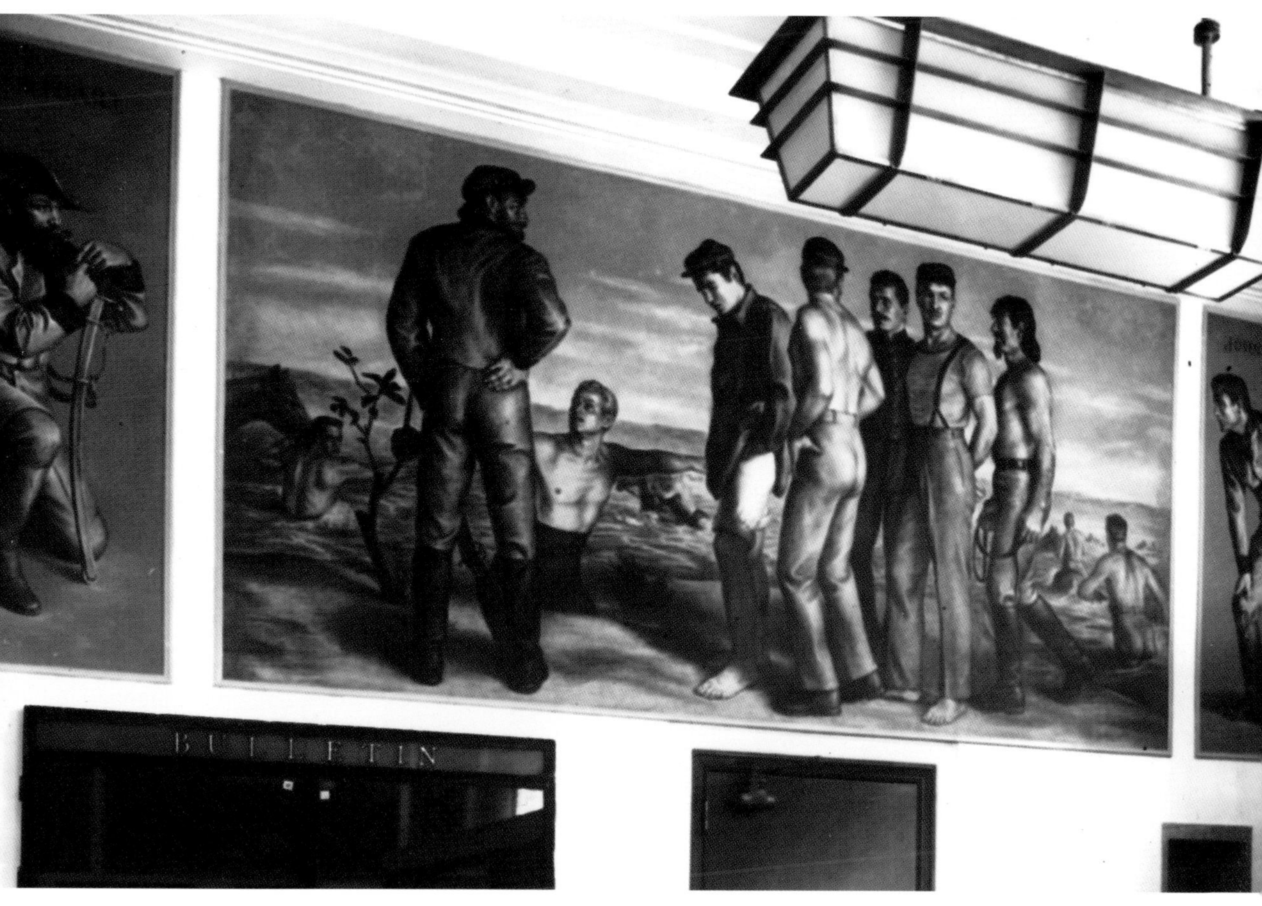

7 Jared French, *Stuart's Raiders at the Swollen Ford* (1938), 7 x 20 ft. Richmond Parcel Post Building (later transferred to the library of the Court House Annex, Richmond, Virginia). Fine Arts Collection, Public Buildings Service, General Services Administration.

an object of the policing of the government or of the Richmond audience. It was nakedness itself that was feared. But why? Arguably, what makes the nudity of both the male and female figures dangerous are the unbounded desires it raises in the viewer—desires that may not conform to the culture's expectations about gender. Yet policing such nakedness doesn't purge the images of desire. On the contrary, it heightens the eroticism of the parts of the body that are not exposed.

It may have been innocent, but French's inclusion of the word "swollen" in the title of the painting has an insider ring to it, as if he were alluding to the male genitals *swollen* in erection, the very genitals that cannot be shown in the mural. French and Cadmus shared a studio as they worked on their respective murals, and the paintings they made were in dialogue with each other. In this sense we can imagine that the men are stripping not to join a fight but to take part in the amorous configurations hinted at in *Pocahontas Rescues Captain John Smith*. That this possibility was missed by the murals' sponsors, I would argue, has to do with their blind spot regarding homosexual desire in such masculine men.

French had to have counted on a similar lack of imagination when he created in 1937–39 a series of murals for a reformatory, the New York Vocational Institution, on the theme of the origins of food. The panel entitled *The Farm* (fig. 8) is outrageous in its sexual connotations. It depicts three burly farmhands. The central figure is shirtless. His chest and biceps are those of a weight lifter. In one hand he holds a husk of corn in a suggestive manner (corn-holing is a euphemism for sodomy). The friend on his right puts his arm around his shoulder, as if signaling his acquiescence, while the other companion gets down on his knees. He too is shirtless, and is holding a bunch of carrots as if they were a surrogate for the male genitals and he were about to perform fellatio (perhaps a lewd pun on the murals' intended location in the unfortunately named town of West Coxsackie, New York). Another kneeling supplicant appears in French's picture *Far West.* He worships another shirtless muscleman, who swirls a lasso over his head, although there are no cattle or horses in sight, just a seductive cowboy leaning against a fence with his buttocks protruding prominently. Appropriately, the background is studded with phallic cacti.

I submit that with this series of murals French was not only gesturing to a gay subculture, he was satirizing the hypermasculinity of so much of 1930s mural art. The fact that French used his friends, many of whom were writers and dancers, as models added another level to the joke, for these men were completely unlike the stereotype of the worker then circulating in mainstream culture. Yet this very masculinity provided the opportunity to make homoerotic desire visible to one audience, made up of homosexuals and other people in the know, while remaining invisible to a larger audience.

The subversive quality of French's murals is more pronounced when we remember that they were meant for the edification of incarcerated young men. Murals in prisons and reformatories were meant to remind the inmates of proper conduct; they were images for emulation. French's *Origins of Food* conforms to the type by demonstrating the way young men from different walks of life and different localities contribute to our agricultural bounty. But such a high-minded narrative is undercut by the mural's references to homosexual contact. It is as though French were purposely raising the question of homosexuality, not on the farm but in the New York Vocational Institution itself. It is well known that sexual contact between men is a common occurrence in the American penal system, where men are forced to live together in crowded quarters without the companionship of women. Ironically, the dominant culture incarcerates those who break its laws in institutions that actually foster forbidden activities. In the context of prison life, homosexual acts are often brutally forced on other inmates as a means of establish-

8 Jared French, *The Farm (Vegetables)* (c. 1938), oil and tempera. Mural for New York State Vocational Institute, location unknown. Photo courtesy of DC Moore Gallery, New York.

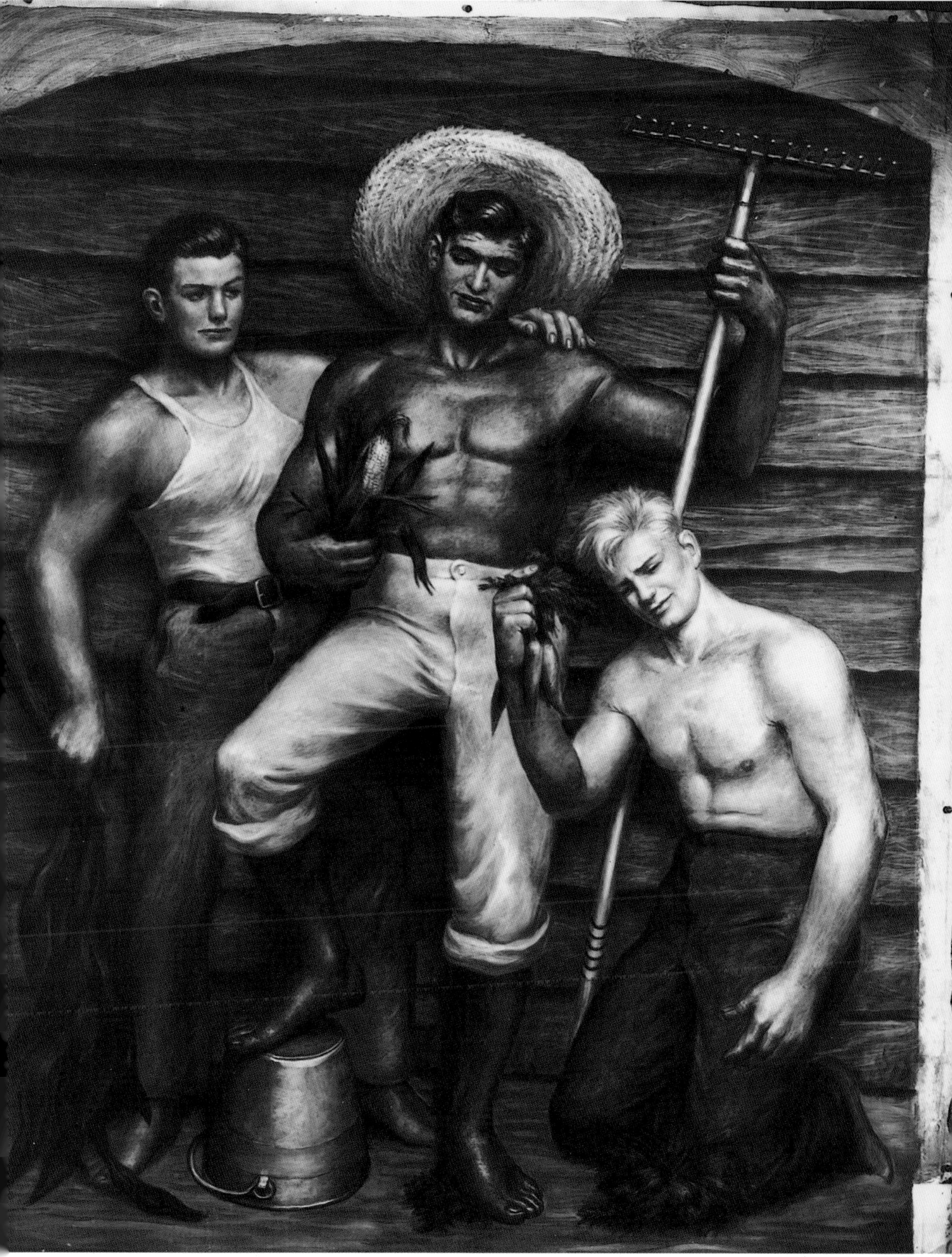

ing dominance. Neither jailer nor jailed is exempt from the brutality and criminality of the penal system.

French's lewd but apt joke on the West Coxsackie reformatory forces us to rethink the automatic equation of regional painting with conservative and nationalist interests. As far as I know, French was no radical. Yet this series of paintings is as questioning of mainstream values as any portrait of Lenin or passage from the *Communist Manifesto*. In any case, its *origins* lie not in the jingoistic rhetoric of a Benton or Craven but in the sometimes leftist, sometimes conservative queer circle in New York City that included Cadmus and Kirstein. Cadmus himself aptly called his own politics and that of his friends "pinkish," a term that nicely suggests both left-leaning inclinations and homosexuality.[26]

On the other hand, there is a reactionary side not only to French's depiction of manly men but to all the works of art I have discussed, including Gellert's. Several authors have commented on the lack of adequate images of women at work in 1930s art. But there is also the fact that in bringing the worker into close view, most male artists of the period distanced him, even exoticized him, through the very exaggerated nature of his musculature. Even more problematic is the absence of images that emphasized the drudgery and danger of work.[27] An exception is Fletcher Martin's controversial study for a mural, *Mine Rescue*, in which two muscular men carry a beautiful young man on a stretcher out of a tunnel cut into the side of a mountain. It is no surprise that this picture was rejected by its intended audience in Kellogg, Idaho, and was denounced "because it cast aspersions on the saga of industry."[28] In his allusion to depictions of Christ's entombment, Martin showed that even the most muscle-bound male body is fragile, incapable of holding up against the overwhelming brutality of such work. Whether a miner succumbs to a catastrophic accident or falls victim to mining dust, his body will give way long before his time. Martin, unlike Gellert, was no communist, but his picture of the male body, beautiful but failing, is perhaps a more apt illustration of the relentlessness of the American industrial system than any of Gellert's musclemen. Martin's picture suggests that what is needed is not more muscle, but a just world in which people's lives and livelihoods are put before the needs of ruthless capital.

MAKING HISTORY:
MALVIN GRAY JOHNSON'S AND EARLE W. RICHARDSON'S STUDIES FOR *NEGRO ACHIEVEMENT*

Jacqueline Francis

In 1934 the African American painters Malvin Gray Johnson (1896–1934) and Earle (Earl) W. Richardson (1912–35) planned a Public Works of Art Project (PWAP) mural entitled *Negro Achievement* for a Harlem library.[1] The project was never realized, but the artists' ambitions are documented in eight preparatory studies. These small, colorful panels are figural representations of black exceptionalism and leadership mapped across the symbolic terrain of the African Diaspora.[2] Buttressed by the literature on the Harlem Renaissance and the Works Progress Administration (WPA), the story of *Negro Achievement* may seem easy enough to relate. With little effort we might assign it to the catalog of images often assembled to illustrate seamless histories of black nationalism from the 1920s onward and of American government patronage of the arts in the 1930s.[3] For certain, Johnson and Richardson were culturally conscious painters keenly interested in African, American, and African Diaspora history; and as PWAP artists they participated in the first wave of New Deal cultural production. Yet, as a project that was arrested and incomplete, *Negro Achievement* should also generate questions about the challenges of mural making, the limits of patronage, and the narration of history.

Negro Achievement is a revealing example of how American artists of the 1930s sought to infuse their murals with direct modernist language. Beyond this, these panels demonstrate Johnson and Richardson's didactic goals for public art. They depict ancient Egypt, abolitionism and

The University of Michigan, Emory University, and the Center for Advanced Study in the Visual Arts, Washington, D.C., provided support for the research and writing of this essay.

armed rebellion against American slavery and European imperialism, and interracial alliances, specifically alliances between blacks and whites involved in "New World" exploration and in the planning and defense of the American nation. Hence "achievement," in this era of social realism, took the forms of critique and celebration, both meant to raise awareness. Richardson and Johnson introduced new black subjects to the American visual canon in order to diversify, trouble, and invigorate it.

Both artists had tragically brief careers. Johnson's most active years were 1927–34, when he participated regularly in the Harmon Foundation's all-black art exhibitions as well as in interracial ones.[4] Like Johnson, Richardson was a prize-winning Harmon Foundation exhibitor; his *Profile of a Negro Girl* (c. 1932) was named best portrait in the foundation's 1933 show. After Johnson's sudden illness and death in November 1934, Richardson continued to work on their mural project.[5] But within a year he too was dead; ill with fever and heart-broken over the death of Johnson, who had been his lover, Richardson leapt from his fourth-floor Harlem apartment window and died of his injuries in December 1935.[6] Their obituaries and periodic mention in publications on black artists indicate that they were respected artists and not readily forgotten by their peers. Artist and art historian James A. Porter (1905–70) wrote a heartrending tribute to Johnson in 1935[7] and artist Stuart Davis (1894–1964) queried the WPA about Richardson's work in 1936.[8]

Richardson and Johnson were "known quantities" during their lifetimes, and yet their profiles were low and their activities modest compared to other artists. More prominent in New York City's black and progressive art circles of the early 1930s were the painters Aaron Douglas (1899–1979), Gwendolyn Bennett (1902–81), and Charles Alston (1907–77). Douglas and Alston were muralists whose projects were sponsored by New Deal art programs; all three were leaders of the Harlem Artists Guild,[9] formed in 1935, and members of the predominantly white Artists Union, formed the year before.[10] Bennett and Douglas were especially vocal activists who picketed to protest the WPA cutbacks, wrote about the guild's goals, and attacked racism, economic exploitation, and fascism in addresses to their progressive colleagues.[11]

While Johnson died just as these progressive movements were getting off the ground, Richardson lived long enough to participate briefly in both the Artists Union and the Harlem Artists Guild. His introduction to politics may have come through his longtime friend Alston, who admired the controversial Mexican muralist Diego Rivera (1886–1957) and strategically joined leftist struggles.[12] Aside from *Negro Achievement*, Richardson made heroic representations of laborers that effectively announce his study of social realism and commitment to proletarian struggle. No published documents link Richardson to the Communist

Party (CP), yet there is mention of him in a CP member's archives; an anonymous writer posthumously praised the artist's energy and his demonstrated promise as an organizer, and mournfully concluded that the party had lost a potential stalwart.[13] Richardson's convictions, or his inclination to display them in realist visual terms, are muted in collaboration with Johnson, whose politics are concealed from us.

Picturing Achievement

Johnson and Richardson created eight panels on the subject of Negro achievement: *Benjamin Banneker* (fig. 1); *Toussaint L'Ouverture* (fig. 2); *Columbus Soldiers—Estavanico* (fig. 3); *Harriet Tubman and Frederick Douglass* (fig. 4); *Nat Turner* (fig. 5); *Negro Pharaoh—Eighteenth Dynasty* (fig. 6); *Negro Soldiers* (fig. 7); and *Art, Music, Literature* (fig. 8). Painted in oil on hardboard and cardboard surfaces, the studies are close to each other in size. Their widths are either twelve or seventeen and a half inches; their lengths range from sixteen to twenty-five and three-quarter inches.

Who painted what? Attribution has been a problem because the record is inconsistent and contradictory.[14] In late April 1934 Johnson asserted authorship of *Toussaint L'Ouverture, Nat Turner, Negro Pharaoh—Eighteenth Dynasty,* and *Negro Soldiers.*[15] These four panels bear

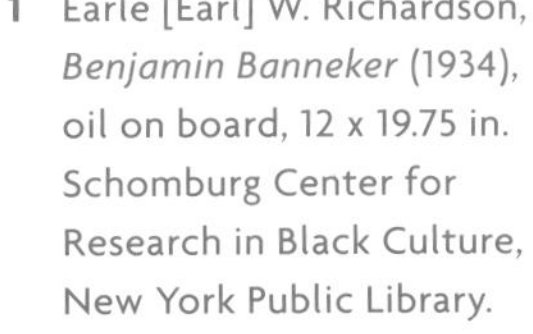

1 Earle [Earl] W. Richardson, *Benjamin Banneker* (1934), oil on board, 12 x 19.75 in. Schomburg Center for Research in Black Culture, New York Public Library.

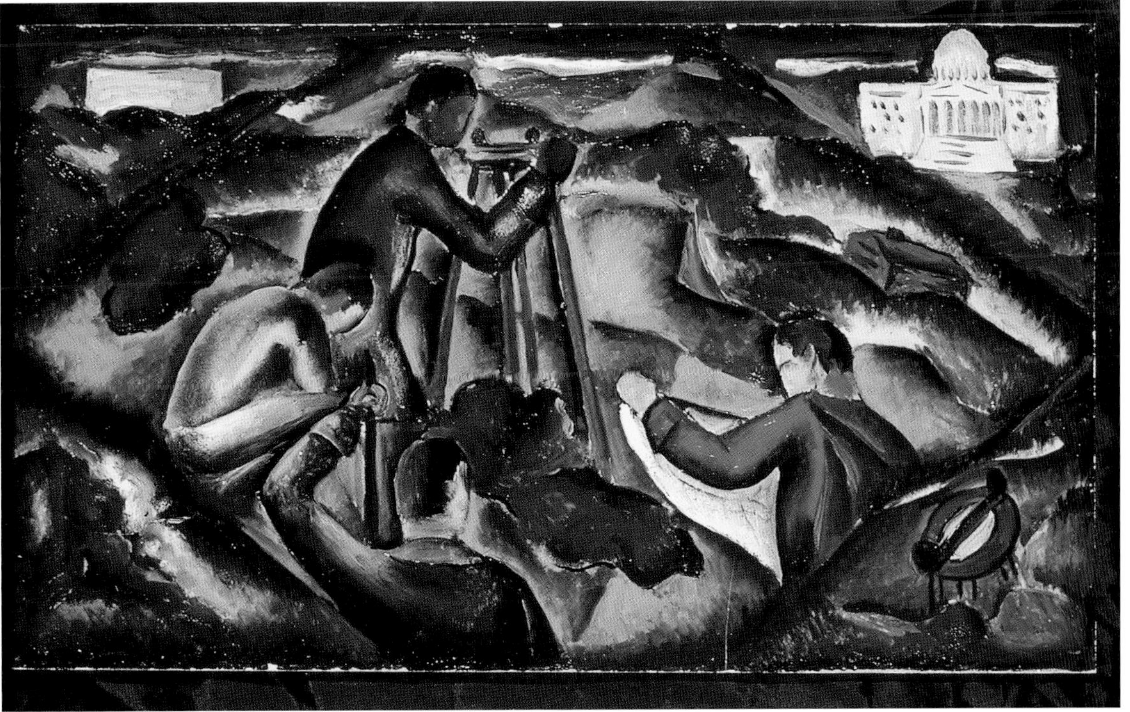

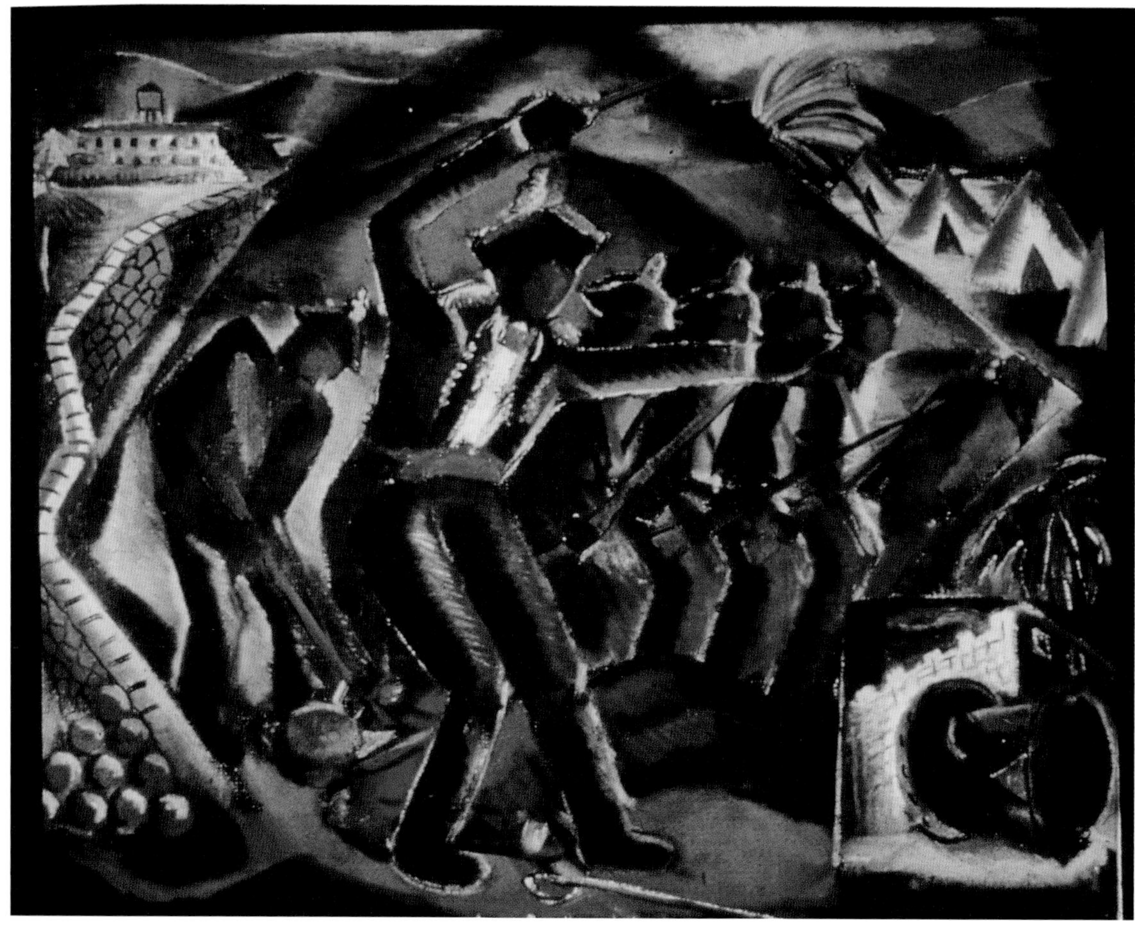

Johnson's signature, and *Negro Soldiers* was signed by Richardson as well.[16] But at the time of Johnson's death in October 1934, his eulogists made no connection between the artist and *Negro Achievement* studies.[17] By June 1936 the PWAP and the press were attributing all the studies to Richardson, who had died the previous December and who had signed *Harriet Tubman and Frederick Douglass* in addition to *Negro Soldiers*.[18]

Based on the textual record and my study of the artists' styles, I assign *Toussaint L'Ouverture, Nat Turner,* and *Negro Pharaoh—Eighteenth Dynasty* to Johnson; *Columbus Soldiers—Estavanico, Benjamin Banneker, Harriet Tubman and Frederick Douglass,* and *Art, Music, Literature* to Richardson; and *Negro Soldiers* to both artists. In Johnson's panels there is a demonstrated preference for low-value hues and compositional simplicity, evident throughout his oeuvre; Richardson's work has qualities that are plainly "un-Johnson-like," namely, a bright palette and a more ambitious approach to both figuration and pictorial organization. Yet, even as I make a case for the individual hands of Johnson and Richardson

2 Malvin Gray Johnson, *Toussaint L'Ouverture* (1934), oil on cardboard, 12 x 22.50 in. Schomburg Center for Research in Black Culture, New York Public Library.

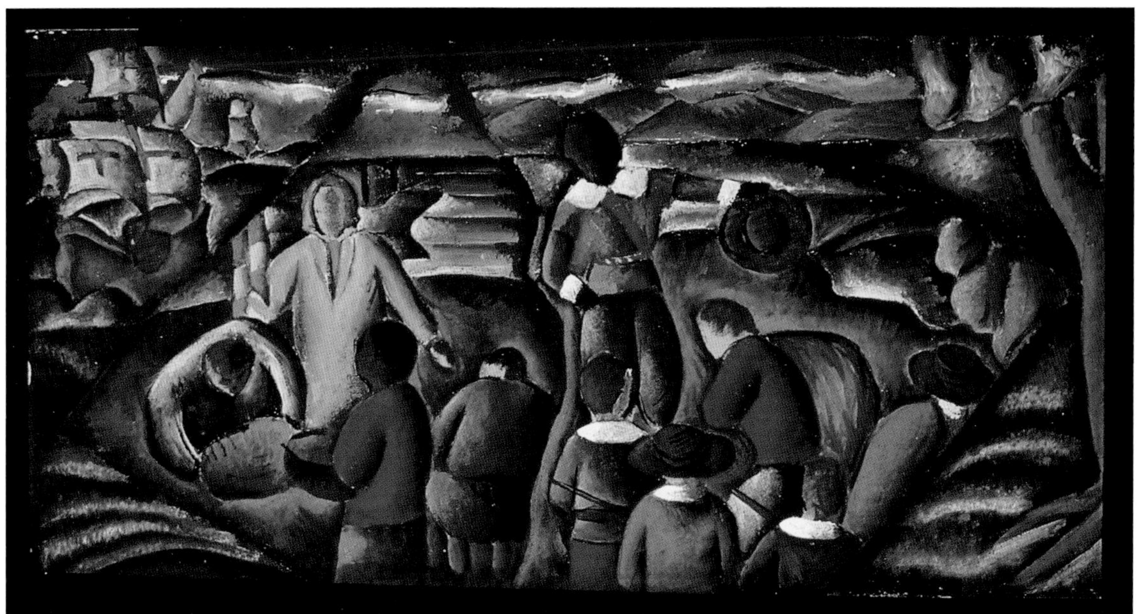

in their respective studies, I also seek to draw attention to the way the artists attempted to fuse their styles into a harmonious plan. Richardson subordinated his lyrical style to Johnson's geometric expressionism. Johnson, in turn, accepted Richardson's ideas for dramatizing subjects as much as possible. As a result, all the studies offer more bodies than are typically found in Johnson's spare, iconic tableau; moreover, they reflect the comparatively complex figural relationships and action that Richardson aspired to create.

Studies are rough constructions, made to present the most important visual ideas in brief, and those for *Negro Achievement* are purposefully schematic, asserting the hallmark quality of Johnson's painting of 1933–34. During this period Johnson developed an expressionist style, one consistent with the modernist tendency toward abstraction. Always inclined to simplify forms, Johnson experimented with figural and spatial abstraction from the early 1930s, a period in which he studied Cézanne's paintings and African sculpture.[19] The most salient aspect of Johnson's art during this period is its geometric figuration and overall organization; he developed and seemed to delight in constructing bodies and spaces as rhymed angles. In *Toussaint L'Ouverture,* acute angles define the bent limbs of the Haitian leader and his troops, tricorn caps, the wall surrounding the Citadel fort, the Haitian countryside, and the army's tents.[20] As is the case with these figures, those in *Negro Pharaoh— Eighteenth Dynasty* and *Nat Turner* are posed to emphasize angularity: the Egyptian ruler sits with arms bent while supplicants kneel and cool him with leafy fans. Likewise, the Turner-led insurgents' flexed limbs

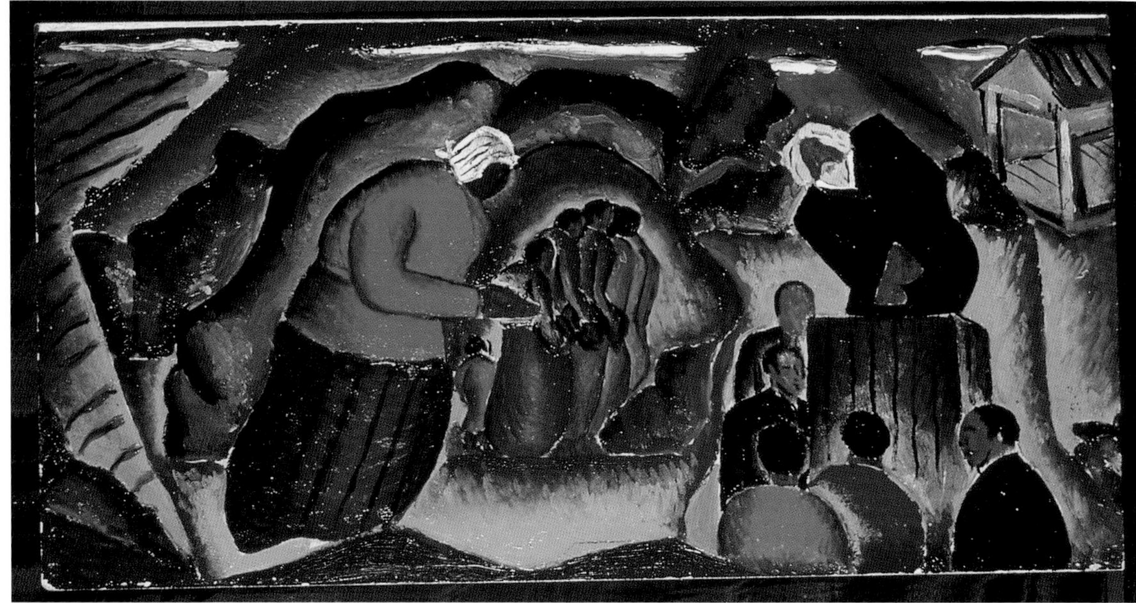

and sharply sloped backs and shoulders are diagonal structures that create a pattern of coherent dynamism in the panel. Enclosing the human actors in all the panels is yet another angularity, a diamond-like frame that Johnson also employed in an undated painting, *Harmony*. It is my guess that Johnson, having tried out this balancing and unifying device in *Harmony*, applied it to his *Negro Achievement* panels and persuaded Richardson to adopt it as well.

Johnson's aesthetic strategies decisively influenced his younger collaborator's panels, which are so markedly different from Richardson's other known efforts.[21] In addition to his studies for *Negro Achievement* and for a separate mural project on black farm workers, Richardson's surviving work consists of four expressionist oil paintings—a landscape, a self-portrait, a still life, and a Retablo-like depiction of a saint—and four expressive charcoal drawings—two genre scenes of laborers, a pietà of a black mother holding her lynched son, and an apocalyptic scene of war and destruction. Considering the brevity of Richardson's career and the paucity of existing work, it would be wrong to assert that he had a defined style. Nonetheless, even in this small body of production, Richardson's predilection for descriptive representation is obvious, as is his ambition for precision and variation. Both artists' approaches might be termed expressionist, but the contrast is seen in Richardson's desire for weighty figures, compressed compositional spaces, and telling details. Notably, where Johnson selects reductive profile views that allow him to make the body a gesturing silhouette, Richardson distinguishes his subjects with a variety of poses and uses a wider, more colorful palette

4 Earle [Earl] W. Richardson, *Harriet Tubman and Frederick Douglass* (1934), oil on board, 12 x 22.50 in. Schomburg Center for Research in Black Culture, New York Public Library.

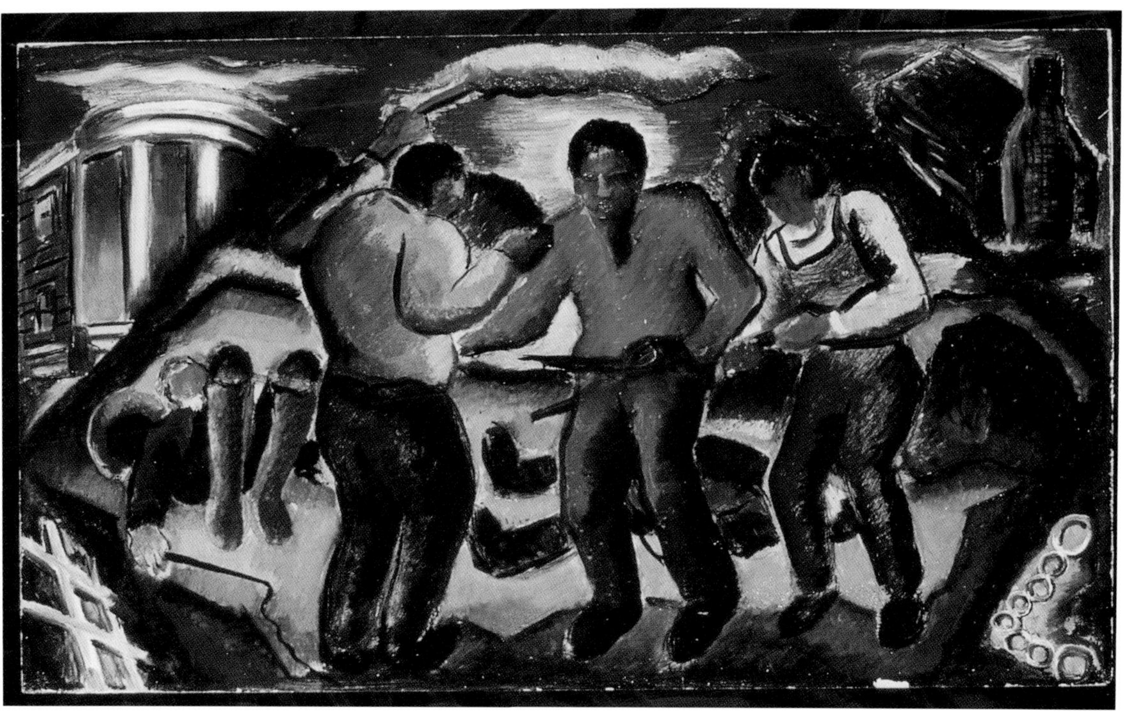

both to imbue them with plasticity and to enliven his panels. Richardson had a decorative sensibility and drafting ability that garnered note. In a review of a group exhibition in which he participated, the New York critic Carlyle Burrows wrote: "Earl Richardson ... shows a pronounced decorative gift. His figure subjects, done in a manner of archaic stylization, are deft and graceful, while his profile portrait of a Negro girl is very tastefully worked out in simple planes of color and with especial feeling for decorative pattern."[22] The portrait to which Burrows referred is the unlocated *Profile of a Negro Girl*. Even in reproduction, this oil painting evinces Richardson's study of the portrait convention and his interest in restating it in antinaturalistic terms.[23] *Profile of a Negro Girl* conveys Richardson's conceptual and artistic talents quite well, and yet these qualities are not fully evident in his *Negro Achievement* studies.

Johnson and Richardson pushed the ideal of collaboration to its limits in *Negro Soldiers,* the panel that bears both their signatures. Its subdued, nearly monochromatic palette and its angled bodies are Johnson's contribution, while the dynamic arrangement resembles the one Richardson employed in *Art, Music, Literature.* Strong diagonals divide the scenes into unequal quadrants and the overall effect is a quilt-like design. In *Art, Music, Literature* there are bare-chested drummers and a tuxedoed jazz musician; readers in a library setting, and others who take a break from field work to open a book; bright, African fabric and

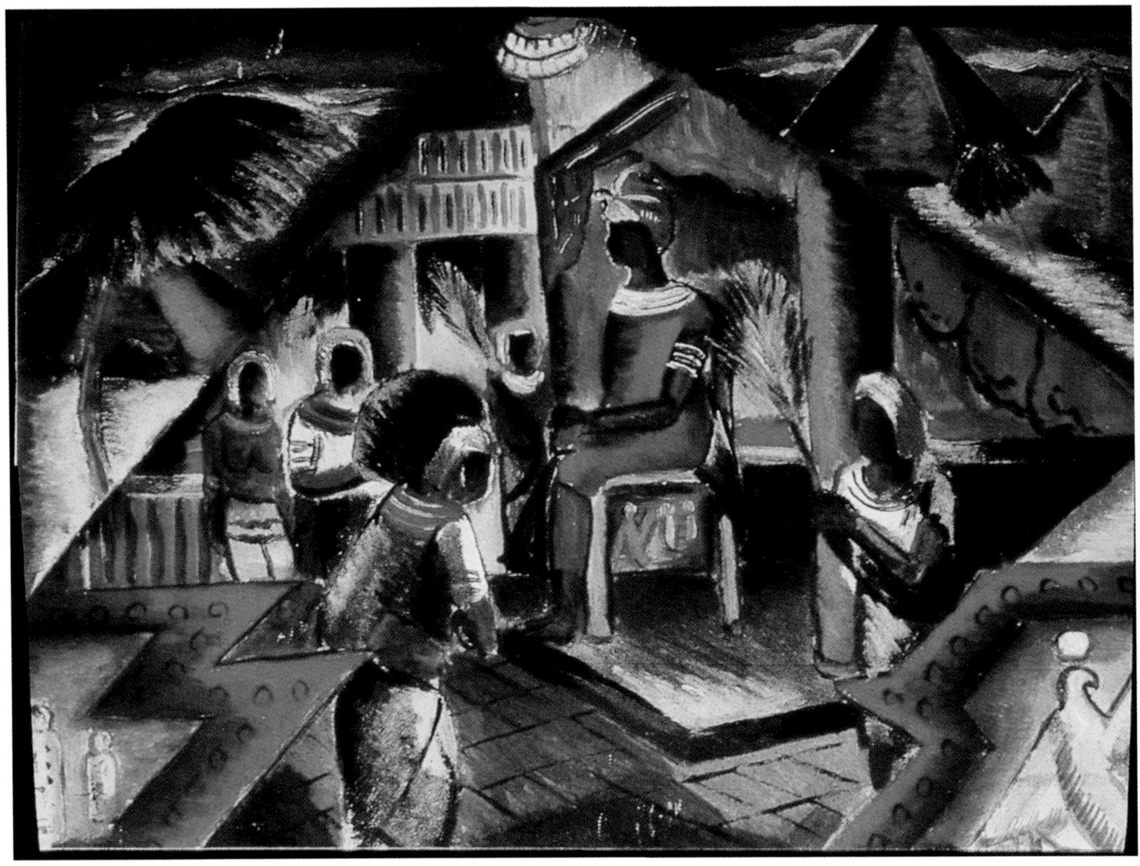

ritual sculpture in silhouette; and African American artists sculpting and painting in a studio. *Negro Soldiers* is similarly crowded with figures: the black protagonists in the Boston Massacre, and in the Civil War, Spanish-American War, and World War I. Johnson favored the motif of men in uniform and costume; he aspired to portray the beauty, order, and prestige of matching dress in *Harmony* and *Toussaint L'Ouverture* and in the genre portraits *Sailor* (1933), *Postman,* and *Negro Soldier* (both 1934). Moreover, as a World War I veteran, he had good reason to suggest the subject of black military service for *Negro Achievement.*[24]

Johnson's recollection of war undoubtedly served Richardson's interest in presenting detail and dramatic action. They worked together to make the figures and terrains historically plausible, enabling the viewer to make deductions about these black subjects—i.e., that the felled man in the upper left is Crispus Attucks, martyred during a colonial protest against British rule in 1770; in the adjacent passage, that it is a black Union army regiment that follows a white officer on horseback; that the palm trees in the right quadrant signify a tropical site, and therefore that the soldiers positioned nearby must be a black cavalry unit preparing to

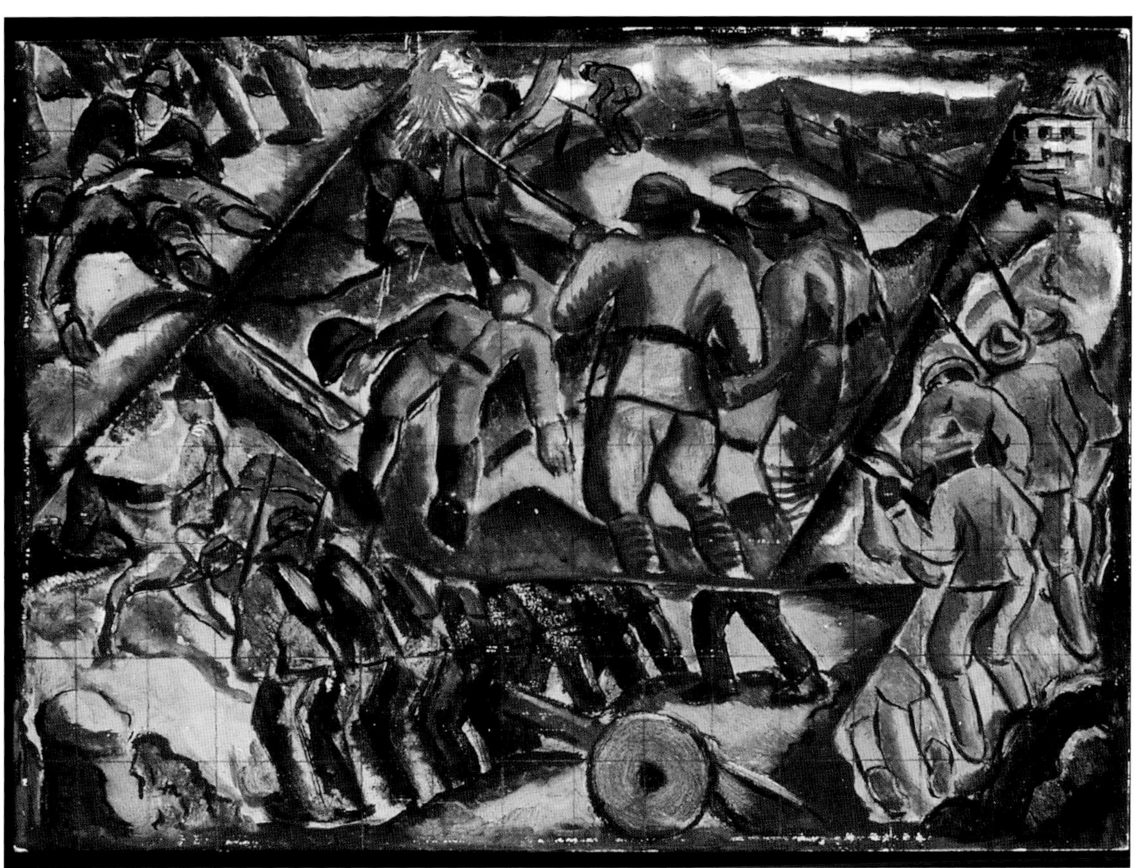

attack a Spanish-held fort in Cuba (perhaps the unit that opened the way for Teddy Roosevelt's Rough Riders on San Juan Hill); and that the large, central panel is a World War I scene of "doughboys" firing on their Axis powers enemies. In the era of its making, *Negro Soldiers* was among the few known depictions of black fighting men.[25] While few African American artists took up this subject, *Negro Soldiers* communicates African Americans' willingness to serve the very nation that failed to deliver their civil rights. This panel, then, is a measure of Johnson and Richardson's investment in ideologies of manhood and patriotism, and, as one writer has put it, the African American struggle for "the right to kill and be killed."[26]

The choppy designs of *Negro Soldiers* and *Art, Music, Literature* are problematic schemes that serve to illustrate the challenge of making murals in the 1930s. Trying to press their case of black citizenship and cultural production, respectively, in these two panels, the artists perhaps summoned too many images. Johnson and Richardson were easel painters who sensed that murals had to surpass the monocular vision of the small-scale genre scene.[27] Arguably, the overarching quality of the other

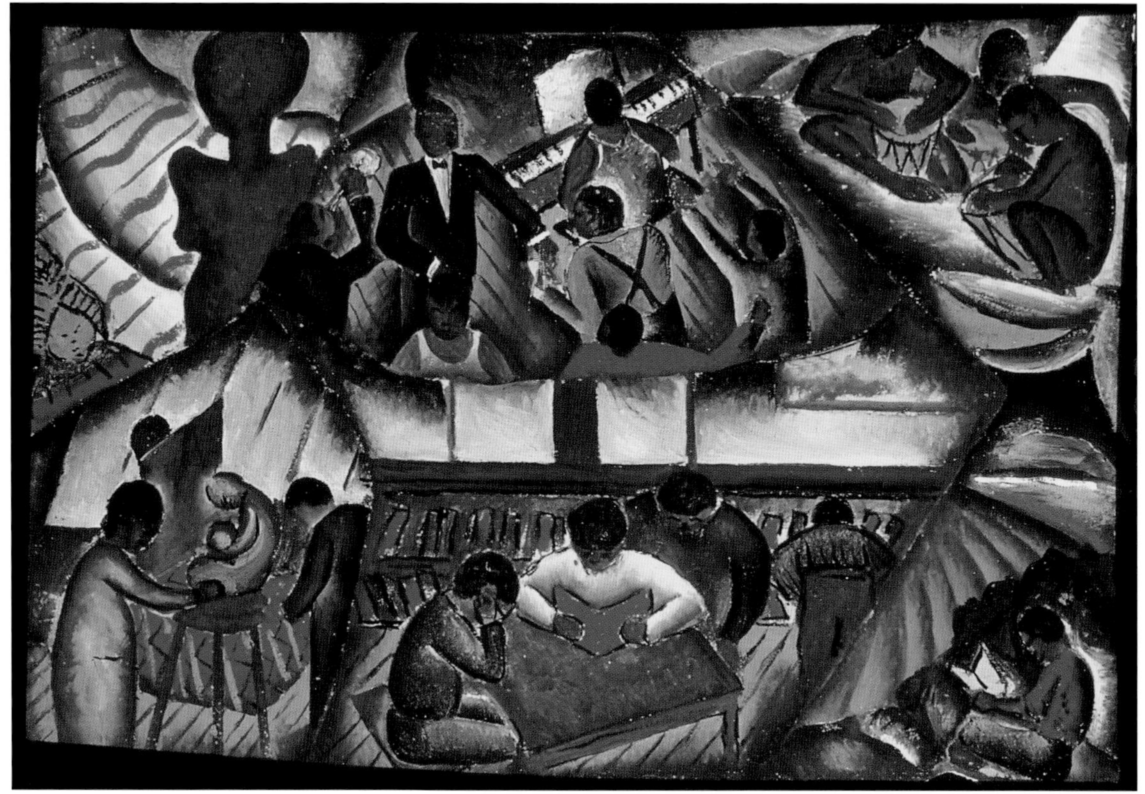

panels of *Negro Achievement* is the result of their direct focus on the subject body; the historical figure is made iconic in *Nat Turner, Toussaint L'Ouverture, Harriet Tubman and Frederick Douglass, Columbus Soldiers—Estavanico,* and *Negro Pharaoh—Eighteenth Dynasty.* As befits their exemplary status, these bodies are conceptually "biographical," set centrally, and made distinct from and superior to the supporting staffage. In contrast, when taking up the sweeping themes of war and culture, Johnson and Richardson looked to represent collectivity. Furthermore, the artists rejected Beaux Arts cycles and realist panoramas that retained authority and currency in the period; numerous American artists, including the African Americans William E. Scott and James A. Porter, embraced these paradigms and Richardson and Johnson had the opportunity to see their murals and mural sketches.[28] In the mid-1930s traditional formats were not necessarily safe bets, for contemporary critics expressed their boredom with academic approaches and neoclassical ideals. To the influential New York writer Henry McBride, many American murals were "the dry husks of other years and other countries without a trace of inspiration and without any relation to the life of our time."[29] Even Thomas Hart Benton's realist epics of the American nation, today presented as the uniformly acclaimed murals of the 1930s, met with ambivalence.[30] The standards for

8 Earle [Earl] W. Richardson, *Art, Music, Literature* (1934), oil on board, 17.50 x 25.75 in. Schomburg Center for Research in Black Culture, New York Public Library.

American murals, and for painting in general, were vague and unsettled, a situation ripe for artistic experimentation and laden with risk as well.[31]

"Men of Prominence"

In the years prior to the planning of "Negro Achievement," Johnson and Richardson had taken the conventional path to becoming professional artists. Both had studied at the National Academy of Design (NAD) in New York City, where a number of African Americans and black immigrants to the United States learned the fundamentals of drawing and painting during the first decades of this century.[32] Each enjoyed modest success at the School of the NAD, where they won student prizes for their work. Nonetheless, the academic imprimatur itself did not bring success to black artists; instead, critical acknowledgment was a direct result of the Harmon Foundation's juried exhibitions of black artists' production in 1928–31, 1933, and 1935.[33] Run by liberal-minded whites in consultation with African American intellectuals (among them the philosopher Alain Locke and the sociologist George S. Haynes), the foundation staged art exhibitions "to show outstanding creativity ... as an approach to better interracial, intercultural understanding."[34] Each Harmon exhibition opened in New York and garnered press comment in the city's newspapers; in the years 1929–34, portions of the Harmon displays were sent on tour throughout the United States, generating even more publicity. Johnson and Richardson participated in other exhibitions—both all-black and integrated—but the recognition they earned as Harmon prize-winners was by far the most substantial light ever shed upon their creative output.[35]

As painters in dire economic straits during the Depression, Richardson and Johnson met the PWAP's need-based criteria; as blacks, their presence helped administrators substantiate their claims of a diverse workforce. In the first project newsletter, published in February 1934, Assistant Technical Director Edward B. Rowan announced the national count of twenty-five Native Americans, 526 women, and "at least ten Negro artists working for the Public Works of Art. There are, no doubt, more but color is seldom designated on the payrolls. In this list are men of prominence, most of them well known in Paris, including Archibald Motley, William Edouard Scott, John Hardrick, Palmer Hayden, Malvin Gray Johnson, Dan Terry Reid, Elton Fax, and Dennis Gross."[36] Enthusiastic and flattering, Rowan's observation was a proclamation of successful pluralism, albeit an uncertain one. Indeed, of the 3,521 PWAP artists, few were African Americans.[37] In the New York division of eight hundred artists, there were only eight African Americans: the above-named painters

Johnson, Hayden, Richardson, and Joseph Delaney, Aaron Douglas, and
Richard William Lindsey, as well as John H. D. Robinson, and the photographer James Latimer Allen.[38]

Their reputations as Harmon exhibitors notwithstanding, Johnson
and Richardson were fortunate to earn a highly sought after PWAP mural
commission. Neither artist had worked on a mural commission prior to
Negro Achievement and there is no indication that either had formally
studied mural painting at the School of the NAD. However, inexperience
was no obstacle to PWAP assignments; the program's primary goal was to
provide income to unemployed artists during the harsh winter of 1933–
34.[39] That is not to say that the PWAP employed rank amateurs, for its
artists, charged with decorating nonfederal public buildings and parks,
had to demonstrate both economic need and artistic competence.[40]

Allotted fifteen hundred square feet, *Negro Achievement* was slated
to be installed in the reading room of the New York Public Library's
West 135th Street branch in Harlem. It would have been the second
of two murals on this site, the first being Aaron Douglas's now more
famous *Aspects of Negro Life* (1934). But in June 1934, when Douglas
was well on his way to completing his mural, Johnson was appealing
to the PWAP/New York administration for funds.[41] To Deputy Chairman Lloyd L. Rollins Johnson wrote that he and Richardson were "both
anxious to know why our part was not approved as we were under the
impression that this project would be done as one job since it was being
done in the same building. ... I am at [a] loss as to what steps to take."[42]
Rollins's prompt reply explained that the PWAP had run out of money
and that only a handful of projects had been picked up by another federal agency.[43] Douglas's *Aspects of Negro Life,* apparently ranked ahead of
Negro Achievement, was one of these.[44]

What went unsaid was that Douglas was an experienced muralist
whose preparatory studies bespoke his confidence with this format. As
their titles suggest, his mural studies *From Slavery to Reconstruction* and
An Idyll of the Deep South (both 1934) represent black enslavement in
the United States, emancipation, and political reorganization. Bent-over
bodies and lank rope as the symbols of the plantation economy and racist terror, respectively, are rendered in Douglas's signature geometric
style. With this scheme the artist not only subverted the well-established
idealization of slavery, he also sought to "document" civilization in Africa
and "African America." Silhouetted southern banjo players and singers
are superimposed over African dancers and their audience, effectively
linking these forms of black cultural production. Throughout Douglas's
frieze-like arrangement, African and African American subjects are inter-
dependent parts of a closely knit theme. If Johnson and Richardson
aimed to make a similar statement about historical continuity, cultural

authority, and unified identities, their studies remain too atomized and their subjects too discrete to sustain such claims.

When the PWAP hired African American artists, its administrators anticipated the depictions of particular "Negro themes." In the same PWAP newsletter item mentioned above, Rowan wrote: "The most hopeful indication of their work is the predominance of Negro themes, one such mural shows the evolution of the Negro race; another, Negro life along the Mississippi; a third, the present state of the Negro. Elizabeth Catlett, in her mural, for Miner Teachers' College brings out the dependence of the masses upon the teacher. One artist has represented a colored Pied Piper followed by his tribe of little pickannies [sic]."[45] As Rowan saw it, the iconography of "the Negro" was long and progressive ("evolution"), geographically specific ("Mississippi"), and in its "present state" too difficult to characterize easily; the figured black body could be pedagogic, variably collective (Marxist masses and primitive tribe), comic ("pickannies"), and dependent.[46] Rowan's statement stands on all too familiar stereotype, and yet it also reflected the ways in which the public arts administrators incorporated the advancing "New Negro" into their politically progressive utopian project. However problematic its conception of African American art production, the New Deal government nonetheless envisioned a participatory role for blacks in a new cultural order, one that saw racial and ethnic particularity as the shared common denominator of all Americans. The gesture of inclusivity inscribed in Rowan's comments was expanded during the Federal Art Project (FAP) years of 1935 to 1943. As Jonathan Harris has argued, FAP discourse was distinguished by the "subjectivities or social roles, such as 'artist,' 'woman,' and 'Negro' [which] could be seen as links in a chain of equivalents articulated by and to the organizing notion of citizenship."[47]

While Richardson apparently did not correspond with the PWAP administrators, Johnson made certain to express his enthusiasm to them. Letters he wrote to them were politic moves, meant to both promote himself and praise the PWAP's initiatives.[48] In response to Rowan's published comments, Johnson professed to the newsletter's editor, "I found much of interest to Art and Artist and it gave me great pleasure to see my name mentioned. ... I am sure that our government will be more than repaid for what it is now doing for its Artists."[49] Perhaps Johnson feigned an interest—metaphorically donning a mask to dupe his patrons— but perhaps he was in some way sincere. Balancing these possibilities endows the history of Johnson and Richardson's situation with a necessary complexity. These painters fashioned ad hoc strategies that were neither separatist nor assimilationist. A decade before Johnson and Richardson started to plot out *Negro Achievement,* Alain Locke wrote in "The New Negro": "The Negro mind reaches out as yet to nothing but

American wants, American ideas. ... The racialism of the Negro is no limitation or reservation with respect to American life; it is only a constructive effort to build the obstructions in the stream of progress into an efficient dam of social energy and power. So the choice is not between one way for the Negro and another way for the rest, but between American institutions frustrated on the one hand and American ideals progressively fulfilled and realized on the other."[50]

Johnson and Richardson's process for visualizing "achievement" was an emblematic negotiation of Negro "racialism" and "American wants." Negro "racialism" is represented through the grandeur of the Egypt of the pharaohs and "New Negro" culture, as well as in the critiques of American slavery and Western imperialism. "American wants" are expressed as the key moments in U.S. national origins and development, notably in the panels *Columbus Soldiers—Estavanico, Benjamin Banneker,* and *Negro Soldiers,* in which blacks are depicted as founders, leaders, and defenders of the soil who subscribe to the majority's ideals.[51] While these three panels depict interracial cooperation as a historical fact, *Tousssaint L'Ouverture* and *Nat Turner* warn of the dire consequences of national and racial oppression. With its narrative voices of protest tempered by accord, the plan for *Negro Achievement* differed from other popular history paintings that shed light on injustices, among them Douglas's *Aspects of Negro Life,* José Clemente Orozco's *Epic of American Civilization* (1932–34), and Ben Shahn's *Passion of Sacco and Vanzetti* (1931–32).

"Your history dates back beyond the cotton fields of the South, back thousands of years before Christ"

English-language histories of Africa and black America were published in modest numbers in the 1930s. In addition to Carter G. Woodson's quarterly *Journal of Negro History* and his Associated Publishers monographs, there is an incomplete record of self-published amateur treatises, yearbooks, and pamphlets.[52] Both types of historical record were decidedly revisionist, meant "to show that Blacks could do the things White Men value."[53] Significantly, professional and amateur historians also published in the black press, where articles, syndicated columns, and cartoons presented the facts and feats of blacks and other people of color. Although some of these newspaper items were hyperbolic (a characteristic of U.S. journalism in the period), many were factual, providing an affordable and accessible course in black history to a wide audience.

The black press features, in particular, were available resources of popular history and models of didacticism for black artists. Joel Augustus

Rogers's offerings—"Ruminations," a *New York Amsterdam News* column, and "Your History," an illustrated series of short biographies run in the nationally distributed *Pittsburgh Courier*—illustrate this point.[54] Each installment of the latter led off with the hortatory subhead: "Your history dates back beyond the cotton fields of the South, back thousands of years before Christ." With this familiar tone of address, Rogers, a self-trained historian, appealed directly to the black reader's sense of racial pride and cultural ownership. Bracketing the period of enslavement, he listed and summarized the highlights of black accomplishment through the ages. Primacy was the "hook," for Rogers routinely situated his black subjects as "firsts." Thus Eugene Bullard was the "first AfraAmerican aviator on record"; Mohammed, the "founder of the religion with the greatest number of followers next to Christianity"; Benjamin Banneker made "the first striking clock in America."[55] This construct served Rogers's preference for biographical writing; he believed that this genre and, undoubtedly, his choice of winning subjects provided black people with "a sense of direction through life's wilderness as well as the courage to press on."

Johnson and Richardson's choices for *Negro Achievement* subjects may have been prompted by Rogers's writings, such as a "Ruminations" column of February 1934. Here, Rogers crowed, "A Negro, Estavanico, discovered Arizona and New Mexico 86 years before the ancestors of the Mayflower blue-bloods touched these shores."[56] For Rogers, achievement boiled down to a contest between whites and blacks (other races were rarely mentioned), a head-to-head competition, and the age-old view of history as the winners' tales. In contrast, Richardson visually paired Estavanico's exploits with Columbus's, suggesting that their feats and leadership qualities were equally admirable.

As contemporary analogues, *Negro Achievement* and Rogers's popular histories shared a discursive approach to history, framed as the decisive action of men. Rogers frequently wrote of black fighting men, from swashbuckling Bedouins to the British boxer Peter Jackson, and his "Your History" accounts were accompanied by realistic line portraits of the subject. Still, representations of blacks were not new to the Western canon; what was provocative is their presence in heroic pantheons constructed by black artists.[57] The inclusion of black fighting men in *Negro Achievement* is significant because Johnson and Richardson bypassed less controversial subjects that would also have served their theme. In the winter of 1934, when Johnson was doing his sketches for *Negro Achievement,* he also produced several portraits of black citizens: *Soldier, Postman, Booker Washington,* and *Jenkins (Orphan) Band.* Of these paintings, only *Jenkins (Orphan) Band* portrays protagonists in action—musicians playing before a street audience; in the others, the "race man"

Washington and the middle-class figures in uniform are sedate studio sitters whose significant labor is the assertion of leadership, social rank, and economic achievement. Apparently *Negro Achievement* demanded a bifurcated male subjectivity that could be expressed through gestures of fraternity and antagonism. There are four instances of the former: the panels devoted to Banneker and his white associates surveying Washington, D.C., to Columbus and Estavanico and their interracial parties,[58] to Toussaint L'Ouverture and his troops, and to Attucks and the uniformed soldiers. These images of male bonding and teamwork—resonant with Johnson and Richardson's artistic collaboration—coexist with stark representations of conflict. The depictions of armed black men standing over the fallen bodies of defeated whites in *Nat Turner* and *Toussaint L'Ouverture* were unprecedented. Pictured as the leaders of bloody insurrections, Toussaint and Turner were volatile subjects. The only comparably unflinching images came later in Hale Woodruff's mural *Amistad Mutiny, 1839,* Robert Savon Pious's oil painting *Slave Ship,* and Jacob Lawrence's tempera series, *Frederick Douglass.*[59] Such scenes of black male resistance against slavery and imperialism had to have been especially dramatic in the 1930s. As Margaret Vendryes has shown, the decade was witness to a rise in the number of southern lynchings, to anti-lynching campaigns and anti-lynching art, and to black fears of white retribution in response to protest.[60] Johnson and Richardson marshaled a panoply of heroes—those who "fought" with their minds, weapons, and oratory—to rebut characterizations of black cowardice and passivity.[61]

Harder to explain is the exaggeratedly oversized rendering of the major female subject in *Negro Achievement:* the Underground Railroad "conductor" and Union army spy Harriet Tubman. Her tall, thick, leaning body overwhelms that of Frederick Douglass, represented in the same panel, and those of the fleeing slaves, which are the smallest figures in the composition. Tubman's physique is drawn bluntly as if to liken it to the boulders depicted behind her, and her skirts are as woodenly fashioned as the podium before the orator Douglass. Richardson's representation had to have been partly influenced by a popular illustration of Tubman, the cover rendering for Sarah H. Bradford's 1869 biography.[62] In this widely distributed image, Tubman wears a striped skirt and holds a rifle whose length almost equals her height.[63] Richardson disarms Tubman, though her hand—indicating the direction toward freedom—is pointed like a pistol. In this account of history, dominated by representations of men's deeds, the very inclusion of Tubman was extraordinary. Richardson's monumentalized Tubman represents an effort to signify her legendary bravery and to establish a female character equal to the men of *Negro Achievement.*[64] Tubman's presence is an exception that

nonetheless reminds us that leadership is generally historicized as a
fraternal body.

Tubman was not the only larger-than-life female protagonist in
Richardson's known production. Around the same time that *Negro
Achievement* was being sketched out, Richardson painted two oil panels for an FAP project, *Employment of the Negro in Agriculture;* one scene
depicts cotton harvesters, the other, workers bearing fruits and vegetables. Among these highly idealized bodies, the female figures are
especially strong and erect. Like chiseled statues, they serve as compositional anchors for each panel, a timeless space of proletarian nobility.
Richardson's figures are as weighty and solemn as African sculptural
forms, a known interest of Richardson's creative circle. In 1932 he had
exhibited with Primitive African Art, a self-described movement of African American artists dedicated to the "serious study" of these forms and
their history.[65] The effects of their investment in African art are manifest
in the *Employment of the Negro in Agriculture* panels and in Richardson's
self-portrait. In the latter, his visage is faceted and mask-like in its brown,
wooden color and solidity, and, as is the case with Malvin Gray Johnson's
Self-Portrait (1934) and Palmer Hayden's still life *Fétiche et Fleurs* (1933),
Richardson's self-portrait exemplifies the manner in which trained
African American painters carefully developed a racially inflected modernism. Never abandoning Western conventions and styles, they made
use of resonant symbols of Africa and the formal qualities of African art,
all absorbed by Cubists, Expressionists, and abstractionists. Indeed, Richardson's figures are as bold as European Renaissance portraits, sources
he may have studied in art school or in art magazines for their solid
physicality and authority.[66]

The classicized interpretation of the worker subject strongly links
the *Employment of the Negro in Agriculture* studies to Diego Rivera's
populist imagery.[67] As a progressive and a leftist, Richardson might
have looked to Rivera's work as a model of activist art, as did his friend
Charles Alston.[68] Richardson's debt to Rivera is broadly evident in the
simplified palette, flattened forms, shallow spaces, massed figures, and
iconic symbols of the *Employment of the Negro in Agriculture* panels. In
these Richardson establishes balance and multiple points of focus, qualities he had attempted in *Art, Music, Literature* and *Negro Soldiers* but
failed to realize in those works.

Doing for History

What is the measure of *Negro Achievement?* Johnson and Richardson's
studies were preliminary working documents that were subject to change.

Today, nonetheless, the panels are oft-displayed public images; they are housed in the Schomburg Center for Research in Black Culture, an archive of black cultural resources adjacent to the 135th Street Public Library, the proposed mural site. They are often exhibited one or two at a time, sometimes without mention of the planned mural that might explain their making and their sketchy and fragmentary quality. They cannot stand in for the mural itself, nor are they finished tableaux. Yet, independent of the art-historical and specific procedural contexts, the panels advance the artists' goal of commemoration. At the least, the story behind *Negro Achievement* underscores the mural's status in the 1930s. Clearly, artists sought to enhance their reputations by creating such public decoration, and yet not all earned the opportunity to do so.

Johnson and Richardson both died before their respective talents could mature fully. But Richardson's decisions in mural design—both in *Negro Achievement* and in *Employment of Negroes in Agriculture*—attest to his ability to rapidly absorb and develop solutions to representational roadblocks. Namely, in the panels of the latter project, he abandoned the demands of textbook history and outlaw heroes, and subsequently cast the anonymous in iconic roles and resonant symbolic space. The squared and linked figures in *Employment of Negroes in Agriculture* are pointedly more descriptive and decorative than those of *Negro Achievement*. While the latter's figures cohere to the ideal of *peripeteia*—the decisive moment of the history painting—the former's group is composed of a frieze, one that could be transformed into a convincing mural passage. Moreover, although employment is a historical issue, Richardson does not treat it as such. The space is conditionally atemporal and generalized. These figures are noble not for what they do but for their monumentalized character and perseverance.

Collaboration on *Negro Achievement* also transformed Johnson's style. More than ever he summoned the figure as an opportunity to distort and exaggerate form; following Richardson, he also enlivened his palette. In *Platform Dance,* a watercolor from mid-1934, Johnson quickly rendered the necessary items of a "clapboard aesthetic": plank floorboards, banjos, a tree stump. *Platform Dance* is assertively more decorative than documentary, for these figures are the most succinct kind of visual shorthand. As representative of the work that Johnson and Richardson produced after *Negro Achievement, Platform Dance* and the *Employment of Negroes in Agriculture* panels speak to the recuperation of the folk in the 1930s by artists and writers—African American and European American both. They are deliberately composed folk spaces that celebrate the vitality of rural southern culture. Above all, such folk images were received as documentary and historical; in other words, viewers saw them as "true" rather than works of representation. Black folk images in particular nearly supplanted the newly conceived black history painting in the 1930s. The distant past was a greater challenge to depict the rural world; rendered as premodern spaces, the backwoods were "historical" indices to the nation's Edenic beginnings. The folk body could document this imagined locale, for the perception was that the rustic had not changed over time and that this body essentially embodied the past. Furthermore, the folk as subject appealed powerfully to the consuming audience's tastes for "racial art" as any figurative style that was bold, colorful, and immediate. The rural milieu was amenable to just such characterization, and this was a ready site in which to locate authentic blackness.

LYNCHING AND ANTI-LYNCHING:
ART AND POLITICS IN THE 1930S

Marlene Park Lynching became a fact of American life after the Civil War, but it only became an important subject for writers of the Harlem Renaissance in the 1920s and for visual artists other than cartoonists in the 1930s. During the Depression, anti-lynching works were first a reaction to the widespread outrage over the Scottsboro case and then part of the political and legislative efforts to make lynching a federal offense. In early 1935 both the National Association for the Advancement of Colored People and the Communist Party's John Reed Club held competing art exhibitions that condemned lynching and supported these groups' legislative objectives.

The historical reality of lynching was more complex and horrifying than any literary or visual account; some knowledge of the history of

This is a condensed, slightly revised version of my article of the same title published in *Prospects* 18 (1993): 311–65. As the title suggests, Helen Langa, in "Two Antilynching Art Exhibitions: Politicized Viewpoints, Racial Perspectives, Gendered Constraints," *American Art* 13 (spring 1999): 10–39, interprets the same exhibitions without new evidence. Since 1993 the literature on lynching has increased greatly. See Norton H. Moses, comp., *Lynching and Vigilantism in the United States: An Annotated Bibliography*, no. 34 in the series Bibliographies and Indexes in American History (Westport, Conn.: Greenwood Press, 1997). For the most scholarly context of the John Reed Club exhibition, see Andrew Hemingway, *Artists on the Left: American Artists and the Communist Movement, 1926–1956* (New Haven: Yale University Press, 2002), 64–67 and passim. For additional images, see Frances K. Pohl, *In the Eye of the Storm: An Art of Conscience, 1930–1970* (San Francisco: Pomegranate, 1995), 48–52; Patricia Phagan, *The American Scene and the South: Paintings and Works on Paper, 1930–1946* (Athens: Georgia Museum of Art, University of Georgia, 1996), 227–41; Robert L. Stevens and Jared A. Fogel, "The Depression in the South: Seymour Fogel's Images of African Americans," *Social Education* 62 (February 1998): 80–83; James Allen et al., *Without Sanctuary: Lynching Photography in America* (Santa Fe: Twin Palms, 2000); Lin Shi Khan and Tony Perez, *Scottsboro, Alabama: A Story in Linoleum Cuts,* ed. Andrew H. Lee (New York: New York University Press, 2002); and Bram Dijkstra, *American Expressionism: Art and Social Change, 1920–1950* (New York: Harry N. Abrams, in association with the Columbus Museum of Art, 2003), 138–50.

lynching and the anti-lynching campaigns provides the best context
for discussing the images. Though there were mob murders in colonial
America, lynching became a major form of deliberate, lawless violence
after the Civil War. The phenomenon was a national one; people were
lynched in forty-four of the forty-eight states. The most dangerous states,
relatively speaking, were in the South, from Virginia to Florida, from
Georgia to Texas. It was in the rural South that the most savage lynchings took place, but the statistics make clear that for many decades
lynchings were a serious threat to civil liberty, to law and order, to
democracy—and a national disgrace.

Lynch victims were mostly men, but also women and children, and
it was not unusual for five people to be lynched at once. The victims
included Native Americans and foreign nationals—Italian, Mexican,
and Chinese.[1] The crimes of which these people were accused included,
first of all, murder, but also "window peeping," "unpopularity," "insulting
women," "being disreputable," and sometimes "cause unknown."[2] A few
early mob murders did take place on the frontier, but many victims were
taken from town or city jails and killed with the complicity or help of
law enforcement officers. Few victims were "strung up" in a hurry; many
more were tortured and burned.

One difference between murder and lynching is that lynching is
committed by a mob, which was usually defined as three or more persons. In most lynchings, the names of the victims are known, but there
is relatively little information about the members of mobs. In the 1930s,
when detailed studies of lynchings were published, mobs sometimes
consisted of "several hundred," or the "community."[3] Lynching was often
a crime in which the guilt was so widespread that prosecution was virtually impossible. But even in instances in which the identities of mob
members were known, they were rarely brought to trial or convicted of
their crimes. A few lynchings were announced well ahead of time by the
press and radio and attended by large crowds, who witnessed the cruelty in a carnival atmosphere. The real horror is conveyed by Arthur F.
Raper's estimate that for twenty-one lynchings in 1930, "The mobs ... had
about 75,000 members—men and women and children who went out to
kill, or to look on sympathetically while others killed." Raper concluded
that "not one of these so-called onlookers is morally or legally guiltless."[4]

The attempts to prevent and to punish lynching began in the courts
and state legislatures, but efforts to prevent lynchings by publicizing
them were also important. In 1892 Ida B. Wells-Barnett (1862–1931)
became the first journalist to crusade against lynching. At the time,
three African American men who had successfully opened a grocery in
a Negro section that already had a white-owned grocery were lynched
in Memphis, Tennessee. After defending themselves from attack, they

were jailed, taken from the jail, and killed. A mob looted and destroyed the store, which was then closed by creditors. Wells-Barnett wrote an editorial exposé, and the *Free Speech* leader advised its readers to flee the area, advice that a large part of the African American population heeded.[5] Such migrations were so predictable that T. Arnold Hill of the Chicago Urban League said, "whenever we read newspaper dispatches of a public hanging or burning ... we get ready to extend greetings to people from the immediate vicinity of the lynchings."[6] Jacob Lawrence made this point in *The Migration of the Negro* series (1940–41, Phillips Collection, Washington, D.C.). In Panel No. 15, an empty noose hangs from a bare branch in a desolate landscape. The caption reads: "Another cause was lynching. It was found that where there had been a lynching, the people who were reluctant to leave at first left immediately after this." Wells-Barnett's subsequent pamphlets, as well as articles on lynchings for the *New York Age,* were direct and forceful, setting a standard for later journalists. She was particularly effective in exposing the truth in cases in which rape was claimed to be the reason for the lynching.

The NAACP, organized in 1909, took up the anti-lynching crusade. The NAACP grew out of meetings held after the 1908 race riots in Springfield, Illinois. The founders were shocked to find that such riots could occur not just in a northern city but in the city most closely associated with the Great Emancipator. The NAACP set out to end segregation and discrimination by both educational and legal means.

Several events in the teens added to the difficulties that the NAACP faced in opposing lynching. In 1915 William J. Simmons reorganized the Ku Klux Klan, and beginning in 1920 two publicists helped expand it into a large secret society. In 1915 Leo Frank was lynched in Atlanta. Frank, a Jewish New Yorker, was superintendent and part-owner of a pencil plant, where a thirteen-year-old female worker had been raped and murdered in 1913. Frank was convicted and condemned to death, but after the governor commuted his sentence to life imprisonment, a mob took him from a state prison and lynched him. When the Supreme Court ruled that there was no reason for the federal government to investigate the trial, the NAACP worked to overturn the decision, because the Court in effect had judged the conviction to be legal even though the Atlanta court had been intimidated by an armed mob. The NAACP recognized that this was a "legal lynching," meaning that the defendant could in effect be legally convicted and sentenced to death by a mob.[7]

Race riots were a feature of the immediate postwar years and many people were killed by mobs during the riots. In 1917, in a riot in East Saint Louis, a great many African Americans, who had recently settled there and been hired to replace union workers, were killed. In the summer of 1919, which the NAACP called the Red Summer, there were seven large race riots, the three worst ones in Washington, D.C., Chicago, and Arkansas. What was different was that this time African Americans fought back.

The anti-lynching campaign was, of course, just one priority of the NAACP. For instance, in 1919, the year the group published its first major attack on lynching, *Thirty Years of Lynching in the United States, 1889–1918,* the first item on the agenda was "a vote for every Negro man and woman on the same terms as for white men and women." "Defense against lynching and burning at the hands of mobs" came fifth.[8] But, as Robert L. Zangrando concluded, "the anti-lynching drive had an urgency, a public visibility, and a dramatic quality that no other civil rights activity quite matched. It was through the anti-lynching struggles that the NAACP gained much of its stability and recognition, learned how to deal with the complex problems of race in America, and placed itself simultaneously in the vanguard of black activism and at the center of national affairs."[9]

The anti-lynching campaign included many approaches—meetings, whether with small groups or political leaders, conferences, rallies, marches, picketing, lawsuits, press releases, publications, publicity, and working with other groups—but perhaps the most important were the attempts to pass federal legislation and the investigations of lynchings. Two different but very talented men in turn led the anti-lynching activities of the NAACP from 1916 until 1955: James Weldon Johnson (1871–1938) of Jacksonville and Walter Francis White (1893–1955) of Atlanta.

In 1918, when the NAACP decided to seek federal anti-lynching legislation, there were two bills on the House floor. The NAACP chose to support the bill put forward by Leonidas C. Dyer (R-Mo.), and for the next five years Johnson devoted most of his time and energy to securing passage. The bill provided for prosecution in federal court for members of mobs, for fines and imprisonment of officials who failed to prevent or prosecute lynchers, and for indemnities to be paid to the heirs of the victim by the counties in which lynchings occurred.

The legal basis cited for the Dyer bill was the Fourteenth Amendment (1868), the amendment intended to give federal protection to newly emancipated African Americans. Under the Constitution the states, rather than the federal government, are responsible for the protection of individual life, liberty, and property, and thus murder is a crime prosecuted under state law. But the amendment noted that people are citizens of both the United States and of a state, and directed that "No State shall make or enforce any law which shall abridge the privileges or immunities of citizens of the United States; nor shall any State deprive any person of life, liberty, or property, without due process of law; nor deny to any person within its jurisdiction the equal protection of the laws."

The Dyer bill passed the House by a vote of 231 to 119 in 1922, but, like all subsequent anti-lynching bills that passed the House, it failed to pass the Senate.[10] As Johnson wrote, even the defeat of the bill was a kind of victory for the NAACP:

> The first prosecution of lynchers under the facts were discussed and brought home to the American people as they had never been before. Agitation for the passage of the measure was, without doubt, one of the prime factors in reducing the number of lynchings in the decade that followed to less than one-third of what it had been in the preceding decade—to one-tenth of what it was in the first decade of the keeping of the record. It served to awaken the people of the Southern states to the necessity of taking steps themselves to wipe out the crime, and this, I think, was its most far-reaching result.[11]

Walter White, in the course of his long career with the NAACP, investigated a total of forty-one lynchings and eight race riots. His accounts were published in both newspapers and magazines, and his anti-lynching activities were so widely known that his portrait appeared on the cover of *Time* magazine on 24 January 1938—when another anti-lynching bill was before Congress. White, like Johnson, also became a literary figure in the Harlem Renaissance. When he received a Guggenheim Fellowship to write a third novel, he wrote instead *Rope and Faggot,* which was published in 1929, the year of the stock market crash. It was, in his words, "a study of the complex influences—economic, political, social, religious, sexual—behind the gruesome, and too little understood, phenomenon of lynching" and was hailed as the first such study.[12] In the introduction White noted that "the deeper one inquires into the subject, the more one must regard lynching as being of only minor importance in itself; it is as a symptom of a malodorous economic and social condition that it is chiefly significant."[13]

White chose as a frontispiece George Bellows's 1923 lithograph *The Law Is Too Slow* (fig. 1). The title refers to a common rationalization summarized by James Harmon Chadbourn: "lynching is often interpreted as a protest against the inefficiency of courts as agencies for the punishment of crime."[14] Bellows, an artist of the Ash Can School before World War I, best known for his paintings of New York City and of boxing, was the major artist-lithographer of the early 1920s. He had been commissioned to illustrate a story called "Nemesis," by Mary Johnston, that appeared in the May issue of *Century* magazine. *The Law Is Too Slow* illustrated a passage that read, "One of the four men lighted the pile, the cane blazed up, and the night turned red and horribly loud—like hell."[15] The black-and-white print is a night scene. In the center a Negro man, chained to a stump, writhes and grimaces in pain as a fire burns his feet and legs. A large group of masked or hooded men surrounds him, most watching but one tending the fire. The stark pattern of dark and light, in which the white light silhouettes the victim, focuses attention on the suffering and horror of the scene and on the indifference of the onlookers in the surrounding darkness. For its dramatic use of black and white, the white being the plain paper, one reviewer compared the print to a Rembrandt.[16]

Bellows's lithograph is actually closer in spirit to James Weldon Johnson's poem "Brothers," published in 1922 in Johnson's anthology of Negro poetry. The poem read in part:

> Enough, the brute must die!
> Quick! Chain him to that oak! It will resist
> The fire much longer than this slender pine.
> Now bring the fuel! Pile it `round him! Wait!
> Pile not so fast or high! or we shall lose
> The agony and terror in his face.
> And now the torch! Good fuel that! the flames
> Already leap head-high. Ha! hear that shriek!
> And there's another! Wilder than the first.
> Fetch water! Water! Pour a little on
> The fire, lest it should burn too fast. Hold so!
> Now let it slowly blaze again. See there!
> He squirms! He groans! His eyes bulge wildly out,
> Searching around in vain appeal for help![17]

Bellows's print records only one second of the grisly scene and thus seems more matter-of-fact than Johnson's poem. But its relation to the poem suggests that the poems of the Harlem Renaissance provided the first anti-lynching images and inspired many sympathetic artists who were not actively part of the movement.

By 1930 the Communist Party of the United States of America emerged as a rival to existing civil rights organizations. From the mid-1920s, under Soviet direction, the party began to change from an organization based on foreign-language federations and concerned primarily with labor questions to a political party with an ambitious agenda. As part of that change, the Comintern directed the establishment, in 1925, of the American Negro Labor Congress, and B. D. Amis published a pamphlet, *Lynch Justice at Work,* attacking the NAACP and the National Urban League as agents of the white ruling class and mis-leaders of Negroes.[18] Such attacks only intensified after the Sixth World Congress of the Communist International in 1928 called for abandoning

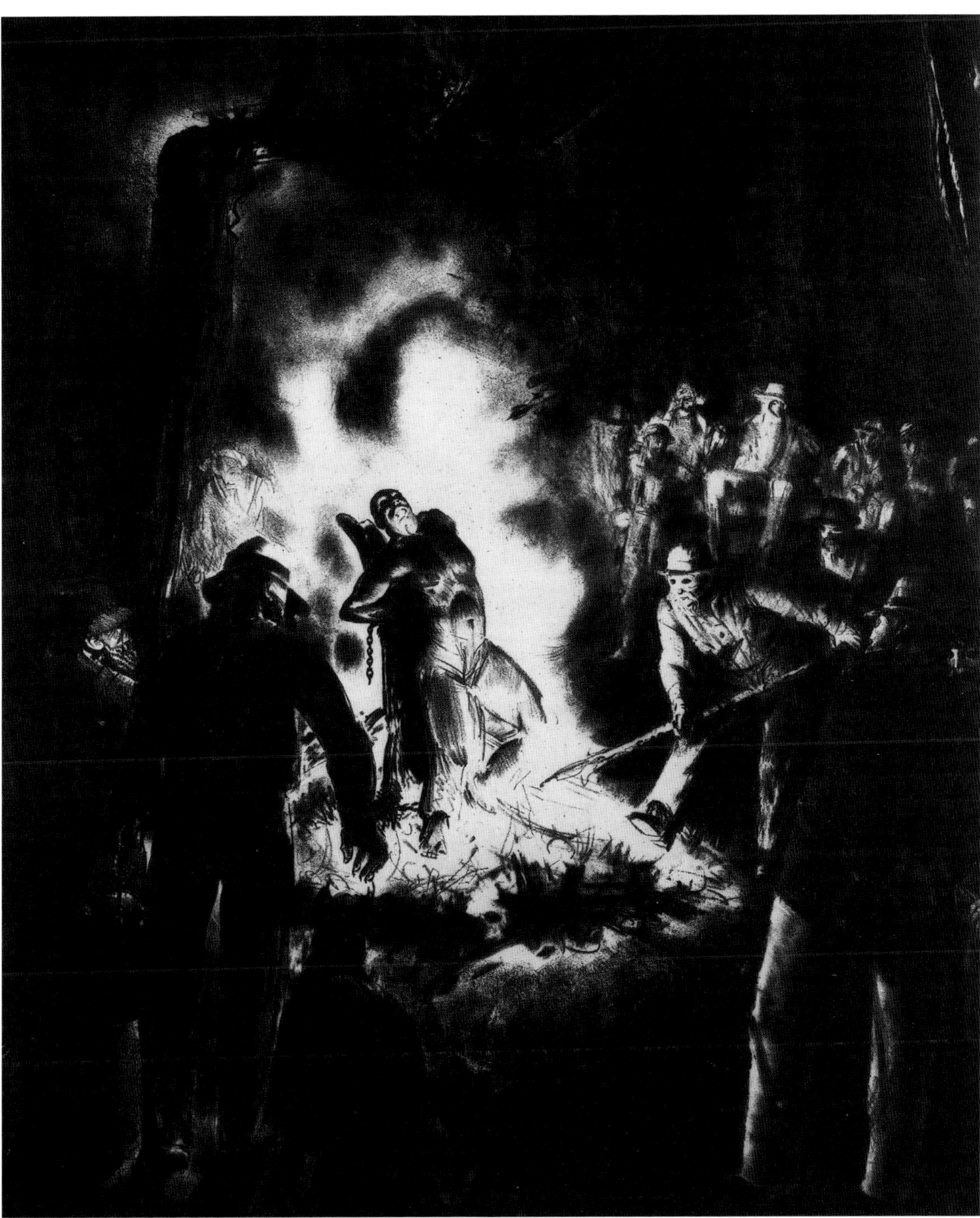

the strategy of taking over existing organizations, and instead decreed
the establishment of separate organizations. The new policies also
included "Self-Determination for Negroes in the Black Belt," and stepped-
up attacks on capitalism, "social fascism," and liberals, including Negro
reform leaders. In 1929 the International Labor Defense (ILD), founded in
1925 as the legal arm of the Communist Party, made Negro rights its central priority. In 1929 the John Reed Club was formed in New York City
under Communist leadership, and its branches in many cities became
centers for lively discussions of the relationships between social and
artistic issues. In 1930 the party organized the League of Struggle for
Negro Rights, the main agenda of which was an anti-lynching campaign.
Langston Hughes was its president.[19]

Thus by 1930 the CPUSA and its affiliates, poised to play a greater
role in racial politics, needed only to seize upon and publicize some great
injustice. The great racial *cause célèbre* of these years, the Scottsboro
case, was ideal because it centered on charges of rape and the possibility
of lynching, actual or "legal." On 25 March 1931 a group of young hoboes
got off a Memphis-bound freight train at Stevenson, Alabama, and told
the stationmaster that they had been beaten and thrown off the train by
a "bunch of Negroes." At the next stop, Paint Rock, a sheriff and his depu-
ties searched the train and found nine Negro boys, one white boy, and
two young white girls dressed as boys. After the youths had been loaded
onto a truck, one of the girls told a deputy sheriff that the nine boys
had raped the girls. They were all taken to nearby Scottsboro. Afraid
of a lynching, the sheriff called the governor, who dispatched National
Guard troops to protect the prisoners. They pleaded not guilty but were
indicted by a grand jury. As Dan T. Carter wrote about the case, "The
nine Negro boys had already been tried, found guilty, and sentenced to
death by the news media."[20] Though the testimony during the trials was
characterized by contradictions and inconsistencies, eight of the boys
were sentenced to death—though never executed. (Only in 1976 did the
governor of Alabama pardon the last Scottsboro survivor.) The ILD immediately sent a telegram to the judge, and the Central Committee of the
CPUSA released a statement charging that the case was a legal lynching
staged by the "Southern ruling class" in order to split the working classes.
The ILD then took charge of the defense in what was to become the first
change of sides in a tug-of-war involving the boys, their parents, the ILD,
the NAACP, and many lawyers. At stake were not only justice and the fate
of the boys but also national and international publicity. The CPUSA used
the case to attract attention, raise money, recruit Negro members and
sympathizers, and discredit Negro reformers. The NAACP was a particular target; its leaders were called traitors and betrayers of the Negro race
and were even accused of collaborating with southern lynchers.

Artists immediately responded to the publicity generated by the Scottsboro case. In addition to numerous drawings and cartoons executed for various publications, artists created works in a variety of media. Philip Guston did several drawings that alluded to lynching. *Conspirators* (Whitney Museum of American Art, which dates it c. 1930) (fig. 2) is in Guston's strange and somewhat surreal style of the 1930s. Like Giorgio de Chirico, Guston uses a perspective grid, invented in the Renaissance for the measuring and ordering of space, to suggest the contrast between rationality and irrationality or between objective and subjective realities. The drawing shows hooded Klansmen silhouetted against a diagonal wall surmounted by masonry shapes that suggest human figures. A large figure in the foreground seems to meditate on a rope he is holding; the rope drapes over blocks that probably represent simplified shapes of the states of Mississippi and Louisiana. The figures behind are grouped in front of a tree from which hangs a nude African American man; a cross with a white figure attached to it is placed diagonally in the background. The reference to Christ's crucifixion is not unusual. It makes the point, common in the literature on lynching, that while southern lynchers professed to be followers of Jesus Christ, who was condemned under Roman law to the slow and painful death of a criminal, they inflicted slow and torturous deaths on Negroes.

Aaron Douglas painted a mural on the first federal art project that included a reference to lynching. The series, *Aspects of Negro Life,* was painted in 1934 on the Public Works of Art Project for the Countee Cullen Branch of the New York Public Library in Harlem. The series, a tribute to the resilience and continuity of African American culture in America, is a quintessential work of the Harlem Renaissance, stressing African roots and incorporating African decorative motifs. Its figures silhouetted against a series of circles and diagonal rays of light, the painting is also stylistically typical of the artist's Harlem Renaissance works. Douglas wrote a caption for the panel: "*An Idyll of the Deep South* portrays Negroes toiling in the fields, singing and dancing in a lighter mood, and mourning as they prepare to take away a man who has been lynched."[21] The reference to lynching, though startling when the viewer discovers it, is visually a very small part of the composition—the pair of feet and a rope dangling from a tree in the upper left.

The new atmosphere of hope and confidence that President Roosevelt himself and the New Deal initiatives inspired was undoubtedly important to the NAACP's decision again to seek federal anti-lynching legislation. In late 1933 Walter White resolved to commit himself to another time-consuming campaign that would last throughout the 1930s. With the aid of two Columbia University Law School professors, the NAACP drafted new legislation. It provided for fines or jail for any official

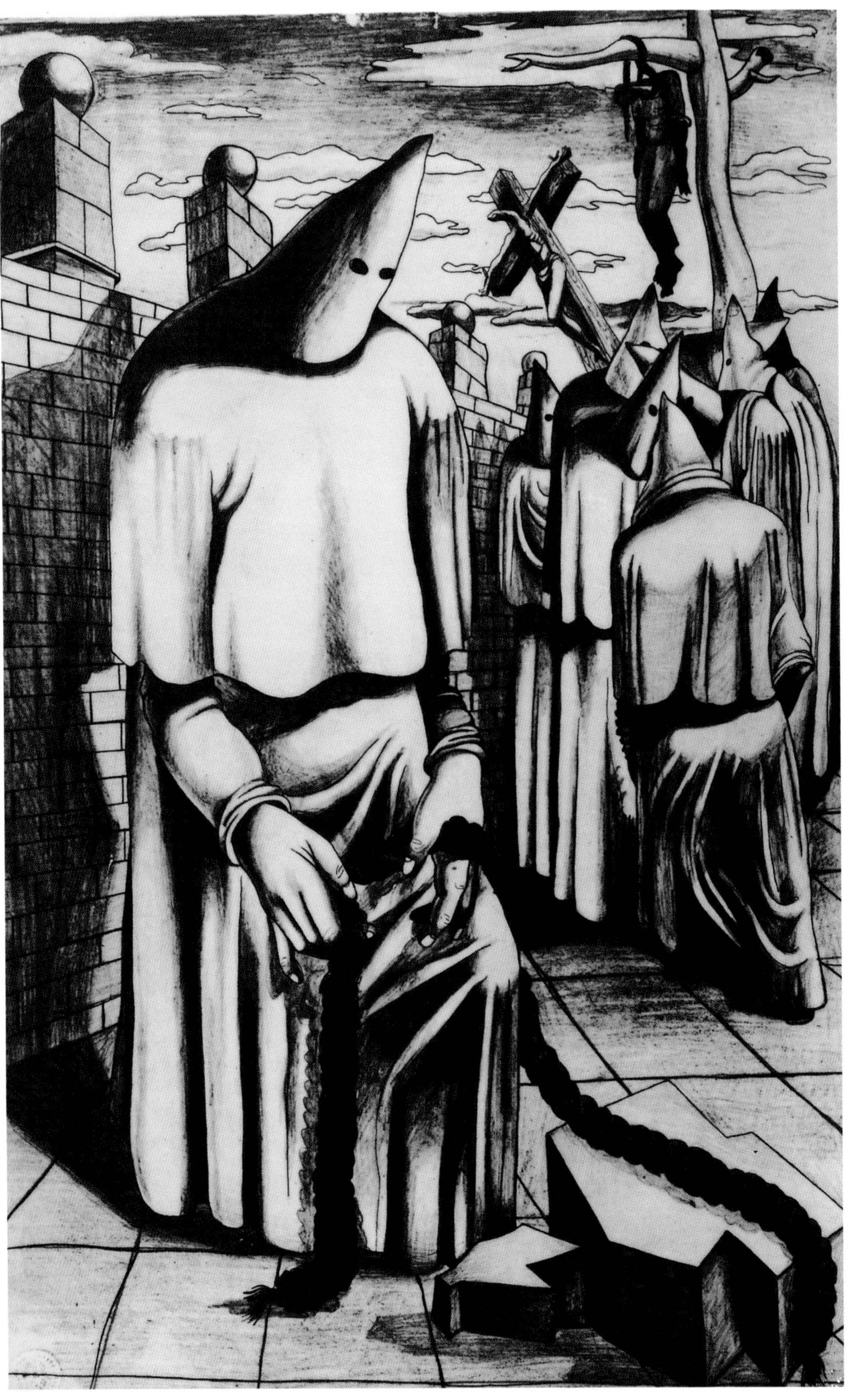

who failed to protect prisoners adequately; fines on the community to be paid to dependents of the victim; and, after thirty days without state prosecution of lynchers, a trial in a federal court under the appropriate state laws. Because of the constitutional objections raised by the Dyer bill, it did not stipulate prosecution of mob members under federal law. Edward P. Costigan (D-Col.) presented the bill in the House and Robert F. Wagner (D-N.Y.) sponsored it in the Senate. It did not pass in 1934 or 1935, but White lobbied hard, and with Mrs. Roosevelt's help met twice with the president, who, though charming and sympathetic, declined to endorse any anti-lynching bill. As Zangrando concluded, "No less than in the days of the Dyer bill, the Costigan-Wagner measure and its later counterparts suffered from southern intransigence and from the higher priorities that national leaders accorded to other aspects of America's domestic and foreign policies."[22]

In the midst of the tug-of-war over the Scottsboro case and all the lobbying for the Costigan-Wagner bill, White began collecting lynching images for the NAACP offices, and then decided to have an exhibition. He wrote to Gertrude Vanderbilt Whitney, founder of the Whitney Museum of American Art, for advice and enclosed a copy of the investigation of the recent lynching in Marianna, Florida. White noted, "even a morbid subject can be made popular if a sufficiently distinguished list of patronesses will sponsor the exhibit and the right kind of publicity can be secured for it." He added, "I fear that I have put this somewhat crudely and inadequately but I trust that you will be able to understand how I am trying delicately to effect a union of art and propaganda."[23]

Working furiously on the exhibition, he wrote to many artists requesting the loan of lynching images or asking them to do one or more for the show. His letters show that he was concerned with the quality as well as the propaganda value of the art. In December 1934 and January 1935 he sent out dozens of letters to artists: cartoonists, Mexican muralists, older artists from the Ash Can School, somewhat younger Regionalists, African American artists associated with the Harlem Renaissance and others, artists with strong political leanings, including radical artists, very young artists who received their first recognition on the first federal art project, and others who are more difficult to categorize. By mid-January he had ten of the forty-nine works in his office.[24]

Besides the speed with which he had to work and the refusal of artists he invited to participate, White had other difficulties. For publicity purposes he wanted the show to be held in the most prestigious gallery possible. It was announced that the exhibit would open on 16 February at the Jacques Seligmann Galleries on Fifty-first Street, and the works were assembled there. At the last minute, Seligmann refused to hang the

show. In an article in the *New York Times* on 12 February he was quoted
as saying, "I took over the show merely on its artistic merit. Some of the
exhibiting artists are well known. However, I was faced with an outburst
of opposition. Since I wish to keep the galleries free of political or racial
manifestations, I thought it better to cancel the show."[25] The *New York
Amsterdam News* was not so reticent in its account of the cancellation:
"The Amsterdam News has learned that the League of Struggle for
Negro Rights and the John Reed Club, Communist Party affiliates, had
protested against the proposed exhibition several weeks ago." Then the
article went right to the heart of the matter: "The Communist groups ...
had charged that the association [NAACP] was using the exhibition to
assist in the passage of the Costigan-Wagner Anti-Lynching Bill, a measure which the Communist Party is opposing. The L.S.N.R. and the John
Reed Club announced an exhibition of their own."[26] Five artists managed
to ignore the antagonism between the John Reed Club and the NAACP and
sent work first to one and then to the other exhibit.

"An Art Commentary on Lynching" opened at the Arthur U. Newton
Galleries at 11 E. 57th Street on 15 February and ran through 2 March
1935. For something put together, at least by today's standards, in great
haste, the results were impressive. Winston Burdett of the Brooklyn
Daily Eagle, who reviewed the show on opening day, summarized the
exhibition: "It includes sentimental glorifications of the martyred Negro,
symbolic analogies between the Negro and Christ, scenes of lustrid-
den mobs at lynching parties and a number of cartoons. The pictures
are particularly good when they satirize less the act of lynching than
the state of mind which makes it possible." The reviewer then praised
California Points with Pride, which satirized Governor Rolph, who had
condoned a double lynching. The cartoon, by Edmund Duffy, had won
a Pulitzer Prize in 1933 and was in the collection of Columbia University. He also praised the satirical drawing by Reginald Marsh, "This Is
Her First Lynching," which showed "a frightened and fascinated girl of
about 8 hoisted up by her mother above the heads of the mob to get a
better view of the gala proceedings."[27] (The drawing had recently occupied a full page in the *New Yorker.*) But he found fault with the scenes
of lynchings. "Perhaps the most disappointing aspect of Mr. Newton's
show is that the actual lynching scenes are the least successful. There
are dramatic and striking compositions, but as propaganda they are
rather innocuous." He thought they should have the gruesomeness of
Goya, and that the artists had failed because "the painters were more
preoccupied with problems of space and coloring than they were with
social issues."[28]

Art News, although it recognized the prominent artists, gave the
most negative assessment:

> Art and propaganda have never to our memory been more unfortu-
> nately wedded than in the group show. ... For although the works of
> many talented artists are to be found, a strong atmosphere of sen-
> sationalism is the prevailing note. ... To make matters worse, the
> current trend towards rather tortured forms finds unrepressed out-
> let in the macabre possibilities of dark bodies twisted in the knotty
> agonies of death. ... Noguchi's sculpture ... unfortunately dominates
> the exhibition. But this pendant mass of silvered realism is only a
> macabre commentary, closely approaching the bizarre. Among the
> few works which seemed to have a certain convincing integrity of
> concept and feeling were Paul Cadmus "On the Way to the Lynch-
> ing," the very simple sculpture by Samuel Becker and Julius Bloch's
> "Lynching."[29]

Paul Cadmus's drawing, *On the Way to the Lynching* of 1935 (Whitney Museum of American Art), has all the overcrowded and raw energy
of his work of the period and a very menacing use of black and white.
The title alludes to the crucifixion, as if this were a station of the cross.
Three writhing men and a horse surround the bound figure of a nude
Negro man whose body falls diagonally toward the lower right corner of
the picture. The foreground and background figures seem intertwined
in a maelstrom of malevolent energy. As in baroque paintings, the forms
seem to project toward the viewer, the blood, the wide-open tooth-filled
mouths dramatizing the violence and even sadism of the scene. There is
no correspondence to indicate that White thought it overdone.

Apparently what the *Art News* critic wanted was a stark, emotionally powerful style to convey the significance of the subject, but found
instead cool, calculated, sensational, or macabre works. The pieces mentioned positively were the most simple and direct ones, which, in the
absence of great works, the critic preferred.

Noguchi's *Death* (1934) (fig. 3), which the *Art News* critic found most
objectionable, was the piece that the critic from *Parnassus,* the publication of the College Art Association, praised most highly. Noguchi had
sent the piece to his solo exhibition at the Marie Harriman Gallery but
obliged Walter White by moving it to the lynching show. The critic
selected it from among all his works to praise: "Noguchi is versatile not
only as to medium but also as to idea. He has dared ... to portray a lynching! ... If there is anything to make a white man feel squirmy about
his color, he has it in this gnarled chromium victim jigging under the
wind-swayed rope."[30] In fact Noguchi, like the Mexican artists José Clemente Orozco and Diego Rivera, based his image on the photograph of
the burned body of George Hughes, lynched by a mob in 1930 in Sher-
man, Texas. The photograph had been reproduced in the *Labor Defender,*

and White had sent Noguchi a copy.[31] (Berenice Abbott's photograph
of Noguchi's sculpture, reproduced here, shows the original installation
and not the more familiar wooden frame.) Noguchi rendered the posture
accurately, not only the tightening of the limbs but their knotted forms,
only changing the charred flesh to a flawless reflective metal. Orozco
lent his lithograph *Negroes* or *Negros ahorcados* (1930) (fig. 4) to both
exhibitions, but it did not attract the attention that Noguchi's sculpture
did. Orozco makes the image hellish by multiplying the hanging figures
and emphasizing the leaping flames. Only the central figure betrays its
origin in the photograph. The flattened forms seem sexless, castrated or
removed to another world.[32] (Rivera's portable fresco panel of 1933 for
the New Workers School was in neither exhibition.)

The review in New York's *Amsterdam News,* a Negro newspaper, was
very different—approving, stronger, and satirical—because the reviewer
understood the references to actual lynchings but was also moved by
symbolic images. It began: "If you've never seen a lynching, by all means
pay a visit to the Arthur U. Newton Galleries. ... There is displayed the
disgrace of so-called Western civilization in all its depraved glory and
stark realism." The reviewer listed the well-known white artists but then
turned to the generally neglected African American artists. He selected
E. Simms Campbell's *I Passed Along This Way* as one of the most striking
pieces. "It depicts a figure of Christ shouldering a huge cross, while walking beside him is a Negro who is being pulled along by a rope around his
neck. This particular piece is powerful both in thought and handling."
His second choice was the etchings by Henry Bannarn, "a young artist
from Minneapolis, who is now studying art in New York." He then mentioned a watercolor by Samuel Brown "that caused so much excitement
recently because of its unusual treatment. It presents an exaggerated
bird's-eye view of a Negro being lynched."[33]

Samuel Brown's watercolor was done in 1934 on the Public Works
of Art Project in Philadelphia. A reviewer for the *Interracial Review*
wrote, "its effect of terror [is achieved] by putting the observer, as it
were, on top of the gallows looking down upon first the victim and then
the crowd. By means of foreshortenings the terrible scene from rope to
ground is all displayed below us."[34] The spatial exaggeration and the cartoon-like distortion, which verge on caricature, are shocking in the way
they force the viewer to confront the reality of lynching. The reviewer
continued by remarking on Allan Freelon's "'Barbecue—American Style'
[which] shows the distorted figure of a Negro burning at the stake, while
a crowd of whites, including children, are looking on." Freelon wrote
to White, "I have not attempted to portray any particular lynching, but
merely to record the horror of what has come to be a major sports event,
with radio announcements and invitations in advance. I have shown

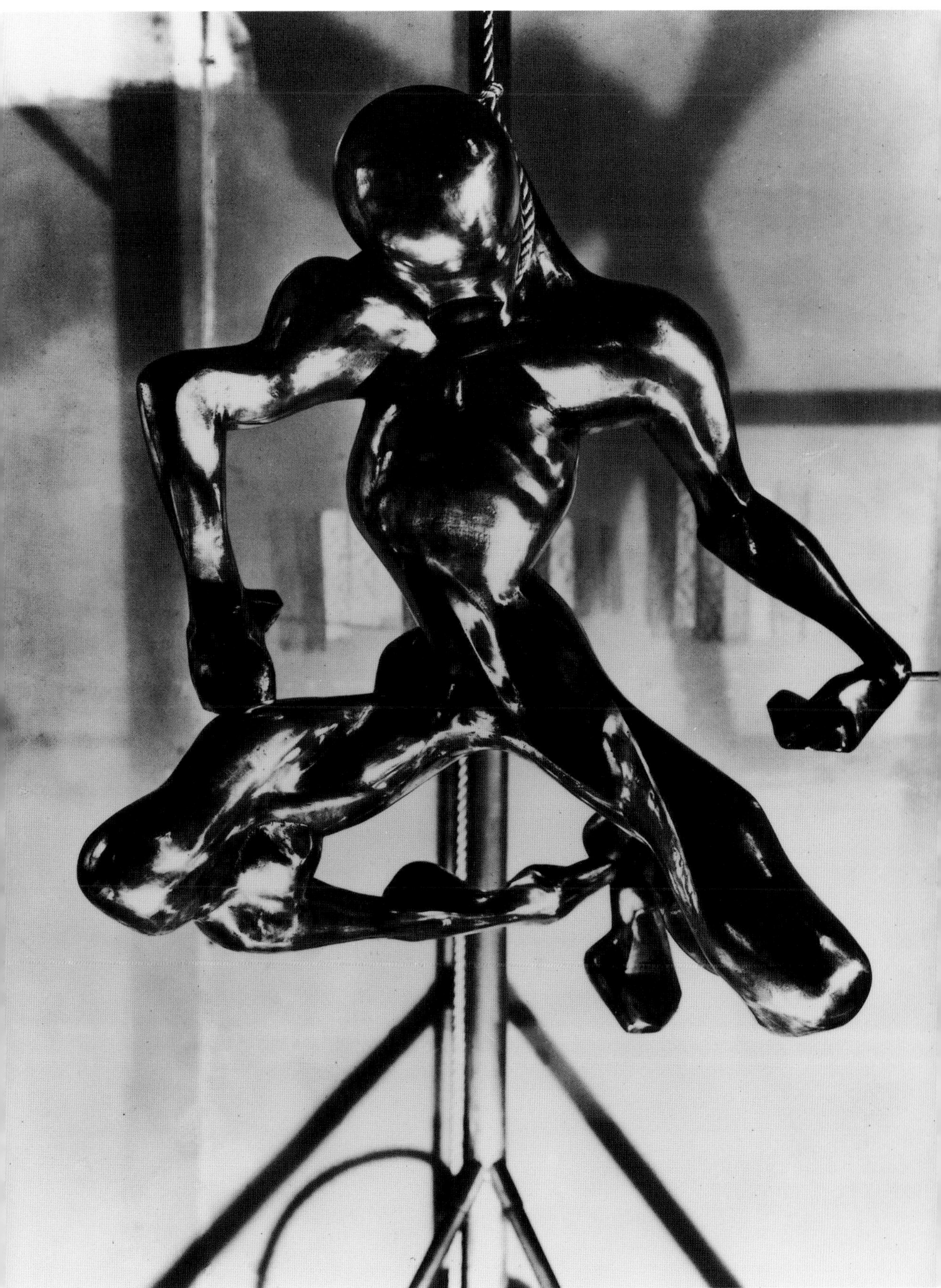

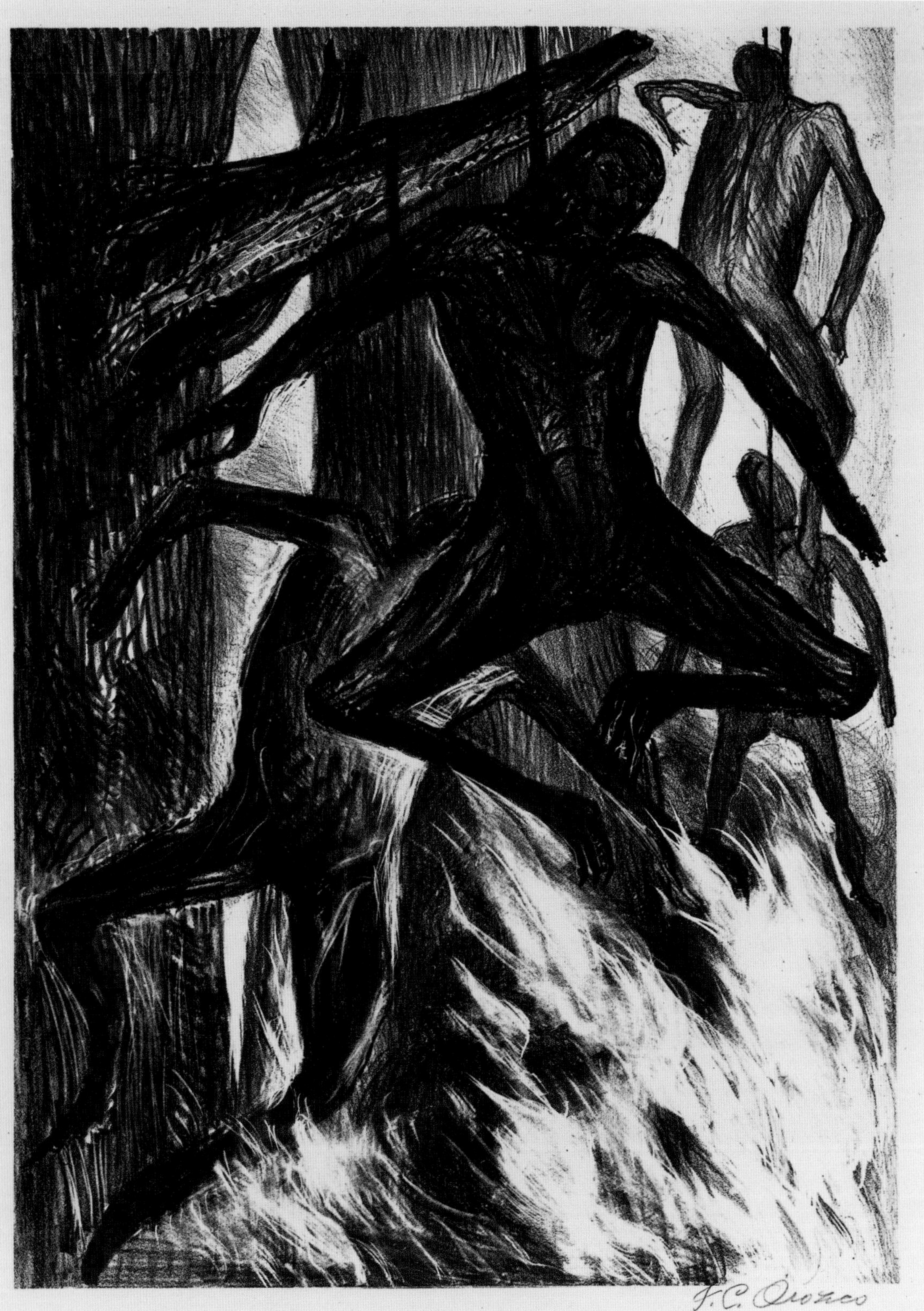

only the feet of the crowd, but by means of this I have expressed their emotions ranging from indifference to squirming discomfort (the feet of the small boy). I have taken that moment when the victim first feels the flames begin to lick at his body."[35]

The *Amsterdam News* reviewer concluded that "Most of the pictures show horrible examples of lynchings and the Negro is in most instances the mob victim." As an example he cited Harry Sternberg's *Southern Holiday,* which "presented one Negro mob victim tied to a post completely deprived of genital organs by a frenzied mob,"[36] as had been the case in the recent lynching of Claude Neal in Florida.

Harry Sternberg sent work to both exhibitions. White had seen Sternberg's tempera painting *Southern Holiday* at the Whitney biennial and wrote to the artist. Sternberg replied that he would send one or two lithographs to the show, one of which was also entitled *Southern Holiday.* The print shows a castrated figure bound to a ruined pillar, broken off at the top and revealing the brick beneath the stone facing. There is a second pillar to the left. Beyond the fields is an industrial landscape whose many phallic forms, in addition to that of the pillars, dramatize the castration. There is the suggestion that industrialization bears some burden of guilt. Andrew Hemingway has also noted that the pillars symbolize a decaying and decadent social order that could give rise to such barbarism.[37] Sternberg recalled, "I was filled with anger and shame as I worked on this stone and evidently transmitted these emotions through the finished print."[38]

The *Crisis,* the NAACP's magazine, devoted three columns to the exhibition and reproduced E. Simms Campbell's *I Passed Along This Way* as a frontispiece, William Mosby's wood carving *Dixie Holiday,* and Thomas Hart Benton's *A Lynching.* Benton's oil was the largest canvas in the show. Benton used his twisting forms to represent a group of white men hastily hanging and burning a contorted figure, which may also be based on the photograph of Hughes.[39] The *Crisis* reviewer took a factual approach, saying that more than three thousand people had seen the show and listing the artists and the visitors from other cities and abroad. The writer noted, perhaps with satisfaction, "The cancellation of the show by the Seligmann Galleries and the attendant publicity served only to increase the number of visitors to the show when it finally opened." Rather than make a judgment about the exhibit, the writer quoted the *New York World-Telegram* critic: "This exhibition may do much to crystallize public opinion. In it are fifty-odd paintings, sculptures, prints, drawings and cartoons depicting the horrors of the practice. It is an exhibition which tears the heart and chills the blood. Remember, this is not an exhibition for softies. It may upset your stomach. If it upsets your complacency on the subject it will have been successful."[40] Apparently the *Crisis* preferred to express its partisanship in someone else's words, but the quotation also suggests that the writer was most interested, understandably, in the political impact of the exhibition.

Another well-known Regionalist, John Steuart Curry, exhibited three works, the painting *Manhunt* (1931) from the collection of Arthur B. Spingarn, and both the painting *The Fugitive* (1933–40) and a lithograph, also entitled *The Fugitive* (fig. 5) of 1935. The painting shows mounted and armed men led by a bloodhound setting off on a chase, while the lithograph shows a large man hiding in a tree in the foreground and the "posse" going by, a vignette in the dense background. Peter A. Juley's photograph of the painting best reveals the artist's sensibility. Curry's swirling brushstrokes contribute to the sense of the relentless momentum of the hunters, but the rhythm of the flitting butterflies in the lower right counters that movement. The similarity of the hunted man's figure to the tree trunk also gives the viewer a sense of natural strength that will triumph. The visual image of *The Fugitive* is close to that in Langston Hughes's poem "Flight," first published in 1930, conveying the terror and isolation of the hunted:

> Plant your toes in the cool swamp mud;
> Step and leave no track.
> Hurry, sweating runner!
> The hounds are at your back.
>
> No I didn't touch her.
> White flesh ain't for me.
>
> Hurry! Black boy, hurry!
> Or they'll swing you to a tree![41]

Several artists did works especially for the exhibit. Wilmer Jennings's linocut, *At The End of the Rope* (1935) (fig. 6), provides a quiet contrast to the violent scenes. (The damaged print is missing two corners.) An oval head seems to lie peacefully in a jungle setting until, suddenly, the viewer recognizes the rope. The metaphor of a tree of death rather than life found its best-known expression in Billie Holliday's song *Strange Fruit,* based on lyrics of 1936 by Lewis Allan.

> Southern trees bear a strange fruit,
> Blood on the leaves and blood at the root,
> Black body swinging in the Southern breeze,
> Strange fruit hanging from the poplar trees.
> . . . .
> Here is a fruit for the crows to pluck,

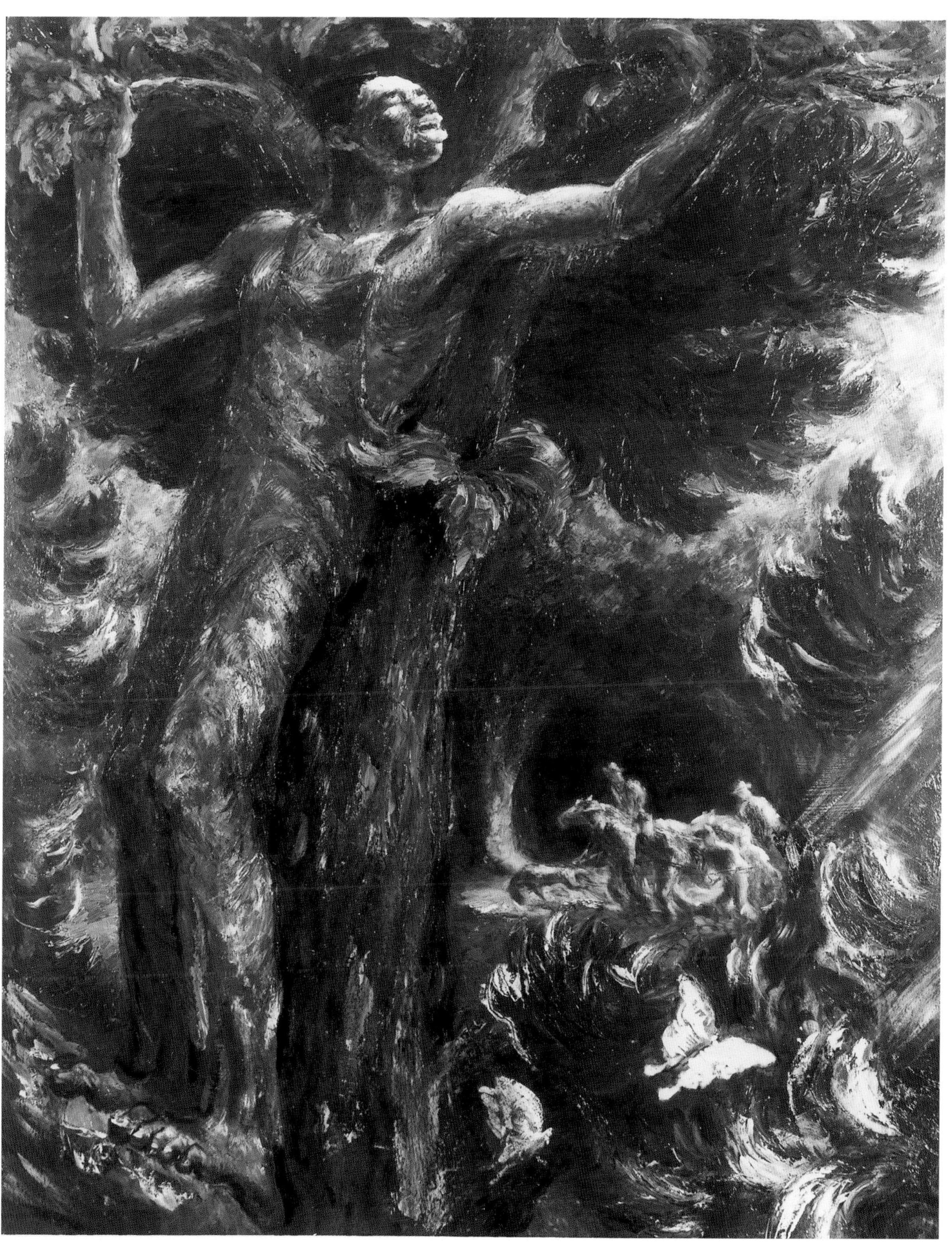

For the rain to gather, for the wind to suck,
For the sun to rot, for a tree to drop,
Here is a strange and bitter crop.[42]

Jennings studied with Hale Woodruff at Morehouse College in
Atlanta. Woodruff, who recalled in an interview that Walter White
"helped make it possible for me to go to Europe to study,"[43] exhibited
two linocuts, *Giddap* and *By Parties Unknown*. In the former onlookers gather to witness the driver of a wagon saying "Giddap" to start the
mule and hang the bound victim standing in the wagon. The victim has
a cross shape on his chest; the mob members are clearly rural people and

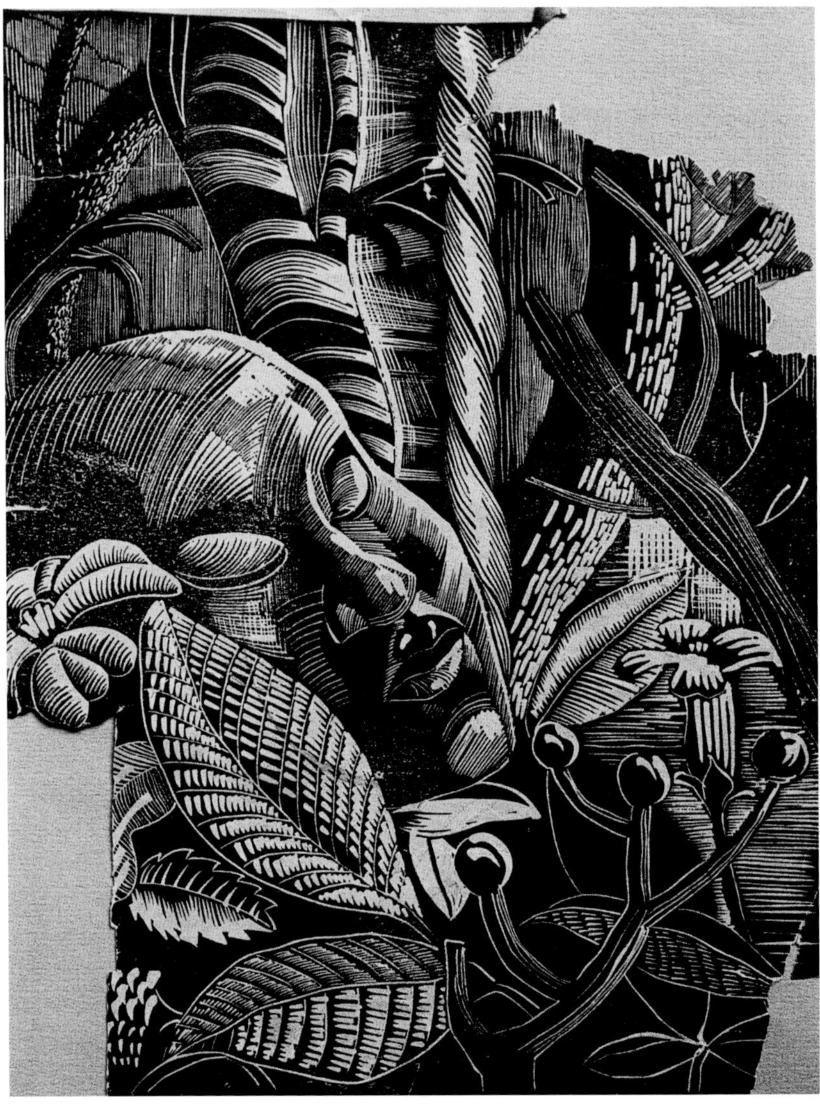

6 Wilmer Jennings, *At the End of the Rope* (1935), linocut, 8½ x 11 in. Courtesy of the Kenkeleba Gallery, New York.

include a young girl who urges on the driver. The other print shows the body of a lynched victim on the steps of a dilapidated frame church.[44] "By parties unknown" was the phrase commonly used when lynchers, however well known, were unidentified and unpunished. Woodruff was literally laying the blame at the doorstep of the poor southern whites who professed to be Christians.

The rival exhibition, "The Struggle for Negro Rights," occupied the ACA Gallery on West 8th Street from 3 to 16 March. It was sponsored by the John Reed Club, the Artists Union, the Artists' Committee of Action, the League of Struggle for Negro Rights (LSNR), the ILD, and the Vanguard. The exhibit opposed the NAACP and the Costigan-Wagner Act and supported another anti-lynching bill that had been sent to Congress in 1933.[45]

The ACA exhibition received far less notice than its rival. Even the Artists Union magazine, *Art Front,* failed to review the exhibition, and Stephen Alexander alone wrote a review comparing the two shows for the *New Masses.* His opening paragraph left no doubt in the reader's mind about which was superior: "If you saw the Theatre Union's production of *Stevedore* you will remember the difference between the two Negroes, Lonny Thompson and Jim Beals. Thompson is a 'bad nigger.' Bad because he won't 'take it lying down.' He fights for his social and economic rights. Jim Beals is a 'good nigger.' Bootlicking and obsequious, he is a spineless traitor to his people and his class. He would rather side with his white boss than with his black fellow-workers." Alexander quickly dismissed the NAACP show: "With a few notable exceptions (Biddle, Cadmus, Duffy, Marsh, Wheelock), there is little attempt to explain lynching or attack the forces responsible for it. Most of it is chalked up against God or human nature. Many of the works are so permeated by religious spirit as to be little more than prayers in graphic and plastic form."

In contrast, Alexander wrote, the ACA exhibit mirrored "the forthright militant character" of the Bill for Negro Rights and Suppression of Lynching. He noted that some pictures were in both shows but found two essential differences between the shows, one the absence of religious pictures, and the other "the presence of 'fighting pictures.'" Alexander then cited six pieces, including Noguchi's, that merited a reproduction, that were sufficiently powerful emotionally, in his view, to constitute anti-lynching propaganda. But he also asserted that, to be completely successful, such images must "carry the fight to a higher political level. ... in order to fight effectively against the oppression of the Negro, it is not enough merely to arouse indignation or sympathy or horror. We must also *explain* lynching graphically and plastically. We must attack the social forces responsible for lynching." Alexander ended his review by citing nine artists who, though using "various approaches," succeeded on this political level.[46]

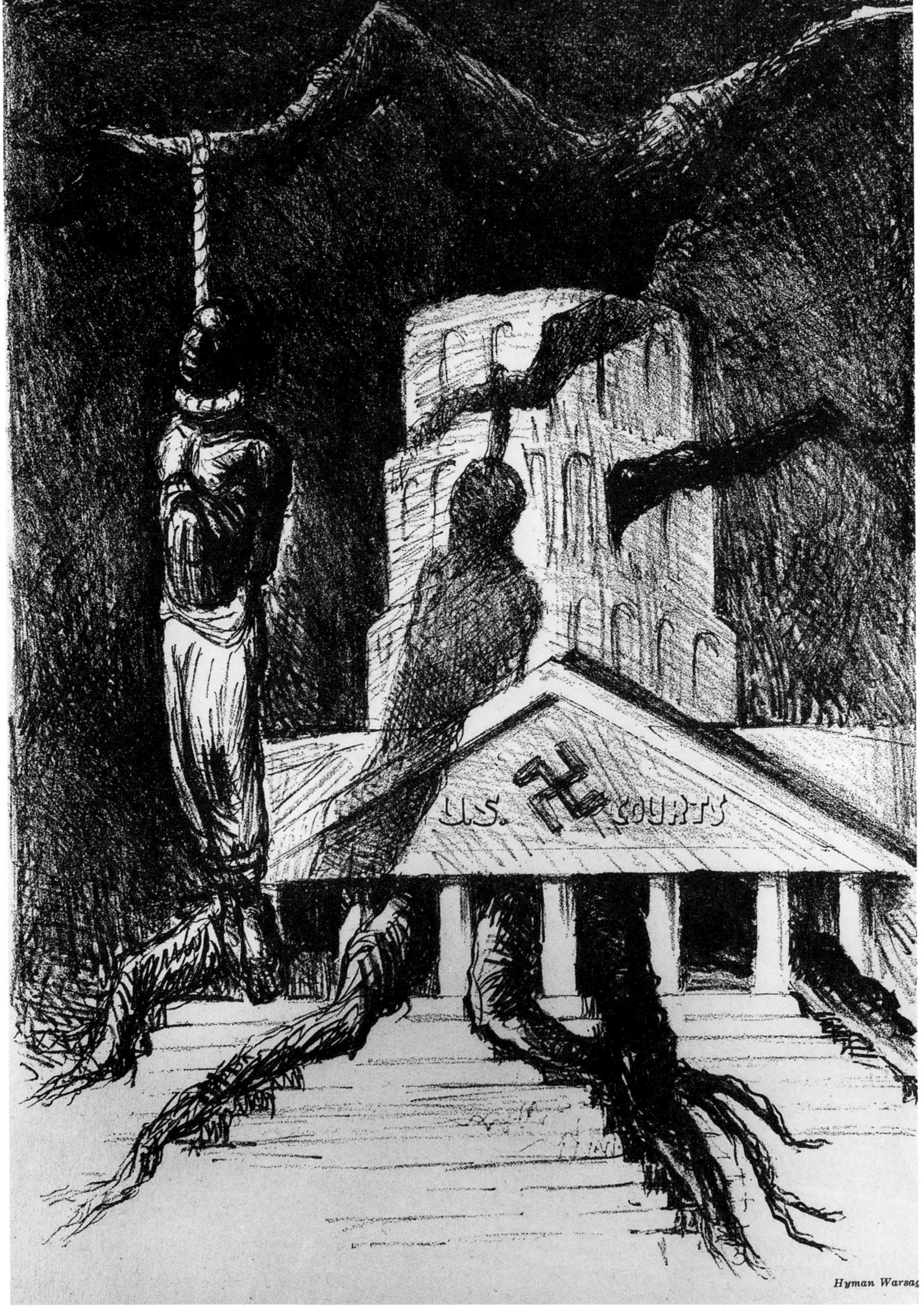

U.S. COURTS
Hyman Warsag

Although Philip Evergood was well known for his left-wing sympathies, his work was not singled out. His *That's the Man,* a drawing from 1935 (Hirshhorn Museum and Sculpture Garden, Washington, D.C.) is an interesting example of a personal style that hovers between realism and caricature to satirize the theme of "the protection of white womanhood." The large heads, lumpy bodies, and spatial ambiguities are accentuated by the eccentric but skillful quality of the draftsmanship. If one is not distracted by the peculiarities of the drawing, one sees a quite accurate scene that refers to alleged rape as a justification for lynching. In a rural landscape a tough, older blonde woman accuses a small, resigned Negro of rape. Three lawmen, one a gleeful sheriff, are about to hang the man, but the ghoulish deputy also threatens the man with a revolver. Apparently Alexander did not think it succeeded on the political level.

Alexander did mention a cartoon entitled *The Law* (fig. 7), by Hyman Warsager, reproduced in *New Masses* on 9 January 1934. The bound figure of a Negro man hangs from a tree whose roots grow through a fantastic edifice in the middle ground labeled "u.s. courts." The shadow of the figure falls ominously across the building and in the center of the pediment is a swastika. The primary meaning is that the American legal and judicial systems are fascist, mere tools of the capitalists and their bourgeois allies to control and destroy the working class and to deny civil rights to Negroes. The secondary meaning is that American racism is the same as Nazism. Warsager, like several of the John Reed Club artists, was Jewish.

After the exhibitions closed, neither the NAACP's efforts to pass an anti-lynching bill nor artists' interest in lynching images ceased, but fewer images were produced. The number of lynchings continued to decline and, as in the case of the lobbying for the Dyer bill, the publicity may have been helpful. What did change was CPUSA policy. Following the Comintern's pronouncement of the Popular Front, the CPUSA disbanded the John Reed Club in 1935, ceased its attacks on Negro reform leaders, and even joined in supporting the NAACP's anti-lynching legislation.

III LABOR AND LABOR CONFLICT

ART AND POLITICS IN THE POPULAR FRONT:
THE UNION WORK AND SOCIAL REALISM OF PHILIP EVERGOOD

Patricia Hills

Buried in the Philip Evergood papers at the Archives of American Art is a scrap of paper on which is penciled a quotation from Lenin: "Art belongs to the people, its roots should penetrate deeply into the very thick of the masses of the people. It should be comprehensible to these masses and loved by them. It should unite the emotions, thoughts and will of these masses and arouse them."[1] Another handwritten note quotes a fragment of a 1937 letter written by Dr. Norman Bethune, the famous Canadian surgeon who developed surgical techniques on the frontlines of Mao Zedong's army in the late 1930s and became in the process a dedicated communist. Bethune expresses sentiments that clearly resonated with Evergood's own deeply felt beliefs. In Bethune's view, the artist had a social mission: "The function of the artist is to disturb. His duty is to arouse the sleepers, to shake the complacent pillars of the world. He reminds the world of its dark ancestry, shows the world its present, and points the way to its new birth. ... In a world terrified of change, he preaches revolution—the principle of life. He is an agitator, a disturber of the peace—quick, impatient, positive, restless and disquieting.

I want to thank the John Simon Guggenheim Memorial Foundation and the Charles Warren Center of Harvard University for their support in 1982–83, when I made a year-long study of socially concerned American artists. I used much of that research in "The Socially Concerned Painters of the 1930s: An Introduction," an essay for the exhibition catalog *Social Concern and Urban Realism: American Painting of the 1930s,* which I organized for the Bread and Roses Cultural Project of the National Union of Hospital and Health Care Employees and which was published by the Boston University Art Gallery.

For the present essay I want to thank Stephanie Taylor for research help and Judy Throm of the Archives of American Art. Alan Wallach offered useful suggestions, and Kevin Whitfield read many drafts of the manuscript with a critical eye.

He is the creative spirit working in the soul of man."[2] The Evergood
Papers contain a number of such scraps with undated notations and
quotations. These saved bits of other people's words had talismanic
power to inspire Evergood's own art. Indeed, the stylistic qualities of his
painting—eccentric line, distortions of perspective and anatomy, garish
color—effectively expressed the revolutionary's aim to arouse and disturb. With Evergood, style and content were to fuse into a visually vivid,
but very personal, social realism.

Evergood, like many other artists of the time, embraced the politics
of the left, which encouraged an art uniting the "emotions, thoughts and
will" of the working classes. Like others, he was sympathetic to radical
social change and gravitated to the Communist Party of the United States
of America (CPUSA), which had grown in popularity and influence during
the Depression years.[3] Once within the orbit of the movement, Evergood
negotiated his way through the changes of party policy and strategy, from
the revolutionary phase (before 1935) to the Popular Front phase (after
1935), a development with its own ambivalences and contradictions.
Thus we find that the radicalism in his art surges and subsides, like the
radicalism of other movement artists and like the party's line itself.

The CPUSA in the 1930s

As a consequence of their association with the Communist Party,
Evergood and his artist friends became imbued with a worldview
that embraced the radical theories and ideas of the time, particularly
Marxism, and became involved themselves with political action on
working-class issues.[4] But communist theories and actions could not
have taken such hold if the artists themselves had not had personal
experiences of the Depression. To Evergood and artist friends such as
Raphael Soyer, William Gropper, Nicholai Cikovsky, and others, the collective character of their social experiences became a prime source of
subject matter. Participation in party discussions and union activities
helped them to gain focus. They chose to create a socially concerned art
not because of any explicit directives from the party but because they
wanted to express through art their genuine engagement with political issues.[5] Comrades within the art world, including dealers and critics,
encouraged them, and internationally known left-wing artists such as
Diego Rivera, David Siqueiros, José Clemente Orozco, Fernand Léger, and
Pablo Picasso served as role models.[6]

During the 1930s the CPUSA changed its political course, following
the lead of the Comintern. The Soviet Union, recognizing the strength
of the fascist onslaught, changed its international strategy. It suspended

its support of local communist revolutions and adopted the policy of building a mass movement of progressive organizations in all countries in order to confront the spread of fascism. The strategy, which became known as the Popular Front, was laid out in August 1935 at the Seventh World Congress of the Communist International, when the Communist Party of the Soviet Union and its international allies, including the CPUSA, met in Kharkov, Ukraine.[7]

A thumbnail sketch of the party might summarize its two main phases as follows: In the first phase, in the early 1930s, the CPUSA was a revolutionary party, unwilling to make alliances with the liberal leadership of other progressive organizations and expressing itself in the rhetoric of confrontational class struggle. In the second phase, as a consequence of the Popular Front line, party members and their friends disbanded those organizations deemed narrowly sectarian, such as the John Reed Clubs and the Film and Photo League, and shifted to a rhetoric of conciliation and reform. Lawrence Schwartz points out in *Marxism and Culture* that when the party gave up its independent revolutionary politics for the sake of a united front, "The politics of the popular front then [became] union organizing, anti-fascist organization building, and the agitation for the immediate relief of depression ills. The basic tactic tied to the strategy ... was the creation and building of *unions*."[8] Indeed, 1935 became a busy year for communists assigned to building mass organizations and unions.

Marxism stresses the importance of practice; artists in the party were called on to work with party leaders to develop and implement the party's plans. To the party, *organizational* practice was of primary importance, but *rhetorical* practice (what the artists said) also mattered. *Artistic* practice (what artists painted or sculpted) was less significant, as long as artists made art that appealed to the masses.[9] These practices, as they affected Communist Party members and their friends, provide the background for Evergood's own need to produce a personal and revolutionary art.

Organizational Practice

The largest organizations in which communist movement artists exerted influence at the beginning of the Popular Front period were the American Artists' Congress (AAC) and the Artists Union (AU).[10] The AAC, like the American Writers' Congress, was initiated by party members in the summer of 1935 to replace the sectarian John Reed Clubs. In order to achieve a broad appeal among nationally known and influential artists and writers, the AAC limited its membership to professional artists who had undergone training and who had exhibited, unlike the John Reed Clubs, which had encouraged and embraced politically earnest amateurs. Moreover, most of the officers of the AAC were reputedly not party members.[11] Thus, at its first convention in February 1936, many members of the national executive committee and many speakers were simply left-leaning liberals, such as Lewis Mumford, Alexander Brook, and Paul Manship.

The Artists Union had a history of involvement with communist movement artists long before the Popular Front. In September 1933 a group of twenty-five artists, then working for the government's Emergency Work Bureau, met to discuss the consequences of the discontinuance of the bureau. One of the artists was Bernarda Bryson, who had helped organize the Unemployed Councils for the Communists. Calling themselves the EWB Artists Group, they soon changed their name to the Unemployed Artists Group. In December they petitioned relief administrator Harry L. Hopkins for relief work for all unemployed artists, to include teaching, mural painting, easel painting, and commercial art jobs.[12] Their petition declared, "The State can eliminate once and for all the unfortunate dependence of American artists upon the caprice of private patronage."[13] This statement is typical of the rhetoric of the CPUSA in the early 1930s. But the petition worked, for in December Hopkins set up the Public Works of Art Project, with Julianna Force, director of the Whitney Museum of American Art, administering the program.[14] Since the Unemployed Artists Group was now representing both employed and unemployed artists, it no doubt seemed appropriate to drop "unemployed" and call the group the Artists Union.[15]

When the government set up the Federal Art Project (FAP) in August 1935, under the administration of the Works Progress Administration (WPA), and put artists on the payroll, the recently employed artists began to swell the ranks of the Artists Union.[16] This coincided with the Popular Front strategy that urged CP members and their friends to become actively involved in unions. By the summer of 1935 the Artists Union was seeking to affiliate with the American Federation of Labor, which at that time was the only large, viable union organization, and one that would give the artists economic clout as well as official visibility. The artists, moreover, did not want the public to view them as an elite group. They had heard that the government planned to cut the wages of workers on other relief programs in order to finance the cultural workers being hired, and they did not want a backlash from those workers.[17] Worker solidarity was, of course, a primary principle of communist organization.

Talks dragged on as the conservative AFL hesitated to take on the artists. The AFL did, however, grant a charter to the Commercial Artists and Designers Union (CADU)—many members of which also belonged to the Artists Union. By 1937, however, the Congress of Industrial Organi-

zations (CIO) was emerging to challenge the AFL. The CIO was especially
receptive to radicals, such as the artists, since many in the CIO leadership,
as well as the rank and file, were communists seeking to boost membership with workers from all walks of life.[18] While still keeping the door
open to the AFL, the Artists Union began talking in earnest with the CIO
during the fall of 1937.[19] Since Evergood had assumed the presidency
of the New York Artists Union in September 1937, he was involved in
working out the affiliation. In January 1938 a charter was drawn up, and
the Artists Union became the United American Artists, Local 60 of the
United Office and Professional Workers of America (UOPWA), itself a CIO
affiliate. Thus Evergood and his friends successfully followed the party
line in their union work—by pushing for reform rather than taking a
revolutionary stand.[20]

Apart from unions, communist movement artists helped to organize many other organizations that brought people together to raise
consciousness—not to discuss capitalism and its effects but to focus on
the victims and other manifestations of fascism.[21] For example, when
the Spanish Civil War broke out in 1936, artists rallied to the Republican
cause. In October 1936 members of the AAC contributed art to an exhibition and benefit entitled "To Aid Democracy in Spain," held at the ACA
Gallery, which raised about $700 for the People's Front in Spain. Another
organization was the American League Against War and Fascism.[22]

Ad hoc demonstrations served to bring people into the orbit of the
party. On 1 December 1936 the Artists Union organized a sit-down strike
at FAP headquarters in New York to protest cutbacks in the WPA. Some
219 people were arrested.[23] On 9 January 1937 a massive protest demonstration in New York was followed by a march on Washington six days
later. The following August a National Job March was held in Washington. Evergood participated in all of these demonstrations.[24]

Rhetorical Practice

The rhetoric of party members during the Popular Front period generally
suppressed references to socialism or revolution.[25] The earlier John Reed
Club, in contrast, had always made reference to revolutionary art; for
example, when the JRC held an exhibition in December 1933, the accompanying checklist stated its expectations of the artist: "He is on one side
or the other of the historic class struggle. The John Reed Club Gallery
shows and encourages artists who take the side of the revolutionary
working class in its fight against hunger, fascism and war."[26]

An example of movement rhetoric that bridges the two periods was
the foreword to the catalog of a John Reed Club–sponsored exhibition on

the theme of lynching, held in April 1935 at the ACA Gallery. Written by Angelo Herndon, a communist, the essay, entitled "Pictures Can Fight," read in part:

> [T]he pictures in the A.C.A. Gallery—they FIGHT! They fight the Scottsboro frame-up and the Klan and the chain-gang. They fight the Negro and white misleaders, who say we can make everything come right by going to the Big Boss.
>
> But the real truth is that we can only stop lynching by STRUGGLE— by mass organization of white and Negro workers, by mass defense, by mass pressure for a real fighting anti-lynching bill like the Bill for Negro Rights and the Suppression of Lynching.[27]

Although the essay sounds the rhetoric of revolutionary agitation, it ends by calling for support of government action. The shift to advocacy of progressive legislation characterizes the Popular Front strategy.

Not surprisingly, the phrase "revolutionary working class" was not in evidence when artists and writers delivered papers at the AAC conference held in February 1936. As art historians Matthew Baigell and Julia Williams have observed in their introduction to a reprint of the AAC papers: "An overarching Popular Front theme was the great necessity of presenting a united face to the world. Reading these papers one is struck by how carefully areas of possible disagreement among artists are avoided. Over and over again issues that might have caused discord were skirted or glossed over quickly."[28] In other words, ideological struggle was avoided. The reformist agenda behind many of the papers was support for a united front in the fight against fascism.

But rhetorical practice during the Popular Front period did not stifle entirely the call to revolution. In fact, a review of leftist literature shows that in the years immediately after 1935 the concept of revolutionary art matured in America, at least among independent leftists. Louis Lozowick, although not a social realist as a visual artist, was a committed Marxist and early theorist. He wrote "Towards a Revolutionary Art" for the July–August 1936 issue of *Art Front,* and the essay advanced a sharp definition of revolutionary art in the context of working-class struggles. This was a full year after the Popular Front policies that downplayed revolutionary rhetoric had been initiated. Lozowick wrote:

> In all parts of the world there are signs of incipient and open revolt against the system. The organized working class, joined by growing numbers of intellectuals, farmers and other elements, and guided by the philosophy of Karl Marx, is the only force that can abolish it. ...
>
> When the revolutionary artist expresses in his work the dissat-

isfaction with, the revolt against, the criticism of the existing state of affairs, when he seeks to awaken in his audience a desire to participate in his fight, he is, therefore, drawing on direct observation of the world about him as well as on his most intimate, immediate, blistering, blood-sweating experience, in the art gallery, in the bread line, in the relief office. But as already indicated, experience to him is not a chance agglomeration of impressions but is related to long training, to habits formed, to views assimilated and entertained at a definite place and time; to him experience acquires a significant meaning by virtue of a revolutionary orientation.

To Lozowick, probably the most sophisticated Marxist artist of the decade, "revolutionary art ... is not due to an arbitrary order from any person or group but is decreed by history, is a consequence of particular historic events."[29] His final remarks were no doubt meant to counter the accusation that cultural commissars from the CPUSA were issuing orders via Moscow to American artists. One of the contradictions of party attitudes during the Popular Front period is that while the leaders did not overtly call for revolution, they covertly encouraged the long-range view that once fascism was defeated, the struggle against capitalist exploitation would be renewed.[30]

Artistic Practice

Actual artistic practice by communist movement artists did not necessarily follow what was expected of them in either the earlier John Reed Club period or the later Popular Front period. One writer, Martha Candler Cheney, in her book *Modern Art in America* (1939), must have had her ear tuned to the implications of the CPUSA line, when she characterized the shift.

> In the United States until 1935, dying strikers, starving children, hungry rioters, the armed force of the law represented by mounted police and machine gunners, Capital and Politics symbolized in the guise of brute force, were familiar subjects in the painting which documented the proletarian struggle for power, and which was frankly designed to incite a Communist revolution. The nationalization of relief for unemployed artists of all kinds in that year, the shift in Marxist policies of aesthetic approach, the organization meetings for the American Artists' Congress, operated together then to change the character of socially conscious art. ...
>
> Since 1935, influences in national and international life have

given it [socially conscious art] the character of New Deal art, with
Peace, Culture, and Democracy as its slogan. Although much of the
total output is shallow, materialistic, and self-assertive, there is a
spreading conviction among artists that issues both in art and in life
are extremely serious and call for a spirit of cooperation.[31]

But movement artists did not march in lockstep to the changes in
the CPUSA line as suggested by Cheney. For example, Stuart Davis and
Raphael Soyer, who otherwise participated in organizational activities,
insisted on being apolitical in their art. Davis continued working in his
abstract style of flat, brightly colored forms; Soyer, although focusing on
the subject matter of homeless men, used a naturalist style free of editorial comment. The CPUSA had neither the power nor the inclination to
coerce them.[32]

Another stock explanation for artists' modification of the political
content of their art after 1936 is that they were responding to guidelines
from government administrators. The WPA/FAP encouraged "American
Scene" paintings because such subjects were understandable to the general public.[33] But it is not the case that project artists only cranked out
pictures extolling Roosevelt, government programs, technological progress, agricultural abundance, nationalism, and the nuclear family, with
its muscular father and its nurturing mother caring for a boy and a girl.[34]
Such "New Deal art" may have been displayed in the government murals
and easel paintings turned in every six weeks to the WPA offices (a condition of employment), but movement artists made other paintings as well,
many of them on radical themes and shown in exhibitions.[35]

Evergood as a Case Study

Philip Evergood serves as a reminder that American artists, while loyal
to party decisions about organizational and rhetorical tactics, remained
fairly independent when it came to their art. His art drew consistently
on his own experiences of struggle—both in the early John Reed Club
phase and the later Popular Front period—but it also represented what
many considered a sharp critique of capitalist society. Harry Gottlieb,
himself an artist and communist organizer, wrote to Evergood in the late
1930s: "I cannot help but contrast your work with that of another comrade's recently shown at the ACA—his rather stiff and detached, yours
glowing and affirmative both in your hatred of evil forces and in your
identity of yourself with the working class. I am very much interested
in this particular question which I feel must be more and more clarified
by us as Communists."[36] By this time Evergood's style of inelegant linear

distortion and brightly colored forms had become his signature.

The beginnings of Evergood's conversion to social realism had come in 1932, when Lincoln Kirstein invited him to participate in the Museum of Modern Art's mural show. Evergood offered the curators a composition typical of his pre-1932 period, *The Angel of Peace Offering the Fruit of Knowledge to the World,* which included symbolic motifs and personifications appropriate for a universal humanist statement. By contrast, many of the other participants, among them Hugo Gellert, William Gropper, and Ben Shahn, presented controversial political subjects that would tweak the sensibilities of the museum's trustees, such as Gellert's *Last Defenses of Capitalism* and *The Triumph of Lenin* or Gropper's *Class Struggle in America Since the War.* Evergood considered this exhibition to be a key event of his life; he recalled that at this time he "began to search for expression in contemporary life and scene" and "lost interest in subjects purely drawn from the imagination."[37] As he formed friendships with communist movement artists, he began to realize the possibilities for a more socially engaged subject matter.

The ideas of these politically engaged artists prepared him to be moved by another experience, which occurred in the winter of 1932–33, the worst of the Depression. He related the incident in a lengthy interview with curator John I. H. Baur, who was preparing the 1960 retrospective of Evergood's work for the Whitney Museum. One winter night, walking down Christopher Street toward the Hudson River, Evergood saw a large city lot dotted with shacks and men warming themselves before small fires. He went over to talk to them: "They didn't seem to resent me, and I felt that they were all very cold so I went through my pockets and brought out two or three dollars and told them to go and get some gin. They bought a big bottle and all had a drink. ... We sat around the fire and talked. ... Old Foot was one, Terrapin another. They were interesting people, but their tragedy hit me between the eyes because I had never been as close to anything like that before."[38] Evergood went home to get sketching materials and returned to sketch them (fig. 1). This epiphanic moment forever changed both Evergood's worldview and his art. He later told Forrest Selvig. "[W]hether the background was proletarian or not, there is a point sometimes in people's lives when something comes along to stir them up and change them a bit. ... I didn't methodically go out and try to become a social painter ... the real urge to paint America ... came when the Depression came and people were actually sitting on the curbs with their tongues hanging out."[39] This experience inspired Evergood's painting *Government Report on North River.*

A chronology he presented to the Whitney Museum charts his growing commitment to socially meaningful art. For 1933–34 he wrote that

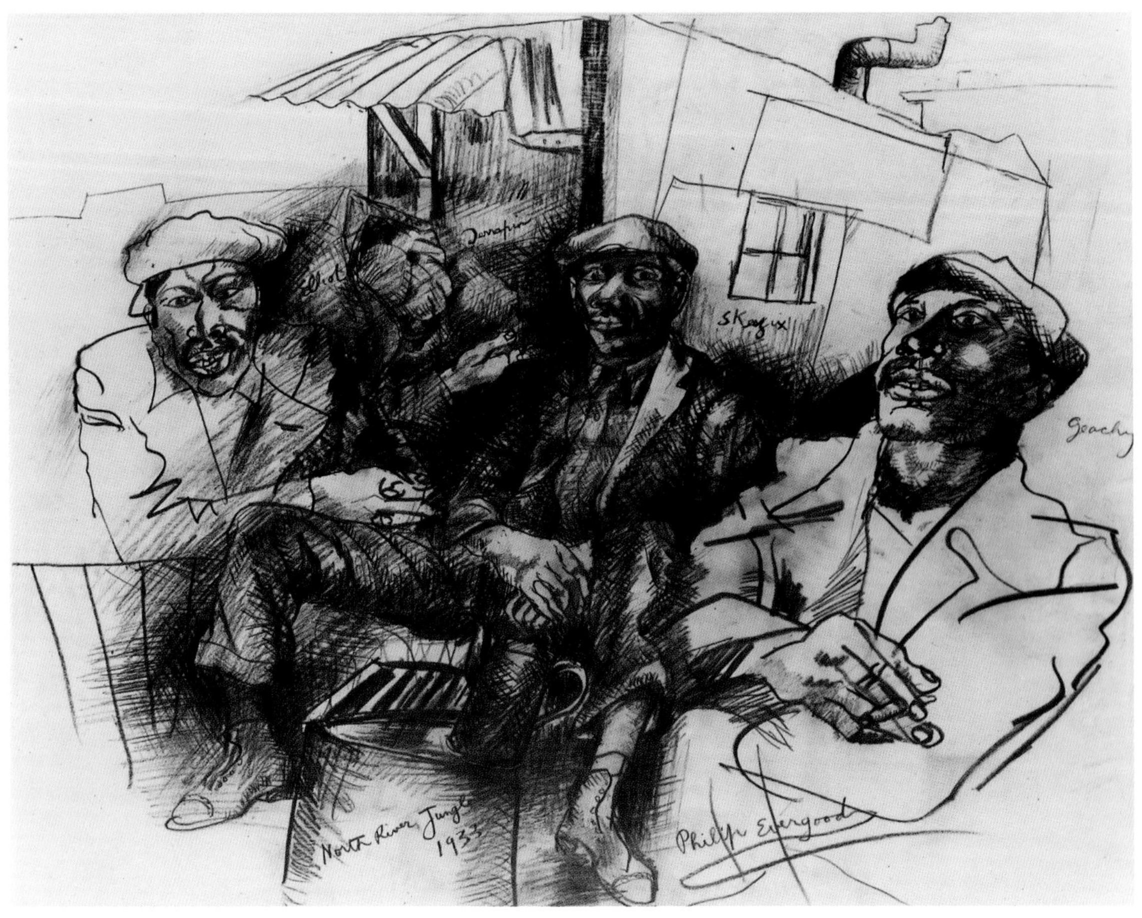

he was becoming "interested in the artist's role in society—social protest art—[and the] potential importance of the artist as a propagandist." As he socialized with the artists at the John Reed Club and the musicians at the Pierre Degeyter Club and moved toward art as social commentary, he became bolder in his color and more expressive in his line.[40]

The John Reed Club encouraged artists to experiment with styles appropriate for revolutionary art. The brochure for the exhibition "The World Crisis Expressed in Art on the Themes Hunger, Fascism, War," held in December 1933, stated: "We cannot say what style, manner, school or form is best suited to the artistic expression of the struggles of the oppressed. That is the artist's problem. We do say however, that it is not sufficient merely to record the scene, to describe it or illustrate it. The artist to be artistically and socially vital must use his art forms to comment, to satirize, to condemn or praise. He is never passive. He takes sides, not only thru his subject matter, but in his treatment."[41]

Evergood's contribution to the JRC show was *Mine Disaster* (fig. 2), a three-part composition. In the left section, *Labor in Darkness,* the

1 Philip Evergood, *North River Jungle* (1933), pencil on paper, 18 ⁷⁄₁₆ x 22 ⁷⁄₈ in. Hirshhorn Museum and Sculpture Garden, Smithsonian Institution.

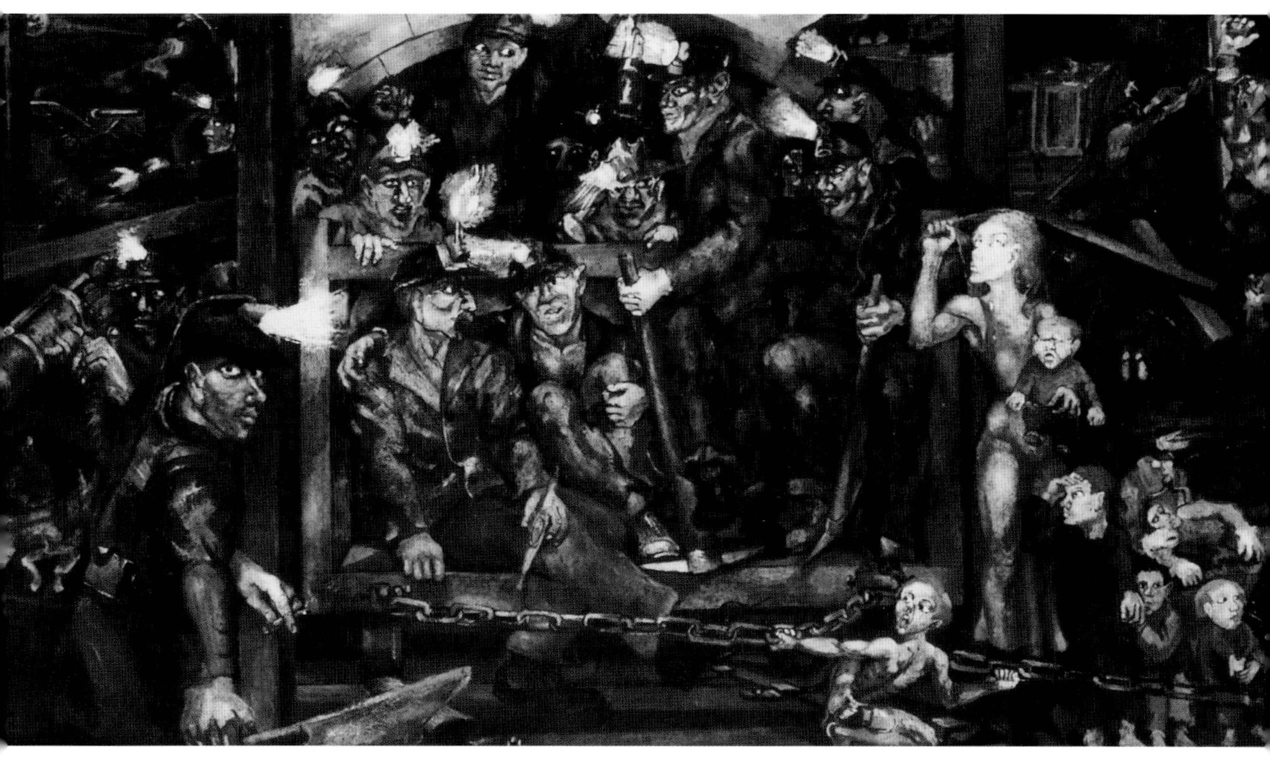

workers toil away. The center section, *Rescue Squad,* is brighter, show-ing the rescuers heroically poised to descend into the shaft to search for their comrades. They are watched by one miner's wife who holds a child as three other children huddle together. In the right section, *Trag-edy of Entombment,* a figure slips under the mine pilings and is buried alive. The casket at lower right foretells the story's end—the death of the miner despite the heroism of his friends.[42]

Although many artists, among them Harry Gottlieb, did scenes of miners and mine disasters in the early 1930s, Evergood heightened the drama; his miners stare at us, and we become engaged in their lives, just as Evergood had been engaged by the homeless men on Christopher Street. By including the whole family, Evergood also commented on the ramifications of mine disasters: a dead miner means a dead father and husband. All these people are enclosed within an iron chain held by the young boy, the worker of tomorrow. The unity of the family parallels the unity of workers—an ongoing theme for the artist—even though their situation in Evergood's picture is grim.

With the FAP/WPA in place in August 1935, Evergood was assigned to the mural section. He began work on a mural for the Richmond Hill branch of the Queensborough Public Library that was to represent the history of the planning of the garden city of Richmond Hill. The finished

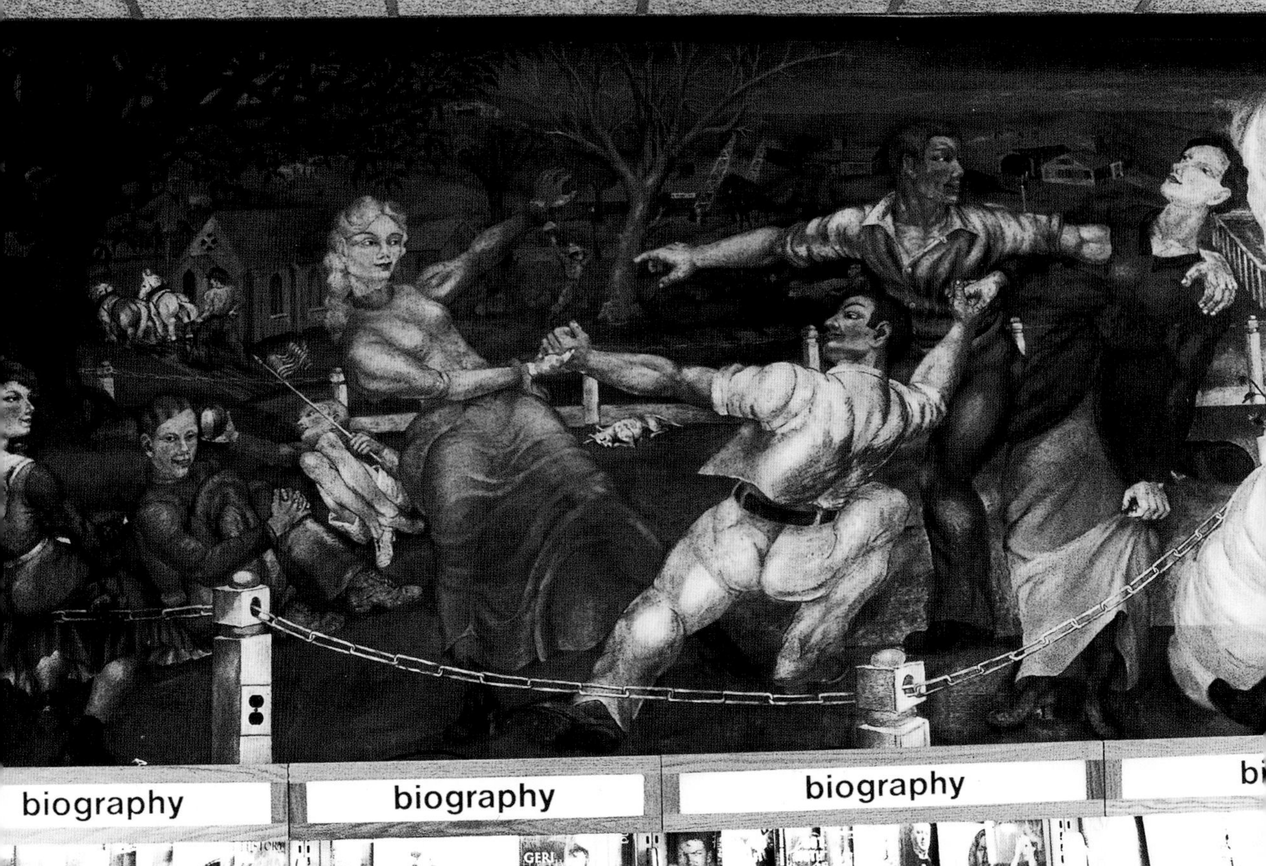

160-square-foot mural, *The Story of Richmond Hill* (fig. 3), depicts the architects and patrons of the project sitting down at a table to discuss their plans. The painting, however, emphasizes the workers, leaving their jobs to travel home on the subways to the joyous community they find in the country-like setting of their homes. Unlike *Mine Disaster* and more typical of FAP/WAP murals, *The Story of Richmond Hill* is upbeat and Popular Front in spirit: enlightened government and private-sector planning will make for happy workers.[43]

Government was not responding very well to the needs of the artist-workers, however. During the summer and fall of 1936, when Evergood was engaged with his Richmond Hill mural, artists had rallied to support Franklin Delano Roosevelt in his bid for re-election. When Roosevelt won by a landslide, the artists were emboldened to petition for a permanent art project. Instead, the government responded by announcing that two thousand jobs would be cut from the art program.[44] Artists felt betrayed and protested the cuts. Evergood helped organize the famous sit-down strike of 1 December 1936, when 219 protesting FAP workers and their friends took over the WPA offices of Audrey McMahon, the New York director of the FAP. Evergood later explained the event to John Baur:

> I was one of the smaller organizers. ... Paul Block, the sculptor who
> was killed in Spain a short time later, was the really brave man and

3　Philip Evergood, *The Story of Richmond Hill* (detail), 1937–38, oil on canvas, 160 sq. ft. Queensborough Public Library, Richmond Hill Branch.

really courageous person in that whole thing. He was conspicuously the revolutionary leader of it, you might say. He stuck his chin right out and put his arms right around that post and they had to beat him insensible to get him out of there. They beat me insensible, but not because I did anything heroic like that but just because I was one of the biggest and then standing in the front line and refused to ungrip my arms with the others around me and refused to leave the building. ... My nose was broken, blood was pouring out of my eyes, my ear was all torn down, my overcoat had been taken and the collar ripped off, and they hardly recognized me when I was pushed out by the police at the bottom of the elevator and thrown into a Black Maria.[45]

According to a news account in *Art Front,* Evergood, Helen West Heller, and Philip Reisman "were brutally beaten."[46]

With those experiences fresh in his mind, Evergood was jolted by the news and photographs of the police attack on striking workers at the South Chicago plant of Republic Steel on Memorial Day 1937 (fig. 4). The circumstances of the attack were that the Steel Workers Organizing Committee (swoc) of the cio had been attempting to get recognized by Republic Steel. Although U.S. Steel had already signed an agreement with the cio, the "little steel" companies, such as Republic, had resisted. Whatever the provoking incident, police panicked and fired tear gas and bullets into the crowds. In labor history the event is referred to as the Memorial Day Massacre, for ten workers were killed and close to a hundred injured. The event inspired Evergood to paint *American Tragedy* (1937) (fig. 5).[47]

Evergood readily confessed to John Baur that his own experiences of the "219" sit-down strike the previous December had motivated the image: "I don't think that anybody who hasn't been really beaten up by the police badly, as I have, could have painted an *American Tragedy.*"[48] The picture is one of the most radically revolutionary of the period; the workers, armed only with sticks, show aggressive solidarity in the face of the police attack. The workforce is integrated and includes African Americans, Latinos, and whites, and both women and men. No "New Deal" or "Popular Front" painting would depict such a scene of determined class struggle. Evergood at this time became even more deeply involved in the Artists Union and labor issues. That summer he was elected president of the au, a post he held from September 1937 to September 1938. Two main jobs had to be accomplished: the first was to affiliate the Artists Union with a larger union, and the second was to push for the Federal Arts Bill (H.R. 8239), which had been introduced by Representative John M. Coffee in August 1937. The bill, published in full in *Art Front*'s October 1937 issue, called for a permanent Bureau of Fine Arts.[49] Evergood

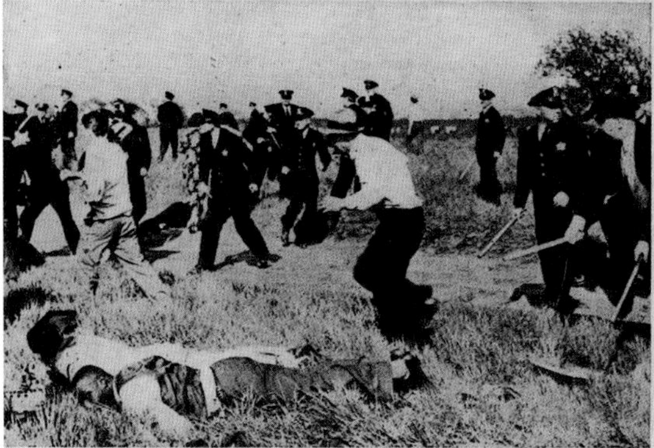

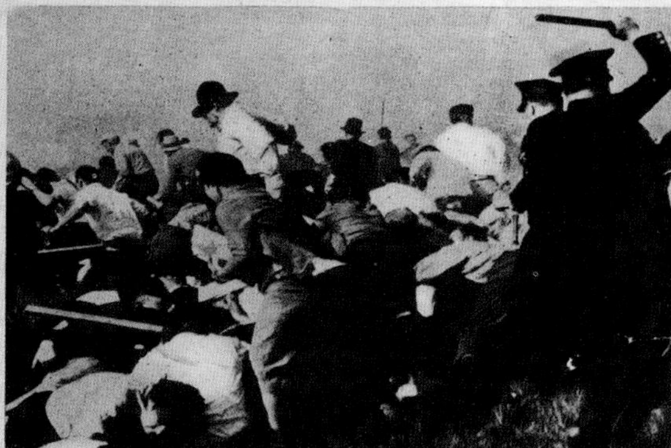

CHICAGO: MEMORIAL DAY MASSACRE

An Eye Witness Account by Meyer Levin

A STRIKE meeting was called for Sunday afternoon in the yard of Sam's Place, a deserted road-café which was strike head-quarters. Being Memorial Day, a lot of the boys' wives came along in their holiday clothes; their kids played in a sandpile in the yard. The meeting wound up with a unanimous vote to proceed and peacefully picket outside the plant of Republic Steel. A line of two hundred cops strung across the prairie barred their way. The strikers stopped, face to face with the police and waited quietly while their spokesman asked Captain Mooney for permission to picket on the public street. "We're citizens, we've got a right. . . . ." Captain Mooney walked toward the edge of the line, where I stood, mumbled the formal notice to "disperse in the name of the law."

Suddenly, shooting sounded. Almost simultaneously, a rock sailed high over the police line. A ball of tear-gas smoke rolled lazily across the high grass. As we ran the rapid shooting sounded oddly distant and insignificant in the bright afternoon.

There had been no attack from the strikers. The police advanced, clubbing, shooting and gassing; the shooting was thick as machine gun fire, then scattered, peppering. I couldn't believe they were firing anything but gas-bombs. Then a white-shirted fellow stumbled out of the smoke, hands over his eyes. I guided him. "The gas effect wears off," I said, but he was mumbling, "I'm shot."

A chunky man leaped over fallen strikers, holding his hands high in the air. Cops chased him. Two, three, five were on him, smashing their clubs on his head. I saw him later in the morgue. His skull was cleft as with an ax. His name was Popovitch.

A man in a blue shirt pitched into the grass at my feet. I heard a kid say, "Pa, I'm shot." It was a boy of about ten, with a bullet through his ankle.

People made crosses on bits of cardboards and stuck them in their car windows. Such first aid cars came pouring from the field, bringing in fifty bullet-wounded. Archie Paterson, a steel worker, came with a half-full car. "We had another man but the cops dragged him out, wouldn't give us time to tie a tourniquet on his leg," he said. "He was bleeding bad. They threw him in a paddy-wagon." That man was next seen at the morgue, listed as "Un-identified, wound in leg, apparently bled to death."

I saw wounded at strike headquarters, and in the hospitals. Shot in the back, in the back of the neck, through the guts from behind. Almost all of the wounds were from behind — men, women, and children shot, chased and shot as they fled.

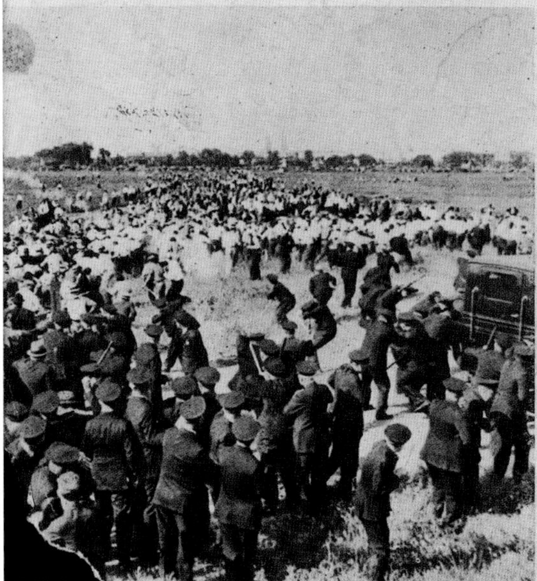

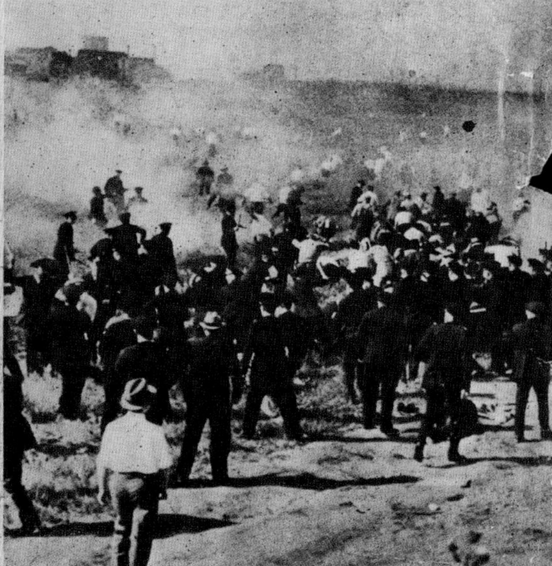

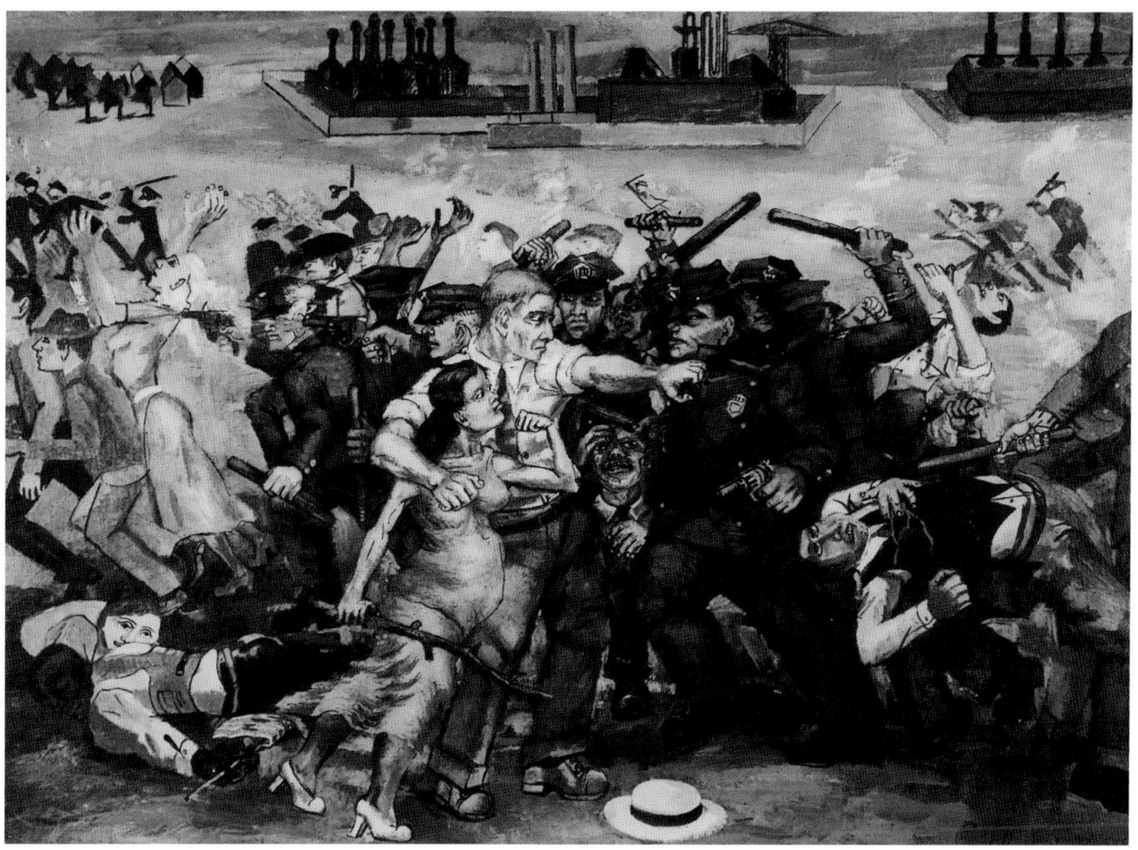

explained to the American Artists' Congress, assembled for its second convention in December 1937, "Artists now look to the establishment of a permanent Bureau of Fine Arts as a logical and necessary step toward a secure and stabilized life for themselves and the building of a great American culture."[50] In his public statements for the Artists Union Evergood was careful to advocate reform, not revolution.

Throughout the winter and spring of 1938 Evergood expended a great deal of energy lecturing and promoting the Federal Arts Bill, which went through several modifications in response to criticism.[51] Meanwhile, an AU committee wrote to members requesting contributions of artwork for a twenty-by-thirty-inch leather-bound volume of fifty to seventy-five drawings, watercolors, prints, or oil paintings to be presented to Roosevelt "in order to impress the President, our legislators, and the public with the quality and importance of governmental art activity."[52] As the presentation project neared completion, Evergood, as the president of the AU, wrote a foreword flattering to Roosevelt. He praised Roosevelt for his "lofty ideals and humanitarian principles and ... warm heart ... [and] recognition of the artist as a human being who needs to eat, and one who can be a powerful uplifting force both moral and spiritual to the people of this Country through beauty and culture." "In dedicating this volume to you," Evergood wrote, "we urge you to continue the great work you have started, by retaining the Federal Art Projects in their entirety, by asking for appropriations sufficient to carry on this noble and necessary work, and sufficient to employ those unfortunate brother artists who are still on the unemployed rolls."[53] The AU's gift to the president was designed to prod him to act on behalf of the artists. Artists such as Evergood now looked to the New Deal—rather than to a workers' revolution—to bring about positive change for all workers. Evergood's enthusiasm seems genuine, but the supplication to politicians is typical of the Popular Front approach.

Evergood clarified his position in "Should the Nation Support Its Art?" an article published in the April 1938 issue of *Direction.* Great art, he argued, had always been a people's art. The phrase "people's art" had replaced "revolutionary art" in the lexicon of movement artists during the Popular Front: "The voices of the people cry for a great American Culture. The Painter, the Sculptor, the Writer, the Actor, the Dancer, the Musician [on] the Federal Art Projects have answered their voices. ... It has set a weight in motion, it has let loose a force that has affected hundreds of thousands of lives. It has made these fuller, happier and better lives." Evergood concluded with a restatement of his view of the function of art in a democracy: "Meanwhile the artist is confident that the American People need him. He knows that his people need a Democratic Culture. ... He knows that if they stand back of him and see that he gets a steady job, that he can give them a great culture and also a great Peoples' Art."[54]

ACA gallery director Herman Baron was himself part of the communist movement. No longer mounting exhibitions such as the anti-lynching show of 1935, Baron now showcased art compatible with upbeat New Deal attitudes. To keep the issue of the Federal Arts Bill alive, the ACA Gallery mounted a group exhibition in August 1938 called "1938—Dedicated to the New Deal." Baron's preface to the catalog reflects the Popular Front sentiments of the moment: "Artists have become aware of the sharpening conflict between reaction and progress; they have definitely aligned themselves with the forces grouped around the New Deal, which they are defending because they realize that its enemies are also the enemies of democracy and culture."[55] All of the works were done on five-by-three-foot panels, to give the exhibition coherence and to suggest the mural-like qualities of the pictures.

Critics gave the show mixed reviews. Several focused their attention on Evergood's *The Artist in the New Deal* (fig. 6). Artist Jacob Kainen, writing for the *Daily Worker,* praised Evergood's panel for the way it "deals with the effects of the New Deal on the artist. Earlier conditions

6   Philip Evergood, *The Artist in the New Deal* (1938), oil on canvas (original image later painted over). Reproduced in ACA Gallery catalog, 1938.

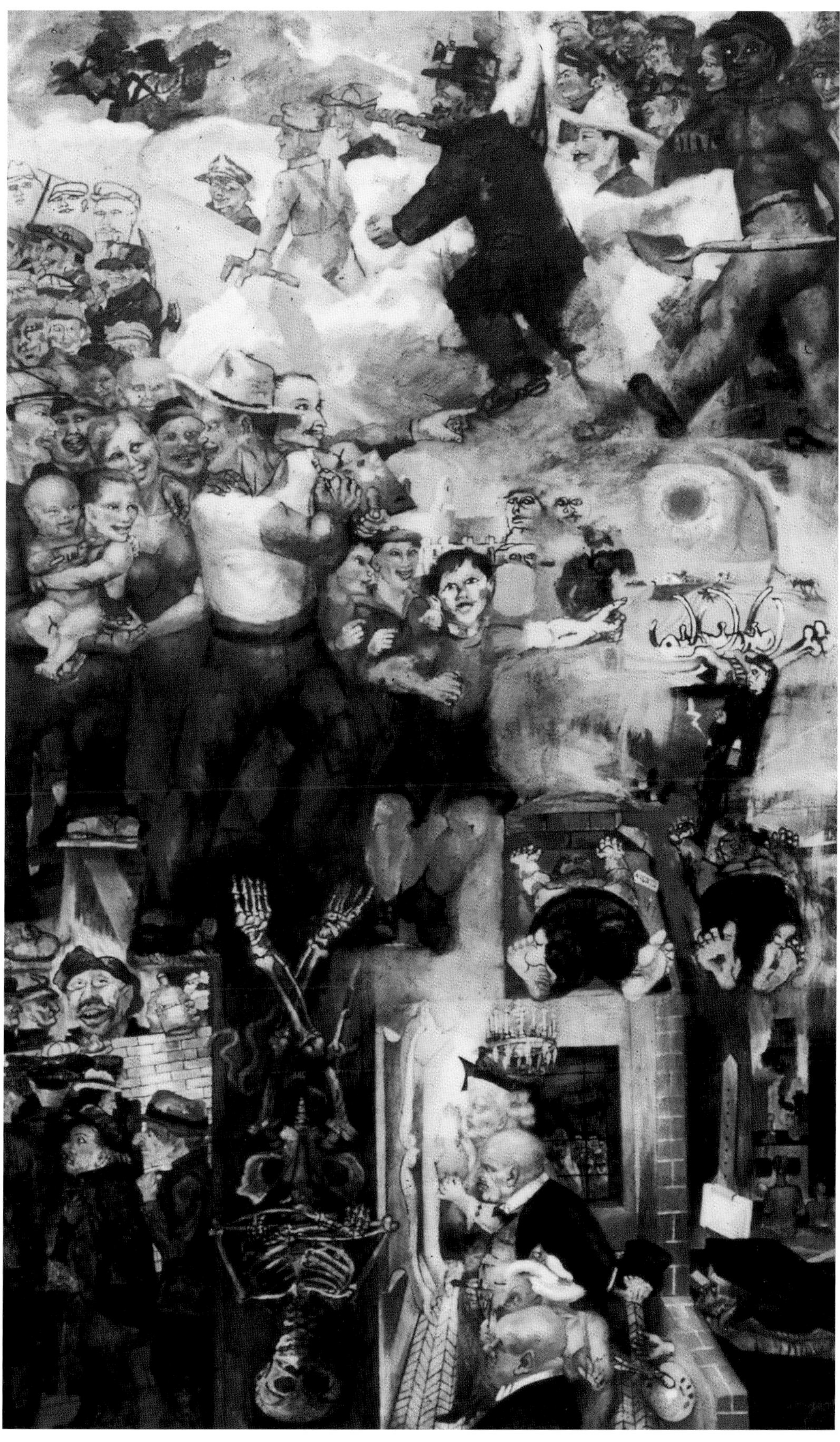

are shown, in which the artist suffered miserably in garrets and on breadlines. Everything culminates in the new artist of today, pointing to the road ahead together with masses of happy workers. A fine mural conception, handled in Evergood's usual super-directed manner."[56] Elizabeth McCausland, who wrote frequently for *Art Front* under the pen name Elizabeth Noble, praised Evergood in her regular column for the *Springfield (Mass.) Sunday Union and Republican:*

> [Evergood] succeeds in filling his canvas with hope and affirmation, even the joy of living—a miracle in this ninth year of the depression and this possible first year of the second world war.
>
> An unmistakable scenario supplies the core around which the picture is built—the artist dead and buried for lack of support; the rich "patrons" of art patronizing his work through lorgnettes; the Federal Art Project giving the artist support and an audience in the American people; the creative release and inspiration of the new social relation between artist and public. Plastically the conflicting elements are integrated in a powerful and happy whole.[57]

John Crosby, writing for the *New York Herald Tribune,* disagreed. He felt that the artists were not showing their best, for most paintings were "windy elocutions, overweighted with symbolism and cluttered with anecdotes." His sharpest criticism was directed toward Evergood, whom Crosby recognized as a talented artist. *The Artist in the New Deal,* Crosby wrote, was "a cleverly handled picture, as cleverly handled as is possible with such material, but as an art work it is clumsy and obvious. A half dozen other pictures are guilty of similar overstatement."[58] The hostile reviewer for the *New York World-Telegram* found Evergood's painting confusing and worthy of ridicule: "The whole conception is as saccharine as the old-fashioned movie silents."[59]

The critics were not unbiased. The positive reviewers, Kainen and McCausland, had allied themselves with the movement and were disinclined to criticize the efforts of well-meaning artists like Evergood. The critics of the mainstream press recognized Evergood's talent but were hostile to the simplistic message.

Evergood must have had doubts about his schematic and propagandistic picture. He later made changes, such as replacing the cannon, which was morphing into a smokestack and a tree, with a dancing boy. He also awkwardly twisted the head of the prominent, mawkishly grinning worker. To our discerning eyes today, the hodgepodge painting is embarrassingly disorganized and lacks either aesthetic or political power.

By September 1938 Evergood's term as president of the Artists Union had ended. He had managed to affiliate the AU with a larger union, but the Federal Arts Bill had died. In that month he also resigned from the project, because his wife had inherited money and he no longer qualified for relief. In December, however, Audrey McMahon hired him back as managing supervisor of the Easel Division, a position that did not require the poverty oath. He continued to stay active in artists' groups and served on the art committee for the New York World's Fair.

In 1939, with massive cutbacks in the WPA programs, the membership of the United American Artists dwindled. Its continuance as a local of the UOPWA was no longer viable. When the war came, artists formed the Artists League of America (ALA). Eventually those members helped to organize Artists Equity in 1946, an organization still in operation today.[60]

By the end of the 1930s it was clear that the Communist Party had abandoned its vanguard leadership, as it became more and more co-opted by the Democratic Party and at the same time came under attack from independent leftists and Trotskyite groups for abandoning its revolutionary political struggle and maintaining its loyalty to the Soviet Union.[61] The American Artists' Congress broke up in April 1941 over the issue of whether or not to contribute funds to Herbert Hoover's relief for the victims of the Soviet Union's invasion of Finland. But Evergood kept the faith and followed the party line by voting for Roosevelt and contributing to the Spanish Civil War victims and Russian relief drives.[62]

Because of his organizational position as president of the Artists Union in 1937–38, Philip Evergood was one of a handful of articulate, socially concerned movement artists in a position to influence his fellow artists. He incorporated Popular Front attitudes and rhetoric into his speeches before the Artists Union, he successfully merged the AU into the United American Artists, he wrote persuasively in defense of the Federal Arts Bill, and he was trusted to make a direct appeal to President Roosevelt on behalf of artists' issues.

When it came to Evergood's practice as an artist, however, he followed no directives or urgings. The imperatives of either Marxist revolution or Popular Front reform were less compelling than his desire to paint what he felt, and what he felt was the sum of both personal and collective experiences up to that moment. These experiences gave him the material to synthesize theory and practice. *American Tragedy,* his response to the 1937 police riot in South Chicago, went further toward Lozowick's ideal of revolutionary art than any of his contemporaries. His picture of workers fighting the police in South Chicago expressed his own revolutionary ideal; eyewitness accounts record no effective worker resistance at the actual Memorial Day Massacre, and such images were no longer encouraged by the Popular Front leadership in 1937.

Evergood continued to paint anticapitalist themes in the late 1930s

and early 1940s that focused on the working classes and that lacked a
New Deal message. He showed a compassionate view of human endur-
ance amid poverty in such works as *Lily and the Sparrows* (1939) and
Don't Cry Mother (1938–44). The drudgery of working-class life amelio-
rated by comradely friendships is the subject of *Through the Mill* (1940).
Racial solidarity, the subject of *The Future Belongs to Them* (1938–53),
was explored by other movement artists of the 1930s. *New Birth, New
Struggle* (1947) (fig. 7) could serve as an illustration for Norman Bethune's remark that the artist "points the way to [the world's] new birth."
A joyous white woman, lying in her hospital bed, passes her biracial
newborn to two white workers, while the proud father, an African American, and a hospital nurse look on. Evergood never could repress his
optimism for worker solidarity, as he showed in *Workers' Victory* (1948),
painted at a time when both unions and the CPUSA were under attack.[63]
Other pictures of the late 1940s are sharply satirical, but most are at the
same time optimistic and humanistic. Without a vigorous Communist
Party and its support for working-class politics, Evergood, like others still
in the movement, gradually drifted away. He never again attempted a
politically revolutionary art.

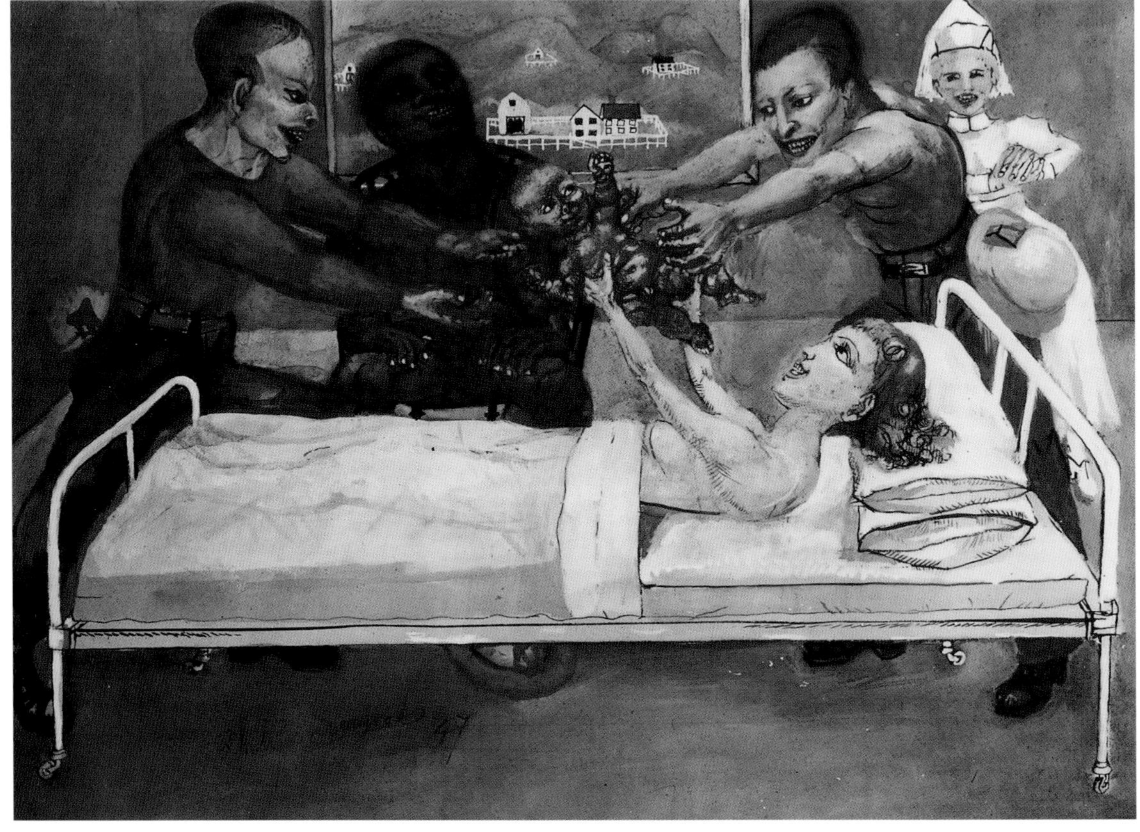

WORKERS AND PAINTERS:
SOCIAL REALISM AND RACE IN DIEGO RIVERA'S DETROIT MURALS

Anthony W. Lee

Looking back from the distance of several decades, the Russian immigrant Victor Arnautoff recalled with great fondness his early years as an assistant to Diego Rivera. He initially had been employed in the unglamorous work of mixing pigments and plastering walls for Rivera's National Palace mural project. Within a few short years, however, he had advanced to transferring sinopia designs, supervising much of the preparatory work, and, when Rivera took extended leaves from the mural site (which was often), even finishing secondary areas. When Rivera was in residence on the project, the two artists regularly worked late into the evening together, discussing not only the details of fresco work but also more expansive topics about the role of art in political revolution, the attitudes of Stalin toward a proletarian visual culture—this, in the late 1920s, when Socialist Realism had yet to be pronounced and made dogmatic—and the relationship between painterly realism and radical political ideology. The image of the two men on the scaffolds, deep in thoughtful discussion, is still able to conjure for us something of the seriousness and possibility of that early moment of public art. Arnautoff's own writings suggest that he kept that image too, even or perhaps especially when forced to endure the anticommunist witch hunts of the 1950s. "Everything that I had learned and achieved in painting before somehow fell into place and took shape under Rivera's guidance," he

This essay owes much to the careful reading and thoughtful suggestions of this anthology's editors, Alejandro Anreus, Diana Linden, and Jonathan Weinberg; the anonymous reader for Penn State University Press; and Andrew Hemingway and James Oles, who heard versions of this paper delivered as public lectures and responded with their usual generosity, incisiveness, and cantankerousness.

wrote. "Being with Rivera confirmed me in the belief that the making of art is not a matter of idle contemplation, it cannot leave the viewer indifferent. Its goal is to move people."[1]

In the 1930s Arnautoff undertook his own projects and became, most famously in 1934, supervising artist for the massive, deeply controversial Coit Tower mural project in San Francisco. Indeed, his attempt to "move people" led to a quarantine of the tower by the police and National Guard and eventually a whitewashing, by the tower's own patrons, of the most explicitly political work.[2] Although his own professional career waxed and (mostly) waned after that, Arnautoff always credited Rivera for whatever success he enjoyed and specifically for helping him develop his sense of a committed social realist practice. He represents an especially poignant case of a leftist artist in America whose career took shape from this early relationship to Rivera and his monumental murals; in a sense, his later work continually worked through the implications of that relationship. He was certainly not alone in this regard, for many American painters gained their sense of themselves as social realists through engagement with Rivera and his work. The great irony is that most were not nearly as leftist as either Rivera or Arnautoff—in fact, many were quite reactionary—and yet claimed inspiration from murals that were, at least to Arnautoff's mind, politically redolent. How do we account for this? How is it that social realism, which today may strike us as a manifestly *undescriptive* term, given the range of artistic and political attitudes it encompasses, so often takes us back to the work of a painter who continually claimed that his work came out of Marxist thinking?

One reason may be an ambivalence at the heart of Rivera's practice itself, an ambivalence that made possible competing, indeed contradictory, social realisms in the works of those who claimed inspiration from him. If Arnautoff pursued a line of thinking and painting that seemed more in keeping with Rivera's stated concerns, he took only the most manifest of a series of possibilities found within Rivera's work. To suggest this ambivalence, I want to pursue a reading of Rivera's perhaps most topically relevant, certainly his most monumental and, as I argue, most metacritical example, his *Detroit Industry* murals, painted in 1932–33 in the Garden Court of the Detroit Institute of Art. There, in a multilevel, multisurround representation of Henry Ford's River Rouge factory, the muralist pictured skilled workers within the confines of America's most advanced industry, and the tenor of that relationship— its various utopian and dystopian inflections—was the regular gristle for this and many other Depression-era artists. I would suggest, however, that the muralist articulates, in a far more self-conscious register than his contemporaries normally did, the leftist fantasy of the American worker.

Rivera understood that worker as a body organized under competing
political sympathies, but he failed to find a more stable and alternative
form for him than the one conventionally presented by American industry itself. That failure was the result of the painter's own confrontation
with the complexity and contradiction of the American working classes,
which he, like so many others who followed him, ended up fabricating rather than addressing. Yet in fabricating, his picture of the worker
allowed, indeed inhered, competing political beliefs about the worker's
place in industrial life. Rivera elaborated on this conceptual and pictorial impasse in response to the invidious events in strike-ridden Detroit,
in which the committed painter came face to face with his own inability
to overcome American labor's racism. The effort to picture the worker in
an environment of racial tension revealed to the painter how much the
worker was a feature of political and cultural desire, a crucial but fictive
and deeply unstable presence in what we know would become the social
realist imaginary.

In what follows, social realism and Socialist Realism—two terms
that are kept rigorously separate today—are folded together and pushed
back to the origin they both share. I will try to recall a moment before
the two became distinct, when there was a feeling among leftists that a
truly activist art was on the horizon and needed to be striven for, before
such a feeling hardened into rigid, deadening orthodoxy.

By the late 1920s Rivera had already had two fallings-out with the Communist Party, punctuated by his membership in the famous October
Group, a collection of radical artists who, among other things, maintained a critical distance from what soon became the Stalinist version of
social realism.[3] The October Group attempted a middle course between
the expressionist and abstract tendencies of the French and Russian
avant-gardes on the one hand and the often flaccid heroic realism of the
Association of Artists of Revolutionary Russia on the other. Its ideas
about specific artistic forms were intentionally ambiguous, attempting to
preserve the autonomy of leftist artistic practice in the face of the growing threat of doctrinal rigidity. In the very early 1930s Rivera regularly
called himself a member of the leftist opposition, not only invoking the
sense of a political challenge to Stalin but also, perhaps more important
to him, support of a free, experimental art.

As Rivera quickly learned, however, the fragile promise of October
was a subtlety generally lost in the United States, itself lacking a strong
tradition of a leftist political avant-garde; and by the mid-1930s it was
moot, given the increasingly rigid ideas about art prescribed by the central organ of the Communist Party, the Comintern, and the views of the
more militant artists of the John Reed Clubs.[4] It was not only pressure

from these two groups that pushed Rivera to think of his work in more doctrinally recognizable terms. As he learned from his prolonged stay in San Francisco in 1930–31, the only way to pursue radical public art in the States seemed to be through some kind of accommodation of the Soviet Union's version of revolutionary art—what later became known as either social or Socialist Realism—and, just as important, the fiction of a coherent, cohesive left that it suggested. California's "united front," or at least the claim for one, had produced the most coherent efforts at a multiracial constituency among skilled labor, and a far more productive relationship between leftist political and cultural spheres than had ever been the case on the West Coast. Certainly it succeeded in the matter of art, for which Rivera, through the example of his protégé Arnautoff, took considerable credit. It was this heady mix of trade unionists, Communists, and Rivera-trained artists that gave rise, for example, to the scandalous, politically powerful Coit Tower murals.

I believe that this wish for unity on the left framed Rivera's effort in Detroit. "I want to be a propagandist for Communism," he wrote in 1932, as he developed sketches for the mural, and explicit in this desire was an image of a stable, coherent communism and the careful erasure of a contentious, sometimes rancorous leftist sectarianism for an American audience.[5] The wish was strategic, perhaps even earnest, though, as we can see in hindsight, valedictory. But what is remarkable was the attempt to grapple, in such a massive work no less, with social and Socialist Realist thinking as they were only then being formulated in the Soviet Union. For *Detroit Industry* anticipates, indeed tries to answer, the famous demand soon put forward by Moscow: "Socialist Realism requires of the artist a true, historically concrete depiction of reality in its Revolutionary development. In this respect, truth and historical concreteness of the artistic depiction of reality must be combined with the task of ideologically transforming and educating the workers in the spirit of Socialism."[6]

As Rivera explained, *Detroit Industry* was the result of his observations in the River Rouge plant, which he toured for a full month in fascinated preparation. His experiences in the factory spurred him to represent it as a complex, polyvalent machine in itself, with its myriad intricate processes, functional interconnectedness, relentless productivity, even something normally so elusive as its startling "speed caused by the structure of the materials which it synthesizes, analyzes and transforms."[7] On the north wall (fig. 1), he pictured the intricate stages of the V-8 engine manufacture; on the south (fig. 2), the assembly of completed engine, chassis, and body; on the east, the embryonic origins of human life; on the west (fig. 3), the "feeder" industries (so called because they fed into automobile production) of aviation, shipping, and rubber-tree harvesting. Congested and bloated with teeming detail, the Rouge as pictured by Rivera resembles anything but the spare, lucid lines of the Model A, the object of all of its frenetic energy. The finished car is hardly visible (a speck on the south wall) and is displaced by a more proper subject matter for a new, distinctly revolutionary age. "Painting," Rivera's biographer Bertram Wolfe suggested in response to the mural, "must absorb the machine if it was to find the style for this age, assimilate it as easily and naturally as it had the still-life objects, landscapes, dwellings, castles, faces, nude bodies."[8] In that technological utopia, where the piston replaced the nude as the stuff of art and where emphasis on the laboring process seemed more proper than the commodities it produced, the painter believed he had found a subject ripe for "true, historically concrete depiction." It seemed to match Marx's suggestion that working-class takeover of an advanced capitalist industry signaled, or at least portended, the triumphant moment of socialist revolution.

This effort, to repeat, tried to give the illusion of a unified left through articulation of the Comintern's program for socialist art. And while the ambition was savvy, perhaps even noble given Rivera's previous erratic behavior in the Communist Party, it does not mean that the

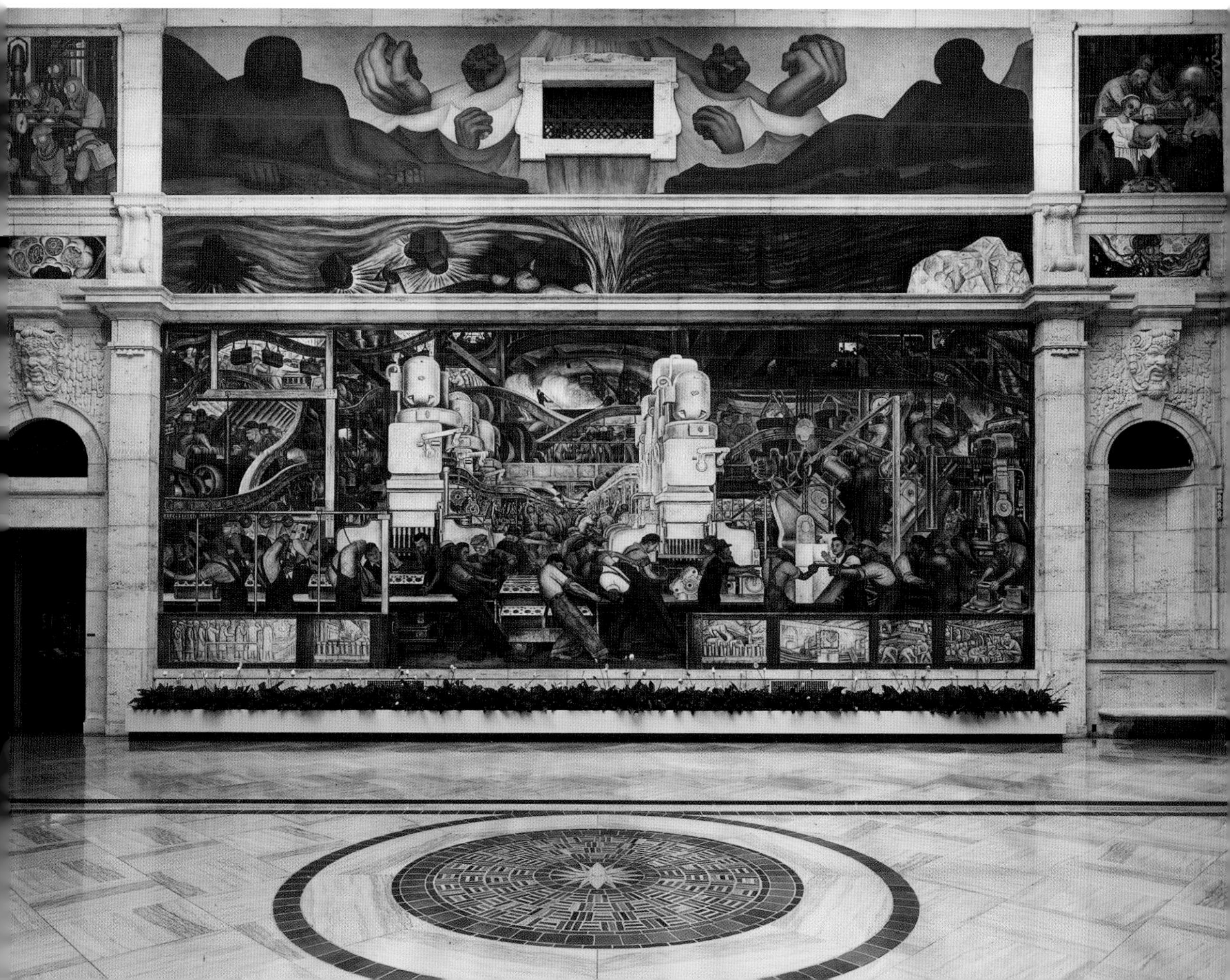

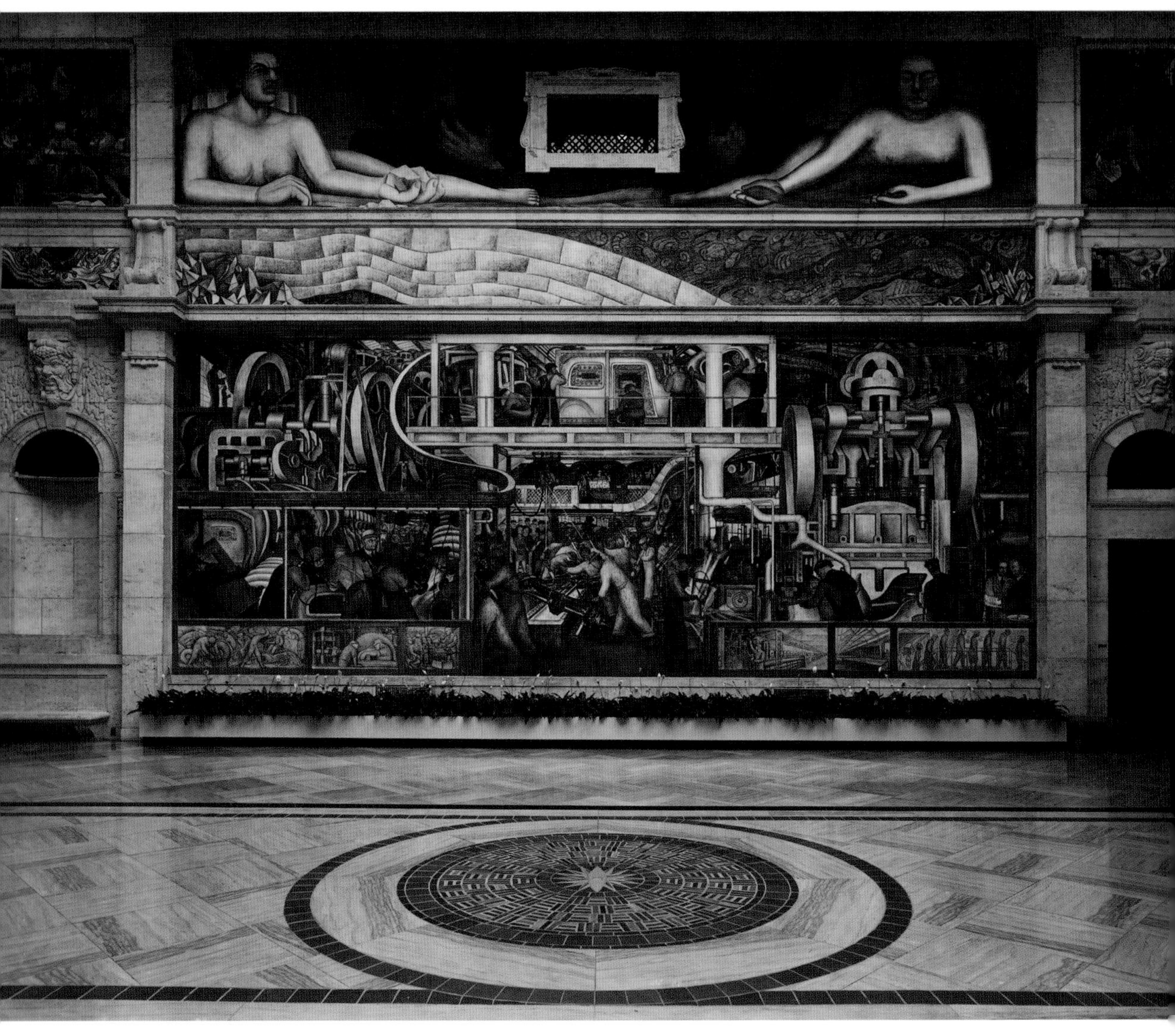

mural actually fulfilled its charge. For Rivera's reading of a "true, historically concrete depiction" permitted quite the opposite possibility—that
the mural not only suggested a left in disarray but might not articulate
a socialist vision to the American worker at all. This ambivalence was
made possible by Rivera's willful acceptance (about which more later)
of the more celebrated socialist belief in unalienated labor. Envisioning
a socialist future devoid of commodity fetishism—providing a com-
mensurate image of "Revolutionary development"—meant insisting on
the use-value and not the exchange-value of the factory's technological
wonders, on the love of industry and industrial work themselves and
not the pleasure of material things the factory produced, as the working
class's new proletarian character. "My childhood passion for mechanical
toys," Rivera later wrote of the main north and south wall panels, "had
been transmuted to a delight in machinery for its own sake and for its

2 Diego M. Rivera, *Detroit
Industry, South Wall*
(1932–33). Gift of Edsel
B. Ford. Photo © 1989 The
Detroit Institute of Arts.

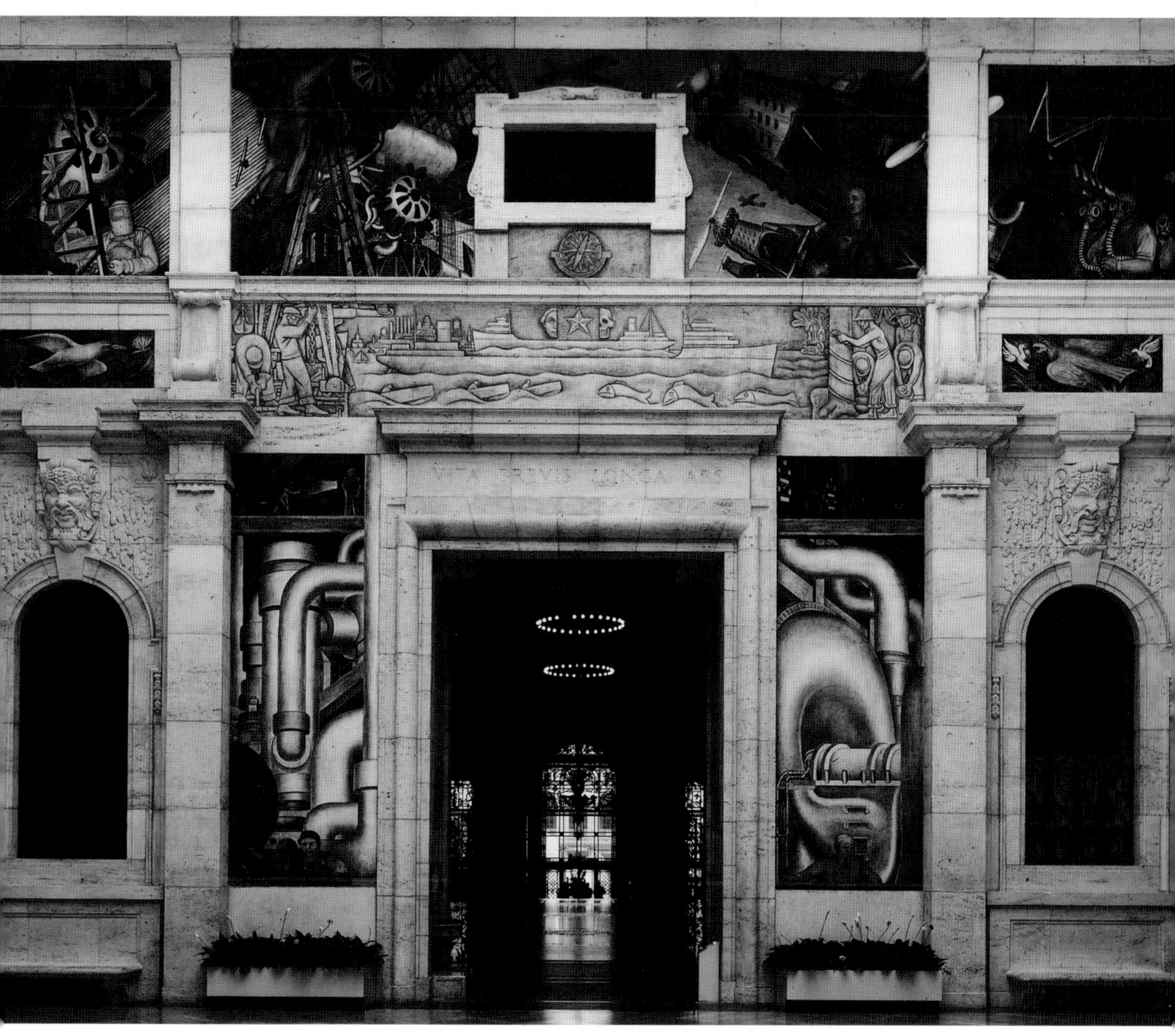

3 Diego M. Rivera, *Detroit Industry, West Wall* (1932–33). Gift of Edsel B. Ford. Photo © 1989 The Detroit Institute of Arts.

meaning to man—his self-fulfillment and liberation from drudgery and poverty."[9] But there was already slippage in the claim. In the attempt at an iconography of the factory machine, the painter assumed that such a description was always already socialist in intent—that the mural's fascinated attention on the factory's wonders was compatible with working-class liberation and that the emphasis on technology was somehow a sign of unalienated labor.

This was nothing if not the standard socialist argument circulating in the Soviet Union in the late 1920s, when Rivera first visited. Technological changes are assumed to determine social relations, and the very "delight in machinery" can, almost by itself, secure proletarian consciousness. Revolutionary art based upon the fetish for the machine was undoubtedly a durable art—for one thing, it avoided the question of what Marx called the superexploited classes; for another, it suggested a

relatively straightforward iconography and pictorial form and allowed
less talented painters to follow easy prescriptions—and it became, most
famously, the basis for dogmatic art under Stalin's cultural commissar, Andrei Zhdanov.[10] But it hardly needs saying that such a vision of
the factory and its assumption about unalienated labor was something
for which the American autoworker generally had little understanding, let alone sympathy, given the taxing conditions on the River Rouge
assembly lines. Indeed, the great irony about this aspect of the "true,
historically concrete depiction" is that its emphasis on the worker's
enthusiastic productivity coincided not with the aspirations of American
trade unionists but with the technophile attitudes of American capitalists, especially with their belief that labor must be absorbed into the
efficiency of the machine and that such an absorption was the basis for
a new relation between the classes, between labor and capital. Rivera's
view of Henry Ford's factory and its workers is an uncanny one, in that
it calls forth a capitalist vision of harmony on the assembly line even as
it tries to articulate a socialist vision, and that it instantiates an industrial
capitalist understanding of the worker even as it tries to liberate him.

Consider again the large central panels of the north and south walls
(figs. 1 and 2). The floor is a veritable beehive of mechanical activity.
Automobile parts move to and fro, undulating up and down conveyor
belts, into the component parts of a singular assembly line. All of that
assembly is dependent on the physical effort of stationed workers, and
as much as the factory floor is a highly organized space of clean metal
surfaces and coursing steel edges, Rivera tries to insist that its quality
of "productivity" is also based on the countless men who move in and
out of its machinery, that the laboring man is a rhythmic and almost
undifferentiated component of advanced industry. The men themselves
are deeply absorbed in their tasks, as evidenced by the careful choreog-
raphy of bodies at work. Muscles bulge and strain; arms crook at taut
angles; legs stiffen to brace against the enormous weight of the engines
themselves. The men lay hands on shiny steel surfaces and massage
their machines, grab hold of bumpers, grinders, polishers, and slag bug-
gies—all of this producing a kind of industrial dance. But the argument
about the worker's joyous place in the factory is, of course, entirely
consonant with American industry's own prevailing understanding of
that worker's seminal place before the assembly line‾ except that scientific management, as embodied in the ideas of its most famous guru,
Frederick Taylor, lamented rather than celebrated it. Taylor notoriously
attempted to instill principles of factory regimentation and mindless efficiency ("it would be possible to train an intelligent gorilla," he claimed
in deadly seriousness, "so as to become a more efficient pig-iron handler
than any man could be").[11] Even more than in the previous decade, when

the image of large-scale industry was built on utopian promises to con-
sumers, the Depression-era automobile factory centered on the worker
as a disciplined body, whose gestures and postures needed to be the
transparent signs of American industry's vitality and logic.[12] To Detroi-
ters so predisposed, the mural's workers can be said to conform to the
image envisioned not by Rivera but by the automobile magnate himself,
who understood (or reinterpreted) the Depression not as a crisis in capitalism's logic but as an opportunity to demand even more productivity
from the lucky few who were picked to work.[13]

The unstable relationship between socialist and capitalist utopias is
evident in Rivera's own review of his experiences in the factory. Out on
a tour of the Rouge, he was astonished by its numbing efficiency, which
led him afterward to recall what might seem to be a completely unrelated subject, a visit to a Russian worker's home. "On a visit to his home,"
Rivera wrote, "I had noticed, hanging on a wall, three separate portraits
above a fourth, of Stalin. The first portrait was of Karl Marx, the center
one of Lenin, and the third, a likeness of my esteemed new friend, Henry
Ford. As my face showed astonishment at this unique ensemble, the
worker had explained, 'Those three make the establishment of socialism
a real possibility. Karl Marx produced the indispensable theory. Lenin
applied the theory with his sense of large-scale social organization. And
Henry Ford made the work of the socialist state possible.'"[14]

It is an astonishing, unexpected image that Rivera brings forth. Yet
that quick shift in his mind, from the American factory's rigors to the
Russian worker's confession of socialist faith, and from the grueling
assembly line to the worker's home, where the muralist's "new friend" is
added to the holy trinity, is partially explained by the Rouge's manifest
abilities to shape and tame its workforce into a productive unit. Like so
many other early leftists, Rivera's image of American industry attended
mostly to its totalizing, systematizing picture of a working class seemingly
free of desire for anything but work, an achievement largely unattained
in practice in either the Russian trade unions of the NEP period or the
Mexican unions of the revolutionary era. In its vision of a Third International world, where revolutionized relations of production could be
achieved on a global basis, this early version of social realism believed that
industry and technology automatically produce a proletarian imagination
and culture. It of course ascribes little to the worker's *current* investments.
His socialist relationship to the Model A will begin anew, and any present
fetish for the car—any intense relation with it that already structures his
desires, actions, and sense of self—will simply evaporate.

Thus, even as it tries to renovate the factory floor for the socialist
imagination, social realism in Rivera's hands remains a view of the floor
afforded from only the purveyor's vantage point—a totalizing, panoptic

view in which, as Michel de Certeau writes, an "immense texturology [is]
spread out before one's eyes."[15] The factory floor is laid out like a blueprint,
a manual for alternately a capitalist or a socialist operation; its worker is
part of a technological, ideological process. The worker is the "collective
hero, man-and-machine," as Rivera explained.[16] He is best understood as a
working body, utterly absorbed in mechanical tasks, as pictured.

I said earlier that Rivera's understanding of revolutionary art's theoretical subtext was willed. Part of the painter's willfulness grew out of
an attempt, as I've suggested, to tackle Soviet art theory in its earliest
moments of formulation, a typically Riveraesque ambition. Part of this,
as I've also suggested, was the belief (momentary, as it turned out) in the
political effectiveness of presenting a unified left through elaboration of
a doctrinaire attitude. But another part, as I describe here, grew out of
an effort to compensate for what seemed a debilitated and fragmented
working class in Detroit, one that was hardly in a position to recognize,
let alone act upon, the call for a united front.

This suggestion contradicts much of what is often described as
the labor scene during Rivera's work in Detroit. In March 1932, three
weeks before the unveiling of Ford's new V-8 engine and just a month
before the muralist arrived, the gap between the divided working classes
seemed instead to be closing for the left. In a demonstration known as
the Ford Hunger March, three to five thousand unemployed autoworkers waved red banners and marched on the River Rouge plant. Near
the factory gates, they confronted a resistant Dearborn police force (by
most accounts a branch of Ford's own service department), which led
to an infamous, violent, and mortal conflict. As one chronicler tells it,
the "police went after them, wielding truncheons to turn them back,
and the marchers retaliated with whatever lay to hand: rocks, lumps of
slag, fence posts."[17] By day's end, four laborers were dead and hundreds
wounded. In the funeral march that followed, the coffins of the four
were draped in red, the procession of fifteen thousand mourners wore
red armbands or carried red flags, and the band played the "Internationale" and the funeral march of the Russian revolutionaries. It seemed as
if, finally, the working classes had been prodded into revolutionary protest and given a measurable, specifically communist identity.

But that identity was not unequivocally and unproblematically leftist,
as Rivera quickly understood during his tours in the factory and among
workers. Despite the red banners and flags, the marchers were primarily
conventional trade unionists, and their demands were far more reformist than revolutionary: the rehiring of laid-off workers, half-rate pay for
the unemployed, a shortened day for lower pay, slowing the manic rate
of assembly-line work, fifteen-minute rest periods, and relief for unem-

ployed Ford workers.[18] As reasonable as these demands may sound, they
are conservative by the standards, in the early 1930s, of the Third International and the left in general. (Indeed, they hardly match the working
class's proletarian character as soon pictured by Rivera.) It was clear
to hardened leftists that the marchers had invoked the specter of communism not to lay claim to a revolutionary identity but to reach the
bargaining table, and the dissimulation brought forth bilious responses.
By mid-March 1932, the Socialist Labor Party condemned the demonstration, and Detroit's small but militant Proletarian Party simply repudiated
it. Just as significant for our concerns, working-class organizing and
activism generally kept people of color—blacks and Mexicans most of
all—outside its ranks. In the case of Mexicans, white workers hankered
for their removal from Detroit altogether. Rather than channel their anger
and rancor against Ford and his thugs, Detroit labor in these early years
also turned against those who were even "lower" on the economic scale.
Their sense of themselves was structured as much by resistance to those
below as by rebellion against those above, making race and racial conflict
a means of solidifying class identity and mediating class conflict.[19]

Racial conflict, a subject to which Rivera was enormously atten-
tive, seemed to distinguish the muralist's experiences in 1932–33 Detroit
and 1930–31 San Francisco and suggested to him the new difficulties
in organizing a united working-class front. In late 1932 the nastiness
of racial politics must have hit home hard. In the aftermath of the Ford
Hunger March, when the ideological seeds for what would become the
United Auto Workers were being planted, Mexican autoworkers were
also expelled from organized labor and returned to Mexico. As the repatriation program's director observed, Mexicans needed to be removed
because they generally received "first consideration in employment" in
the auto industry's hiring logic; their enforced removal permitted "residents and citizens"—potential trade unionists who demanded more
wages but also claimed ballot box rights—assembly line jobs.[20] Rivera's
own activism among Mexican autoworkers never came close to overcom-
ing the racial divide; his calls for a collective working-class identity, one
in which class solidarity mended or simply elided racial tension, seemed
to Mexican repatriates blindly utopian or plainly misguided as they were
being shipped out of the country.[21]

When Rivera and Frida Kahlo sent off the first round of Mexican
repatriates at Union Depot in late 1932, the sight must have been disheartening. Reports tell us that the day was unusually gray; the 432
repatriates crammed into a single Wabash Railroad passenger train;
and none of the nonpaying passengers (that is, all of the children) was
provided food for the ten-day journey. How ironic it must have seemed
to the muralist that most of the repatriates were being sent to hastily

arranged agricultural worker cooperatives in Mexico (one cooperative even named "Diego Rivera," where a "great tract of land" had been promised), when he himself was trying to imagine a distinctly technologized utopia.[22] How even more disheartening when reports reached him a month later that the repatriates had been transferred like farm animals to boxcars, shipped to regions of the Mexican countryside where the land was arid and unirrigated, and never given the proper tools and seeds to raise crops. Some of the former autoworkers resorted to begging; others tried to find ways to return to Detroit, only to be caught and returned. By the end of the year, Rivera was denouncing repatriation as an effort to stave off the Mexican autoworkers' dismal existence on his native soil, only this time he himself was being denounced by the Communist Party for having acquiesced in the program in the first place.

In such a scenario, to picture a multiracial working class in *Detroit Industry* required a much larger, more generic figuration in an effort to keep it from being read too concretely, perhaps too casually, against the backdrop of Detroit's racial tensions. The subject is thus offered in the form of the famous great goddess figures in the upper registers of the north and south walls. Let me signal how this view of the goddesses— seen from the perspective of Detroit's own racial conflicts, reintegrating them with the series of events into which Rivera was himself pulled, seeing them as a way to make the utopianism of social realism seem somehow not absurd in such an unequal working-class society—differs from the ways in which they have been regularly construed. Their presence has generally been interpreted, as Rivera himself once tried to do, as an "organic" balance to the factory-as-machine in the main panels. On the north wall (fig. 1), for example, although the basic components for the engine are being assembled from the "ground up," so to speak, conventional wisdom has it that they are actually being produced, as visually and compositionally presented, from the top down, their origins in the monumental, mythic space where racialized goddesses dwell. Indeed, this view of the goddesses' function has tremendous explanatory power and helps to organize the layers of visual information. In the topmost register, allegorical figures of the red and black races hold iron ore and coal, respectively. Their giant hands are duplicated several times in the dry mountain behind them, as if the ingredients of the natural world are their gifts to industry. Just below, in a long horizontal tableau, the iron and coal have been embedded by them in geological strata, waiting to be mined by human hands. Below these top two registers, the factory vision of industry finally begins, the manufacturing process becomes more detailed, the division of labor more acute and rationalized, and the intervention of assembly line logic more obvious. (At the top center, for example, a blast furnace transforms the raw iron ore, coke, and limestone into useable iron. To the right, giant ladles mix molten iron with steel scraps to produce molten steel, which is then poured into casting boxes. Those boxes have been prepared at the far left, where rows of workers mix sand for engine molds and then pack it into mold cores. In its new forms as engine blocks and parts, the iron-steel travels on conveyor belts, winding its way down onto the factory floor, where the blocks will have excess metal shaved, holes honed or smoothed out, and cylinder heads added. By the time the assembled engines have reached the central foreground space, where they are loaded onto carts and heaved into place by autoworkers, they are ready to be added to the chassis and body, as pictured on the south wall.)[23] The whole downward flow of the mural—the slow transformation of the goddesses' gifts into engine parts—seems to emphasize a "world-historical ancientness of industry."[24] In this vision of the factory, the ancient races combine to generate industry's very structure and, more important, the conditions for socialism's concrete development.

It is not that this reading is inaccurate or insufficient, only that it takes race as an unproblematic basis for conceiving of the socialist factory's "origins." The question we might pose is not whether race was effectively used to organize an image of the Rouge, but *why* it seemed necessary at all—why race became a determining issue for imagining the socialist factory. The answer, as we have seen, lay just outside the factory gates and near the train tracks, where unwanted Mexicans were being squashed into Wabash railroad cars. Thus, whereas the ancient world and its carnivalesque goddesses are regularly understood to help generate a critical, socialist meaning, we can suggest that they complicate such meaning.[25] Not that the goddess panels are ancillary, but that in the painter's attempt to address the conditions of working-class life in American industry, the invocation of mythic, racialized bodies seemed the only way to do so. In the context of 1932, the goddesses permitted Rivera a means by which to represent race and working-class race relations as a *symbolic* as opposed to an *actual* instrument of change, the imaginary basis of the modern industrial process and not its actual force in the contemporary factory. We can also therefore stress the goddesses' distancing function, their strategic impossibility of racial identification with the workers in the panels below or in the factory outside.[26] Our reading of the murals might suggest how this early version of social realism, the new visual language that aimed for "historical concreteness," actually organized a *compensatory* picture of the working classes in an effort to avoid, perhaps even overcome, the sticky problem of American working-class racism.

This much of the River Rouge factory regimen is now a commonplace: for those who stood on the assembly line (especially those who were

lucky enough to work during the Depression), the items to be attached
came at an insanely manic pace; the tasks became more robotically and
hypnotically repetitive; the production goals increased to what must
have often seemed nearly impossible levels.[27] The new assembly line
seemed to require a new kind of worker, one more inured to repetition
and less devoted to the traditional craftsmen's sensibility than those
who had once made up the automobile factory before the advent of
the assembly line. Ford originally stocked his workforce with the more
settled working-class inhabitants of Detroit—the sons of Anglo-Saxon,
German, Irish, French, and Polish immigrants—but by the late 1920s and
early 1930s he hired the more recent Slavic and Italian immigrants, and
especially the newly transplanted Mexicans and blacks. Such hiring practices afforded him workers with little or no prior skill—a benefit since,
as one machine operator recognized, they "have nothing to unlearn, ...
no theories of correct surface speeds for metal finishing, and will simply
do what they are told to do, over and over again, from bell-time to bell-
time."[28] In practice, that demand often meant foraging further afield for
unskilled work and importing men from distant places.

One result of the new hiring practices was to transform the workplace into a new social mixture. Despite the aggressive Americanization
programs instituted by Ford (which Rivera pictured as a polemical lecture in a south wall grisaille panel), the workers on the line were often
foreigners to each other, not only in the ways of each other's habits but
also even in basic familiarity with their fellow assemblers' cultures.[29] It
was not at all uncommon for recent immigrants to come face to face with
members of other races for the first time, as most Poles, Ukrainians, and
Russians had with newly arrived southern blacks. Although that mixture
of races and cultures on the Rouge floor potentially made for social segregation (Ford often exacerbated this by dividing the assembly line and
its various specializations along racial lines—blacks and Mexicans, for
example, invariably wound up in the more dangerous foundry work),
one can just as easily say that such a factory floor yielded a spectrum of
specifically *social* accommodations on the part of automobile workers
to each other. As much as the factory floor could be viewed from above
in a totalizing panopticism, it contained a social practice from below. "It
was not until I came to Detroit ... that I was introduced to black people," a
Polish autoworker remembered; but despite his initial awkwardness, he
soon became an important conduit for whites among blacks because, as
he declared with a certain amount of swagger, "I speak their language."[30]
While Ford's policy of part-time employment and the frequent turnover
of his workforce produced a constantly shifting set of faces—and therefore made any attempt at political or ideological cohesiveness among
workers enormously difficult for leftist organizers—the assembly line

also permitted a new, not necessarily political means of developing working-class consciousness. The resulting social bonds may be called social *hybridity,* a "heterodox merging of elements usually perceived as incompatible."[31] This term has the benefit of naming a wide range of relations between workers and, furthermore, can be understood as a potentially collectivizing act in the alienating atmosphere of the Rouge.

This basis for working-class solidarity is also, by now, a commonplace in labor histories, but it has not often been seen in relation to the leftist artistic efforts of the period. What seems clear is that social hybridity inverts, contradicts, or in some fashion offers an alternative to the factory floor envisioned by social realism, since it fosters relations generally policed, censored, and even repressed by the insistence on "work."[32] Furthermore, social realism's underlying belief in the transformative power of technology and in the fantasy of unalienated labor created a blind spot for those who followed its tenets, for they were generally insensitive to precisely these new social bonds between workers, bonds that the more conservative trade unionists understood and eventually capitalized on.

The remarkable feature about *Detroit Industry*—another part of what I am calling its ambivalence—is that this more social aspect of working-class bonds found a ghostly presence in the mural. Social hybridity is summoned by other hybrid forms, as if the factory's social life could not be completely suppressed and its fundamentally conservative political nature needed to be staged in order to be contained. The most obvious instance of this is in the main foreground scenes, where the mural reinterprets the worker's actual social relations into technological ones, into the social realist man-machine. The workers bend and dance in unison in their repetitive tasks, as in the cylinder head assembly on the north wall. They tilt this way and that over stamping presses and welding bucks, as in the south wall. The working body is a self-regulated body that has internalized the ideology of productivity by carrying out its commands. And it has also put that ethos of work in the service of a communal body, whose homosocial skills are organized around the machine. Indeed, the men are given what few social gestures they have according to the logic of the assembly line, which now can be understood as a way not only to discipline proletarian bodies but to organize social relations.

Take, as another example, the huge figure of the stamping press in the right foreground of the south wall. Almost from the moment of its making, the stamping press has assumed a pictorial significance, not only because of its massive size, its beginning point for the south wall's assembly line, and its sense of an intimate relationship with its operators, but also, more significantly, because of its strange hybrid look.[33]

Between the earliest sketches and the final version, Rivera anthropo-
morphized the press, adding protrusions to the head to look like ears
and divets on the face to look like eyes, accentuating its wheels into
shoulders and arms, lengthening its pistons and rods to make collar-
bones and ribs. The whole press is a hybrid creature, part mechanical
and part organic, half-modern and half-ancient, situated within the
American factory but strongly pre-Columbian, recalling the monumental stone sculptures of the ancient Aztec god Coatlicue.[34] That tendency
to unite the iconography of modern and ancient cultures was prevalent
in Rivera's work, but we are now in a position to suggest some of its
specific historical purposes, particularly in the sensitive area of working-
class race relations.[35] The mural prefers to *technologize* those relations
and give them a mythic cast. The stamping press is grotesque not in the
sense proposed by the goddess figures but in a particularly industrial
manner, where the somatic limits of the human form are now indistin-
guishable from the machine's own functional logic.

As such, the stamping press's compositional importance is full
of a certain kind of historicity. As pictured, it literally pumps life into
the south wall assembly line: pipes and conveyor belts are attached to
it like umbilical cords; its broad shoulders structure the shape of the
rotating wheels at left; its piston torso is duplicated in the platform at
center. The press operators catch punched steel sheets as they emerge
from its bottom, like infants from a gigantic mechanical mother. Indeed,
the stamping press helps to organize the south wall's pictorial and figural design and, just as important in an ideological register, the way the
diverse social constituencies of the Rouge can be imagined.[36]

The depiction of labor in the Rouge has far more to do with Rivera's
understanding of how the new revolutionary art, as an experimental
(and very soon centralized and doctrinaire, from the Comintern's point
of view) pictorial and political language, might (or in fact might not)
address the conditions of the American working class. If Detroit's racial
tensions caused Rivera to reconsider how his art might generate a usable
public language for the left, we should attend to the ellipses and gaps in
the mural, the omissions and oddities that make its political ideology less
than coherent. And if the mural inspired other painters who professed
none of Rivera's political radicalism—painters with a working-class
desire to be productive, to erase difference within the working classes, to
harness economic production for decidedly social and reformist (not necessarily revolutionary) ends—then those artists took what lay wedged
in the mural itself. That is one of *Detroit Industry*'s ironic legacies. It follows that since the leftist painter had to stake a claim about what could
be represented in the shifting labor climate of the early 1930s, his status

as a voice for the left always remained debatable, unsettled, and open to challenge. (Rivera was soon denounced as a "renegade from the Communist Party," as Detroit's chapter of the International Labor Defense charged in late 1932, in an effort to strip him of his credibility, an "opportunist [who sold] his talent," not a true party man.)[37] The radical social realist was a constructed identity, whose political integrity depended on the works he created and, in the early 1930s, on the image of labor he was able to stabilize in relation to growing Soviet orthodoxy. In the States, he was produced out of the problematic relationship between the Comintern vision and American conditions, and in his attempt to represent the complex subject of the American worker, he argued for his standing and the legitimacy of his concerns.

In such a construction, the social realist is an illusory, transitory identity, and also, in this case, a unity founded *above* the factory and its laboring force. The leftist painter of American labor paints from a position always already over that of the fray, and yet is deeply dependent on its tension. The fragile construction of the socialist factory—its rigorous erasure and displacement of actual conflicting, contradictory labor relations—is the very grounds for "social realism."[38] The great pathos of *Detroit Industry,* however, lies in Rivera's growing understanding that such an artistic project is a process of separation from, rather than an indication of his engagement with, the factory space. He seems to have recognized the fantasy of his image of the workers, that his identification with labor merely registered his own desire. We are able to see that most clearly in a series of missing, censored, and truncated self-portraits in the murals themselves.

In early sketches for the museum's walls, Rivera initially pictured himself in various guises throughout the factory. On the south wall, for example, he placed himself in the lower right section, immediately next to the stamping press. But as the press took on hybrid details in later sketches, he absented himself from the scene, and in the final version he eliminated himself altogether in favor of patron portraits of Edsel Ford and William Valentiner, the museum's director. As class relations became necessarily more symbolically construed in the stamping press itself, Detroit's industrialist sons came to seem a more fitting set of companions to the figures of the press operators. Rivera placed himself instead in the upper left section on the north wall, which he had no intention of doing in the sketches. There, in the engine mold foundry to which blacks and Mexicans were most often relegated, he found himself most appropriately situated. He looks out at the viewer with long, sagging eyes; his whole complexion, like those of the workers around him, is a ghastly green, like the color that the mold-making process gave off but also, metaphorically, the color induced by ideological suffocation.

Part of the disavowals and transformed self-portraits was the result
of the contradiction between the myth of socialist working-class coherence and the fact of its fragmentation. But part also was the simple
fact that Rivera himself was the object of scrutiny, which made him
deeply self-conscious of his own place within a representation of the
River Rouge factory. Ford company photographer W. J. Stettler accompanied the muralist on his factory tours, ostensibly in an effort to help
the painter visualize and record his experiences. But Stettler's camera
was regularly turned on the muralist, as a photograph of Rivera painting before a rapt audience attests (fig. 4). There, the camera tells us, the
painter works alone, with no assistance from his army of helpers. (In
another photograph, unintentionally comic, he is shown at work with
only a faithful dog for a companion.) Stettler knew, of course, that Rivera
reached this moment of solitary labor only after others had prepared
the way. His many assistants had already tested, ground, and mixed the
pigments for his palette—all of it specially imported from France and
Mexico. Like Arnautoff before them, they had enlarged his preparatory
drawings and pinned the cartoons to the wall. They pounced the trac-
ings, drew the sinopia, and then spread three coats of plaster, including
the final, most delicate skim coat, just before Rivera mounted the scaffolds. The materials for the plaster itself required a month of careful
preparation—lime sifted, slaked, aged, cooled, shaved, mixed with lake-
bed sand, and finally kneaded into the consistency of modeling clay. As
pictured by Stettler, however, all of that preliminary work has already
been completed for this section of the south wall; and Rivera's own
sketches have been neatly tacked nearby (or in some pictures, placed on
a chair next to him), ready to be consulted for the more nuanced and
improvisational details, as if the actual "creative" work on the mural
could finally commence. Surely one reason Rivera insisted on the earthly
origins of the industrial process was that the slow transformation of the
earth's minerals so characterized his own work. But, just as surely, the
painter was not insensitive to his own factory-like procedures, where
he was the intersection of a whole range of preliminary, largely hidden efforts, and where, in his commanding moment on the scaffolds, he
obscured an entire economy of labor.

By late February 1933, as he neared the completion of the entire
project, Rivera's sense of his place within the representation of the factory must have been particularly conflicted. On the west wall portal
(fig. 3), he had originally toyed with the idea of picturing himself as a
worker tending the steam pipes. But when he began putting the finishing touches on the panel, he opted instead for a composite portrait with
features only vaguely reminiscent of his own. He could not, it seems,
imagine himself in that fiction as an automobile worker. The gesture

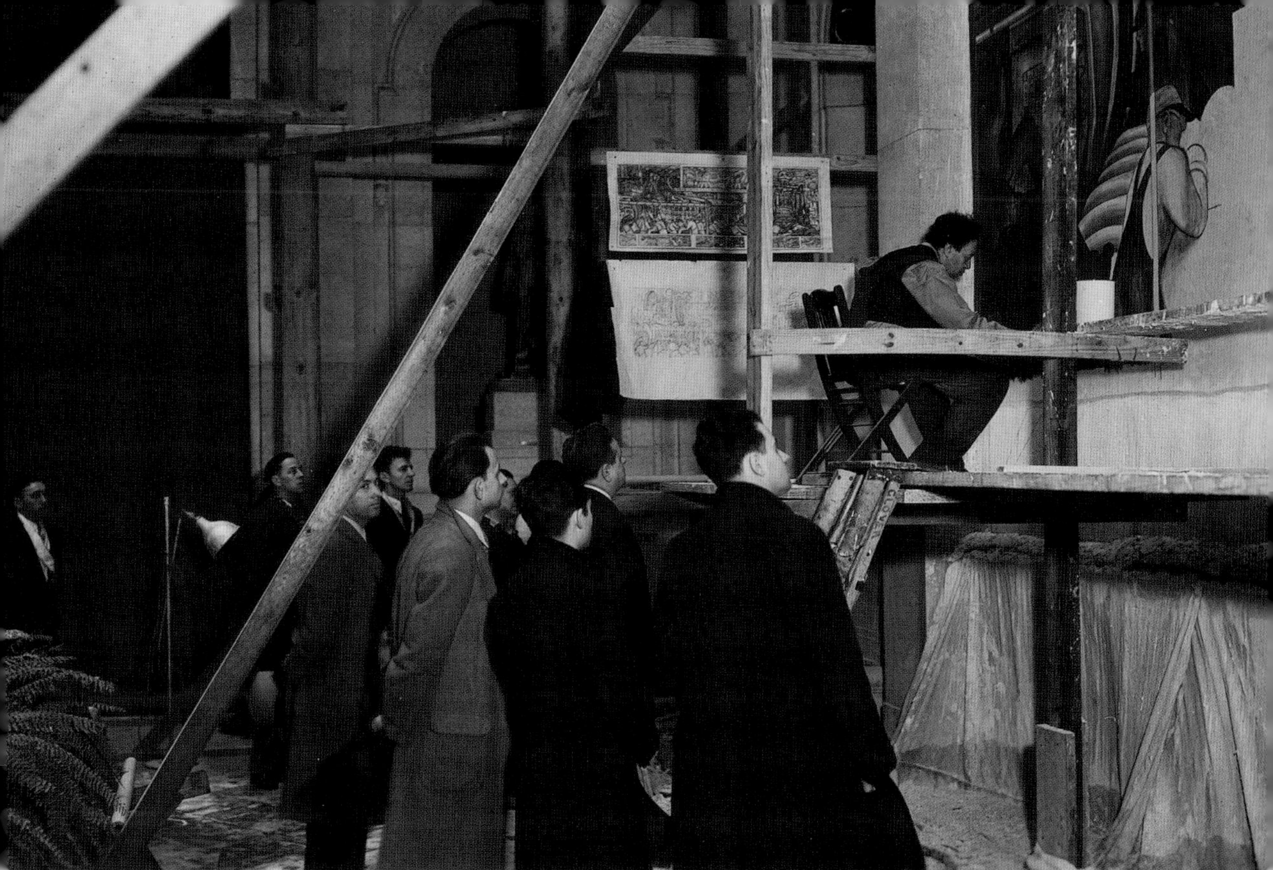

would have seemed far too gratuitous just after the developments in January, when some Mexican repatriates began to straggle back into Detroit. They had sold off most of their personal belongings to obtain transport, only to find no employment in the factories, no help from Rivera, and only the cold streets on which to live and beg. Equally, by that date, Rivera could not imagine himself unequivocally part of the Communist Party and what would soon become its unyielding Zhdanovian demands of artists. He gave his composite worker a hammer to hold and a red star for his glove. It is a covert identification for the worker (the red star was also the insignia of the glove manufacturer), but it was also one he could not claim unproblematically for himself.

So it is with more careful understanding than ridicule that we should read Rivera's own hyperbolic statement about the value of his Detroit murals to the working classes themselves. "We are Detroit workers from different factories," he imagines a man from the crowd calling to him on the scaffolds, "and belonging to different political parties."

> Some of us are Communists, some are Trotskyites, others plain Democrats and Republicans, and still others belong to no party at all. ... [Y]ou're reported to have said that, as long as the working class does not hold power, a proletarian art is impossible. You have further qualified this by saying that a proletarian art is feasible only so long as the class in power imposes such an art upon the general popula-

tion. So you have implied that only in a revolutionary society can
a true revolutionary art exist. All right! But can you show me, in all
these paintings of yours, a square inch of surface which does not
contain a proletarian character, subject, or feeling? ... If you cannot,
you must admit before all these men, that here stands a classic example of proletarian art created exclusively by you for the pleasure of
the workers of this city.[39]

The picture of a proletarian art ahead of its time, of a socialist culture
before social relations had been transformed, was possible only if technology were fetishized and the differences within the working classes
willfully ignored. But even in Rivera's seemingly prosaic account, it is
clear that the workman standing before him is as flat, as unabashedly
fictional, as the wall on which the mural is painted. He is conjured, as
he would continue to be in the era of the Great Depression, by a febrile
imagination.

IV VOICES ON THE MARGINS

"COME OUT FROM BEHIND THE PRE-CAMBRIAN SHIELD":
THE POLITICS OF MEMORY AND IDENTITY IN THE ART OF PARASKEVA CLARK

Natalie Luckyj

In the late 1930s Toronto artist Paraskeva Clark (1898–1986) was one
of a small number of Canadians who publicly challenged the nation's
wholesale rejection of political art.[1] Given the conditions of Clark's personal and professional life at the time, this challenge was remarkable.
Born in Russia, Clark arrived in Canada in 1931, at the beginning of the
Depression. Her position was immediately ambivalent. On the one hand
Clark was an immigrant, not only from her native Russia, which she left
in 1923, but also from France, where she had lived from 1923 to 1931.
In Russia she had witnessed the political and social upheavals of a communist revolution and regime. In both Moscow and Paris she had been
directly engaged with pivotal modernist art practices. These experiences
set Clark apart in Toronto in the early 1930s as an exotic foreigner and as
a critic of the parochial nature of the local art world.

At the same time, Paraskeva Clark had come to Toronto as the wife
of a successful businessman, Philip Clark, whom she had met in Paris in
the late 1920s. Philip Clark's financial position both provided his wife
with the comforts of a bourgeois lifestyle and protected her from the
xenophobia that was rampant in Toronto in the first half of the twentieth century.[2] By 1933, as the mother of two children, Paraskeva Clark
also had serious domestic responsibilities. Furthermore, and somewhat
ironically, Philip Clark introduced his wife to Toronto's insular and self-
admittedly apolitical art scene, to which he himself had serious social
connections. As a result, within two years of Paraskeva Clark's arrival in
Canada she had exhibited with the staid academicians of the Royal Canadian Academy and with the Canadian Group of Painters, whose members

may reasonably be described as conservative modernists engaged in landscape and figural painting.[3]

These contradictions within Paraskeva Clark's personal and professional lives undoubtedly account for the fissure or dichotomy that is clearly represented in her work of the 1930s. And it is within this liminal space, between the personal and the political, that the multiplicity of Clark's identities coexists, that autobiography, memory, and current events are mapped. Clark's paintings and drawings of the early 1930s consist of landscapes, domestic still lifes, portraits of friends and family, and self-portraits. As Clark herself said in an interview in 1980 about this work: "I wasn't terribly political in those days, that came ... later."[4] Nevertheless, even at this time Clark's approach to her work could be described as what cultural theorist Dorothy Holland has defined as "the space of authoring." As Holland argues, "The space of authoring, of self-fashioning, remains a social and cultural space, no matter how intimately held it may become. And it remains, more often than not, a contested space, a space of struggle."[5]

Paraskeva Clark's dramatic self-portrait *Myself* (1933) (fig. 1), exhibited in the Canadian Group of Painters' 1933 exhibition in Toronto, is an example of the artist's "space of authoring." Almost life-size, it was Clark's largest painting to date. Its cubo-modernist style, a legacy of her study under Kuzma Petrov-Vodkin (1878–1939) in the "Free Studios" of Russia's Petrograd Art Academy, confirmed Clark as one of the leading modernists in Toronto.[6] The bold posture that Clark gave herself in this image confronts the viewer with assurance and confidence. Diminutive in stature, Clark maximized her painted persona, at a time when Canada's art world was male-dominated, by scaling her female figure to fill the canvas and using the schematic door behind the figure to thrust herself into the viewer's space.[7]

At the same time, Clark provided *Myself* with double-edged signifiers. The position of her arms, crossed over her swelling belly, may be interpreted as a means of obscuring her pregnant state (her second son, Clive, was born two months later) at a time when pregnancy was not publicly emphasized. But it may also be interpreted as a protective gesture of a joyous state. Similarly, the black dress may refer to the tumultuous period of her prior widowhood (her first husband, Oreste Allegri Jr., had died within two years of their marriage), or it may simply adorn an elegantly and stylishly dressed European woman. As a glamorous, exotic, and powerful "other," Clark's image may easily be read as a challenge to Torontonians' ideas of passive femininity and private maternity in the 1930s. Metaphorically and symbolically, *Myself* engages the viewer in a subtle but theatrical encounter with Clark's public and private personas and with issues of gender and memory. Intersections between "intimate

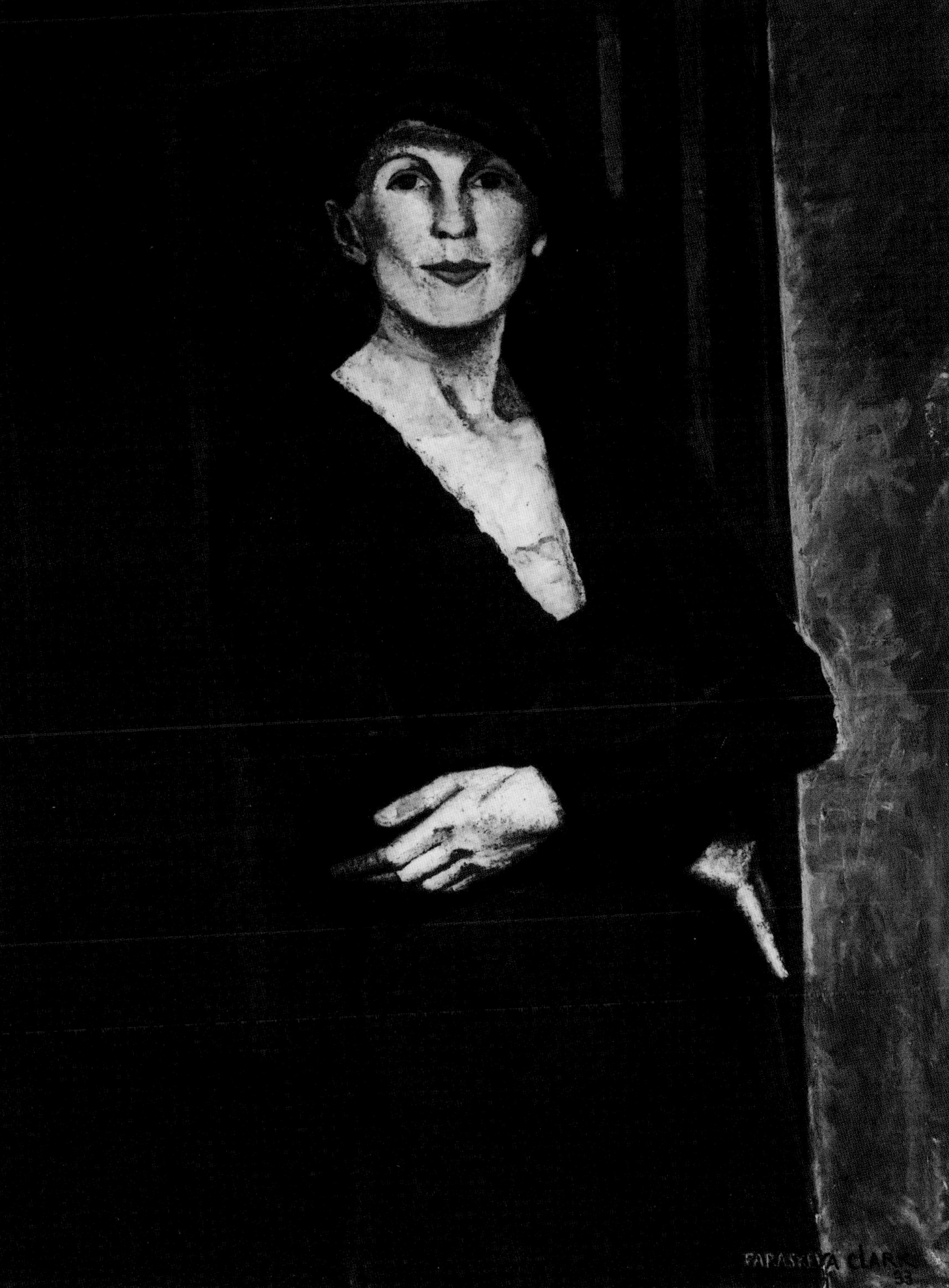

or personal world[s]" and "the collective space of cultural forms and social relations"[8] are conceived poignantly as self-reflections on her identity as outsider, immigrant, wife, artist, woman, mother. Past desires are reimagined as indices of her newly found identity in fashionable society.

Clark's refashioning of self through the intersection of her public and private lives began soon after the untimely death, in 1923, of her husband, Oreste Allegri Jr., a set designer in Moscow. Clark then moved with her young son to live outside Paris with her in-laws. While working as a sales clerk in the fashionable Parisian interior design shop Maison D.I.M. (where she would meet Philip Clark), she sought out time to paint—"just a few hours, now and then, stolen from housework."[9] Struggling to negotiate a position between dependence and independence in her roles as widow, mother, artist, and store clerk, Clark internalized conventional notions of femininity. As she later commented, "the whole history of painting was against Women Painters ... [their] whole physical and mental make up is not suited to gather these forces—necessary to produce a really important work of art—comparable to the World of Art—created by men."[10]

In 1937, however, only six years after arriving in Canada and only four years after exhibiting with the Royal Academy and the Canadian Group of Painters, Clark began to produce a provocative group of drawings and paintings that addressed the disastrous social, political, and economic conditions of the decade. Given the absence of political strife and financial difficulties in Clark's own life in Canada, her family ties to the conservative art world of Toronto, the widespread rejection of political art in Canada at this time, and Clark's own lack of previous artistic engagement with the troubles of the decade, there is little doubt that her new work was galvanized not only by her Russian past but also by her newly formed association with the charismatic and pro-communist Canadian surgeon Norman Bethune (1890–1939). Clark was introduced to Bethune in the summer of 1936 by painter Pegi Nicol MacLeod (1904–49). At this time Bethune was in Toronto raising funds for his medical mission to the Spanish front. Openly subversive in his political stance (he had recently returned from Russia as a member of the Communist Party), Bethune ardently believed that "the function of the artist is to disturb ... to arouse the sleeper, to shake the complacent pillars of the world."[11] As Clark's friendship with Bethune quickly blossomed into a love affair (curiously acknowledged and supported by her husband),[12] her engagement with social and political issues gained ground. Indeed, Bethune's fundamental belief in the power of the artist to transform society seemed to have rekindled in Clark memories of the revolutionary ferment from her student days in St. Petersburg and renewed her sense of personal agency in the public sphere.

In 1937 Clark painted her first exploration of a public political subject, a watercolor called *Presents from Madrid* (fig. 2). Representing her rejection of fascism and her support for communism, it depicts a number of objects related to the war against fascism in Spain and to Canada's role in that war: a cap from the Canadian Mackenzie-Papineau Brigade, a red scarf with three men representing the Spanish Popular Front, a page from a medieval Spanish missal, and a Republican pamphlet.[13] But these objects were also keepsakes or mementos that Bethune had sent from the Spanish Front. Furthermore, the choice of still life, a genre associated traditionally with domestication and female accomplishments, becomes a poignant metaphor for the realities of everyday existence in a war zone. Critics, for the most part, were patronizing and dismissive in their assessment of this painting: "Mrs. Clark excels particularly in still life. ... But sometimes whimsy seizes her, and she throws at you a bunch of civil war knickknacks from Madrid."[14] Clark's subtle intervention into the impersonal male modernist aesthetic went unnoticed. *Presents from Madrid* remained in Clark's personal collection until 1942, when it was

2 Paraskeva Clark, *Presents from Madrid* (1937), watercolor over graphite on wove paper, 51.5 cm. x 62 cm. The National Gallery of Canada, Ottawa.

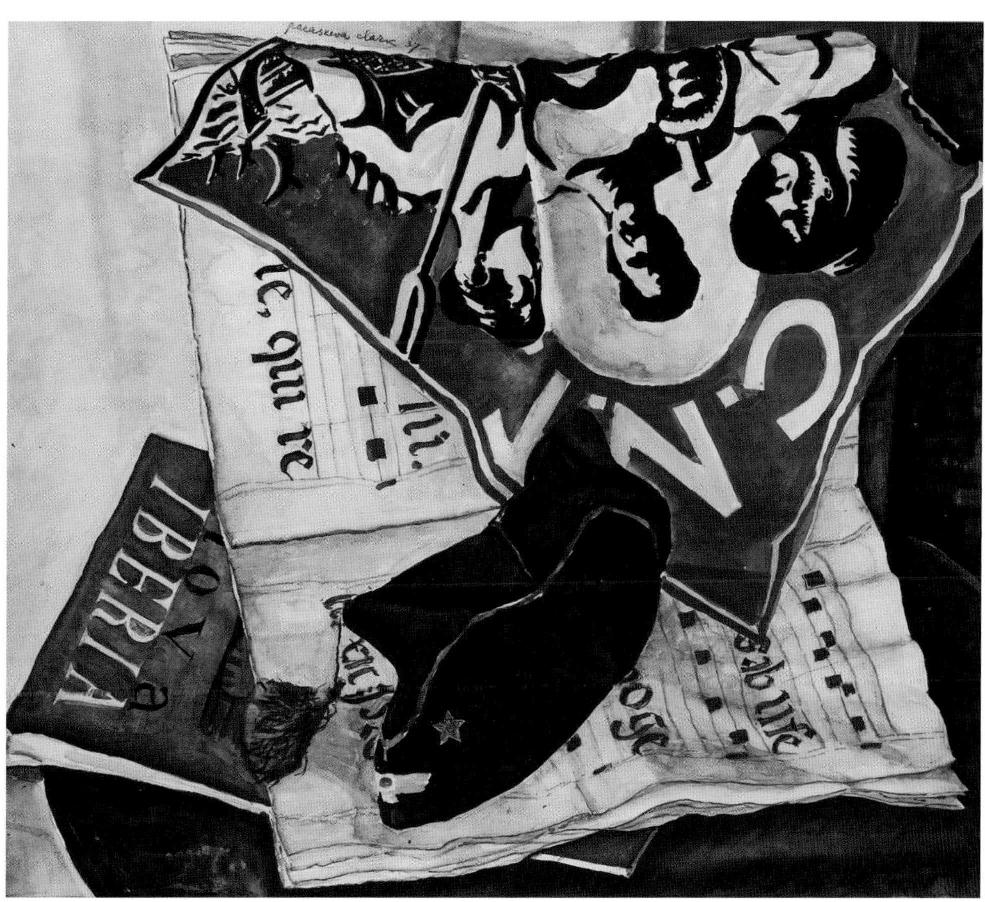

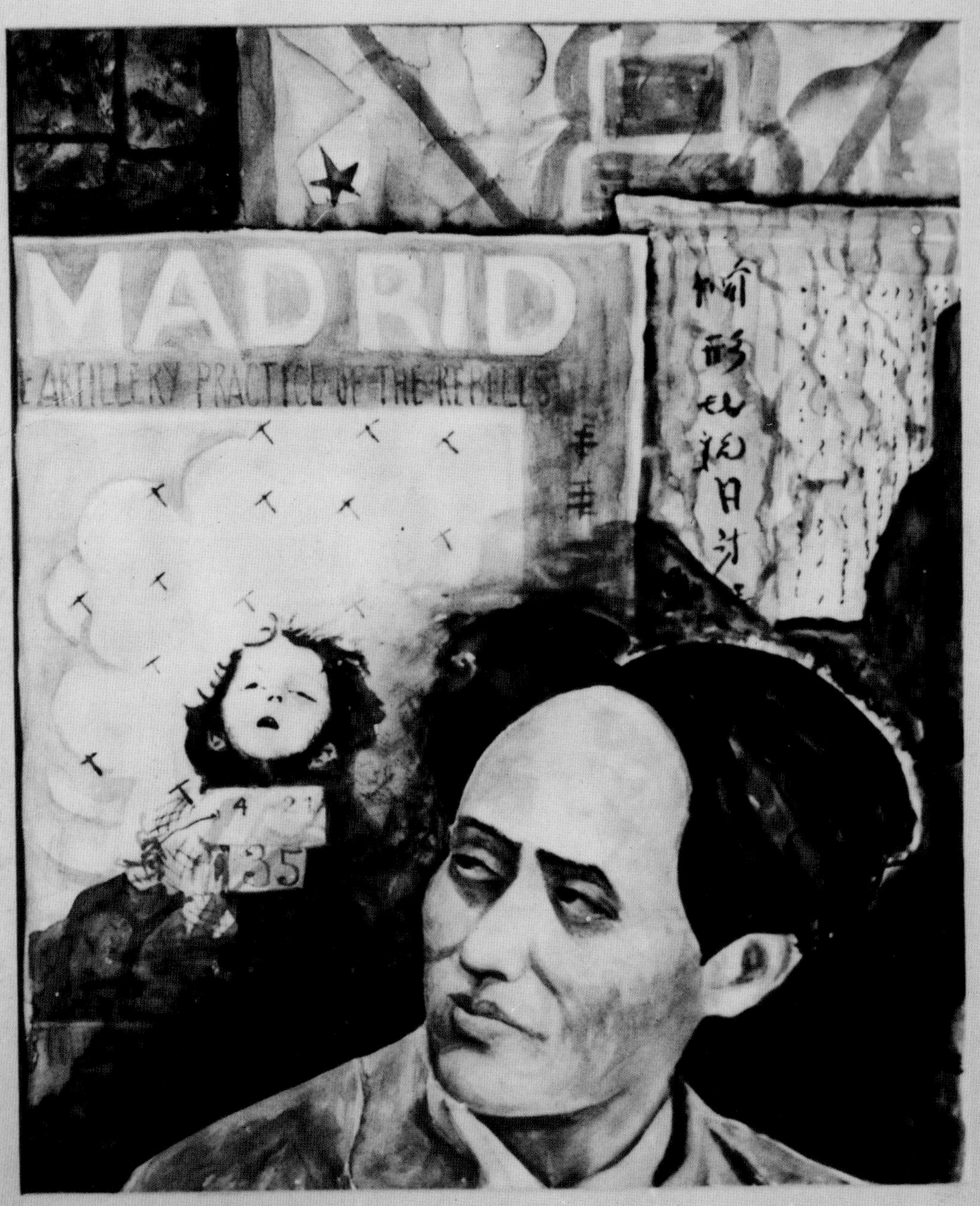

MADRID
ARTILLERY PRACTICE OF THE REBELS
135

sold to a private collector from an exhibition organized by Clark to support Canadian aid to Russia.[15]

Clark employed the same strategy of intervention in her 1938 watercolor *Portrait of Mao* (fig. 3). Once again personal mementos from Bethune—a poster from the Spanish Civil War, a photograph of Mao Zedong, and a fragment of Chinese calligraphy—are carefully juxtaposed to create a complex, multilayered modernist narrative space.[16] By using montage-like techniques in the "portrait," Clark affirmed her identity as a female modernist whose art practice was transformative. Her imagery, drawn from popular and mass culture traditionally associated with the feminine, produced a fusion of the personal with the privileged space of masculine modernist high art practice. The technique of overlapping images without apparent rational connection permitted a subtle conflation between personal intimacy and the public discourse of male action, signified overtly by Mao and covertly by Bethune's pervasive emotional presence. The representation is nuanced and elegiac. Mao gazes sorrowfully, even apprehensively, at the dead child victim of Franco's brutal Nazi-assisted bombings of defenseless citizens. Juxtaposing Chinese and English texts ("Madrid: Artillery Practice of the Rebells [*sic*]") with the faint outlines of a Republican banner bearing the star of the International Brigade allowed Clark to imbed multivocal narratives replete with private internalized references.[17] The "portrait" became a way to orchestrate identity, a "space of authoring," through the sequencing of images, transformed by Clark's imagination. As a *bricoleur* she shared an affinity with Russian modernist Alexander Rodchenko (1891–1956) in her use of montage to create "a complex multi-layered world of poetic imagination and private references."[18] Unlike other political artists of the 1930s who based their montage work on photographs and clippings from newspapers and government publications, such as the American Ben Shahn (1898–1969),[19] Clark drew primarily from personal mementos and keepsakes sent by Bethune who, as lover and hero, signified the "contact zone"—one of the primary locations of her artistic identity. The resulting *frisson* in her images speaks eloquently to issues of gender and difference, and to the "double-voiced discourse" identified by Gloria Orenstein as one "containing both a 'dominant' and 'muted' story."[20]

The insider/outsider duality that Clark experienced burdened her with ongoing conflict. The struggle to engage both Russian and Canadian identities meant going "through life with this major ... problem of being a foreigner and lacking acceptance."[21] But Clark herself was also quick to realize that painting, too, was but one side of another duality—the professional/domestic. As she stated, "It was all done in 'stolen time'—as my main occupation is bringing up my two sons [and] looking after my house and family."[22]

With *Presents from Madrid* and *Portrait of Mao*, Clark also contested the modernist yet still conservative landscapes produced by members and followers of the Toronto-based Group of Seven, Canada's most famous and most popular artists from the 1920s until well after World War II. Positive although patronizing in his assessment, art critic Graham McInnes, who was also a friend of Clark's, confirmed Clark's distinctive positioning within the Canadian artistic field of the 1930s when he wrote: "Her work has a combination of two qualities unusual in a woman painter—extreme sensitivity and wiry strength. ... She is completely and inevitably of her age."[23]

Clark's seemingly newly roused belief in the social responsibility of the artist is demonstrated most strongly in *Petroushka* of 1937 (fig. 4), her first large-scale oil painting to address a social and political subject. Multilayered and subversive, it is the definitive work in Clark's oeuvre. As Clark said, this painting was her "most important" work.[24] It brought her "great satisfaction in having struggled in the direction of ideals" cherished "in my soul."[25] The painting represents a puppet show taking place in a Moscow street. Like Stravinsky, who had drawn inspiration for his 1911 ballet *Petroushka* from the same source, Clark's painting evokes the everyday energy and noise of the urban crowd as it gathers around the puppet stage. The title, *Petroushka,* draws upon memories of the public spectacle of performances by "Peter puppet," a cherished figure in Russian folklore, comparable to the British "Punch" and Italian "Pulchinello," and the domestic space of her family's one-room apartment in Moscow, pictured behind the puppet show. Yet, in Russian, "petroushka" is also the word for parsley—making possible a seamless conflation of the domestic and the political. Clark's use of bright, even garish, colors, flat diagonal planes for the workers' apartment buildings, and compressed spatial sequences speaks not only to her experience with European modernism and her exposure to and love of the theater, but also to her growing confidence in tackling new compositional forms. Some of this confidence came from her work on a series of decorative paintings commissioned by another émigré, designer Réné Cera (b. 1896), for the windows of the Timothy Eaton Company, downtown Toronto's preeminent bourgeois department store. Working on these "huge stage like decoration panels" over a period of five years (1933–38) forced Clark to confront "new problem[s]" which gave "me the nerve to try [experimentation] in my easel painting [and] watercolours."[26]

Significantly, the subject matter of Clark's *Petroushka* is no longer directly dependent on Bethune. Rather, it is a response to the brutal police suppression of striking workers at the Republic Steel Corporation in South Chicago on Memorial Day 1937, the same event that inspired American artist Philip Evergood's *American Tragedy* of the same year

4 Paraskeva Clark, *Petroushka* (1937), oil on canvas, 122.4 cm. x 81.9 cm. The National Gallery of Canada.

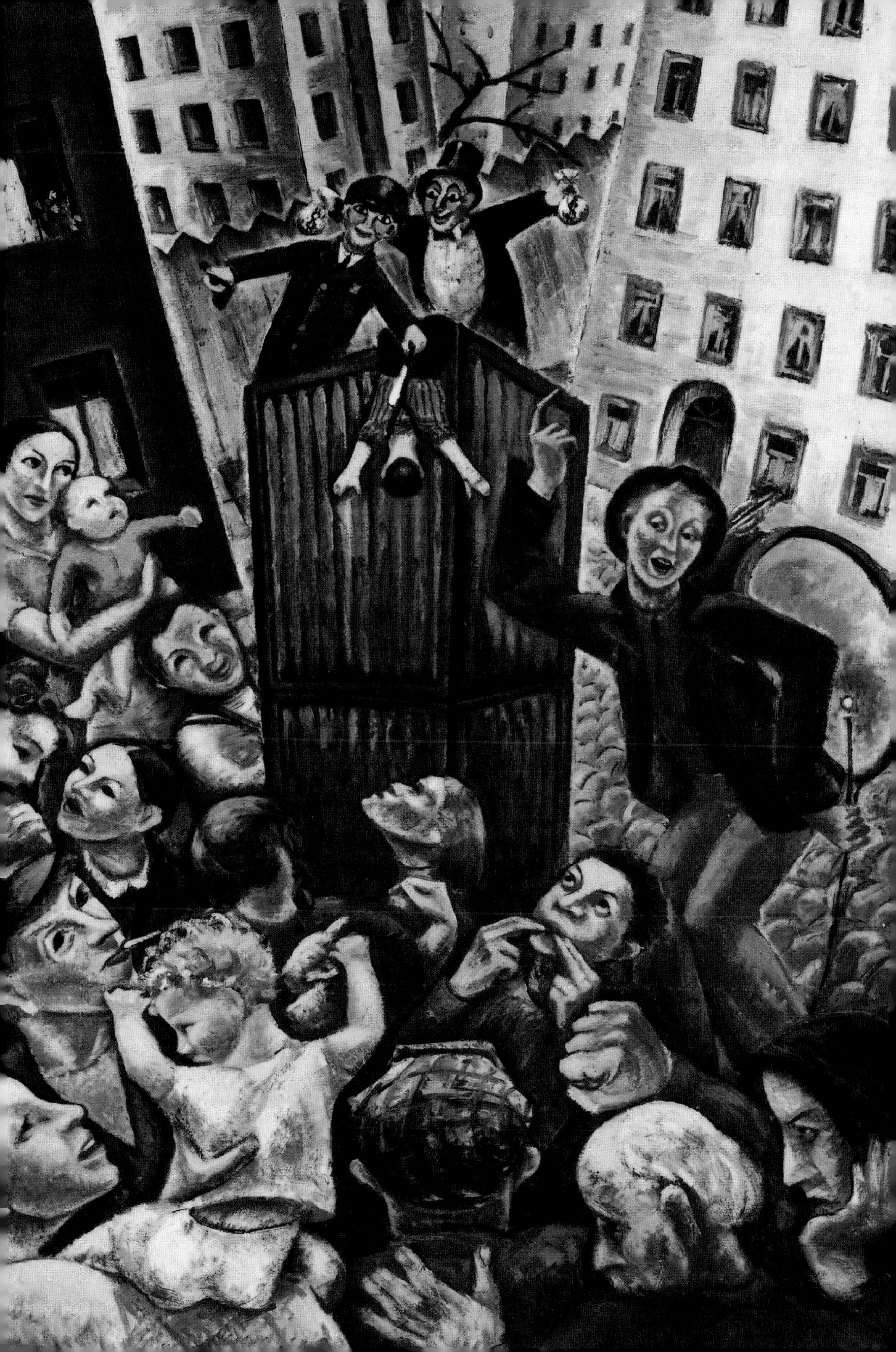

(see Patricia Hill's chapter). More specifically, Clark's painting was based on graphic newspaper images—which Clark attached to the back of the frame—of the murder of five strikers by Chicago police featured in the 1 June 1937 edition of the *Toronto Daily Star* (fig. 5). At the same time, Clark's reference to the American strike remains covert, imbedded in puppets who stand for the people involved in the particular incident: "I made the dolls ... [the] main social characters: Capitalist, police [and] worker."[27] For example, the clenched fist, which a number of the street figures who watch the puppet show seem to display as a gesture of applause, is the universally recognized symbol of Europe's antifascist Popular Front movement.[28] The puppet in formal attire, including top hat, resembles the "robber barons" in cartoons in Canadian leftist publications of the 1930s. But Canadians could also identify this puppet as R. B. Bennett, one of Canada's prime ministers during the 1930s, who wore similar clothing and, according to many leftist Canadians, was ineffective in solving the problems of the Depression.[29]

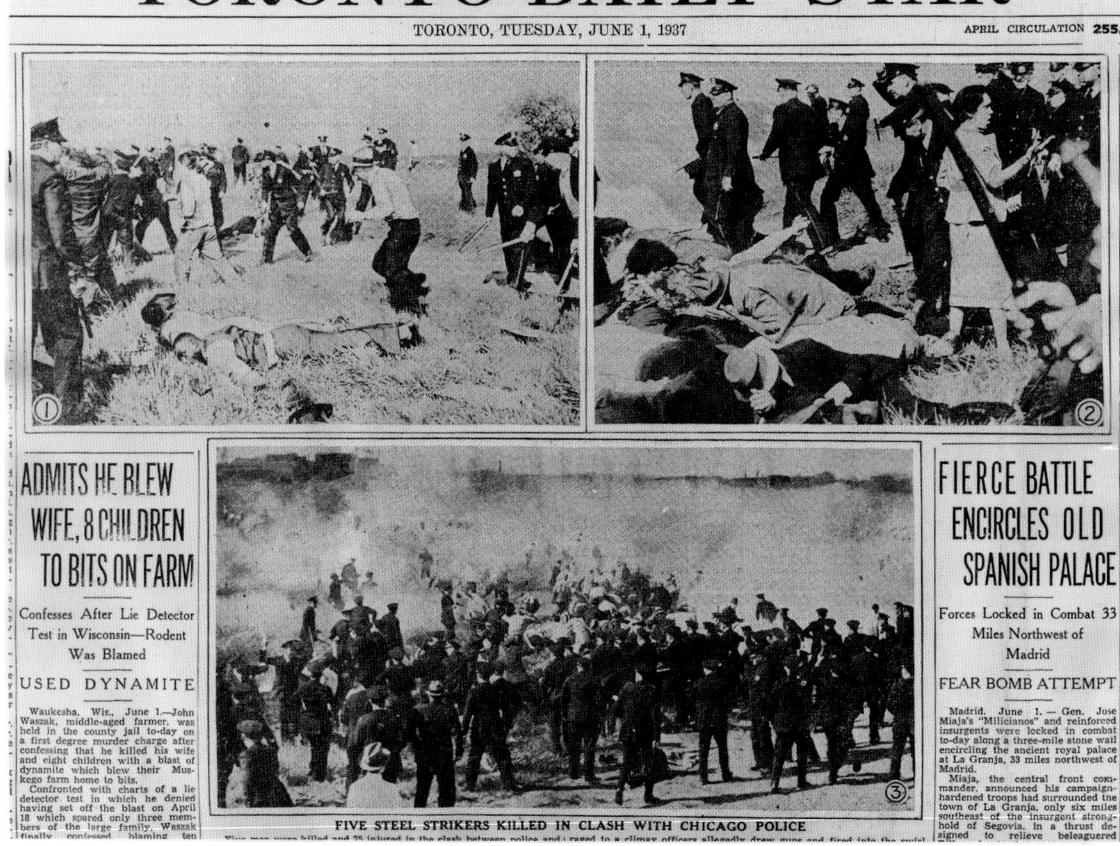

Clark's covert approach to the political subject matter of *Petroushka* produced what may be described as a multivocal bricolage of past histories and present realities that elude fixed readings and mediate a sense of agency and map her "history-in-person."[30] In the Toronto of the time, concealment of this type was not unjustified. Indeed, the Canadian government's determination to stamp out "revolutionary" elements[31] still haunted Clark years later. In a 1979 interview she said she had concealed the newspaper source for *Petroushka* out of fear of being arrested and jailed.[32] Clark was thinking specifically of the trial of Canadian trade unionist and Communist Party leader Tim Buck and seven others who were charged with sedition under the notorious section 98 of the criminal code.[33] Clark's status as an outsider and a woman, in addition to being a Communist sympathizer, made her especially wary of speaking openly, in *Petroushka* or elsewhere. The complex depiction of ethnicity and modernity we see in *Petroushka* was Clark's way of presenting herself as a communist-leaning Russian émigré to an Anglo-Canadian audience.[34]

Not surprisingly, *Petroushka* attracted the attention of critics when it was shown in the 1938 Canadian Group of Painters' exhibition. Their responses ranged from the banal—"a Punch and Judy mob scene against perilously leaning skyscrapers"[35]—to a more astute perception of the link between modernist composition and political content: "*Petroushka* with its distorted perspective, will cause dissent, but it has definite quality and says something."[36] Clark had great ambitions for this painting. As she said years later, she had "dreamt [of a] U.S. public for *Petroushka*," and was delighted when the work was selected for the Great Lakes Exhibition in 1938. In a letter to H. O. McCurry, director of the National Gallery of Canada, Clark enthused about the significance of the American exposure: "[It] was the happiest experience in my painting career. ... I am curious and hopeful for results. [C]razy enough maybe—but we all have great ambition in our heart—one time or another."[37] To have the work validated by appreciative and politically informed audiences and critics would be a refreshing change from Toronto. Paradoxically, Clark's very concealment of the source of *Petroushka* resulted in misguided commentary by the American press, which characterized the work as a "primitive fantasy" rather than a work of social or political import.[38] Nevertheless, as the sole illustration for the review in the *New York World-Telegram*, and touted as the most telling example of "dynamic ... vital and young and imaginative" art produced in Canada, *Petroushka*'s modernity had been validated internationally.[39]

Unlike the United States, where both public and private funds permitted social realism to become the dominant mode of artistic expression in the 1930s, Canada had very few artists who could be described as socially engaged. Those, like Clark, who could be, were most often situated on the margins of mainstream nationalistic art and rarely exhibited. Many of these artists provided left-wing magazines like Toronto's *Canadian Forum* and *New Frontier* with graphic illustrations openly critical of the situation of factory workers and the unemployed.[40] Not surprisingly, most of the artists whose work appeared in these journals were males with first-hand experience of the political and social issues they portrayed. Often commercial artists and members of the Workers Unity League and Artists Union, they inhabited spheres usually inaccessible to upper-middle-class women like Clark. Nevertheless, because of her political background, Clark felt a sense of camaraderie with artists, such as Leonard Hutchinson (1896–1980), who were responsive to the economic plight of their fellow citizens. Hutchinson documented, among other things, the male strikers' public protests and lockout at the Dominion Foundry and Steel Company in Hamilton, Ontario, in 1937.[41] Clark took a different approach to the economic problems of the decade. In her small watercolor *Evening Walk on Yonge Street* (1938) (fig. 6), she puts the harsh realities of the Depression in the foreground. The dark silhouettes of a family group—father on crutches and mother clutching a child to her breast—brace themselves against an unseen force and struggle bravely to move forward, oblivious to the glittering, luminous world of bourgeois fashion on display in the store window behind them.

Clark expressed dismay at most other Canadian artists' lack of interest in social and political subject matter. In particular she criticized the emphasis on landscape ("in Canada it's landscapes, landscapes, landscapes, a kind of a national form of art"),[42] referring to this work as "amateur or backward."[43] Clark's view echoed precisely the critiques presented in a number of short-lived Marxist journals published in Toronto. These critiques, while generally focusing on the bleak mood of the nation (one in four Canadians was unemployed, and more than 250,000 families had no option but "the dole"),[44] at times offered rare insights into the contested terrain of art. *Masses* (1932–34), for example, openly challenged the wilderness landscape popularized by members and followers of the Group of Seven, as well as the nostalgic, picturesque landscapes of other contemporary Canadian artists: "Little rural houses on still suburban streets, rural churches on barren country hills. ... Is this Canada? Is this what even bourgeois newspapers reflect? Is this industrialism, depression, bankruptcy, oppression and struggle? Or is it the medieval peace of a mythical Quebec village?"[45] Similar rhetoric appeared in the *Daily Clarion* (1936–39).

Like other committed socialists in Canada, Clark applauded her friends' contributions to such publications and their support of the newly formed League for Social Reconstruction, whose efforts helped transform the political landscape by uniting unemployed farmers and

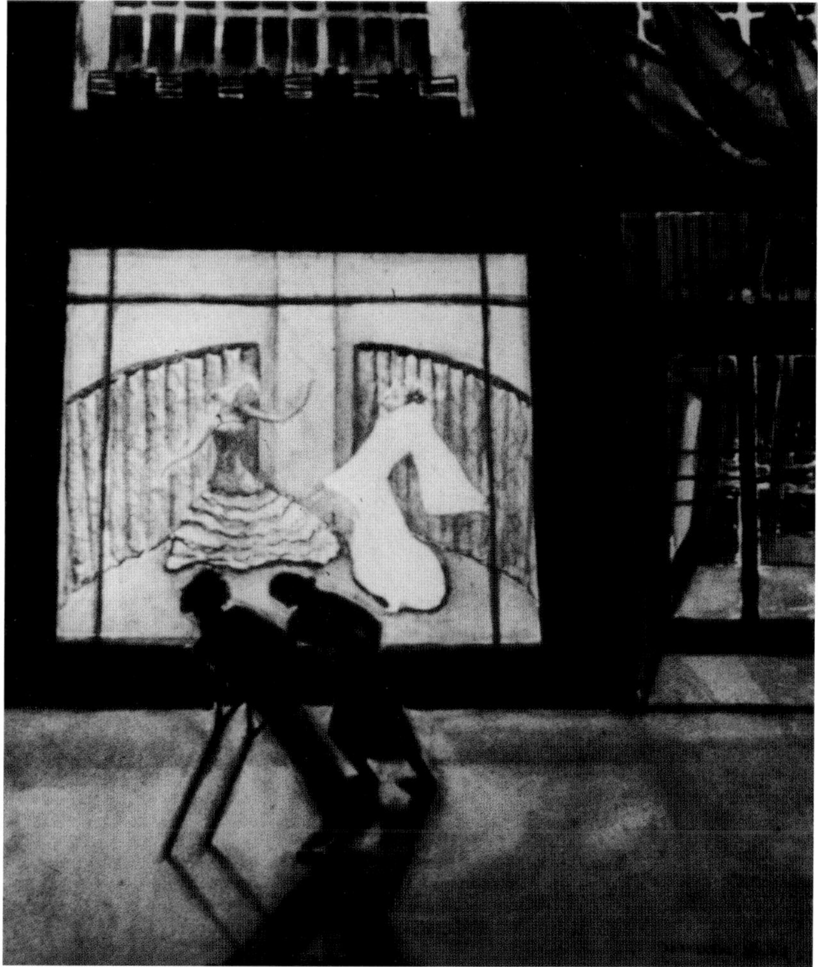

middle-class intellectuals in new regional parties.[46] Several months before Clark produced *Petroushka* (and somewhat parodoxically, given her fear of openly expressing her political beliefs in *Petroushka*), Clark wrote an article for the *New Frontier* that bluntly described what she saw as the proper political role for artists and offered a blistering attack on artists who refused to fulfill this role.[47] Here she confirmed her allegiance with left-wing progressives of the day and challenged members of the Group of Seven and their followers to "come out from behind the Pre-Cambrian shield,"[48] that is, to abandon their rugged landscapes and become socially active artists. Clark's was responding to a *New Frontier* article by a supporter of the Group of Seven, Toronto sculptor Elizabeth Wyn Wood (1903–66).[49] Clark's polemic carried the full weight of one who had witnessed revolution firsthand. Written in collaboration with art critic Graham McInnes (the byline reads "as told to"), Clark speaks directly about the role of the artist: "think of the human being: take actual part in your own times, find their expression and translate it, help your fellow man in the struggle for the future."[50] Her challenge was unequivocal: "I cannot imagine a more inspiring role than that which the artist is asked to play for the defence and advancement of civilization." She urged Wood and other artists "to come down from [their] ivory tower[s], to come out from behind [their] pre-Cambrian Shield and dirty [their] gown[s] in the mud and sweat of conflict."[51]

Henceforth, challenging the social and artistic establishment became central to Clark's identity in Anglo-Canadian Toronto. Her basement studio, decorated with Russian flags, Soviet propaganda, a portrait of Lenin, personal keepsakes, and "civil war knick-knacks," marked her difference from her bourgeois Toronto neighbors. So did her friendship with Tim Buck (who, as well as serving as Communist Party president, co-chaired the Committee to Aid Spanish Democracy with Graham Spry, a member of the League for Social Reconstruction and a committed socialist); the socialist art critic and academic Walter Abell (Clark lent him G. V. Plenkhanov's 1937 book *Art and Society* and copies of her *New Frontier* article); and poet Dorothy Livesay and other members of the *New Frontier* editorial board.[52]

During the late 1930s Clark also used her social and artistic capital to engage with women whose circumscribed lives limited their opportunities for direct political engagement. With members of the Heliconian Club and the Lyceum's Women's Art Committee, Clark organized art auctions to raise funds for the Committee to Aid Spanish Democracy and helped arrange the homecoming of the Mackenzie-Papineau Battalion from Spain, acting out her challenge to contemporary artists to "think of the human being: take actual part in their own times, find their expression and translate it, help your fellow man in the struggle for the future."[53]

In 1941 Graham McInnes commissioned Clark to produce her first published graphic work—a series of drawings satirizing the "foibles and virtues" of "Toronto the Good" for the *New World Illustrated*.[54] By then Clark's "vivid interest in contemporary life ... expressed, with technical excellence and honesty ... and sincerity of artistic emotion"[55] confirmed her place within the vanguard of young modernist Canadian artists. In her acerbic *New World* vignettes (accompanied by equally caustic captions written by McInnes) Clark approached Toronto society with "the objectivity of a complete outsider."[56] Unlike the Group of Seven and their followers, who "for too long ... have had their eyes resolutely fixed on the Pre-Cambrian Shield with its rocks and lakes and spruce," Clark's satire of Torontonian "goodness" used parody and humor as a way of establishing an other's view of the city.[57] By this time Clark was obviously becoming more comfortable with expressing her political views openly, aided in

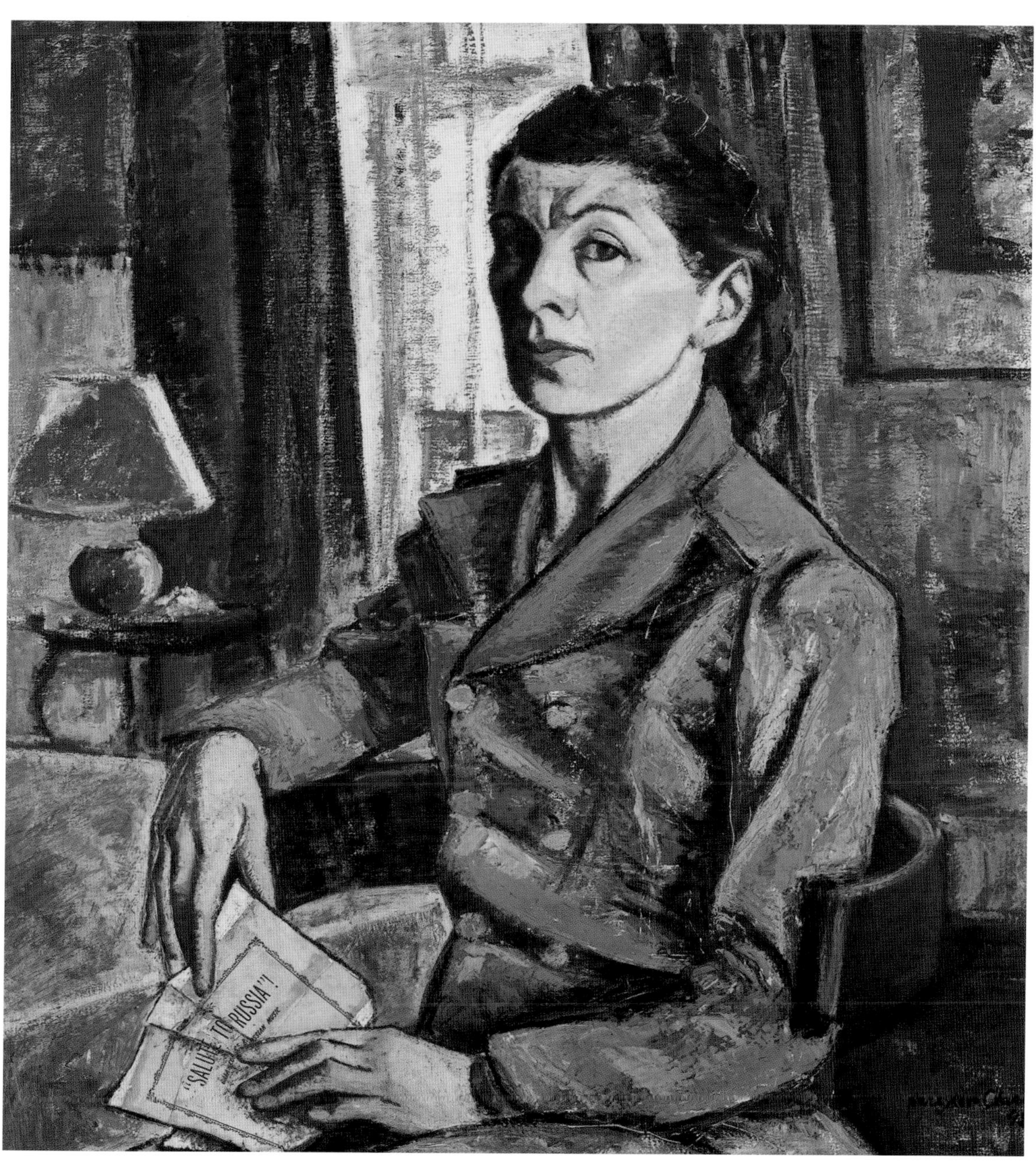

7 Paraskeva Clark, *Self-Portrait with Concert Program* (1942), oil on canvas, 76.6 cm. x 69.8 cm. The National Gallery of Canada.

this by Russia's status as a beleaguered ally. In 1942, during the siege of Leningrad, Clark organized an exhibition of her work (Canadian Aid to Russia Exhibition and Sale) to support her home city, where family members still lived: "If I can transform even some of my paintings into food, clothing and medicines for Russia I shall be content. ... I am holding this exhibition and sale because I believe wholeheartedly in the cause of the Russian people. ... Sometimes I feel I should be working side by side with the women of my homeland. Since this is not possible I must help them in any way I can."[58] Throughout the 1940s Clark continued to work at fostering relations between Russia and Canada by writing articles for *Vesnick*, a Russian-language newspaper published in Toronto, and, in 1944, by winning election as national vice president of the Federation of Canadian Russians. In this position she delivered passionate lectures on the history of Russian art to Canadians in several cities, including Hamilton, Toronto, and, Montreal.[59] When the celebrated Russian army sniper, Lieutenant Ludmilla Pavlichenko, visited Toronto in 1943, Clark was not only a member of the welcoming committee but recorded the event in her painting *Pavlichenko at City Hall*. Next to her signature she added the following inscription, an open expression of her patriotism: "February 21, 1943 / 25th Anniversary of the Heroic Red Army." The work was exhibited at the annual Ontario Society of Artists in a section devoted to war art. In another work, *In a Toronto Streetcar* (1942), Clark took great delight in documenting the wave of public enthusiasm for the Russian victory over the Germans at Leningrad. This painting later went to Russia as a part of exhibition sponsored by the Writers', Broadcasters' and Artists' War Council and was eventually acquired by the City of Leningrad. In August 1943 Clark was responsible for overseeing an exhibition of Russian photographs, handicrafts, and other art sponsored by the National Council for Canadian-Soviet Friendship.[60]

By 1942 Clark was finally able to use her art to represent a liminal space, a site of declaration—a "contact zone"—in which an open fusion of private and public identities was possible. For example, in her *Self-Portrait with Concert Program* of 1942 (Figure 7), Clark is shown seated in her fashionable living room, looking uncompromisingly at the viewer. Her hands hold the program for "Salute to Russia" (collaged onto the surface of the painting), a benefit concert in support of the victims of the Nazi siege of Leningrad. She appears serious and confident, refusing to dramatize her pose as she did in *Myself*. Here, identity and personal agency are openly conveyed. No longer fearful of reprisals, Clark frankly identities herself as a Russian patriot *and* a Canadian wife and mother. The portrait seamlessly connects the social, the political, and the artistic within her own domestic space. Her private anxieties ("I felt very terrifically about Leningrad being besieged, it's my home town") are now made public ("by the pose and expression of my face I wanted to point out the seriousness of that great moment with the whole world at war").[61] This "active practising of place" restored to the domestic sphere notions of public and political agency.[62] For it is in the "memories, dreams and the contacts of [her] lived life" that Clark, the outsider, constructs a "web of diaspora crossings," challenging middle-class conventions of gender and domesticity.[63]

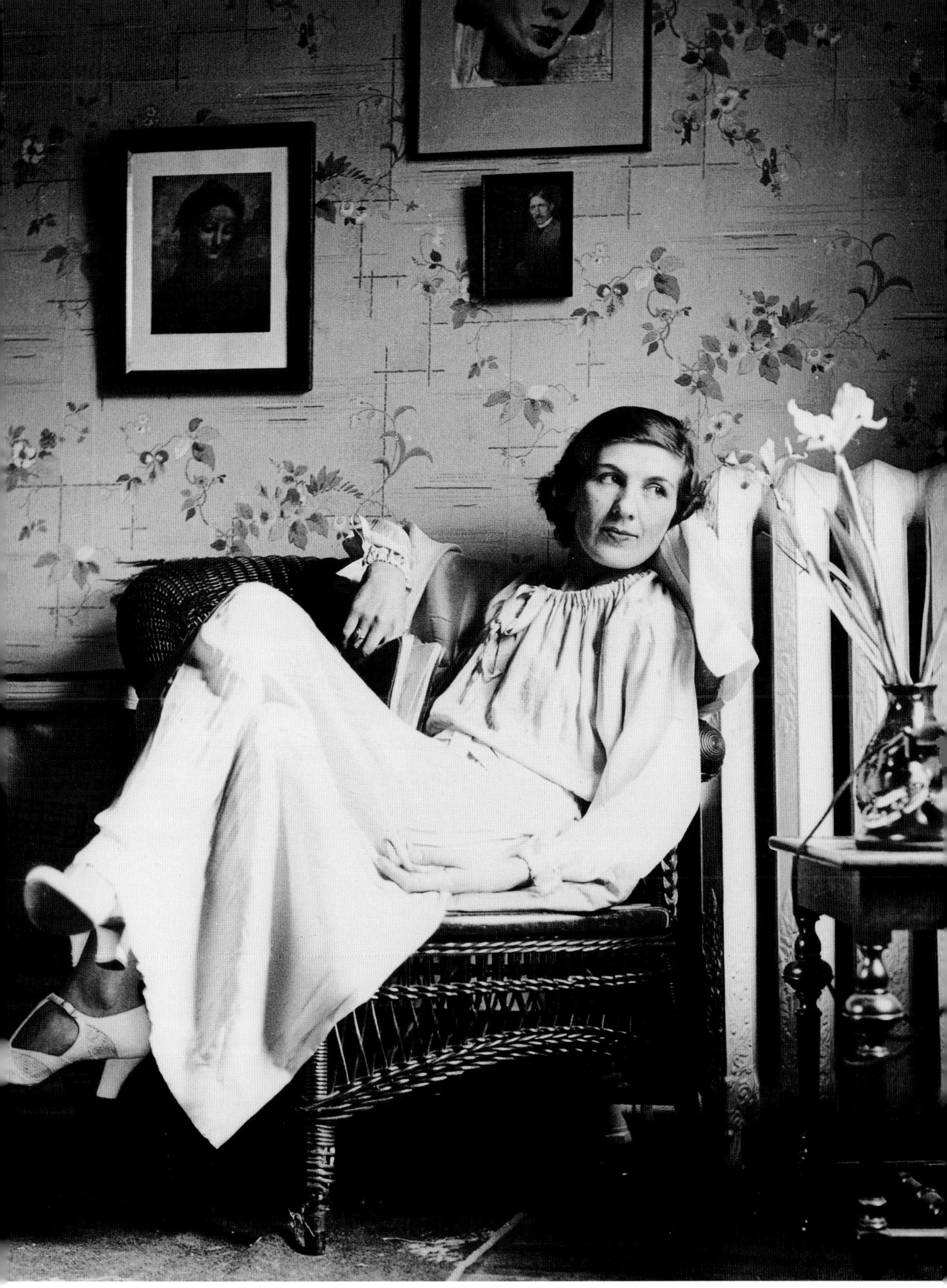

Clark's response as mother, wife, society matron, artist, socialist, communist supporter, and immigrant are marked by her gender, ethnicity, and class. Being an outsider, her negotiation of the social and political is complex, shifting, multilayered, and ultimately conflicted. Compelled by her belief in the need for artists to engage actively with the political and social issues of their time, Clark's struggle to balance her obligations as wife and mother in her adopted country resulted in a unique intersection in which the private/domestic and the public/political sphere informed each other in her art practice.

BEN SHAHN'S NEW DEAL MURALS:
JEWISH IDENTITY IN THE AMERICAN SCENE

Diana L. Linden

Although scholars and the public alike often categorize Ben Shahn (1898–1969) as a Jewish artist, we lack a consensus as to what Jewishness meant in his life and in his work—this despite several recent exhibitions and publications devoted to the artist.[1] Some argue that Shahn's turn to the American Scene of the 1930s, the period under consideration here, required him to forego Jewish content in his New Deal murals (1933–43) in deference to federal art standards. Others believe that Shahn's commitment to depicting the social ills of the 1930s evidences a distinctly Jewish sensibility, the natural outgrowth of his early Talmudic training and ethnic heritage. Such disagreements among art historians and the public parallel the continuing debate over the very nature of Jewish identity itself—is Jewishness a religion, a race, a culture, or an ethnicity?[2] Ben Shahn painted his murals in response to the often anxious experience of American Jewish life during the Great Depression, a period since overshadowed in the historical literature by the Holocaust. A broader cultural definition of Jewishness reveals that Shahn's murals refer to the sociopolitical conditions of the working-class American Jewish community that was redefining itself culturally, economically, and politically.[3] Shahn's mural for the Jersey Homesteads (1937–38) (fig. 1); the controversy over his *Resources of America* (1938–39), painted for the Bronx Central Post Office; his proposed series on constitutional freedoms and

An earlier version of this essay appeared in *Common Man, Mythic Vision: The Paintings of Ben Shahn,* exh. cat., ed. Susan Chevlowe (Princeton and New York: Princeton University Press and the Jewish Museum, 1998), 37–66. I would like to thank Frances K. Pohl and Matthew Baigell for their assistance over the years. Michelle Hermann Raheja offered helpful comments, as did Peter W. Ross. Many thanks to my co-editors, Alejandro Anreus and Jonathan Weinberg.

241

immigration (1939) for the St. Louis Post Office; and the related one-panel *First Amendment* (1940–41) for the Woodhaven Station, Queens, Post Office illustrate as a group Shahn's dedication to liberal social policy, his support for immigration reform, and his desire for political freedom, positions that, although not exclusive to American Jews, were strong markers of American Jewish identity during the interwar years.

Shahn's Early Career

Between 1933 and 1943 the federal government funded numerous art programs to employ artists, maintain American culture during the depths of the Depression, and make the arts accessible to a greater portion of the public. The government provided artists—whose training, style, and concerns varied—with specific thematic and stylistic guidelines. They were to depict the American Scene, to create celebratory images of the nation's past and present in a legible, narrative, and realist style.[4] Shahn was one of many artists employed by the federal programs, and experts today consider his murals some of the finest of the New Deal. By the time the federal arts programs were established, Shahn had earned a reputation as a socially critical artist. In the early 1930s Shahn's desire to "tell a story and his search for subject matter relating to his own personal experience" led to his first works to depict social injustices.[5] For inspiration, Shahn looked to both recent Jewish secular history and Jewish religious traditions. He began with a series on the Dreyfus Affair and a Haggadah (both 1931), the latter portraying the story of the Exodus. Shahn was still developing a style strong enough to convey his social message, which he achieved with his gouache-and-tempera series *The Passion of Sacco and Vanzetti,* (1931–32) and his subsequent series on labor leader Tom Mooney (1932). Mexican muralist Diego Rivera (1886–1957) wrote the catalog essay for Shahn's Mooney series; he then invited the younger artist to assist with his fresco *Man at the Crossroads* (1933) for Rockefeller Center, which Nelson Rockefeller, infamously, ordered destroyed.[6] Shahn later helped Rivera on his murals for the New Workers' School (1933). Through working with Rivera, Shahn became one of the few New Deal muralists to learn the demanding technique of fresco painting. Inspired by Rivera's technical prowess and commitment to an art of social change, Shahn was determined to paint his own murals.

Ben Shahn pursued eight separate mural commissions under the federal arts programs and established a pattern notably different from those of his contemporaries.[7] He chose not to enroll in the New Deal's easel division, as many painters did, but instead worked as a photographer for the Resettlement Administration/Farm Security Administration

(RA/FSA). Shahn was highly ambitious in his choice of mural commissions. He sought out officials to whom he could propose his mural projects rather than wait for them to announce competitions, and he only applied to the most prestigious national competitions. In order to paint his multifigured, compositionally complex murals, Shahn did extensive preparatory study and research, drawing upon books and articles, his travels, his own prior work, and popularly reproduced photographs.[8] Shahn wrote lengthy descriptions detailing his mural's iconography and storyline, showing that he conceived his murals both conceptually and visually. Shahn and other left-leaning artists envisioned their murals as a way to spur their audiences (both real and imagined) to political and social action. Yet, simultaneously, Shahn created an iconography of nation building and civic pride. He sought to confront America's social problems but also to reaffirm Jewish life in America—in other words, to paint Jews into the American Scene.

Jews Without Money

During the years of Shahn's mural production, American Jews expressed great anxiety about their immediate economic situation, the employment, education, and housing barriers they faced, and the rapid growth of fascism and anti-Semitism globally. Anti-Semitism, with its violence, restrictions, and resulting sense of danger and uncertainty about the future, set the American Jewish experience apart from that of other white working-class ethnic groups. Even before the Depression, modernization and acculturation had destabilized Jewish institutions and communities in the United States. Secularization weakened communal bonds previously cemented by shared languages, religious traditions, and social interdependence; yet, in America, Jews built new bonds through cultural, fraternal, and political institutions.[9] Labor unions, leftist organizations, and the Democratic Party became important institutions through which Jews could organize and participate in American public life.[10] Shahn, whose *Jersey Homesteads* fresco contains one of the few images of Franklin D. Roosevelt in a federal mural, was devoted to the president and to the New Deal. In hindsight, scholars have proposed that such Jewish devotion was undeserved in light of FDR's refusal to intervene on behalf of European refugees.[11]

With the creation of the Popular Front (1935), the Communist International openly proclaimed an antifascist position, supporting democratic governments opposed to fascism and becoming more tolerant toward ethnic expression among its members. The Popular Front's support

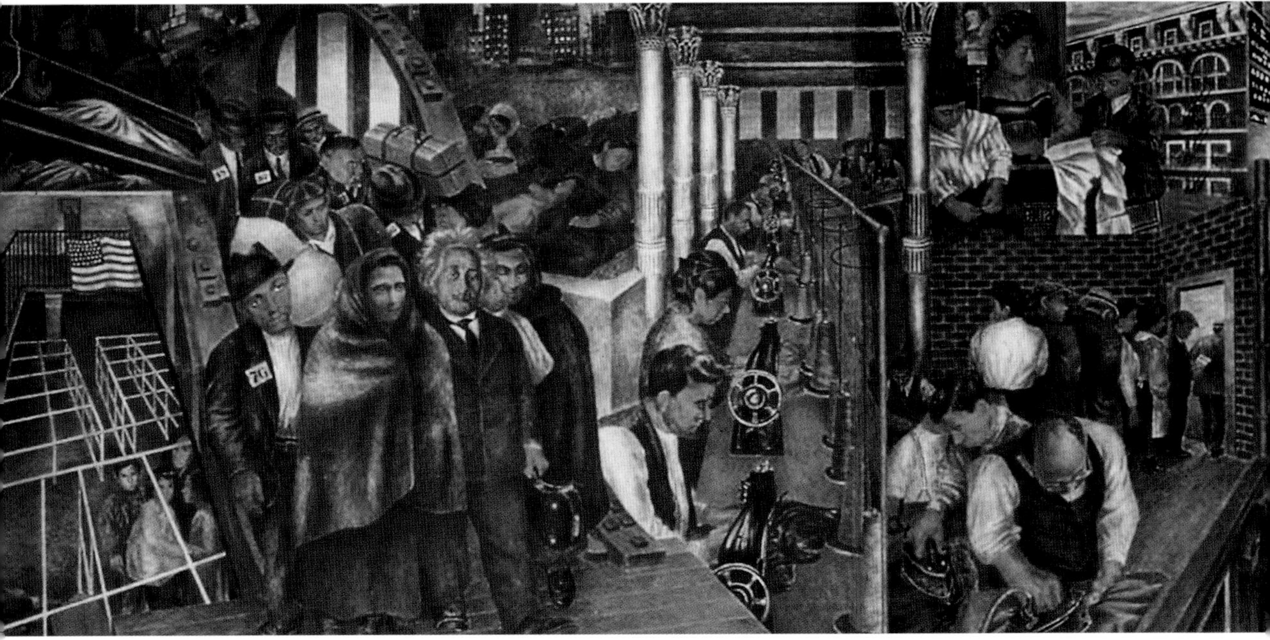

for FDR and the New Deal was particularly appealing to Jews who could
now support both FDR and socialism. Previously, the American Communist Party (CPUSA) stressed that members should "Americanize," since
ethnicity was a barrier to working-class unity and the class struggle.[12]
With the Popular Front, the CPUSA formed new ethnic bureaus—the
largest being the Jewish bureau—that hosted a variety of cultural and
political activities. Shahn supported FDR, the New Deal, and the Popular Front's antifascist campaign. He was concerned about the increase
in American nativism and European fascism and hoped that as an artist he could positively inform and reform society. Although the federal
government initiated the art projects in 1933 (as the Public Works of Art
Project) and Shahn applied for commissions immediately, it was several
years before he saw a commission through to completion. In 1936 officials selected Shahn to paint a mural for the Jersey Homesteads, which
was not only his first mural but also his most open expression of the
American Jewish experience.

The Jersey Homesteads: Zion in the Garden State

Established by the Resettlement Administration, the Jersey Homesteads
(now Roosevelt, New Jersey) was a subsistence homesteading commu-
nity created to house Jewish garment workers from nearby New York
City. Shahn moved to the town in 1939 and lived there until his death.
The needle trades were important to the Jewish economy for decades.
By the early 1930s the garment industry employed one-third of New
York's Jews, who were left devastated by layoffs during the Depression.[13]

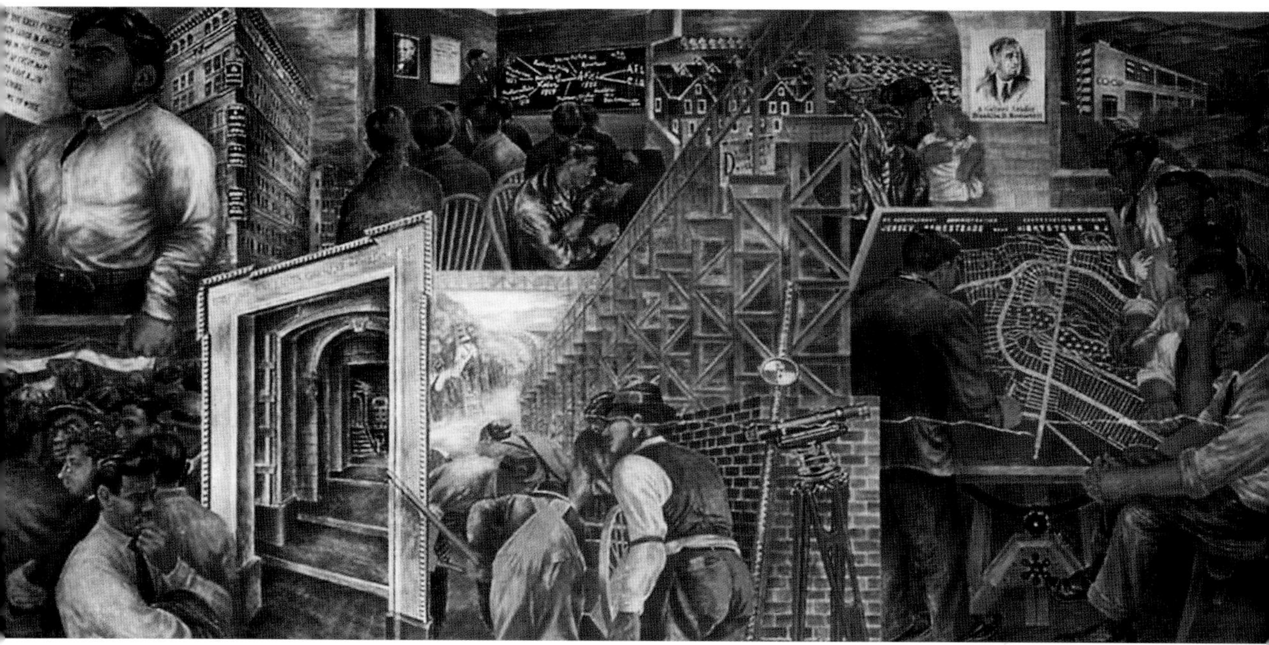

1 Ben Shahn, *Jersey Homesteads* (1937–38), mural, full view, fresco 12 x 45 ft. Commissioned by the Farm Security Administration. Photo courtesy of VAGA. © Estate of Ben Shahn, licensed by VAGA, New York.

To counter such dependence on one industry, the Jersey Homesteads was to have a dual economy based on both agriculture and garment production. The majority of homesteaders, including Shahn, were Eastern European émigrés. Shahn's untitled fresco recounts the story of mass East European Jewish immigration to the United States—a major event in American history; the oppressive labor and living conditions that Jews found in exploitive sweatshops and tenements; the better lives they created for themselves through trade unionism; and the labor reforms and social programs of the New Deal.

Although two-thirds of Shahn's mural focus on urban imagery, the setting for the mural—the Jersey Homesteads—was in fact rural. American Jewish history is often presented as solely an urban experience, centralized in New York's Lower East Side, which has been mythologized into a Jewish Plymouth Rock.[14] Jewish agricultural and rural utopias, such as the Am Oylom Movement, were an important part of the American experience that saw a revitalized interest during the 1930s.[15] Birobidzhan, in the Soviet Union's Jewish Autonomous Region established by Stalin, was one important prototype for the Jersey Homesteads.[16] Benjamin Brown, the key organizer of the Jersey Homesteads, was involved with the establishment of Birobidzhan and with earlier Jewish American farming cooperatives.

A U.S. Interior Department press release revealed the government's expectations for the Homesteads, which were both social and economic:

> [I]t is popularly thought to be unusual for Jewish people to engage in a rural or semi-rural undertaking. The Jewish people are known as a gregarious race who have been highly urbanized for the past

two thousand years, in large measure as the result of European laws, which prohibited them from owning land. What is not so well known is that some 120,000 Jews are on farms in this country today. Attempts by other countries to settle Jewish families on the land have failed largely because they neglected the social side of life which is so important to the Jew. The Jew is a sociable citizen. He sets great store by family, friends, and community. He flees from isolation. The Jersey Homesteads plan promises him a semi-rural or suburban life, but one in which neighbors and the community are strongly emphasized. In such a community, the advantages of subsistence homesteading are to be enjoyed with no loss of these fine social activities which go to make up the well-rounded life which the Jewish family demands.[17]

Contradictions are many within the Homesteads press release and indeed within the notion of the town itself. The author of this press release describes Jews as "sociable citizens," notable for their gregariousness, family ties, and communal aspects, all of which runs counter to the strong strain of individualism celebrated in American thought. While labeled pioneers and homesteaders, terms that would resonate with the concept of American individualism, the Homesteads actually segregated Jews by placing them in an artificial community based on shared ethnicity and occupation. Wanting to avoid such conflicts and contradictions over his mural's content, Shahn proposed an advisory panel of consultants: Felix Adler (1851–1933), founder of the Ethical Cultural movement; Rabbi William Fineschreiber (1878–1968), outspoken opponent of Zionism and the establishment of a Jewish state in Palestine; art historian and activist Meyer Schapiro (1904–96); and (Baruch) Charney Vladeck (1886–1938), socialist, founder of the American Labor Party, former editor of the *Jewish Daily Forward,* and champion of public housing. It is doubtful that the panel ever convened, however, for Adler had died several years earlier. But the makeup of the proposed group speaks nevertheless to the pluralism of the American Jewish community during the 1930s, and to Shahn's receptivity to such diversity.

Shahn's notes, sketches, and correspondence establish that as he worked on the mural he changed both its overall theme and its particular details. He replaced a Passover scene set in the Pale of Settlement with an image of busy garment workers doing piecework in a New York tenement. While Passover is a festival of freedom, it also signified danger, because pogroms and anti-Jewish violence, fueled by false accusations that Jews were performing blood rituals, often erupted at this time. Shahn therefore removed the Passover scene not to deny or camouflage religion, or his and the homesteaders' identity as Jews, but rather to

concentrate on the hardships experienced by workers in America.[18] By
the time Shahn began work on the mural, he had become very active in
the American labor movement and the newly formed Congress of Industrial Organizations (CIO).[19] Labor unions, including the garment unions,
were strong centers of both ethnic and political identification for Jews.[20]
Shahn's mural program sets forth his belief that American Jews should
affiliate with other workers and build a broader base of support for
themselves in this way. Charney Vladeck similarly urged Jewish workers to build coalitions based on class and labor rather than on ethnicity.[21]
Yet neither Shahn nor Vladeck believed that Jews should renounce their
heritage in order to assimilate into mainstream culture. What they envisioned was a new type of Jew and a new kind of American: a strong
American worker-Jew, protected by the New Deal and by labor unions.[22]

Shahn designed his mural's tripartite structure as an unfolding tale
of the past, present, and future that he labeled "background," "immigration," and "unionization." In a lengthy handwritten outline, Shahn began
his narrative in the Pale of Settlement, noting the repressive conditions for Jews under czarist rule and the frequent accusations that Jews
practiced blood rituals (i.e., in the Mendel Beilis case).[23] Zionism, immigration, or retreat into religion as solace were the options Shahn saw for
Old World Jews who sought a better, safer life. Immigration—Shahn's
choice, brought Jews to America; and in this new country, he wrote,
generational tensions between the older Jews, raised in East European
shtetls, and the new breed of American Jews soon developed. Looking
warily at contemporary Germany, Shahn warned all Jews, young and old,
against assimilation and disunity. In a later but undated essay, Shahn
developed his ideas for the mural further, filling in the details presented
in the first, sketchy, list. He remained committed to the best path for
Jews to follow toward a better future. He imagined a cloud "in which
the horrors of Jewish persecution in Hitler Germany are shown," hanging perilously above a young Jewish worker who has reached a divided
pathway in the road. Deciding that his future is not in Palestine, Shahn's
worker instead ventures forth as an American Jew, returning to the land
by living communally (in the Jersey Homesteads), practicing his trade
but not "sacrificing his racial and cultural treasures."

For the final fresco Shahn created a storyline that departed from a
strictly linear chronology, one constructed of images both personal and
public, full of densely stacked figures, rapid perspectival shifts, and the
use of architectural elements to enclose and divide scenes (all evidence
of Rivera's stylistic influence). Shahn began his mural in 1930s Germany,
where, at upper left, in the darkest portion, the small figure of a Nazi soldier stands with signs that warn in German: "Germans beware: don't buy

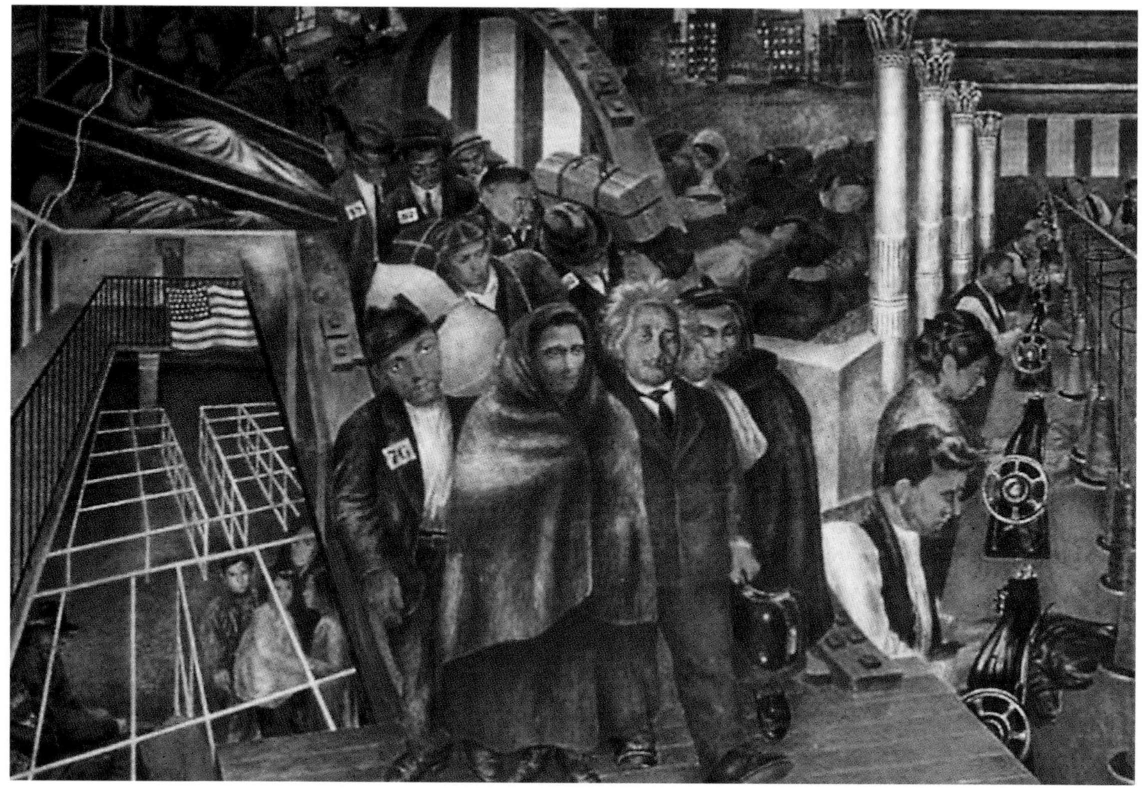

from Jews" and "Attention Jews, visit forbidden," referring to the 1933 Nazi boycott and the Nuremburg Laws of 1935 (fig. 2). To the right of the Nazi, Shahn makes a temporal shift back to 1927. Two Jewish women raise their arms in anguish as they mourn beside the open caskets of the executed political martyrs Sacco and Vanzetti, who for Shahn symbolize the vulnerability of all radicals and immigrants in America. Holding up the coffins, directly below, is the Ellis Island registry hall, shown almost empty of émigrés to indicate that the setting is post-1924, when government imposed its immigration restrictions.[24]

Shahn created a pastiche of immigrants coming off a ship's gangplank (fig. 2), mixing the anonymous arrivals with portraits of his family, friends, and historical figures—all of whom had arrived at different times and from different countries. Shahn painted his mother, who arrived in the United States in 1906, standing near the artist Raphael Soyer (1899–1987), who had actually arrived in 1912 as a teenager (Shahn shows Soyer as a grown man in the 1930s) because his father, a Hebrew scholar, was fleeing persecution. One row behind stands the socialist German-Jewish electrical engineer Charles Steinmetz, who arrived in 1889 at Castle Gardens, not Ellis Island as depicted. Shahn painted Albert Einstein, who had just arrived in 1933, as the leader of

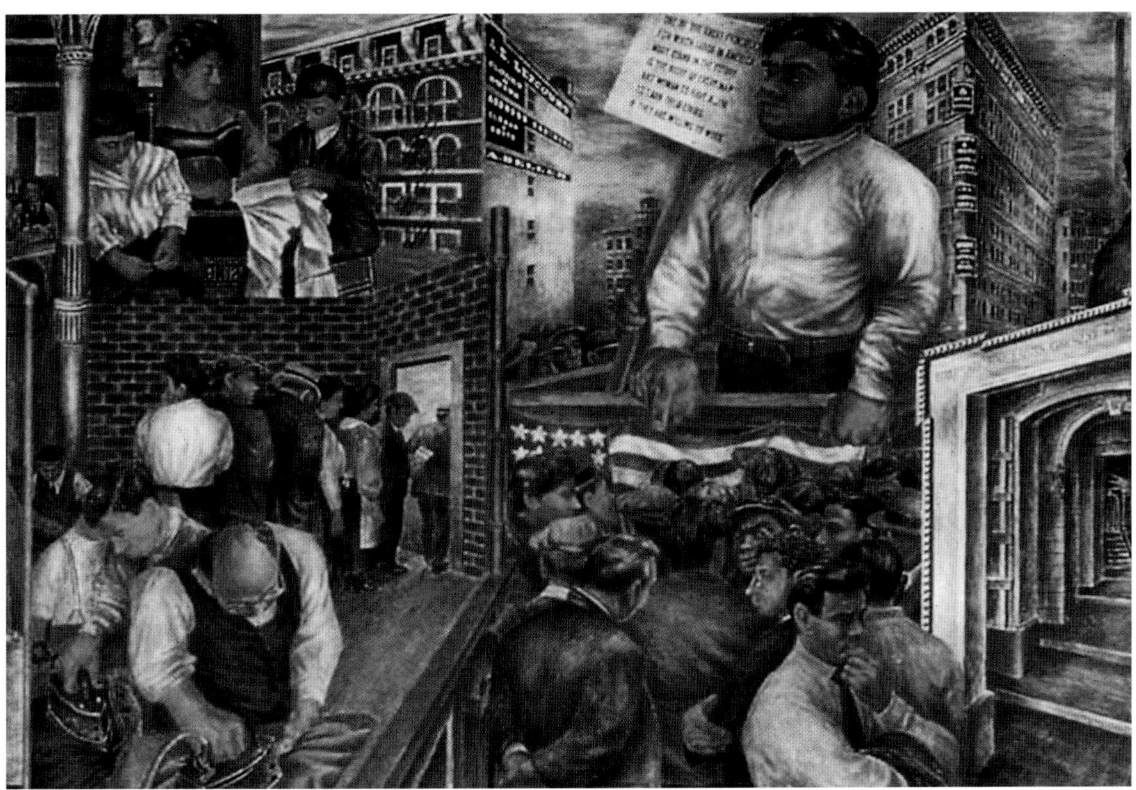

3 Ben Shahn, *Jersey Homesteads* (center detail). © Estate of Ben Shahn, licensed by VAGA, New York.

the group. Unlike the residents of the Homesteads, who were from Eastern Europe, Einstein had recently renounced his German citizenship to settle in Princeton, near the Homesteads.[25] Significantly, Shahn suggests that immigration to America is open, when in fact restrictive policies barred refugees and exiles from entering.

The montage of images spilling out of the darkness of Nazi Germany culminates with the arrival of this group of immigrants. These new Americans stride forward, commanding the greatest space within the composition to symbolize freedom breaking loose from oppression. The common cause behind their flight to America, namely, persecution on either religious or political grounds, takes precedence over the actual dates of entry to the United States. Together, such celebrated individuals as Einstein, Steinmetz, and Soyer, joined by Shahn's friends and relatives and by other, anonymous, figures symbolize Jewish refugees who have sought freedom through in the United States throughout American history.

Shahn concentrates on labor history and labor unions for the mural's central panel (fig. 3). Whereas the Nazi figure in the first panel warns viewers of the horrors in Germany, Shahn's includes the Triangle Shirtwaist Company building (indicated by company signs painted on its façade), site of the tragic 1911 fire, to remind viewers that America,

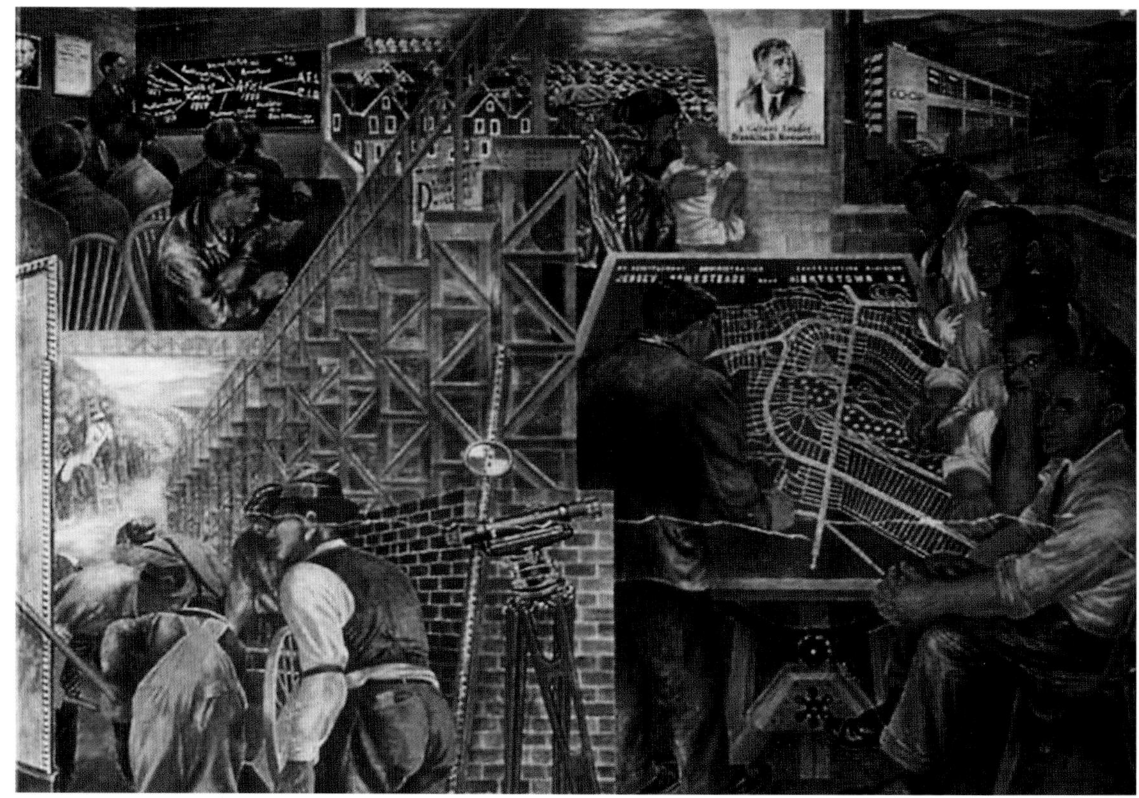

too, knows horror and injustice.[26] In front of the building stands a
union organizer who bears a strong resemblance to John L. Lewis and
dominates the scene, pushing back against and diminishing the factory
building. On his sign, Shahn wrote the following message: "One of the
great principles for which labor and America must stand in the future
is the right of every man and woman to have a job, to earn their living
if they are willing to work." In a preparatory study entitled *East Side
Soap Box* (1936) Shahn painted Yiddish text on the signboard. In the
mural, Shahn painted a quotation from Lewis's closing address at the
CIO's 1937 conference in Atlantic City. Below the grandstand a group of
workers mill about, each looking off in a different direction; they have
yet to form a collective body of workers. Still Shahn depicts the men in
thought, closely bound together, pausing, all to indicate the potential of
Lewis's message taking hold.

In the mural's concluding panel, Shahn displays the benefits brought
about by organized labor and the New Deal. Viewers gain entrance to
the final panel and its promise of a better life by first standing on line
with the other workers that Shahn has painted outside a doorway
marked "ILGWU" (International Ladies' Garment Workers' Union); Shahn
follows this entrance with other doorways, each inscribed with the name

4 Ben Shahn, *Jersey
Homesteads* (right detail).
© Estate of Ben Shahn,
licensed by VAGA,
New York.

of a different union (fig. 4). Clearly, Shahn's message is that the efforts of organized labor have made a better life possible. To paraphrase Mary K. Coffey's essay in this volume, as viewers move alongside the expanse of Shahn's mural, they enact a historical walk, moving from the horrors of Europe to the safety of America. Shahn's audience must now pass through one final painted doorway and stand silently behind workers seated in a classroom who are learning the history of American labor. In the concluding scene of the Homesteads mural, Shahn rendered a tabletop on which are spread the blueprints for the Jersey Homesteads. Seated around the table, as if patrons in a Renaissance triptych, are John Brophy, director of the CIO; Sidney Hillman, president of Amalgamated Clothing Workers of America; David Dubinsky of the ILGWU; Heywood Broun of the American Newspaper Guild; and New York senator Robert F. Wagner, who drafted crucial labor-reform legislation during this period. The picture window view just to the left of these men shows fertile land, families, and a cooperative factory. Following the mural's progression from the dark scenes of Nazi Germany to this land of growth and plenty, Shahn has delivered his viewers to a new Eden, a place of safety and economic self-sufficiency for Jewish workers in America.

Confronting Censorship: The Bronx Central Post Office Mural

Shahn decided to make American labor and its workers the theme of his next mural, *Resources of America,* for the Bronx Central Post Office (1938–39).[27] Shahn covered the walls of the Bronx Central Post Office with a panoramic suite of workers, thirteen monumental frescos painted in tawny tones celebrating Americans at work in a variety of agricultural and industrial jobs. Despite the recent economic fluctuations, this mural is extremely optimistic, showing worker productivity and pride.[28] On its central panel, Shahn depicts the American poet Walt Whitman lecturing to a group of workers. With his flowing beard, Shahn's Whitman resembles a composite of Karl Marx and Moses, as he gestures to lines of his poetry written on a blackboard (fig. 5). In Shahn's original plans, he selected a verse from Whitman's "Thou Mother with Thy Equal Brood" (1872).[29] When officials put Shahn's mural studies on display in the lobby of the Bronx Post Office, they were met with an unanticipated protest by local Catholic clergy against Whitman's words and Shahn's vision. The objectors made their opinions known not only in the Bronx Post Office building but also in letters to local newspapers and in their Sunday sermons.

The Reverend Ignatius W. Cox, a professor of ethics at Fordham University in the Bronx, led the protest against Whitman's words and

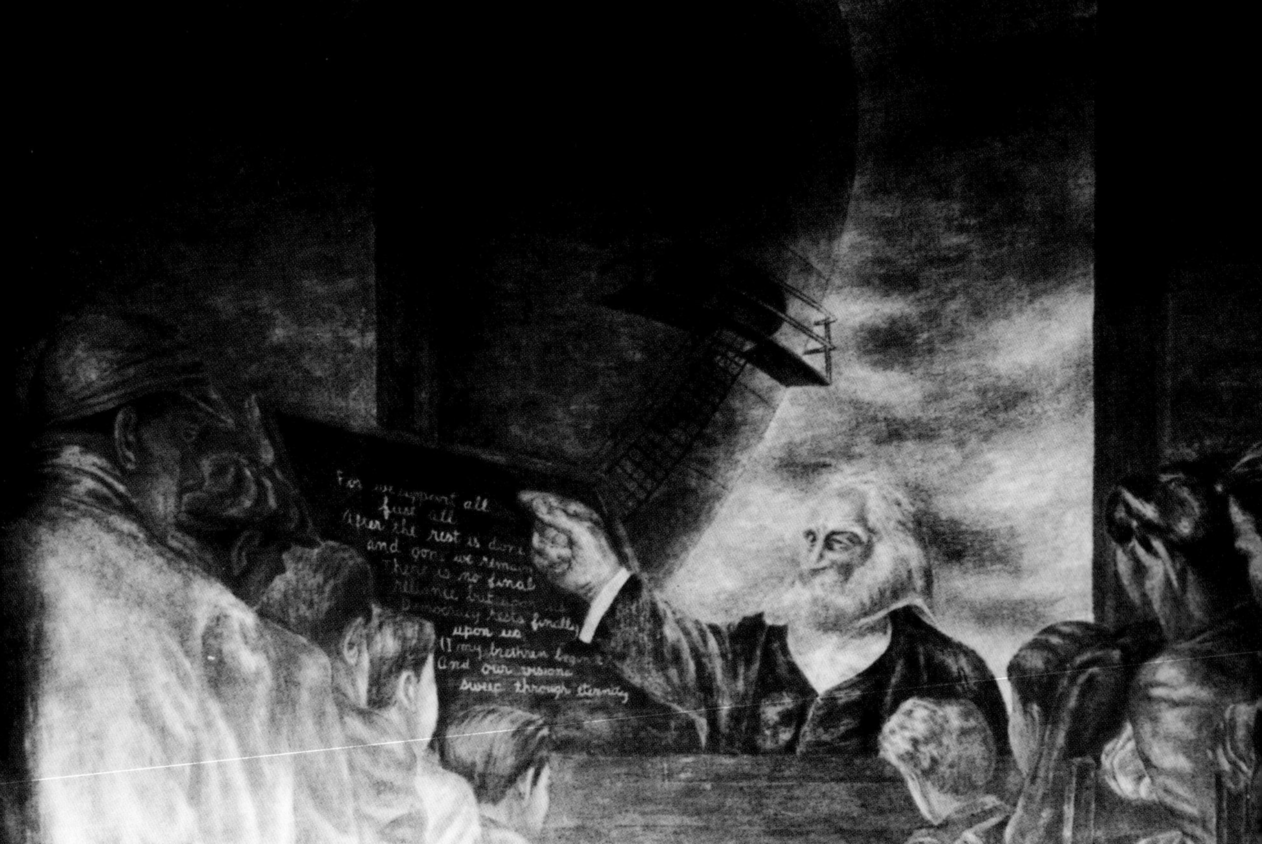

Shahn's murals. In a Brooklyn church, Cox delivered a sermon entitled "Is Government Sponsoring Irreligion in Art?" in which he described Shahn's work and Whitman's words as an insult to Christians. Cox encouraged parishioners to write letters demanding that the commissioners cancel the project. Brooklyn, it should be mentioned, was the national stronghold for supporters of the right-wing priest Father Charles "The Radio Priest" Coughlin, the most visible representative of American fascism and anti-Semitism and the subject of a Shahn caricature.[30] The official newspaper of the Catholic archdiocese in Brooklyn, the *Brooklyn Tablet,* openly supported Coughlin, attacked Jews and leftists, and opposed immigration reform. Changes would have to be made, or the mural would have to go.

Shahn countered the proposed cancellation, arguing against the right of a single group to dictate public taste in art and noting that "with democracy rather on its mettle these days, it gives one quite a shock to hear 'verboten' directed against a traditionally American poet."[31] Shahn's intentionally chose the word *verboten,* which he had recently painted in the upper-left corner of his Jersey Homesteads mural. In this semantic choice Shahn shrewdly aimed to create discomfort among reporters, officials, and the objectors themselves.

Nonetheless, in the interest of finishing his mural, Shahn acquiesced and replaced the "objectionable" lines from Whitman with a stanza from the poet's "As I Walk These Broad Majestic Days." Shahn compromised

5 Ben Shahn, *Resources of America: Walt Whitman* (detail of center panel) (1938–39), egg tempera on plaster. Bronx Central Post Office. © Estate of Ben Shahn, licensed by VAGA, New York.

in order to save the commission and probably also for the sake of the money he so badly needed. But he did not walk away unscathed by this inflammatory encounter with small-minded censors. Freedom became his most pressing artistic theme—informed by the mounting global crisis, which Shahn would interpret in his proposal to the city of St. Louis.

Immigration and Freedom: St. Louis and Queens

In the spring of 1939, the Treasury Section art program officials in Washington announced the national competition for the decoration of the St. Louis Post Office lobby.[32] While Missouri should have been Shahn's sole focus, the growing crisis in Europe influenced his concepts and mural designs more strongly. Shahn received from Treasury officials a thick bibliography on St. Louis history, legends, and lore designed to help in preparing proposals. The sponsors suggested that "A continuous story based on the colorful history of the mail in and around St. Louis would offer fascinating subject matter for frescoes." Shahn instead grouped the nine required studies into three distinct themes: regional history, with scenes of Missouri river traffic, wagon trains, and frontier life; the freedoms guaranteed by the Bill of Rights; and immigration to America.[33] Shahn painted two preliminary studies, both entitled *Immigration,* a subject unrelated to the sponsor's guidelines.

An urgent, violent mood pulses through the first *Immigration* scene, a montage Shahn divided into three parts (fig. 6). In the first third, a family arrives in America, babies and bundles in hand, to begin a new life. This hopeful scene brushes up against that of a crude prison or concentration camp enclosed by barbed wire, which holds a half-dozen semi-clad despondent men. The ominous background, darkened sky, and bare ground create a bleak mood but do not establish the precise

6 Ben Shahn, *Immigration* (1939), tempera on board, 5½ x 15½ in. Private Collection. Photo courtesy of Kennedy Galleries. © Estate of Ben Shahn, licensed by VAGA, New York.

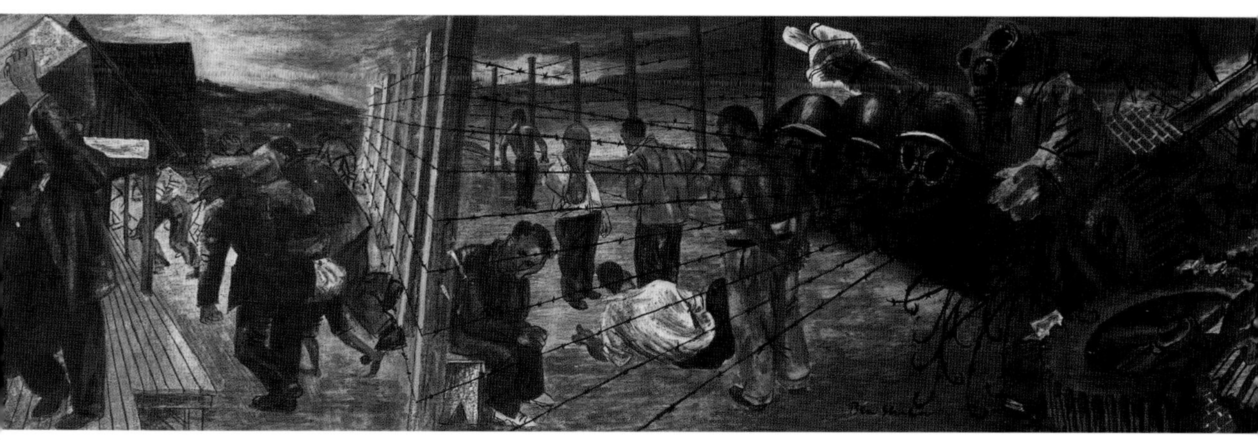

time or location of the scene. However, Shahn has created an image that, through the barest of symbols, eerily suggests what later would become the iconic forms and elements of a Nazi concentration camp—the wire fence, the despondent figures, the slender (although not emaciated) bodies.[34] In the concluding panel, Shahn painted a gas-masked military figure who reaches back toward the image of the camp and with his left hand pulls taut the barbed wire. With this sharp gesture, Shahn established the contrast between immigration (freedom, safety, new lives), and detention and war.

Shahn opened his second panel, *Immigration #2,* with scenes of war (fig.7). Anonymous soldiers clad in metal helmets flank a bombed-out building. At center, from a dizzying overhead perspective, Shahn painted people scurrying about chaotically, perhaps victims of a pogrom. Toward the right, the lean figure of a man wearing the long coat and beard of an Orthodox Jew catches the viewer's eye. This man is no Missourian but an East European Jew, one of the mass of people who fled Europe during the late nineteenth and early twentieth centuries, the period of Shahn's own arrival.[35] Shahn concludes this panel with a picture of a nineteenth-century immigrant newly arrived from Europe, his meager belongings in hand, standing in front of the Statue of Liberty and Castle Garden. Instead of joyfully celebrating American immigrants and their successes, Shahn somberly tells the story of exodus, pogroms, chaos, and refugees.

Shahn intended his panel *Freedom of Religion* (1939) to open his submission to the St. Louis competition. Within its horizontal frame, Shahn assembled identifiable symbols, people, and structures that represented America's dominant religions. The Statue of Liberty's uplifted torch occupies the center, painted as if made of stained glass rather than three-dimensional bronze, in order to fuse together the ideas of immigration and religious freedom. Shahn next interpreted the clauses of the First Amendment that provide for freedom of speech and freedom

7 Ben Shahn, *Immigration #2* (1939), tempera on board, 5½ x 15½ in. Private Collection. Photo courtesy of Kennedy Galleries. © Estate of Ben Shahn, licensed by VAGA, New York.

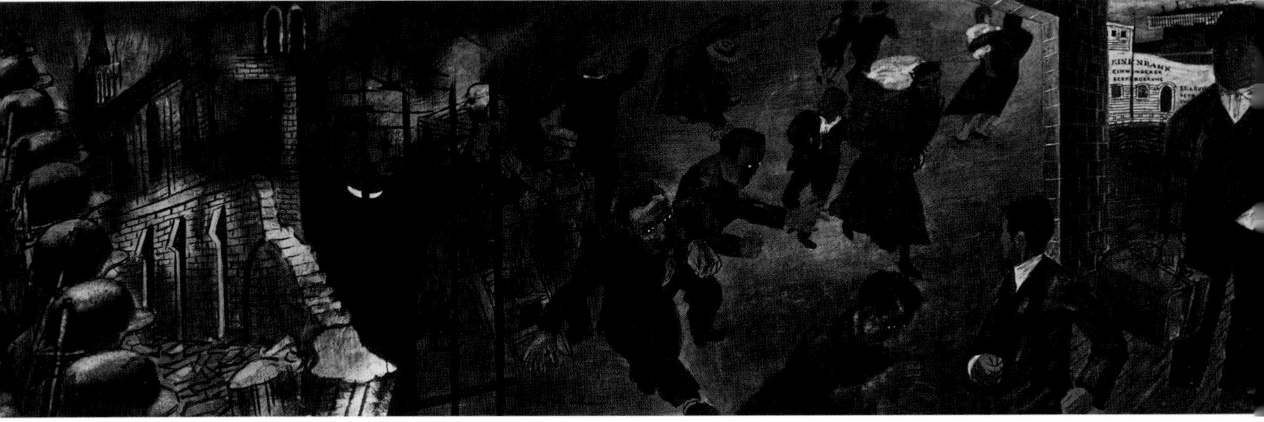

of the press, and depicted citizens actively setting the course of their government by means of the ballot and grassroots activism. In his St. Louis proposal, Shahn chose to focus on the nation's heritage of civil and political rights—now especially pertinent to Jews—and on such relevant issues as immigration rather than regional boosterism.

Between 1936, when Shahn began his Jersey Homesteads mural, and 1939, when he was working on his St. Louis proposal, American Jews became increasingly concerned over the fate of Europe's Jews and the barriers to their entering the United States. Franklin D. Roosevelt, the president Shahn and so many other Jews so admired, chose not to lift the immigration quotas and remove obstacles to immigration and safety for European refugees. FDR's inaction was consistent with the worldwide reluctance to help Jews. In 1939, against this tide of indifference, New York senator Robert F. Wagner spoke out for lifting America's immigration quotas. Wagner, whom Shahn portrayed in his Jersey Homesteads mural, introduced a bill on the Senate floor that would have facilitated the entry of twenty thousand refugee children into America under a special dispensation of the quota. Wagner's strategically referred to the children as "German" rather than "Jewish" so to any deflect anti-Semitic opposition to the bill. Although Wagner's bill was a humanitarian measure designed to rescue children, Congress opposed it; with no active presidential endorsement, the bill was defeated in committee.

When Congress voted down the measure, Wagner took to the airwaves in a final effort to build popular support for his bill. In a dramatic radio address he compared the plight of the refugee children to that of the passengers on the ill-fated SS *St. Louis* to exemplify the desperate nature of the situation. In mid-May 1939, the *St. Louis* had left Germany for Havana, carrying 907 German-Jewish refugees en route to safety in the United States. On 27 May, while Shahn was still working on his St. Louis mural studies, the ship docked in Havana. The ship's passengers attempted to disembark, but Cuban officials blocked them. The passengers were thrown into diplomatic limbo and waited several weeks onboard while officials negotiated on their behalf; their ordeal was covered extensively by the press.[36]

The German government had deliberately orchestrated what ultimately became a human tragedy. The Germans arranged with the Cuban government to invalidate the Jews' landing permits, and also calculated, correctly, that the United States would turn the refugees away. This, of course, was all unknown to the Jewish voyagers. For the refugees on the *St. Louis,* Cuba was to have been only a temporary respite en route to the United States and safety.[37] As the weeks dragged on, newspapers reported the testimony of relatives waiting onshore and printed impassioned letters from refugees onboard the ship. Jewish relief agencies

gathered these reports, letters, and testimonies in the hope of persuading
the United States to validate the refugees' papers, but they were unsuccessful. The United States' inaction forced the ship to return to Europe,
where the crew distributed the passengers among various countries,
many of which soon were overtaken by the Nazis. Several hundred of the
passengers were eventually killed in the death camps.[38] Nazi propaganda
fully exploited the United States' refusal of the *St. Louis,* wryly commenting in the August 1939 issue of *Der Weltkampf:* "We are saying openly
that we do not want the Jews while the democracies keep on claiming
that they are willing to receive them—and then leave the guests out in
the cold! Aren't we savages better men after all?"

In his St. Louis proposal, Shahn neither directly answered the rhetoric of the Nazis nor confronted American inaction, nor did he explicitly
narrate the events of the refugee crisis and the *St. Louis.* Instead he
emphasized the values of liberty, civil and human rights, and the opportunities for life—including his own—made possible because of America's
liberal immigration policies in the past, as contrasted with the growing
possibility of war, concentration camps, and religious persecution abroad.
While the jury never fully explained their rejection of Shahn's mural,
they remarked that the work "contained political distractions."[39]
Shahn soon had the opportunity to condense his nine St. Louis studies
into a one-panel mural. In early 1940 Treasury Section officials invited
Shahn to submit mural designs for the Woodhaven Branch Post Office in
Queens.[40] Freed from the constraints of having to tailor his ideas to Missouri history, Shahn concentrated on his message of American freedom
and immigration. To symbolize these dual and related concerns, Shahn
placed the Statue of Liberty's oxidized green hand and uplifted torch
prominently at the composition's center. The powerful hand at the center of Shahn's Queens mural calls to mind another representation of a
hand by the artist. As part of his 1931 *Haggadah,* Shahn represented the
"mighty hand" and "outstretched arm" of God. Where a Haggadah retells
the story of the Exodus, Shahn's Woodhaven Station mural narrates the
impetus for immigration—in particular, Jewish immigration—to the
United States.

In his Queens mural, Shahn focused on the Bill of Rights, and
beneath the Statue of Liberty's torch he inscribed the words of the First
Amendment. Officials objected to this inscription, which they judged
unnecessary to convey the mural's message. Shahn challenged the officials, ultimately persuading them, and wrote: "The thing that I have tried
to put into this mural, I feel very strongly. I feel that it has profound
significance for every American, more significance every day because of
increasing threats to our rights and liberties. I feel that if I, as an artist,
can bring home to the people who see this work any added realization

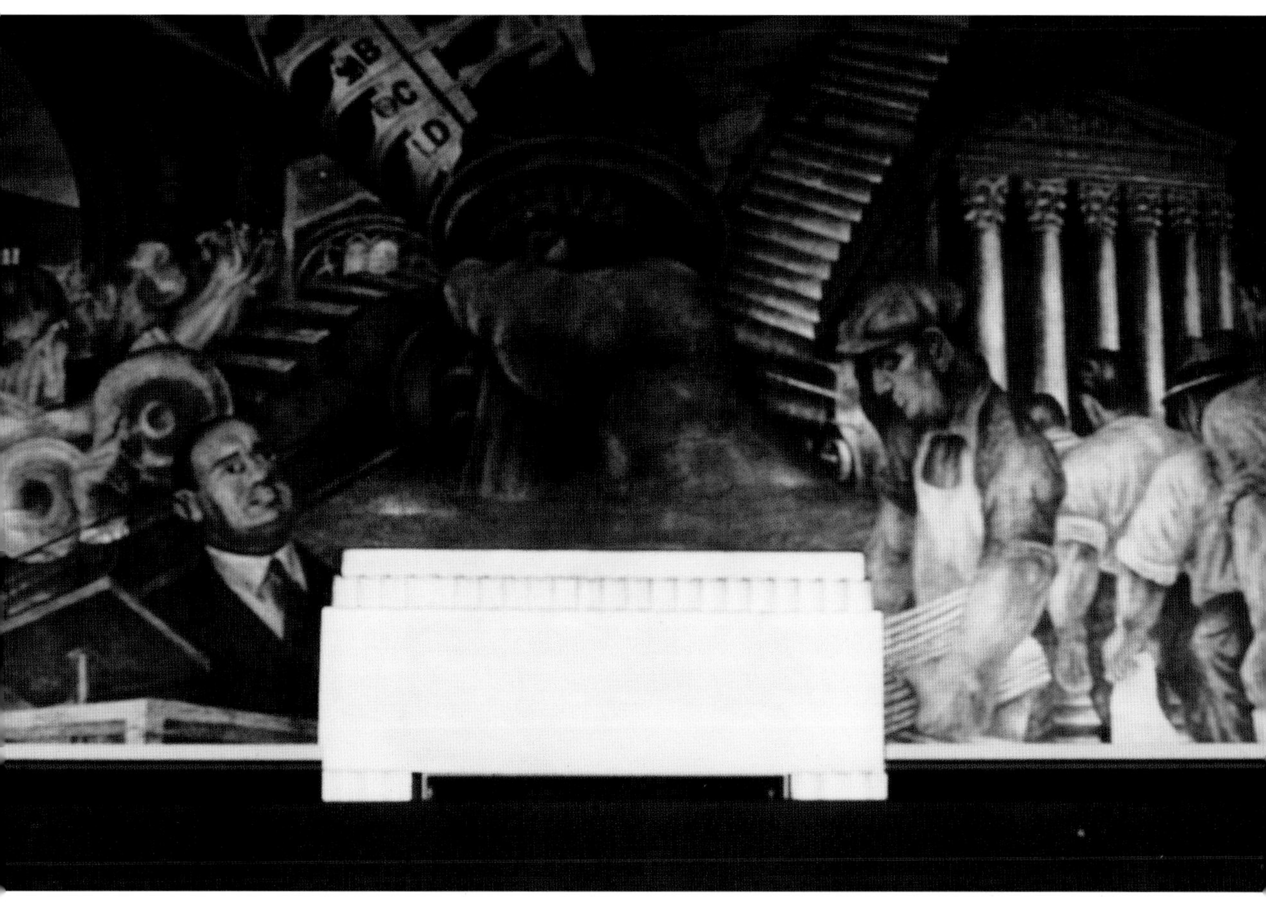

8   Ben Shahn, *The First Amendment* (1940–41), egg tempera on canvas, 8 ft. 6 in x 16 ft. Woodhaven Branch Post Office, Queens, New York. Photograph by David Linden.

of how these basic rights project into their lives and activities, then I've done as good a piece of work as I want to, and don't much mind breaking the rules for pure art."[41] On 6 January 1941 President Roosevelt addressed Congress in his annual message, noting the "unprecedented" threat to American security from outside its borders and the consequent need for a "world founded upon four essential human freedoms."[42] Shahn installed the Woodhaven Station mural in 1941, at a time when both the national and international climate was precarious. According to historian Henry L. Feingold, the year 1941 concluded the "refugee phase of the Holocaust"; the time and opportunity for rescue had ended.[43] In this light, Shahn's St. Louis and Queens murals offered a moral and legislative direction that the United States chose not to follow.

For Ben Shahn, the New Deal art programs were a singular opportunity to explore and depict in a public forum themes of Jewish history and political concern, in the hope of effecting positive change for his community and country. The dismantling of the New Deal and America's

entrance into the war were followed in the postwar era by dramatic
changes in American Jewish life. Whereas during the interwar years a
disproportionate number of Jews were active on the radical left, afterward geographic dispersion and rapid upward social mobility weakened
such Jewish commitment. Many on the radical left renounced their
former anti-Zionist stance once the truth of the Holocaust and Stalin's
murderous rampage were made known. In the postwar era, Israel, the
Holocaust, and liberalism, rather than labor or leftist politics, became
the main focal points of Jewish communal identification for many. The
end of the New Deal programs meant the end of ready patronage for
mural projects, and Shahn never painted a mural again. In the 1950s
and 1960s Shahn's few works on a monumental scale were wall mosaics
created either for synagogues (on biblical themes), or for educational and
cultural institutions (on science and knowledge in the postnuclear age).
Throughout his career, Shahn spoke out on human rights, American
freedoms, and progressive politics, and he continued to make his art and
his home as a Jew in America.

V EXTENDING THE DISCOURSE

BETWEEN ZHDANOVISM AND 57TH STREET:
ARTISTS AND THE CPUSA, 1945–56

Andrew Hemingway

Revisionist art history, so-called, has effectively rewritten the history of American art in the 1940s and 1950s, so that Greenberg's oft-quoted sketch for a narrative of "how anti-Stalinism which started out more or less as Trotskyism turned into art for art's sake, and thereby cleared the way, heroically, for what was to come" has become a kind of received wisdom about the period. This new story, in its several variants, seeks to show how the rise and "triumph" of the American avant-garde was closely bound up with political realignments among left-leaning artists and intellectuals that accompanied their disenchantment with Soviet communism and the hard choices forced upon them by the coming of the cold war. It is certainly a better story than the one in which a group of heroic artists forged a new American art that represented a profound sense of the human condition in the modern world, and were able to do so because they had the good fortune to reside in the most democratic of polities. By "better" I mean that it offers a more comprehensive, a more adequate, explanation of what occurred. In that sense it is an advance in historical knowledge.

Having said this, however, the revisionist history has some limitations of its own, limitations that probably derive from the new-left perspective of those who developed it in the 1970s and 1980s. First, it assumed that the key problem was establishing the grounds for the supremacy of the postwar American avant-garde. This was obviously a resonant concern at a moment of widespread critique of metropolitan

This essay is a much condensed version of material in my book *Artists on the Left: American Artists and the Communist Movement, 1926–1956* (New Haven: Yale University Press, 2002). Research for it was funded by the British Academy, Leverhulme Trust, Central Research Fund (University of London), and Dean's Travel Fund (University College London).

261

museum culture among left-wing critics, historians, and artist-activists in the United States itself, and it corresponded to an imperative to unmask the effects of U.S. cultural imperialism shared by new left activists and scholars everywhere. But this definition of the problem also contained within it a presumption that it was avant-garde culture alone that really mattered. In this respect, those concerned effectively reproduced hegemonic definitions of what was aesthetically significant even if now the aesthetically significant was (arguably) shown to be complicit in some sense with cold war liberalism. Further, the new history did nothing to end the invisibility of the kinds of art that had been marginalized by the avant-garde's triumph. The reasons for this, one may surmise, were as much political as aesthetic, in that the new left generally felt it had nothing to learn from the old left, the culture and politics of which were irredeemably discredited by their association with Soviet totalitarianism.

It is not possible in a brief essay to lay out and defend a story different from the revisionist one, but by focusing on the history of the communist cultural movement in the later 1940s I hope to point up something of what has been missed as a result of this oversight. My argument falls into two parts. In the first I sketch the institutional base through which communist and fellow-traveling artists operated in the 1940s, and the phases of its demise. In the second, I show that the communist movement was still producing a relatively sophisticated critical discourse around the arts in this period. Whatever our judgments on the value of these phenomena, they were an important aspect of the American artistic scene of the 1940s and are crucial to understanding its politics.

The Institutional Base

It is conventionally assumed that the combined effects of the Nazi-Soviet Pact and the Soviet invasion of Finland effectively destroyed the American Artists' Congress (AAC). Yet this was not quite the case, for the Congress, working in conjunction with the League of American Writers, managed to organize a conference at the Hotel Commodore in New York in June 1941, accompanied by an exhibition of works by 101 artists, among whom were Philip Evergood, William Gropper, Louis Lozowick, Ad Reinhardt, Joseph Solman, Moses and Raphael Soyer, David Smith, and Paul Strand.[1] The Artists Union, which was also a sponsor of the conference, lost most of its *raison d'être* with the winding down of the Federal Art Project, and in May 1942 it fused with the AAC to form the Artists' League of America (ALA). Rockwell Kent, a staunch communist supporter who had been president of the union, was elected president of the new organization.

The ALA perpetuated the thirties model of artist activism. ALA contingents marched in New York May Day parades, and members made signs for striking workers and stood on picket lines themselves. The organization campaigned for progressive legislation such as that setting up the Fair Employment Practices Commission and was involved in the Committee to Abolish the Un-American Committee. It also openly advocated the principle of peaceful coexistence with the USSR. Unsurprisingly, the ALA followed the CP line in 1946 in abandoning the Democrats and backing the American Labor Party in the congressional elections in New York State, and in 1948 it endorsed Wallace against Truman.

In addition to its political allegiances, the openness of the ALA's membership (it had no membership prerequisites) probably discouraged prominent artists from joining. It had no prestige to offer them, and they did not need its exhibitions or other services. Neither was it a truly national body in the way the American Artists' Congress had been. Rockwell Kent characterized it in March 1945 as a "movement of the 'discontented masses' in art" and already sensed that, since it was incapable of having any real political clout, it would wither away.[2] In January 1947 its secretary, Norman Barr, estimated that there were 276 paid-up members, with a substantial number who had been members but were behind with their dues.[3] Although the ALA had its own gallery and art school, neither seems to have been much of a success, and its annual membership exhibitions were mainly small affairs in which little-known artists predominated. In 1949 it effectively fizzled out.

One of the long-term problems of the ALA was that its aims overlapped with that of two broader-based bodies, the Independent Citizens' Committee of the Arts, Sciences and Professions (ICCASP) and the Artists' Equity Association (AEA). The first of these began life in 1944 as the Independent Voters' Committee of the Arts and Sciences for Roosevelt (IVCASR), set up to work for the president's fourth term under the leadership of the international portrait sculptor Jo Davidson. It was essentially a wing of the National Citizens' Political Action Committee (NCPAC), which had been initiated by Sidney Hillman to extend the social reach of the CIO's Political Action Committee beyond organized labor and create what Steven Fraser has called "a united front against reaction." In the aftermath of Roosevelt's re-election, IVCASR was reformed as ICCASP, a permanent body with a paid professional staff, dedicated to campaigning for the extension of democracy (both within the United States and without), worldwide peace through the agency of the United Nations, full employment, and "a decent living standard for all." Members were organized into subcommittees concerned with theater, radio, literature, films, art, science and technology, music, education, medicine, and journalism. ALA members participated in ICCASP from the beginning, and the execu-

tive board of the art division was packed with leftists, many of whom
were also in the League.

The role of communists within the CIO's Political Action Committee
was a highly controversial issue in the 1944 presidential election campaign.[4] Communists probably played an even more important role in the
ICCASP, although the claim that it was set up as a "front" takes the claims
of ex-communist informers too much for granted and underestimates
the integrity of the "social liberalism" of the 1940s.[5] From its officers
and the list of "initiating sponsors," ICCASP appeared to be an organization dominated by entertainers and Hollywood celebrities, and its ability
to get glitterati such as Frank Sinatra to endorse liberal political stances
was the object of much pointed comment.

As things worked out, the hopes leftists invested in the ICCASP were
misplaced, for the kind of Popular Front strategy the organization represented became unworkable in the climate of the postwar period, as
the liberal camp became increasingly divided. At the end of 1946 the
National Citizens' Political Action Committee and ICCASP merged to form
Progressive Citizens of America (PCA); and a week later the Union for
Democratic Action, which had been founded in 1941 and consistently
refused any cooperation with communists, changed its name to Americans for Democratic Action. The long-standing split in liberal ranks
had finally crystallized around support for or opposition to the Truman
administration as it hardened its stance toward the USSR.[6]

By the time of the 1948 Progressive Party campaign, ICCASP had
become the National Council of the Arts, Sciences, and Professions
(NCASP), and artists involved with that body were mainly responsible
for the insertion of a cultural plank into the party's platform at its convention in Philadelphia in July 1948. This was believed to cover the
setting up of a department of fine arts on a permanent basis to realize
the promise of the WPA arts projects and initiate a national cultural program.[7] Sponsors of the cultural agenda of the NCASP included not only
the familiar roster of artists with longstanding communist connections,
but also less expected figures such as Paul Cadmus, Katherine Dreier,
and Baroness Hillar Rebay. Many of the same names had appeared in
the committee of "Artists for Wallace," a shadowy body launched in June
1948 with the veteran leftist Max Weber as chairman and the communist Robert Gwathmey as acting secretary.

The defeat of the Progressive Party in 1948 did not bring to an end
the NCASP. Its last major act was the organization of the Cultural and Scientific Conference for World Peace, held at the Waldorf Astoria Hotel in
New York, 25–27 March 1949, which was addressed by Soviet cultural
figures (Shostakovitch among them), while noisy anticommunist demonstrations took place outside. Although the executive committee of

the NCASP told themselves that the Waldorf Conference had been a great
success, it further contributed to the organization's reputation as a communist front and saddled it with crippling debts.[8] The NCASP limped on
into the early fifties, but in 1954 no annual convention was held, and the
national organization seems to have been on the verge of collapse.

The ALA's other rival, the Artists' Equity Association, was set up in
1947 as a purely professional organization, without political affiliation, to
assist artists in their relations with dealers and museums. Some of those
involved in its creation were also members of the League, but the executive of that body was not entirely approving of what it conceived to be a
new apolitical organization, the economic functions of which overlapped
with its own.[9] By 1948 Artists' Equity had thirteen hundred members,
and the following year it had fifteen hundred, spread over thirty-eight
states.[10] Moreover, with Yasuo Kuniyoshi as its president and such
respectable figures as John Taylor Arms, William Zorach, and Eugene
Speicher among its vice presidents, it was able to attract precisely the
kind of established artists the ALA could not. However, the composition
of its leading officers and the prohibition on activities of a "partisan aesthetic or political character"[11] do not tell the whole story. While the list
of fifty-three founding members of the organization included prominent
artists who had never associated with the left, around half had been signatories of the call for the American Artists' Congress in 1935 or had
otherwise distinguished themselves as leftists. Moreover, while by no
means an overwhelming presence, CP members and sympathizers such
as Harry Gottlieb, Joseph Hirsch, Mitchell Siporin, and Harry Sternberg
were to figure prominently in its executive committees.

Just how significant their influence was is difficult to evaluate, partly
because so many artists were probably still attached to some form of
New Deal liberalism at this stage. The political stances the AEA took were
entirely consonant with such a position. At the first regular membership
meeting in April 1947, resolutions were passed condemning the cancellation of the State Department's Advancing American Art exhibition
and calling for the establishment of state and federal art projects.[12] The
following year the honorary president, Leon Kroll, read a resolution to
the annual meeting condemning the tactics of the House Un-American
Activities Committee and supporting the Stop the Censorship Committee.[13] At the 1950 meeting, director Jack Levine tabled a resolution calling
for the AEA to go on record as opposed to the infamous Mundt-Nixon
Bill, which became the basis of the McCarran Internal Security Act,
although after much discussion the issue was referred to the directors.[14]
None of these resolutions represented positions that Roosevelt liberals
would have found difficulty in endorsing, but by the late 1940s liberals
were increasingly being tarred as communist sympathizers by the con-

gressional right and its allies. On 25 March 1949 Representative George
Dondero (R-Mich.) gave a lengthy denunciation of Artists' Equity before
the House, claiming that of its officers, directors, and governors, sixty-
nine had "left-wing connections," and that most of its members were
"soldiers of the revolution—in smocks"(!). Dondero could indeed show
that some of those he cited, such as Evergood, Gropper, Gwathmey, and
Weber, had longstanding links with communist-sponsored organizations
and publications. However, some of his accusations about communist
influence in the art press were ludicrous, and he did not distinguish
between membership in Popular Front bodies such as the American Artists' Congress (to which many liberals belonged) and genuine communist
commitments.

In the aftermath of Dondero's attack, Hudson Walker visited him in
Washington in an attempt to explain that AEA was concerned only with
artists' "economic problems," but met with a hostile reception: "Mr. Dondero replied that he was interested in doing away with any organization
if it has even a few Communists."[15]

Dondero's attacks did not destroy the AEA, and indeed in the
early 1950s its New York chapter seemed to be going from strength
to strength. In 1951 it put on an innovative fund-raising exhibition at
the Whitney Museum that raised $52,000, and subsequently took out
a mortgage on a building at 13 East 67th Street that became a center
for exhibitions, forums, lectures, and workshops.[16] However, divisions
arose over the running of the center and there were accusations about
factional maneuvering within the chapter that were accompanied by
political name-calling.[17] As a result, the national organization took over
the New York chapter and its building in 1954, and New York members
did not regain their status as an autonomous chapter until 1956.

The repercussions of all this are indicated by notes for a talk from
the mid-1950s, in Harry Gottlieb's papers. Gottlieb observed that the AEA
had ceased to be a "coalition" organization and was now "right led," and
that the progressives within it were subject to red-baiting. The new situation obliged communist artists to "work with anyone who agrees with
us on a minimum program," and he urged them to do the "normal things
artists do" so that they did not appear to set themselves apart.[18] In effect,
communists were marginalized in the AEA in the same way that they
were in the trade union movement over the years 1948–50.

Finally, we should note the continuing presence of Herman Baron's
ACA Gallery, which had been a key support for the left artistic groupings
of the thirties and remained a self-proclaimed "people's art gallery." In
March 1944 Baron launched a small monthly magazine, *American Contemporary Art,* which ran until early 1946, and in 1945 took over another
floor of the building on East 57th Street to expand his exhibition space.

Baron certainly intended the gallery to function as "a vital center" where lectures would be given and from which publications would issue,[19] but the ACA's position was an increasingly beleaguered and marginal one as the decade progressed.

On 17 May 1949 Representative Dondero, who had already described the ACA as "a definitely communistic place" before the House, devoted a whole statement to exposing the links between the gallery and organizations such as the John Reed Club and American Artists' Congress. He referred to Baron repeatedly as "Comrade Baron," and also claimed to show the "Red record" of such associates as Evergood, Gwathmey, and Elizabeth McCausland. In one particularly lurid passage he asserted, "I believe it to be the hub, the gathering point of Marxists in art, whose subtle, nefarious un-American schemes receive their prime incitement. It should be shunned like a plague center of infection."[20]

Dondero's remarks received significant coverage in the New York press, and in an interview with the *New York Sun* Baron explicitly denied his charges as "just stupid," claiming disingenuously that he did not know or care about the political affiliations of his artists. However, while he claimed to be "interested only in artists," he refused to answer the question as to whether he had ever been a Communist Party member.[21] In July Baron produced a six-page statement saying that to be attacked by Dondero was an honor and defending the record of the AAC and cognate organizations. Yet, as he noted privately, "one can die very heroically in a nightmare," and it is clear that he was deeply disturbed by the climate of fear.[22] Nonetheless, the ACA remained the main showcase for what Baron called "pro-objective art" until his death in 1961.

All these dwindling efforts to combat the conservative turn in U.S. politics and culture were ultimately unavailing, and increasingly the party's cultural workers were isolated within their own small clubs. However, their struggle to create an alternative "people's culture" did not founder only because of harassment by federal, state, and city agencies, House and Senate committees, and self-appointed private bodies— although all that was real enough.[23] They also foundered because of the party's own defensive responses to persecution, which led it to purge any who showed signs of dissent or were inactive, and eventually, in 1951, to send leading cadres underground.[24] Corresponding to this was an increasingly intransigent line on culture, a subject to which I now turn.

Cultural Criticism Between Zhdanovism and 57th Street

At the height of the grand alliance, the CPUSA, under Earl Browder's leadership, dissolved itself, reemerging as a pressure group committed to working within the American political system. As the war drew to a close and tensions between the allies increased, it became evident that this move was premised on a disastrous miscalculation of the chances for peaceful coexistence. The reconstitution of the CPUSA in July 1945 under the leadership of William Z. Foster and Eugene Dennis had major implications for the party's cultural workers.[25] The rejection of what was termed Revisionism or Browderism and the return to a Leninist vanguard position led to a revival of the slogans and stances of the Third Period. Yet, while there were those such as Mike Gold who had never adapted to the relative pluralism of the Popular Front, there were also many sincere and committed members who had either joined at that time or embraced the more expansive vision of progressive culture it promoted. These elements did not just adapt passively to the new line. Moreover, after the turmoil surrounding Browder's ouster, the party needed to rebuild its membership base, within which middle-class elements were an important component. This meant there could be no simple return to the slogan of proletarian culture, which in any case had long been discredited within Soviet aesthetics. Having said this, it should be noted that in the leadership's view postwar capitalism was in a phase of terminal crisis and desperate imperialist expansion, the corollary to which was an interpretation of contemporary culture as essentially decadent—a decadence epitomized by Hollywood cinema. In this climate of crisis, intellectuals had to choose sides.[26]

The Maltz Affair

The key episode in defining differences over cultural strategy (and, by extension, aesthetic principles) in the postwar period was the so-called Maltz Affair.[27] Albert Maltz was a talented novelist and screenwriter who was later imprisoned as one of the Hollywood Ten. He inadvertently became the focus of a major policy debate because of an article he wrote entitled "What Shall We Ask of Writers?" which appeared in *New Masses* in February 1946 and in which he suggested that much committed writing had suffered from the shallow approach of critics who demanded of art an "immediate political utility," while the slogan of the proletarian phase "art is a weapon" had contributed to a vulgarization of Marxist aesthetics. Maltz stressed the distinction between the value of artworks and the political stance of their authors, citing as instances the novels of J. T. Farrell and Richard Wright, both one-time communists who were now fiercely critical of the party and whose writing had become completely discredited in communist eyes as a result.[28] Although Maltz was not the only communist writer to articulate such views, his article became the object of a whole string of attacks in both *New Masses* and the *Daily Worker.* The sum of these was that his arguments were "anti-Marxist" in their attempt to make some space between art and politics, and that he had not recognized the organic connection between progressive political ideas and literary achievement. Samuel Sillen set out the logic of this critique clearly: "The artists who ally themselves with the degenerating forces in our society, themselves degenerate *both* as 'citizens' and as 'artists,' both in terms of 'ideology' and of 'art.'"[29]

Art *was* necessarily a weapon in the Manichean struggle between capital and the progressive forces of the proletariat, and all talk of "pure art" was simply a delusion promoted by the ruling class.[30] It was only because of the party's errors under Browder's leadership that the slogan had been abandoned.

The assault on Maltz was in part a ritual of atonement through which the party's cultural workers purged themselves of Browderism, but it also related to genuine differences of opinion between hardliners like Sillen and those with more expansive views. In April Maltz's recantation appeared, in which he advised those who had approved the original article that it was an example of revisionist thinking and that Browderism could not promote a healthy working-class culture.[31] Effectively the debate was closed later that month by a statement on cultural policy by party chairman Foster that rehearsed familiar Stalinist platitudes and called on communist and "other democratic artists" to identify with the "basic artistic strivings of the masses."[32]

However, the promulgation of a policy was not the same as its enactment. The party had to work with those writers and artists who were prepared to give it their allegiance, and many of these seem to have paid lip service to the new line while continuing to produce work that suggested a broader and more intelligent vision. Here I can illustrate the quality and character of debates on the visual arts through only two instances: the criticism of "Marion Summers" and that of Joseph Solman. Inevitably these debates centered around the status and value of modernism to the proletarian cause.

"Marion Summers"

The party's "central organ," the *Daily Worker,* had been the major forum for its cultural workers since the early 1930s. In the immediate postwar period most of its art criticism was written by "Marion Summers," in actuality the art historian Milton W. Brown.[33] One of the striking features of Summers's criticism is its acceptance that much of the most significant art of the twentieth century had been modernist.[34] Artists such as Brancusi,

Klee, Lipchitz, Matisse, Mondrian, and Picasso should, he argued, be regarded as akin to research scientists revealing new possibilities of artistic form.[35] For Summers, however, this phase of healthy experimentation was now over, and the conditions of the epoch put new demands on artists. Thus, while he praised the early Cubist works of Picasso and Braque as "rational expressions of fundamental artistic ideas," he was critical of the "bitterness and cruelty" of Picasso's recent work, which showed "a basic disregard for human values."[36] (Picasso was thus not judged simply by his newly advertised political commitments.) What gave urgency to Summers's judgments on modernism was his perception of the increasing dominance of abstract art in galleries and exhibitions, and the worry that "This type of art is now in a position to dominate the entire field."[37] In June 1946 he devoted a series of four articles to its critique.

Summers was no ill-informed observer. He understood the variety of what went under the name of "abstract art" and also something of the range of its meanings, and, as we have seen, he took a positive view of its formal achievements. But now there was an "offensive" to restrict all art to painting of this type and to "enthrone" its theories as a "universal aesthetic." Summers asserted that many of the theories of abstraction were "half-truths with limited validity," while others were "sheer nonsense," and he ridiculed the argument that the two-dimensionality of the medium demanded abstraction, pointing out that *trompe l'oeil* and the denial of surface had not been the aim of naturalism. For all its "fancy verbiage" and "pretense," abstract art was now "merely another docile expression of bourgeois culture."[38] He was particularly scathing on the mythmaker wing of Abstract Expressionism, which framed its products in a pretentious discourse of irrationalism that he could only see as obscurantist.[39]

Attempting to define a progressive aesthetic in a two-part article of July 1946, Summers distinguished between realism as "a purely stylistic term" (meaning "fidelity to natural appearances") and realism as a broader attitude, implying the search for "the real, the truth about nature, man or society" that was always tied to the progressive forces in human history. Because of the modernist break with the post-Renaissance tradition, realism was now "almost purely an attitude," and social realists no longer felt tied to naturalistic techniques but made use of "symbolism, expressionism and even elements of abstract art." It could encompass "many variations in style" but had to be broadly concerned with the "reflection of social reality." What also distinguished realist art was the artist's concern with communication.[40] Social art was "unequivocal and outspoken propaganda for social progress." To achieve this end, the artist had to temper "his" concern with freedom with awareness of the need to develop a "common language." Such a language did not yet exist, for, as Summers perceptively observed, "There is no body of folklore nor any coherent storehouse of common symbols upon which the social artist can draw. He is often forced to express himself in a purely personal symbolism. In some cases these symbols explain themselves, in others they remain obscure." Art of such broad ambition could not flourish in the "hot house atmosphere of 57th Street." It needed a mass audience, and artists must thus look to the unions and workers' organizations. They should seek more direct contact with the working class. Public support was a necessary precondition for a vigorous social art—private patronage did not provide the conditions necessary to its growth.[41]

When it came down to particulars, Summers was compelled to acknowledge the limitations of the work of many artists of the left in relation to his ideal. Thus, while Max Weber had "a deep sympathy for humanity and an understanding of social events," this did not get into his art "except perhaps vaguely as a lyrical feeling."[42] When he turned to the social artists with more active commitments, such as Evergood, Gropper, Hirsch, and Siporin, his judgments were often quite critical of what he saw as overgeneralized symbolism and inadequate technique. Ironically, the contemporary on whom Summers bestowed the highest praise, Ben Shahn, was a social liberal and neither a communist nor a fellow traveler. For Summers, Shahn was "one of the few men who has successfully used the visual language of Modern Art to express social meaning," having formed "a personal style unique in American art, cold, precise and acidly sharp. It has all the impersonality of a police line-up photograph coupled with a haunting lyricism." The spareness of this style enabled the artist to avoid sentimentality, and he had the ability to make obvious symbols unforgettable through his organization of shapes and "tart, flat" color.

Summers contrasted Shahn with Siporin, whose "Haymarket" drawing series of 1934–35 and frescos in the post offices at Decatur, Illinois, and St. Louis were among the major achievements of thirties social art. Yet after the war (in which he served with the Information and Historical Service of the Fifth Army), Siporin turned to more broadly symbolic subjects, rendered in a style in which figures appeared like mannequins, and scale and perspective were relatively arbitrary. Comparing his *Endless Voyage* (fig. 1) with Shahn's work, Summers found its symbolism "too generalized and abstract," so that it recalled "not the thing but the idea of the thing." "In Shahn we recognize the very quality and nature of a particular condition, while in Siporin we are merely reminded that it exists." Siporin's somber canvas of a "huddled mass of Jews adrift on a limitless sea, placing faith in the flimsy sail of their hope" was simply too "tragic," too infused by the "pessimism" that was "a dominant note in bourgeois culture," to be satisfactory as politically engaged art, whereas

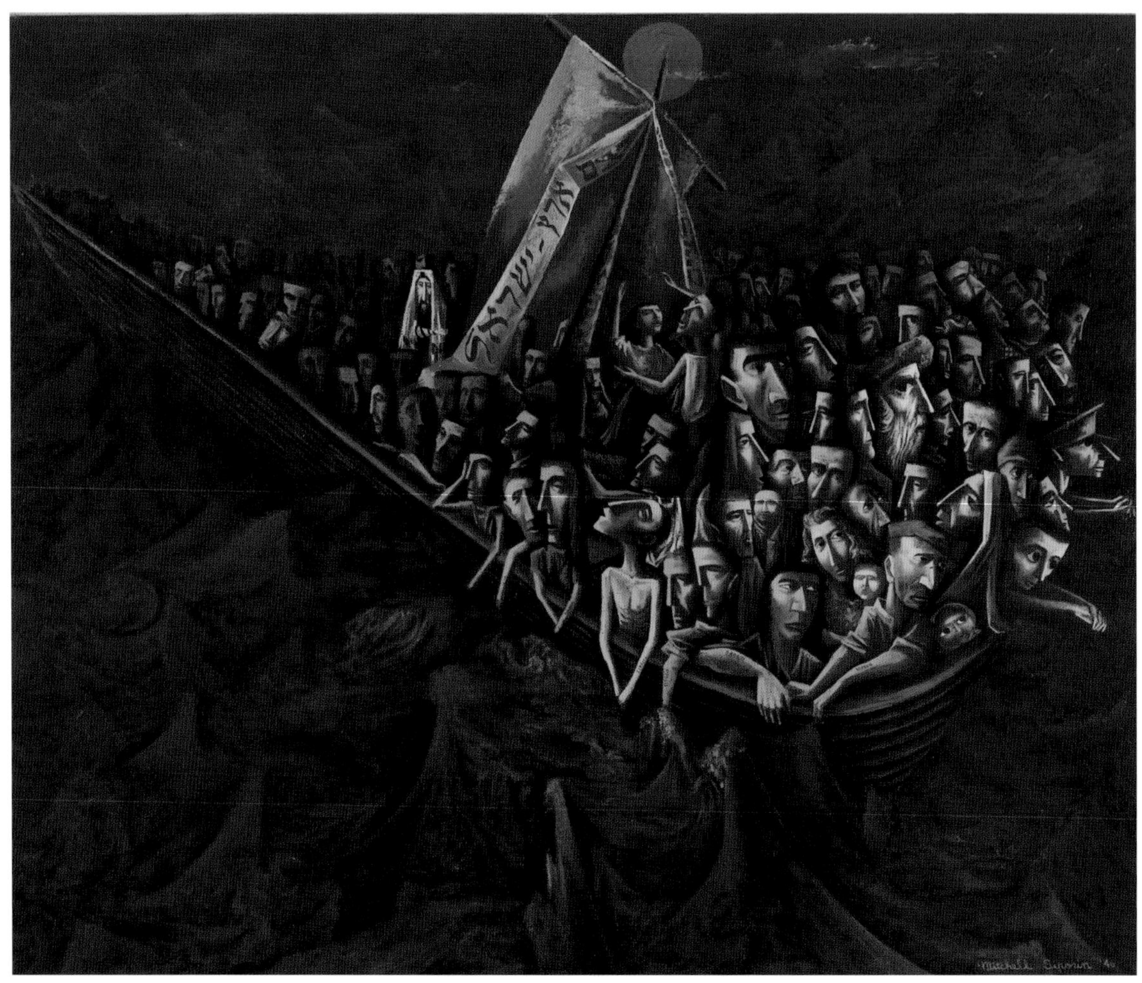

the "astringency" of Shahn's work redeemed it from this tendency to "romantic pathos." In fact, what Summers admired most were Shahn's posters for the CIO's Political Action Committee and the American Labor Party, in which pessimism was displaced by the enjoinment to action.[43] Given the increasingly anticommunist atmosphere in the American labor movement in the late 1940s, however, the chances of any artist with communist affiliations working within it were fast diminishing.

1 Mitchell Siporin, *Endless Voyage* (1946), oil on canvas, 34.5 x 39.4 in. University of Iowa Museum of Art. Museum Purchase.

Joseph Solman

For Charles Humboldt, one-time editor of *Art Front* and one of the most gifted cultural critics associated with the Communist Party, Summers's pronouncements on abstraction were too doctrinaire, and he wrote to the *Daily Worker* to advise that they could potentially alienate abstract artists associated with the party.[44] One of those "abstract artists" he had in mind may well have been Joseph Solman (another *Art Front* veteran), since, although Solman's work contained recognizable naturalistic forms, its overt modernist techniques and lack of obvious social themes put it close to what Summers encompassed by "abstraction."[45] Solman himself commented on the Summers/Humboldt exchange in *New Masses,* arguing for an expanded conception of realism that could draw on modernist innovations: "The concept of realism changes with the social demands and discoveries in each epoch. To reveal the fundamental reality of our day is the challenge facing the modern artist."

Solman denied that there was any "framed formula" for a Marxist aesthetic. There was, however, "a direction and a belief." While "all creative work should move in the direction of the 'socially purposeful,'" this allowed the politically committed artist a broad brief: "All art that is affirmative and alive with the meaningful symbols of our day, art that has a directness and simplicity unfettered by nineteenth century mystic-romanticism or the newer brands of metaphysics, an art that faces the universe with perception and courage and meant for the broadest communication, all such art can forge a truly social expression."[46] Between December 1946 and the end of 1948 Solman elaborated these views in a sequence of reviews for *New Masses* and its successor, *Masses & Mainstream.*

For an artist with Solman's aesthetic commitments, it was crucial to distinguish between "semi-abstract art" and "non-objective art." Thus, in his first review for *New Masses,* he argued, in contrast to Summers's erroneous view, that Cubist still-life painting had *not* implied "eliminating the subject." But he too was highly critical of the "pure design" of Mondrian and other nonobjective painters, which was connected with various forms of philosophical idealism. He was equally impatient, however, with social painters who viewed "all abstract art as outdated," for "No vital painter today can ignore the tremendous contribution made by abstract painting in the last thirty years."

It will be evident that Solman had assumed the mantle of Stuart Davis as defender of modernism within communist criticism, although he did not seek to achieve such a tight fit between the logic of artistic form and the progressive forces in history as Davis had in his formulations of the 1930s. This position meant that he accorded a positive value to the works of such artists as Carl Holty, Byron Browne, and Balcomb Greene, which Summers would not have done.[47] In contrast to him, he also saw Picasso's recent paintings as "his greatest work" and thus as "the greatest in our time." This was because of what he regarded as the expanded range of Picasso's subjects and a new expressive richness in his color and paint textures,[48] a point that indicates that Solman placed less emphasis than Davis did on form as the progressive aspect of modernism, and placed correspondingly more on expression and the human figure.[49]

Of all the artists associated with the communist left, Solman was the best placed to pass judgment on emergent Abstract Expressionism. Not only did he have a wide knowledge of modern art, he also knew Gottlieb and Rothko from his involvement with The Ten group. In a comment on Rothko's work in 1947 he scathingly evoked the inflated rhetoric of the "mythmaker" wing of the movement. This was an art "made up of biomorphic shapes and hieroglyphs searching to attach themselves to symbols" and "bent on resurrecting the ancient corpse of mythology." For Solman, it represented "a flight from reality," "a new mysticism," encouraged by commercial galleries and some of the major museums.[50] Writing a year later in *Masses & Mainstream,* he divided the "new cult" into those who drew on "totemic, ritualistic symbols" (Gottlieb and Newman) and the "'subjectivist school' which believes that the inner urge is the only valuable asset in art" (Pollock and Hofmann). Yet the two sides shared tenets in "setting irrationality over reason, urge over concept, symbol over representation, and in making intuition the sole guiding principle of design." For Solman, Gottlieb's claim that "the painting of nature and man has been thoroughly exhausted" nullified "[t]wenty centuries' recorded evidence of the visual world renewing art," and he referred scathingly to Newman's assertion that "[t]he basis of an esthetic act is the pure idea." He liked the work of Pollock and Hofmann still less. Referring to Motherwell and Rosenberg's famous statement about the extremity of the political situation in *Possibilities,* he equated such art with a retreat into "despair," which was effectively a submission to those forces in society that wished to "bind the artist and intellectual to obscurantism."[51] The promotion of this art by museum curators and critics represented a specious cult of "Individualism" to counterpose to the bogey of "Red collectivism."[52]

The dual foundations of Solman's criticism were a sophisticated post-Cubist approach to form and a belief that significant expression was fundamentally dependent on recognizable naturalistic references that connected with common experience. Indeed, what Solman could not abide was the "corrupted realism" he saw in the works of artists such as Blume, Cadmus, Tchelitchew, and the Albright brothers, who used a meretricious technique to deal in ideas of a "coarse bourgeois venality."[53] By contrast, in 1946 Solman gave high praise to Anthony Toney's ambitious canvas *Four Corners* (fig. 2) at the annual ALA exhibition, one of a series of paintings in which the artist sought to represent his experience of the war and its aftermath. *Four Corners,* he told Solman, was intended to "render the terrifying apathy many GIs meet on their return home" through the depiction of "a typical main street peopled with symbols and

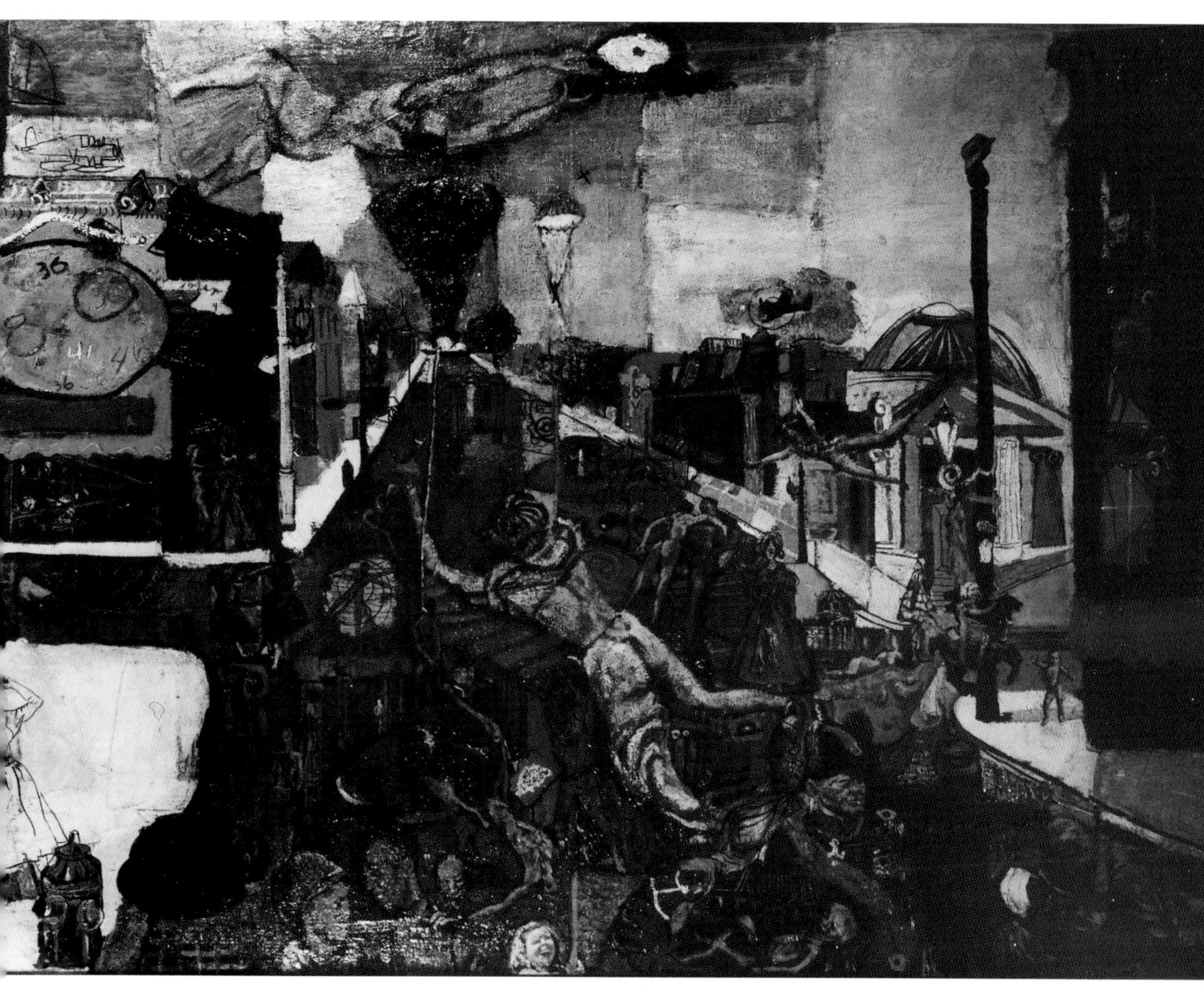

2 Anthony Toney, *Four Corners* (1946), oil on canvas, 37.75 x 51.4 in. Robert Hull Fleming Museum, University of Vermont. Gift of Dr. and Mrs. Arthur Kahn.

scenes of bigotry and persecution, apathy and despair." It is not an easy picture. The coloring is cacophonous, as are the stylistic disjunctions, and there are also disconcerting variations in texture, with dense globs of impasto on some areas of the surface, thin paint and schematic outlines elsewhere. Correspondingly, the symbolism is intricate and dense, and the work arguably tries to do too much. Nonetheless, it is an impressive conception, and Solman singled it out as the highlight of the show. Significantly, Marion Summers did not even mention it in his review.[54]

Solman gave an equally sympathetic judgment on Evergood, who also often failed in his attempts to develop a symbolic lexicon adequate to postwar conditions. In his view, Evergood's work could best be understood as a development of the northern Renaissance tradition of moral satire and fantasy enlivened by modern Expressionist techniques. Sometimes, however, Evergood's conceptions were over-elaborate and whimsical, and Solman was appropriately critical of some of the more fanciful works in the artist's 1948 ACA show. But he also gave generous acknowledgment of the originality and wit of paintings such as *Dream Catch* (fig. 3), a poignant dreamscape in which an African American child escaping the white world to catch an enormous fish is projected through startlingly acid contrasts of blue and red.

Yet Solman did not develop any sustained connection between art and political engagement in his criticism, and he praised some paintings

3 (below) Philip Evergood, *Dream Catch* (1946), oil on canvas, 30 x 20.9in. Hirshhorn Museum and Sculpture Garden, Smithsonian Institution, Washington, D.C. Gift of Joseph H. Hirshhorn.

4 (opposite) Ben-Zion, *Seated Prophet* (c. 1950), oil on canvas, 17.1 x 12.2 in. Hirshhorn Museum and Sculpture Garden, Smithsonian Institution, Washington, D.C. Gift of Joseph H. Hirshhorn.

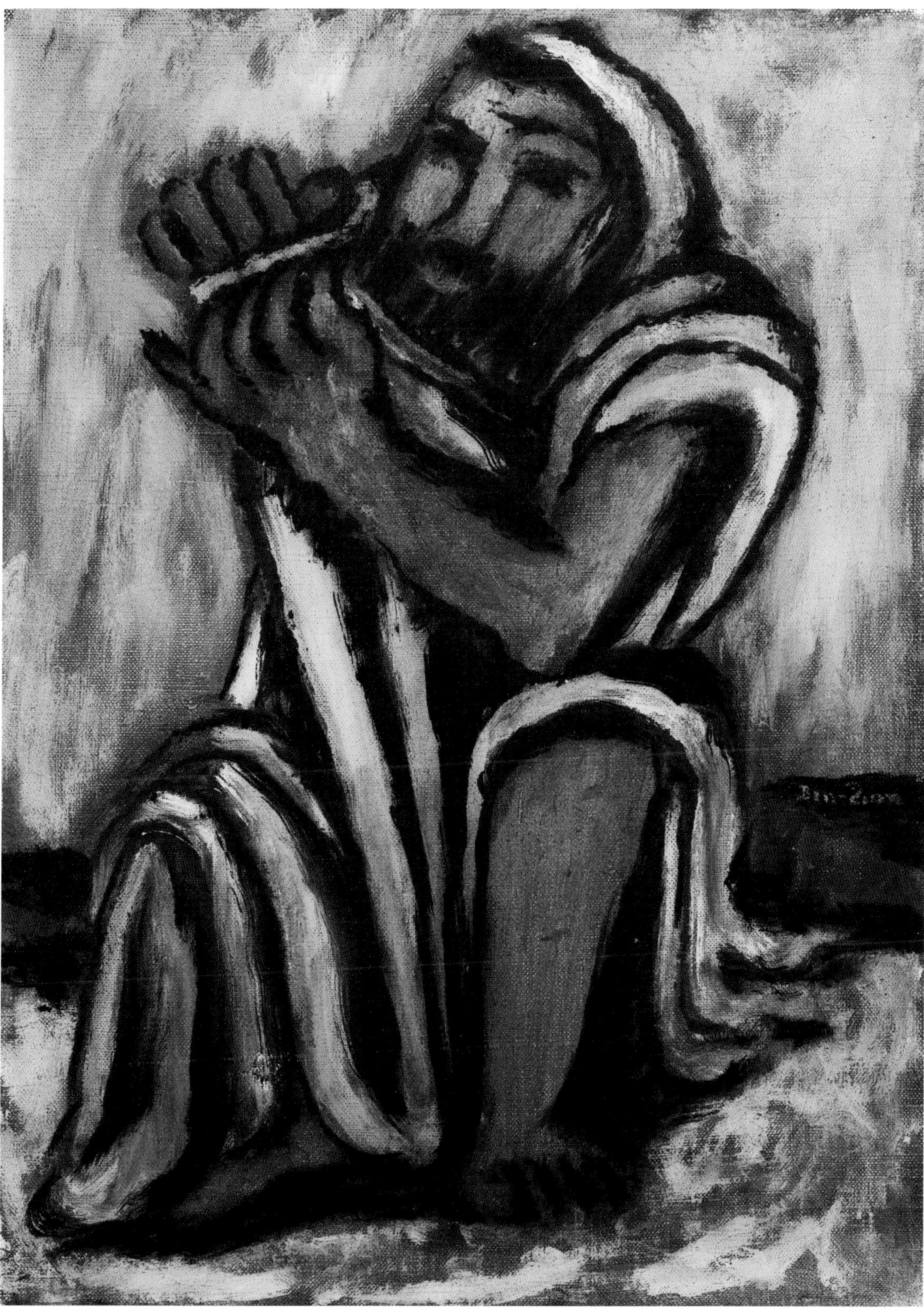

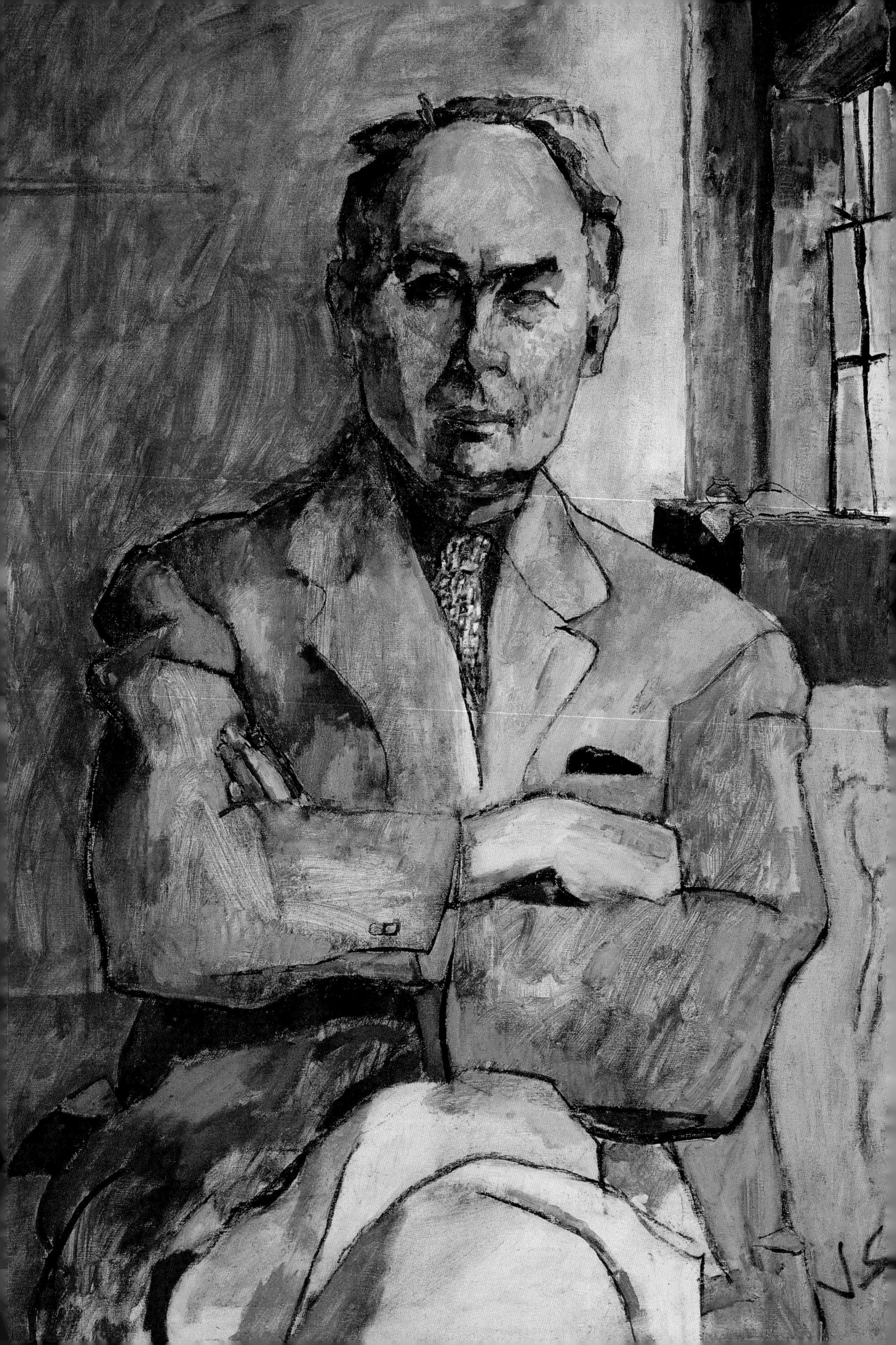

on primarily formal grounds. Reviewing the work of Ben-Zion (fig. 4), another graduate of The Ten group, in 1948, he hailed his images of Jewish prophets as "projections of the will and conscience of mankind," while claiming that his "elemental" designs and original use of color showed him as "one of the few imposing figures in American art today."[55] Whatever the merits of Ben-Zion's work, it did not integrate art and politics in the way that of Evergood and Toney repeatedly and insistently did. In this respect it resembles the work of Solman himself, who concentrated primarily on portraits, still lifes, and interiors in these years (fig. 5). Solman certainly regarded his art as realist, but he did not seek to solve "social problems with a paintbrush," as he had put it in a letter of 1939.[56] Perhaps it was his inability to accept the implications of the current communist line on culture that caused him to give up art criticism after March 1949, although he continued to exhibit with the ACA Gallery throughout the 1950s. At any rate, by this point the movement had certainly become increasingly hostile to his kind of position.

The Impact of Zhdanovism

As the criticism of Summers and Solman illustrates, the Maltz Affair had not brought aesthetic debate to an end in communist circles, nor had it led to the acceptance of a narrow instrumentalist aesthetic. The artistic disputes of the Popular Front continued, and they were not resolved until 1950, by which time the extreme polarization of cold war politics and corresponding developments in the Soviet line on culture meant that the choices for artists would be posed in much starker terms than in 1946. The text that finally forced these choices was Sidney Finkelstein's *Art and Society* (1947), one of two book-length studies in aesthetics published by the CP press in the postwar period.[57] Conceived and drafted in the 1930s, *Art and Society* is a quintessential Popular Front statement that attempts to ground the healthy and progressive tendencies that distinguish great art throughout history in folk culture and popular forms, as these emerge in particular national contexts. For Finkelstein, realism was not equivalent to naturalism but was to be judged according to its function in promoting the self-understanding of a "people."[58] Classicism and romanticism were perennial tendencies in the arts that marked departures from realism, yet within both "a partial grasp of reality" could be manifested.[59] On this basis, Finkelstein also argued for the value of a wide range of modernist works, from Picasso, Joyce, and Stein through Schoenberg and Hindemith. Although capitalism is bad for art, leading to its isolation from common life and an unhealthy degree of individualism, *Art and Society* does not present art as a stake in the class struggle, which scarcely figures in its pages.

Initially the book was well received in the Communist Party press,[60] and it apparently prompted much discussion, some of it critical. It was not until 1950 that this criticism took printed form, when *Art and Society* was attacked in a number of letters and articles in the *Daily Worker,* and in a long article in *Political Affairs,* the party's theoretical journal. The substance of these attacks was that Finkelstein's position rested on "a gross theoretical error" and was non-Marxist. He had failed to register that art was always linked with class power, and his view of art as "communication" had led him to formalism. Given the moralistic tenor of communist critiques, what most outraged his critics was, predictably, his failure to register the intrinsic connection between form and ideology, so that he wrote about writers such as Eliot and Joyce as if the formal qualities of their work were separable from its political tendency.[61] Like Maltz, Finkelstein was forced to recant, and in a letter replying to his critics he acknowledged that he had been led astray by a desire to define "some universal principle of 'good art.'" He also suggested that his softness on "extreme 'modern' tendencies" arose from the fact that the book was conceived in the days of the WPA, when such art had a false "air of social militancy."[62]

What is striking about the debate over *Art and Society* is the breast-beating that it occasioned. Samuel Sillen, editor of *Masses & Mainstream,* and V. J. Jerome, editor of *Political Affairs,* both felt it necessary to issue mea culpas for their failure to publish criticisms of the book when it appeared and to exercise sufficient vigilance in the elimination of Browderism.[63] This is probably indicative of that wrenching process of self-criticism and purgation with which the party responded to the prosecution of its leaders under the Smith Act. Also significant are Sillen's and Jerome's invocations of "the brilliant cultural critiques of Andrei Zhdanov" and the appeal to the example of Soviet Socialist Realism as the model for progressive art.[64] This was a new turn in the cultural discourse of the American party and is linked with the circulation of articles by Zhdanov and others in translation.[65]

We can register the impact of the new Zhdanovite line on communist artistic circles from a mimeographed document circulated in the party's New York artists' club in 1947.[66] This consisted of a translation of an article from *Pravda,* a commentary entitled "American Communist Artists Discuss the 'Pravda' Article," and an unsigned and untitled rebuttal of the commentary by some higher-up. The *Pravda* article, "Toward the Flowering of the Soviet Art," announced the decision to turn the All-Russian Academy of Fine Arts into the Academy of Fine Art of the USSR and accompanied this with a statement about the functions of the new institution in building Soviet culture. What affronted the authors of the commentary was its incipient anti-Westernism, and its blanket assertions that there was "a collapse of art" in Western Europe and that the art of bourgeois societies was "rotten," "decadent," and "formalistic." To counter the example of Matisse and Picasso et al., the article held up that of "a highly spiritualized Russian realistic art" deriving from Repin and Surikov.

As the authors of the commentary pointed out, the *Pravda* article displayed "an oversimplified and non-Marxian concept of the relation between art and society." Marx had specifically rejected the idea that ideology and culture mechanically reflected "economic needs and processes." The commentary sought to distinguish between art that was produced in bourgeois society and art that served bourgeois interests, and it rehearsed the familiar arguments about the relative isolation of the artist under capitalism as the root cause of formalism. But while the modern artist was "isolated from the main political currents of society" and could not produce an art that conveyed "specific social messages," this did not mean that "his" work had no relation to social experience. The works of Cézanne, Van Gogh, Matisse, and Picasso had contributed to "the enlargement of human vision and feeling," and the study of non-Western art had led to the development of "a new visual language with international and universal characteristics" that provided a rich resource for those who wished to use art as a weapon. Western art was "anything but 'collapsed,'" and "in the ranks of progressive and communist artists throughout capitalist countries there are great numbers whose work in varying degrees is connected with the 'formalist' tradition." In sum, the author of the *Pravda* article had "a static and limited approach to the question of realism."[67]

Like Finkelstein, to whose *Art and Society* they referred, the authors of the commentary saw art generally as standing for values antithetical to capitalism, and could therefore envisage a broad alliance of artists working in different modes who were all threatened by the current crisis. However, while this had been the vision of the Popular Front, it was a position quite out of kilter with that of the party leadership in the late forties. The critique of the artists' statement accused them of arrogance toward their Russian comrades and of ultimately falling into the camp of defenders of Western culture against the regimentation of "eastern Communism." However, even this acknowledged that in looking to the Russian national heritage, *Pravda*'s writer had been "diverted" from "the more vital realist tradition of non-Russian painters of the 19th and 20th centuries" and had failed to recognize "the vital developments of social art in Mexico and the United States." The author further implied that there was something to be learned from the work of Picasso and the School of Paris, and he tried to qualify *Pravda*'s "brash statement" that Soviet realist art was "the most advanced in the world" by suggesting this did not mean "the best in an esthetic sense" but only that which was "at least ideologically, and in direction, the most advanced." However, he expressed shock at the temerity of the artists in daring to question the Marxism of the CPSU. *Pravda* was correct in its critique of formalism, which was premised on the bourgeois myth of a classless art. It was not only art that directly propagated bourgeois ideals, such as reactionary political cartoons and advertising that served the interests of the bourgeoisie as a class. It was also any art that did not directly ally itself with the proletarian movement.

For all the attempt to mitigate the stark crudity of the Soviet position, the critique of the artists' statement could not disguise the fact that modernist techniques were now viewed as highly suspect, and communist artists should not be indulging themselves in work with no direct political end. Charles Keller, whose studio on East 14th Street was a meeting place for one of the CP artists' clubs, has recalled that the statement was sent in to the *Daily Worker,* which refused to print it, and that the whole episode had the effect of alienating abstract artists from the party.[68] In fact, some whose works clearly displayed modernist features, such as Evergood, Gwathmey, and Toney, continued to associate closely with it. However, the cost of the emergence of Zhdanovism within the CPUSA was that it could no longer articulate an effective critical discourse to embrace their work, or anything that could provide the basis for further development of a Marxist aesthetic. After March 1950 *Masses & Mainstream* ceased to carry art criticism, and in 1954 Finkelstein published a book-length study of the visual arts that marked a complete capitulation to the Soviet line, and was sharply critical of the adoption of modernist forms by "the social-minded artists of the 1930s."[69] Crushed between Zhdanovism and 57th Street, committed artists had nowhere to turn for a support system. By the time the shocks of 1956 finally tolled the party's death knell,[70] there was no communist cultural movement left to speak of—only a few aging activists who clung to the ideal of a collective democratic culture that had briefly seemed within reach in the 1930s, but that the ensuing decade proved to be unrealizable.

I hope that this essay has established two main points. First, the communist cultural movement did not collapse because of a crisis of moral legitimacy in the late 1930s but because of direct political repression and a much larger historical shift in the ensuing decade. And second, that the depletion of Marxist critical discourse, with all its repercussions, came about because of what the Communist Party did to itself in response to this repression and to the anti-Western turn in Soviet cultural policy of 1947–53. This is a story of losers, but it remains one worth telling, for without it a substantial body of ambitious art will continue to be neglected, and the extent of the negation that had to occur for the avant-garde to triumph will continue to be underestimated.

THE PRESIDENT'S TWO BODIES:
STAGINGS AND RESTAGINGS OF THE NEW DEAL BODY POLITIC

Sally Stein **The Art of Recovery**

"Candidate with a cane" could easily serve as generic title for a 1928 news photograph of Franklin D. Roosevelt that appeared without caption in a pictorial survey of U.S. presidents in 1969 (fig. 1).[1] Viewed in passing among countless other official poses, it seems on first glance hardly remarkable: a full-length frontal portrait of a white, middle-aged, well-dressed man with a cane. Yet this image offers a twist on the typical modern representations of our politicians. The persistent hagiographic rhetoric of presidential triumph over adversity has hardly prepared us to find on closer inspection that more than one cane supports this pose. Rising above the photographer, the figure almost succeeds in projecting an air of rock-solid confidence by assuming a quite contorted version of *contrapposto,* in which he balances himself on a second cane positioned behind him.

If the perception of a second cane causes some viewers to strain themselves by trying to rotate one shoulder and arm backward while

A more extensively illustrated version of this essay was published in the March 2004 issue of *American Art.* This article extends research I presented in the January 1995 CAA panel organized by James D. Herbert, "Acts of Representation, Semiotic and Political." I thank him for encouraging me to pursue issues I raised tangentially in "Peculiar Grace: Dorothea Lange and the Testimony of the Body," in *Dorothea Lange: A Visual Life,* ed. Elizabeth Partridge (Washington, D.C.: Smithsonian Institution Press, 1994), 57–89. Thanks also to Annetta Kapon, Laurie Monahan, Ellen Nasper, Allan Sekula, and Jonathan Weinberg for their comments on drafts of this essay. I dedicate this effort to the memory of Valerie Lloyd (1945–99), whose passion for photography was matched at the end of her life by a personal commitment to thinking socially about disability.

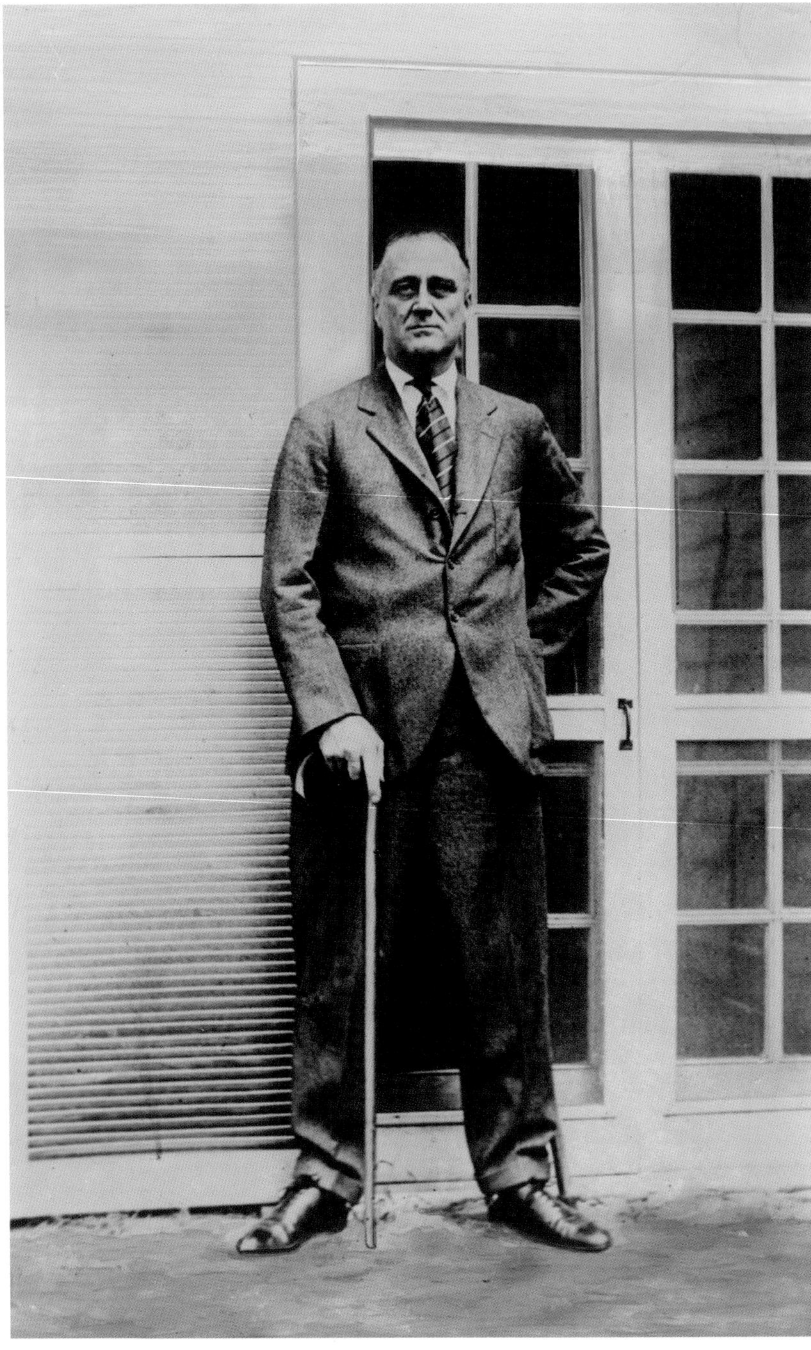

continuing to face straight ahead, it may be owing to the imaginary relations that draw the public to the political leader. Particularly in electoral politics, we judge the representative according to our capacity to identify, and to imagine his or her counteridentification. Paraphrased colloquially, we put ourselves in the politician's shoes and wonder whether the politician can put him- or herself in our shoes. The shoes, in this figure of speech, bring us back to the body as the most familiar measure of political fitness.

According to Hobbes, "sovereign power is achieved either by force or by assent."[2] In the latter case, the sovereign achieves voluntary submission by means of the confidence he inspires to provide protection against all others. Modern mass media may generate a certain atavism in the way they encourages us to scrutinize the bodies of leaders and would-be leaders for signs inspiring confidence or, conversely, signs disabusing us of any such hope. Over time the signs change, but some visual indices, standing included, are so deeply embedded that we barely recognize the way they form the ground for judgment. Absolute monarchs may sit, but even they are often depicted in athletic stances.[3] Leaders who lack absolute authority but depend upon popular mandate must demonstrate their "good standing" quite literally by rising to present themselves to their constituents.[4]

In keeping with the theatrical conventions of modern democracy, the U.S. electorate has exhibited little variation in the type of national political leader it has found acceptable: usually male, nearly always WASP, ostensibly heterosexual (and until very recently monogamous, or at least discreet), of sound mind (little public tolerance of even minor psychological doubts, though spiritual doubts requiring religious consultation are tolerable, even reassuring), and of sound body. On this last count, FDR departed conspicuously from the norm. When first elected president in 1932, Roosevelt had not walked or stood without some form of external support for more than a decade, following an attack of poliomyelitis in 1921, when he already was middle-aged. The issue of his political success seems even more noteworthy when one considers the countervailing tendency, in this period of international crisis, to seek out and embrace "strong leaders."[5]

To reconcile this apparent departure from magisterial type, historians have fashioned a variety of explanations for the New Deal architect's success. Some have proposed that the disability mattered little to Roosevelt and was equally inconsequential to his political associates, who either had more important issues to contemplate or else were blinded by admiration for their leader's political skill and authority. As for the nation at large, a similar claim for the relative insignificance of the president's paralysis suggests that most citizens in this period were too preoccupied with their own problems to pay much attention to superficial aberrations in their leader's physical condition. A conspiratorial variation on the insignificance thesis argues that the issue attracted minimal public attention because FDR and his associates made a point of masking his disability (a "closet" argument that implicitly attests to the fundamental significance of the issue). Finally, there is the quite different interpretation that disability was of considerable significance in making Roosevelt seem more empathic or impressive given his own vulnerability; according to this argument, polio was FDR's "log cabin," which, if it did not actually humble him, appeared to do so.[6]

There are compelling aspects of each of these arguments that draw upon disparate political notions, from the Oz-like machinations of presidential propaganda to mythical notions of the natural selection of leaders following superhuman tests of courage. What these models share is the tendency to attribute knowledge and power either to the leader and his circle or to the people. I propose a less unilateral model, allowing more equivocation and interaction on both sides of the equation. In the case of FDR's political career, the public was exposed to sufficient evidence of his handicap that complete ignorance was impossible. Indeed, it was the public as much as the leader that produced a "cover-up." Thus, instead of trying to assign blame to one party or another for acts of political deception, it may be more productive to examine the long-term collaborative process of recovering the president's ailing body. The resulting image of Depression-era leadership in the United States may help us better comprehend the ideological underpinnings of the unheroic, merely ameliorative New Deal politics of recovery.

Mirror Stage

At no time in a political era are images invested with such importance as during the period of the electoral campaign—which, drawing on Lacan's model of the grandiose first steps toward subject formation, we might call the "mirror stage" of the body politic.[7] Accordingly, we see the greatest fixation on and adjustment of FDR's image at the beginning of the 1930s, as he started up his first presidential campaign. After a period of extended convalescence and rehabilitation in the first half of the 1920s, Roosevelt returned to active political life in New York State, winning election as governor in 1928 as the designated successor to Al Smith, who that year waged an unsuccessful campaign against Herbert Hoover for the presidency. But the efforts FDR made in the 1920s to project an image of successful rehabilitation pale in comparison with the extravagantly mystified image of virtually complete recovery that was created once he set his sights on the White House.

Anticipating the suspicions he would face outside his home state of New York, Roosevelt began his national campaign efforts in 1931 by covertly commissioning a press story that headlined the presumptive fundamental question, "Is Franklin Delano Roosevelt Physically Fit to

Be President?" Though stage-managed, the story was largely accurate. It stretched the truth in asserting that swimming was restoring partial use of FDR's legs, a claim bolstered by a portrait of an athletic-looking FDR seated on the ground in a swimsuit. But this view was offset by another photograph of the paraplegic politician at work in his office, with a caption pointedly acknowledging the bright metal leg braces extending below his trousers to clamp around his shoes. Moreover, the body of the article contained some revealing details that the captions had belied: after conceding that once installed at his desk he could not move easily, Roosevelt remarked that being effectively chained to his work at least prevented him from indulging in "the fidgets."[8] Thus, for a brief period, the prospective candidate was fairly candid about his physical condition, while tacitly proposing ways that disability might be converted into a productive virtue. Soon after this interview appeared in the popular Macfadden magazine *Liberty*, Roosevelt must have been advised that the discipline he had so cheerfully internalized was less than inspiring. In seeking to present himself as a tireless public servant with limited possibilities for distraction or even mobility, he had run the risk of appearing more prisoner than master of circumstances.

Once the "race" for the presidency was underway, a contrary course was charted, with the candidate downplaying both discussion and evidence of his physical disability. To conceal the braces, FDR began wearing trousers long enough to cover the heels of his shoes. Since even this tailoring trick could not conceal the steel braces when he was seated, the braces were painted black to avoid detection or at least glaring prominence in photographs.[9] Instead of leaning on canes or crutches, the president appeared to stand on his own and to walk, in both instances by relying heavily on human attendants; Roosevelt's sons in particular filled that role until the war, for their presence by the father's side could be rationalized in terms of filial devotion rather than physical assistance. Consistent with these efforts to simulate recovery, Roosevelt, though a great patron of the Warm Springs polio clinic, almost never appeared in pictures with fellow rehab patients.[10] And except for the "fireside chats" (so named, perhaps, to discourage expectations of formality by either speaker or listeners), until 1945 Roosevelt went to great lengths to deliver all of his public speeches from a standing position. In the absence of other supports, he would grip the podium that invariably had been reinforced in advance to ensure its function as a physical support.[11]

That FDR succeeded in projecting an image of wondrous resilience was due partly to his painstaking efforts to appear inexhaustibly active and in command, as well as to a cooperative press that generally agreed not to depict him as immobilized or confined to a wheelchair, and finally to a nation that desperately wanted to believe in miraculous recoveries.[12]

Though historians are more inclined to stress the value of a cooperative press in this matter, or alternately to emphasize the White House staff's close monitoring of the press, we should not overlook the weight of public opinion. On one occasion, during Hoover's "lame duck" period, after FDR's election in 1932 but before his inauguration, *Time* magazine referred in passing to the president-elect's "shriveled legs." A few weeks later, the magazine admitted receiving five hundred letters in response to its word choice. Although the editors claimed that half the letters supported the magazine's plainspokenness, most of the letters published suggest that people considered discretion in this context the better part of journalistic and presidential valor. These letters of protest had their effect, for after this episode the news weekly avoided similarly blunt references to the president's physical condition.[13]

Just as rare as *Time*'s frank description were photographs documenting the everyday effects of the president's physical impairment. No more than a couple of snapshots made by family and friends show FDR in a wheelchair, and these scant visual records surfaced decades after his death. During his four terms in office just one press photograph appeared in print that offered any clue about the usual way the president was wheeled around Washington. That one rather fuzzy and distant photograph of the president, on the grounds of the D.C. naval hospital, immediately provoked official objections when *Life* magazine published it in a double-page album-style layout of relatively ordinary scenes in the life of FDR and his family. The scarcity of such images, though most commonly attributed to careful press management by White House staff, seems equally attributable to public tastes and aversions. Surely numerous press photographers equipped with a small-format 35mm Leica or Contax camera could have managed much more revealing scoops had there been a lucrative market for such pictures.[14]

If anyone was calling for full disclosure by 1933, it was Roosevelt, and he was speaking rhetorically. We need only consider his first inaugural speech to appreciate the skill with which this politician managed the desire to confront and simultaneously disavow his disability. Most of us today can recite just the famous line, "the only thing we have to fear is fear itself." The longer passage is more explicit. After noting that fear itself posed the greatest social danger, Roosevelt underscored the point with opposing tropes of mobility, both to describe the ultimate symptoms and to prescribe a likely remedy: "nameless, unreasoning, unjustified terror which paralyzes needed efforts to convert retreat into advance."[15] It was a deft way of reminding his listeners, who could not see him, that he deserved the public's confidence on the basis of his personal experience with paralysis and his own apparent ability to propel himself forward by sheer force of will.

Even more than the words he employed or his animated face and quick grin, jutting chin, and rakishly angled cigarette, there was his voice that broadcast so well. Probably FDR could not have managed a successful return to politics without the prosthetic assistance of broadcast sound in the new era of national radio. After hearing Roosevelt's inaugural address, Lillian Gish, the veteran silent picture star, exclaimed that the president seemed "to have been dipped in phosphorus." One historian links Gish's comment to the gray blustery weather shrouding the Washington inauguration on 4 March 1933.[16] But her remark as plausibly reflects the eerie dissonance between the projected voice—vibrant, forceful, inviting—and the guarded body.

Bodies Lost and Found

Compensatory visual representations arose with the official shielding of the president's body. A time-honored strategy was the portrait bust or head shot.[17] In retrospect, the White House's use of these conventions—and also much New Deal art's use of them—frequently looks rather strained, particularly when accompanied by conspicuous efforts to justify the body's exclusion. Including without literally incorporating FDR was Ben Shahn's solution in his 1937 mural for the newly created Jersey Homesteads resettlement community. For this commission Shahn depicted a number of contemporary luminaries—Albert Einstein, Rexford Tugwell, Robert F. Wagner, John L. Lewis, Sidney Hillman, and others—in major scenes of immigration and the forging of new workplace and residential communities.[18] Roosevelt, however, was not integrated into these densely packed segments, unified visually by an overall field of reddish hues accented by blue, white, and black. Instead, FDR hovers above this patriotic schema in the form of a monochrome poster portrait bearing his name and the encomium "A Gallant Leader."

This strategy of enshrining FDR by shelving him on high risked the appearance of prematurely retiring the president from active political life when he had only begun his second term after a landslide re-election in 1936. Perhaps for this reason, the depiction of Roosevelt's head, framed as a picture within a picture, remained relatively rare, especially compared with the recurrence of two compensatory strategies noteworthy for their attempts at contained but dynamic embodiment. One such strategy aimed to convey the supercharged power of head and hands alone (see right-hand page in fig. 2). This semiotic condensation recalls Roosevelt's self-characterization as being chained to a desk. But the rendering now is far more euphemistic, with the exclusion of the entire lower body while deploying candid photography, montage layouts (and

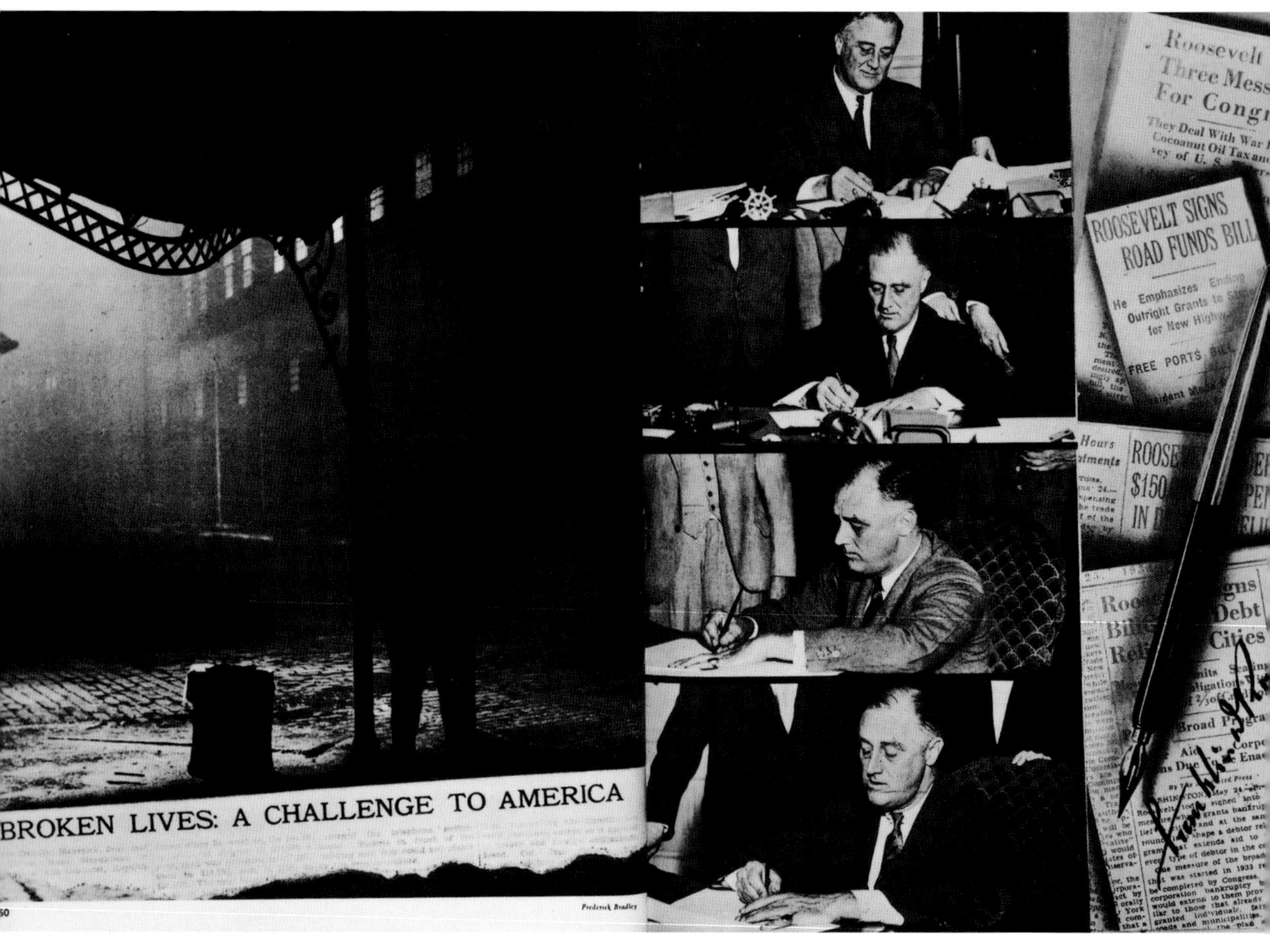

2 Double-page spread from
M. Lincoln Schuster, ed.,
*Eyes on the World: A
Photographic Record of
History-in-the-Making*
(New York: Simon &
Schuster, 1935), 50–51.

in special contexts color photography) to underscore the vitality in the leader's upper extremities.[19]

In many respects the image of the desktop executive was a fitting symbol for depicting the frenetic pace of legislation that characterized the first years of the New Deal. Occasionally, however, the prohibition against depicting more than FDR's upper body turned parodic. A full-page photomontage entitled "A Laughing Cavalier," published in the October 1933 issue of *Vanity Fair,* clusters so many smiling FDR head shots into a media hydra that Roosevelt appears as insubstantial as the bubbly froth produced by soap, or by the newly legalized beer. The accompanying caption, "For the first time in many years the Nation's Chief Executive is a man who understands the value of a grin," added its own hollow ring to the theme of guarded optimism.[20]

The unsigned montage (perhaps by art director M. F. Agha) was just strange enough to fit nicely into the American vernacular section of the Museum of Modern Art's 1936 exhibition, "Fantastic Art, Dada, Surrealism." Maybe it was judged too irreverent, for MOMA's wide-ranging survey found room for a celebratory composite portrait of FDR, also made in 1933, by a little-known contemporary illustrator, C. C. Beall (fig. 3). In Beall's depiction of the Depression-era reformer, the head of Roosevelt is superimposed on various figures intended to symbolize New Deal targets and goals: "elimination of child labor" at nose and mouth; "new dawn" on forehead; cornucopia at Adam's apple, etc. In the MOMA exhibition, the closest precedent for this fusing of political symbols was the sixteenth-century imperial allegories of Arcimboldo. In contrast to Arcimboldo's witty rendering of the principle of the *corpus mysticum,* Beall's composite portrait was striving far more earnestly to fashion the modern equivalent of the king's mystical body, which European historian Ernst Kantarowicz traced from early modern statecraft back to medieval Christian doctrine.[21] If the melding of leader and people into the figure of the collective body politic reminds us of the oft-reproduced frontispiece to Hobbes's *Leviathan,* Beall's work confines this overlapping to the area of the leader's head. Bodies, however, are not absent altogether. The child's body is especially conspicuous; less prominent but arguably more arresting is the trace of a hand holding a cane insinuated in the shadow of the president's cheek. Here we have a textbook case of disavowal, for the legend accompanying this puzzle picture directs the viewer to associate the cane not with Roosevelt but with the "forgotten man," the figure of need invoked by FDR in his first presidential campaign.

This leads us to an alternative semiotic strategy, in which the shielded body of the president was disclosed, but on other figures. Such transposition satisfied the need to behold a complete body in the contemporary symbolism of the body politic, the organically unified nation, and simultaneously to uphold the leader's dignity. *Dignitas,* according to Kantarowicz, served the jointly cohesive purpose of ensuring continuity in the succession of the sovereign and the perpetuity of the social community.[22] However much the vestigial principle of *dignitas* helps explain the impulse to conceal the leader's impairment in a period obsessed with the specter of prolonged crisis and the possibility of popular revolt, we still should not be surprised that in a culture obsessed with physical appearance the banished body would reappear in other forms. One cartoon, published on the day of Roosevelt's nomination in July 1932, made multiple references to canes and physical infirmity but scrambled the symbols to alter their meaning. The scene presents a neatly constructed Democratic Party platform looking comparatively sturdy in front of the heap of planks identified as the GOP platform. The Democratic platform remains unoccupied but supports an armchair, implying that the nominee who mounts it may need to sit. Below the platform stands a male figure, hat outstretched in one hand while he leans on a cane with the other. But this expectant figure is not Roosevelt. Cartoonist Rollin Kirby deliberately identified him with the generic label "voter." Thus the cane that Roosevelt sought to dispense with in public was transferred from

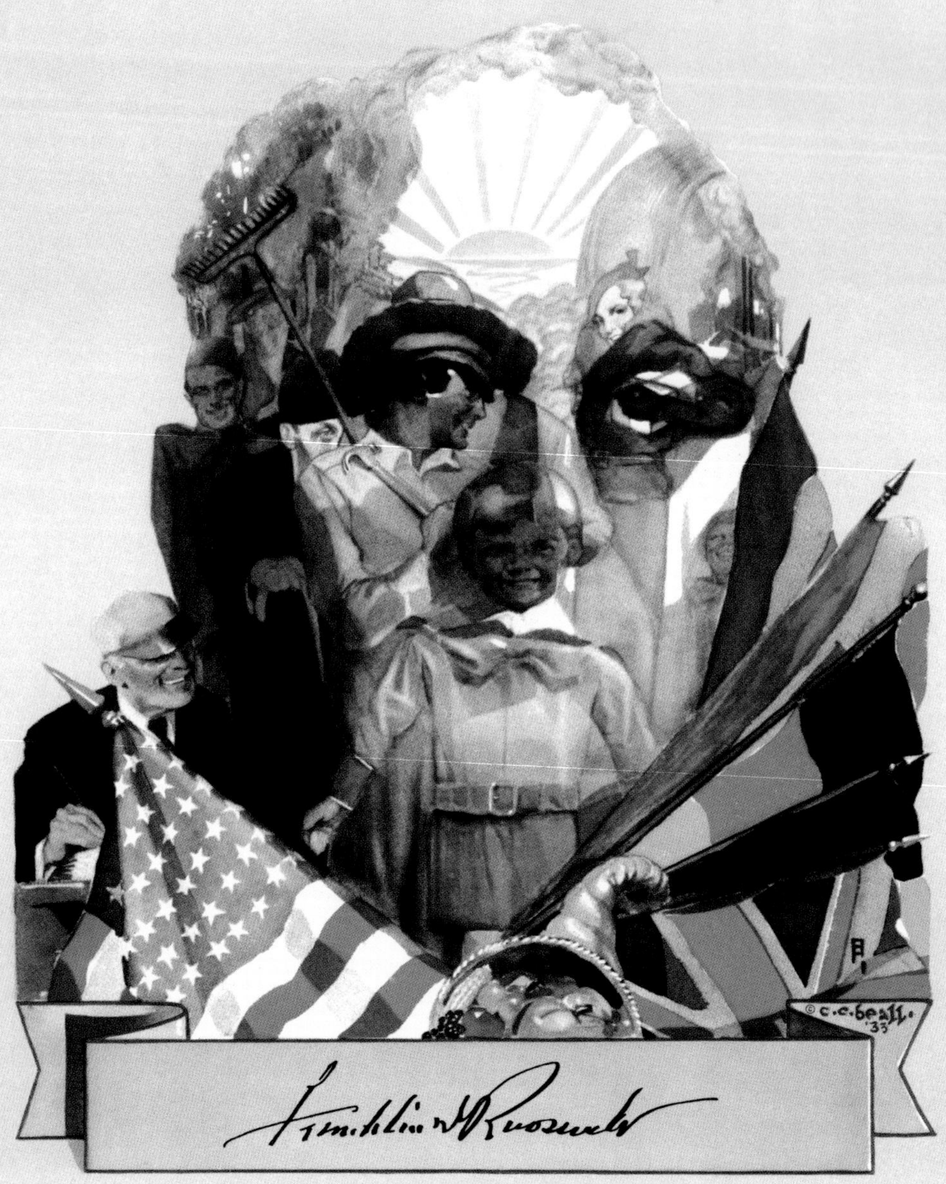

BORN JANUARY 30, 1882 • 32ND PRESIDENT OF THE UNITED STATES • INAUGURATED MARCH 4, 1933

Find WHAT ROOSEVELT MEANS TO THE U. S. A. *in this Picture*

1. ELIMINATION OF CHILD LABOR *(see nose and mouth).*
2. RIGHTS OF LABOR *(see his right eye).*
3. OPPORTUNITY FOR FARMER *(see his right eyebrow).*
4. OLD AGE PENSIONS *(see his right cheek-bone).*
5. BIGGER NAVY AND REFORESTATION *(see hair on right side of his head).*
6. WOUNDED VETERAN RELIEF *(see his right ear).*

7. THE NEW DAWN *(see his forehead).*
8. CONSERVATION OF WATER SUPPLY *(see his left forehead).*
9. REVIVAL OF INDUSTRY *(see his left temple).*
10. INCREASED PURCHASING POWER *(see his left eye).*
11. BETTER INTERNATIONAL RELATIONS *(see flags under his chin).*
12. RENEWED PROSPERITY *(see horn of plenty).*

13. THE FORGOTTEN MAN *(see his right shoulder).*

3 C. C. Beall, "Find What Roosevelt Means to the U.S.A. in This Picture," 1933. Reproduced as plate 523 in the exhibition catalog edited by Alfred H. Barr Jr., *Fantastic Art: Dada Surrealism* (New York: Museum of Modern Art, 1936).

the absent figure of the candidate to the constituents he sought to represent by identifying their pressing social needs.[23]

Other cartoonists, graphic artists, and photographers adopted similar strategies of dissociating the cane from Roosevelt and grafting it onto diverse figures intended to symbolize the common man, the forgotten farmer, or the down-and-out man on the street. Indeed, the depiction of FDR as desktop executive makes use of this grafting strategy when we recall that the image is the right-hand side of a double-page spread in which FDR's signing of multiple bills answers the listing figure on the left-hand page, which carries the headline, "Broken Lives: A Challenge to America" (fig. 2).[24] As the cane was bandied about, passed from one figure to another, the signs of physical infirmity became in effect generic symbols that served to affiliate diverse groups under the institutional rubric of New Deal reform. Call it a purposeful confusion that likened those who could not support themselves physically with those who could not do so economically, by visualizing the etymological link between pathology and pathos. If the affinities thus forged depended more on analogy than on strict equation, affinities invariably work to obscure internal disparities; in this case, the socially dispossessed served as surrogate bodies for the leader's unspeakable, unapproachable body, while the president's carefully managed physical handicap rationalized his position as commanding political spokesman. Yet even as the cane and the postures of dependency came to be commonplace figures, they retained a measure of poignancy—propping up the idea of suffering as widespread, unpredictable, and best endured by a mix of personal adjustment and gradual social consolidation.

The extremely partial presentation and representation of the president's body became over time normative, as did the Depression itself for more than a decade. Just once, toward the end of his life, did Roosevelt dispense with formality and present the public with a quite different image of its president. Returning from Yalta, he allowed himself to be wheeled in to Congress to deliver an address while seated. On this occasion he began, "I know you will realize it makes it a lot easier for me ... not having to carry about ten pounds of steel around the bottom of my legs." The pointed reference to his usual public posturing reportedly met with laughter from the Congress.[25] Neither then nor following FDR's death, six weeks later, was anyone eager to dismantle the myth of a "freestanding" leader.

Vanishing Acts

Notwithstanding FDR's parting acknowledgment of the heavy weight of the braces he constantly carried, the posthumous representational strategies attest that public disavowal of FDR's physical condition continued strong for many decades. The first official memorial representation was the Roosevelt dime, struck in 1946. In a period striving for peacetime reconversion without a concomitant return to Depression hardships, the numismatic portrait exceptionalizes Roosevelt by withholding any indication of a body below the head. Coins admittedly offer cramped spaces for portraiture, the small size of the dime being most restrictive. Even so, the physiognomy on the Roosevelt dime stops unnecessarily short with the chin, especially compared to the way necks and sometimes shoulders figure as prominent supports in the case of the Lincoln penny, the Jefferson nickel, and the Washington quarter.

The other side of the coin of such selective posthumous renderings was the physical destruction of those necessary material props that had enabled Roosevelt to serve as president. For many years the braces were considered too unsightly to be exhibited with other FDR memorabilia at his former family home on the Hudson River, which after his death was designated the official library housing his papers and other personal effects. Likewise, as soon as Harry Truman assumed the presidency, the ramps installed for his predecessor were removed from most public buildings. Thus even access to Hyde Park became difficult for those who have trouble walking. And until the 1968 Bartlett Act mandated that federal buildings be made accessible to the handicapped, it must have been hard to imagine anyone—past, present, or future—wheeling through the halls of power to command authority without standing.

FDR would not have been surprised by this outcome. Just as the four-term president fully appreciated that the semblance of physical autonomy was essential to his public acceptance, so too he envisioned that even after his death few would elect a more explicit depiction of either his physical impairment or his need to manage it carefully. During his exceptional third term in office, FDR anticipated the monumental dilemmas that commemorative efforts would face. During his second term, he had witnessed political and artistic controversy surround and nearly swamp the building of the Jefferson Memorial.[26] To avoid similar controversy when he no longer could oversee its resolution, the president dictated to Justice Felix Frankfurter the following guidelines for any future memorial in his name: "placed in the center of that green plot [in front of the Archives Building] ... a block about the size of this (putting his hand on his desk). I don't care what it is made of, whether limestone or granite or what not, but I want it to be plain, without any ornamentation, with the simple carving 'In memory of. ...'"[27] If this plan sounds suspiciously low-key—a parody of less-is-more modernism from a president who exhibited no love for modernism—posthumous events demonstrate that anything more would only magnify the extreme difficulty his image posed for memorials on a grand scale. Apart from FDR's self-designated memorial, efforts to produce a public memorial during the second half of the twentieth century resulted in two successive projects being aborted and a third proceeding fitfully. However much they varied in plan and style, the designs successively favored for a major FDR memorial share a symptomatic tendency to repeat earlier efforts to evade or gloss over the particularities of a body that could not conform to conventional postures of leadership.

Even a cursory review of the memorial's checkered history reveals both how much and how little has changed. A congressional resolution in July 1946 first approved the concept of a FDR memorial, but ten years elapsed before the formation of a Franklin Delano Roosevelt Memorial Commission, which in 1958 finally designated a site in West Potomac Park not far from the Jefferson Memorial. An early monograph on the 1960 competition, which drew five hundred submissions, notes that the winning proposal, by the architectural team of William F. Pedersen and Bradford S. Tilney, was one of many featuring tall shafts "to express the inspiration and hope that Roosevelt gave to world." Theirs definitely stood out as well as up, with the principle of uplift extending to the landscape design that was terraced with many steps (fig. 4). Had the memorial proceeded according to plan, the ubiquitous terracing would have restricted all others who were similarly handicapped. At the center, soaring white slabs were meant to serve as upright tablets, bearing inscriptions from the speeches of the president. As solo supplement to abstract form, text underscored the absence of a body. In defense of this form of abstraction, one critic declared that the spare design of simple incised slabs "quite literally made FDR's words his monument."[28] That claim recalled the eerie effect of a disembodied voice, an effect made more strange by the ultra-luminous slabs themselves. The plan made a point of specifying a crystalline surface of crushed white marble mixed with concrete, which some warned might be blinding on sunny days. Architects involved in subsequent plans must have recognized the quest for shimmering effects as fetishistic, choosing instead to work with dark, unpolished materials. The first architectural team sought to dispel criticism by cutting the height and adding a rather ungainly figurative depiction of FDR at the base of these shafts. But these compromises placated few critics and ultimately led members of the Roosevelt family to declare their fervent opposition to the original design and all efforts at modification, leading Pedersen and Tilney to resign the commission in 1965.[29]

The next year the Memorial Commission began anew, this time avoiding an open competition. After consulting more than fifty architects, the commission invited Marcel Breuer to develop a proposal. In collaboration with Herbert Beckhard, Breuer submitted a design that the commission accepted in December 1966, only to face immediate

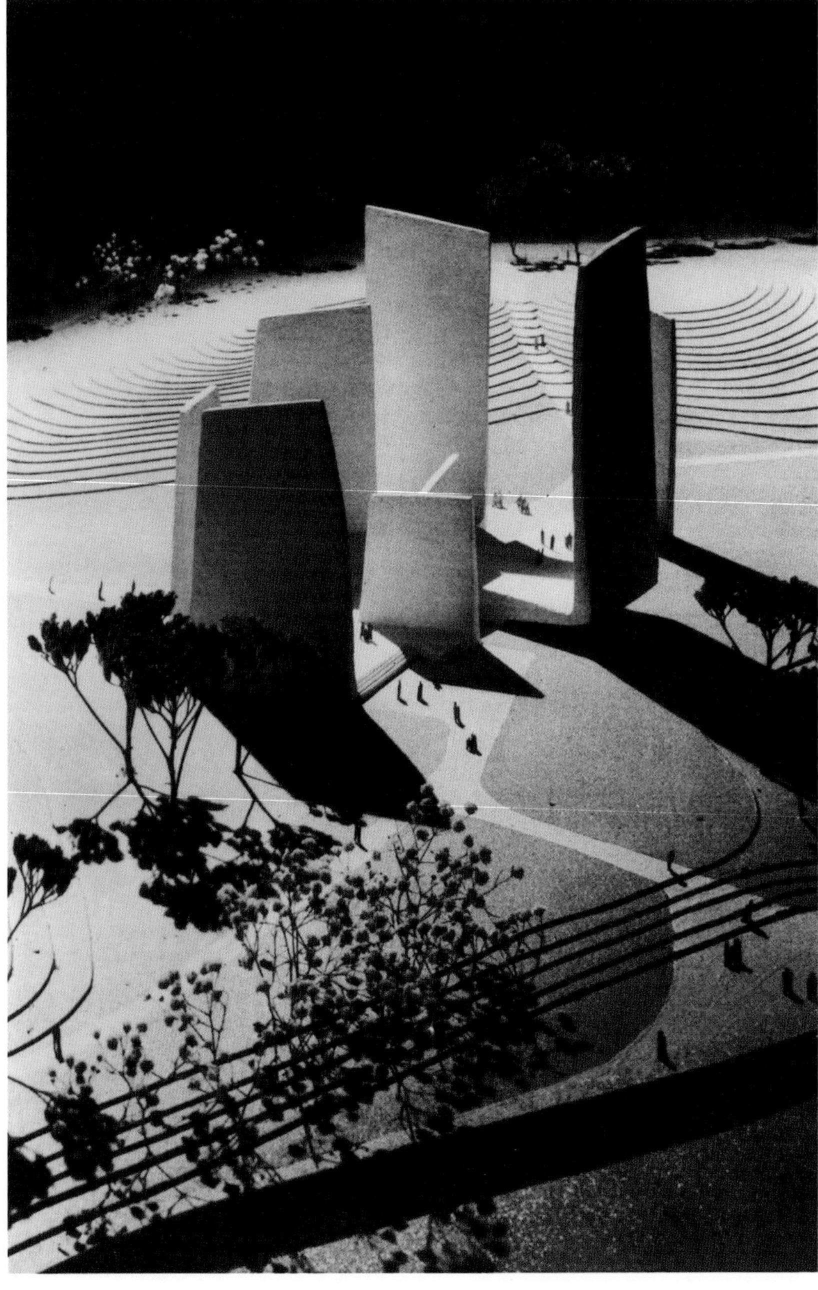

4 Louis Checkman,
photograph of 1960 model
in winning plan by William
F. Pederson and Bradford
S. Tilney, as reproduced
in Thomas H. Creighton,
*The Architecture of
Monuments: The Franklin
Delano Roosevelt
Memorial Competition*
(New York: Reinhold,
1962), 32.

rejection by the D.C. Commission of Fine Arts early in 1967. The new
plan contained obvious references to Pedersen and Tilney's earlier plan,
which Breuer respected, but with major changes. Seven triangular shapes
replaced the objectionable towering shafts, and they no longer threatened to compete with adjacent monuments, as these triangles sixty feet
in height in dark granite (fig. 5). Integrated in the plan from the start

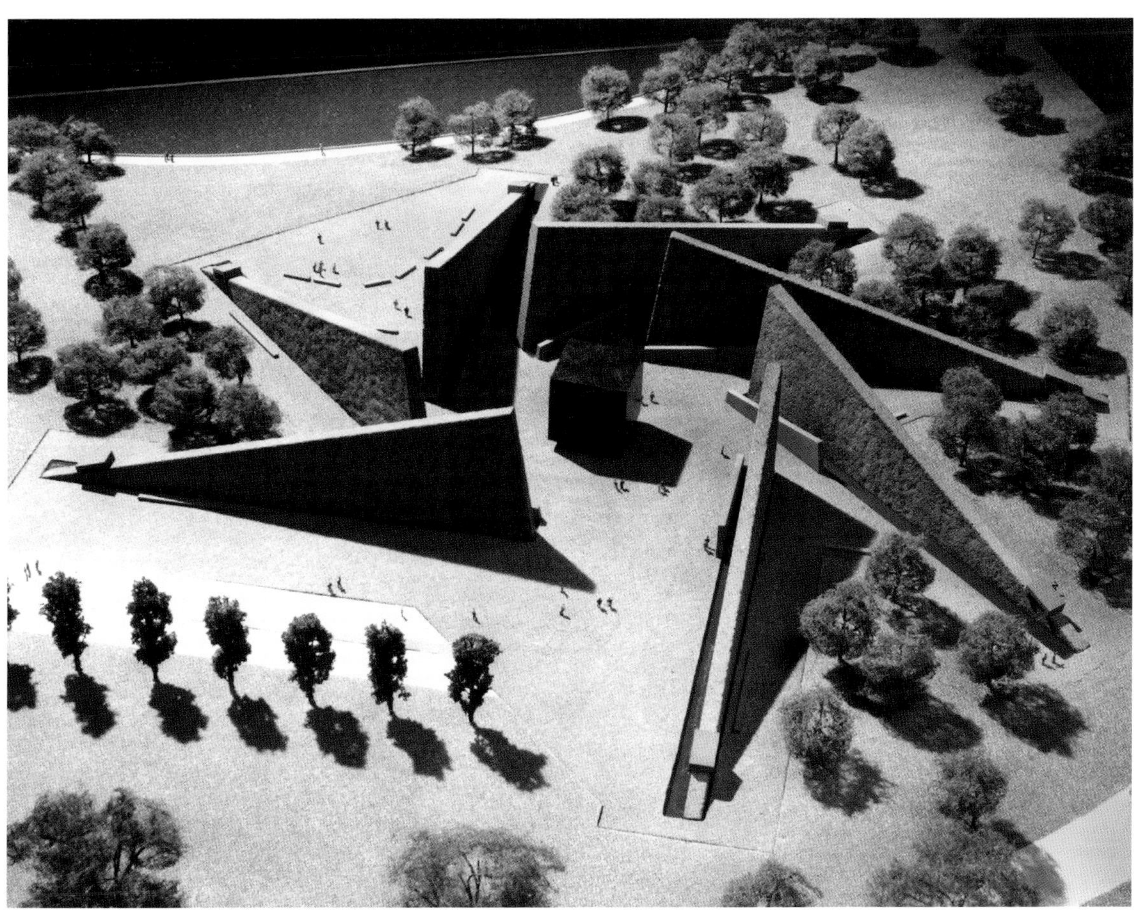

was a familiar likeness, drawn in style as well as substance from newspaper sources. At the center of the seven wedges, angled like spokes in a wheel, stood a cube measuring thirty-two feet incised with a hugely enlarged reproduction of a photojournalistic portrait. As with most halftones, the viewer's distance would vary the degree to which the dots would merge into a recognizable image.[30]

The official grounds for rejection were mainly aesthetic. According to architectural historian Isabelle Hyman, most objectionable was the plan's eclecticism, inviting charges of being both too modernistic (which in the second half of the 1960s meant old-fashioned) and too trendy in its references to Pop Art.[31] But aside from aesthetics, there may have been as grave concern about the design's "significance," its manifest refusal to soar loftily. Although this plan revolved around a conventional portrait, the surrounding triangles were positioned like sentries to deflect attack, even frontal exposure. As for the halftone image, FDR-turned-Ben-Day-dotty all but proclaimed the leader's inaccessibility except via mass media. Regarding his choice of the cube as centerpiece, Breuer's

essentially formal explanation contained its own notable slippages:
"I chose the cube because it is the very center, the very base of form—
practically perfect. ... The globe is comparable, but it isn't static; it moves
too much. I preferred the great stability, the 'standing power,' of the
cube. FDR had 'standing power' too."[32] I assume he meant to say "staying power." As the only president elected to four terms, FDR had great
staying power despite his limited standing power. The contradiction was
indirectly acknowledged by Breuer, who envisioned this block mounted
on a nearly invisible pedestal, so that it "seemingly floats above the
ground." Given these equivocations, the plan may have seemed more
canny than uncanny in its invocation of the supremely skillful politician.
Breuer resigned his commission in 1969.

Pork-Barrel Postmodernism

Following this second stalemate, the Memorial Commission delayed for
a half decade before proceeding a third time to identify a design concept that promised to pass the multistage review process. This time the
commission avoided consulting outside architects. Oregon senator Mark
Hatfield, a member of the commission, championed West Coast landscape architect Lawrence Halprin on the basis of a plaza he had designed
for downtown Portland. Halprin's initial proposal won approval from the
commission in 1975 and then, with surprising speed, obtained preliminary approval from the D.C. Commission of Fine Arts in 1976. Funding
took far longer to materialize. The initial cost projection of $50 million
was especially unwelcome during the domestic recession at the end of
the Vietnam War. Though Halprin scaled back his design, it was only at
the end of the 1980s, after Claude Pepper, the last congressional veteran
of the New Deal era, made the FDR memorial his final cause, that the
government committed funds for the project. Following three decades of
monumental ambivalence, ground was broken in 1991 and construction
of the FDR Memorial finally began in 1994.

No doubt Maya Lin's spare Vietnam Veterans Memorial (design
1981, dedication 1982) helped pave the way for the realization of the
FDR Memorial.[33] By contrast, Halprin's plan was far more expansive,
appearing to offer something for everyone, which partly recalls the
Popular Front of the 1930s and partly the conciliatory sensibility of the
nineteenth-century *juste milieu,* a middle-of-the-road compromise strategy that certainly had an appeal in the war-weary post-Watergate era.
Anyone looking for abstraction in Halprin's plan could find bits of it, but
without the rigor that gave Lin's design its edge, and mixed liberally with
quite traditional figurative sculptures. Instead of rising high, it would

extend, park-like, over 7.5 acres on one side of the Tidal Basin. "As you approach West Potomac Park, you might even suspect it's not there," is how one supporter praised its low profile.[34]

Halprin was eminently suited to devise a solution that harmonized with the existing environment of monuments, park, and tidewater swamp. Since the 1960s Halprin's projects had been notable for their ecological tone. Water is one of the elements he most liked working with, particularly in dense, noisy environments, where he demonstrated that pocket parks containing fountains, pools, and falls could achieve the semblance of microsanctuaries. Religious currents were even more prominent in his proposal for the FDR Memorial. Halprin referred to the central memorial area as a "sacred space," within which he envisioned a sequence of four "outdoor rooms" corresponding to FDR's four presidential terms. Uplift would result not from verticality but from a carefully structured shrine-like procession through a chain of open-air galleries linked by narrower passageways. Along the way, visitors would pause to read excerpts from FDR's speeches carved into the granite walls, this inclusion of multiple texts being one of the only elements his design shared with previous proposals.[35]

Where the earlier designs were essentially circular in shape, Halprin's plan was quite elongated. Still, his design did not strive for radical decentering. Halprin always intended to balance the idea of linear movement with a strong figurative element that would conceptually unify the memorial space: "In his notes from 12 March 1974 [Halperin] indicated that he would like something 'bigger than life, standing with cape and cane and braces—because that's how most of us remember [FDR].' Four days later, Halprin changed his mind ... [and] also admitted to himself, 'The statue issue is a tough one in terms of scale. Also should [FDR] be seated as he normally was when we saw him or standing ... I think sitting is better—but how?'"[36] According to this account, the architect gradually recognized that the memories he had long harbored of a standing New Deal leader were closer to wish fulfillment than reality. The artifactual evidence of a president who was hardly ever seen directly in a standing posture also left him uncertain as to what kind of seated pose might work in a comparable commanding fashion (for in many historic images, FDR, even when seated, is visible only from the chest up). Only after turning the walls of his studio into an "image bank" of historic photographs of FDR did Halprin accept that he could find no typical image of Roosevelt seated that he felt confident could withstand the demands for reasonable accuracy while providing a formal and symbolic pillar of strength.[37] The standing versus sitting dilemma stalled Halprin for a year. Finally, in March 1975, he resolved to end the impasse by embracing the "principle of multiples." With this declaration of pluralism, no single figure cast "bigger than life" would dominate the space, but rather "a number of pieces by many sculptors," presenting diverse iconic depictions of ordinary Depression citizens as well as their leader.[38]

Halprin must have been hoping that amid a throng of figures— some standing, others sitting—relativity would prevail, thereby distracting viewers from the still vexing issue of how to depict the four-term leader's inspiring power to govern. The group of sculptors first assembled to realize this scheme of multiples included Robert Graham (with whom Halprin had previously worked), Leonard Baskin, and George Segal. Already diverse, the group became even more so when Congressman Eugene Keogh, while serving as chair of the Memorial Commission, urged the addition of Neil Estern, a traditional sculptor of official likenesses who happened to reside in Keogh's congressional district.[39] Though Estern's inclusion had its basis in the time-honored exchange of favors, he worked hard to contribute his mimetic skills, volunteering to fashion the major depictions of FDR and Eleanor when none of the other sculptors expressed interest in these portrait assignments. The original three men all preferred to render anonymous New Deal scenes and subjects. Graham opted to produce the relief depicting the first inauguration, in which scene FDR appears riding in an open car, visible only from the chest up, and a separate set of reliefs on the theme of New Deal social programs; Baskin elected to produce two reliefs, one of the funeral cortege, and another, later dropped, of FDR standing with what appears in the sketch to be the faint trace of a supporting hand entering at the edge (though that third hand rests on FDR's elbow, reversing the way FDR, in order to appear standing without crutch or cane, needed to lean his weight on the arm of another);[40] Segal applied his lifecasting methods to three scenes of ordinary Depression-era Americans struggling to cope—a breadline, a farm couple, and a solitary man seated beside a period radio as if listening to one of FDR's "fireside chats."

Crowding the memorial in this way resonates metaphorically with the massive impact of the economic crisis that Roosevelt's New Deal aimed to resolve. It resonates also with the historiographical turn away from biographies of Great Men toward "history from below." But underlying the apparent commitment to social history is a very traditional ode to the Great Man, albeit one whose physical presence has been, in posthumous art as in life, kept under wraps. Notwithstanding the populist rhetoric mobilized to advance Halprin's plan, there was never any risk that the motley assortment of figures would undermine the fundamentally magisterial chronicle. The walls of this extensive memorial are scored with words, but the anonymous figures are mute. Their muteness is far from inevitable. The Roosevelt archives contain an unprecedented volume of letters to the White House. Literally millions of ordinary citizens (including those barely literate) were inspired by FDR's political invocation of the "forgotten man" to register their personal observations, complaints, demands, and thanks.[41] Yet that popular impulse to speak out is forgotten anew in this memorial. The only words incised in the granite that roughly delineates the four open-air rooms are those of FDR, accompanied by the ubiquitous sound of falling water.

Even the course of water in this memorial is monologic in its effect, enhancing the president's singular authority without fixing attention on him. As a pragmatic instrument, the loud "natural" sound of moving water muffles the noise of jets on their flight path to nearby National (now Reagan) Airport (itself a major New Deal construction project). But the water's sounds are carefully modulated, and the way Halprin orchestrated this fluid element belies the ostensible significance of the social landscape in this monument. The first, inaugural, outdoor room features a waterfall to herald the start of FDR's four-term presidency. For the entry space marking the early years of the Depression, a barely running stream would have been more evocative of privation in general, and in particular of the major drought exacerbating the economic and social crisis.

In like manner, Halprin's arrangement of iconic scenes reinforces traditional notions of historical causality and the flow of power. Just as Halprin referred to his deployment of water as "waterplay,"[42] we might consider his use of multiple sculptures a form of "historyplay." While the structural principle of four linked rooms lends itself to the easy narration of FDR's political progress, the placement of iconic scenes within this plan scrambles the order of major social events to avoid upstaging the presidential chronicle. To reinforce the image of heroic solitary leadership, first lady Eleanor Roosevelt makes her appearance only after FDR's funeral cortege, as the first U.S. delegate to the United Nations. There is no sign of her unprecedented political role in the Depression era—as FDR's most prominent domestic ambassador and simultaneously as an independent voice championing politics far more progressive than her husband's. On the front end of Halprin's plan, the breadline is curiously absent from the first room, appearing instead in the second room. Like a waiting stage, the first courtyard is left nearly empty, so as to highlight FDR's entry into the national spotlight. This sequence places the cart before the horse. If the presidential architect of the New Deal came to be viewed by many as a modern-day democratic savior, it is because the breadlines and shantytowns (called "Hoovervilles" in 1932) were such common sights in the first years of the Depression. Had Roosevelt been elected president four years earlier, he probably would have been voted out of office, just as Hoover was in the 1932 election.[43] In other words, the breadlines and the widespread despair they represented laid the foundation for FDR's election and inauguration to power.

Notwithstanding the memorial's decentered form and accompanying claims to commemorate the times as well as the leader, the overall effect of this space is profoundly monographic, even though the formal principle of "multiples" makes it far from monolithic.

All populist claims are dropped in the third courtyard, where Roosevelt presides over the spectacle of war, suggested formally by broken blocks of granite heaped like rubble. In this theatrical setting FDR, previously appearing only in relief, is now "fleshed out" in three dimensions. And in contrast to all the other memorial figures that are life-size or smaller, this sculpture is scaled nearly double life-size, so that even in a seated posture the figure on its low platform rises nine feet high (fig. 6). All these visual cues direct the viewer's gaze to the figure of the president, at the same time that both figure and gaze are cleverly veiled. Neil Estern's sculptural portrait derives primarily from one photographic source, specifically selected because it shows FDR wearing a military cape. Choosing this image as the basis for the major sculptural rendition makes it possible to present the wartime president in massive volume while exposing little of his body. The final sculpture includes minor allusions to FDR's physical impairment—the tiny wheels added discreetly to the high-backed armchair; the disproportionately thin legs, one of which juts out awkwardly from beneath the cape; the rather abrupt postural shift between the arrangement of legs off to one side and the torso, hands, and head facing forward—without ever acknowledging the handicap directly. As one children's book on Estern's presidential sculpture explains, "Neil wants to suggest the disability but doesn't want it to be the first thing that people notice."[44] In the hope that other aspects of the portrait would be noticed first, Estern lavished attention on the elaborately braided closures of the naval officer's cape, the carving on the signet ring that adorns the left hand, the deep ridges of wrinkles in both hands and face, and the rhythmic waves of hair.

Beyond (but not far from) the cape and accessory details that cloak the commander-in-chief, there is no overlooking the obsessively sculpted dog. Pound for pound, Fala does the heaviest lifting in the entire monument. The iconography of fidelity provides one starting point for solving the riddle of the dog.[45] Halprin has expressly noted that Fala's presence should remind us of the president's constant good humor in the face of adversity.[46] Yet is simple "good humor" reason enough to risk having a dog detract from the solemn scene of war? Just as Estern's inclusion was the result of political patronage, so Estern added a dog to his assignment at the urging of another politician. Construction of the memorial depended on congressional support. After reviewing plans at a relatively late stage, Senator Carl Levin sensed something lacking in the maquette for this portrait (among other things, the outstretched fingers betrayed the absence of a cigarette that the president had been holding in the source photo).[47] After the senator recommended adding Fala, the compliant Estern took a mannerist tack, adding a cascade of tresses to make the rather scruffy dog more inviting.[48] Halprin must have considered Estern's sculptural improvisation a key addition. Though he refers to Fala's placement at FDR's feet,[49] FDR actually was pushed to the right half of the niche to give the pet ample space. And why not sideline the

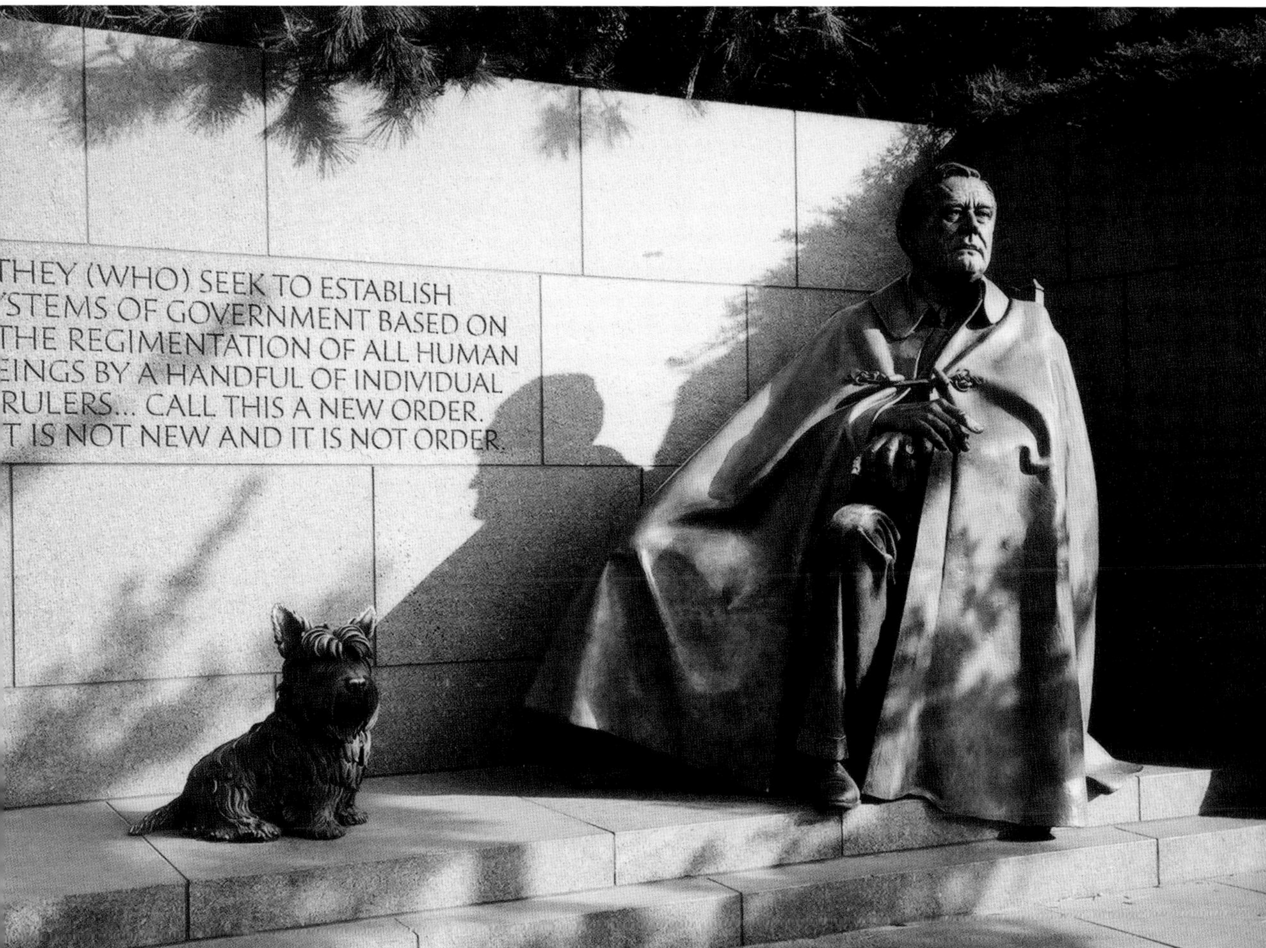

6 Photograph of Neil Estern sculpture of FDR in the FDR Memorial designed by Lawrence Halprin.

commander-in-chief, when the bronze Fala serves double duty as perch and guard—inviting the innocent to approach (for rest, a bit of play, perhaps a snapshot pose) while maintaining vigilant watch?

There is considerable historical justice in this descent from landscape architecture to petting zoo. FDR constantly used Fala as a media prop to deflect attention from himself, especially at the faltering end of his life. Some have argued that the final fourth-term election was clinched only after FDR denounced all attacks on himself as injurious to his pet. What came to be marveled at as "that Fala speech" worked like a charm in September 1944. The Republicans quickly dropped the personal attacks, hoping to avoid what the Democrats now welcomed as "a contest of Dewey versus Fala."[50] But this time the pet ruse did not perform the same trick. Visitors cozy up to Fala, but the guarded pose of his master was not saved from attack.

Habeas Corpus

Attacks commenced while the memorial was under construction, once major details of the overall design were made public. In an era of intense identity politics, one might expect quite a few groups to find fault with diverse aspects of this panoramic depiction of two decades of depression and war. Nevertheless, feminists did not publicly protest the way this memorial marginalized Eleanor Roosevelt by downplaying her vital public role in the 1930s. Nor did Japanese Americans publicly assail the hypocrisy of carving in stone Roosevelt's rhetorical commitment to civil rights while sweeping under the rug the infamous internment camps established in 1942 by Executive Order 9066. Nor did historians challenge the scrambled chronology. Rather, criticism immediately coalesced around just one aspect of this wide-ranging memorial: the figurative depiction of FDR.

Particularly around questions of disability, the political stakes had changed radically during the two decades that Halprin's memorial was awaiting approval, funding, and construction. The early 1980s witnessed the emergence of the disability rights movement, based on the principles of unapologetic self-advocacy while drawing on a widening constituency who insisted on being fully heard, seen, and accommodated by the mainstream. Concomitant with demands for social recognition, political lobbying for protective federal legislation resulted in the passage of the 1990 Americans with Disabilities Act (legislation achieved with the somewhat surprising support of conservative Republicans, until one considers that a significant portion of the disabled are military veterans). Throughout the 1990s activists continued to fight for proper enforcement of this bill, while also turning to the memorial under way as a site of symbolic struggle.[51] A decade earlier, Roosevelt had not been universally viewed as a role model for the disabled.[52] But in the 1990s, it was more pragmatic to overlook any differences in political strategy and hail FDR as a pioneering advocate. After so claiming him, the movement had good reason to contest the way this fundamental physical aspect of his life was retrospectively rendered invisible once again.

In the mid-1990s disability activists lobbied for alteration of Estern's sculptural model of FDR, advocating that the president's reliance on wheelchairs, braces, or canes correspond to the condition of "millions of others living with disability." With construction underway after many stages of revision, the commission was reluctant to make any but minor changes (which seems to be how, in a gesture of token appeasement, tiny wheels came to be added to the chair on which FDR is seated—even though a similar chair used at Hyde Park is not the chair on which he sits when photographed in his naval cape; and a more conventionally serviceable "obvious" wheelchair was added to the small educational display in the visitor center that mainly serves as gift shop). Finding the commission unresponsive to major revisions, the activists went public with their objections. One spokesperson on the board of the National Organization on Disability invoked the "50 million disabled people living in this country" as corollary to his argument that FDR "lived in a wheelchair and history should record it."[53]

Over the next two years, those demanding a new depiction of FDR and those defending the approved ones exchanged charges and countercharges of "political correctness" and "revisionism." Both sides claimed the banner of historical accuracy, with each side marshaling select bits of evidence that bolstered its arguments for disparate versions of mimetic authenticity.[54] As there was some merit to each side of this debate, President Clinton's conclusion that the resolution was a "no-brainer" sounded a false note. Then again, in the spring of 1997 Clinton was referring less to the debate itself than to the need to forestall activists threatening to disrupt the scheduled dedication. Just as the memorial was nearing completion, the movement upped the ante, publicly staging preliminary rallies with promises of a major turnout for the ribbon-cutting ceremonies. In the press photos of these public rehearsals, the activists had enlarged one of two recently unearthed photos of FDR in a wheelchair (see fig. 7). As photos tend to do, this one seemed to speak for itself. Even though this was such an atypical depiction that it did not even circulate among FDR's friends in his lifetime, it now carried the weight of published evidence, thereby implying that any other depiction was an evasion. In a battle over visual representation, it should come as no surprise that the decisive weapon would be a photograph.

To fend off similar demonstrations at the memorial's dedication, President Clinton announced at the eleventh hour that he would ask Congress to mandate the inclusion of a statue of FDR in a wheelchair.[55] Legislation authorizing such an addition passed both Houses of Congress within three months. Distilling the tenor of identity politics while once again conflating physical and socioeconomic impediments, one politician contended, "it took a disabled president to lead a disabled nation." As for the mimetic accuracy and simultaneously the didactic efficacy of such a depiction, another advanced the following paired points: "Contrary to popular belief, President Roosevelt did at times purposely display his disability to inspire wounded veterans, persons with polio, and other groups of Americans. A statue portraying his disability will stand as a reminder to current and future generations of Americans that disability is a natural part of the human experience that in no way diminished the ability of a person to fully participate in all aspects of American life."[56]

Setting aside his initial resistance to further changes, Halprin began working with a new advisory group, convened by the Secretary of the Interior, that included a considerable number of disability activists. Preferring to avoid having a separate sculpture that might stand in dissonant relation to the memorial, Halprin resolved that any change be incorporated so seamlessly as to appear part of the original conception. Along

7 Photograph of demonstration in Washington, D.C., protesting the soon-to-be-dedicated memorial to Roosevelt that included no representation of him "in a wheelchair or braces."

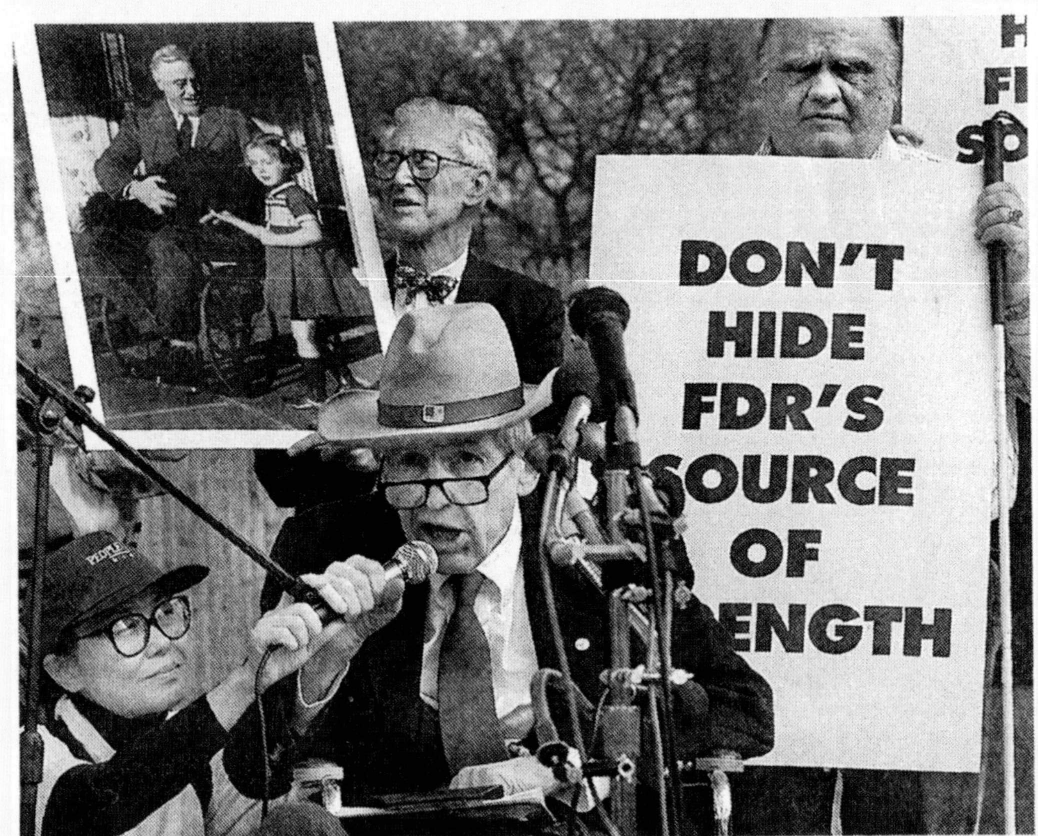

Associated Press

Calling for F.D.R.'s Wheelchair

About 75 disabled people protested yesterday at the Franklin D. Roosevelt Memorial in Washington, angry that none of the statues shows the President, a polio victim, in a wheelchair or braces. Justin Dart, director of Justice for All, was among the speakers. The memorial is to be dedicated on May 2.

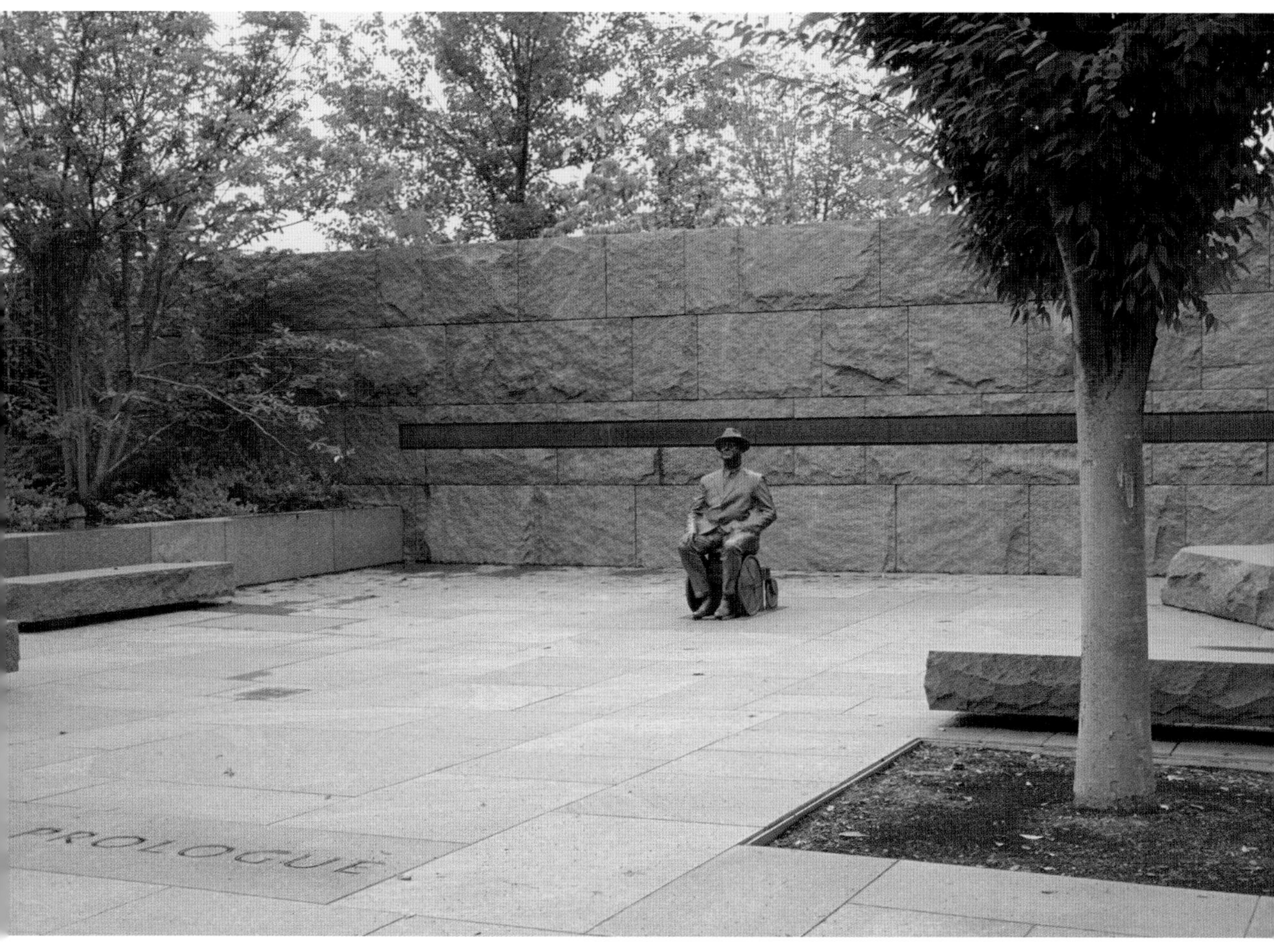

8 Photograph of Robert Graham sculpture of FDR shortly after its installation in the added forecourt of the FDR Memorial designed by Lawrence Halprin.

with insisting that any alteration be called an "enhancement," the architect made sure that the new sculpture was produced by a member of his original team, Robert Graham, with the surrounding "forecourt" composed of the same materials used in the rest of the memorial.[57] Nearly four years later, Clinton presided over the unveiling of this addition, which had been designed to not disclose itself as such (fig. 8). In the new space preceding the first "room," which had been incised in its granite paving with the word "Prologue," appeared a second three-dimensional rendering of Roosevelt, now seated at ground level in a wheelchair.

Anticlimax

With the unveiling of the expanded memorial taking place the same week as the inauguration of Clinton's controversial successor, George W. Bush, the installation of the sculpture was understandably eclipsed by the installation of a new Republican administration. Apart from competing controversies, there may be other reasons why the resolution of this heated representational debate produced so little commentary. On its own, Robert Graham's sculptural addition is quite competent, even inspired, given the paucity of sources showing FDR seated in this manner. Yet possibly because of the intensity of debate that provoked this change, I felt let down on first seeing the addition, which seemed less definitive than diminutive. At ground level and in an otherwise empty forecourt, Roosevelt appears small and his chair even smaller. Maybe it is the paradox of mimesis that the quest for faithful resemblance leads not to perfect correspondence but rather to endless quibbling over details. Nevertheless, what most impressed me was that after so much struggle over showing Roosevelt in a wheelchair, the chair itself seems to have shrunk in size, so that FDR looks as if he could risk sliding out of it.

Roosevelt had tried designing a chair less cumbersome than the clinical models available at the time. But his jerry-rigging of wheels to a kitchen chair while striving for discretion was not intended to be so toy-like that an adult of his medium size could not be seated securely. Cast in bronze, the closed wheels at the base of Graham's sculpture seem particularly anachronistic, closely resembling the most advanced contemporary handicap vehicles made of lightweight alloys. The newest designs in wheelchairs are fitted with elegantly cambered wheels in the rear for nimble self-propulsion. The large wheels in the chair designed by FDR make his jerry-rigged model look like an early prototype for those nimble models, but the big front wheels are neither tall enough nor counterweighted to permit much automobility. In other words, FDR, so seated, still needed constant help getting around; yet here he appears alone, accompanied only by an inscription from Eleanor's memoir, written after his death, in which she recalls the way his illness compelled him "to think out the fundamentals of living and learn the greatest of all lesson—infinite patience and never-ending persistence."

At the very least, this "prologue" adds one other voice to the otherwise monologic monument (although it was not the quotation advocated by the consulting group of disability activists).[58] But the addition produces more visible and distinctive changes in the monument. Iconographically, it makes the FDR Memorial the first to honor a modern political leader with a depiction emphasizing that his body did not conform to the sovereign stereotype. As remarkably, it will be the first modern memorial to commemorate a past leader with two major depictions of his person.

Cynics may argue that however costly this addition, it is far cheaper than substantive accommodation of the disabled population in terms of full access to education, jobs, housing, transportation, and all other forms of public space and services. It is also arguable that FDR, thus depicted, could come to stand as a rebuke to those who lacked the compensatory class and gender privileges that enabled him, notwithstanding, to achieve so much. And champions of modernism may respond that that the truest form of populism would be to avoid all figurative depiction. But defenders of the alteration could respond that abstraction fails to address the long-standing fantasies of normative ideals, evading the particularly vexing problem of how a society comes to term with disability and difference. According to this logic, symbolic victories such as the recasting of FDR in a wheelchair may significantly advance the cause of disability rights. By the same token, a monument to FDR and the New Deal, though it was funded and erected in a period of drastic cutbacks in social services (the second sculptural rendering was installed just as the Supreme Court radically curtailed the Americans with Disabilities Act),[59] may yet edify future generations about the civic benefits of public policy and programs that reduce the disparity of opportunity between poor and rich, and likewise between physically impaired and able-bodied citizens.

Like memories, memorials reflect the present through which the past is refracted.[60] Even more, with this stealth addition, the FDR Memorial is sure to speak distinctively about the era in which it developed. Literally, the president will have been endowed with two bodies, one frail, accessible, and rather diminutive, the other draped and commanding. Still, while just beginning to reflect on the effect of this dichotomized result, I continue to wonder how the two major sculptural depictions will interact and alter the overall space. Graham's depiction is designed to augment rather than counter Estern's sculpture. Surely the latter will carry more weight, figuratively as well as literally. By dint of coming second in the chronological procession (and thus, in effect, having the last word), it should be more memorable. Unlike Graham's mandate for a life-size depiction, Estern's commander-in-chief looms larger than life, surrounded by symbols of war and state power. And those wanting some buoyancy need only turn to Fala, already a proven crowd-pleaser.

So instead of a provocative clash of symbols, visitors encountering these two major sculpted portraits may experience less the tension between the private and public personae than the triumph of the symbolic body politic over the highly individuated leader. Such an outcome would come close to replicating the theological vision of the king's two bodies that was enunciated most strongly in the late medieval period. In that vision, there was a perfect splitting of the private mortal body of the leader and the divine immortal figuration of the social body, the body politic that ideally the ruler had incorporated in his prime. In the early fifteenth century, the ruler's death occasioned a practice of doubling to make manifest that distinction between mortal ruling body and the per-

petuity of the body politic. By the sixteenth century, the sovereign image
had eclipsed the effigy of the mortal body, articulating a new triumphal
element for the public sphere and modern statecraft.[61]

To the extent that the FDR Memorial recapitulates this fissure of private and social roles, with one clearly dominating the other, the ironic
legacy of the era known for its social realism will be that it is monumen-
tally recalled in a way that emphasizes not crisis and conflict but the
maintenance of power and order. This will not constitute a new argument. In essence Barton J. Bernstein propounded it more than three
decades ago in an essay taking issue with prevailing characterizations of
the New Deal as radically innovative.[62] Yet while Bernstein's proposition
aimed to expose the fundamental lack of change produced by the New
Deal, in this memorial context the solid weight of architecture will probably have a less critical effect, paving the way to reconstruct the recent
past in the frame of a much older story of dualism and its transcendence.
The unintended consequence of this gerrymandered sculptural program
may be a narrative that promotes political activity not for the way it can
address the needs of particular bodies and constituencies but rather as a
form of self-renunciation for the greater good.

But this conclusion is far from inevitable. If the "enhanced" monument offers a classic splitting of vision and values, it also invites us to
resolve this split in new as well as old ways. For a long time, while the
debate raged, I thought it would be more appropriate to scrap the Estern
statue and replace it with a sculptural rendering of Roosevelt appearing to stand, as we see him in the full-length photograph made during
his first gubernatorial campaign (fig. 1). Such a solution would resist the
clear-cut dichotomies of whether we see the leader as physically handicapped or not, presenting instead a more ambiguous scenario in which
the sphere of politics is made manifestly theatrical. Another possibility for innovative figuration would be FDR leaning on another figure,
serving as a sign that power is never monolithic. And of course a third
possibility would be simply to reject all figuration of the president.
Increasingly I have come to think the double figuration an apt reflection
of the fierce schism of opinion that such recollections provoked in the
more than half a century since FDR's death. Optimally, this monumental form of body doubling will help realize what architectural historian
James Young has described as "the dialogical quality of ... memorial
space."[63] In that case, the FDR Memorial, despite its efforts to perform
consensus, just might succeed in re-creating the best contentiously popular aspects of the New Deal.

Introduction

1. David Alfaro Siqueiros "The Mexican Experience in Art," in *Artists Against War and Fascism: Papers of the First American Artists' Congress,* ed. Matthew Baigell and Julia Williams (New Brunswick: Rutgers University Press, 1986), 208–12. Julia Codesido represented Peruvian artists, and Antonio Gattorno represented Cuban painters (212).

2. For the impact of Mexican art, which primarily came during the 1940s, on Canadian art, see Christine Boyanoski, *The Artists' Mecca: Canadian Art and Mexico* (Toronto: Art Gallery of Ontario, 1992).

3. Gilbert Wilson, "A Mural Painter's Conviction," in Baigell and Williams, *Artists Against War and Fascism,* 129. Born in Terre Haute, Indiana, Wilson trained at Indiana State University, the Art Institute of Chicago, and Yale University. An apprentice to Rockwell Kent in the 1940s, Wilson devoted a significant portion of his career to stage designs, illustrations, and a short art film, all on Melville's *Moby-Dick.*

4. Charmion Von Wiegand, "Mural Painting in America," *Yale Review,* n.s. 23 (June 1934): 788–99.

5. Paul Wood, "Realisms and Realities," in *Realism, Rationalism, Surrealism: Art Between the Wars,* ed. Briony Fer, David Batchelor, and Paul Wood (New Haven: Yale University Press, 1993), 254.

6. See Andrew Hemingway, "American Communists View Mexican Muralism: Critical and Artistic Responses," *Crónicas* 2–3 (March 2001–March 2003): 13–43.

7. "Los vehículos de la pintura dialéctico-subversiva," lecture given by Siqueiros at the Los Angeles John Reed Club on 2 September 1932. The complete text is in Raquel Tibol, ed., *Palabras de Siqueiros* (Mexico City: Fondo de Cultura Económica, 1996), 62–78.

8. Because the term social realism wasn't used during the 1930s, some scholars are beginning instead to use more historically accurate terms. For example, art historian Helen Langa uses the term "social viewpoint." See her *Radical Art, Transient Opportunities: New York Printmakers, Cultural Democracy, and the Left in the 1930s* (Berkeley and Los Angeles: University of California Press, 2003).

9. See Charles Hill, *Canadian Painting in the Thirties* (Ottawa: National Gallery of Canada, 1975).

10. Barry Lord, *The History of Painting in Canada: Towards a People's Art* (Toronto: NC Press, 1974). See as well Esther Trepanier, "Modernite et Conscience Sociale: La Critique d'Art Progressiste des Annees Trente," *Journal of Canadian Art History* 8 (1984): 80–109.

11. David Alfaro Siqueiros, *Manifesto at the Union of Mexican Workers, Technicians, Painters, and Sculptors* from El Machete, 1923. Translation reprinted from Dawn Ades, *Art in Latin American* (New Haven: Yale University Press, 1989), p. 323–324.

12. David Shapiro, ed. *Social Realism: Art as Weapon* (New York: Frederick Unger Publishing Co., 1973), 3.

13. Patricia Hills, "Painting 1900–1940," in Patricia Hills and Roberta K. Tarbell, *The Figurative Tradition and the Whitney Museum of America Art: Paintings and Sculpture from the Permanent Collection,* exh. cat. (New York: Whitney Museum of American Art in association with University of Delaware Press, 1980), 84. In his *Socialism and American Art* (Princeton: Princeton University Press, 1967), Donald Drew Egbert uses the phrase "social protest" art; Milton W. Brown prefers "social art." Brown quoted in ACA Galleries, *Social Art in America: 1930–45* (New York: ACA Galleries, 1981), 6.

14. Cecile Whiting, *Antifascism in American Art* (New Haven: Yale University Press, 1989), 43–44.

15. Matthew Cullerne Bown, *Socialist Realist Painting* (New Haven: Yale University Press, 1998).

16. Michael Denning, *The Cultural Front: The Laboring of American Culture in the Twentieth Century* (London: Verso, 1996).

17. John Kwait, "John Reed Club Exhibition," *New Masses* 8 (February 1933): 23–24.

18. Jacob Burck, "Sectarianism in Art," *New Masses* 8 (April 1933): 26–27.

19. For a discussion of the history of realism in nineteenth-century European and American art, see Linda Nochlin, *Realism* (New York: Penguin Books, 1971). In fact, during the 1920s and `30s, artists and critics referred to the art of Courbet, Daumier, and others when discussing the work of contemporary political artists. See also Andrew Hemingway, "Critical Realism in the History of American Art," in *Visions of America Since 1492,* ed. Deborah L. Madsen (London: Leicester University Press, 1994), 111–44; see 133–41 for information on social realism and critical realism in the 1930s and the CPUSA.

20. See Bill Mullen and Sherry Lee Linkon, "Introduction: Rereading 1930s Culture," in *Radical Revisions: Rereading 1930s Culture,* ed. Bill Mullen and Sherry Lee Linkon (Urbana: University of Illinois Press, 1996), 1–12, which asks comparable questions of the decade's literature and draws on recent theories of gender, class, race, representation, and ethnicity.

21. Aaron Douglas, "The Negro in American Culture," in Baigell and Williams, *Artists Against War and Fascism,* 84.

22. Barbara Foley, *Radical Representations: Politics and Form in U.S. Proletarian Fiction, 1929–1941* (Durham: Duke University Press, 1993), viii.

23. Ibid., x.

Trachtenberg

1. Roy Emerson Stryker and Nancy Wood, *In This Proud Land: America 1935–1943 as Seen in the FSA Photographs* (Boston: New York Graphic Society, 1973), 7. My view of the FSA owes a good deal to Maren Stange, *"Symbols of Ideal Life": Social Documentary Photography in America, 1890–1950* (New York: Cambridge University Press, 1988). See also Maurice Berger, *The Illiterate Eye: Photographs from the Farm Security Administration* (New York: Hunter College Art Gallery, 1985), and Hank O'Neil, *A Vision Shared: A Classic Portrait of America and Its People* (New York: St. Martin's Press, 1976).

2. James Agee and Walker Evans, *Let Us Now Praise Famous Men* (Boston: Houghton Mifflin, 1960), 11.

3. Harvey Swados, ed., *The American Writer and the Great Depression* (New York: Bobbs-Merill, 1966), xv. A classic study of Depression writing is William Stott, *Documentary Expression and Thirties America* (New York: Oxford University Press, 1973).

4. Swados, *American Writer and the Great Depression*, 43–45.

5. F. Scott Fitzgerald, *Babylon Revisited and Other Stories* (1937; rept. New York: Simon & Schuster, 1996), 25.

6. Robert S. McElvaine, *The Great Depression: America, 1929–1941* (New York: Times Books, 1984), 206–7.

7. Nathaneal West, *Miss Lonelyhearts* and *The Day of the Locust* (New York: New Directions, 1962), 39.

8. Swados, *American Writer and the Great Depression*, xv.

9. Warren I. Susman, *Culture as History: The Transformation of American Society in the Twentieth Century* (New York: Pantheon Books, 1984), 164. See also Michael Denning, *The Cultural Front* (New York: Verso, 1996).

10. Stryker and Wood, *In This Proud Land*, 17.

11. F. Jack Hurley, *Portrait of a Decade* (Baton Rouge: Louisiana State University Press, 1972), 36. See also the essays by Lawrence W. Levine and Alan Trachtenberg in *Documenting America, 1935–1943*, eds. Carl Fleischauer and Beverly W. Brannon (Berkeley and Los Angeles: University of California Press, 1988).

12. Stryker and Wood, *In This Proud Land*, 14.

13. Ibid., 15.

14. Walker Evans, "The Reappearance of Photography, *Hound & Horn* 1 (October–December 1931), 128.

15. Quoted in Thomas H. Garver, *Just Before the War* (Balboa, Calif.: Newport Harbor Art Museum, 1968), no page numbers.

16. Jerry L. Thompson, ed., *Walker Evans at Work* (New York: Harper & Row, 1982), 98.

17. Ibid., 113.

18. Ibid., 112.

19. James A. Miller, *Harlem: The Vision of Morgan and Marvin Smith* (Louisville: University Press of Kentucky, 1998); Bonnie Yockelson, *Berenice Abbott: Changing New York* (New York: New Press, 1997); Miles Barth, *Weegee's World* (Boston: Little, Brown, 1997); Lew Thomas, *The Restless Decade: John Gutmann's Photographs of the 1930s* (New York: Henry N. Abrams, 1984); Margaret R. Weiss, *Ben Shahn, Photographer* (New York: Da Capo Press, 1973).

20. Edward Steichen, "The F.S.A. Photographers, in *U.S. Camera 1939*, ed. T. J. Maloney (New York: William Morrow, 1938), 44.

21. Ibid.

22. Dorothea Lange quoted in Elizabeth Partridge, ed., *Dorothea Lange: A Visual Life* (Washington, D.C.: Smithsonian Institution Press, 1994), 111, and Sally Stein, "Peculiar Grace: Dorothea Lange and the Testimony of the Body," in *Dorothea Lange: A Visual Life*, ed. Elizabeth Partridge (Washington, D.C.: Smithsonian Institution Press, 1994), 57–90.

Martínez

1. Alvaro Medina, "La Revista de Avance y la plástica cubana de los años 20," *Cuba les étapes d'une libération* (Toulouse: University of Toulouse Press, 1980): 2:26.

2. Most studies on Cuban modernist art have emphasized formal issues regarding European artistic sources or symbolic ones regarding national identity. One notable exception is the work of art historian Yolanda Wood, who has published essays on muralism and on the free art studio of the 1930s. See her "El muralismo en la proyección social de la vanguardia en Cuba," *Temas* 14 (1987): 158–65; "50 años del Estudio Libre de Pintores y Escultores," in *Exposición 50 años del Estudio Libre, 1937–1987* (Havana: Museo Nacional, 1987). Both articles are reproduced in her book *De la Plástica Cubana y Caribeña* (Havana: Editorial de Letras Cubanas, 1990). I am indebted to her work and to the help of Ramón Vázquez, curator of Cuban art of the 1930s and 1940s at the Cuban National Museum in Havana, and to Luz Merino, a senior art historian at the University of Havana.

3. Texts on the Cuban vanguardia movement are few. For works in English, see my *Cuban Art and National Identity: The Vanguardia Painters, 1927–1950* (Gainesville: University Press of Florida, 1994), and Giulio V. Blanc, "Cuban Modernism: The Search for

a National Ethos," in *Wifredo Lam and His Contemporaries, 1938–1952,* ed. Maria R. Balderrama (New York: Studio Museum in Harlem, 1992). For works in Spanish, see Ramón Vázquez Diaz, *La Vanguardia: Surgimiento del arte moderno en Cuba,* exh. cat. (Havana: Museo Nacional, 1988); "Amelia Peláez," in *Tarsila Do Amaral, Frida Kahlo, and Amelia Peláez,* ed. Asunción Cabrera and Casilda Mora (Barcelona: Centre Cultural de la Fundació la Caixa, 1997); Luz Merino Acosta, *La pintura y la ilustración: dos vias del arte moderno en Cuba* (Havana: Universidad de La Habana, 1990); and Wood, "El muralismo en la proyección social."

4. Ana Cairo, *El Grupo Minorista y su Tiempo* (Havana: Ediciones de Ciencias Sociales, 1978), 67–68. All translations are my own.

5. "Manifesto de Artistas y Escritores Revolucionarios," *La Palabra* 2 (3 February 1935).

6. The Platt Amendment was a clause in the Cuban constitution of 1902 that declared that the United States had the right to intervene in Cuban affairs to preserve law, order, and (most ironically) independence. It also allowed the U.S. government to maintain military bases on the island. See Louis A. Pérez Jr. *Cuba Between Reform and Revolution* (New York: Oxford University Press, 1988).

7. The study of Cuban muralism in the 1930s is a problematic task, for some of these mural projects did not advance beyond the conceptual stage, and most of those that were completed have been lost and are known mostly through photographs in contemporary magazines. Yet it is essential to reconstruct such projects for a better understanding of Cuban social and political art of the decade.

8. Among the numerous articles published in *Social* and *Carteles* on contemporary Mexican art from 1925 to 1930, the following are noteworthy: Alejo Carpentier, "Diego Rivera, Pintor Mexicano," *Carteles* (11 July 1926); Alejo Carpentier, "El Arte de Clemente Orozco," *Social* 11 (October 1926); Diego Rivera, "Datos sobre los pintores mexicanos de hoy," *Social* 11 (November 1926): 40; and *Social* 11 (August 1926), which issue is dedicated to Mexico. The editors of *Revista de Avance* also dedicated an issue to Mexican culture—vol. 3 (15 November 1928).

9. "Figuras de Broadway," *Social* 13 (May 1928): 29; "El Pintor Carlos Merida," *Social* 10 (October 1925): 20.

10. Antonio Gattorno, "La Pintura Mural y el Cuadro de Caballete," *Revista de la Habana* 4 (November 1930): 150.

11. Wood, "Muralismo en la proyección social," 163.

12. Ibid.

13. Hugh Thomas, *Cuba or the Pursuit of Freedom* (New York: Da Capo Press, 1998), 656.

14. There are various theories about Mella's assassination. The most often mentioned is that he was assassinated on the orders of Machado, whom Mella was conspiring to overthrow (see ibid., 588). Another theory blames the Mexican Communist Party, which suspected Mella of supporting Trotsky; and another points to the Mexican government, which feared his capacity to arouse students and workers to antigovernment action. See Margaret Hooks, *Tina Modotti* (New York: Pandora, 1993), 162–63.

15. For a reproduction of this photo, see Hooks, *Tina Modotti,* 158. The photo was often reproduced after Mella's death. For instance, *El Machete* printed a poster-size version of it in a special edition dedicated to Mella, and postcards of the photo were distributed in a protest rally at Madison Square Garden.

16. José Lezama Lima, *Arístides Fernández* (Havana: Dirección de Cultura, 1950), no page numbers.

17. Ibid.

18. Enrique Carreño, *Arístides Fernández: Narrador y Pintor* (Matanzas: Ediciones Matanzas, 1992), 45.

19. *Selecta* 2 (9 October 1937): 51.

20. For reproductions of most of these murals, see *Carteles* 30 (17 October 1937): 45; and *Selecta* 2 (9 October 1937): 51.

21. *Selecta* 2 (9 October 1937): 51.

22. See the issues for 30 June, 15 August, and 15 September 1927.

23. Enríquez, "El arte puro como propaganda ha fracasado plenamente," *El País* (2 September 1936).

24. Ibid.

25. Ibid.

26. According to Juan Sánchez, the mural measured twelve meters in length. See *Carlos Enríquez* (Havana: Editorial Letras Cubanas, 1996), 101.

27. Ibid., n. 58. I have found no published information on the restoration itself of these mural projects.

28. Thomas, *Cuba or the Pursuit of Freedom,* 601.

29. Pogolotti was drawn to the Futurist interest in developing an art of the industrial age, but did not care for their involvement with fascism and thus left the movement relatively soon. See Pogolotti, *Del Barro y las Voces* (Havana: Editorial Letras Cubanas, 1982), 293.

30. Pogolotti, "De lo Social en el Arte," *Exposición Pogolotti: Nuestro Tiempo (Dibujos),* exh. cat. (Havana: Frente Nacional Anti-Facista, 1944).

Coffey

1. See Barry Carr, "The Fate of the Vanguard Under a Revolutionary State: Marxism's Contribution to the Construction of the Great Arch," in *Everyday*

Forms of State Formation: Revolution and the Negotiation of Rule in Modern Mexico, ed. Gilbert M. Joseph and Daniel Nugent (Durham: Duke University Press, 1994), 326–54; Octavio Paz, "Re/Visions: Mural Painting," in *Essays on Mexican Art,* trans. Helen Lane (New York: Harcourt, Brace & Co., 1993), 113–68; and Mary Kay Vaughan, *The State, Education, and Social Class in Mexico, 1880–1928* (DeKalb: Northern Illinois University Press, 1982), 239–66.

2. This is Guillermo Bonfil Batalla's term, from his book *México Profundo: Una Civilización Negada* (Mexico City: SEP, CIESAS, 1987), in which he asserts the indigenous or "deep Mexico" as the essential nation in an attempt to reorient representative politics around Mexico's most subjugated populations.

3. Octavio Paz, "Will to Form," in *Mexico: Splendors of Thirty Centuries* (New York: Metropolitan Museum of Art, 1990), 32–33.

4. In this essay, I use the word "native" despite its pejorative connotations. As part of the discourse I am reconstructing, it captures the disciplinary and paternalistic flavor of the literature on the "Mexican problem." Furthermore, the term means something different in the Americas, where it has been maintained in such phrases as "Native Americans" or "native peoples." The newer term—"First Nations"—has not been adopted by scholars or indigenous populations in Mexico. While I prefer the term "indigenous" and use it whenever possible, it too is a product of the disciplinary project I trace in this essay, as will become clear.

5. Benedict Anderson, *Imagined Communities: Reflections on the Origin and Spread of Nationalism* (London: Verso, 1983).

6. David A. Brading, "Manuel Gamio and Official Indigenismo in Mexico," *Bulletin of Latin American Research* 7, no. 1 (1988): 89.

7. The literature on Mexican muralism is vast. However, some recent and notable contributions not cited elsewhere include Alejandro Anreus, *Orozco in Gringoland: The Years in New York* (Albuquerque: University of New Mexico Press, 2001); Olivier Debroise, ed., *Otras Rutas Hacia Siqueiros* (Mexico City: INBA and Curare, Espacio Crítico para las Artes, 1996); Renato González Mello and Diane Miliotes, eds., *José Clemente Orozco in the United States, 1927–1934* (New York: Hood Museum of Art, Dartmouth College, in association with W. W. Norton, 2002); Marjorie L. Harth, ed., *José Clemente Orozco: Prometheus* (Los Angeles and Santa Barbara: Perpetua Press, for the Pomona College Museum of Art, 2001); and Anthony Lee, *Painting on the Left: Diego Rivera, Radical Politics, and San Francisco's Public Murals* (Berkeley and Los Angeles: University of California Press, 1999).

8. The most important literature on the relationship between Mexican modernism and postrevolutionary modernization remains Karen Cordero Reiman, "Constructing a Modern Mexican Art, 1910–1940," in *South of the Border: Mexico in the American Imagination, 1914–1947,* ed. James Oles (Washington, D.C.: Smithsonian Institution Press, 1993), 11–48; Olivier Debroise, *Figuras en el Tropico: Plastica Mexicana, 1920–1940* (Barcelona: Océano, 1984); and Olivier Debroise, ed., *Modernidad y Modernización en el Arte Mexicano, 1920–1960* (Mexico City: INBA, 1991). A recent noteworthy contribution to this scholarship is Rick Anthony López, *Lo más mexicano de México: Popular Arts, Indians, and Urban Intellectuals in the Ethnicization of Postrevolutionary National Culture, 1920–1972* (Ph.D. diss., Yale University, 2001). Each of these studies firmly documents the relationship between artists and the modernizing and nationalizing projects of the postrevolutionary government. While Debroise and Cordero trace this history by situating mural art within the other vanguard art movements of the period, López focuses exclusively on the elevation of artesanías, or folk art, as part of what he calls the "ethnicization" of the national. In this essay I elaborate on this scholarship by situating mural art within a broader governmental context.

9. While the analysis of culture and politics in this essay has been informed by Ernesto Laclau and Chantal Mouffe's theory of hegemony in *Hegemony and Socialist Strategy: Towards a Radical Democratic Politics* (London: Verso, 1985), my orientation is fundamentally Foucauldian. I avoid Gramsci's terminology because I am wary of the tendency to collapse the complexities of hegemony into simple class domination. The scholarship on Mexico in particular tends to identify class interest with essentialized racial and ethnic categories and to attribute the political effects of cultural initiatives to an overdetermined Creole privilege. This oversimplifies postrevolutionary society and cultural politics. I am more compelled by Foucault's critique of ideology theory as an "economy of untruth" (elaborated by Michele Barrett in *The Politics of Truth: From Marx to Foucault* [Stanford: Stanford University Press, 1991]). Consequently, I emphasize the production of truths about the nation and its origins. Instead of trying to resuscitate what certain cultural products meant prior to their distortion by one dominating power or another, I explore the epistemological character of mural art and ask how it functioned within governmental apparatuses such as educational projects and national-culture initiatives. For a more extensive discussion, see my essay "Representation, Institutionalization, and the State:

Marxist and Post-Structural Approaches to Mexican Muralism and the Popular," in a forthcoming issue of the journal *Historical Materialism.*

10. Michel Foucault, "Governmentality," in *The Foucault Effect: Studies in Governmentality,* ed. Graham Burchell, Colin Gordon, and Peter Miller (Chicago: University of Chicago Press, 1991), 87–104.

11. Nikolas Rose, "Governing 'Advanced' Liberal Democracies," in *Foucault and Political Reason: Liberalism, Neo-Liberalism, and Rationalities of Government,* ed. Andrew Barry, Thomas Osborne, and Nikolas Rose (Chicago: University of Chicago Press. 1996), 41.

12. Ibid.

13. Mitchell Dean, "Foucault, Government, and the Enfolding of Authority," ibid., 211.

14. Ibid., 210.

15. Ibid., 42.

16. José Vasconcelos, *The Cosmic Race: A Bilingual Edition,* trans. Didier T. Jaén (1925; rept. Baltimore: Johns Hopkins University Press, 1979), 31.

17. Ibid., 40.

18. José Vasconcelos, "The Race Problem in Latin America," in *Aspects of Mexican Civilization: Lectures on the Harris Foundation* (Chicago: University of Chicago, 1926), 92.

19. Ibid., 95.

20. Ibid., 100.

21. Manuel Gamio, "The United States and Mexico," ibid., 173.

22. Manuel Gamio, "Incorporating the Indian into the National Population," ibid., 127.

23. William Rowe and Vivian Schelling, *Memory and Modernity: Popular Culture in Latin America* (London: Verso, 1991), 184.

24. José Vasconcelos, *A Mexican Ulysses: An Autobiography,* trans. W. Rex Crawford (Bloomington: Indiana University Press, 1963), 157.

25. Ibid., 170.

26. In addition to Vasconcelos and Caso, other members included Alfonso Cravioto, Alfonso Reyes, Pedro Henriquez Ureña, Gómez Robledo, Eduardo Colín, and Julio Torri.

27. Caso's educational theory combined religious values, ethics, and aesthetic pleasure. Speaking for the Athenaeum, he wrote, "We resolve to achieve the realization of a complete man by education. ... To create men who are good and shining spirits, apt living centers of artistic disinterest and moral abnegation (charity), this is the law and the prophets summarized: love for one's neighbor as for oneself." Quoted in John H. Haddox, *Antonio Caso: Philosopher of Mexico* (Austin: University of Texas Press, 1971), 74.

28. See Jean Franco, *The Modern Culture of Latin America: Society and the Artist* (New York: Frederick A. Praeger, 1967); John H. Haddox, *Vasconcelos of Mexico: Philosopher and Prophet* (Austin: University of Texas Press, 1967); Patrick Romanell, *The Making of the Mexican Mind: A Study in Recent Mexican Thought* (Lincoln: University of Nebraska Press, 1952); and Vaughan, *State, Education, and Social Class in Mexico,* 239–66.

29. The members of the Athenaeum were influenced by José Enrique Rodó's *Ariel.* Many of them contributed to the journal *Revista Moderna,* which promoted the growing Hispanist literary movement by linking the Spanish generation of 1898 with Latin American writers like Rodó and Manuel Ugarte.

30. This reversal of values was particularly cogent within a cultural context saturated with Justo Sierra's rationalization of Mexico's social and political history. According to his social Darwinist history of the Americas, the British and Dutch colonists had established capitalist-oriented "modern" colonies, while the Spanish had established "feudal" ones. The qualitative distinction between "modern" and "feudal" explained Mexico's belated national development as well as the United States' relatively advanced state of evolution. Sierra was the high priest of liberal positivism during the *Porfiriato.* While he was a mentor and hero to the Athenaeum of Youth, their rejection of social Darwinism and preference for fin-de-siècle spiritual humanism needs to be understood as a reaction to the Díaz regime and the national inferiority complex that had fueled his industrialization of the country through foreign investment. See Justo Sierra, *The Political Evolution of the Mexican People,* trans. Charles Ramsdell (Austin: University of Texas Press, 1969).

31. See Antonio Caso, *La Existencia Como Economía y Caridad* (Mexico City: Editorial Porrua, 1916).

32. Vaughan, *State, Education, and Social Class in Mexico,* 239–67.

33. Vasconcelos, *Cosmic Race,* 30.

34. Ibid.

35. Vasconcelos favored the late nineteenth-century neoclassicism of the French Symbolists, decorative motifs drawn from the Mesoamerican traditions, and national allegory for subject matter. This kind of art dominated the Mexican Salon of 1910, a fin-de-siècle reaction to the retrenchment of the Mexican Academy and to the Porfirian regime's preference for European art. For a synthetic discussion of this first phase of Mexican modernism, see Reiman, "Constructing a Modern Mexican Art."

36. Vasconcelos, *Mexican Ulysses,* 180.

37. Bertram D. Wolfe, *Diego Rivera: His Life and Times* (New York: Knopf, 1939), 160.

38. These identifications are Rivera's, from his explanatory notes transcribed by Wolfe. Ibid., 150–53.

39. Ibid., 152.

40. Ibid.

41. Leonard Folgarait, *Mural Painting and Social Revolution in Mexico, 1920–1940* (Cambridge: Cambridge University Press, 1998), 41.

42. Ibid.

43. Ibid.

44. For a discussion of this early group commission, see Anita Brenner, *Idols Behind Altars* (New York: Harcourt, Brace & Co., 1929); Jean Charlot, *The Mexican Mural Renaissance* (New Haven: Yale University Press, 1963); and Debroise, *Figuras en el Tropico,* 45–62.

45. In addition to these artists, Fermín Revueltas, Emilio García Cahero, and Ramón de la Canal also executed murals in this building.

46. Desmond Rochfort, *Mexican Muralists: Orozco, Rivera, Siqueiros* (San Francisco: Chronicle Books, 1993), 36. For a discussion of the early cycle, see Laurance P. Hurlburt, "José Clemente Orozco," in *The Mexican Muralists in the United States* (Albuquerque: University of New Mexico Press, 1989), 13–25.

47. Laurence E. Schmeckebier, *Modern Mexican Art* (Minneapolis: University of Minnesota Press, 1939), 40.

48. Wolfe, *Diego Rivera,* 156.

49. David Siqueiros, "Lectures to Artists," *New University Thought* (winter 1962), no page numbers.

50. Rochfort and Folgarait attribute the weaknesses of the first murals to Vasconcelos's influence. Wolfe, a Red, argues that Rivera had not yet been radicalized by the Communist Party. Schmeckebier suggests that this phase reflects Obregón's political program. Each favors the later murals, either as more "original" or as more politically astute, and all articulate the shift from juvenilia to maturity to national politics.

51. Siqueiros, "Lectures to Artists."

52. David Alfaro Siqueiros, Diego Rivera, Xavier Guerrero, Fermín Revueltas, José Clemente Orozco, Ramón Alva Guadarrama, Germán Cueto, and Carlos Mérida, "Manifesto of the Union of Mexican Workers, Technicians, Painters, and Sculptors," *El Machete* (1923), reprinted in Dawn Ades, *Art in Latin America: The Modern Era, 1820–1980* (New Haven: Yale University Press, 1989), 323–24.

53. Ibid., 324.

54. Originally, Rivera was given the first courtyard, and his fellow muralists, Amado de la Cueva, Jean Charlot, and Xavier Guerrero, were given the second. When Vasconcelos resigned in 1924, however, the new secretary of Public Education gave Rivera control over the entire commission. Rivera subsequently whitewashed some of the work done by the other three and

subjugated them to his design. Folgarait, *Mural Painting and Social Revolution,* 81.

55. Diego Rivera, with Gladys March, *My Art, My Life* (New York: Dover Publications, 1960), 79.

56. See Mary K. Coffey, "The Two Fridas: (A)Dressing the National Body" (master's thesis, University of Illinois, 1996).

57. An important exception is David Craven, who analyzes Rivera's mural cycles as narrative epics. But Craven focuses on formal qualities and iconography rather than the architecture that houses, and thus structures, the viewer's experience of these frescos. Furthermore, his emphasis is on the artist's vanguardism and its legacy in the cultural and social movements of revolutionary Russia and Mexico. In this essay, I am locating the artist's work within a different sphere of influence, namely, the political rationality of postrevolutionary reformers and the emergent institutions of the postrevolutionary state. See David Craven, *Diego Rivera: As Epic Modernist* (New York: G. K. Hall, 1997).

58. In his recent book, Andrew Hemingway has significantly complicated received notions about the art produced by communists and fellow travelers throughout the 1930s, `40s, and even the `50s. He demonstrates that there was as much stylistic as political variation among artists working in social realist idioms. Furthermore, he complicates overly reductive condemnations of nationalism in mural art, and especially in New Deal murals allied with the Popular Front. While Hemingway emphasizes artists' engagement with radical politics in the U.S. context, in this essay I am focusing on artists' relationship to the postrevolutionary state within the Mexican context. See Andrew Hemingway, *Artists on the Left: American Artists and the Communist Movement, 1926–1956* (New Haven: Yale University Press, 2002).

59. Guanajuato is where Father Hidalgo uttered his "Grito de Dolores" (Cry of Dolores). Therefore, visual references to this regional architecture conjure up the memory of Mexico's struggle for independence.

60. An anonymous guard working at the ministry pointed this out to me in 1997, when I first saw and photographed these murals. I have to admit that before our talk I had never noticed the skull. Furthermore, it has not been a standard iconographic identification within the literature on this mural. To my knowledge, Leonard Folgarait was the first to mention it. While one can't generalize about the entire Mexican population, this guard's nuanced understanding of Rivera's mural reveals that for some Mexicans this art speaks volumes.

61. See Octavio Paz, *The Labyrinth of Solitude: Life and Thought in Mexico,* trans. Lysander Kemp (New York: Grove Press, 1961).

62. The belief that the communitarian values of Mexico's pre-Hispanic and contemporary indigenous cultures were protosocialist in their organization was common in postrevolutionary intellectual circles. The Zapotecs of the Isthmus of Tehuantepec, in particular, were discussed in this way. See Miguel Covarrubias, *Mexico South: The Isthmus of Tehuantepec* (1946; rept. New York: Knopf, 1967).

63. Wolfe, *Diego Rivera,* 181–96.

64. Vasconcelos, "Similarity and Contrast," in *Aspects of Mexican Civilization,* 3–43.

65. See Homi K. Bhabha, "Introduction: Narrating the Nation," in *Nation and Narration,* ed. Homi K. Bhabha (London: Routledge, 1990), 1–8; Ernest Renan, "What Is a Nation?" ibid., 8–22; Martin Thom, "Tribes Within Nations: The Ancient Germans and the History of Modern France," ibid., 23–43.

66. For a telling discussion of nationalism from the period, see Ernest Barker, *National Character and the Factors in Its Formation* (London: Methuen, 1927). Barker's book, published while Rivera was working at the ministry, makes explicit what is often tacit in Rivera's imagery. While there is no indication that Rivera ever read Barker's book, the consonance of their views on national progress demonstrates just how pervasive this logic was during the first half of the twentieth century.

67. Vasconcelos, "Similarity and Contrast," 5–7.

68. See *La población del Valle de Teotihuacán, el medio en que se ha desarrollado; su evolución étnica y social; iniciativas para procurar su mejoramiento, por la Dirección se Antropología, seindo director de las investigaciones, Manuel Gamio,* 2 vols. (Mexico City: Dirección de Taller Gráfico, Secretaría de Educación Pública, 1922).

69. Bertram Wolfe, *Portrait of Mexico* (New York: Covici, Friede Publishers, 1937), 21.

70. Ibid., 22.

71. Ibid., 25.

72. Ibid., 45.

73. Foucault's notion of "problematization" helps to bring together the discourse on nationalism and governmental initiatives in the fields of education and anthropology, as represented by Vasconcelos and Gamio, and the artistic project of muralism, here represented by Rivera and Wolfe. In a 1984 interview with François Ewald, Foucault said, "Problematization doesn't mean representation of a pre-existing object, nor the creation by discourse of an object that doesn't exist. It is the totality of discursive or non-discursive practices that introduces something into the play of true and false and constitutes it as an object for thought (whether in the form of moral reflection, scientific knowledge, political analysis, etc.)." Michel Foucault, "The Concern for Truth," in *Politics, Philosophy, Culture: Interviews and Other Writings, 1977–1984,* ed. Lawrence D. Kritzman (New York: Routledge, 1988), 257.

74. See Alejandro Anreus, *Orozco in Gringoland: The Years in New York* (Albuquerque: University of New Mexico Press, 2001).

75. See Shifra M. Goldman, "La Pintura en el Decenio de la Confrontación: 1955–1965," *Plural* 6 (October 1978): 33–44.

76. See Emanuel Eisenberg, "Battle of the Century," *New Masses* (10 December 1935): 18.

77. My translation from the Spanish, which reads, "El pueblo mexicano levanta esta monumento en honor de las admirables culturas que florecieron durante la era precolombiana en regions que son, ahora, territorio de las republica. Frente a los testimonios de aquellas culturas el México de hoy rinde homanaje al México indigena, en cuyo ejemplo reconoce caracteristicas esenciales de su originalidad nacional."

78. Nestor García Canclini, *Hybrid Cultures: Strategies for Entering and Leaving Modernity,* trans. Christopher L. Chiappari and Silvia L. López (Minneapolis: University of Minnesota Press, 1995), 135.

McKay

1. For a history of the role of the Catholic Church in French Canada up to 1960, see John A. Dickinson and Brian Young, *A Short History of Quebec,* 2d ed. (Montreal: McGill-Queen's University Press, 2000).

2. For Fortin, see Dennis Reid, *A Concise History of Canadian Painting,* 2d ed. (Toronto: Oxford University Press, 1988), 207; for Des Clayes, Natalie Luckyj, *From Women's Eyes: Women Painters in Canada* (Kingston, Ontario: Agnes Etherington Art Centre, Queen's University, 1975), 31; for Desrosiers, Maria Tippett, *By a Lady: Celebrating Three Centuries of Art by Canadian Women* (Toronto: Viking Press, 1992), 78, 85; for Leduc, *Ozias Leduc: An Art of Love and Reverie* (Montreal: Montreal Museum of Fine Arts, 1996), 214, 263.

3. Nicole Cloutier, *Laliberté* (Montreal: Montreal Museum of Fine Arts, 1990), 192; Rosemary Donegan, *Industrial Images* (Hamilton: Art Gallery of Hamilton, 1987), 17.

4. Paraskeva Clarke [*sic*], "Come Out from Behind the Pre-Cambrian Shield," *New Frontier* 1 (April 1937): 16–17.

5. For information on Norman Bethune, see, e.g., *The Politics of Passion: Norman Bethune's Writing and*

Art, ed. Larry Hannant (Toronto: University of Toronto Press, 1998). For a biography of Paraskeva Clark, see Mary MacLachlan, *Paraskeva Clark: Paintings and Drawings,* exh. cat. (Halifax: Dalhousie University Art Gallery, 1982).

6. Hyde's drawing, *Still Life,* was published in *New Frontier* 1 (April, 1937): 15.

7. See, e.g., Helen Duffy, *The Brave New World of Fritz Brandtner* (Kingston, Ontario: Agnes Etherington Art Centre, Queen's University, 1982); Monique Nadeau-Saumier and Pierre L'Allier, *Muhlstock* (Quebec: Musée du Québec, 1995).

8. Patricia Ainslie, *Images of the Land: Canadian Block Prints, 1919–1945* (Calgary: Glenbow Museum, 1984), 56–57, 66–67; Donegan, *Industrial Images,* 66–67.

9. Alex Mogelon, *Miller Brittain in Focus* (Toronto: S. Dresdnere, c. 1980).

10. See Donald W. Buchanan, "Embryology on a Wall," *Canadian Forum* 15 (January 1935): 154–55; Donald W. Buchanan, "The Haydon Mural at Pickering College, Newmarket, Ontario," *Saturday Night* 50 (15 December 1934): 2, 11.

11. This mural was destroyed. For an illustration, see *Shawnigan Lake School Magazine* (1934): 15.

12. Neil Stuart, "Where Do You Stand? Teachers, Doctors, Artists," *Daily Clarion* 15 (23 December 1936): 4.

13. John Fairfax, "Art for Man's Sake," *Canadian Forum* 16 (August 1936): 23.

14. Charles Hill, *Canadian Painting in the Thirties* (Ottawa: National Gallery of Canada, 1975), 21.

15. Lorna Farrell-Ward, "Tradition/Transition: The Keys to Change," in *Vancouver: Art and Artists, 1931–1983,* exh. cat. (Vancouver: Vancouver Art Gallery, 1983), 27–28.

16. Esther Trépanier, "Modernité et Conscience Sociale: La Critique d'Art Progressive des Années Trente," *Journal of Canadian Art History* 8 (1984): 109.

17. Tippett, *By a Lady,* 97.

18. John Herd Thompson and Allen Seager, *Canada, 1922–1939: Decades of Discord* (Toronto: McClelland & Stewart, 1985), 267.

19. Illustrated in Hill, *Canadian Painting in the Thirties,* 142.

20. Donegan, *Industrial Images,* 10.

21. Quoted in Miller Brittain, *Miller Brittain, 1912–1968: Paintings and Drawings, 1930–1967; Galerie Dresdnere, Toronto, 4–25 October 1975,* exh. cat. (Toronto: The Galerie, 1975), 8.

22. See Arthur Lismer, "Mural Painting," *Journal of the Royal Architectural Institute of Canada* 10 (July 1933): 128.

23. Ibid.

24. *Proceedings of the Conference of Canadian-American Affairs, Queen's University, Kingston, Ontario, June 14–18* (Boston: Ginn and Co., 1937), 136. For a discussion of Canadian interest in Mexican art, which occurred mostly after 1940, see Christine Boyanoski, *The Artists' Mecca: Canadian Art and Mexico* (Toronto: Art Gallery of Ontario, 1992).

25. Farrell-Ward, "Tradition/Transition," 28.

26. Thompson and Seager, *Canada, 1922–1939,* 226.

27. Michiel Horn, *The League for Social Reconstruction: Intellectual Origins of the Democratic Left in Canada, 1930–1942* (Toronto: University of Toronto Press, 1980), 13; Thompson and Seager, *Canada, 1922–1939,* 227.

28. Caren Irr, *The Suburbs of Dissent: Cultural Politics in the United States and Canada During the 1930s* (Durham: Duke University Press, 1998), 162.

29. Quoted in Horn, *League for Social Reconstruction,* 6.

30. Maria Tippett, *Making Culture: English-Canadian Institutions and the Arts Before the Massey Commission* (Toronto: University of Toronto Press, 1990), 73.

31. For a discussion of arts funding in Canada before World War II, see ibid.

32. Mogelon, *Miller Brittain in Focus,* 16, 64.

33. Ray Collett, interview by author, Lakefield, Ontario, 14 June 2001.

34. Seymour Martin Lipset, *Continental Divide: The Values and Institutions of the United States and Canada* (New York: Routledge, 1990), 1.

35. Quoted ibid., 8.

36. Quoted in J. Russell Harper, *Painting in Canada: A History* (Toronto: University of Toronto Press, 1966), 331. For Lyman, see Louise Dompierre, *John Lyman, 1886–1967* (Kingston, Ontario: Agnes Etherington Art Centre, Queens University, 1986); for Roberts, see Goodridge Roberts, *Goodridge Roberts* (Ottawa: National Gallery of Canada, 1969).

37. Bertram Brooker, ed., *Yearbook of the Arts in Canada 1936* (Toronto: Macmillan, 1936), xv–xxiii.

38. Quoted in Guy Robert, *Lemieux,* trans. John David Allan (Toronto: Gage Publishing, 1975), 44.

39. Ibid., 48.

40. Joan Murray, *Daffodils in Winter: The Life and Letters of Pegi Nicol MacLeod* (Moonbeam, Ontario: Penumbra Press, 1984).

41. Esther Trépanier, *Marian Dale Scott: Pionnière de l'art moderne* (Quebec: Musée du Québec, 2000), 115–18.

42. Quoted in Alicia Boutilier, *Four Women Who*

Painted in the 1930s and 1940s (Ottawa: Carleton University Art Gallery, 1998), 28. See also Joan Murray, *The Art of Yvonne McKague Housser* (Oshawa, Ontario: Robert McLaughlin Gallery, 1995), 23.

43. Christine Boyanoski, *Loring and Wyle: Sculptors' Legacy* (Toronto: Art Gallery of Ontario, 1987), 104.

44. Patricia Ainslie, *Margaret Shelton: Block Prints, 1936–1984* (Calgary, Alberta: Glenbow Museum, 1985), 13; Tippett, *By a Lady*, 97.

45. For Evans's and Wolcott's mining photographs, see Leah Bendavid-Vol, *Propaganda and Dreams: Photographing the 1930s in the USSR and the US* (Washington, D.C.: Corcoran Gallery of Art, 1999).

46. Karen Lucic, *Charles Sheeler and the Cult of the Machine* (London: Reaktion Books, 1991), 15.

47. Melissa K. Rombout, "John Vanderpant. A Modernist Vision of Canada," *History of Photography* 20 (summer 1996): 131.

48. Mural paintings relocated to the new Toronto Stock Exchange. See *Designing the Exchange: Essays Commemorating the Opening of the Design Exchange,* ed. Nelda Roger (Toronto: Design Exchange, 1994).

49. Dennis Reid, *Edwin Holgate* (Ottawa: National Gallery of Canada, 1976), 20.

50. These murals were destroyed. Later versions of two of the panels, *Mining* and *Shipping and Railroads,* are in the Provincial Archives of British Columbia. Farrell-Ward, "Tradition/Transition," 28; Donegan, *Industrial Images,* 105–6.

51. Margaret Gray et al., *Charles Comfort* (Toronto: Gage Publishing, 1976), 20.

52. Quoted in Laurance P. Hurlburt, *The Mexican Muralists in the United States* (Albuquerque: University of New Mexico Press, 1989), 107.

53. Masha Zakheim Jewett, *Coit Tower, San Francisco: Its History and Art* (San Francisco: Volcano Press, 1983), 70–71.

54. For Bond, see Tippett, *By a Lady,* 89, 97. For Daly, see *Retrospective: Kathleen Daly, George D. Pepper* (Baie-Saint-Paul, Quebec: Le Centre d'art de Baie-Saint-Paul, 1996), no page numbers. For Holgate, Harris, Muhlstock, Ogilvie, and Stevens, see Carmine Nelson, *Through An-other's eyes: White Canadian Artists—Black Female Subjects* (Oshawa, Ontario: Robert McLaughlin Gallery, 1998), 14, 15, 20, 21, 25, 27. For Heward, see Natalie Luckyj, *Expressions of Will: The Art of Prudence Heward* (Kingston, Ontario: Agnes Etherington Art Centre, Queen's University, 1986), 27, 30, 31. For Housser, see Murray, *Art of Yvonne McKague Housser,* 60–61.

55. For Reisman, see Patricia Hills, *Social Concern and Urban Realism: American Painting of the 1930s*

(Boston: Boston University Art Gallery, 1983), 20. For Wolcott, see Bendavid-Vol, *Propaganda and Dreams,* 173.

56. For widespread support for this point of view in Canada in the thirties, see Marylin McKay, *A National Soul: Canadian Mural Painting, 1867–1939* (Montreal: McGill-Queen's University Press, 2002), chapter 7.

57. Two of these panels are in storage in the Public Archives of Canada; two others were destroyed. Robert Stacey, *C. W. Jefferys* (Ottawa: National Gallery of Canada, 1985), 20–21.

58. *Catalogue of Historical Paintings in the Legislative Building* (Regina: Government of Saskatchewan, 1933), no page numbers.

59. This mural is now in the Confederation Centre Art Gallery, Charlottetown, Prince Edward Island.

60. Gray et al., *Charles Comfort,* 19, 74. For information on potlatches, see James R. Miller, *Skyscrapers Hide the Heavens: A History of Indian-White Relations in Canada* (Toronto: University of Toronto Press, 1989), 140–41. For recent racist interpretations of this mural, see Ray Cronin, "Captain Vancouver by Charles Comfort: Four Native Perspectives (David Neel, Edward Poitras, Teresa Marshall, Joane Cardinal-Schubert)," *Arts Atlantic* 15 (fall–winter 1997): 20–21.

61. For discussions of antimodernism, see T. J. Jackson Lears, *No Place of Grace: Antimodernism and the Transformation of American Culture* (New York: Pantheon Books, 1981); and Lynda Jessup, *Antimodernism and Artistic Experience: Policing the Boundaries of Modernity* (Toronto: University of Toronto Press, 2001).

62. For Daly, see *Retrospective: Kathleen Daly, George D. Pepper;* for May, Morris, and Seath, Tippett, *By a Lady,* 68, 81; for Robinson, *Albert H. Robinson (1881–1956): A Retrospective Exhibition,* exh. cat. (Montreal: La Galerie Walter Klinkhoff, 1994).

63. Elizabeth Wyn Wood, "Art and the Pre-Cambrian Shield," *Canadian Forum* 16 (February 1937): 13.

64. Robert Linsley, "Landscapes in Motion: Lawren Harris, Emily Carr, and the Heterogenous Modern Nation," *Oxford Art Journal* 19 (1996): 80–95.

65. Lawren S. Harris, *Revelation of Art in Canada* 7 (15 July 1926): 86–87.

66. Linsley, "Landscapes in Motion," 86.

67. Harper, *Painting in Canada,* 310.

68. Tippet, *By a Lady,* 76

69. Ibid., 97; Doris Shadbolt, *The Art of Emily Carr* (Toronto: Clarke, Irwin, 1979), 143, 162.

70. Hill, *Canadian Painting in the Thirties,* 35.

71. Tippett, *By a Lady,* 84.

72. David P. Silcox, *Painting Place: The Life and*

Work of David B. Milne (Toronto: University of Toronto Press, 1991), 231, 248, 273.

73. Maria Tippett, *F. H. Varley: A Biography* (Toronto: McClelland & Stewart, 1998), fig. 9.

74. Reid, *Concise History of Canadian Painting,* plate 175.

75. Luckyj, *Expressions of Will,* 53, 61.

76. Quoted ibid., 51.

77. Reid, *Concise History of Canadian Painting,* 187.

78. For Humphrey, see ibid., 200; for Holgate, Reid, *Edwin Holgate,* 50, 67, 69; for Smith and Newton, Tippett, *By a Lady,* xii, 89, 97, 98, 107, and 66, respectively.

79. Frank Underhill, review of the *Yearbook of the Arts in Canada Canadian Forum* 16 (December 1936): 27–28.

80. Clarke [*sic*], "Come Out from Behind the Pre-Cambrian Shield," 17.

81. Barker Fairley, "Canadian Art: Man vs. Landscape," *Canadian Forum* 19 (December 1939): 284, 286.

82. Tippett, *By a Lady,* 97; Gray et al., *Charles Comfort,* 20.

83. Linsley, "Landscapes in Motion," 91–92.

84. Hill, *Canadian Painting in the Thirties,* 11.

Anreus

1. Mark Falcoff, "Argentina," in *Encyclopedia of Latin American History and Culture,* ed. Barbara A. Tenenbaum (New York: Charles Scribner's Sons, 1996), 1:153–55.

2. Lilí Berni (daughter of Antonio Berni), interview by author, 26 May 1997, New York.

3. Museo Nacional de Bellas Artes, *Antonio Berni: Obra Pictórica, 1922 1981* (Buenos Aires: Museo Nacional de Bellas Artes, 1984), 85.

4. Ibid., 86.

5. The best discussion of political radicalism and the working class in Argentina is Jacov Oved, *El Anarquismo y el Movimiento Obrero en Argentina* (Buenos Aires: Losada, 1978). For a thorough discussion in English of the Modern School in the United States, see Paul Avrich, *The Modern School Movement: Anarchism and Education in the United States* (Princeton: Princeton University Press, 1980).

6. Spilimbergo had submitted his work to the Salón Nacional as early as 1920. In Italy in the late 1920s he executed a series of neoclassical paintings of Italian peasant women. Back in Argentina in the 1930s, he continued to work in a figurative, volumetric manner that was very neoclassical. Spilimbergo's work could be stylistically uneven, and between more avant-garde periods he repeatedly returned to traditional landscape painting throughout his career. Spilimbergo worked with Berni, Juan Carlos Castagnino, Enrique Lázaro, and Siqueiros in the execution of the mural *Plastic Exercise* in 1933. In 1934 Spilimbergo would be one of the founders of the Sindicato de Artistas Plásticos (Artists' Union), and together with Berni he would be active in the antifascist Agrupación de Intelectuales, Artistas, Periodistas y Escritores (AIAPE). In 1948 Spilimbergo became the director of the School of Fine Arts at the University of Tucumán. He taught art for many years, both in his studio and at the university. Among his students was the extraordinary draftsman and painter Carlos Alonso. Art historian Diana B. Wechsler's *Spilimbergo y el Arte Moderno* (Buenos Aires: Fondo Nacional de las Artes, 1999) is essential reading on the artist.

7. Museo Nacional de Bellas Artes, *Berni: Obra Pictórica,* 87.

8. Lilí Berni, interview. Lilí Berni recalls her father's disgust with Aragon for his allegiance to Stalinism. For years they were not in touch with each other. They renewed their friendship when Berni exhibited *The Massacre of the Innocents* in Paris in 1971. At the time Aragón wrote a brief text about Berni's work.

9. Ibid. Henri Lefebvre's important pre–World War II publications are *Nationalism Against Nations* (1937) and *Dialectic Materialism* (1939), and his postwar anti-Stalinist statements are *Marx and Liberty* and *Marxism,* both published in 1947. In March 1949 Lefebvre published the self-criticism expected by the French Communist Party, where he accused himself of excessive idealism and neo-Hegelianism in his interpretation of Marx. His *Problems of Marxism* (1957) is a rigorous attack on Stalinism and a critique of rigid and unimaginative interpretations of Marx. Yet Lefebvre remained theoretically attached to Leninism—not realizing that Stalinism developed straight out of Leninism. Lefebvre joined the French Communist Party in 1928 and followed the party line for several years. He was officially expelled from the party in 1958. Scholars agree that his two most important works are *A Critique of Everyday Life* and *The Sociology of Marx.* For a biographical and philosophical portrait of Lefebvre, see Michael Kelly, "Henri Lefebvre, 1901–1991," *Radical Philosophy* 60 (spring 1992), and Arthur Hirsh, *The New French Left: An Intellectual History from Sartre to Gorz* (Boston: South End Press, 1981).

10. Lilí Berni, interview. According to Lilí Berni, "they were simply close friends, who liked eating and drinking together, conversing and discussing books." The following account of the friendship is based on my interview with Lilí Berni.

11. Lilí Berni, interview.

12. Lilí Berni recalled her father's love of de Chirico's "espacio infinitamente meláncolico."

13. The first of these is a pencil drawing from 1924. The second is a small oil painting from 1929. The third, which I shall discuss, is also from 1929. There are others.

14. Briony Fer, David Batchelor, and Paul Wood, *Realism, Rationalism, Surrealism: Art Between the Wars* (New Haven: Yale University Press, 1993), 6–12.

15. Mark Falcoff, "Argentina," in Tenenbaum, *Encyclopedia of Latin American History and Culture,* 1:152–55.

16. Robert J. Alexander, "Communism," ibid., 2:232–33.

17. Lilí Berni, interview.

18. Ibid. Berni did adhere to certain Communist Party positions, particularly in regard to U.S. foreign policy in the Americas and the threat of nuclear war after World War II. He also maintained a friendship with fellow painter Juan Carlos Castagnino (1908–72), who was a member of the Argentinean Communist Party until his death. In France, Henri Lefebvre had warned Berni of the practical impossibility of being both an independent Marxist and a member of the Communist Party. At the same time, Lefebvre felt that with the threats of nationalism and fascism, both the intellectual and working classes had an obligation to join the Communist Party.

19. Museo Nacional de Bellas Artes, *Berni: Obra Pictórica,* 88, 107.

20. Lilí Berni, interview.

21. Museo Sala de Arte Publico Siqueiros, *Cronologia Mínima de Siqueiros* (Mexico City: Museo Sala de Arte Publico Siqueiros, 1994), 14.

22. David Alfaro Siqueiros, *Me Llamaban el Coronelazo,* 3d ed. (Mexico City: Editorial Grijalbo, S.A., 1987), 409–16. At this time Siqueiros was not in the Mexican Communist Party; he had been expelled in 1930 and was not readmitted until 1946—after plenty of public proof of his loyalty to the party and Stalin. For a discussion of Siqueiros's many activities, and his significance, see Olivier Debroise, ed., *Otras rutas hacia Siqueiros* (Mexico City: Instituto Nacional de Bellas Artes y CURARE, 1996). Of particular significance are the essays by Gabriel Peluffo Linari (dealing with Uruguay) and Marcelo E. Pacheco's essay on Berni.

23. David Alfaro Siqueiros, "Call to Argentinean Artists" (Un Llamamiento a los Plasticos Argentinos), in *Palabras de Siqueiros,* ed. Raquel Tibol (Mexico City: Fondo de Cultura Económica, 1996), 86–87. Originally published in the Buenos Aires daily *Critica* on 2 June 1933.

24. Museo Sala de Arte Publico Siqueiros, *Cronologia Mínima de Siqueiros,* 14.

25. Siqueiros, *Me Llamaban el Coronelazo,* 410.

26. Antonio Rodríguez, *Siqueiros Mural Painting* (Mexico City: Fondo Editorial de la Plástica Mexicana, 1992), 26–28.

27. Museo Nacional de Bellas Artes, *Berni: Obra Pictórica,* 17–19.

28. Siqueiros, "Un Llamamiento a los Plasticos," 86–100, 111–12. This is a selection of writings by Siqueiros while in Argentina. It includes a letter to Berni, asking him to continue the struggle for mural painting in Argentina.

29. Antonio Berni, untitled and unpaginated typed manuscript, n.d., in possession of Lilí Berni, Buenos Aires, Argentina. Also see Berni, "Siqueiros y el arte de masas," 14. Berni's comment on the importance of the print as an alternative to the mural in Argentina appears in this article, and also in an interview with Rafael Squirru published in *Américas* magazine 17, November 1965, 20–29.

30. Museo Sala de Arte Publico Siqueiros, *Cronologia Mínima de Siqueiros,* 15.

31. Museo Nacional de Bellas Artes, *Berni: Obra Pictórica,* 89.

32. Ibid.

33. Over the years, a number of persons (art critic José Gómez Sicre, former diplomat Juan Mathé, and art dealer Ruth Benzacar) who knew all three artists have spoken to me about the "more middle-class" background of Spilimbergo and Castagnino, as well as their lack of political "depth" in comparison to Berni. These same persons stressed Berni's down-to-earth personal qualities and working-class sense of humor, as well as his extraordinary and critical knowledge of Marxism.

34. A good discussion of Argentinean literature and its politics is David Viñas's *Literatura Argentina y Realidad Política: De Sarmiento a Cortázar* (Buenos Aires: Siglo Veinte, 1971).

35. Lilí Berni, interview.

36. Ibid. While in Europe, Berni discovered the clear and solid depiction of form, as seen not just in the work of a modern painter like de Chirico but also in the work of masters like Mantegna and della Francesca.

37. Antonio Berni, "El nuevo realismo," *Forma* (August 1936), unpaginated. He would restate his "new realist" position again in the article "El neuvo realismo," published in *Ars* (March 1941): 13. Berni began using the term "nuevo realismo" in 1936.

38. Ibid. All translations from the Spanish in this essay are my own.

Weinberg

1. *New Masses* 10 (13 March 1934): 2.

2. For a discussion of Gellert's career, see James Wechsler, "From World War I to the Popular Front: The Art and Activism of Hugo Gellert," *Journal of Decorative and Propaganda Arts* 24 (spring 2002): 198–229. For a recent discussion of the erotics of images of labor that uses many excellent examples from the Wolfsonian Collection, see Erika Doss, "Looking at Labor: Images of Work in 1930s American Art," ibid., 230–55.

3. *New Masses* 8 (November 1932): 26.

4. For a discussion of Kalish's and Hine's images of labor in the 1920s, see Melissa Dabakis's *Visualizing Labor in American Sculpture: Monuments, Manliness, and the Work Ethic, 1880–1935* (Cambridge: Cambridge University Press, 1999). I am indebted to Dabakis's discussion of the depiction of labor at the turn of the century.

5. See Eve Kosofsky Sedgwick, *Between Men: English Literature and Male Homosocial Desire* (New York: Columbia University Press, 1985).

6. Martin Berger, *Man Made: Thomas Eakins and the Construction of Gilded-Age Manhood* (Berkeley and Los Angeles: University of California Press, 2000), 10.

7. For a discussion of masculinity and anxiety about work, see, for example, Michael S. Kimmel, *Manhood in America: A Cultural History* (New York: Free Press, 1996). Kimmel also discusses Americans' growing fascination with bodybuilding in the twenties and thirties.

8. See Dabakis's discussion of organized labor and Robert Aitken's Samuel Gompers Memorial in her *Visualizing Labor in American Sculpture*, 212–24.

9. The work by Mukhina that seems closest in spirit to Gellert's figures is her colossal *Worker and Collective Farm Girl*, which stood atop the USSR Pavilion in Paris in 1937. See Sarah Wilson, "The Soviet Pavilion in Paris," in Matthew Cullerne Brown and Brandon Tayler, eds., *Art of the Soviets: Painting, Sculpture, and Architecture in a One-Party State, 1917–1992* (Manchester, Eng.: Manchester University Press, 1993).

10. Barbara Melosh, *Engendering Culture: Manhood and Womanhood in New Deal Public Art and Theater* (Washington, D.C.: Smithsonian Institution Press, 1991), 89–90. For the most part, when blacks were depicted in public murals and sculptures it was for government projects in which the viewers were thought to be primarily African American, as in the sculpture by Heinz Warneke (with the assistance of Richmond Barthé) for the Harlem-Macombs Place Housing Project.

11. Labor organizer Daniel Smokler has written an excellent essay on Hugo Gellert entitled "Illustrating the Artist in 1930's Art and Politics: The Life and Art of Hugo Gellert" (History of Art Department, Yale College, 2001), in which he explores the question of race relationships in Gellert's work. Smokler is particularly interested in Gellert's response to the case of the Scottsboro Nine, in which nine African American youths were wrongly accused of rape. While Smokler celebrates Gellert's attempt to forge labor alliances across racial boundaries, he is critical of Gellert's lack of "delicacy" in dealing with the complexity of race relationships.

12. Thomas Craven, *Modern Art* (New York: Simon & Schuster, 1934), 367.

13. Jonathan Harris, *Federal Art and National Culture: The Politics of Identity in New Deal America* (New York: Cambridge University Press, 1995), 10.

14. Hugo Gellert, "Fascism, War, and the Artist," in *Artists Against War and Fascism, Papers of the First American Artists' Congress*, ed. Matthew Baigell and Julia Williams (New Brunswick: Rutgers University Press, 1986), 174–75.

15. See Dan Burne Jones, *The Prints of Rockwell Kent: A Catalogue Raisonné* (Chicago: University of Chicago Press, 1975).

16. See Kent's autobiography, *It's Me, O Lord: The Autobiography of Rockwell Kent* (New York: Dodd, Mead, 1980).

17. See Frances K. Pohl, "Rockwell Kent and the Vermont Marble Workers' Strike," *Archives of American Art Journal* 29, nos. 3–4 (1989): 50–60.

18. Lincoln Kirstein, *Mosaic: Memoirs* (New York: Farrar, Straus and Giroux, 1994), 174.

19. It was actually Henry Roosevelt, assistant secretary of the navy and FDR's cousin, who took the step of removing the painting from the exhibition of WPA art at the Corcoran, but Admiral Hugh Rodman made the most publicized defense of the navy's action. For a detailed analysis of the scandal, see Philip I. Eliasoph, "Paul Cadmus: Life and Work" (Ph.D. diss., State University of New York at Binghamton, 1979). See also my *Speaking for Vice: Homosexuality in the Art of Charles Demuth, Marsden Hartley, and the First American Avant-Garde* (New Haven: Yale University Press, 1993), and "Cruising with Paul Cadmus," *Art in America* 80 (November 1992): 102–9.

20. Harry Salpeter, "Paul Cadmus: Enfant Terrible," *Esquire* (July 1937): 105–11.

21. Rodman's letter was printed in the *New York Times,* 18 April 1937, 1, 9.

22. "Should Sailors Be Sissies?" editorial, *New York Daily News,* 20 April 1934, 37, cited in Eliasoph, "Paul Cadmus," 49.

23. The navy had been involved in a major scandal that centered on male hustling in Newport in the mid-1920s. See George Chauncey Jr., "Christian Brotherhood or Sexual Perversion? Homosexual Identities and the Construction of Sexual Boundaries in the World War One Era," *Journal of Sexual History* 19 (winter 1985): 189–211.

24. Lincoln Kirstein, *Paul Cadmus* (San Francisco: Pomegranate, 1992), 40.

25. Karal Ann Marling recounts the story of what she calls "the most heavily retouched and scrupulously expurgated murals in Section history." She claims that when Cadmus's and French's pictures were unveiled they met with heavy criticism from locals, but that this had little to do with their supposed lewdness. Marling believes that any work commissioned by northerners would have met with disapproval. She quotes Mrs. B. A. Blenner, president of the United Daughters of the Confederacy, who writes, "I think that the Confederate period should not be depicted unless the pictures are painted by Southern artists who know the spirit and traditions of the South." Karal Ann Marling, *Wall-to-Wall America: A Cultural History of Post-Office Murals in the Great Depression* (Minneapolis: University of Minnesota Press, 1982), 282–92.

26. I had the honor of knowing Paul Cadmus, and in one of our many conversations in the 1990s he referred to his politics as "pinkish."

27. To get a more adequate sense of the hardships of labor in the 1930s, one must turn away from public murals and sculpture and look at photographs—for example, Margaret Bourke-White's pictures for *You Have Seen Their Faces,* in which a narrative is created between the opening shots of boyhood laborers and the closing pictures of older women and men brutalized by the unbearable conditions of tenant farming. But more indicative of the sheer repetition and boredom of labor are the pictures, by Gordon Parks, of an African American woman who cleaned the offices every night. Parks's pictures acknowledge not only that much labor is done in America by African Americans and women: it refuses to glorify that work.

28. Marling, *Wall-to-Wall America,* 174.

Francis

1. The PWAP operated from December 1933 to May 1934, funded by a $1 million Civil Works Administration grant. As PWAP secretary Edward Bruce wrote in 1934: "The objective of the Project was to give artists employment at craftsmen's wages in the embellishment of public property with works of art." Bruce, "Foreword," *National Exhibition of Art by the Public Works of Art* (Washington, D.C.: Corcoran Gallery of Art, 1934), 2.

2. Throughout this essay, I use "black" to refer to people of African descent, regardless of their birthplaces or citizenship.

3. For example, see Marlene Park and Gerald E. Markowitz, *New Deal for Art* (Hamilton, N.Y.: Gallery Association of New York State, 1977), 86; and Alvia Wardlaw, *Black Art: Ancestral Legacy* (Dallas and New York: Dallas Museum of Art and Harry N. Abrams, 1989), 151.

4. Johnson participated in group exhibitions with the Society of Independent Artists (1924, 1925); at the Times Gallery, a Madison Avenue operation (1932); at Washington Square Outdoor Art Exhibition (1932–34); and at the Salon of America (1934)—venues that I describe as integrated as a result of Johnson's and other nonwhite artists' participation. Richardson participated in the all-black Primitive African Art group exhibition at the Urban League in New York (1932) and the integrated Wanamaker Department Store exhibition (c. 1931).

5. "Young Artist Passes Away," *New York Amsterdam News,* 3 November 1934, 4.

6. "Artist Dies in Plunge," *New York Times,* 20 December 1935, 8; Dr. Bobbye Booker (Richardson's niece), telephone interview by author, 25 August 1996; Alleyne Richardson Booker (Richardson's sister), interview by author, Medford, Mass., 6 December 1996.

7. James A. Porter, "Malvin Gray Johnson," *Opportunity* 13 (October 1935): 117–18; on Richardson, see "Survey of the Month—Art," *Opportunity* 14 (January 1936): 32; and "Work of Dead Artist Displayed at Theater," publication not known, c. 1936, in Richardson vertical file, Schomburg Center for Research in Black Culture, New York.

8. A WPA official replied to Davis's query letter regarding Richardson: see unsigned letter, U.S. WPA, New York City, to Stuart Davis, 26 June 1936, in Richardson vertical file, National Museum of American Art, Smithsonian Institution, Washington, D.C. The query letter that Davis must have written to the WPA is not included in Richardson's file, nor does it exist in WPA/FAP records at the National Archives or in Davis's files at the Archives of American Art, Smithsonian Institution, Washington, D.C. (hereafter AAA). I believe that Davis, a leftist activist, either knew Richardson from the interracial, politically progressive circles in which they both traveled or, once he was exposed to Richardson's work after the artist's death, sought more information about him.

9. The Harlem Artists Guild was also known as

the "Negro Artists Guild." The interesting referential shift—from the racial body to the racial geography—occurred soon after the organization's formation in March 1935. By 1937–38 the guild had more than one hundred members. See Gwendolyn Bennett, "The Harlem Artists Guild," *Art Front* 3 (April 1937): 20; "Harlem Artists Guild and Harlem Community Art Center, November 17, 1985," *Artists and Influence* 5 (1987): 35–47; Romare Bearden and Harry Henderson, *A History of African-American Artists* (New York: Pantheon Books, 1993), passim.

10. Diana L. Linden and Larry A. Greene, "Charles Alston's Harlem Hospital Murals: Cultural Politics in Depression Era Harlem," *Prospects* 26 (2001): 26, 391–422.

11. "The Harlem Artists Guild," *Art Front* 2 (April 1936): 4–5; "The Harlem Artists Guild," *Art Front* 3 (April 1937): 20. While the earlier article is unsigned, Bearden and Henderson have suggested that Bennett was its author (*History of African-American Artists,* 233). Douglas's 1936 speech, "The Negro in American Culture," is reprinted in *American Artists' Congress,* ed. Matthew Baigell and Julia Williams (New Brunswick: Rutgers University Press, 1986), 78–84.

12. Alleyne Richardson Booker, interview by author. A family photo shows young Earl Richardson and an adolescent Alston in their roles as mascot and player for St. Jude's Chapel (New York) basketball team. Of his politics in the 1930s and his peers', Alston said in retrospect: "You supported a lot of things that you knew were Communist-backed. ... You had to be supportive because they dealt with Negro rights and changes in situations in the South. How could you not do it?" Quoted in Camille Billops and Ivie Jackman, Transcript of interview with Charles Alston, 27 January 1975, Billops-Hatch Archives, 419 Broadway, New York, 27, 32.

13. Richardson is mentioned in the archives of his contemporary, James Yeargans (1908–71), a New York–based painter, CP activist, editorial board member of the Artists Union periodical *Art Front,* and a founding member of SPIRAL, an African American artists' group formed in 1963. His papers are privately held in Montreal, Canada.

14. In a 1981 checklist of the Schomburg's holdings, *Nat Turner, Negro Pharaoh, Negro Soldiers,* and *Toussaint L'Ouverture* are credited to Johnson; *Benjamin Banneker, Columbus Sailors—Estavanico,* and *Harriet Tubman and Frederick Douglass* to Richardson. For *Negro Pharaoh—Eighteenth Dynasty,* which has been assigned to Richardson for the last decade, see Wardlaw, *Black Art,* 151.

15. Malvin Gray Johnson's "Receipt Cards for Works of Art, 1933–1934" folder, PWAP/FAP, RG-121, Records of the Public Buildings Service, box 2, entry 113, National Archives, College Park, Md.

16. Although Johnson typically placed his signature in the bottom right quadrant of his paintings and drawings, he signed *Negro Pharaoh—Eighteenth Dynasty* on its back. Penciled in capitals, his signature has been partly erased, but his unmistakable handwriting remains.

17. "Young Artist Passes Away," 4; James A. Porter, "Malvin Gray Johnson, Artist," *Opportunity* 13 (April 1935): 117–18; Alain Locke, *Negro Art: Past and Present* (Washington, D.C.: Associates in Negro Folk Education, 1936), 75–76.

18. "Artist Dies in Plunge," 8; Locke, *Negro Art,* 81; "Work of Dead Artist Displayed at Theater," and unsigned letter, U.S. WPA/N.Y. to Davis.

19. Porter mentions Johnson's study of Cézanne in "Malvin Gray Johnson," 118. Johnson's oeuvre includes an African mask drawing (c. 1930–34, Amistad Research Center, New Orleans) and the painting *Negro Masks* (1933, Hampton University Museum).

20. Johnson did a larger version of this composition, also entitled *Toussaint L'Ouverture* (1934); it is an oil painting in the collection of Hampton University Museum.

21. It could be argued that Richardson's palette influenced Johnson's last body of work: vivid watercolors, executed in the summer of 1934 in rural Virginia. These drawings are held in the collections of the Hampton University Museum, Fisk University, and the Amistad Research Center.

22. "Harlem Artists Make Bid for Recognition," *New York Herald Tribune,* 17 June 1932, sec. 7, p. 8. Edward Alden Jewell also praised Richardson's painting in "Art in Review: Sargent Johnson Wins Chief Prize at Exhibition by Negro Artists," *New York Times,* 21 February 1933, 22.

23. The painting is reproduced in *Exhibition of Work by Negro Artists* (New York: Harmon Foundation, 1933).

24. Johnson served in the 184th Infantry Brigade of the Ninety-second Division of the U.S. Army. Sent to northeastern France, the Ninety-second Division fought the German army in August and September 1918. See Arthur E. Barbeau and Florette Henri, *The Unknown Soldier* (New York: Da Capo Press, 1996), 148–49.

25. Edwin A. Harleston's portrait, *The Soldier* (1919) and Horace Pippin's *The End of War: Starting Home* (c. 1930) are among the handful of interpretations of the fighting black man.

26. Jim Cullen, "Gender and African American Men," in *Divided Houses: Gender and the Civil War,* ed.

Catherine Clinton and Nina Silber (New York: Oxford University Press, 1992), 82.

27. A typical comment was New York critic Margaret Breuning's dismissal of a contemporary American mural exhibition at the Museum of Modern Art in 1932 as "bad paint and worse composition." "Critics Unanimously Condemn Modern Museum's Mural Show," *Art Digest* 7 (15 May 1932): 7. Many critics defined the problem in general as the failed application of easel painting technique to muralism. The progressive writer Elizabeth McCausland surmised: "A nation of easel painters has been turned loose on the walls of our schools, jails, courthouses, libraries, hospitals, with the result that some very good talent has been revealed. ... But ... from the artistic point of view ... these ambitious undertakings must be though[t] of rather as education by trial-and-error than as finished works of art." "Opening of Federal Art Project Gallery," *Springfield Sunday Union and Republic,* 5 January 1936, no page number, in McCausland Papers, AAA, microfilm roll D-374.

28. Scott and Porter exhibited sketches for murals at the Harmon Foundation exhibitions in 1928 and 1929, respectively. See Porter's mural sketch (c. 1928) for a hemicycle mural in *James A. Porter, Artist and Art Historian: The Memory of the Legacy,* exh. cat. (Washington, D.C.: Howard University Gallery of Art, 1992), 34. A typical Scott mural sketch is *Three Magi and the Star in the East* (c. 1915, private collection), reproduced in Edward Barry Gaither, "The Mural Tradition," in *Shared Heritage: Art by Four African Americans* (Indianapolis: Indianapolis Museum of Art, 1996), 130. For an account of a representative realist mural conception by a European American artist in the 1930s, see "[Francis Scott] Bradford, Rome Fellow, Paints American Epic," *Art Digest* 6 (1 January 1932): 4.

29. "Critics Unanimously Condemn Modern Museum's Mural Show," *Art Digest* 7 (15 May 1932): 7.

30. Benton's representations are generally distinguished by spatial distortions and figural exaggeration, differing from the naturalism American critics and audiences expected in art. For example, an unidentified journalist offered ambiguous praise for Benton's murals, attributing to them a "nervous electric quality" that some found "loud and disturbing." "U.S. Scene," *Time* magazine 24, 23 December 1934, 24.

31. Surveying the scene, Samuel Kootz wrote in 1932, "Artists are at liberty to paint anything they find interesting. ... Technique is something that should vary with every picture; it cannot be routinized." "'Uber Alles?'" *Art Digest* 6 (1 January 1932): 8.

32. Johnson studied at the School of the NAD in 1916–17, 1923–25, and 1927, Richardson in 1929–31. Among the other black NAD students during the first

four decades of this century were William H. Johnson, Albert Alexander Smith, James Lesesne Wells, and James Yeargans.

33. Established in 1922 by the midwestern realtor William E. Harmon (1862–1928), the foundation built urban playgrounds, granted student loans, and supported artists—white, black, and Asian—until its closing in 1969. See David Driskell, "Mary Beattie Brady and the Administration of the Harmon Foundation," in *Against the Odds: African-American Artists and the Harmon Foundation,* exh. cat. (Newark: Newark Museum, 1989), 59–69; and *Breaking Racial Barriers: African Americans in the Harmon Foundation Collection* (Washington, D.C., and San Francisco: Smithsonian Institution Press and Pomegranate, 1997).

34. Mary Beattie Brady, executive director of the Harmon Foundation, to Cuthbert Lee, Asheville, N.C., 22 July 1965, in Johnson folder, box 76, Harmon Foundation Papers, Library of Congress, Washington, D.C.

35. Johnson's oil painting *Swing Low, Sweet Chariot* (1928) was reproduced on the front page of *Art Digest* in 1929, accompanying an article comparing it to "the master works of Albert P. Ryder." "*Swing Low, Sweet Chariot* Will Be Popular," *Art Digest* 3 (mid-January 1929): 1. Richardson's *Profile of a Negro Girl* is reproduced in Evelyn Brown, "The Harmon Awards," *Opportunity* 11 (March 1933): 78–80. Harmon exhibitor and writer Edward J. Brandford offered conditional praise for Richardson's painting: "Though his work is modern and clearly defined in outline, yet still, it lacks a 'certain something' which is undefinable." "Harmon Foundation Announces Awards to Negro Artists," *New York Age* (25 February 1933): 1, 7.

36. "About the Artists," PWAP *Bulletin* 1 (February 1934): 6, in PWAP, AAA, roll NDA-3. Of the women artists Rowan wrote: "In many instances, they are setting a higher standard for most of the men." He also offered that a special provision was made for the employment of "Indian artists." All of the artists named by Rowan were Harmon Foundation exhibitors. Scott, Motley, and Hayden studied and worked in Paris during the teens and twenties; nonetheless, Scott, who exhibited in the 1912 Salon, was the only one of whom it might be said that he "was known in Paris."

37. Romare Bearden and Harry Henderson list ten African American artists on the PWAP across the United States: painters Lester Matthews (San Francisco), Samuel J. Brown (Philadelphia), Allan Rohan Crite (Boston), Wilmer A. Jennings (Atlanta), Elton Fax (Baltimore), Palmer Hayden and John H. D. Robinson (New York), Archibald J. Motley Jr., Dan Terry Reid, and Charles Dawson (Chicago). *History of African-American Artists,* 229.

38. My count is based on artists' biographies in Harmon Foundation, *Negro Artists: An Illustrated Review of Their Achievement* (New York: Harmon Foundation, 1935), and on Alain Locke, ed., *The Negro in Art* (1940; rept. New York: Hacker Art Books, 1968).

39. See Richard D. McKinzie, *A New Deal for Artists* (Princeton: Princeton University Press, 1973), 3–33.

40. On the required competency tests, see McKinzie, *New Deal for Artists,* 8–11. Jonathan Harris, in *Federal Art and National Culture: The Politics of Identity in New Deal America* (New York: Cambridge University Press, 1995), argues that PWAP administrators expected highly competent art to be produced under their auspices (24–25). Nonetheless, PWAP director Edward Bruce did not consider all his employees deserving of the rank of "artist." See the 1934 exchange between Bruce and San Francisco poet and activist Kenneth Rexroth in "Correspondence with Artists" folder, National Archives, College Park, Md., RG 121, box 4, entry 108.

41. *Negro Achievement* was one of fifty-seven uncompleted projects; only four projects, Douglas's among them, had secured funding as of June 1934. Malvin Gray Johnson to Lloyd L. Rollins, New York, 7 June 1934, in WPA/FAP Region 2 (New York) Papers, 1933–34, AAA, roll DC-113. Douglas completed his mural in November 1934. See "Aaron Douglas Work Unveiled at Library: Murals Viewed as Program Is Given to Mark Official Opening of Branch," *New York Amsterdam News,* 17 November 1934, 15.

42. Johnson to Rollins, 7 June 1934.

43. Rollins to Johnson, 12 June 1934, in WPA/FAP, Region 2 (New York) Papers, 1933–34, AAA, roll DC-113.

44. The Temporary Emergency Relief Administration (TERA) took over five of fifty-seven mural projects: Douglas's *Aspects of Negro Life;* a sculpture project at Brooklyn's Prospect Park Zoo by Allen Saalsburg, Hunt Diedrich, and F. G. R. Roth; murals at Charles Evans Hughes (formerly Straubenmueller Textile) High School by Mons Breidvik, Geoffrey Norman, and Jean Charlot; F. G. R. Roth's sculpture project at Manhattan's Central Park Zoo; and Salvatore Morani and Frederick Stahr's mural at Staten Island's Borough Hall. See Park and Markowitz, *New Deal for Art,* 154–68.

45. "About the Artists," 6. The mural of the "the evolution of the Negro Race" may refer to Johnson's or Douglas's studies. The mention of "Negro Life along the Mississippi" and "the present state of the Negro" probably refers to Baltimore painter Elton Fax's two-panel mural decoration for Dunbar Junior High in that city. Henry Hudson, a Washington, D.C., artist, painted *Pied Piper,* which was in the Corcoran Gallery of Art's exhibition of PWAP art in 1934.

46. The "Negro" was required staffage for representations of the Old South. See, for instance, a 1932 news item, "Birmingham Murals," describing a decoration project in the Alabama city: two panels representing the "old"—"a cotton field, Negro mammies, and a steamboat"—and the "new"—"a man, around whom arises the New South, with steel plants, cotton mills and modern transportation." *Art Digest* 6 (1 July 1932): 4. In a related way, Elton Fax's panels demarcate, first, a southern space of black dock workers and a banjo player set backed by a river steamboat; this milieu stands in contrast to the second panel's urban, presumably northern, realm of black industrial workers, a mother and child, a scientist, an intellectual, and an easel painter backed by skyscrapers. Fax's panels are reproduced in Anna Roosevelt Dall, "America by America: Under the CWA Genuinely Natural Art Has Been Developed," *Today,* 5 May 1934, in "Magazine Publicity #1" folder, PWAP/FAP, National Archives, College Park, Md., RG 121, box 1, entry 110.

47. Harris, *Federal Art and National Culture,* 9.

48. See Johnson to Juliana Force, December 1933, in WPA/FAP, Region 2 (New York) Papers, AAA, roll DC 113; Johnson to Edward Bruce, 21 July 1934, in Johnson folder, "Central Office Correspondence with Artists, 1933–1934," PWAP/FAP, National Archives, College Park, Md., RG-121, box 2. Johnson was a dutiful correspondent, determined to keep his name before patrons, among them the Harmon Foundation, the Harlem librarian and exhibition coordinator Louise Latimer, and ACA Gallery owner Herman Baron.

49. Johnson to Ann Craton, 12 March 1934, in Johnson folder, "Central Office Correspondence with Artists, 1933–1934," PWAP/FAP, National Archives, College Park, Md., RG-121, box 2.

50. Alain Locke, "The New Negro," in Alain Locke, ed., *The New Negro* (1925; rept. New York: Atheneum, 1992), 11–12.

51. While the U.S. occupation of Haiti (1916–34) elicited protest from African American progressives, they voiced little opposition to other instances of American imperialism, notably the Spanish-American War (1898), the annexation of the Panama Canal zone (1903), and the occupation of the Dominican Republic (1916–24). The economic, political, and social restrictions on African American life and African American patriotism worked against the expression of empathy for the black and colored populations of these seized nations and regions.

52. Woodson founded the Association for the Study of Negro Life and History, which began publishing the *Journal of Negro History* in 1916. A university-trained historian, Woodson differentiated his publications

from the amateur efforts, stating that "if the story of the Negro is ever to be told it must be done by scientifically trained Negroes. Men of other races cannot function efficiently because they do not think black." Quoted in Peter Novick, *That Noble Dream: The "Objectivity Question" and the American Historical Profession* (Cambridge: Cambridge University Press, 1988), 475.

53. Ronald G. Waters, "The Negro Press and the Image of Success, 1920–1939," *Midcontinent American Studies Journal* 11 (fall 1970): 39.

54. See Valerie Sandoval, "The Bran of History: An Historiographic Account of the Work of J. A. Rogers," *Schomburg Center for Research in Black Culture* 1 (spring 1978): 5–7, 16–19. Rogers's columns and the characteristic trajectories of African American history are taken up in Wilson Jeremiah Moses, *Afrotopia: The Roots of African American Popular History* (Cambridge: Cambridge University Press, 1998).

55. Joel Augustus Rogers, "Your History," *Pittsburgh Courier,* 7 December 1935, sec. 2, p. 1; 29 February 1936, sec. 2, p. 1; 4 January 1936, sec. 2, p. 1.

56. Joel Augustus Rogers, "Ruminations," *New York Amsterdam News,* 28 February 1934, 6.

57. Rogers's illustrator, George E. Lee, frequently annotated his drawings with "From Portrait," a practice employed by nineteenth-century illustrators to assure their readers of the fidelity of their images. Part of this earlier discourse, Lee's drawings index the sustained authority of realistic portraiture in the popular media of the 1930s.

58. Christopher Columbus (1451?–1506) sailed to the Americas in 1492, and some accounts mention a black man, Pedro Alonso Niño, among his crew. Estavanico (a.k.a. Estevanico), identified as a black explorer, traveled with Spanish explorer Alvar Nuñez Cabeza de Vaca (1490?–1577) across North America, c. 1527–36. See John Hope Franklin, *From Slavery to Freedom* (New York: Knopf, 1980), 33–34.

59. Influence and exchange among the New York–based artists—Johnson, Pious, Lawrence, and Richardson—is a topic for further research. Lawrence (1917–2000) may have developed an interest in narrative history and modernist styles through his exposure to Harmon Foundation exhibitions and PWAP decoration planned for his neighborhood library, i.e., the 135th Street branch in Harlem. Lawrence, in fact, studied at a College Art Association workshop held at the library. See Ellen Harkins Wheat, *Jacob Lawrence: American Painter* (Seattle: University of Washington Press, 1986), 28–30. Pious (1908–83) and Richardson were close friends and sketching partners who may have first met at the School of the NAD. After four years of study at the NAD (1931–35), Pious focused on

a career in commercial illustration. See "Robert Savon Pious," in *Against the Odds,* 242. Regarding the images of vanquished whites, the frequently reproduced Dartmouth College mural (1932–34) by José Clemente Orozco was an available source for these artists; the mural's "Hispano-American Society" section is particularly provocative for its depiction of a brown-skinned, rifle-wielding Mexican peasant standing over his elite and corrupt "Anglo" countrymen.

60. Margaret Vendryes, "Hanging on Their Walls: 'An Art Commentary on Lynching,' the Forgotten 1935 Art Exhibition," in *Race Consciousness,* ed. Judith Jackson Fossett and Jeffrey Tucker (New York: New York University Press, 1997), 153–76. On the burst of anti-lynching representation in art in the 1930s, see Marlene Park, "Lynching and Anti-Lynching: Art and Politics in the 1930s," in this volume.

61. Sociologist Robert E. Park's famous characterization of blacks in the first half of the twentieth century, in "The Conflict and Fusion of Cultures," *Journal of Negro History* 4 (April 1919), was typical: "Everywhere and always the Negro has been interested rather in expression than in action. ... The Negro is, so to speak, the lady among the races" (130).

62. See Ellen Harkins Wheat, "The Harriet Tubman Series, 1939–1940," in *Jacob Lawrence: The "Frederick Douglass" and "Harriet Tubman" Series of 1938–1940,* exh. cat. (Hampton, Va.: Hampton University Museum, 1991), 33; Sarah H. Bradford, *Scenes in the Life of Harriet Tubman* (Auburn, N.Y.: W. J. Moses, 1869).

63. A Tubman biography published after Richardson's death described her as a small woman of about five feet in height; see Earl Conrad's eponymously titled treatment *Harriet Tubman* (Washington, D.C.: Associated Publishers, 1943).

64. In 1930 Aaron Douglas painted a mural, *Harriet Tubman,* for Bennett College. As Bennett, a historically black women's college, was located in Johnson's hometown of Greensboro, North Carolina, both he and Richardson may have known the mural. Several years later Jacob Lawrence's *Harriet Tubman* narrative series (1939–40) presented a heroic and monumentalized protagonist, which may have been influenced by the *Negro Achievement* panel.

65. Richardson exhibited at the Primitive African Art Center in July 1932. Carlyle Burrows's review of this group show of African American artists' work also mentioned "African wood carving, jewelry, metalwork, and textiles" from the Newark Museum and a private collection that were on view. "African Art Center Will Be Launched in 'Village,'" *New York Amsterdam News,* 4 June 1930, 9.

66. Italian Renaissance art was regularly discussed and reproduced in English-language art journals during the period 1929–35. For example, see E. L. Johnson, "Artist Goes to Italy," *Arts* 17 (May 1931): 556–57, and reproductions of Piero della Francesca's Duke and Duchess of Urbino portraits in *American Magazine of Art* 21 (November 1930): 629.

67. On Rivera's influence in North and South America, see Francis V. O'Connor, "The Influence of Diego Rivera on the Art of the United States During the 1930s and After," in Detroit Institute of Arts, *Diego Rivera: A Retrospective* (Detroit and New York: Detroit Institute of Arts Founders Society and W. W. Norton, 1986), 157–83.

68. On Alston and Rivera, see Harry Henderson, "Remembering Charles Alston," in his *Charles Alston: Artist and Teacher* (New York: Kenkeleba House, 1990), 7–9.

Park

1. James Elbert Cutler, *Lynch-Law: An Investigation into the History of Lynching in the United States* (1905; rept. Montclair, N.J.: Negro Universities Press, 1969), 172.

2. See the National Association for the Advancement of Colored People, *Thirty Years of Lynching in the United States, 1889–1918* (1919; rept. New York: Arno, 1969). For the most recent complete account, see Philip Dray, *At the Hands of Persons Unknown: The Lynching of Black America* (New York: Random House, 2002). Dray mentions the NAACP exhibit on 353–54.

3. Jessie Daniel Ames, *The Changing Character of Lynching: Review of Lynching, 1931–1941* (1942; rept. New York: AMS, 1973), 23–26, 31–32. Ames was the executive director of the Association of Southern Women for the Prevention of Lynching. For the role of women, see Mary Jane Brown, *Eradicating This Evil: Women in the American Anti-lynching Movement, 1892–1940* (New York: Garland, 2000).

4. Arthur F. Raper, *The Tragedy of Lynching* (1933; rept. Montclair, N.J.: Patterson Smith, 1969), 47.

5. Ida B. Wells-Barnett, *Crusade for Justice: The Autobiography of Ida B. Wells,* ed. Alfreda M. Duster (Chicago: University of Chicago Press, 1970), 51–52. See Patricia A. Schechter, *Ida B. Wells-Barnett and American Reform, 1880–1930* (Chapel Hill: University of North Carolina Press, 2001), 81–168.

6. Quoted in Claudine L. Ferrell, *Nightmare and Dream: Antilynching in Congress, 1917–1922* (New York: Garland, 1986), 90.

7. In 1923 the Supreme Court decision in *Moore v. Dempsey* reversed the legal damage of the Leo M. Frank ruling. See Robert L. Zangrando, *The NAACP Crusade Against Lynching, 1909–1950* (Philadelphia: Temple University Press, 1980), 90. Citing the figures from the Archives at Tuskegee Institute, Zangrando gives a total of 4,742 persons lynched, of whom 3,445 were African American.

8. Albert P. and Robert L. Zangrando, eds., *Civil Rights and the American Negro: A Documentary History* (New York: Trident, 1968), 338.

9. Zangrando, NAACP *Crusade,* 21.

10. See Ferrell, *Nightmare and Dream,* and Zangrando, NAACP *Crusade.*

11. James Weldon Johnson, *Along This Way: The Autobiography of James Weldon Johnson* (New York: Viking Press, 1933), 373.

12. Walter Francis White, *A Man Called White* (1948; rept. New York: Arno, 1969), 94.

13. Walter Francis White, *Rope and Faggot* (1929; rept. New York: Arno and the *New York Times,* 1969), viii.

14. James Harmon Chadbourn, *Lynching and the Law* (Chapel Hill: University of North Carolina Press, 1933), 5. For a recent legal history, see Christopher Waldrep, *The Many Faces of Judge Lynch: Extralegal Violence and Punishment in America* (New York: Palgrave Macmillan, 2002).

15. Quoted in Lauris Mason, *The Lithographs of George Bellows: A Catalogue Raisonné* (Millwood, N.Y.: KTO, 1977), 189.

16. James W. Lane, "Lynching—As the Artist Sees It," *Interracial Review* 8 (March 1935): 36.

17. James Weldon Johnson, "Brothers," in *The Book of American Negro Poetry,* ed. James Weldon Johnson (New York: Harcourt, Brace & Co., 1922), 86–88.

18. Zangrando, NAACP *Crusade,* 94.

19. For the ILD and the LSNR, see Mark Naison, *Communists in Harlem During the Depression* (Urbana: University of Illinois Press, 1983).

20. Dan T. Carter, *Scottsboro: A Tragedy of the American South* (Baton Rouge: Louisiana State University Press, 1969), 20.

21. "Notes from Aaron Douglas, October 27, 1949," Aaron Douglas file, Schomburg Center for Research in Black Culture, New York Public Library.

22. Zangrando, NAACP *Crusade,* 114–25, 129.

23. Walter White to Mrs. Harry Payne Whitney, 13 December 1934, NAACP Papers, Library of Congress, Manuscript Division, Group I, C206 (hereafter NAACP Papers). The papers are available on microfilm.

24. "In Mr. White's Office, 1/16/35," NAACP Papers.

25. "Protests Bar Show of Art on Lynching," *New York Times,* 12 February 1935, 23.

26. "Protests Fail to Halt Lynch Art Show," *New York Amsterdam News,* 16 February 1936, NAACP Papers.

27. Marsh's preliminary unpublished drawing, captioned, "It's her first lynching," is in the Print Collection of the New York Public Library.

28. Winston Burdett, "Artists Call Attention to the Gentle Art of Lynching," Brooklyn *Daily Eagle,* 15 February 1935, NAACP Papers.

29. M. M., "Art Commentary on Lynching," *Art News* 33 (23 February 1935): 13.

30. J. W. L., "Current Exhibitions," *Parnassus* 7 (March 1935): 22.

31. A. Jakira, "As If to Slaughter," *Labor Defender* 5 (June 1930): 126 (rept. in *Equal Justice,* New York: Greenwood Repr. Corp., 1968). "Lynching as a Japanese Sculptor Sees It," *Christian Century* 51 (13 February 1935): 196–97 identified the source.

32. See Alejandro Anreus, *Orozco in Gringoland: The Years in New York* (Albuquerque: University of New Mexico Press, 2001), 88–89, and Renato Gonzalez Mello and Diane Miliotes, eds., *José Clemente Orozco in the United States, 1927–1934* (Hanover, N.H.: Hood Museum of Art, Dartmouth College, in association with W. W. Norton, 2002), 85–86.

33. J. T., "Lynching Art Show Lauded," *New York Amsterdam News,* 23 February 1935, NAACP Papers.

34. Lane, "Lynching—As the Artist Sees It," 36.

35. Allan Freelon to Walter White, 2 February 1935, NAACP Papers.

36. *New York Amsterdam News,* NAACP Papers.

37. Hemingway, *Artists on the Left,* 65.

38. Harry Sternberg, *Harry Sternberg: A Catalogue Raisonné of His Graphic Work,* exh. cat. (Wichita: Edwin A. Ulrich Museum of Art, Wichita State University, 1975), no. 117. See Ellen Fleurov, *No Sun Without Shadow: The Art of Harry Sternberg* (Escondido: California Center for the Arts, 2002), 19–20.

39. See James M. Dennis, *Renegade Regionalists: The Modern Independence of Grant Wood, Thomas Hart Benton, and John Steuart Curry* (Madison: University of Wisconsin Press, 1998), 63–66.

40. "An Art Exhibit Against Lynching," *Crisis* 42 (April 1935): 106.

41. Langston Hughes's "Flight" was published in *Opportunity* 8 (June 1930): 182, and reprinted in his anthology, *Dear Lovely Death* (Amenia, N.Y.: Privately printed at the Troutbeck Press, 1931), no page numbers.

42. See David Margolick, *Strange Fruit: Billie Holiday, Café Society, and an Early Cry for Civil Rights* (Philadelphia: Running Press, 2000).

43. Hale Woodruff, interview by Al Murray, 18 November 1968, Archives of American Art, Smithsonian Institution, Washington, D.C., transcript, 3.

44. See Alain Locke, *The Negro in Art* (1940; rept. New York: Hacker Art, 1971), 57.

45. Harry Haywood's 1934 report to the CPUSA compares the two bills. See Philip Foner and Herbert Shapiro, eds., *American Communism and Black Americans: A Documentary History, 1930–1934* (Philadelphia: Temple University Press, 1991), 249–319.

46. Stephen Alexander, "Art," *New Masses* 14 (19 March 1935): 29. *Stevedore* was a play presented in 1934 by the Theater Union. See Mark Solomon, *The Cry Was Unity: Communists and African-Americans, 1917–36* (Jackson: University Press of Mississippi, 1998), 279.

Hills

1. Evergood's copy of the English translation of Lenin's letter to Clara Zetkin; Philip Evergood Papers, roll 1354, frame 1183, Archives of American Art, Smithsonian Institution, Washington D.C. (hereafter Evergood Papers).

2. Evergood Papers, roll 1354, frames 1175–76. Evergood's source was Sydney Gordon and Ted Allan, *The Scalpel, the Sword: The Story of Dr. Norman Bethune* (London: Robert Hale, 1954), 128. Bethune, also a talented artist, went to Spain in 1937 to aid the Republicans as a battlefield surgeon. The letter is published in full in Larry Hannant, ed., *The Politics of Passion: Norman Bethune's Writing and Art* (Toronto: University of Toronto Press, 1998), 161–65.

3. Throughout this essay I use the somewhat awkward term "communist movement artists" to indicate those artists who were deeply committed to the goals of the CPUSA, whether or not they were card-carrying members. I prefer this phrase to "fellow traveler," made pejorative during the witch hunts of the late 1940s and 1950s. Because of anticommunist sentiment, then and now, artists typically declined to reveal whether they had a formal affiliation with the party; many are now deceased and reliable secondary sources must therefore be used. Regarding Evergood, Helen Sloan (the widow of John Sloan) told me that the artist "made no secret" of his membership in the Communist Party. "He would pull his card out at cocktail parties," she said. Helen Sloan, telephone interview by author, 28 March 1983. Kendall Taylor, in *Philip Evergood: Never Separate from the Heart* (Lewisburg: Bucknell University Press, 1986), avoids the issue of Evergood's politics and the word "communist" in general. A useful reassessment of the negatively biased historiography of communism that developed during the cold war era can be found in *New Studies in the Politics and Culture of U.S. Communism,*

ed. Michael E. Brown, Randy Martin, Frank Rosengarten, and George Snedeker (New York: Monthly Review Press, 1993).

4. The Communist Party's appeal to Evergood and other artists confronting the hardships of the Depression is understandable. To these artists, communist organizers seemed adept at both practice and theory. The artists applauded the party for actively representing the unemployed and protesting housing evictions. The communists knew how to plan for demonstrations, strategize for strikes, and articulate the issues with coherent and persuasive logic. And, moreover, they offered an explanation for the failures of capitalism that had led to the economic crisis.

5. Some artists, such as Hugo Gellert, temporarily gave up art altogether in order to be more effective organizers; others, such as Stuart Davis, continued to paint, but their production suffered because of their political activities. Still others, such as Phil Bard, volunteered for the international brigades that went to Spain to aid the Republican cause in the Spanish Civil War.

6. Rivera, Orozco, Siqueiros, and Léger were all in New York during the 1930s, and Siqueiros ran a workshop there. Picasso's *Guernica* toured the country in 1937, and Picasso also delivered a telephone message to the Second American Artists' Congress, held in December 1937.

7. See Georgi Dimitroff, *The United Front Against Fascism: Speeches Delivered at the Seventh World Congress of the Communist International, July 25-August 20, 1935* (New York: New Century Publishers, 1935).

8. Lawrence H. Schwartz, *Marxism and Culture: The CPUSA and Aesthetics in the 1930s* (Port Washington, N.Y.: Kennikat Press, 1980), 56. Malcolm Sylvers, in "American Communists in the Popular Front Period: Reorganization or Disorganization?" *Journal of American Studies* 23 (December 1989), agrees: "During the Popular Front Communists tended to function primarily as trade union militants rather than Party builders. ... Acting as trade union leaders of non-communist workers would have been difficult for Party militants had they also insisted on building in the factories a stronger Communist organization" (378). See also Malcolm Sylvers, "Popular Front," in *The Encyclopedia of the American Left,* ed. Mari Jo Buhle, Paul Buhle, and Dan Georgakas (New York: Garland, 1990), 591–95.

9. My own research and observations concur with Sylvers, "American Communists in the Popular Front Period," that the "fetish of organization" has historically been "a general American tendency which, increasingly in the nineteenth century with the advance of corporate capitalism, indicated organization as the only way to effect material change. ... The importance of orga-

nization as a concept did not have to be imported and represents a broad area of contact between US communism and at least a part of contemporary American historical experience and ideology" (389–90).

10. Roberg Keeran, "The Communist Influence on American Labor," in Brown et al., *New Studies in the Politics and Culture of U.S. Communism,* 165, has pointed out that an assessment of communist "influence" often overlooks the impact that the party actually had on the day-to-day activities of workers. Keeran notes that "influence itself is not a unitary thing but occurs in different ways and to different degrees," and can occur at the levels of policy initiatives, policy making, and policy implementation.

11. As Sylvers, "American Communists in the Popular Front Period," notes: "[A]t least officially, Party factions within the trade unions were dissolved" (378). This means that the party refrained from having a separate coterie of party members planning tactics unbeknownst to the membership at large—at least "officially." Under any ideology and in almost all institutions there are always internal power struggles and factional intrigue over ends and means. Nevertheless, historically, communists have fallen under greater suspicion—perhaps because of the "orders from Moscow" or "outside agitators" stereotypes. Recent scholarship on the CPUSA credits it for far greater independence and more sensitive responses to actual local conditions than previously believed.

12. "History of the Artists Union," *Art Front* 1 (November 1934), 4. By 1934 artists' unions had sprung up across the country; see "National Artists Union" in the same issue, also on p. 4.

13. Quoted in Gerald M. Monroe, "The Artists Union of New York" (Ph.D. diss., New York University, 1971), 39. The petition (Monroe calls it a "Manifesto") was given to Monroe by one of the organizers, Max Spivak. Monroe quotes extensively from movement artists he interviewed in 1969–71.

14. The artists kept constant watch over Mrs. Force, who at first hired only the well-known artists she knew, whereas the Unemployed Artists Group wanted the PWAP to address the needs of all unemployed artists; see "History of the Artists Union."

15. In November 1934 *Art Front* began publication, a joint effort of the Artists Union and the Artists' Committee for Action, a group that had grown out of demonstrations against the destruction of Diego Rivera's Rockefeller Center mural. *Art Front* was the liveliest publication for artists of the mid-1930s and consistently reported on AU activities.

16. The FAP had four sections: art, music, theater, and writers. Holger Cahill headed up the agency for

art; he hired Audrey McMahon of the College Art Association, who had set up a temporary program for artists in late 1932, to head up operations for the WPA/FAP art section in New York. Within a few months she had put artists, artists' assistants, models, framemakers, arts administrators, and secretaries on the payroll. Eventually there would be many divisions in the art program to which artists could be assigned: murals, easel painting, sculpture, graphic and poster designers, and even a stained-glass studio, as well as the Index of American Design, a division that employed artists to copy the designs of American folk art. The most succinct description and chronology of the art programs can be found in Marlene Park and Gerald E. Markowitz, *New Deal for Art* (Hamilton, N.Y.: Gallery Association of New York State, 1977), xii–xiii. Also useful is Francis V. O'Connor, *The New Deal Art Projects: An Anthology of Memoirs* (Washington D.C.: Smithsonian Institution Press, 1972). Jonathan Harris analyzes the projects in terms of the contradictions within New Deal politics in *Federal Art and National Culture: The Politics of Identity in New Deal America* (New York: Cambridge University Press, 1995).

17. See Phil Bard, "The Union," *Art Front* 1 (July 1935): 2.

18. Regarding the negotiations with the CIO, see Gerald Monroe, "The Artists Union of New York," 187–243.

19. When artists' unions across the country held their first convention, in May 1936 in New York, their report, published in *Art Front* 2 (June 1936), stated, "Artists' Unions should cooperate locally with the A.F. of L. on all possible measures. Affiliation will have to pend the formation of National Organization. As the building trades are opposed to the artists, while the other unions such as the musicians and teachers and bookkeepers, etc., favor us, it is probable our best opportunity is through the Committee for Industrial Organization [Congress of Industrial Organizations] (Lewis). We will only enter on the basis that we maintain our own jurisdiction" (6).

20. At that time the Cartoonists' Guild and Commercial Artists and Designers Union also voted to join the CIO; see *Time* magazine, 27 December 1937, 18. Meanwhile, the Mural Artists Guild joined the United Scenic Artists of America, Local 829, an AFL affiliate. The charter officers of the muralists included George Biddle, a liberal, as president, but also men known to be party members and fellow travelers: Rockwell Kent and William Gropper, as first and second vice presidents, respectively, and Hugo Gellert as a member at large. Hence, even though the CIO was known as the more radical labor organization, the AFL had overcome its earlier reluctance to admit artists. See "Muralists

Unionize," *Art Digest* (1 January 1938): 12. The Artists Union journal, *Art Front,* published its last issue in December 1937.

21. Before the Popular Front, R. Palme Dutt had written the widely read *Fascism and Social Revolution* (New York: International Publishers, 1934), in which he argued that fascism was the logical result of capitalism in crisis. During the Popular Front the connections between fascism and capitalism were not made.

22. See Matthew Baigell and Julia Williams's introduction to *Artists Against War and Fascism: Papers of the First American Artists' Congress,* ed. Matthew Baigell and Julia Williams (New Brunswick: Rutgers University Press, 1986), 25. See also *Art Front* 2 (December 1936): 3.

23. See Patricia Hills, "Philip Evergood's *American Tragedy:* The Poetics of Ugliness, the Politics of Anger," *Arts Magazine* 54 (February 1980): 138–42.

24. See Taylor, *Philip Evergood,* 92–93.

25. Sylvers, "American Communists in the Popular Front Period," 386–88, has analyzed the classes given at the CPUSA schools and notes that in the Popular Front period socialism was deemphasized: "The loss of a specific Marxist or Marxist-Leninist content to Party education for new members engrossed those disturbed by the general drift of the CP line."

26. Exhibition brochure for John Reed Club exhibition, December 1933. Evergood Papers, unmicrofilmed.

27. Brochure lent to me by Mrs. Lila Refregier in 1982. Herndon was a black communist organizer in Birmingham, Alabama; see the many references to him in Robin D. G. Kelley, *Hammer and Hoe: Alabama Communists During the Great Depression* (Chapel Hill: University of North Carolina Press, 1990). On the lynching exhibitions in New York in 1935, see Marlene Park, "Lynching and Antilynching: Art and Politics in the 1930s," *Prospects* 18 (1993).

28. Baigell and Williams, *Artists Against War and Fascism,* 14. They give the example of Aaron Douglas's paper, "The Negro in American Culture." Douglas admires the fact that in revolutionary art the African American was "sincerely represented," but he adds, "But here the portrayal is too frequently automatic, perfunctory and arbitrary. He becomes a kind of proletarian prop, a symbol, vague and abstract." Baigell and Williams conclude from Douglas's example: "But, in the spirit of the congress, Douglas mutes the impact of his critique of revolutionary artists by praising them for 'pointing a way and striking a vital blow at discrimination and segregation, the chief breeding ground for Fascism.' As if to cement the solidarity of the artists present, Douglas reminds his audience of their common enemy, fascism."

29. Louis Lozowick, "Towards a Revolutionary Art," *Art Front* 2 (July–August 1936): 12–13.

30. Lozowick may or may not have been an actual member of the Communist Party. The party had open members, but it also had secret members who may have been given license to express the old rhetoric. To the inner cadre of the CPUSA the "Popular Front" strategy was akin to a war measure; once fascism was defeated, they assumed they would return to planning for communist revolution. They did not at the time reckon on postwar anticommunism and the government's passage of the Smith Act, which made any revolutionary rhetoric a punishable offense. As an independent Marxist, Meyer Schapiro maintained a revolutionary line in the face of the CPUSA's reformism; see Patricia Hills, "1936: Meyer Schapiro, *Art Front,* and the Popular Front," *Oxford Art Journal* 17, no. 1 (1994): 30–41.

31. Martha Candler Cheney, *Modern Art in America* (New York: McGraw-Hill, 1939), 128–29, 136.

32. Jack Levine remarked in conversation with the author, 22 September 1979, that the party was pleased when artists participated in picket lines for striking artists. During the earlier period the John Reed Club cast a broad net and encouraged amateurs as well as professionals to make proletarian art. Meyer Schapiro, however, was sharply critical when the exhibitions fell short of expectations. In his *New Masses* review of the JRC exhibition, "The Social Viewpoint in Art," held in early 1933, he declared (using the pen name John Kwait) that the exhibition was not a success because "more than half the objects shown express no revolutionary ideas" (*New Masses* [February 1933]: 23). Schapiro felt that "of the rest, only a few reenact for the worker in simple, plastic language the crucial situations of his class." The Schapiro/Kwait essay is reprinted in David Shapiro, ed., *Social Realism: Art as a Weapon* (New York: Frederick Unger Publishing Co.), 66–68.

33. Park and Markowitz, *New Deal for Art,* 26–27, discuss the relative lack of guidelines.

34. For another analysis of communist movement artists in the New Deal, see Helen A. Harrison, "John Reed Club Artists and the New Deal: Radical Responses to Roosevelt's 'Peaceful' Revolution," *Prospects* 5 (1980): 241–68. On themes in New Deal murals, see Marlene Park and Gerald E. Markowitz, *Democratic Vistas: Post Offices and Public Art in the New Deal* (Philadelphia: Temple University Press, 1984), and Barbara Melosh, *Engendering Culture: Manhood and Womanhood in New Deal Public Art and Theater* (Washington, D.C.: Smithsonian Institution Press, 1991).

35. Evergood's *American Tragedy* (1937) is an example.

36. Harry Gottlieb to Philip Evergood, undated, Evergood papers, box 1, quoted in Taylor, *Philip Evergood,* 86. Taylor's dating of the letter to the late 1930s seems correct, since both Evergood and Gottlieb then worked together for the Artists Union.

37. Chronology prepared for the Whitney Museum of American Art. Archives of the Whitney Museum of American Art, New York.

38. The interview was held in June 1959; quoted in John I. H. Baur, *Philip Evergood* (New York: Harry N. Abrams, 1975), 30.

39. Transcription of Forrest Selvig interview, December 1968, Archives of American Art, Smithsonian Institution; quoted in Kendall Frances Taylor, "Philip Evergood and the Humanist Tradition" (Ph.D. diss., Syracuse University, 1979), 36.

40. Evergood was sent an invitation to join the John Reed Club in March 1933 but declined because he was already a member of the Pierre Degeyter Club (Evergood Papers, box 1). The Pierre Degeyter Club was the name given by musicians to their John Reed club. Pierre Degeyter was a French worker with little formal education who managed to study music at a conservatory. In 1888 the choir of the French Worker's Party asked him to compose music for Eugene Pottier's rousing poem "L'Internationale," written at the time of the defeat of the Paris Commune. Degeyter later joined the Communist Party of France, and when he died there was a massive turnout for his funeral. See Tom Gill, "The International," *Guardian* (Australia) (3 June 1998); reprinted on the Internet at http://www.geocities.com/ CapitolHill/7078/inter.txt.

The new content of social concern guided Evergood's decisions for choosing an appropriate style. The shifts in his handling of color and line were noted by art critic Edward Alden Jewell, who reviewed Evergood's fourth solo exhibition at the Montross Gallery for the 24 September 1933 issue of the *New York Times.* Jewell reminded his readers of Evergood's earlier "classical themes" and now praised the artist for his "brave new surge of color." The exhibition included such works as *Negro Communist* and *Concert by the El.*

41. John Reed Club brochure, December 1933. Evergood Papers.

42. In a draft of a letter written in the summer of 1933 to Holger Cahill, then working for the Museum of Modern Art, Evergood named the three sections. Evergood Papers, unmicrofilmed.

43. Some local residents objected to the anatomical renderings of some of the figures, specifically the way the bodies were revealed beneath their clothing. On the controversy, see Greta Berman, "The Lost Years: Mural Painting in New York City Under the Works Progress Administration's Federal Art Project, 1935–

1943" (Ph.D. diss., Columbia University, 1975), 70–73.

44. Morris Neuwirth quoted Elmer Englehorn, business administrator of the Federal Art Project, as stating callously: "Let the artist dig ditches ... let him be absorbed in other industries" ("219," *Art Front* 2 [January 1937]: 4).

45. Quoted in Baur, *Philip Evergood,* 35. A "Black Maria" is a paddy wagon.

46. Neuwirth, "219," 4. See also Hills, "Philip Evergood's *American Tragedy,*" 138–42.

47. The history of the SWOC's organizing efforts in small steel companies and the Memorial Day Massacre is told in Robert H. Zieger, *The CIO, 1935–1955* (Chapel Hill: University of North Carolina Press, 1995), 60–63; see Zieger's endnotes for more detailed secondary histories. Newsreel films taken of the incident, never released to the public, were shown to the La Follette Committee investigating labor issues.

48. Quoted in Baur, *Philip Evergood,* 35.

49. See *Art Front* 3 (October 1937): 5–9. The very first issue of *Art Front* (November 1934) outlined a structure for a permanent federal art project.

50. Quoted in "Democracy Aided by World Figures at Art Congress," *New York Post,* 18 December 1937, clipping in Evergood Papers. The proposed plan of H.R. 8239 did not require artists to take a poverty oath (a requirement for the FAP), but H.R. 8239 did give priority to artists who needed "relief."

51. The changes in the bill and the opposition to it were reported in *Art Digest* between January and July 1938; the editors of *Art Digest* were opposed to the bill. For the context of the situation, see Richard D. McKinzie, *A New Deal for Artists* (Princeton: Princeton University Press, 1973), 151–55. McKinzie discusses the various rewritings of the bill and the futile efforts to get it passed in Congress at a time when conservative legislators were accusing the theater and writers' projects of being "a hotbed for Communists." Hostile congressmen continually attacked the projects.

52. Leo Fischer to Evergood, form letter dated 7 December 1937, Evergood Papers, box 1 (correspondence 1937).

53. Copy in Evergood Papers, box 1.

54. Philip Evergood, "Should the Nation Support Its Art?" *Direction* 1 (April 1938): 2–5.

55. See ACA Gallery Papers, roll D304, frames 673–74, Archives of American Art, Smithsonian Institution, Washington D.C.

56. Jacob Kainen, clipping from the *Daily Worker,* dated 5 September 1938. Evergood Papers, unmicrofilmed.

57. Elizabeth McCausland, clipping from the *Springfield (Mass.) Sunday Union and Republican,* dated 14 August 1938. Evergood Papers, unmicrofilmed.

58. John Crosby, clipping from the *New York Herald Tribune,* dated 21 August 1938, Evergood Papers, unmicrofilmed.

59. Unsigned, clipping from the *New York World-Telegram,* dated 21 August 1938. Evergood Papers, unmicrofilmed.

60. See Raymond J. Steiner, "Artists Equity Association: A Look Back," *Art Times: A Literary Journal and Resource for All the Arts* (Mt. Marion, N.Y.), printed in the Woodstock Artists Association Beaux Arts Catalogue (August 2003), available at http://www.art-timesjournal.com/rjs%20Lectures/artist%20Equity.htm.

61. André Breton and Leon Trotsky wrote "Manifesto: Toward a Free Revolutionary Art," published in *Partisan Review* in fall 1938 under the byline of Breton and Diego Rivera; using the term "revolutionary" was one way the anti-CPUSA contingent could sharpen the differences between themselves and the party in its reformist phase.

62. In 1943 Evergood was invited to join ten other artists on an overseas trip as artist-correspondents for various magazines under the auspices of the U.S. military. But he, Anton Refregier, and William Gropper were rejected because they had been "premature anti-fascists," in spite of their vigorous protests and their declarations of their patriotism. "Premature anti-fascists" was the phrase the government used for communists. Evergood's FBI file purports to document his activities throughout the 1940s and 1950s.

63. *Lily and the Sparrows* and *Through the Mill* are owned by the Whitney Museum of American Art, New York; *Don't Cry Mother* is owned by the Museum of Modern Art, New York; *The Future Belongs to Them* is owned by Terry Dintenfass, New York; and *Workers' Victory* was formerly in the collection of Robert Gwathmey.

Lee

1. Victor Arnautoff, *A Life Renewed* (Donetsk: Izdatel'stvo Donbas, 1972), 29–30.

2. The whitewashed panel was painted by Clifford Wight. For details of the Coit Tower paintings and the controversies they engendered, see my *Painting on the Left: Diego Rivera, Radical Politics, and San Francisco's Public Murals* (Berkeley and Los Angeles: University of California Press, 1999), 128–59.

3. On the October Group and its artistic attitudes, see John Bowlt, ed., *Russian Art of the Avant-Garde: Theory and Criticism* (New York: Viking Press, 1988), 274–79.

4. There are certainly instances of a politicized avant-garde in the States, but in general it was select writers rather than painters who can be more easily likened to the members of the October Group. A good example might be Kenneth Rexroth, the San Francisco poet, whose early combination of political activism and experimental poetry regularly chafed at the Zhdanovian bit. See the expanded version of his *Autobiographical Novel* (New York: New Editions, 1991). Recently Andrew Hemingway has very usefully complicated the picture of American artists grappling with Soviet demands, pointing specifically to the various readings and often misreadings of the conditions and ambitions of Soviet art, and opening up the possibility of seeing American artists in the mid-1930s as operating in an October Group–like manner. See his *Artists on the Left: American Artists and the Communist Movement, 1926–1956* (New Haven: Yale University Press, 2002).

5. Diego Rivera, "The Revolutionary Spirit in Modern Art," *Modern Quarterly* 6, no. 3 (1932): 64. The statement was probably also an overture to the CPUSA and an attempt at reconciliation or at least loose affiliation. That is often the argument made for Rivera's next commission, the Rockefeller Center mural. See Laurance P. Hurlburt, *The Mexican Muralists in the United States* (Albuquerque: University of New Mexico Press, 1989), 162.

6. "Charter of the Union of Soviet Writers of the USSR, First Section," in Bowlt, *Russian Art of the Avant-Garde*, 297. For a brief but very useful discussion of the complex Soviet debates about social realism in the 1920s, see Paul Wood, "Realisms and Realities," in Briony Fer, David Bachelor, and Paul Wood, eds., *Realism, Rationalism, Surrealism: Art Between the Wars* (New Haven: Yale University Press, 1993), 251–331. For the debates in the 1930s and after, see the essays collected in Miranda Banks, ed., *The Aesthetic Arsenal: Socialist Realism Under Stalin* (New York: Institute for Contemporary Art, 1993).

7. Diego Rivera, "Dynamic Detroit—An Interpretation," *Creative Arts* (April 1933): 289.

8. Bertram Wolfe, *The Fabulous Life of Diego Rivera* (New York: Stein and Day, 1969), 306.

9. Diego Rivera, *My Art, My Life* (New York: Citadel Press, 1960), 183.

10. The debate about the *form* of a Marxist aesthetics has been traced more carefully in the literary Brecht-Lukács debates. For a good summary, see Eugene Lunn, *Marxism and Modernism: An Historical Study of Lukács, Brecht, Benjamin, and Adorno* (Berkeley and Los Angeles: University of California Press, 1982), 75–145. Briefly, beginning in the 1930s, Lukács was a proponent of the continuity of a European classical culture and adhered to what were fundamentally nineteenth-century realist conventions; Brecht proposed a modernist aesthetic more attuned to a technical, collectivist experience. One might say that, in the visual arts, Socialist Realism anticipated (to some degree, obviated) the debate by hinging realist traditions to an iconography built around the machine.

11. Frederick Taylor, *Principles of Scientific Management* (New York: Harpers, 1911), 40.

12. When Ford turned his new plant over to the production of the Model A in 1928, he imagined that it would transform not only the market but also the very procedures for car manufacture, and it was precisely this new object for the factory, the car and its new V-8 engine, that shaped and adapted Taylor's logic. For an extremely useful discussion about this aspect of the River Rouge plant's design, see Terry Smith, *Making the Modern: Industry, Art, and Design in America* (Chicago: University of Chicago Press, 1993), 15–92. Much of the factory's perceived "vitality" drew upon the claim, much publicized at the time, that River Rouge was the final intersection of a whole circuit of Ford capital and the automobile worker the processor of a larger traffic of Ford goods. There was certainly a measure of truth in this claim: the Model A's nearly six thousand parts were produced almost completely within the factory's walls, and the car fulfilled Ford's dream of a "universal crucible," where raw materials imported from afar entered at one end of the factory and a natty car emerged from the other. Even the latex for the tires came entirely from his own Brazilian rubber plantations, as pictured by Rivera in a monochrome panel on the west wall (fig. 3). (Ford reacted in predictable rage when, in January 1933, in the midst of Rivera's work, men on the assembly line went on strike at the nearby Briggs Body Company, whence, alas, a few non-Ford parts for his Model A still came.)

13. The number of Ford plant workers dropped from 100,500 in 1929 to 37,000 in 1931, with half the workers on only three-day work weeks, as tallied by Zaragosa Vargas, *Proletarians of the North: A History of Mexican Industrial Workers in Detroit and the Midwest, 1917–1933* (Berkeley and Los Angeles: University of California Press, 1993), 172.

14. Rivera, *My Art, My Life*, 188. As is often the case with Rivera's retrospective accounts, he probably did not recall this event but manufactured it.

15. Michel de Certeau, *The Practice of Everyday Life*, trans. Steven Rendall (Berkeley and Los Angeles: University of California Press, 1984), 92.

16. Rivera, *My Art, My Life*, 183.

17. Robert Lacey, *Ford, the Men, and the Machine* (Boston: Little, Brown, 1986), 343.

18. I am simplifying the complicated relationship between the March and the Detroit left. For a more nuanced view, see Christopher Johnson, *Maurice Sugar: Law, Labor, and the Left in Detroit, 1912–1950* (Detroit: Wayne State University Press, 1988), 116–24.

19. The idea that the white working classes organized themselves and to some degree understood themselves as a coherent body with like-minded needs and concerns, by imagining what they were not—the colored working classes—has a long history in American labor. See, for example, David Roediger, *The Wages of Whiteness: Race and the Making of the American Working Classes* (London: Verso, 1991); and Alexander Saxton, *The Indispensable Enemy: Labor and the Anti-Chinese Movement in California* (Berkeley and Los Angeles: University of California Press, 1971).

20. John Zubrick, Detroit district director of Immigration, to Harry Hull, U.S. commissioner general of Immigration, 20 October 1932, U.S. Immigration and Naturalization Service Archives, record group 85. Zubrick's other goal in repatriation was also to make possible a "system … to remove indigent Europeans who are not deportable."

21. Most of Rivera's attempts at political indoctrination came through La Sociedad Cultura, which he helped to establish in 1932, and in the community newspaper *La Prensa Libre,* which he helped to reorganize in the same year. On the "cool reception" of Rivera's ideas, see Vargas, *Proletarians of the North,* 179. Rivera's frustrations must have mounted, for he occasionally spouted highly uncharacteristic, almost trade-unionist pleas ("they [Mexican workers] must act with other Americans to achieve a betterment of their economic position"). See Marietta Baba and Malvina Abonyi, *Mexicans of Detroit* (Detroit: Wayne State University Press, 1979), 59.

22. George Pierrot and E. P. Richardson, *Diego Rivera and His Frescoes of Detroit* (Detroit: Detroit Institute of Art, 1934), 14.

23. For a detailed iconography of the entire mural series, see Linda Downs, "The Rouge in 1932: The *Detroit Industry* Frescoes by Diego Rivera," in *The Rouge: The Image of Industry in the Art of Charles Sheeler and Diego Rivera,* exh. cat. (Detroit: Detroit Institute of Arts, 1978), 47–91; and also her more recent *Diego Rivera: The Detroit Industry Murals* (New York: W. W. Norton, 1999).

24. Smith, *Making the Modern,* 216.

25. In an effort to read Rivera's murals as picturing a contemporary form of carnival—when, that is, the social order is momentarily turned upside down—some art historians have pointed to the painter's use of the "grotesque," "carnivalesque" body. This requires

some explanation and revision. In the 1930s Mikhail Bakhtin, the great Russian philosopher, literary theorist, and contemporary of Rivera (one wonders if they ever met during Rivera's trips to Russia), described carnival as a festive moment in popular culture that had socially transgressive overtones. Central to his conception of carnival is the ancient, grotesque body—an excessive, spewing, rollicking body, through which social transgression is given a condensed, public visibility. Carnival's emphasis on and display of the body's somatic limits, concavities and convexities, pleasures and processes (the "acts of bodily drama," as Bakhtin wrote) celebrates that which had been repressed and degraded by officialdom. Indeed, in *Detroit Industry* the mural's goddesses seem to insist that the world they inhabit is not classical or even necessarily Western but, rather, carnivalesque, since their forms are far more grotesque than the classical standards of beauty would allow. They are distended and disproportionate; their legs disjointed and tapering off into mere flesh; their torsos mere sacks for protuberant breasts; their hands exaggeratedly large. Furthermore, in relation to the topmost registers, where the goddesses reign, and in the upper reaches of the east wall, where a human embryo takes form, the industrial world of the main panels is turned upside down, literally placed in the "lower," debased register. In organizing the mural thus, Rivera seems to provide a transhistorical sensibility for the working classes by appealing to an ancient past, and to qualify the authority of Ford and capital as contemporary, momentary. The goddesses' specific subversive force is gauged by their ability to link past with future and to reinterpret, even momentarily erase, the conditions of the present.

This particular invocation of carnival, whatever other historical or biographical links might be summoned as justification, has actually obscured the real value of Bakhtin's ideas for reading Rivera's murals. For Bakhtin, carnival is a festive moment of popular renewal, carried on by members of a given long-standing community. It emphasizes in ritualistic form the persistence of communal life, especially during moments when that life is on the verge of transformation—hence its appearance in Bakhtin's study of Rabelais, when a late-medieval folk culture gave way to a Renaissance courtly one. Bakhtinian carnival, as such, has actually ceased to survive in the modern world as a potent force in popular culture. But as *Detroit Industry* shows, it has continued to survive as an important *symbolic* force. Moreover—and here is the crucial point—carnival is adopted as a mode of representation not by the working classes but by those above it and in many respects constituted by it. In this particularly imaginary form, carnival does not bring forth the communal, rebellious life of the lower orders but in fact the *desire* for one. On this reading of Bakhtin's carnival, see Peter Stallybrass and Allon White, *The Politics and Poetics of Transgression* (Ithaca: Cornell University Press, 1986).

26. My understanding of the goddesses' allegorical function borrows much from Paul de Man's more general critique of allegory. See his "The Rhetoric of Temporality," in *Blindness and Insight: Essays in the Rhetoric of Contemporary Criticism* (Minneapolis: University of Minnesota Press, 1983), 187–228.

27. The literature on the experiences of automobile workers is vast, but see especially Joyce Shaw Peterson, *American Automobile Workers, 1900–1933* (Albany: State University of New York Press, 1987), and Nelson Lichtenstein and Stephen Meyer, eds., *On the Line: Essays in the History of Auto Work* (Urbana: University of Illinois Press, 1989).

28. Quoted in Horace Arnold and Fay Faurote, *Ford Methods and Ford Shops* (1915; rept. New York: Arno, 1972), 41–42.

29. On Ford's "normalization" programs, see Thomas Klug, "Employers' Strategies in the Detroit Labor Market, 1900–1929," in Lichtenstein and Meyer, *On the Line,* 42–72.

30. Stanley Nowak quoted in Elaine Moon, ed., *Untold Tales, Unsung Heroes* (Detroit: Wayne State University Press, 1994), 128.

31. Stallybrass and White, *Politics and Poetics of Transgression,* 44.

32. Barbara Babcock, *The Reversible World: Symbolic Inversion in Art and Society* (Ithaca: Cornell University Press, 1978), 14. Babcock speaks of "symbolic inversion" in a more general sphere of culture, though the definition is certainly applicable here.

33. Nearly all descriptions of the mural mention this, beginning with Walter Pach's eyewitness account as recorded in "Relaciones entre la cultura norteamericana y la obra de Diego Rivera," in *Diego Rivera: 50 Años de su Labor Artística* (Mexico City: Instituto Nacional de Belles Artes, 1951), 207–10.

34. On the relation to Coatlicue, see Betty Ann Brown, "The Past Idealized: Diego Rivera's Use of Pre-Columbian Imagery," in *Diego Rivera: A Retrospective,* exh. cat. (Detroit: Detroit Institute of Arts, 1986), 139–55.

35. The use of hybrid cultural forms has generally been understood in different terms. On its "Pan-Americanism," see the painter's own description of his so-called *Pan American Unity* mural in San Francisco, "Marriage of the Artistic Expression of the North and South on This Continent," in *Diego Rivera,* exh. pam-

phlet (San Francisco: City College of San Francisco, n.d.). On its "alternative modernism," see Smith, *Making the Modern,* 199–228. On its "postcolonialism" or "epic modernism," see David Craven, *Diego Rivera as Epic Modernist* (New York: G. K. Hall, 1997), esp. 50–51.

36. I want to leave open the possibility that the stamping press is an uncanny sign of a distinctly Mexican absence. In the moment of trade unionist racism, when Mexican workers were repatriated to the south, the Aztecan body calls forth a working-class racial minority in the nativist factory. Its hybrid nature provides a vehicle for race to remain, even only as a palimpsestic presence, and to have a place in a representation of the collectivizing American working classes. It is a corrective force, for it operates as a critique of an existing hierarchy—in this case, designated higher and lower racial positions in the labor force. Or, as Rivera put it, "the South penetrated into the North" and all of the unsettling, potentially subversive meanings such a penetration might now suggest (Rivera, *My Art, My Life,* 245). As more partial evidence for this reading, I point to the ways the stamping press's racial presence found life in contemporary criticism of the work as a whole. Was the wall too communistic for detractors? Was it too secular? Or, in fact, was "the Mexican color of it and the painter's Mexican conception of human form [the basis for] the antipathy of the Anglo-Saxon?" See "Will Detroit, like Mohammed II, Whitewash Its Rivera Murals?" *Art Digest* 7 (April 1933): 30.

37. Vargas, *Proletarians of the North,* 186. For a longer account of Rivera's diminishing status among New York and Detroit leftists in 1932–33, see Albert Halper, "Comrade Rivera Gets the Business," in *Goodbye Union Square: A Writer's Memoir of the Thirties* (Chicago: Quadrangle Books, 1976), 89–97.

38. I nearly quote Stallybrass and White verbatim in their conception of "authorship." See their *Politics and Poetics of Transgression,* 60–61.

39. Rivera, *My Art, My Life,* 198.

Luckyj

1. For biographical details of Clark, see Mary MacLachlan, *Paraskeva Clark: Paintings and Drawings,* exh. cat. (Halifax: Dalhousie Art Gallery, 1982).

2. Richard J. F. Day, *Multiculturalism and the History of Canadian Diversity* (Toronto: University of Toronto Press, 2000), 144.

3. Founded in 1933, the Canadian Group of Painters' stated goal was to encourage art of "a national

character, not necessarily of time and place, but also expressive of its philosophy, and a wider appreciation of the right of Canadian artists to find beauty and character in all things." Quoted in the forward to *Canadian Group of Painters*, (Toronto: Art Gallery of Toronto, 1933). Clark became a full member in the CGP in 1937. She also held membership in the Canadian Society of Painters in Watercolour.

4. MacLachlan, *Paraskeva Clark*, 44n50. This exhibition catalog also illustrates many of Clark's other works of the 1930s, the landscapes, portraits, and still lifes.

5. Dorothy C. Holland, *Identity and Agency in Cultural Worlds* (Cambridge: Harvard University Press, 1998), 282.

6. A conservative modernist painter who had been a member of the symbolist Blue Rose group and had studied abroad in Munich and Paris, Petrov-Vodkin was an influential teacher in postrevolutionary Russia. He was the greatest single influence on Clark's mature style as it developed in Canada. Clark recalled those years in the draft of her Guggenheim application: "His colour restricted but brilliant and luminous ... was not like anything I had been used to—not naturalistic nor realistic; it was classic in its simplicity—reaching almost to the point of abstraction—but with the warm emotion of life within it ... In those two terms that I spent in this studio ... my soul and mind became forever imbued with the most advanced-modern ideology in painting, with aspirations directed mainly to the School of Paris." See "Accomplishments," Paraskeva Clark Papers, Library and Archives of Canada, MG 30 D398 (hereafter Clark Papers), vol. 6, file 6-24, Guggenheim Application, sec. 3, 7. Picasso, whose Cubist work was discussed in the studio, became her ideal of the artist who is fully integrated with society. From 1916 to 1918, amid the civil and economic unrest of revolutionary Russia, Clark continued her art studies at the Petrograd Academy and supplemented these with private classes from landscape painter Savely Seidenberg. One assumes that she witnessed the spectacle of the Carnival of the Arts —a parade of brightly decorated buses—staged by poets, writers, painters, and musicians in the streets of Petrograd in the winter of 1917, and that she joined others in marveling at the colossal Futuristic constructions erected at the Winter Palace in celebration of the first anniversary of the Revolution on 8 November 1918. The most direct effect of the Revolution on Clark was the authorities' closure of the Petrograd Art Academy in the summer of 1918 and its reopening in October as the Svomas, or Free Studios. With a radical change in conditions of access and program, the academy provided free art training

to anyone over the age of sixteen. Clark jumped at the chance to quit her office job, to become part of a serious artistic community. She studied illustration under Vassily Shukhayev and then joined a more progressive group of older student-disciples in the studio of Kuzma Petrov-Vodkin. Recruited together with students from the Free Studios to paint scenery for the Maly Theater, Clark met Oreste Allegri Jr., whose father was in charge of set decoration for the theater. They married in 1922. A year later the birth of a son, Ben, was quickly followed by tragedy—the sudden death of Oreste, who drowned while swimming. Three months later Clark and her son moved to the outskirts of Paris to live with the Allegri family in the village of Chatou. Her father-in-law, Oreste Allegri Sr., chief decorator of the St. Petersburg Imperial Theater in 1908, maintained a flourishing theatrical business in Paris.

7. For further discussion of the metaphorical use of the door, see Aleksandra Alund, "The Stranger, Ethnicity, Identity, and Belonging" in *The Future of the Nation State: Essays on Cultural Pluralism and Political Integration,* ed. Sverker Gustavsson and Leif Lewin (London: Routledge, 1996), 79–106.

8. Holland, *Identity and Agency in Cultural Worlds,* 5.

9. Clark, "Accomplishments," Clark Papers, sec. 1, 8. Deborah Burrett notes the recurrent theme—"time stolen from housework"—in Paraskeva's draft Guggenheim application in an unpublished graduate paper of 1996, "Paraskeva Clark: Portrait of the Artist Betrayed by the 'Artist,'" for Carleton University in Ottawa, Ontario. Katherine O'Rourke documents Paraskeva's maternal responsibilities after her eldest child, Ben, was diagnosed as schizophrenic in 1943, in "Labours and Love: Issues of Domesticity and Marginality in the Works of Paraskeva Clark" (master's thesis, Concordia University, Montreal, 1991), 70–71. See also MacLachlan, *Paraskeva Clark,* 13.

10. Clark Papers, vol. 6, file 24. Clark's acerbic commentary on motherhood as an impediment to artistic creation ("What did the Lord create us for? Just to produce more men, I can't forgive him for that") is a leitmotif in Gail Singer's film on Clark, *Portrait of the Artist as an Old Lady,* produced for the National Film Board of Canada in 1983.

11. In a letter ("An Apology for Not Writing Letters") written on the eve of his departure for Spain in October 1936, Bethune speaks eloquently of the role of the artist in society, and more particularly in the defeat of fascism, "the enemy of the creative artist." Quoted in Larry Hannant, *The Politics of Passion: Norman Bethune's Writing and Art* (Toronto: University of Toronto Press, 1998), 164. A Canadian artist, activist, surgeon, and inventor, Bethune journeyed to Spain in 1936

as part of the Canadian Committee to Aid Spanish
Democracy. There he established the first mobile blood-
transfusion service. Awarded an honorary military
commandante, the highest rank held by a foreigner, he
resigned as head of the transfusion unit in April 1937
and returned to Canada to lecture and raise funds for
the antifascist cause in Spain. Two years later he set out
for the Shanxi-Hobei border region in China, where he
once again established frontline mobile blood-trans-
fusion clinics. His death from blood poisoning on the
battlefront in northern China in 1939 was acknowledged by Mao Zedong himself. Bethune remains a hero
today in China. As a well-known painter in Montreal
literary and art circles, Bethune, together with newly
arrived German painter Fritz Brandtner (1896–1969),
set up the Children's Creative Art Centre in 1935 to
provide a creative space for underprivileged children.
See Helen Duffy and Frances K. Smith, *The Brave New
World of Fritz Brandtner* (Kingston, Ontario: Agnes
Etherington Art Centre, 1982), 34–37; and Esther
Trépanier, *Marian Dale Scott: Pioneer of Modern Art,*
(Quebec: Musée du Québec), 102–3.

12. Concerning Philip Clark's understanding of
his wife's relationship with Bethune, their son Clive has
stated: "He [Philip] did everything he could to support
her development as an artist. If that's what she needed,
fine." Quoted in Judy Stoffman, "The Rediscovery of
Paraskeva Clark," *Chatelaine* (August 1983): 104.

13. The Mackenzie-Papineau Brigade was formed
in August 1937 to celebrate the hundredth anniversary
of populist uprisings in Upper and Lower Canada led
by William Lyon Mackenzie and Louis-Joseph Papineau
and resulting in the establishment of responsible government. The "Mac-Paps" consisted of thirteen hundred
Canadians who joined forces with the English-speaking
International Brigade to fight Franco's fascist regime in
Spain.

14. Unidentified newspaper clipping, December
1942, Paraskeva Clark Artist File, Art Gallery of Ontario.

15. The work was acquired by the National Gallery
of Canada in 1980.

16. Although Bethune met Mao only once, he
corresponded with him. Mao's eulogy, "In Memory of
Norman Bethune" (21 December 1939) confirmed his
admiration for Bethune. In 1939 *Portrait of Mao* was
exhibited in an international exhibition of watercolor
paintings in Chicago. Its present location is unknown.
Clark donated the items in the painting to the Norman
Bethune Museum in Gravenhurst, Ontario, in 1975.
MacLachlan, *Paraskeva Clark,* 26; O'Rourke, "Labours
and Love," 54n119.

17. Nathan Petroff, in his 1937 watercolor *Modern
Times,* included a similar reference to media depictions
of the bombing of Madrid. See Barry Lord, *The History
of Painting in Canada: Towards a People's Art* (Toronto:
NC Press, 1974), 183.

18. Margaria Tupitsyn, "From the Politics of
Montage to the Montage of Politics: Soviet Practice,
1919–1937," in *Montage and Modern Life 1919–1942,* ed.
Matthew Teitelbaum (Cambridge: MIT Press, 1992), 88.

19. See Laura Katzman, "The Politics of Media:
Painting and Photography in the Art of Ben Shahn,"
American Art (winter 1993): 70–84; Deborah Martin
Kao et al., "Ben Shahn and the Public Use of Art," in
Ben Shahn's New York: Photography of Modern Times
(Cambridge: Harvard University Art Museums, 2000),
39–74.

20. Quoted in Susan Rubin Sulieman, *Subversive
Intent: Gender, Politics, and the Avant-garde* (Cambridge: Harvard University Press, 1990), 27. Orenstein's
discussion is centered on women who were linked
to well-known Surrealists. Susan Stanford Friedman
argues that "narratives of encounter in the contact
zone often exhibit a contradictory oscillation between
the establishment of firm boundaries between self
and others ... and the transgression of fixed borders,"
in *Mappings: Feminism and the Cultural Geographies
of Encounter* (Princeton: Princeton University Press,
1988), 154.

21. Clive Clark quoted in O'Rourke, "Labours and
Love," 35.

22. Clark, "Accomplishments," Clark Papers, sec. 1, 4.

23. G. Campbell McInnes, "Contemporary Canadian Artists: No.7—Paraskeva Clark," *Canadian Forum*
17 (August 1937): 166.

24. Clark, "Accomplishments," Clark Papers, sec. 3,
12.

25. Paraskeva Clark, Draft of application to the
Guggenheim, 1941, Clark Papers, sec. 1, 11–12.

26. Ibid.

27. Clark, "Accomplishments," Clark Papers,
sec. 4, 4.

28. Clark Papers, "Miscellaneous Lecture Notes,"
undated (c. 1937), vol. 5, file 11.

29. John Herd Thompson and Allen Seager,
Canada, 1922–1939: Decades of Discord (Toronto:
McClelland & Stewart, 1985), 261.

30. The term "history-in-person" is based on the
recent work of Dorothy Holland and others who, in
drawing upon the work of Bakhtin and Vygotsky,
theorize identities as continuous formations "living
in, through and around the cultural forms practiced
in social life." Their notion of "history-in-person" as
the "sediment from past experiences upon which one
improvises, using the cultural resources available, in
response to the subject positions afforded one in the

present" (18) is particularly appropriate for an understanding of the complex interrelationships between Clark's past and present life-narratives. Holland, *Identity and Agency in Cultural Worlds*, 8.

31. Lita-Rose Betcherman, *The Little Band: The Clashes Between the Communists and the Canadian Establishment, 1928–1932* (Ottawa: Deneau Publishers, 1982).

32. Paraskeva Clark, interview by Janice Mann, 1979. Archives of Canadian Women Artists, Carleton University, Ottawa. In Quebec the notorious Padlock Act (1937) made publication and distribution of material used to promote communism or bolshevism punishable by imprisonment for up to a year without appeal.

33. Five months after Clark arrived in Toronto, in 1931, the Communist Party of Canada, which had been active since 1922, was declared illegal (it was banned in 1939) Section 98 of the criminal code made it illegal to champion "governmental, industrial or economic change within Canada by use of force, violence or personal injury to person or property," with the burden of proof placed on the accused—thus presuming guilt rather than innocence. The section was finally repealed in 1936. See Thompson and Seager, *Canada, 1922–1939*, 227.

34. For a detailed discussion of art criticism in mainstream and left-wing journals and newspapers, see Esther Trépanier, "Modernité et Conscience Sociale: La critique d'art progressive des années trente," *Journal of Canadian Art History* 8 (1984): 80–109.

35. Muriel Adams, "Modernistic Trend Strong in National Gallery Show by Contemporary Canadian Artists," *Globe and Mail* (16 February 1938): 9.

36. E. W. H., "Canadian Group of Painters at Gallery," *Ottawa Evening Citizen* (15 February 1938): 22.

37. Paraskeva Clark to H. O. McCurry, 24 June 1938, National Gallery of Canada Archives, Correspondence with Artists: Paraskeva Clark, 7.1-C.

38. The unidentified reviewer commented, "We've seen Canadian art shows before and they've been full of tight, conservative, banal pictures painted by men who never really gave themselves to the country, who held tightly to the rigid tenets handed down by academicians who are in ivory towers in England, America, France, and the rest of the world, and are touched only by the rarified air around them. These, however, by the Canadian Group of Painters, are vital and young and imaginative. ... Some of the artists are rather more expressionistic ... still others are more interested in highly inventive sophisticated pattern, among them Rody Kenny Courtice with his [sic] *Just Cows,* or in near-primitive fantasy, like Paraskeva Clark." "Fair

Offers Two New Exhibitions," *New York World-Telegram,* 26 August 1939, 12. The stylistic analogies with Florine Stettheimer's and Marc Chagall's paintings, although the American critics did not mention them directly, could well have been the inferred by the classification of *Petroushka* as a "near-primitive fantasy."

39. Ibid., 12.

40. The graphic work of German-born Fritz Brandtner (1896–1969), Polish-born Nathan Petroff (1916–), Montrealer Louis Muhlstock (b. 1904), and Hamiltonian Leonard Hutchinson (1896–1980) was often featured in the *Canadian Forum* and *New Frontier.* Lithographs of women and children by Ellen Rosalie Simon (b. 1916) were also included in *New Frontier,* although with less regularity than the work of her male peers.

41. Hutchinson, one of organizers of the Hamilton Local 104 of the Artists Union, had several wood engravings rejected by exhibition juries because of perceived revolutionary content. For a broader discussion of the links between socialist unions and artists, see Lord, *History of Painting in Canada,* chapter 4, and Rosemary Donegan, *Industrial Images* (Hamilton: Art Gallery of Hamilton, 1988), 52–53.

42. Lawrence Sabbath, "Artists in Action Series: 3 Paraskeva Clark," *Canadian Art* 17 (September 1960): 292.

43. Clark later recalled her despondency: "I was really downhearted upon first seeing painting in Canada ... I was appalled how easily the name 'artist' was attached to people." Paraskeva Clark, "Thoughts on Canadian Painting," *World Affairs* (February 1943): 17.

44. In January 1935 Conservative Prime Minister R. B. Bennett, a supporter of big business, delivered a series of five so-called New Deal radio broadcasts detailing changes to Canadian society and the role of the federal government. By late spring these initiatives had stalled or been watered down, revealing the paucity of Bennett's plans. See H. Blair Neatby, *The Politics of Chaos* (Toronto: Macmillan, 1972), 51–70; Thompson and Seager, *Canada, 1922–1939,* 193–221.

45. Quoted in Lord, *History of Painting in Canada,* 182. An organ of the Progressive Arts Clubs under the aegis of the Workers' Unity League, *Masses* actively urged artists and writers to join the proletarian struggle. It was discontinued in late 1934.

46. Historian Frank Underhill (1889–1971) and poet-lawyer F. R Scott (1899–1985), together with other academics and intellectuals, formed the League for Social Reconstruction in January 1932. Nineteen months later the first of several new political parties, the Co-operative Commonwealth Federation, drawing its membership from "radicalized farmers, small labour

parties and white collar social democrats," adopted a formal platform called the Regina Manifesto, named after the prairie provincial capital and based largely upon the liberal ideals of Frank Underhill and the League for Social Reconstruction. Two years later the Co-operative Commonwealth Federation entered the national stage by electing seven members to the House of Commons in Ottawa—all representing the agrarian West. At the same time, the Social Credit Party, under the leadership of Albertan evangelist "Bible Bill" (William Aberhart, 1878–1943), was even more successful, gaining seventeen seats in western Canada. The shape of Canadian politics changed dramatically and permanently with the advent of these political forces, and began advocating new social demands, some of which resonated with those of the older, ill-fated Communist Party of Canada (1922–39). See Michiel Horn, *League for Social Reconstruction: Intellectual Origins of the Democratic Left in Canada, 1930–1942* (Toronto: University of Toronto Press, 1980).

47. Founded in April 1936, the journal aimed "to acquaint the Canadian public with the work of those writers and artists who are expressing a positive reaction to the social scene; and to serve as an open forum for all shades of progressive opinion." "Editorial," *New Frontier* 1 (April 1936): 1. Fritz Brandtner, a member of the editorial board who had exhibited his work under the sponsorship of the Canadian League Against War and Fascism in February 1936, epitomized these ideals.

48. Paraskeva Clarke [*sic*], "Come Out from Behind the Pre-Cambrian Shield," *New Frontier* 1 (April 1937): 16.

49. Elizabeth Wyn Wood (1903–66), one of the leading modernist sculptors in Canada, admired and supported the Group of Seven painters. Her article "Art and the Pre-Cambrian Shield" appeared in the February 1937 issue of the *Canadian Forum* in response to Frank U. Underhill's review of Bertram Brooker's *Yearbook of the Arts in Canada,* published in the December 1936 issue of the same journal. The choice of *New Frontier* as the vehicle for Clark's attack on Wood broadens the engagement of left-wing publications in this widely known controversy. See Victoria Baker, *Emanuel Hahn and Elizabeth Wyn Wood: Tradition and Innovation in Canadian Sculpture* (Ottawa: National Gallery of Canada, 1997).

50. Clarke [*sic*], "Come Out from Behind the Pre-Cambrian Shield," 17.

51. Ibid., 16.

52. Tim Buck (1891–1973), machinist, trade unionist, and founding member of the Canadian Communist Party, spent two years in jail (1932–34) and continued to work actively underground when the party was banned in 1939. Graham Spry (1900–1983), a multitalented journalist, political activist, diplomat, and business executive, co-founded the Canadian Radio League (forerunner of the Canadian Broadcasting Company), published the *Farmer's Sun* (later renamed the *New Commonwealth*), was an active member of the League for Social Reconstruction, and chaired the Ontario Co-operative Commonwealth Federation. See Rose Potvin, ed., *Passion and Conviction: The Letters of Graham Spry* (Regina: Canadian Plains Research Centre, 1992). Walter Abell (1897–1956), who had studied art in Europe and America, was professor of art at Acadia University, Wolfville, Nova Scotia (1928–43) and in 1940 became the founding editor of *Maritime Art* (later *Canadian Art*). His writings included articles on art and aesthetics and the book *Representation and Form: A Study of Aesthetic Values in Representational Art* (New York: Charles Scribner's Sons, 1936). See Hélene Sicotte, "Walter Abell au Canada, 1928–1944: Contribution d' un critique d'art américain au discours canadien en faveur de l'intégration sociale de l'art," *Canadian Journal of Art History* 11, nos. 1–2 (1988): 88–106. See also Dorothy Livesay, *Right Hand, Left Hand* (Erin, Ontario: Porcepic Press, 1977).

53. More than ten thousand Torontonians welcomed home the surviving member of the battalion. Clark's name appeared on the list of Friends of the Mackenzie-Papineau Brigade who organized the welcome and sponsored a rally with posters produced by the Artists' Branch of the Communist Party of Canada. In the same year Clark tried unsuccessfully, on behalf of the Art Gallery of Toronto and the Toronto committee, to aid Spanish refugees in bringing Picasso's *Guernica* and sixty-five additional items to Toronto. Industrialist J. S. MacLean (president of Canada Packers, Ltd.) financed Clark's visit to see the Picasso retrospective in New York. MacLachlan, *Paraskeva Clark,* 30–31.

54. Graham C. McInnes, "Street Scenes: Toronto, Drawings by Paraskeva Clark," *New World Illustrated* 2 (September 1941): 12. Toronto acquired the epithet "the Good" in the late nineteenth century, partly as a result of the large number of churches in the city.

55. G. C. McInnes, "New Horizons in Canadian Art," *New Frontier* 2 (June 1937): 20.

56. Ibid., 13.

57. Ibid., 12.

58. "Women [*sic*] Artist Hopes to Aid Native Russia by Her Paintings," *Toronto Star* (4 December 1942): 7. The exhibition, *Canadian Aid to Russia,* was held 5–19 December at the Picture Loan Society in Toronto, an artists' cooperative. Modeled on Picture Hire Limited in England, the Toronto Society began operation in December 1936; Douglas Duncan, a wealthy supporter of the arts, put up the initial capital. Clark maintained

a long-standing friendship with Duncan based on a shared love of the French language and French painting. Clark acknowledged his pivotal role in the artistic life of Canadian artists in a memorial service years later. "Nobody did as much as Douglas," she said, "in encouraging women artists. ... Douglas Duncan was the centre of inspiration, encouragement, and spiritual and often financial help for artists, particularly young ones." Quoted in Alan Jarvis, *Douglas Duncan: A Memorial Portrait* (Toronto: University of Toronto Press, 1974), 61.

59. O'Rourke, "Labours and Love," 37–39; MacLachlan, *Paraskeva Clark,* 33–34. More than twenty versions of these lectures exist in the Paraskeva Clark Fonds in the Library and Archives of Canada.

60. MacLachlan, *Paraskeva Clark,* 35.

61. Sabbath, "Paraskeva Clark," 293.

62. Michel De Certeau, cited in Lesley Johnson, "'As Housewives we are worms': Women, Modernity, and the Home Question," in *Feminism and Cultural Studies,* ed. Morag Shiach (New York: Oxford University Press, 1999), 489.

63. Alund, "Stranger, Ethnicity, Identity," 79.

Linden

1. For differing opinions on the Jewish aspect of Shahn's late work, see Matthew Baigell, "Ben Shahn's Postwar Jewish Paintings," in *Artist and Identity in Twentieth-Century America Art* (New York: Cambridge University Press, 2001), 213–31, 282–84; and Frances K. Pohl, "Allegory in the Work of Ben Shahn," in Chevlowe, *Common Man, Mythic Vision.* Recent exhibitions include Alejandro Anreus, ed. *Ben Shahn and the Passion of Sacco and Vanzetti,* exh. cat. (Jersey City: Jersey City Museum, distributed by Rutgers University Press, 2002); and Deborah Martin Kao, Laura Katzman, and Jenna Webster, eds., *Ben Shahn's New York: The Photography of Modern Times,* exh. cat. (New Haven: Yale University Press, 2000).

2. Useful texts include Jon Stratton, *Coming Out Jewish* (London: Routledge, 2000); David Biale, Michael Galchinsky, and Susannah Heschel, eds., *Insider/Outsider: American Jews and Multiculturalism* (Berkeley and Los Angeles: University of California Press, 1998); and Laurance J. Silberstein and Robert L. Cohn, eds., *The Other in Jewish Thought and History: Constructions of Jewish Culture and Identity* (New York: New York University Press, 1994).

3. Beth S. Wegner, *New York Jews and the Great Depression: Uncertain Promise* (New Haven: Yale University Press, 1994).

4. Marlene Park and Gerald E. Markowitz, *Demo-cratic Vistas: Post Offices and Public Art in the New Deal* (Philadelphia: Temple University Press, 1984), 125, 139–42.

5. Frances K. Pohl, *Ben Shahn with Ben Shahn's Writings* (San Francisco: Pomegranate Books, 1993), 11.

6. For the Rockefeller Center mural, see Laurance P. Hurlburt, *The Mexican Muralists in the United States* (Albuquerque: University of New Mexico Press, 1989), 159–74.

7. Shahn completed four New Deal murals: a fresco for the Jersey Homesteads (c. 1937–38); *Resources of America* (1938–39) for the Bronx Central Post Office, New York; *The First Amendment* (1940–41) for the Woodhaven Branch Post Office, Queens; and *The Meaning of Social Security* (1940–42) for the Social Security Building, Washington, D.C. Officials and juries rejected his satirical *Prohibition Era* (c. 1933–34), for the Central Park Casino, New York; his *The Great State of Wisconsin* (c. 1937), for the planned community of Greendale, Wisconsin; and a series submitted to the 1939 post office competition in St. Louis, Missouri. Officials canceled his project for Riker's Island Penitentiary, New York, c. 1933–35, as Shahn was beginning work on the site.

8. Laura Katzman, "The Politics of Media: Painting and Photography in the Art of Ben Shahn," in Kao, Katzman, and Webster, *Ben Shahn's New York,* 97–117.

9. Henry L. Feingold, *Bearing Witness: How America and Its Jews Responded to the Holocaust* (Syracuse: Syracuse University Press, 1995), 210.

10. Jews primarily voted the socialist ticket until November 1932, when 85 to 90 percent of them voted Democrat. See Lawrence Fuchs, "American Jews and the Presidential Vote," in *American Ethnic Politics,* ed. Lawrence Fuchs (New York Harper TorchBooks, 1968), 52–54.

11. Verne W. Newton, ed. *FDR and the Holocaust* (Hyde Park, N.Y.: Franklin and Eleanor Roosevelt Institute, 1996).

12. See Harvey Klehr, *The Heyday of American Communism: The Depression Decade* (New York: Basic Books, 1984), 381–85; Michael Denning, *The Cultural Front: The Laboring of American Culture in the Twentieth Century* (New York: Verso, 1996); Theodore Draper, *American Communism and Soviet Russia* (New York: Viking Penguin, 1960), 22, 87, 110–11, 190–91.

13. Wegner, *New York Jews and the Great Depression,* 15, 18.

14. Wegner, "Memory as Identity: The Invention of the Lower East Side," *American Jewish History* 85 (March 1997): 3–28; and Hasia R. Diner, *Lower East Side Memories: A Jewish Place in America* (Princeton: Princeton University Press, 2000).

15. See Abraham Menes, "The Am Oylom Movement," *YIVO Annual of Jewish Social Science* 4 (1949); Ellen Eisenberg, *Jewish Agricultural Colonies in New Jersey, 1882–1920* (Syracuse: Syracuse University Press, 1995); and Gertrude Dubrovsky, *The Land Was Theirs: Jewish Farmers in the Garden State* (Tuscaloosa: University of Alabama Press, 1992).

16. Robert Weinberg, *Stalin's Forgotten Zion: Birobidzhan and the Making of a Soviet Jewish Homeland* (Berkeley and Los Angeles: University of California Press, 1998).

17. U.S. Department of Interior, press release, 10 March 1935, Ben Shahn Papers, Archives of American Art, Smithsonian Institution, Washington, D.C. (hereafter Ben Shahn Papers).

18. Ziva Amaishi-Maisels disagrees and claims that Shahn denied his Jewish identity in the Roosevelt mural. See her article "Ben Shahn and the Problem of Jewish Identity," *Jewish Art* 12–13 (1986–97): 304–19.

19. James R. Green, *The World of the Worker: Labor in Twentieth-Century America* (Urbana: University of Illinois Press, 1998), 151–67, 170–77, and passim.

20. See Draper, *American Communism and Soviet Russia*, 191.

21. Quoted in Bruce Bliven, *The Jewish Refugee Problem* (New York: League for Industrial Democracy, 1939), 4.

22. Irwin Yellowitz, "Jewish Immigrants and the American Labor Movement, 1900–1920," *American Jewish History* 71 (December 1981): 188–217; and Daniel Bender, "'A Hero … for the Weak': Work, Consumption, and the Enfeebled Jewish Worker, 1881–1924," *International Labor and Working-Class History* 56 (fall 1999): 1–22. The image of the new American Jewish worker invites comparison with Israel's Sabra. See Oz Almog, *The Sabra: The Creation of the New Jew* (Berkeley and Los Angeles: University of California Press, 2000).

23. Albert S. Lindemann, *The Jew Accused: Three Anti-Semitic Affairs (Dreyfus, Beilis, Frank), 1894–1915* (New York: Cambridge University Press, 1991).

24. See Mae N. Ngai, "The Architecture of Race in American Immigration Law: A Reexamination of the Immigration Act of 1924," *Journal of American History* 86 (June 1999): 67–92.

25. For information on the representation and imagery of Einstein, see Michael Berkowitz, *The Jewish Self-Image in the West* (New York: New York University Press, 2000), 86–92.

26. See David Von Drehle, *Triangle: The Fire That Changed America* (New York: Atlantic Monthly Press, 2003).

27. For important discussions of *Worker with an Electrical Drill* in Shahn's mural, see Karal Ann Marling, "A Note on New Deal Iconography: Futurology and the Historical Myth," *Prospects: An Annual of American Cultural Studies*, vol. 4 (New York: Burt Franklin & Co., Inc, 1979): 423; and Barbara Melosh, *Engendering Culture: Manhood and Womanhood in New Deal Public Art and Theater* (Washington, D.C.: Smithsonian Institution Press, 1991), 84.

28. See Ben Shahn, interview by Saul Benison, 29 October 1956, Columbia University Oral History Research Office, transcript.

29. Whitman was celebrated by many on the left, including Mike Gold, who saw Whitman's writings as a prototype for proletarian writing. Art historian Andrew Hemingway, in his discussion of New Deal murals by members of the CPUSA, identifies Whitman as a central cultural figure for communist writers and artists. See Hemingway, *Artists on the Left: American Artists and the Communist Movement, 1926–1956* (New Haven: Yale University Press, 2002), 167–91. Other studies that discuss the importance of Whitman to the American left include Bryan K. Garman, "'Heroic Spiritual Grandfather': Whitman, Sexuality, and the American Left, 1890–1940," *American Quarterly* 52, no. 1 (2000): 90–126; Sam Roberts, "On Walt Whitman: The Great Bard's Contempt for Prudery and Bigotry," *Daily Worker*, 25 May 1938, 5; Sam Roberts, "Poet of Democracy: Great American Bard Loved the Workingman," *Daily Worker*, 31 May 1938.

30. See Alan Brinkley, *Voices of Protest: Huey Long, Father Coughlin, and the Great Depression* (New York: Knopf, 1982). For Shahn's caricature of Coughlin, see Chevlowe, *Common Man, Mythic Vision*, 53.

31. "Protest Halts Whitman's 'Irreligious' Verse for Post Office Mural," *New York Herald Tribune*, 12 December 1938, 1, 7.

32. For analyses of the Section's procedures and iconography, see Hemingway, *Artists on the Left*; Karal Ann Marling, *Wall-to-Wall America: A Cultural History of Post-Office Murals in the Great Depression* (Minneapolis: University of Minnesota Press, 1982); Park and Markowitz, *Democratic Vistas*; and Melosh, *Engendering Culture*.

33. For a more detailed account of Shahn's work for both the St. Louis commission and the Queens Post Office, please see my "Ben Shahn, the Four Freedoms, and the SS *St. Louis*," in *American Jewish History* 86 (December 1998): 419–40, which reproduces all of Shahn's nine studies for the St. Louis proposal. I must acknowledge that I erroneously cited the title of the Queens mural as *The Four Freedoms* (1940–41).

34. See Barbie Zelizer, *Remembering to Forget:*

Holocaust Memory Through the Camera's Eyes
(Chicago: University of Chicago Press, 1998). The
central passage of this panel has been identified as the
prototype for Shahn's *Concentration Camp* (1944); see
The Mural Art of Ben Shahn, exh. cat. (Syracuse: Lowe
Art Gallery, Syracuse University, 1977).

35. See Arthur A. Goren, *The American Jews* (Cambridge: Harvard University Press, 1982), 1, 37; and
Moses Rischin, *The Promised City: New York's Jews,
1870–1914* (Cambridge: Harvard University Press,
1962), 20, 33.

36. See "Fear Suicide Wave on Refugees' Ship,"
New York Times, 1 June 1939, 16; "Cuba Orders Liner
and Refugees to Go," *New York Times,* 2 June 1939, 1;
and "Man's Inhumanity," *New York Times,* 9 June 1939,
20.

37. See Robert M. Levine, *Tropical Diaspora:
The Jewish Experience in Cuba* (Gainesville: University Press of Florida, 1993), chapter 4, for a complete
account of the voyage of the SS *St. Louis.*

38. Sarah Ogilvie, director, Division of Education,
U.S. Holocaust Memorial Museum, letter to author, 26
June 2003. The museum is currently researching the
fate of all the passengers and will soon publish its findings.

39. Forbes Watson to Edward B. Rowan, 22 September 1939, National Archives, Washington, D.C.,
Record Group-121. For an excellent discussion of
Mitchell Siporin's and Edward Millman's winning
murals for the St. Louis Post Office, see Hemingway,
Artists on the Left, 166–68.

40. Edward B. Rowan to Ben Shahn, 6 January
1940, National Archives, Washington, D.C., Record
Group-121.

41. Ben Shahn to Edward B. Rowan, 18 June 1940,
Ben Shahn Papers.

42. Samuel Rosenman, ed., *The Public Papers and
Addresses of Franklin D. Roosevelt* (New York: Macmillan, 1941), 672.

43. Feingold, *Bearing Witness,* 7.

Hemingway

1. League of American Writers Congress, American Artists' Congress, and United American Artists, CIO,
In Defense of Culture, program of the Fourth American
Writers Congress and Congress of American Artists,
6–8 June 1941 (New York, 1941).

2. Rockwell Kent to Alvena Seckar, 15 March 1945,
copy, Rockwell Kent Papers, unmicrofilmed, Archives
of American Art, Smithsonian Institution, Washington
D.C. (hereafter Kent Papers).

3. Norman Barr to Rockwell Kent, 24 January
1947, Kent Papers.

4. See Steven Fraser, *Labor Will Rule: Sidney Hillman and the Rise of American Labor* (New York: Free
Press, 1991), 515–26; Maurice Isserman, *Which Side
Were You On? The American Communist Party During
the Second World War* (Middletown: Wesleyan University Press 1982), 208–13.

5. On "social liberalism," see Norman D. Markowitz, *The Rise and Fall of the People's Century: Henry A.
Wallace and American Liberalism, 1941–1948* (New
York: Free Press, 1973).

6. On these developments, see Alonzo L. Hamby,
*Beyond the New Deal: Harry S. Truman and American
Liberalism* (New York: Columbia University Press,
1973), chapter 6; Markowitz, *Rise and Fall of the People's Century,* chapter 6.

7. *A Platform for Artists: The Federal Fine Arts
Program of the New York State Art Division, National
Council of the Arts, Sciences and Professions* (pamphlet
in Kent Papers).

8. On the financial crisis of NCASP, see Clark Foreman to Harlow Shapley, 14 September 1949 (Shapley
Papers, Harvard University Archives, box 10b, file
"Clark Foreman"). Foreman refers to debts of more
than $25,000.

9. Norman Barr to Rockwell Kent, 24 January 1947
(misdated 1945), Kent Papers.

10. *AEA Newsletter* 1 (June 1948): 1; *AEA Newsletter* 2 (June 1949): 1. Copies in Harry Gottlieb Papers,
Archives of American Art, Smithsonian Institution,
Washington, D.C. (hereafter AAA), D343:226, 228.

11. Article X of the constitution of the Chicago
AEA, AAA, D343:338.

12. *AEA Newsletter* (May 1947), AAA, D343:358–61.

13. *AEA Newsletter* 1 (June 1948): 2.

14. "Resolution proposed by Jack Levine, Director,
at the Annual Meeting held in New York City on Friday,
April 28," Harry Gottlieb Papers, AAA, D343:298. On the
Mundt-Nixon Bill and Internal Security Act, see William R. Tanner and Robert Griffith, "Legislative Politics
and 'McCarthyism': The Internal Security Act of 1950,"
in *The Specter: Original Essays on the Cold War and the
Origins of McCarthyism,* ed. Robert Griffith and Athan
Theoharis (New York: New Viewpoints, 1974), 174–89.

15. Minutes of AEA board of directors, 6 April
1949, AAA, D343:323.

16. *Exhibition of Paintings and Sculpture by
Members of the New York Chapter of Artists' Equity
Association for the Building Fund,* exh. cat., Whitney
Museum, 28 May–10 June 1951; Mara Leff, "History
of the NY Chapter of AEA, 1949–59," files of AEA, 498
Broome Street, New York. I am grateful to Mara Leff

for showing me the AEA files and discussing these developments with me.

17. Confidential circular from Lincoln Rothschild, executive director of AEA, to membership, New York chapter, 1 June 1953, AEA files.

18. "Equity," manuscript notes, probably for an address to a CP artists' club, Harry Gottlieb Papers, AAA, 3889:885–98. The notes are datable through their reference to the Eisenhower administration.

19. Circular letter from Herman Baron, 2 July 1945, Harry Gottlieb Papers, AAA, 3887:388. Statement on back cover of *American Contemporary Art* (winter 1946).

20. *Congressional Record—House* (17 May 1949): 6486–90.

21. "Art Gallery Called 'Red': Congressman Dondero Says ACA Veils Propaganda," *New York Sun,* 18 May 1949.

22. Herman Baron, "American Art Under Attack," typescript, AAA, D304:846–52.

23. See David Caute, *The Great Fear: The Anti-Communist Purge Under Truman and Eisenhower* (New York: Simon & Schuster, 1978), and Ellen Schrecker, *Many Are the Crimes: McCarthyism in America* (Boston: Little, Brown, 1998).

24. See Joseph Starobin, *American Communism in Crisis, 1943–1957* (Cambridge: Harvard University Press, 1972), chapters 8–9; Michael Bellknap, *Cold War Political Justice: The Smith Act, the Communist Party, and American Civil Liberties* (Westport, Conn.: Greenwood Press, 1977), chapter 7. Bellknap claims that the party still had a membership of 54,174 at the end of 1949, but this had dropped to 24,796 by early 1953 (190).

25. Isserman, *Which Side Were You On?* chapter 10.

26. See, for instance, the pamphlet by the party's "cultural commissar," V. J. Jerome, *Culture in a Changing World: A Marxist Approach* (New York: New Century Publications, 1947).

27. See Starobin, *American Communism in Crisis,* 136–38. Most contributions to the debate are listed in Lee Baxandall, *Marxism and Aesthetics: A Selective Annotated Bibliography* (New York: Humanities Press, 1973), 174–76.

28. Albert Maltz, "What Shall We Ask of Writers?" *New Masses* 58 (12 February 1946): 19–22.

29. Samuel Sillen, "The Main Issue for the Literary Left," *Daily Worker,* 24 February 1946.

30. Samuel Sillen, "Art as a Weapon," *Daily Worker,* 13 February 1946.

31. Albert Maltz, "Moving Forward," *New Masses* 59 (9 April 1946):8–10, 21–2; and *Daily Worker,* 7 and 8 April 1946.

32. William Z. Foster, "Elements of a People's Cultural Policy," *New Masses* 59 (23 April 1946): 6–9.

33. This information was given me by a CP cultural activist from the 1940s. Summers's column appeared between 6 March 1946 and 7 May 1947.

34. Marion Summers, "A Disturbing Vagueness in New Weber Show," *Daily Worker,* 17 March 1946; "Social Art Must Breathe the Air of the Common Man," ibid., 7 April 1946.

35. Marion Summers, "The Question of Decadence in Art," ibid., 9 June 1946.

36. Marion Summers, "A Glimpse of Early Cubism," ibid., 10 November 1946; "Kootz Exhibits Ten New Works by Picasso," ibid., 9 February 1947.

37. Marion Summers, "Little Fenced-in Visions of Unreality," ibid., 13 March 1946; "Luxury Goods for Sensuous Enjoyment," ibid., 23 June 1946.

38. Marion Summers, "Abstract Art: Highway or Dead End?" ibid., 12 June 1946; "The Tyranny of Purity in Art," ibid., 16 June 1946; "Abstract Art Is a Denial of Social Content," ibid., 20 June 1946; "Luxury Goods for Sensuous Enjoyment," ibid., 23 June 1946.

39. For instance Brown on Adolph Gottlieb's pictographs: Marion Summers, "A Quick Tour of the Galleries," ibid., 23 January 1947.

40. Marion Summers, "Realism, Handmaiden of Progress," ibid., 14 July 1946; "Behind the Anti-Realist Attitude," ibid., 21 July 1946.

41. Marion Summers, "Three Problems of the Social Artist," ibid., 7 April 1946; 14 April 1946; 21 April 1946; "One Man's Reaction to Nature," ibid., 6 March 1946.

42. Marion Summers, "A Disturbing Vagueness in New Weber Show," ibid., 17 March 1946.

43. Marion Summers, "Pessimism Is Not Enough," ibid., 3 October 1946; "PAC Posters—Propaganda and Art," ibid., 17 November 1946. Frances K. Pohl, *Ben Shahn: New Deal Artist in a Cold War Climate, 1947–1954* (Austin: University of Texas Press, 1989); Rose Art Gallery, Brandeis University, *Mitchell Siporin: A Retrospective* (Waltham, Mass., 1976).

44. Charles Humboldt, "Disagrees with Review of Ralston Crawford Show," *Daily Worker,* 17 December 1946; "The Question of Abstract Art," ibid., 14 January 1947.

45. On Solman, see A. L. Chanin, *Joseph Solman* (New York: Crown Publishers, 1966).

46. Joseph Solman, "Art," *New Masses* 62 (4 February 1947): 30.

47. Joseph Solman, "A Look at Abstract Art," ibid., 61 (3 December 1946): 25–26; "Art" (for Balcomb Greene), ibid., 63 (8 April 1947): 30–31.

48. Joseph Solman, "Art," ibid., 62 (18 February

1947): 29–31; "Apples and Guns," ibid., 62 (4 March 1947): 25–26.

49. See, for instance, his admiring review of the Museum of Modern Art's 1947 Henry Moore exhibition: Joseph Solman, "Henry Moore," ibid., 62 (28 January 1947): 28–29.

50. Joseph Solman, "Art," ibid., 63 (1 April 1947): 30–31. This comment was probably prompted by Rothko's one-man show at the Betty Parsons Gallery.

51. Joseph Solman, "Totem and Tattoo," *Masses & Mainstream* 1 (March 1948): 86–88.

52. Joseph Solman, "*Life's* Mad-Hatters," ibid., 1 (December 1948): 83–84.

53. E.g., on Blume's ludicrously portentous painting *The Rock* (Chicago Art Institute), see Joseph Solman, "Rock Candy," ibid., 2 (March 1949): 89–91.

54. Joseph Solman, "Art," *New Masses* 61 (17 December 1946): 30; Marion Summers, "Art Today," *Daily Worker,* 8 December 1946. Cf. Solman's comments on Toney's 1948 one-man show in "Painters with Ideas," *Masses & Mainstream* 1 (April 1948): 85–87. My thanks to Anthony and Anita Toney for helping me locate the picture.

55. Joseph Solman, "Three American Painters," *Masses & Mainstream* 1 (July 1948): 87–88. Cf. his "Art," *New Masses* 63 (8 April 1947).

56. Joseph Solman to Jacob Kainen, 26 February 1939, Kainen Papers, AAA, 565:172; Dorothy Secklar, "Solman Paints a Picture," *Art News* 50 (June–July–August 1951): 42–45, 62.

57. The other was Louis Harap's *Social Roots of the Arts* (New York: International Publishers, 1949).

58. Sidney Finkelstein, *Art and Society* (New York: International Publishers, 1947), 104–14.

59. Ibid., 169.

60. E.g., Charles Humboldt, "The Best Kind of Critic," *New Masses* 65 (25 November 1947): 17–18.

61. For references, see Baxandall, *Marxism and Aesthetics,* 176–77, 179.

62. Sidney Finkelstein, "Finkelstein Replies to Criticism of His Book," *Daily Worker,* 18 May 1950.

63. Samuel Sillen, "Art in the Struggle Today," ibid., 20 June 1950; V. J. Jerome, "On Finkelstein's "Art and Society," ibid., 7 and 8 August 1950.

64. This is also a marked feature of Harry Martel and Marvin Reiss, "Art and Class," *Political Affairs* 29 (September 1950): 79–96.

65. E.g., an abridged version of Zhdanov's speech against the literary journals *Zvezda* and *Leningrad* was published in *Political Affairs* 25 (December 1946): 1112–31. For Zhdanovism and the visual arts, see Aleksandr Kamenski, "Art in the Twilight of Totalitarianism," in *Art of the Soviets: Painting, Sculpture, and Architecture in a One-Party State,* ed. Matthew Cullerne Brown and Brandon Taylor (Manchester, Eng.: Manchester University Press, 1993), 154–60.

66. A copy of this document is in the Tamiment Library, New York University—file on Workshop of Graphic Art. I am grateful to Charles Keller for first drawing my attention to the episode and discussing it with me. The translator of the *Pravda* article does not wish his identity to be revealed. Keller believes that those who wrote the commentary were Herzl Emmanuel, Daniel Koerner, and Anthony Toney. (Conversation with author, 23 June 1992). My guess is that the rebuttal of the artists' statement was by Jerome.

67. One of the striking aspects of this exchange is the range of Marxist authorities who were invoked, from Lenin, Lifshitz, Lunacharsky, and Plekhanov to Friedrich Antal, Christopher Caudwell, and Ralph Fox.

68. Charles Keller, conversation with the author, 23 June 1992.

69. Sidney Finkelstein, *Realism in Art* (New York: International Publishers, 1954), 172–73.

70. On 1956, see Starobin, *American Communism in Crisis,* 224–30.

Stein

1. Although many photographs of FDR are reproduced repeatedly, I have encountered this picture in just one context where it was published not only without caption but without source identification, and was positioned chronologically to suggest that it was a presidential campaign photograph; see Stefan Lorant, *The Glorious Burden: The American Presidency* (New York: Harper & Row, 1969), 600. However, Lorant's picture collection has been deposited in the archives of the International Center of Photography (ICP) in New York City, which made it possible to identify the location and date of this Wide World Press photograph as "home of Franklin D. Roosevelt / Warm Springs, Ga. /10-5-28." Thanks to Brian Wallis at ICP for researching this information.

2. Thomas Hobbes, *Leviathan* (1651; New York: Penguin Books, 1968), 228.

3. Regarding the culture of ancient Mesopotamia, Irene J. Winter notes a close correlation between the divine body and concepts of divine kingship, thereby imbricating admiration and inspiration. Irene J. Winter, "Sex, Rhetoric, and the Public Monument: The Alluring Body of Naram-Sin of Agade," in *Sexuality in Ancient Art,* ed. Natalie Boymel Kampen (New York: Cambridge University Press, 1996), 11–26.

4. The ritual of standing before the electorate,

already familiar in nineteenth-century America,
became a well-worn convention in the twentieth century; see copious illustrations on this score in Lorant,
Glorious Burden. As of 2001 the postural mandate
extends to the world of mass media, where newscast-
ers and pundits have been directed to stand before
the camera; see Elizabeth Jensen, "Anchors Stand and
Deliver: In today's TV news, forget about chairs," *Los
Angeles Times,* 21 July 2001, F1, 16. Jensen quotes one
female anchor, Judy Woodruff of CNN, who observes
that this change in presentational mode will "prevent
us from having interesting people with significant disabilities."

5. For an implicit comparison, see Martin Loi-
perdinger, Rudolf Herz, and Ulrich Pohlmann, eds.,
*Führerbilder: Hitler, Mussolini, Roosevelt, Stalin in Foto-
grafie und Film* (Munich: Piper, 1995); alas, the essays
in this collection consistently refrain from crossing
national boundaries in their consideration of interwar
mass media political portraiture, leaving the work of
sustained cross-cultural comparisons for future scholars. For a provocative start in that direction, see George
L. Mosse, *The Image of Man: The Creation of Modern
Masculinity* (New York: Oxford University Press, 1996),
155–80. Mosse even introduces the politics of posture
when he notes Mussolini's lament that "Italians walked
as if they were crippled; they must learn to walk
straight" (161).

6. For an extended consideration of the variety
of positions adopted to manage and interpret FDR's
image, see Geoffrey C. Ward, *A First Class Temperament: The Emergence of Franklin Roosevelt* (New York:
Harper & Row, 1989), 732–94. Ward expressly acknowledges his debt to Hugh Gregory Gallagher, *FDR's
Splendid Deception* (New York: Dodd, Mead, 1985), the
first study of FDR to look frankly at the many effects
of his illness. For further discussion of the "log cabin"
effect, see Robert S. McElvaine, *The Great Depression:
America, 1929–1941* (New York: Times Books, 1984),
97, 106; Michael E. Parrish, *Anxious Decades: America
in Prosperity and Depression, 1920–1941* (New York: W.
W. Norton, 1992), 278.

7. Jacques Lacan, *Ecrits,* trans. Alan Sheridan (New
York: W. W. Norton, 1979), 1–7.

8. Earle D. Looker, "Is Franklin D. Roosevelt Physically Fit To Be President?" *Liberty* (25 July 1931): 6–10.
In support of his contention that the "Liberty" piece
was a "cooked-up affair," Gallagher notes that Looker on
previous occasions had actually ghostwritten articles
for FDR. *FDR's Splendid Deception,* 84.

9. The painted braces are most apparent in a 1936
photograph of FDR attending ceremonies at Harvard
University. Reproduced in Lorant, *Glorious Burden,* 621.

10. Photographic evidence suggests that FDR
rarely permitted himself to be depicted beside fellow
polio patients; in the one group photo I have found
that shows FDR and Eleanor with four children in
wheelchairs, he is the only patient who is sitting in a
chair that is not obviously a wheelchair. Photo in Frances Perkins, *The Roosevelt I Knew* (New York: Viking
Press, 1946), facing 110.

11. These appearances were not only scripted but
also just as carefully choreographed to minimize the
distance over which the president would be visible to
press and public before reaching a podium. To traverse
short distances in a semi-ambulatory fashion, FDR
leaned on trusted attendants while slowly advancing
by throwing one stiffly braced leg in front of the other.
Gallagher, *FDR's Splendid Deception,* 64–66, 93–95.
In nearly all photographs of FDR delivering speeches
while standing, you can find one of his hands gripping
the lectern.

12. On the range of efforts to manage the president's image, see the previously cited studies from the
last two decades by Gallagher and Ward. One émigré
photographer's retrospective essay includes a recollection of visiting the White House in 1936 that confirms
that FDR, when not appearing in public, was "wheeled
around the White House," and also that candid cameras
were "forbidden around the president." Lucien Aigner,
Lucien Aigner (New York: ICP, 1979), 21–23.

13. *Time* magazine, 5 December 1932, 9; 2 January
1933, 2–4; 16 January 1933, 2.

14. One revealing photograph of FDR in a wheelchair, which was shot from behind by FDR's personal
doctor and confidant, was first published in Gallagher's
FDR's Splendid Deception; on the White House's close
supervision of press photographers, see 93–94. The
offending publication referred to by Gallagher appears
as one of a dozen "snapshots" laid out album-style in
Life magazine, 16 August 1937, 26–27.

15. Annotated typescript of speech, reproduced in
Lorant, *Glorious Burden,* 604–5.

16. Parrish, *Anxious Decades,* 289.

17. On the long tradition in both secular and religious art of the half-length portrait connoting divine or
semi-divine status, see Rona Goffen, *Icon and Vision:
The Half-Length Madonnas of Giovanni Bellini* (Ann
Arbor: University of Michigan Microfilms, 1976), 76.

18. For additional discussion of this mural, see
Frances K. Pohl, "Constructing History: A Mural by Ben
Shahn," *Arts Magazine* 62 (September 1987): 36–40;
and, with pointed consideration of ethnicity and Jewish
identity, see Diana Linden, "Ben Shahn, the Four Freedoms, and the SS *St. Louis,*" *American Jewish History* 86
(December 1998): 419–40.

19. Interestingly, the relatively novel use of color photography to portray FDR appears on the cover of *Time* magazine's first issue of 1933. This issue acknowledged the rash of protests provoked by the magazine's earlier description of the president's "shriveled legs." Intentionally or not, the use of color for a head shot here constituted a form of compensatory apology or "making up" for the earlier objectionable description of the president's handicapped body; see the rather florid cover portrait of FDR captioned "Photographed in Natural Color by O. J. Jordan." *Time* magazine, 2 January 1933.

20. Caption facing unsigned photomontage, *Vanity Fair,* October 1933, 14–15.

21. A print of Arcimboldo's *Summer* (1563) appears as Plate 5 in Alfred H. Barr Jr.'s catalog for the 1936 MOMA exhibition "Fantastic Art: Dada Surrealism." On Arcimboldo's wit, see Thomas DaCosta Kaufmann, "The Allegories and Their Meaning," in *The Arcimboldo Effect* (New York: Abbeville Press, 1987), 89–110. On the "corpus mysticum," see Ernst Kantarowicz, *The King's Two Bodies: A Study in Mediaeval Political Theology* (Princeton: Princeton University Press, 1957), 193–272.

22. Kantarowicz, *King's Two Bodies,* 424–44.

23. Rollin Kirby, "Comparative Workmanship," *New York World-Telegram,* 2 July 1932, 12.

24. Regarding generic images of physical dependency that coincided with FDR's emergence on the national political scene, see, in addition to Kirby's cartoon, Charles MacCauley's "A Message of Hope," *New York Mirror,* 4 July 1932 (though the farmer in this scene is supported by his wife rather than by cane or farm implement); Carey Cassius Orr's "The Crop Outlook," *Chicago Daily Tribune,* 6 July 1932, 1; and Miguel Covarrubias's cover graphic for the October 1933 issue of *Vanity Fair.* The recurrent depiction of physically depleted bodies in the New Deal photography of Dorothea Lange has multiple resonances, since this leading documentary photographer had also been stricken with polio, though with less severe lasting consequences. Still, as I have argued in "Peculiar Grace: Dorothea Lange and the Testimony of the Body," this private issue only surfaced prominently in her photography after FDR emerged on the national political scene, so that even in Lange's case the photographic preoccupation with the body seems to be mobilized by the broad public anxiety around the president's aberrant physical condition.

25. Gallagher, *FDR's Splendid Deception,* 207.

26. John W. Reps, *Monumental Washington: The Planning and Development of the Capital Center* (Princeton: Princeton University Press, 1967), 173–76; Sue A. Kohler, *The Commission of Fine Arts: A Brief History,* *1910–1995* (Washington, D.C.: U.S. Government Printing Office, 1996), 66–74.

27. Felix Frankfurter, "What FDR Wanted," *Atlantic Monthly,* March 1961, 39–40, as quoted in David Dillon, *The Franklin Delano Roosevelt Memorial: Designed by Lawrence Halprin* (Washington, D.C.: Spacemaker Press, 1998), 20. As Dillon documents, a very modest memorial executed according to this plan was installed in the mid-1960s (after the first major memorial plan stalled in 1962), although the horizontal "desktop" surface was not set flat but upright, perpendicular to the ground, even though Frankfurter's notes of the conversation suggest that FDR's plan sought lower visibility.

28. Ogden Tanner and Frederick Gutheim, respectively, as quoted in Thomas H. Creighton, *The Architecture of Monuments: The Franklin Delano Roosevelt Memorial Competition* (New York: Reinhold, 1962), 42, 39.

29. Dillon, *Franklin Delano Roosevelt Memorial,* 27. In strictly formal terms, Dillon provides an excellent summary of the original competition and the subsequent two memorial plans, though he, like Creighton, pays no attention to the way the prolonged debates about figuration and likeness were overshadowed by the issue of disability.

30. *Architectural Forum* (January–February 1967): 124.

31. Isabelle Hyman, "Marcel Breuer and the Franklin Delano Roosevelt Memorial," *Journal of the Society of Architectural Historians* 54 (December 1995): 446–58.

32. Lucy Lippard (quoting Marcel Breuer from an interview about his recently rejected design) "Homage to the Square," *Art in America* 55 (July–August 1967): 51.

33. On Maya Lin's Vietnam Veterans Memorial, see Mary McLeod, "The Battle for the Monument: The Vietnam Veterans Memorial," and Charles L. Griswold, "The Vietnam Veterans Memorial and the Washington Mall: Philosophical Thoughts on Political Iconography," both in *The Experimental Tradition,* ed. Helene Lipstadt (New York: Princeton: Architectural Press, 1989), 115–37 and 71–100, respectively; see also Kohler, *Commission of Fine Arts,* 125–35. Few writers have compared the two memorials, though David Dillon notes briefly in his monograph on the FDR memorial that Halprin's is the softer of the two, and he suggests that Lin would have taken a softer tack had Halprin's design been available as a precedent. Dillon, *Franklin Delano Roosevelt Memorial,* 40.

34. Phyllis Tuchman, "The Franklin Delano Roosevelt Memorial," in *Lawrence Halprin: Changing Places,* exh. cat. (San Francisco: San Francisco Museum of Modern Art, 1986), 84.

35. For an overview of Halprin's career, see ibid.

36. Tuchman, quoting Halprin, "Franklin Delano Roosevelt Memorial," 98.

37. A portrait of Halprin studying a wealth of FDR photographs and photocopies tacked to his studio wall is reproduced (laterally reversed) ibid., 100. The same photograph is reproduced (with the reversal corrected) in Halprin's book on the memorial, again to add documentary authenticity to the sculpture. Halprin, *Franklin Delano Roosevelt Memorial,* 25.

38. Tuchman, "Franklin Delano Roosevelt Memorial," 98.

39. Of the many publications on the memorial, only Dillon's monograph mentions this salient political fact. Dillon, *Franklin Delano Roosevelt Memorial,* 37.

40. A photograph of the unrealized Baskin study maquette of Roosevelt in a standing position appears in the Tuchman catalog essay (written and published before that sleight of hand was deemed too obvious a job of fudging to pass muster). Tuchman, "Franklin Delano Roosevelt Memorial," 99.

41. For a large selection of such letters with a valuable introduction that notes the surge of unsolicited correspondence to the FDR White House, see Robert S. McElvaine, ed., *Down and Out in the Great Depression: Letters from the "Forgotten Man"* (Chapel Hill: University of North Carolina Press, 1983).

42. Halprin used this term when paraphrasing the official guidelines for the memorial, yet it is clearly his, expressive of a long career in which water is deftly introduced in his landscape "score"; *Franklin Delano Roosevelt Memorial,* 8.

43. This is one of the carefully reasoned arguments, countering both the demonization of Hoover and the idealization of FDR, developed in the opening chapters of McElvaine, *Great Depression,* 51–137.

44. Kelli Peduzzi, *Sculpting for the Roosevelt Memorial* (Brookfield, Conn.: Millbrook Press, 1997), 8. It is a strange statement for a children's book, when children are apt to notice a disability right off the bat and, frequently, respond more matter-of-factly than most adults. On the sometimes malicious but usually more accepting reactions of children to her abnormally small size, see Katherine Butler Hathaway, *The Little Locksmith* (1943; rept. New York: Feminist Press, 2000), 152–66.

45. See Erwin Panofsky's canonical essay, "Jan van Eyck's Arnolfini Portrait," *Burlington Magazine* 64 (1934): 117–27. In a recent revisionist monograph on this painting, Edwin Hall takes issue with much of Panofsky's interpretation, in the process marshaling impressive evidence to counter the claim that the dog in the painting was a conventional symbol of marital faith. Nevertheless, Hall allows that Panofsky's interpretation was so persuasively presented that it convinced students and teachers for much of this century of the dog's venerable symbolism. Edwin Hall, *The Arnolfini Betrothal: Medieval Marriage and the Enigma of van Eyck's Double Portrait* (Berkeley and Los Angeles: University of California Press, 1994), 112–15. Thanks to art historian and dog connoisseur Laurie Monahan for pointing out that the dog in the Arnolfini portrait was almost a ringer for FDR's "Scotty."

46. Halprin, *Franklin Delano Roosevelt Memorial,* 107.

47. The greatest amount of published background information about Fala's fairly late inclusion in the memorial plan appears in Kelli Peduzzi's children's book, *Shaping a President,* 20. Senator Carl Levin agreed to a telephone interview with me in August 1999 in which he elaborated on what bothered him about earlier maquettes of this presidential portrait. In the same interview, Levin acknowledged that as a child he listened avidly to a recording of FDR speeches that included the famous Fala speech discussed below.

48. Peduzzi explains why the final rendering of Fala departed notably from the memorial's realist style: "Neil [did] not want to make Fala's hair spiky enough to poke a child who sits on his back." Peduzzi, *Shaping a President,* 20.

49. Halprin, *Franklin Delano Roosevelt Memorial,* 107.

50. Extended quotations from FDR's speech of 23 September 1944, which key Roosevelt advisor and speechwriter Judge Samuel Rosenman considered "the greatest campaign speech of his career," appear in Robert E. Sherwood, *Roosevelt and Hopkins* (New York: Harper and Brothers, 1948), 820–22 (which also recounts this episode); see also John Gunther, *Roosevelt in Retrospect* (New York: Harper and Brothers, 1950), 92. Further details, and the transcript of the entire speech, appear in the *New York Times,* 14 September 1944, 25 (on the congressional inquiry into the Aleutian trip); 24 September 1944 1, 12 (including news coverage, speech transcript, and summary); 25 September 1944, 18 (on enormous response to the speech).

51. A pioneering history of this new civil rights movement is Joseph P. Schapiro's *No Pity: People with Disabilities Forging a New Civil Rights Movement* (New York: New York Times Books, 1993). For a sense of the rich and challenging diversity of that movement-information, see also Lennard J. Davis, ed., *The Disability Studies Reader* (New York: Routledge, 1997), and Paul K. Longmore and Laurie Umanky, eds., *The New Disability History: American Perspectives* (New York: New York University Press, 2001).

52. As recently as 1987 one historian argued to the contrary that Roosevelt could and should have done much more for the cause of disability by being more open about his own disability and by making the status of the disabled a programmatic priority of the New Deal era. See John Duffy, "Franklin Roosevelt: Ambiguous Symbol for Disabled Americans," *Midwest Quarterly* 29 (autumn 1987): 113–35.

53. Mike Deland, as quoted in Meghan Mutchler, "Roosevelt's Disability an Issue at Memorial," *New York Times,* 10 April 1995, A8.

54. Echoing past ways of downplaying the president's handicap, those seeking more particularized depiction of FDR made diverse arguments: FDR was not embarrassed by his disability but only disguised it for political expediency; alternately, FDR was more forthright about his disability than most realize and at times made no attempt to hide it, occasionally even displaying it quite openly to inspire others (particularly, when visiting wounded soldiers during World War II); or, the experience of disability was a crucial part of his life and a "source of strength," either personally or politically; furthermore, had FDR lived longer or in a later period, he would have had no misgivings about being more open about his handicap, many implying that he surely would have supported (and might even have led) the new disability movement; finally, regardless of what FDR did or wanted, such direct identification of his disability at this time would be an inspiration to others. Those opposing alteration made equally speculative and sometimes contradictory points: this was not how we saw him or recall him; not only does such revisionism conflict with personal memories but it threatens to whitewash the reality of the past. As for biographical accuracy, a number of commentators noted that FDR's own brand of identity politics was patrician: he wanted to be seen as a friend of the afflicted, not as one of the afflicted himself. To remember him as afflicted would be to violate his express wishes and thus risk making a travesty of a celebratory memorial.

The article cited above, summarizing the debate (*New York Times,* 10 April 1995), captures many of these positions; others are summarized in C. Todd Stephenson, "Depicting Disability: The Franklin D. Roosevelt Memorial in Washington, D.C.," *Social Education* 60 (September 1996): 299–300. Some of the more conservative arguments are cogently propounded in Sandy Grady, "Memorial shouldn't put FDR in wheelchair," *San Jose Mercury News,* 27 April 1997, C3; see also the expression of one wheelchair-bound citizen fervently opposed to the sculptural addition of the wheelchair: "Memorialize F.D.R., Not His Disability,"

letter to editor from William J. Rochelle 3d, *New York Times,* 13 April 1995, A14.

55. *San Francisco Chronicle,* 21 April 1997, 8.

56. From transcript of Senate debate in *Congressional Record,* 1 May 1997, 41, leading to enactment of Public Law 105 29 (111 Stat 246).

57. U.S. Department of the Interior Press Release, "Babbitt Announces Appointment of FDR Memorial Committee: The Committee Will Help Determine How an Addition to the Memorial Will Show That FDR Used a Wheelchair," 12 September 1997, Washington, D.C.

58. Disability activists selected a very progressive quotation from a mid-1936 speech FDR delivered in Little Rock, Arkansas: "We know that equality of individual ability has never existed and never will, but we do insist that equality of opportunity still must be sought." Halprin and officials in the National Park Service rejected that choice on the grounds that it was redundant, echoing a later quotation advocating the defense of civil liberties already inscribed between the second and third "rooms," even though the consulting scholars strenuously objected to using only Eleanor's words in this context because of the way they reinforced traditional notions that the disabled needed others to speak for them. This late controversy was summarized incisively by one member of the consulting committee, Rosemarie Garland-Thomson, in "Making Meaning with Monuments: Politics and Aesthetics in the FDR Memorial," paper delivered at the annual conference of the American Studies Association, 8 November 2001. I thank Garland-Thomson for making her paper available, and another member of the committee, Scott Sandage, for sharing additional information about the source of the FDR quotation and the dispute between Halprin and the committee.

59. David E. Rosenbaum, "Ruling on Disability Rights Called a Blow by Advocates," *New York Times,* 22 February 2001, A20.

60. See Andreas Huyssen, "Monuments and Holocaust Memory in a Media Age," in Andreas Huyssen, *Twilight Memories: Marking Time in a Culture of Amnesia* (New York: Routledge, 1995), 250–60; and James E. Young, *Holocaust Memorials and Meaning* (New Haven: Yale University Press, 1993).

61. Kantarowicz, *King's Two Bodies,* esp. 383–494.

62. Barton J. Bernstein, "The New Deal: The Conservative Achievements of Liberal Reform," in *Toward a New Past: Dissenting Essays in American History,* ed. Barton J. Bernstein (New York: Pantheon Books, 1968), 263–88.

63. Young, *Holocaust Memorials and Meaning,* xii.

The Social and the Real is the first anthology to deal with the painting, sculpture, graphic arts, and photography of the 1930s in a hemispheric context. We take as axiomatic Cuban poet, journalist, and political theorist José Martí's (1853–95) definition of "America" as a hemispheric, multiracial, and multiethnic entity in which the United States is one nation among many. Although many of the individual essays have a relatively narrow focus, as an aggregate they begin the process of forging a Pan-American perspective on the art of the period, encouraging the reader to compare and contrast the experiences of artists across national boundaries and reconsider familiar narratives. Thinking about art and politics in a hemispheric context expands the very chronology of social realism. Whereas scholars in the United States locate the origins of the movement with the economic crash of 1929 and conclude it with the advent of World War II, the story really begins in Mexico in the early 1920s and continues during the 1940s and 1950s throughout the hemisphere.

ALEJANDRO ANREUS is Associate Professor of Art History and Latin American Studies at William Paterson University.

DIANA L. LINDEN is a Visiting Assistant Professor, Pitzer College, Claremont, California.

JONATHAN WEINBERG is an artist and Fellow, Vera List Center for Art and Politics, New School University.